NAOKI URASAWA

Volume. 1

◆MONSTER◆

Perfect Edition

NAOKI URASAWA

MONSTER

Perfect Edition

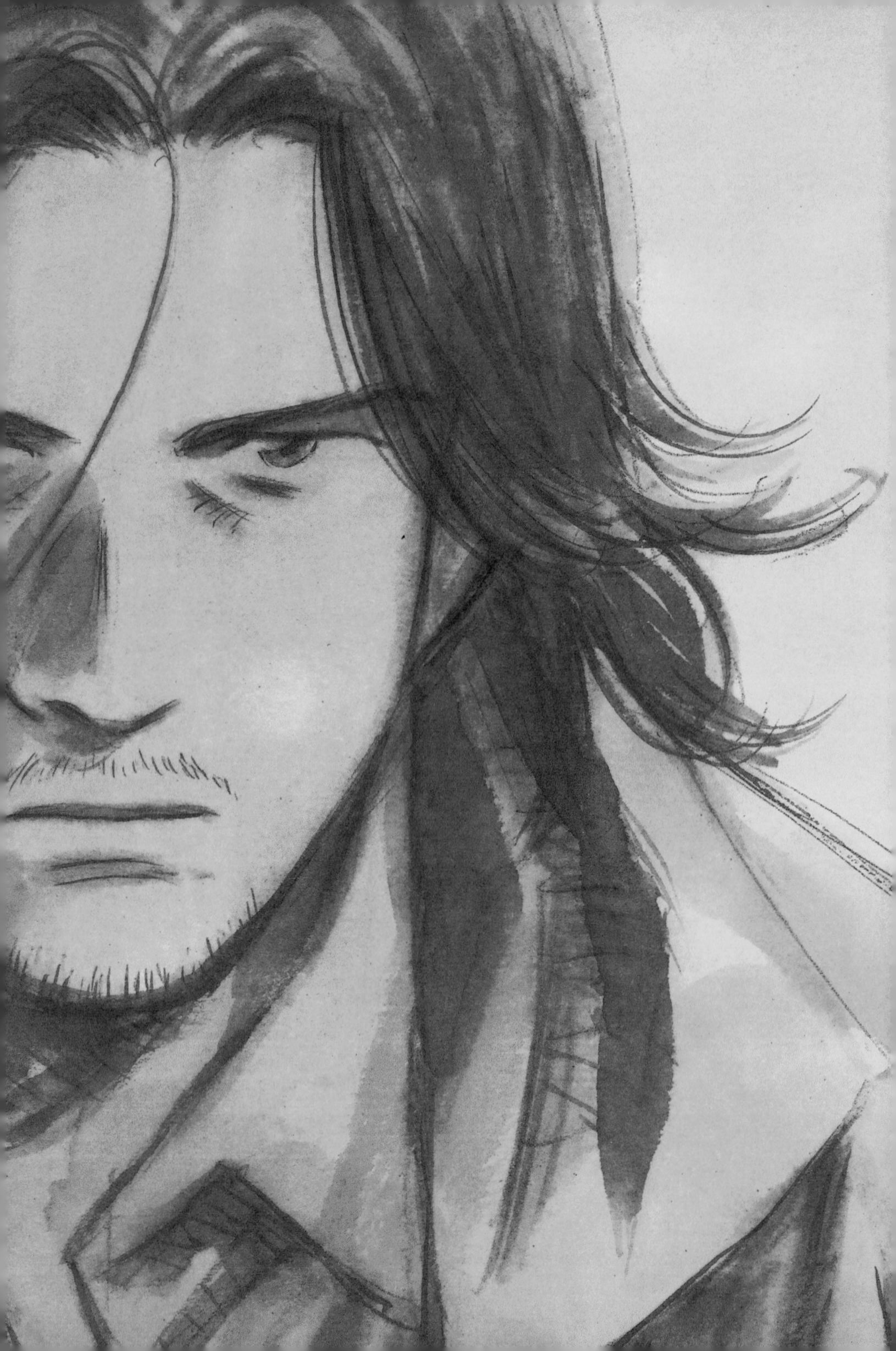

Contents

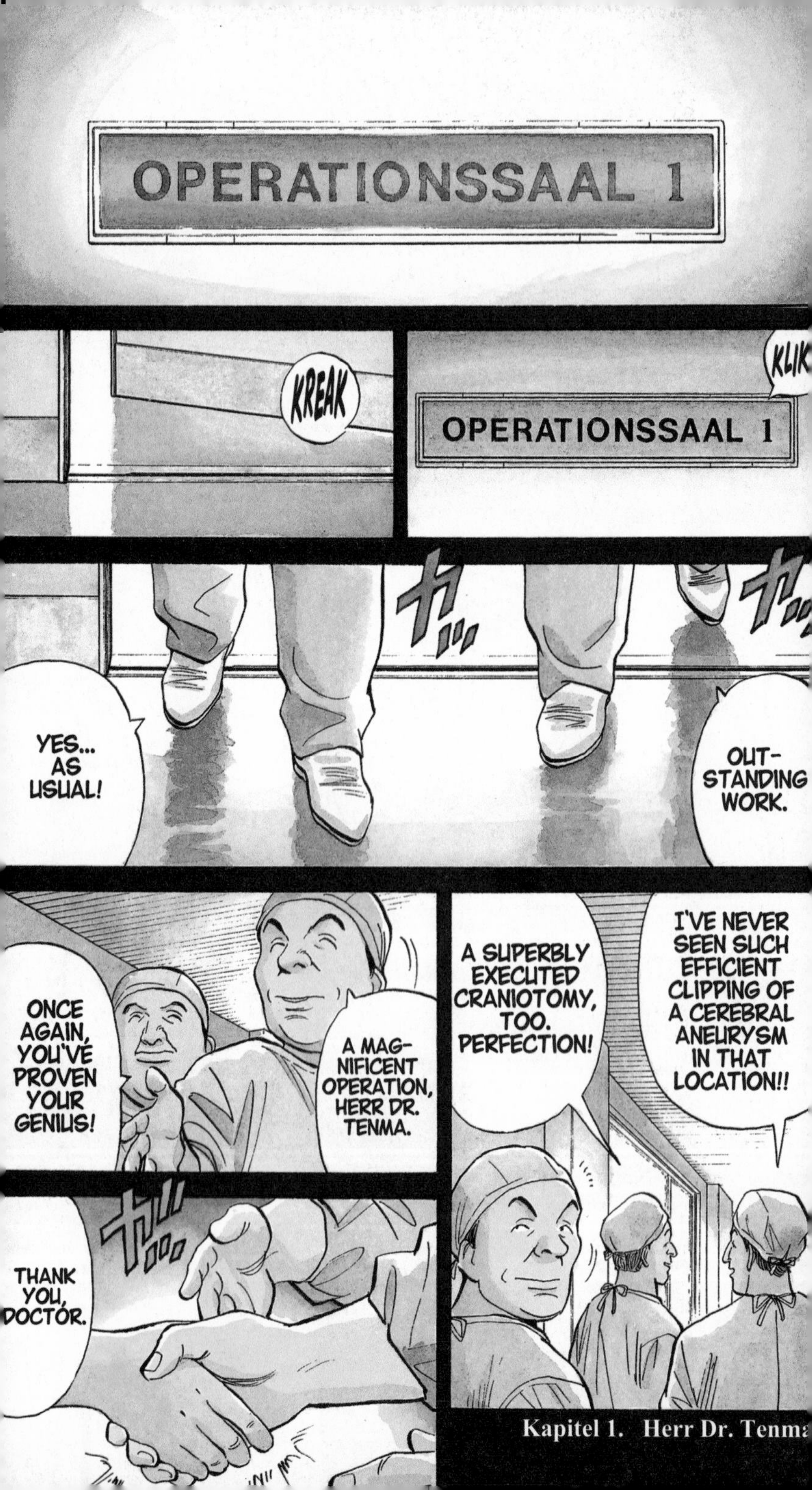
OPERATIONSSAAL 1
KLIK
OPERATIONSSAAL 1
KREAK
OUT-STANDING WORK.
YES... AS USUAL!
I'VE NEVER SEEN SUCH EFFICIENT CLIPPING OF A CEREBRAL ANEURYSM IN THAT LOCATION!!
A SUPERBLY EXECUTED CRANIOTOMY, TOO. PERFECTION!
Kapitel 1. Herr Dr. Tenma
A MAG-NIFICENT OPERATION, HERR DR. TENMA.
ONCE AGAIN, YOU'VE PROVEN YOUR GENIUS!
THANK YOU, DOCTOR.

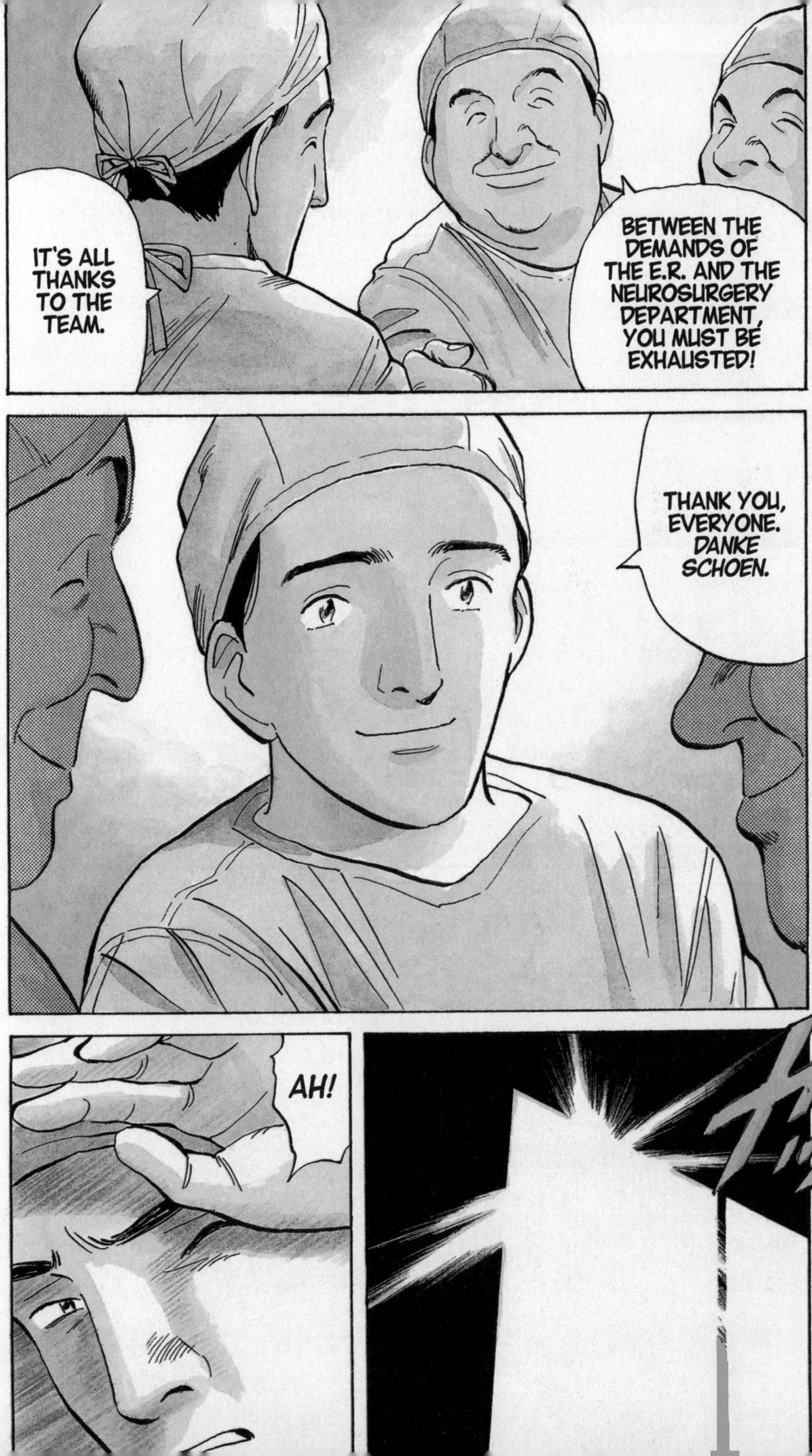
BETWEEN THE DEMANDS OF THE E.R. AND THE NEUROSURGERY DEPARTMENT, YOU MUST BE EXHAUSTED!
IT'S ALL THANKS TO THE TEAM.
THANK YOU, EVERYONE. DANKE SCHOEN.
AH!

And I saw a beast rise up out of the sea,
Having seven heads and ten horns, and upon his horns ten crowns,
And upon his heads the name of blasphemy.
And they worshipped the dragon which gave power unto the beast:
And they worshipped the beast, saying,
"Who is like unto the beast?"
"Who is able to make war with him?"
—The Revelation of Saint John the Divine, 13:1-4

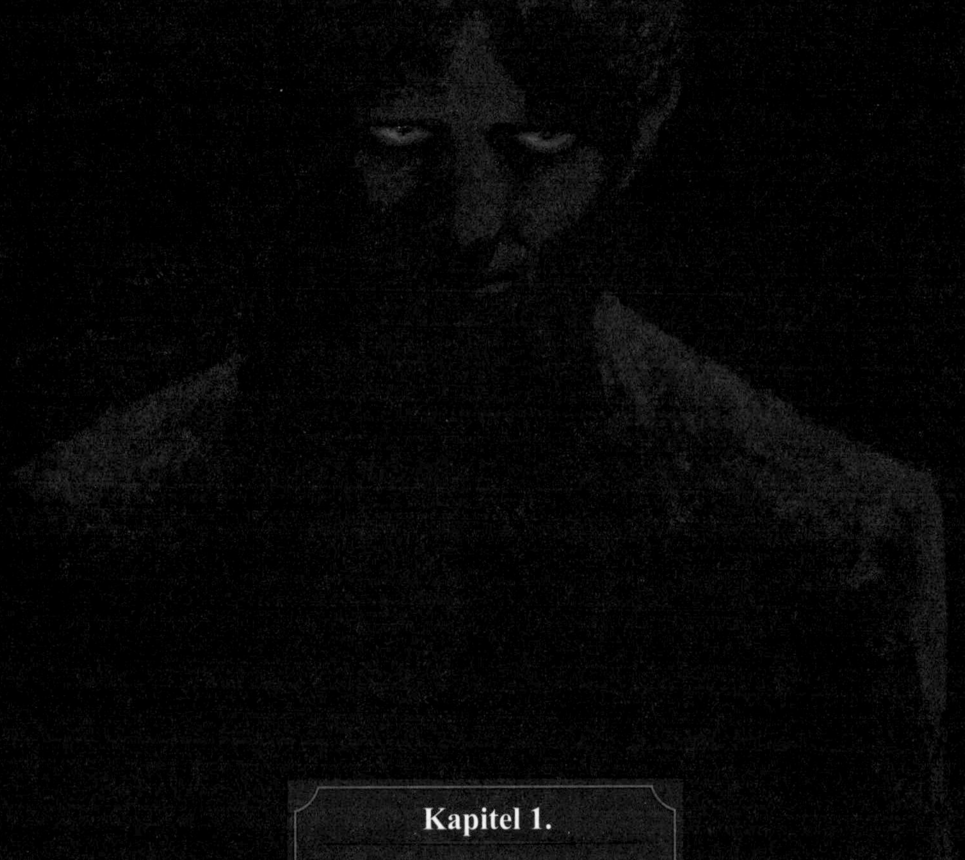

Kapitel 1.

Herr Dr. Tenma

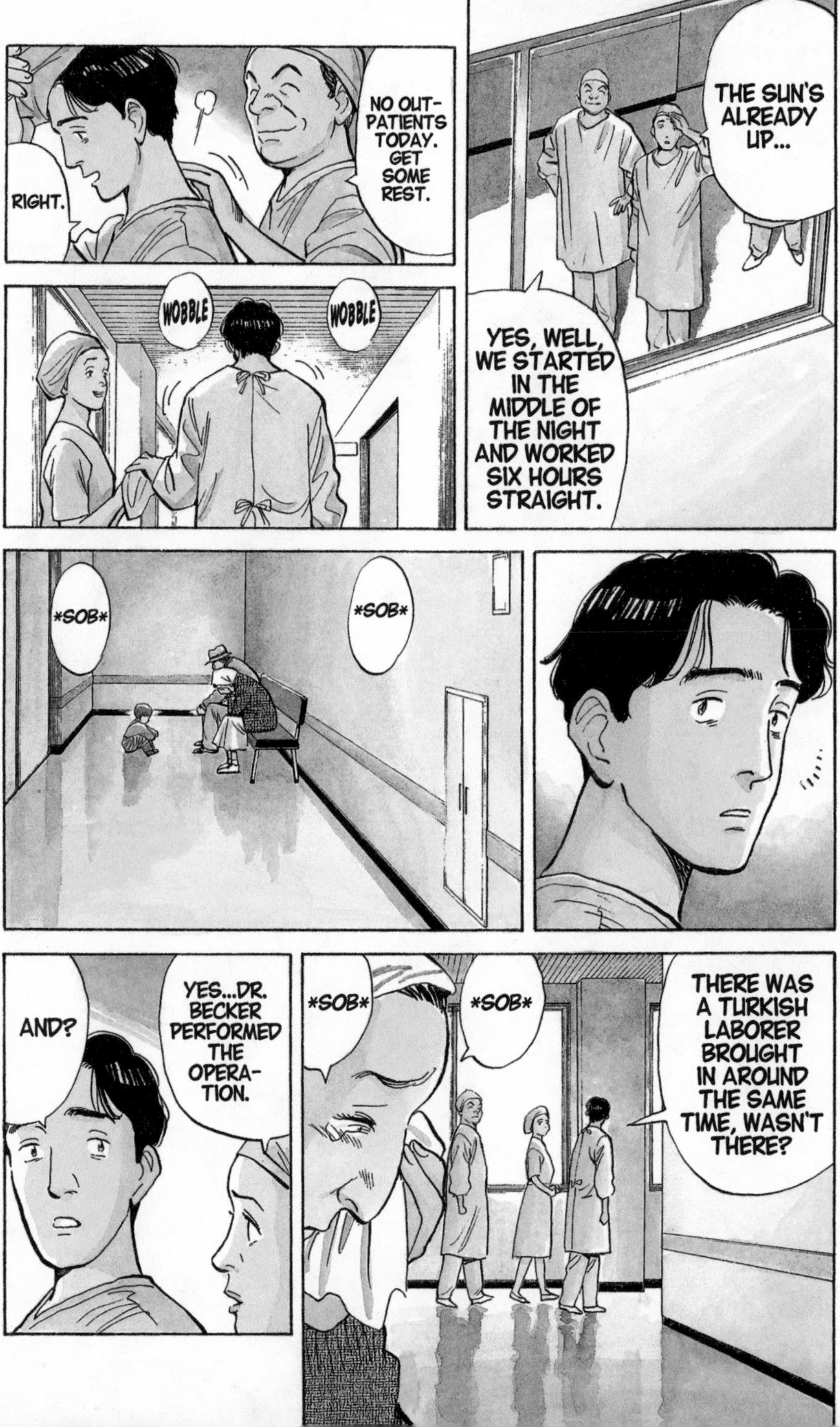
THE SUN'S ALREADY UP...
YES, WELL, WE STARTED IN THE MIDDLE OF THE NIGHT AND WORKED SIX HOURS STRAIGHT.
NO OUT-PATIENTS TODAY. GET SOME REST.
RIGHT.
WOBBLE
WOBBLE
SOB
SOB
THERE WAS A TURKISH LABORER BROUGHT IN AROUND THE SAME TIME, WASN'T THERE?
SOB
SOB
YES...DR. BECKER PERFORMED THE OPERATION.
AND?

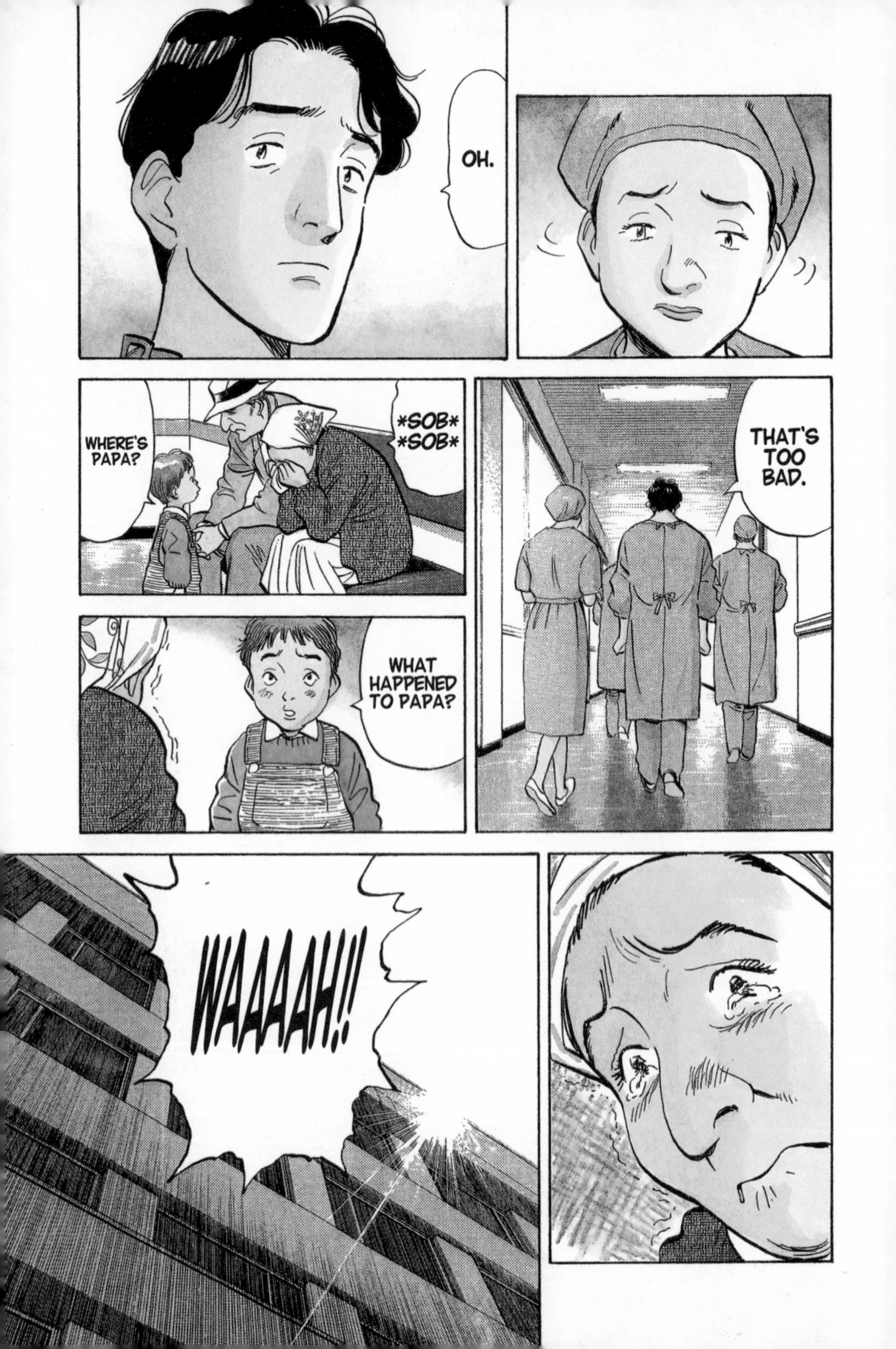
OH.
THAT'S TOO BAD.
SOB *SOB*
WHERE'S PAPA?
WHAT HAPPENED TO PAPA?
WAAAAH!!

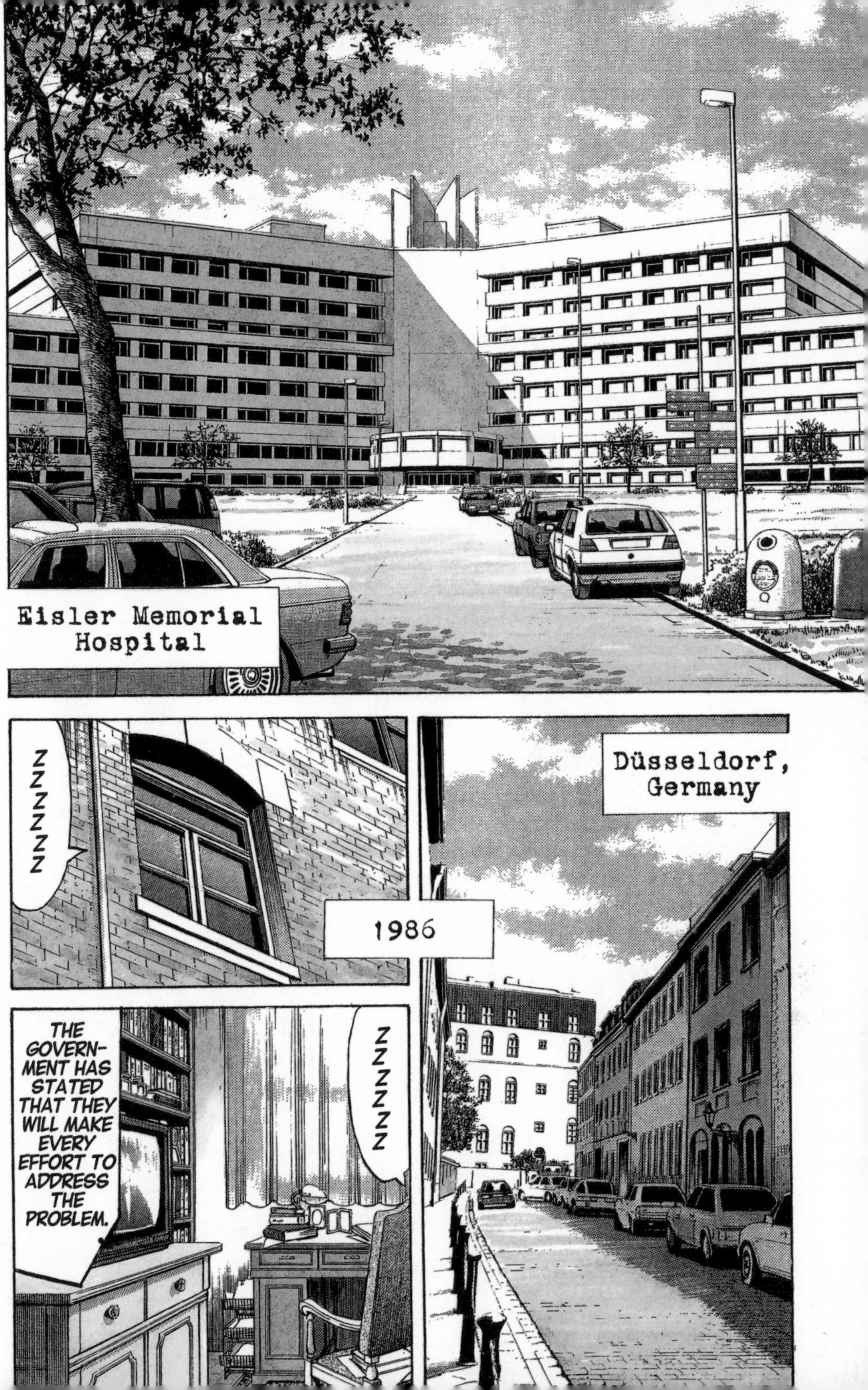

Eisler Memorial Hospital
Düsseldorf, Germany
1986
ZZZZZZ
ZZZZZZ
THE GOVERNMENT HAS STATED THAT THEY WILL MAKE EVERY EFFORT TO ADDRESS THE PROBLEM.

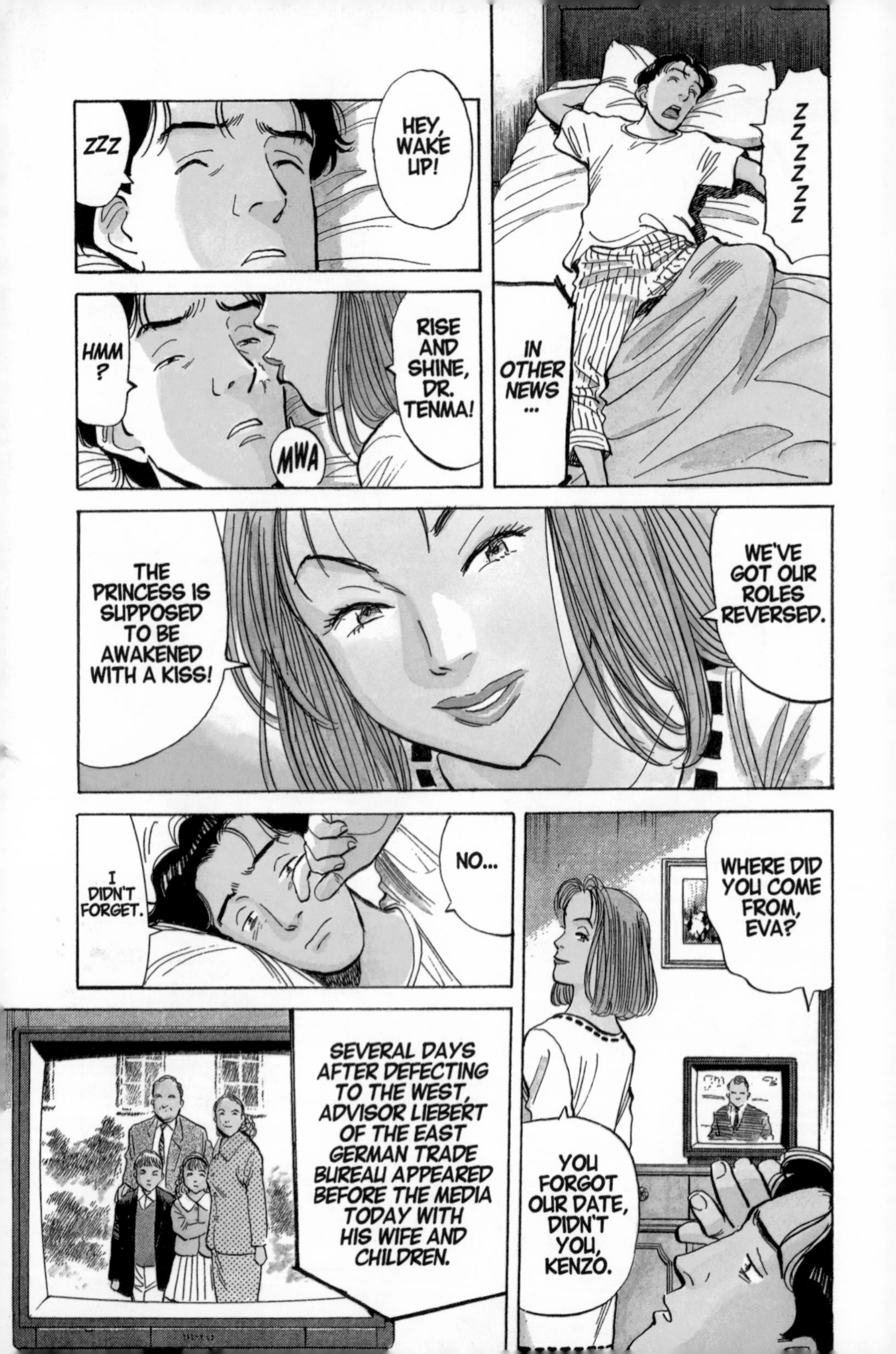
ZZZZZZ
IN OTHER NEWS...
HEY, WAKE UP!
ZZZ
RISE AND SHINE, DR. TENMA!
MWA
HMM?
WE'VE GOT OUR ROLES REVERSED.
THE PRINCESS IS SUPPOSED TO BE AWAKENED WITH A KISS!
WHERE DID YOU COME FROM, EVA?
YOU FORGOT OUR DATE, DIDN'T YOU, KENZO.
NO...
I DIDN'T FORGET.
SEVERAL DAYS AFTER DEFECTING TO THE WEST, ADVISOR LIEBERT OF THE EAST GERMAN TRADE BUREAU APPEARED BEFORE THE MEDIA TODAY WITH HIS WIFE AND CHILDREN.

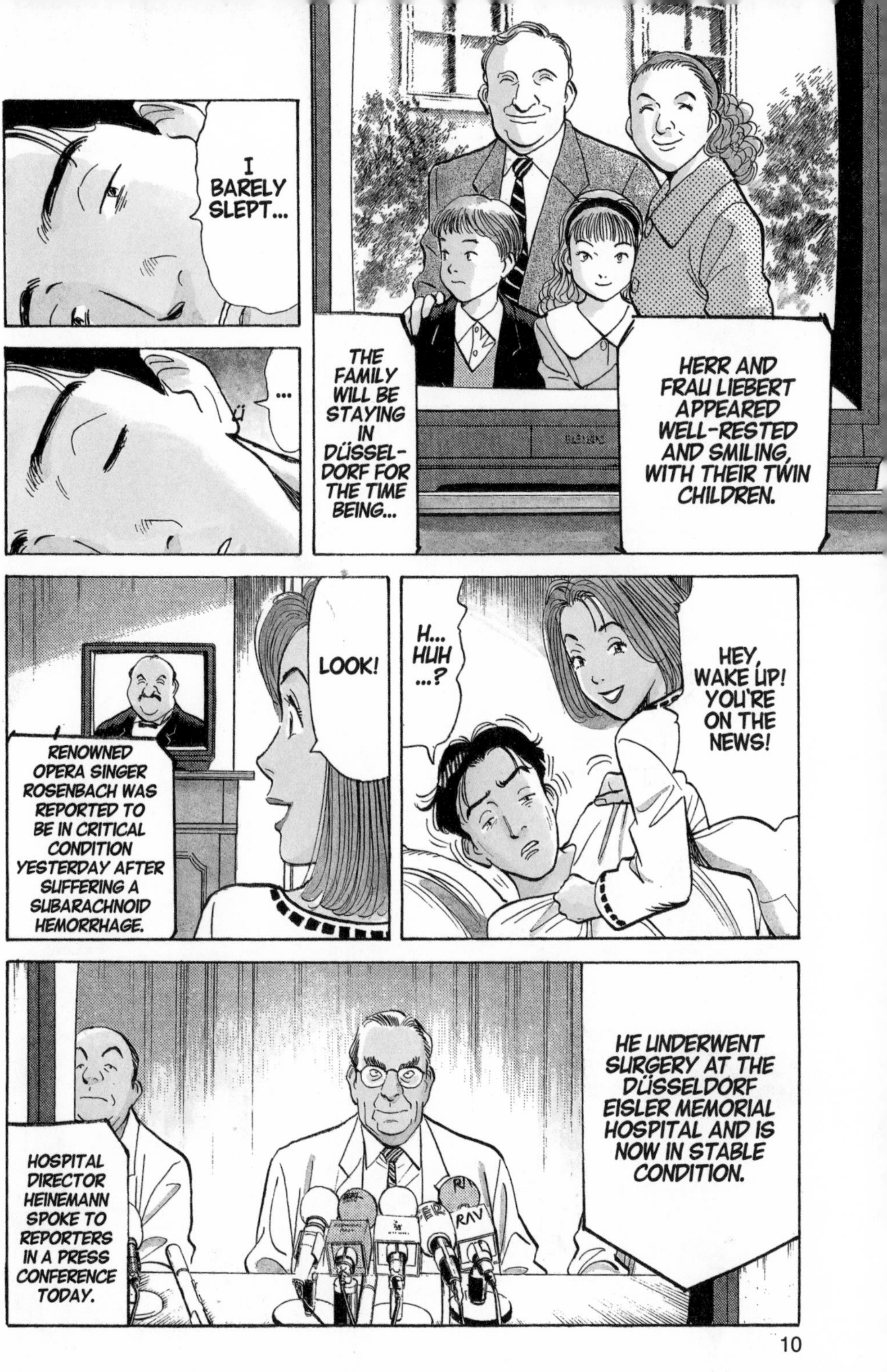
HERR AND FRAU LIEBERT APPEARED WELL-RESTED AND SMILING, WITH THEIR TWIN CHILDREN.
THE FAMILY WILL BE STAYING IN DÜSSELDORF FOR THE TIME BEING...
I BARELY SLEPT...
...
HEY, WAKE UP! YOU'RE ON THE NEWS!
H... HUH ...?
LOOK!
RENOWNED OPERA SINGER ROSENBACH WAS REPORTED TO BE IN CRITICAL CONDITION YESTERDAY AFTER SUFFERING A SUBARACHNOID HEMORRHAGE.
HE UNDERWENT SURGERY AT THE DÜSSELDORF EISLER MEMORIAL HOSPITAL AND IS NOW IN STABLE CONDITION.
HOSPITAL DIRECTOR HEINEMANN SPOKE TO REPORTERS IN A PRESS CONFERENCE TODAY.

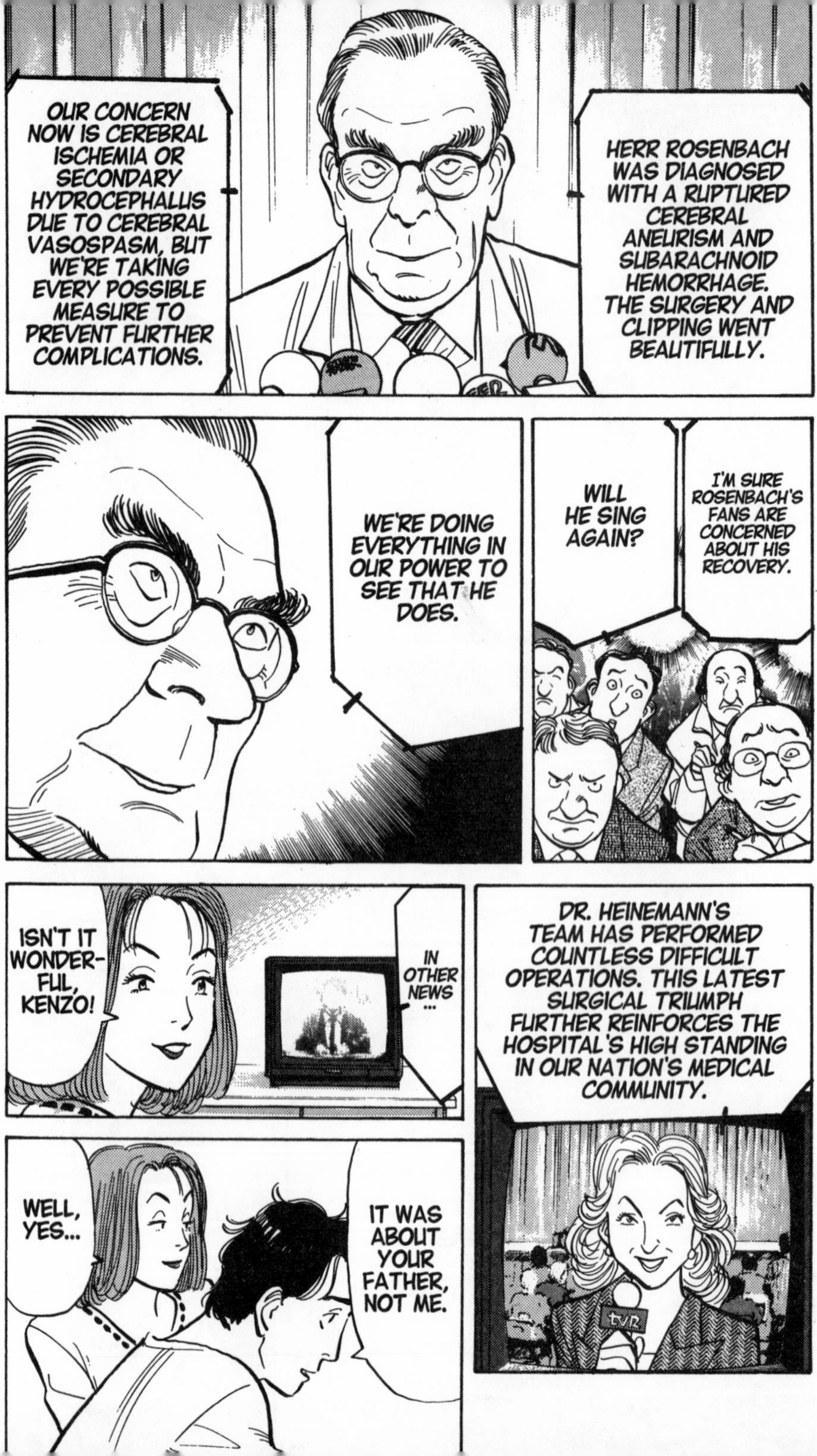
HERR ROSENBACH WAS DIAGNOSED WITH A RUPTURED CEREBRAL ANEURISM AND SUBARACHNOID HEMORRHAGE. THE SURGERY AND CLIPPING WENT BEAUTIFULLY.
OUR CONCERN NOW IS CEREBRAL ISCHEMIA OR SECONDARY HYDROCEPHALUS DUE TO CEREBRAL VASOSPASM, BUT WE'RE TAKING EVERY POSSIBLE MEASURE TO PREVENT FURTHER COMPLICATIONS.
I'M SURE ROSENBACH'S FANS ARE CONCERNED ABOUT HIS RECOVERY.
WILL HE SING AGAIN?
WE'RE DOING EVERYTHING IN OUR POWER TO SEE THAT HE DOES.
DR. HEINEMANN'S TEAM HAS PERFORMED COUNTLESS DIFFICULT OPERATIONS. THIS LATEST SURGICAL TRIUMPH FURTHER REINFORCES THE HOSPITAL'S HIGH STANDING IN OUR NATION'S MEDICAL COMMUNITY.
IN OTHER NEWS...
ISN'T IT WONDER-FUL, KENZO!
IT WAS ABOUT YOUR FATHER, NOT ME.
WELL, YES...

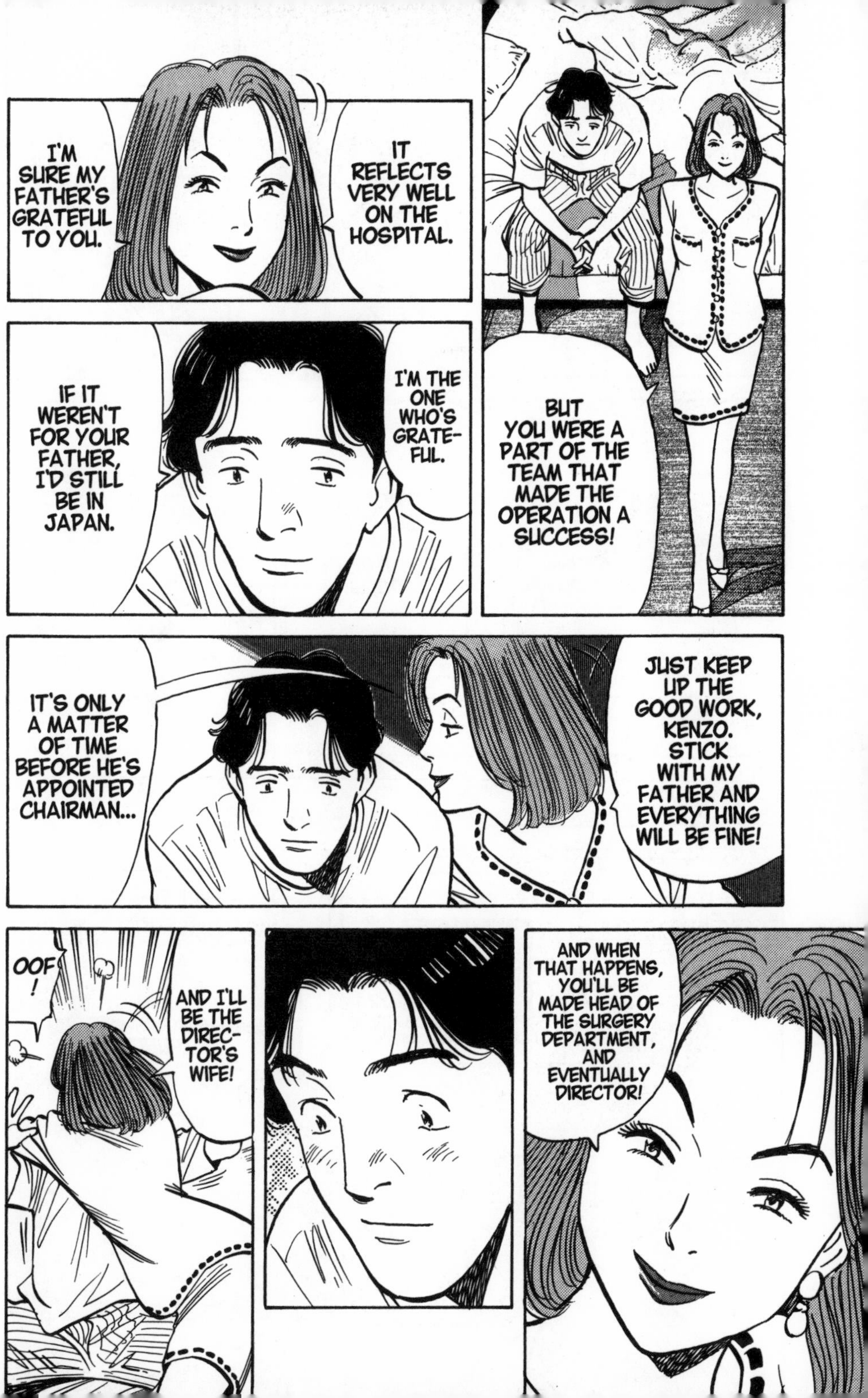
BUT YOU WERE A PART OF THE TEAM THAT MADE THE OPERATION A SUCCESS!
IT REFLECTS VERY WELL ON THE HOSPITAL.
I'M SURE MY FATHER'S GRATEFUL TO YOU.
I'M THE ONE WHO'S GRATEFUL.
IF IT WEREN'T FOR YOUR FATHER, I'D STILL BE IN JAPAN.
JUST KEEP UP THE GOOD WORK, KENZO. STICK WITH MY FATHER AND EVERYTHING WILL BE FINE!
IT'S ONLY A MATTER OF TIME BEFORE HE'S APPOINTED CHAIRMAN...
AND WHEN THAT HAPPENS, YOU'LL BE MADE HEAD OF THE SURGERY DEPARTMENT, AND EVENTUALLY DIRECTOR!
AND I'LL BE THE DIRECTOR'S WIFE!
OOF!

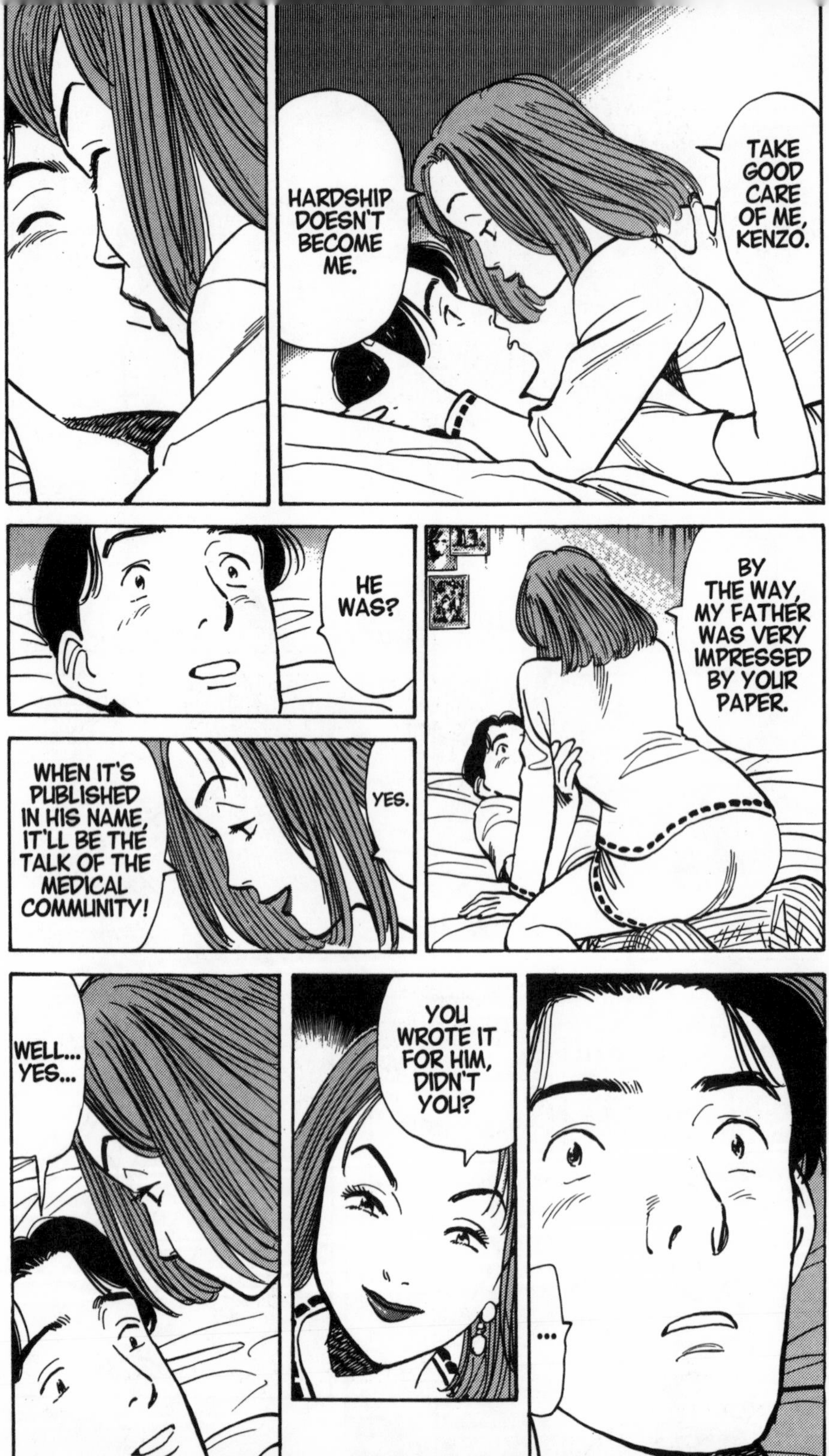
TAKE GOOD CARE OF ME, KENZO.
HARDSHIP DOESN'T BECOME ME.
BY THE WAY, MY FATHER WAS VERY IMPRESSED BY YOUR PAPER.
HE WAS?
YES.
WHEN IT'S PUBLISHED IN HIS NAME, IT'LL BE THE TALK OF THE MEDICAL COMMUNITY!
...
YOU WROTE IT FOR HIM, DIDN'T YOU?
WELL... YES...

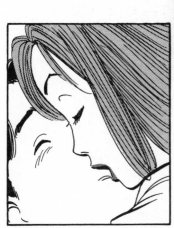

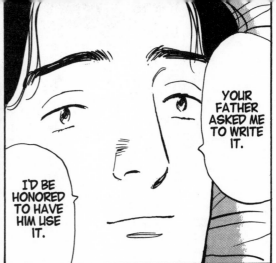

YOUR FATHER ASKED ME TO WRITE IT.

I'D BE HONORED TO HAVE HIM USE IT.

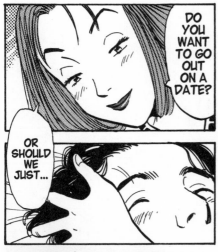

DO YOU WANT TO GO OUT ON A DATE?

OR SHOULD WE JUST...

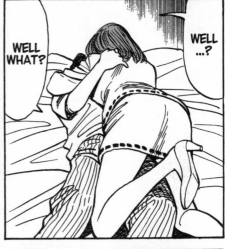

WELL WHAT?

WELL ...?

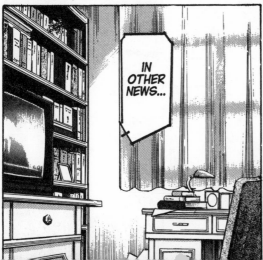

IN OTHER NEWS...

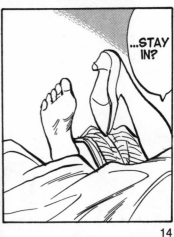

...STAY IN?

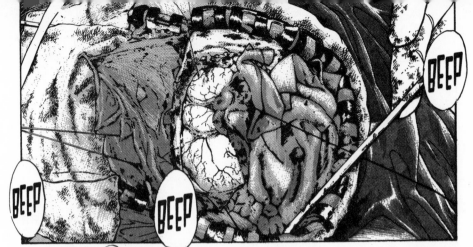

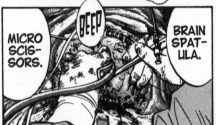

BEEP
BEEP
BEEP
BEEP
BEEP
BLOOD PRES-SURE 128 OVER 64.
BRAIN SPAT-ULA.
BEEP
MICRO SCIS-SORS.
BEEP
SCRAPING PYRAMIS...
BEEP
BEEP

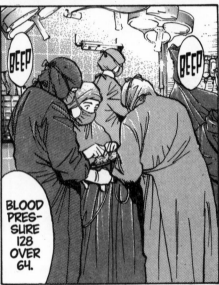

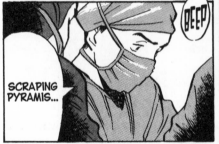

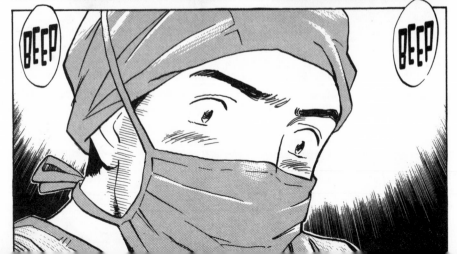

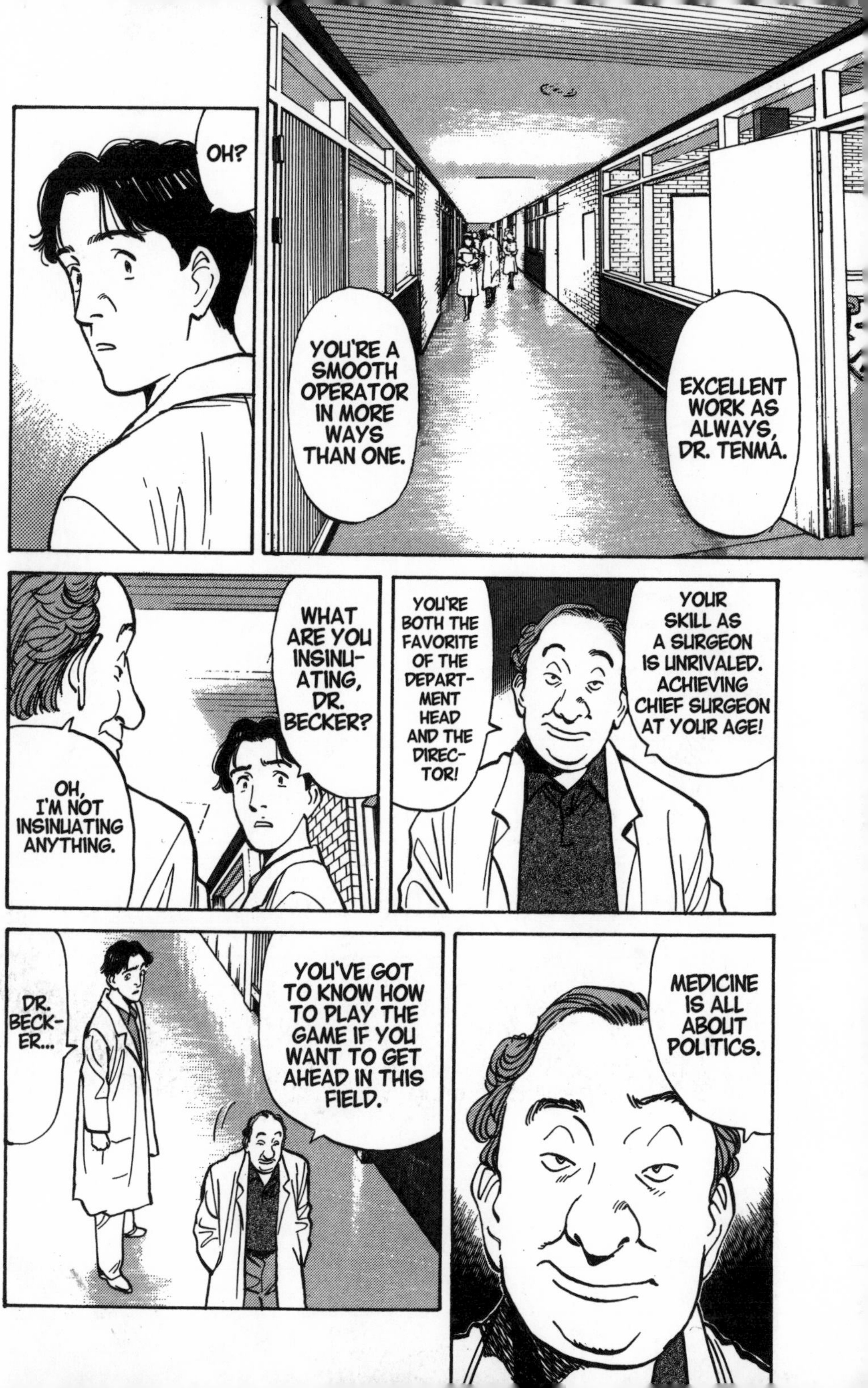
EXCELLENT WORK AS ALWAYS, DR. TENMA.
YOU'RE A SMOOTH OPERATOR IN MORE WAYS THAN ONE.
OH?
YOUR SKILL AS A SURGEON IS UNRIVALED. ACHIEVING CHIEF SURGEON AT YOUR AGE!
YOU'RE BOTH THE FAVORITE OF THE DEPARTMENT HEAD AND THE DIRECTOR!
WHAT ARE YOU INSINUATING, DR. BECKER?
OH, I'M NOT INSINUATING ANYTHING.
MEDICINE IS ALL ABOUT POLITICS.
YOU'VE GOT TO KNOW HOW TO PLAY THE GAME IF YOU WANT TO GET AHEAD IN THIS FIELD.
DR. BECKER...

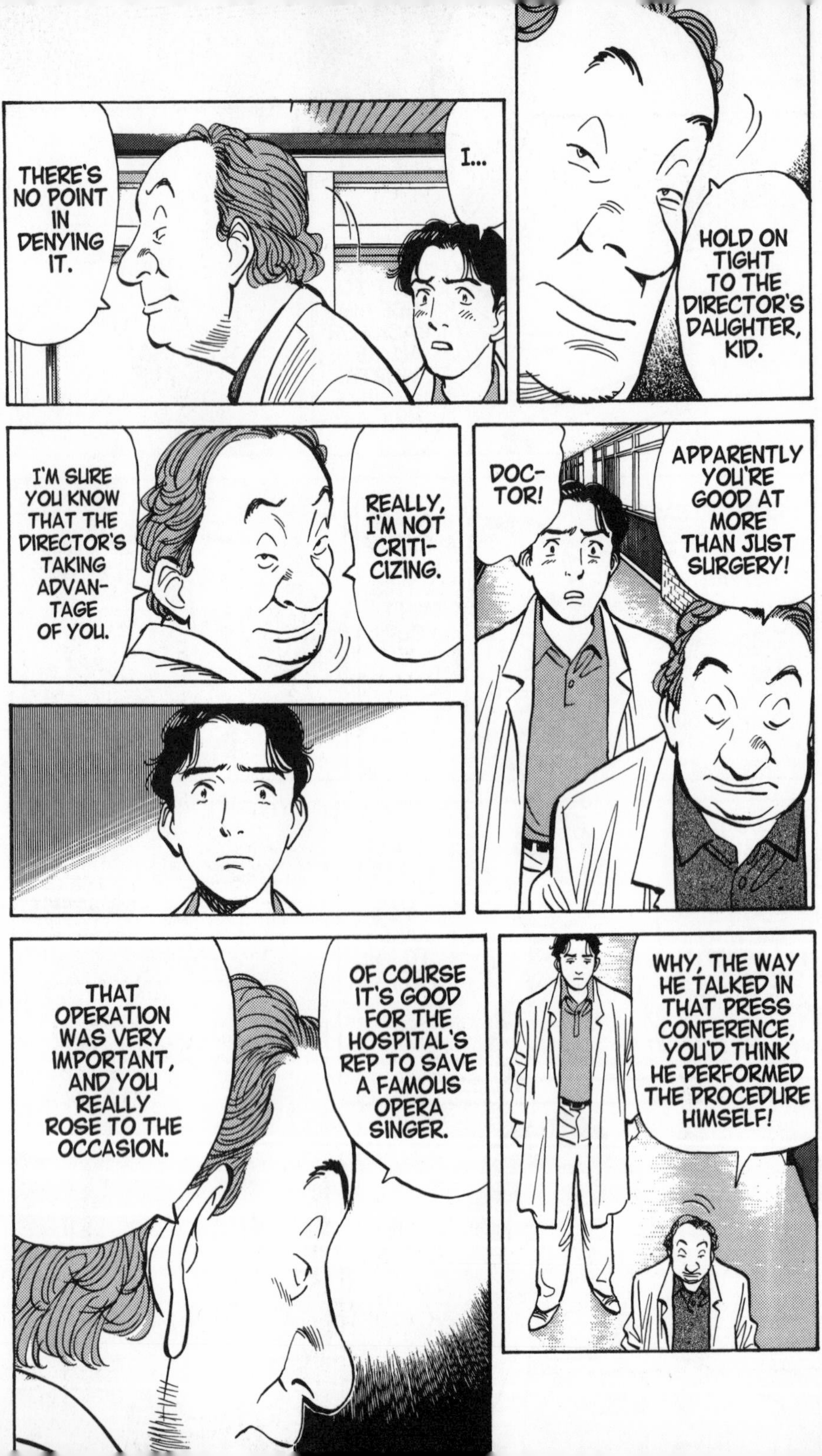
HOLD ON TIGHT TO THE DIRECTOR'S DAUGHTER, KID.
I...
THERE'S NO POINT IN DENYING IT.
APPARENTLY YOU'RE GOOD AT MORE THAN JUST SURGERY!
DOC-TOR!
REALLY, I'M NOT CRITI-CIZING.
I'M SURE YOU KNOW THAT THE DIRECTOR'S TAKING ADVAN-TAGE OF YOU.
WHY, THE WAY HE TALKED IN THAT PRESS CONFERENCE, YOU'D THINK HE PERFORMED THE PROCEDURE HIMSELF!
OF COURSE IT'S GOOD FOR THE HOSPITAL'S REP TO SAVE A FAMOUS OPERA SINGER.
THAT OPERATION WAS VERY IMPORTANT, AND YOU REALLY ROSE TO THE OCCASION.

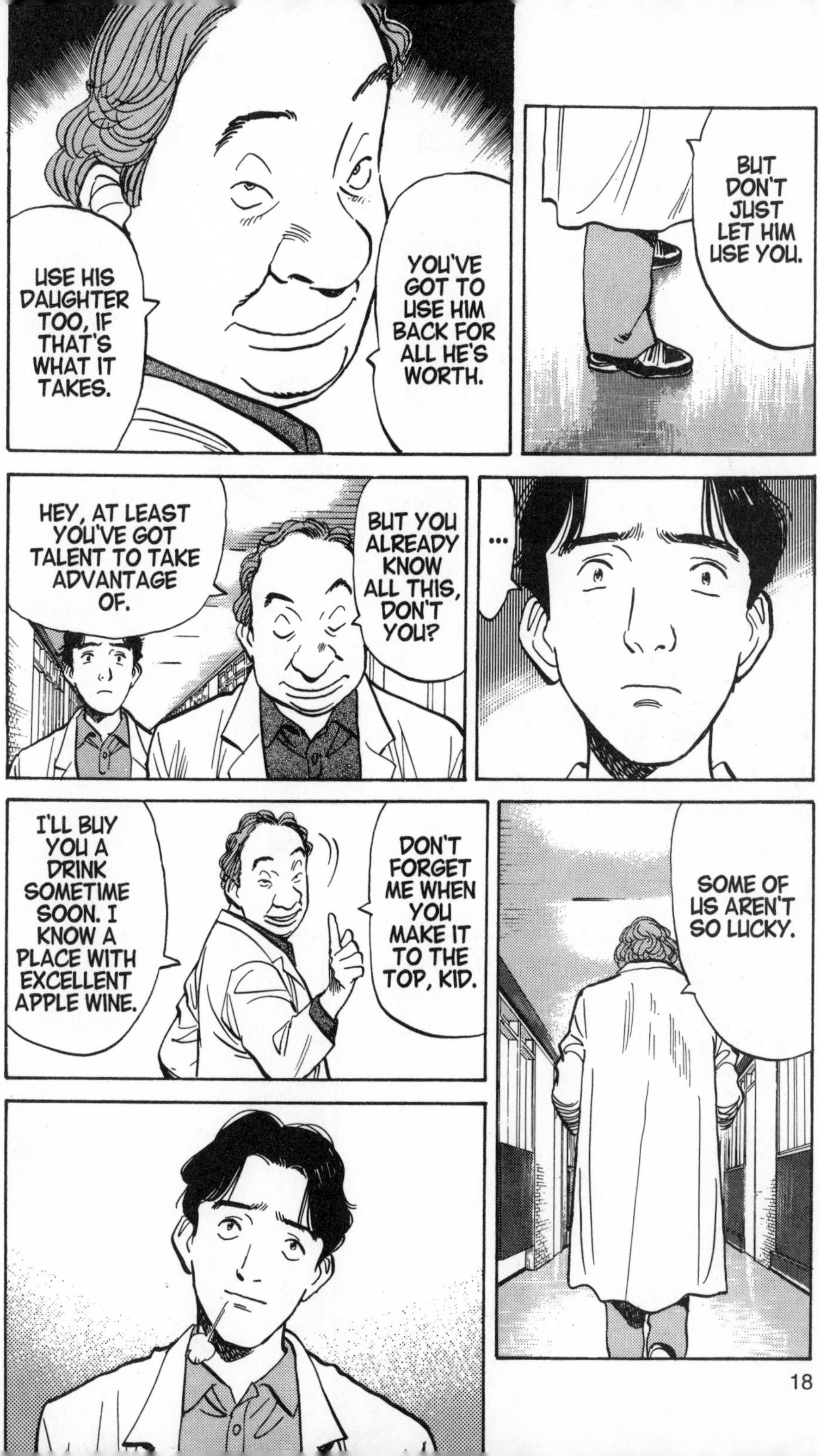

BUT DON'T JUST LET HIM USE YOU.
YOU'VE GOT TO USE HIM BACK FOR ALL HE'S WORTH.
USE HIS DAUGHTER TOO, IF THAT'S WHAT IT TAKES.
...
BUT YOU ALREADY KNOW ALL THIS, DON'T YOU?
HEY, AT LEAST YOU'VE GOT TALENT TO TAKE ADVANTAGE OF.
SOME OF US AREN'T SO LUCKY.
DON'T FORGET ME WHEN YOU MAKE IT TO THE TOP, KID.
I'LL BUY YOU A DRINK SOMETIME SOON. I KNOW A PLACE WITH EXCELLENT APPLE WINE.

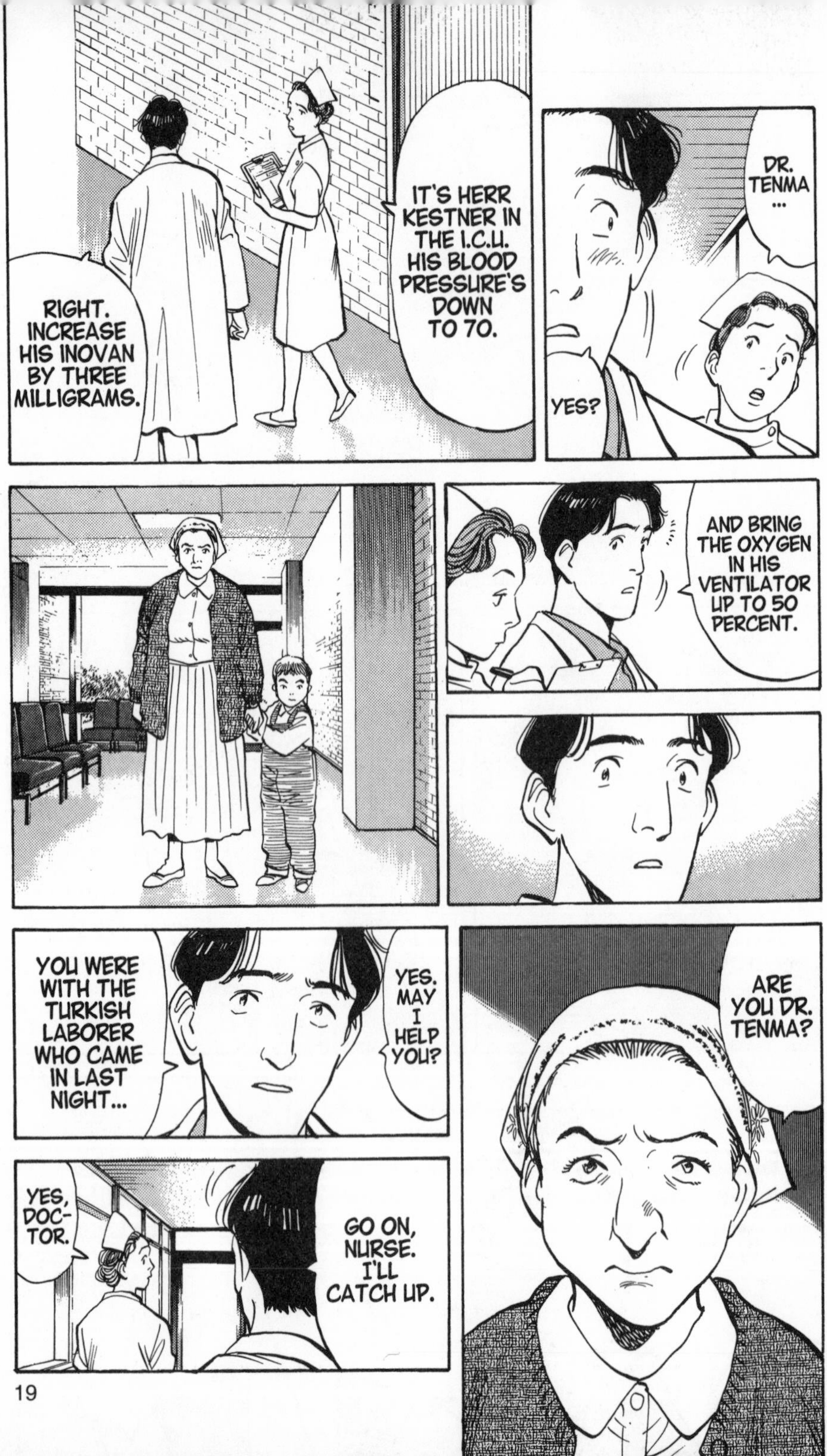
DR. TENMA ...
YES?
IT'S HERR KESTNER IN THE I.C.U. HIS BLOOD PRESSURE'S DOWN TO 70.
RIGHT. INCREASE HIS INOVAN BY THREE MILLIGRAMS.
AND BRING THE OXYGEN IN HIS VENTILATOR UP TO 50 PERCENT.
ARE YOU DR. TENMA?
YES. MAY I HELP YOU?
YOU WERE WITH THE TURKISH LABORER WHO CAME IN LAST NIGHT...
GO ON, NURSE. I'LL CATCH UP.
YES, DOC-TOR.

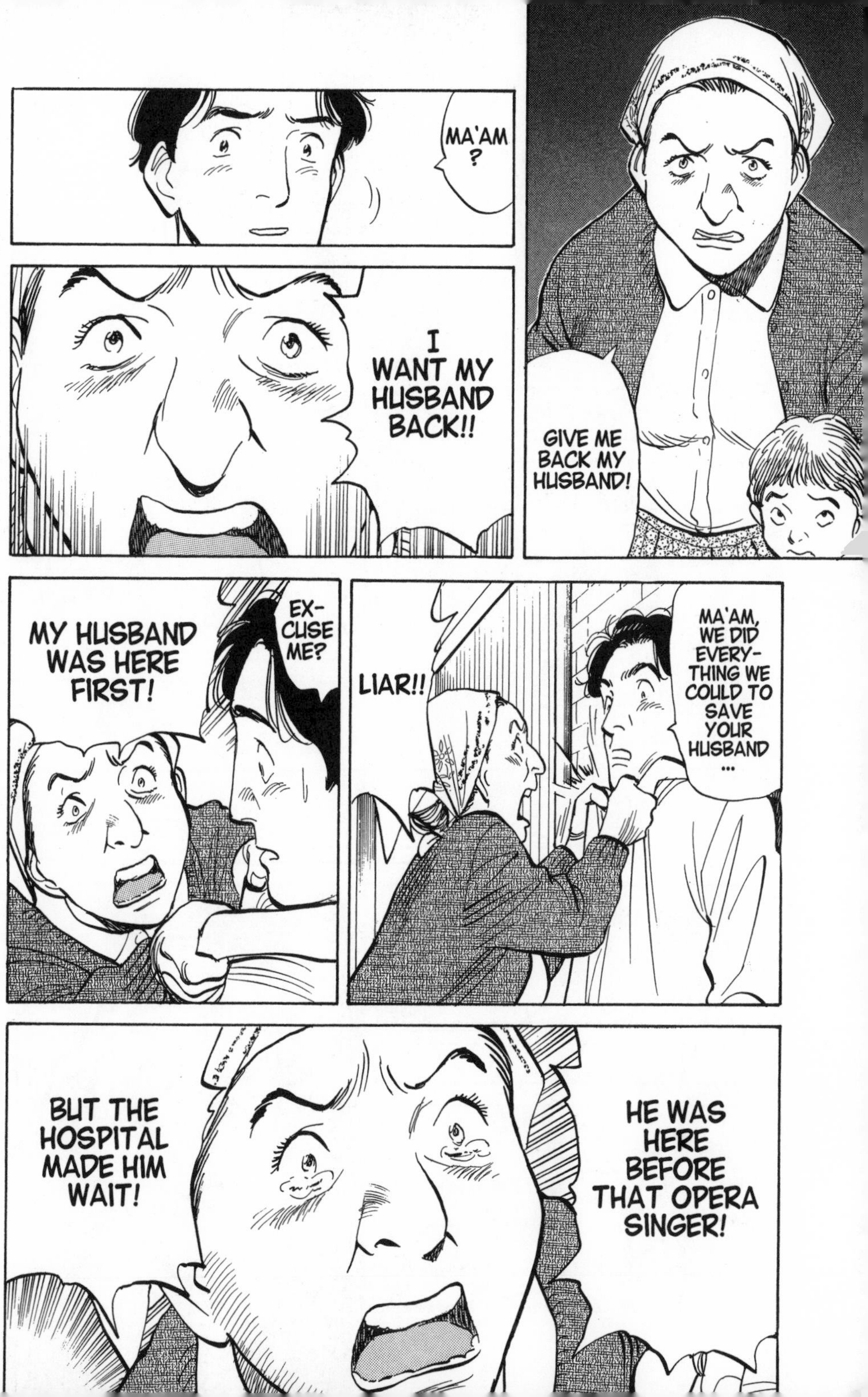
GIVE ME BACK MY HUSBAND!
MA'AM ?
I WANT MY HUSBAND BACK!!
MA'AM, WE DID EVERYTHING WE COULD TO SAVE YOUR HUSBAND ...
LIAR!!
EXCUSE ME?
MY HUSBAND WAS HERE FIRST!
HE WAS HERE BEFORE THAT OPERA SINGER!
BUT THE HOSPITAL MADE HIM WAIT!

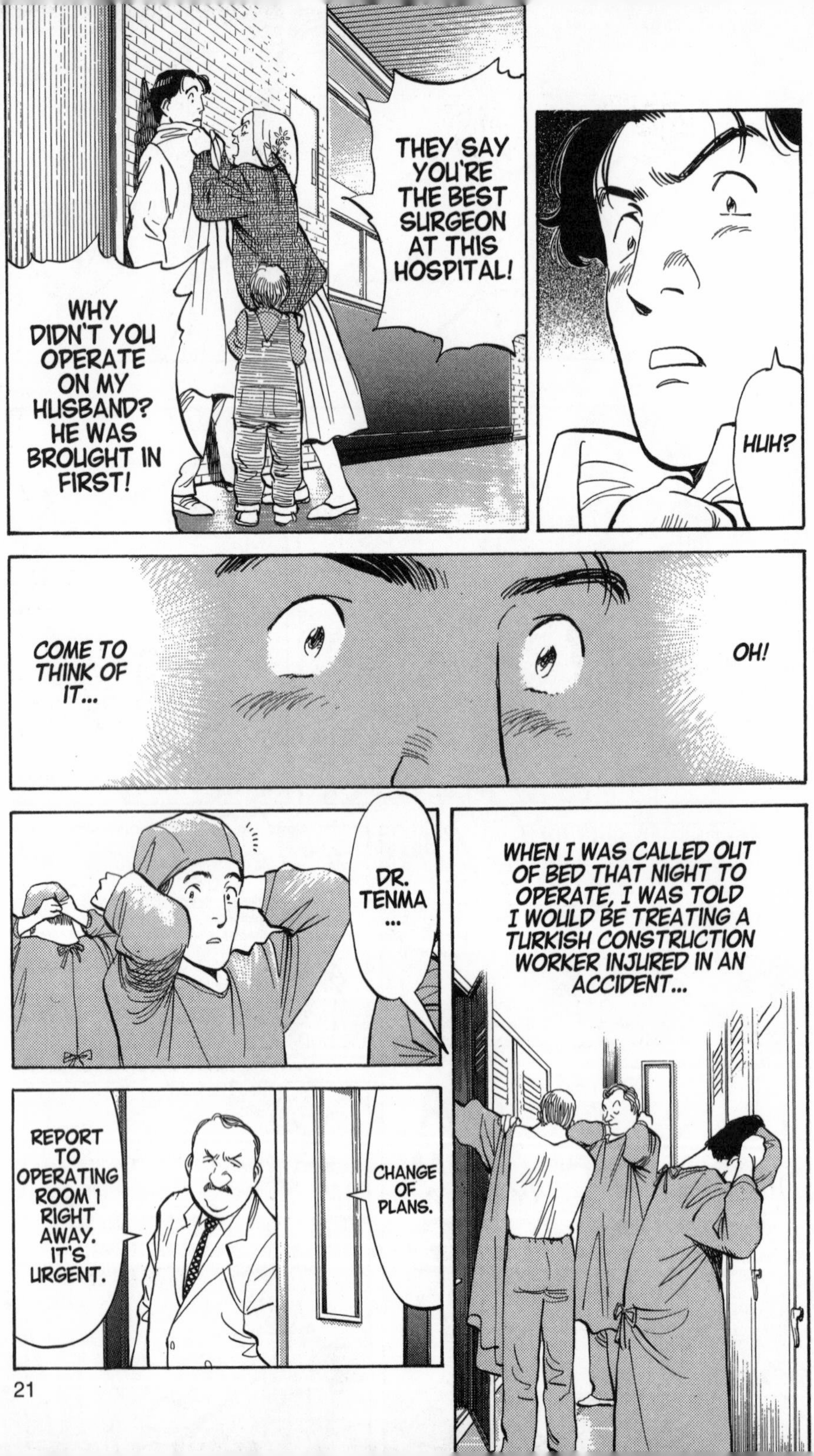
HUH?
THEY SAY YOU'RE THE BEST SURGEON AT THIS HOSPITAL!
WHY DIDN'T YOU OPERATE ON MY HUSBAND? HE WAS BROUGHT IN FIRST!
OH!
COME TO THINK OF IT...
WHEN I WAS CALLED OUT OF BED THAT NIGHT TO OPERATE, I WAS TOLD I WOULD BE TREATING A TURKISH CONSTRUCTION WORKER INJURED IN AN ACCIDENT...
DR. TENMA ...
CHANGE OF PLANS.
REPORT TO OPERATING ROOM 1 RIGHT AWAY. IT'S URGENT.

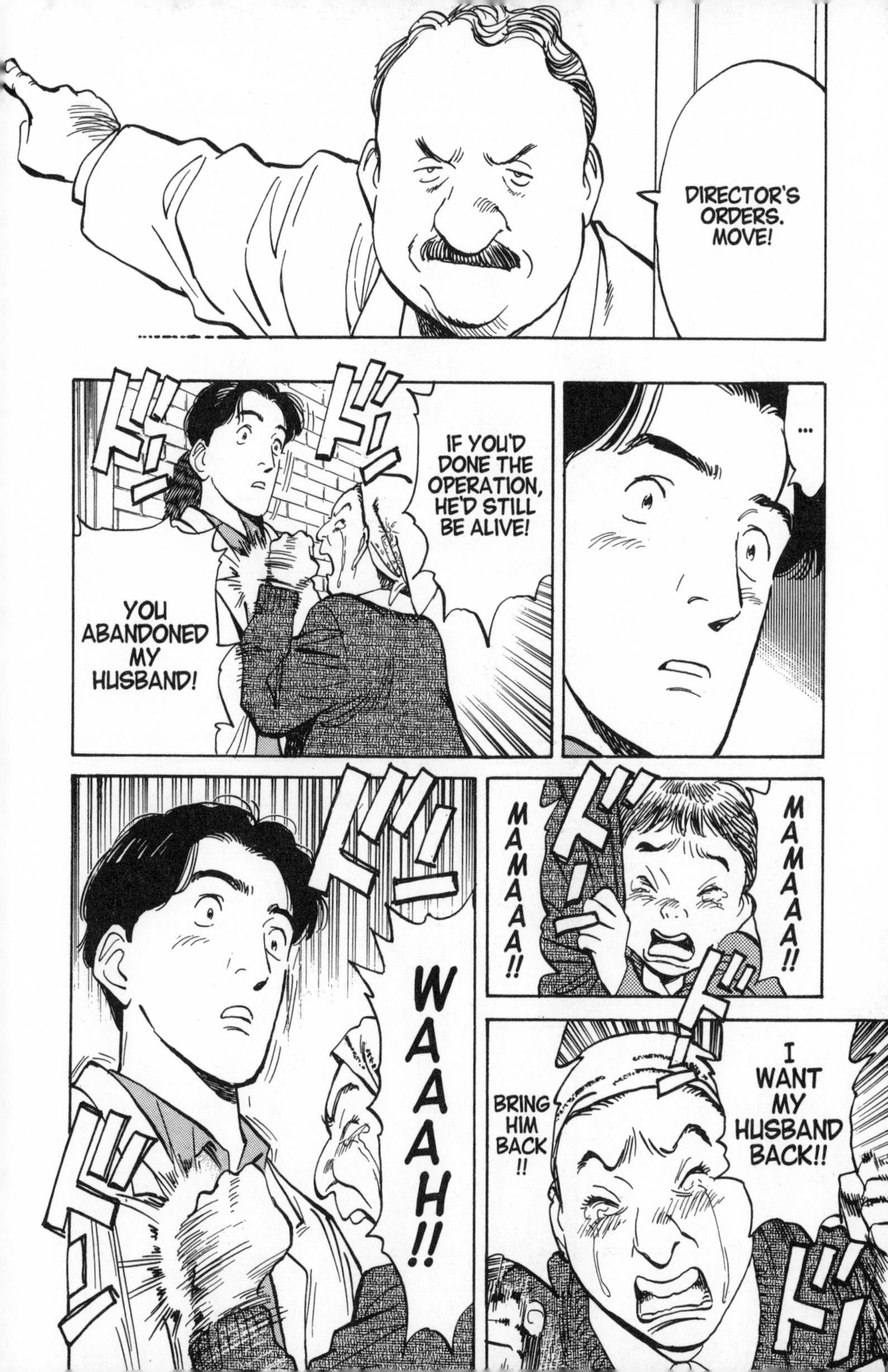
DIRECTOR'S ORDERS. MOVE!
...
IF YOU'D DONE THE OPERATION, HE'D STILL BE ALIVE!
YOU ABANDONED MY HUSBAND!
MAMAAAA!!
MAMAAAA!!
I WANT MY HUSBAND BACK!!
BRING HIM BACK !!
WAAAAH!!

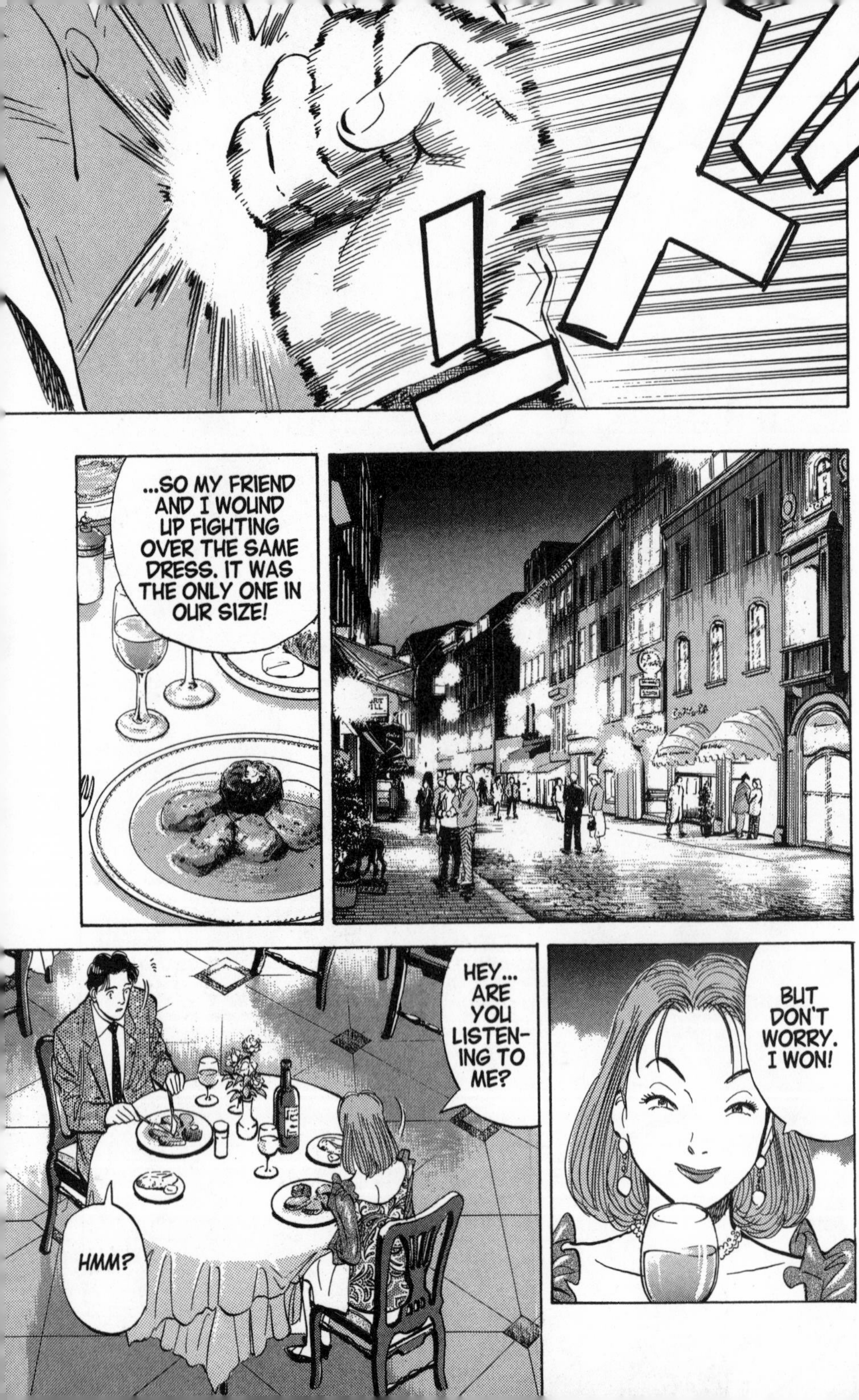
...SO MY FRIEND AND I WOUND UP FIGHTING OVER THE SAME DRESS. IT WAS THE ONLY ONE IN OUR SIZE!
BUT DON'T WORRY. I WON!
HEY... ARE YOU LISTENING TO ME?
HMM?

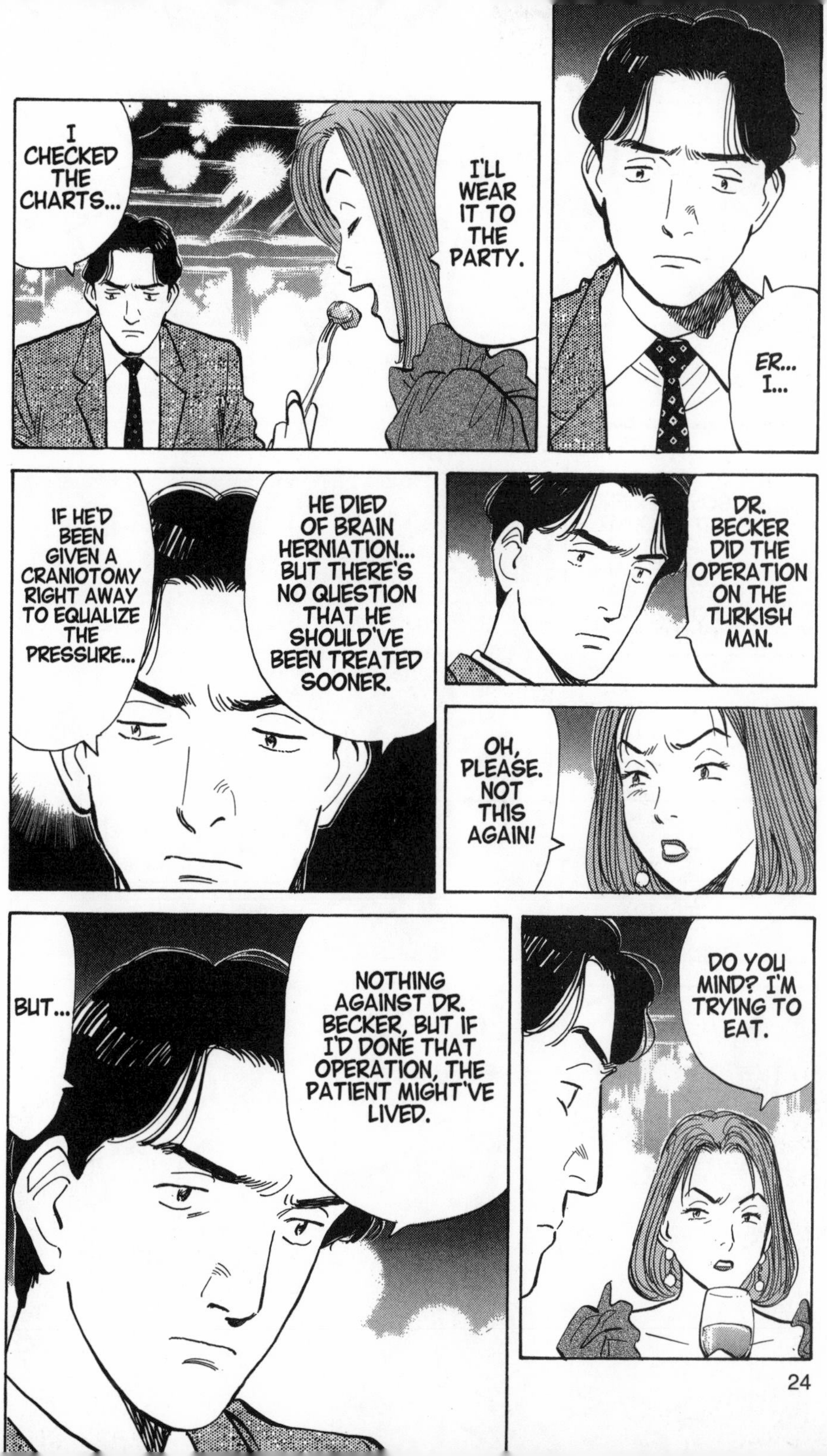
ER... I...
I'LL WEAR IT TO THE PARTY.
I CHECKED THE CHARTS...
DR. BECKER DID THE OPERATION ON THE TURKISH MAN.
OH, PLEASE. NOT THIS AGAIN!
HE DIED OF BRAIN HERNIATION... BUT THERE'S NO QUESTION THAT HE SHOULD'VE BEEN TREATED SOONER.
IF HE'D BEEN GIVEN A CRANIOTOMY RIGHT AWAY TO EQUALIZE THE PRESSURE...
DO YOU MIND? I'M TRYING TO EAT.
NOTHING AGAINST DR. BECKER, BUT IF I'D DONE THAT OPERATION, THE PATIENT MIGHT'VE LIVED.
BUT...

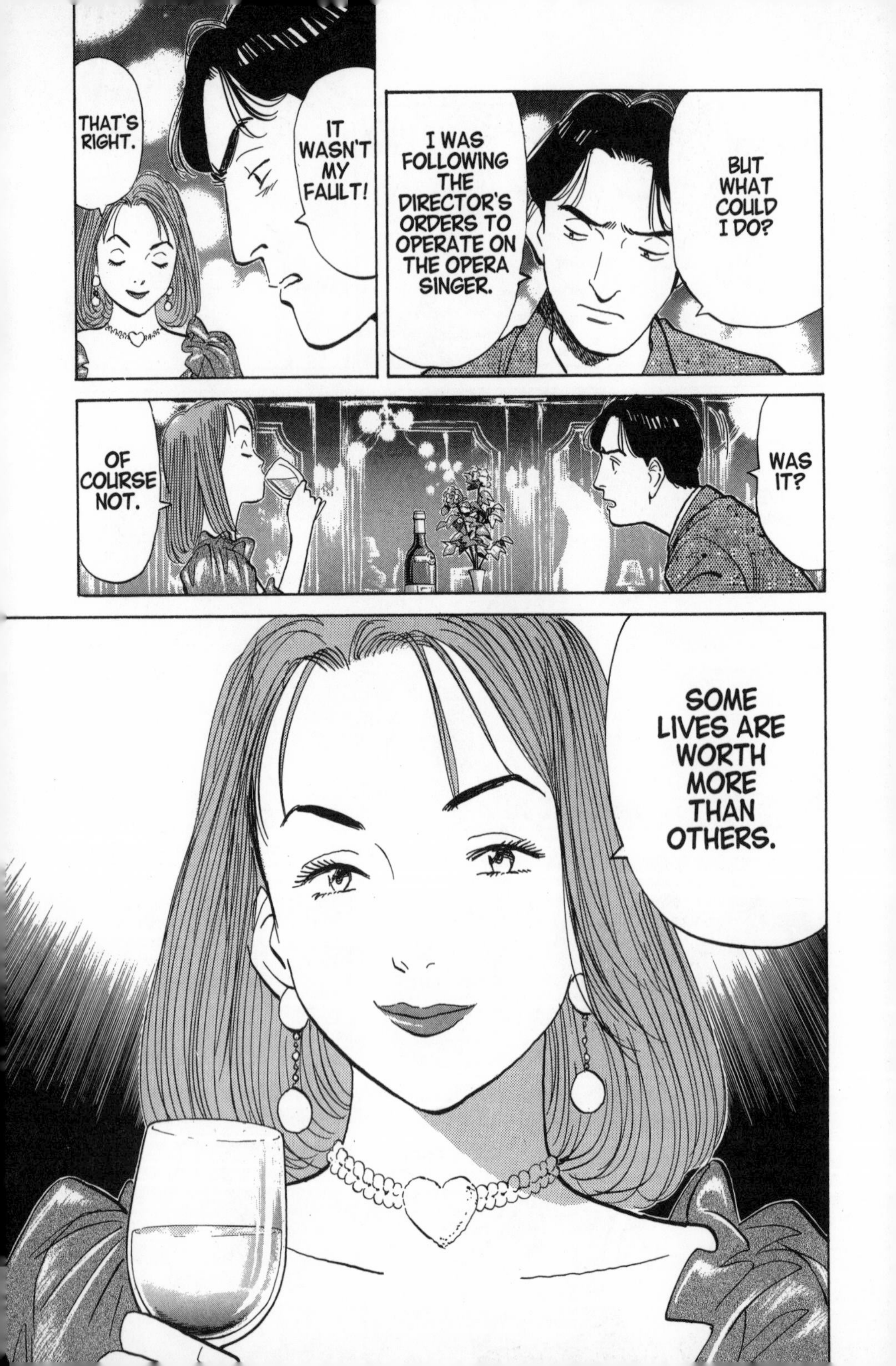
BUT WHAT COULD I DO?
I WAS FOLLOWING THE DIRECTOR'S ORDERS TO OPERATE ON THE OPERA SINGER.
IT WASN'T MY FAULT!
THAT'S RIGHT.
WAS IT?
OF COURSE NOT.
SOME LIVES ARE WORTH MORE THAN OTHERS.

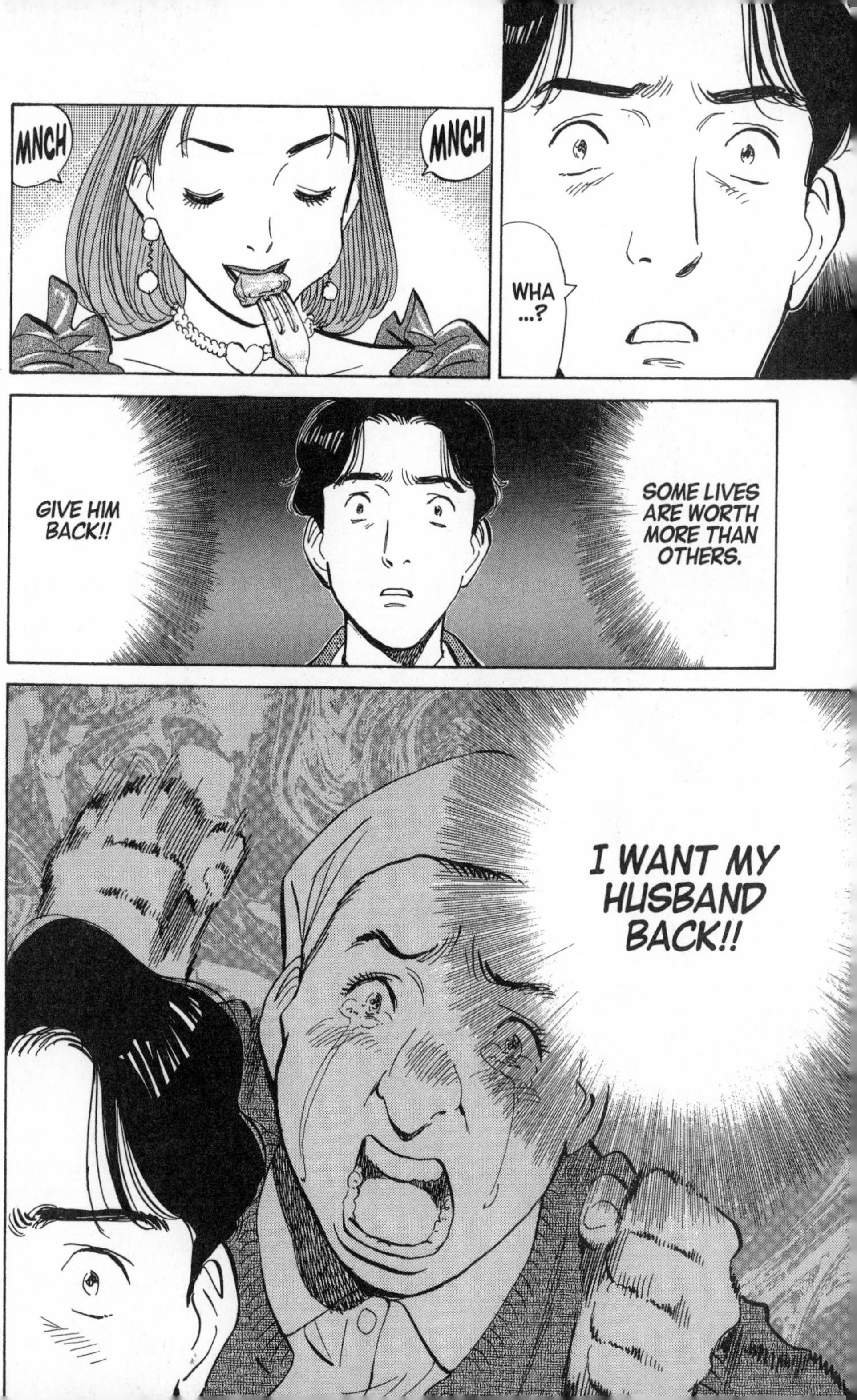
WHA ...?
MNCH
MNCH
SOME LIVES ARE WORTH MORE THAN OTHERS.
GIVE HIM BACK!!
I WANT MY HUSBAND BACK!!

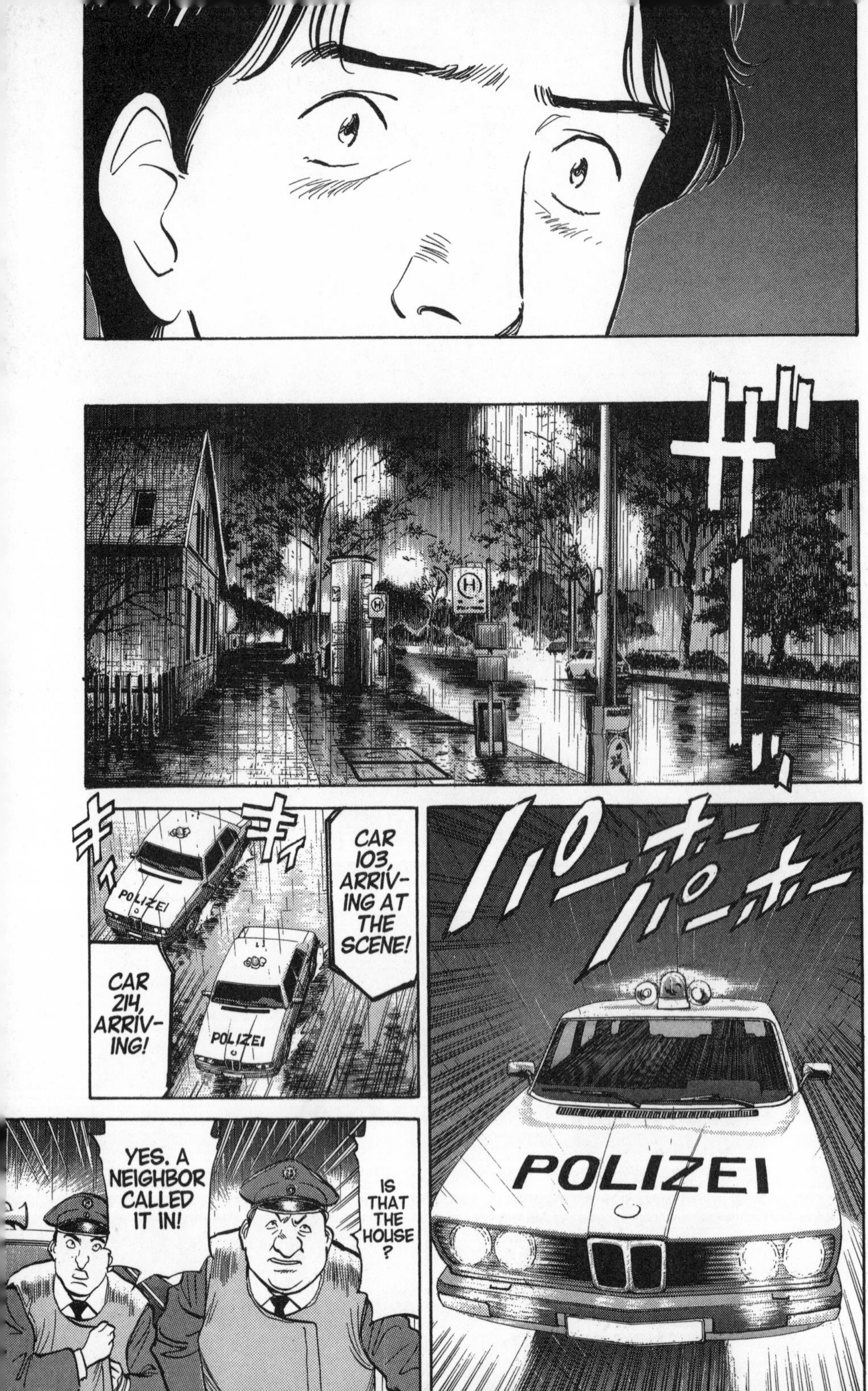
ザザーッ
キィ
キィ
CAR 103, ARRIVING AT THE SCENE!
CAR 214, ARRIVING!
IS THAT THE HOUSE?
YES. A NEIGHBOR CALLED IT IN!
POLIZEI

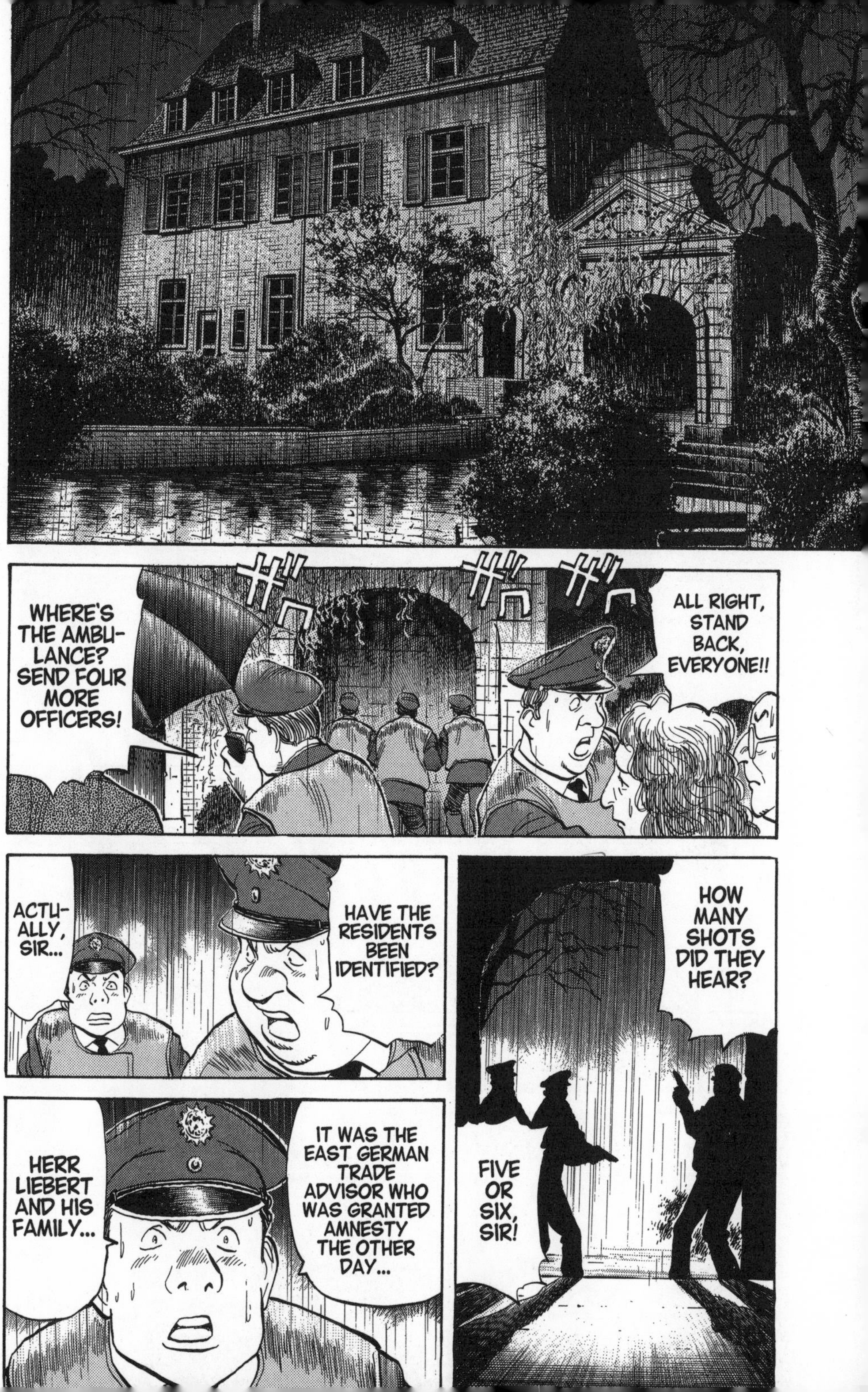
ALL RIGHT, STAND BACK, EVERYONE!!
WHERE'S THE AMBULANCE? SEND FOUR MORE OFFICERS!
HOW MANY SHOTS DID THEY HEAR?
FIVE OR SIX, SIR!
HAVE THE RESIDENTS BEEN IDENTIFIED?
ACTUALLY, SIR...
IT WAS THE EAST GERMAN TRADE ADVISOR WHO WAS GRANTED AMNESTY THE OTHER DAY...
HERR LIEBERT AND HIS FAMILY...

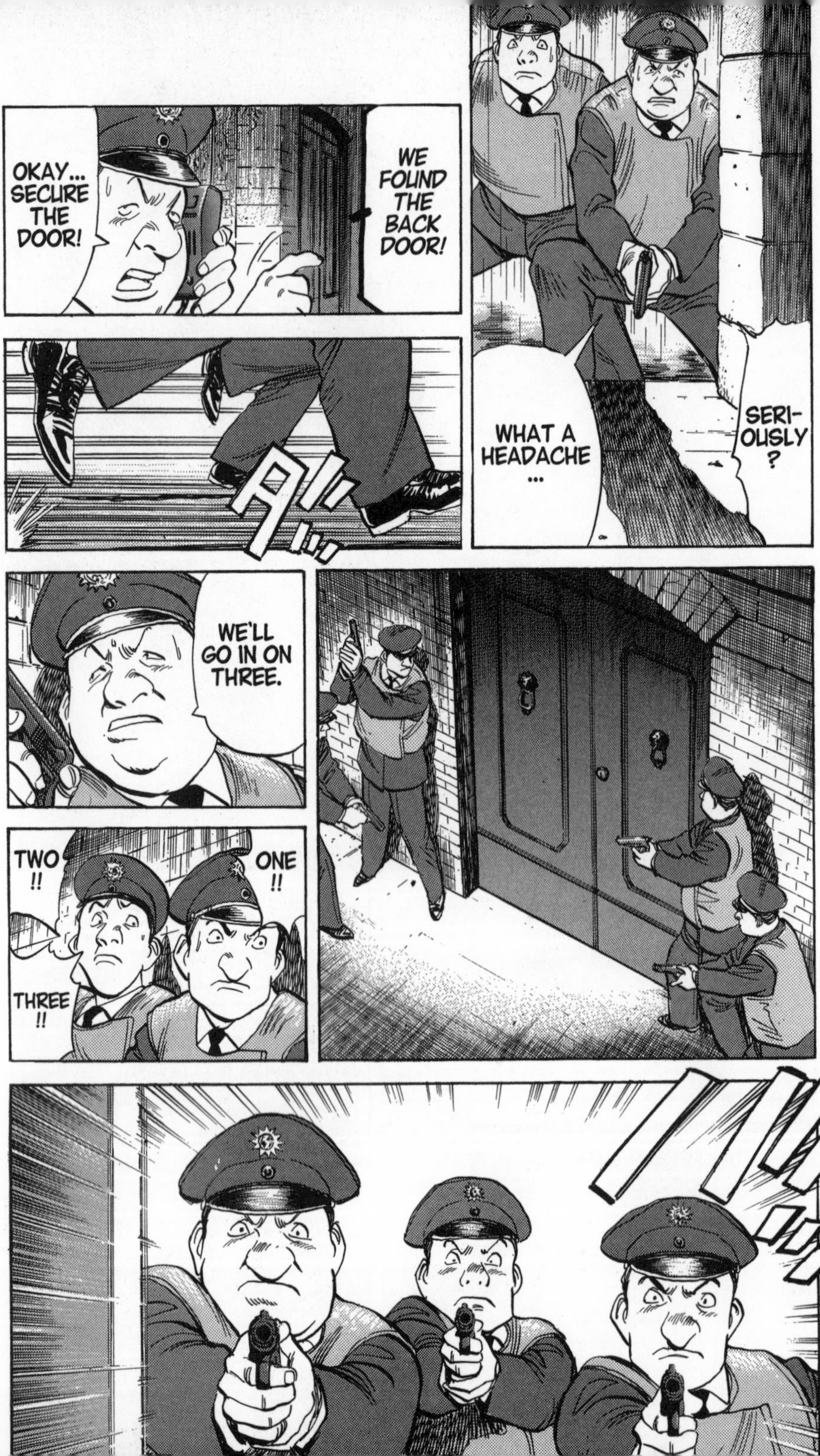
SERI-OUSLY?
WHAT A HEADACHE...
WE FOUND THE BACK DOOR!
OKAY... SECURE THE DOOR!
WE'LL GO IN ON THREE.
ONE!!
TWO!!
THREE!!

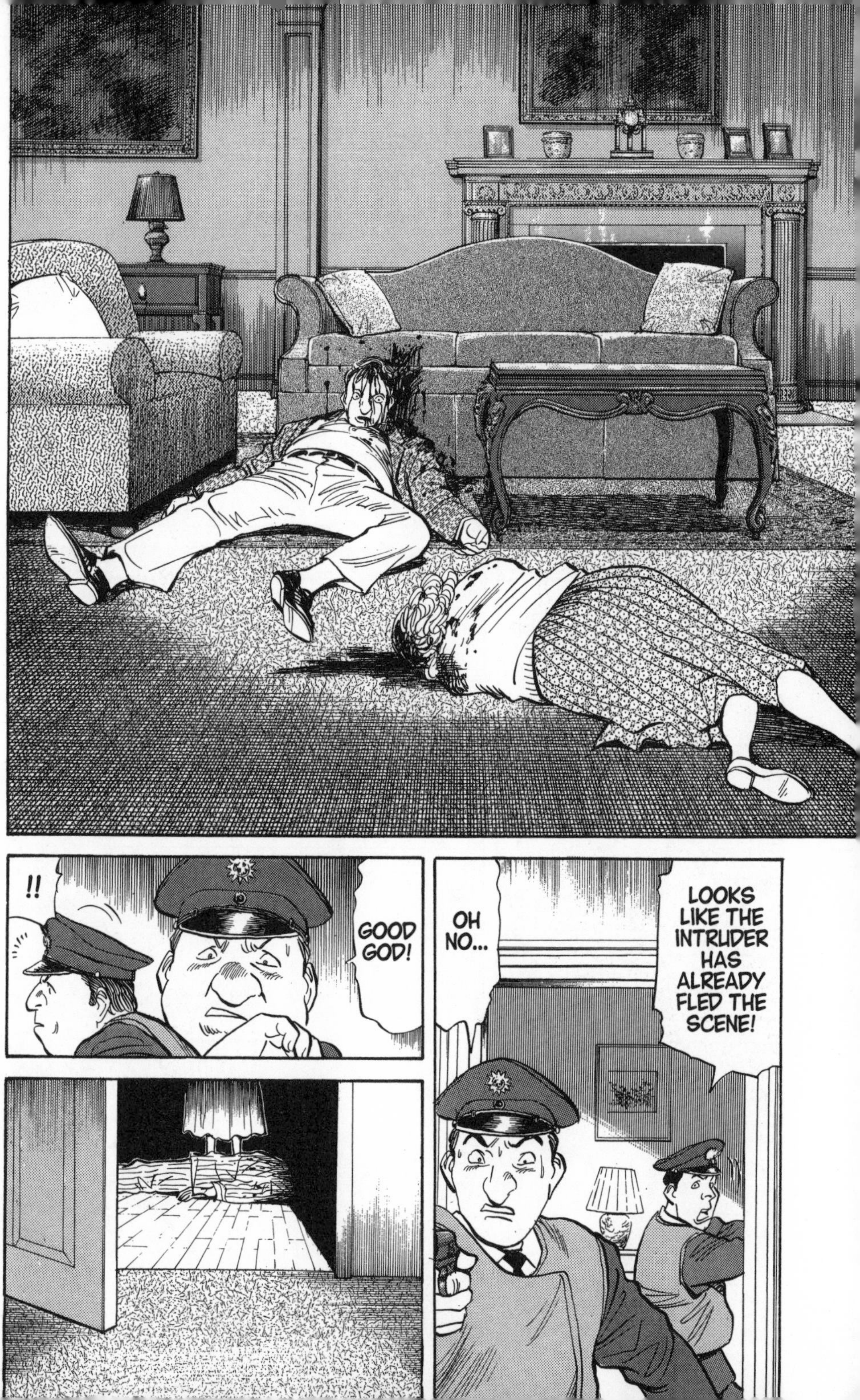
LOOKS LIKE THE INTRUDER HAS ALREADY FLED THE SCENE!
OH NO...
GOOD GOD!
!!

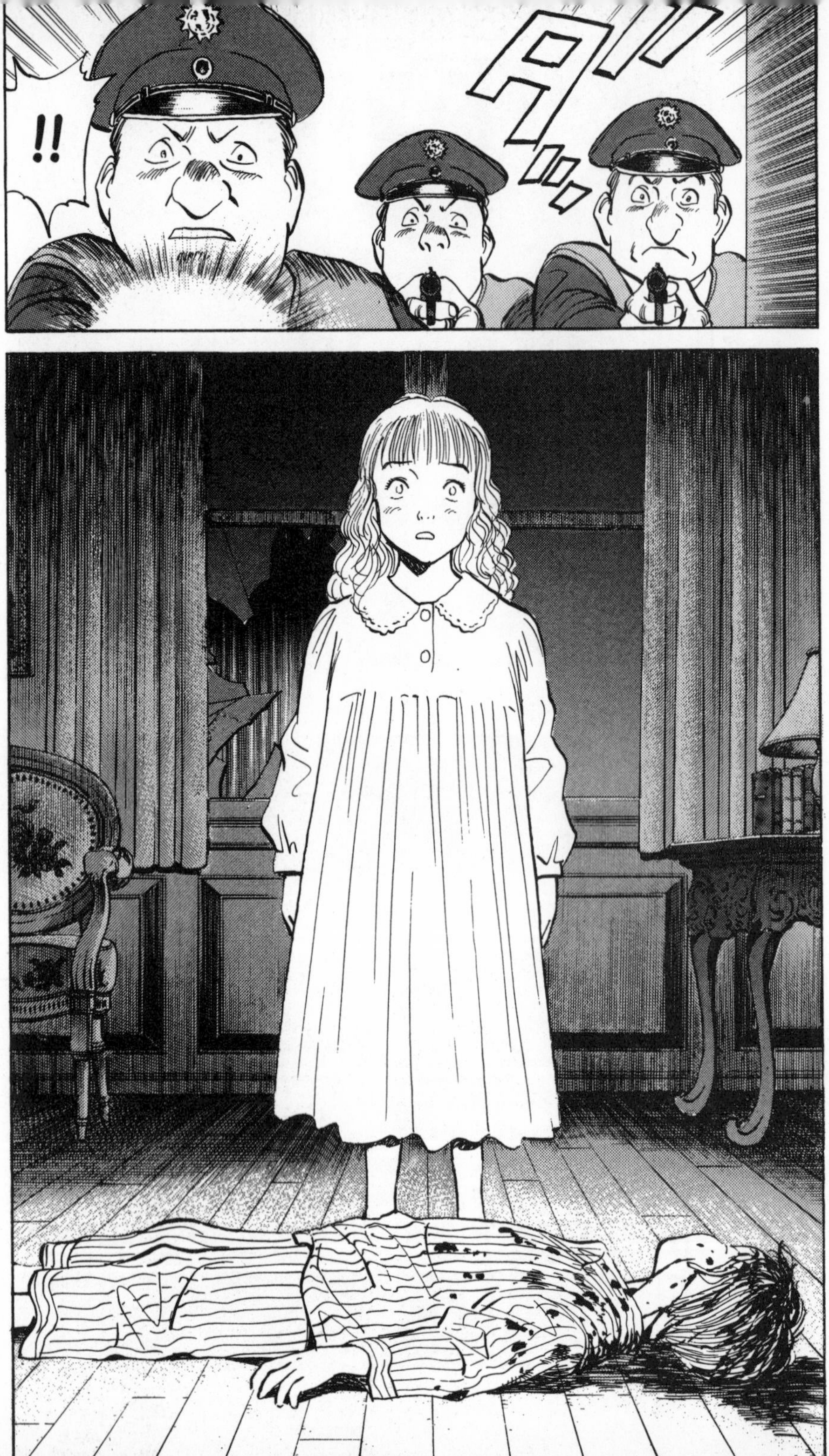
ダッ
!!

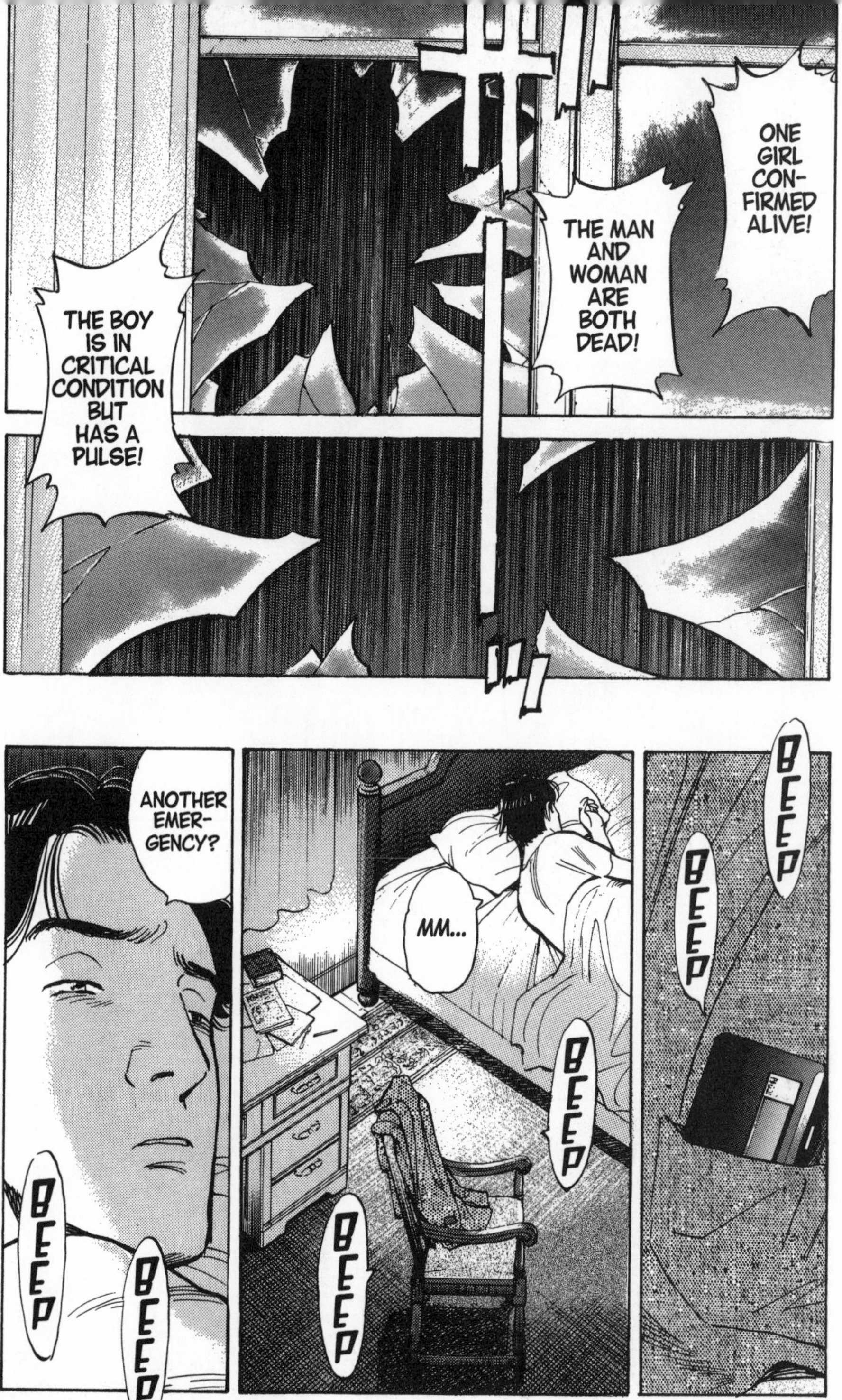
ONE GIRL CONFIRMED ALIVE!
THE MAN AND WOMAN ARE BOTH DEAD!
THE BOY IS IN CRITICAL CONDITION BUT HAS A PULSE!
BEEP
BEEP
BEEP
MM...
BEEP
ANOTHER EMERGENCY?
BEEP
BEEP

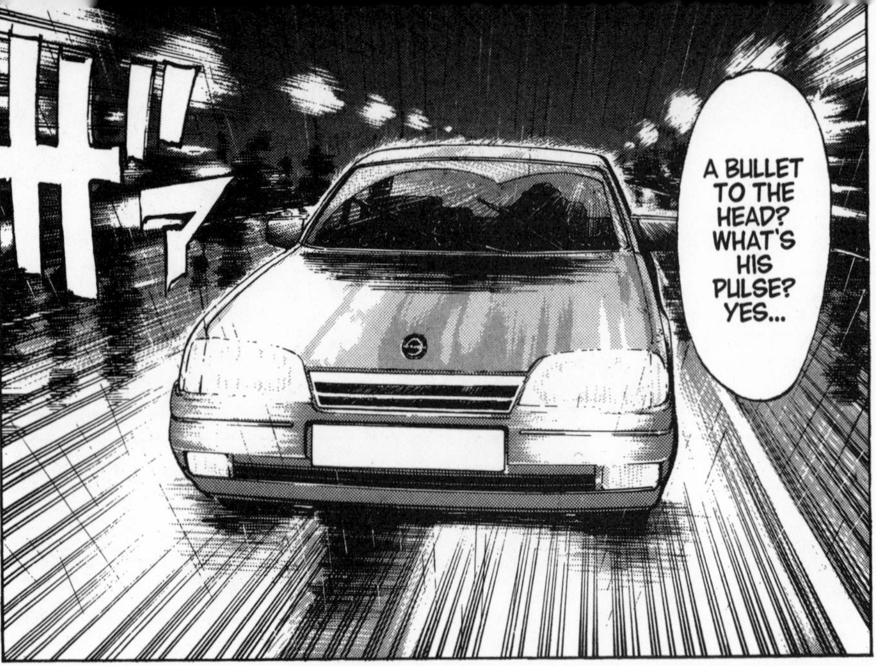
A BULLET TO THE HEAD? WHAT'S HIS PULSE? YES...

Kapitel 2.

Kill

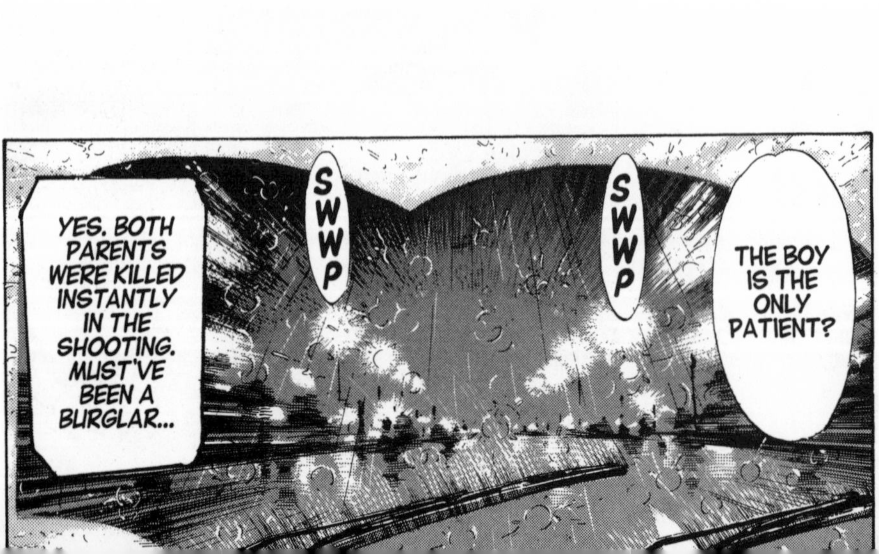
THE BOY IS THE ONLY PATIENT?
SWWP
SWWP
YES. BOTH PARENTS WERE KILLED INSTANTLY IN THE SHOOTING. MUST'VE BEEN A BURGLAR...

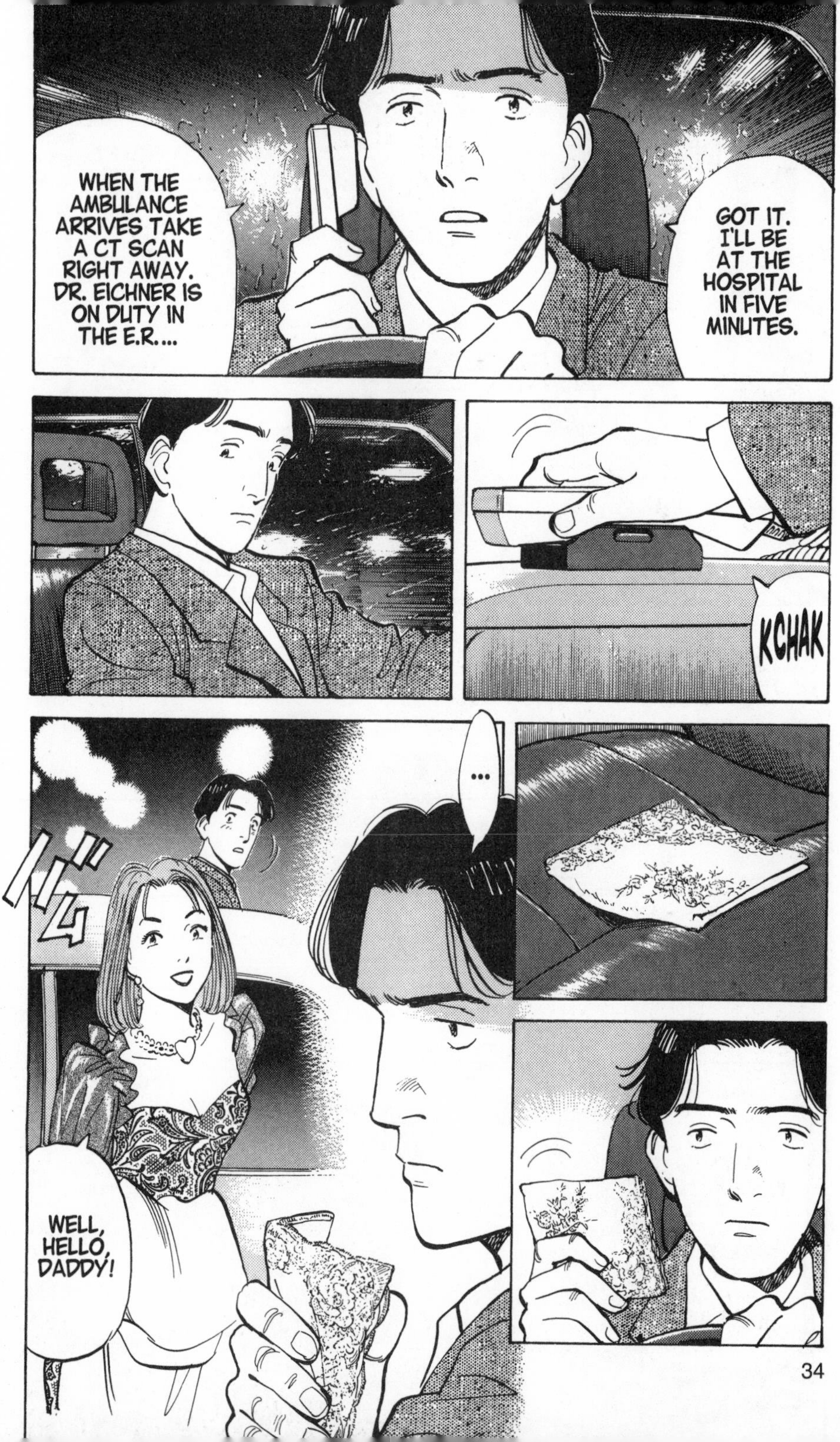
GOT IT. I'LL BE AT THE HOSPITAL IN FIVE MINUTES.
WHEN THE AMBULANCE ARRIVES TAKE A CT SCAN RIGHT AWAY. DR. EICHNER IS ON DUTY IN THE E.R....
KCHAK
...
WELL, HELLO, DADDY!

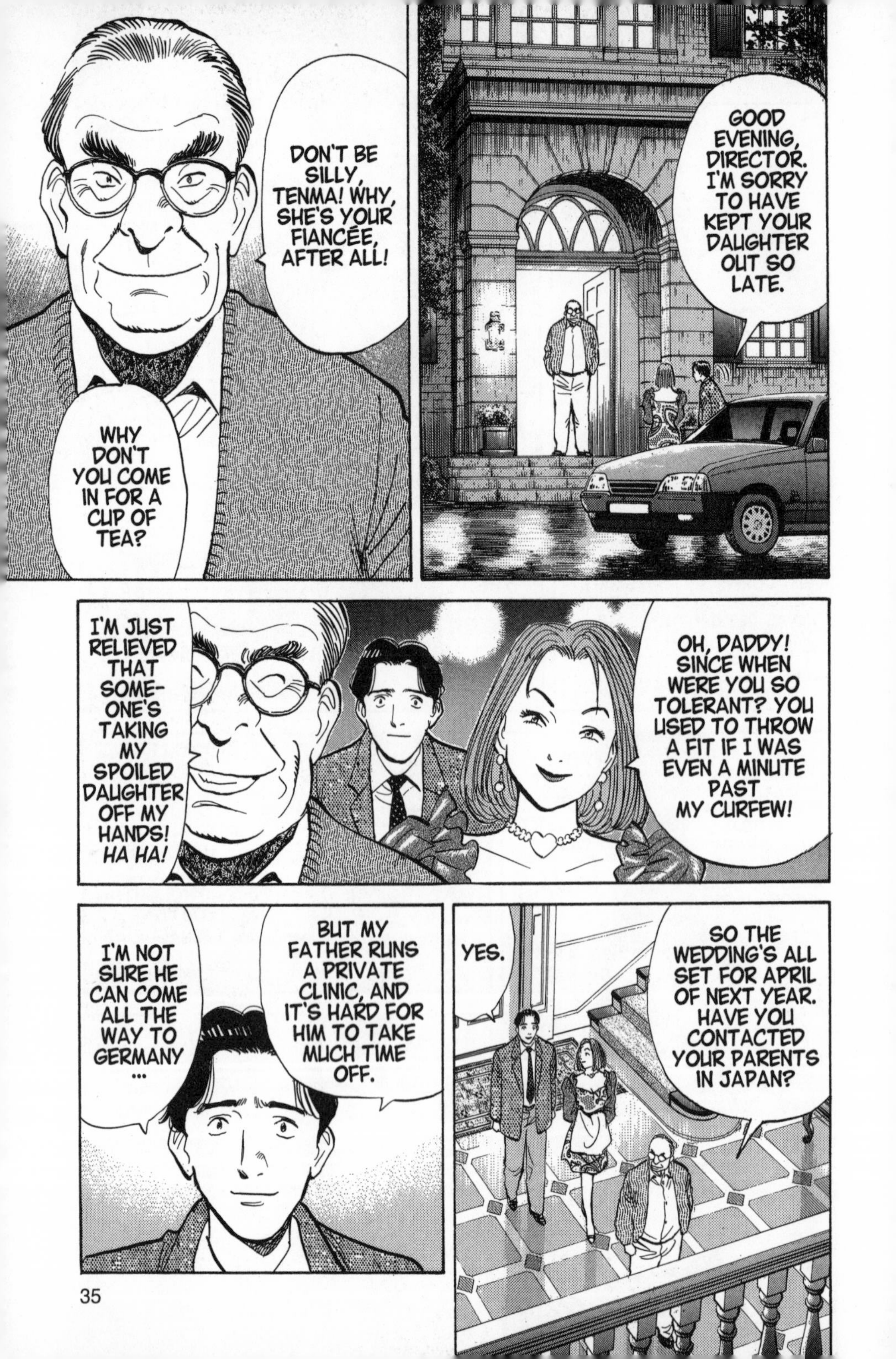
GOOD EVENING, DIRECTOR. I'M SORRY TO HAVE KEPT YOUR DAUGHTER OUT SO LATE.
DON'T BE SILLY, TENMA! WHY, SHE'S YOUR FIANCÉE, AFTER ALL!
WHY DON'T YOU COME IN FOR A CUP OF TEA?
OH, DADDY! SINCE WHEN WERE YOU SO TOLERANT? YOU USED TO THROW A FIT IF I WAS EVEN A MINUTE PAST MY CURFEW!
I'M JUST RELIEVED THAT SOME-ONE'S TAKING MY SPOILED DAUGHTER OFF MY HANDS! HA HA!
SO THE WEDDING'S ALL SET FOR APRIL OF NEXT YEAR. HAVE YOU CONTACTED YOUR PARENTS IN JAPAN?
YES.
BUT MY FATHER RUNS A PRIVATE CLINIC, AND IT'S HARD FOR HIM TO TAKE MUCH TIME OFF.
I'M NOT SURE HE CAN COME ALL THE WAY TO GERMANY ...

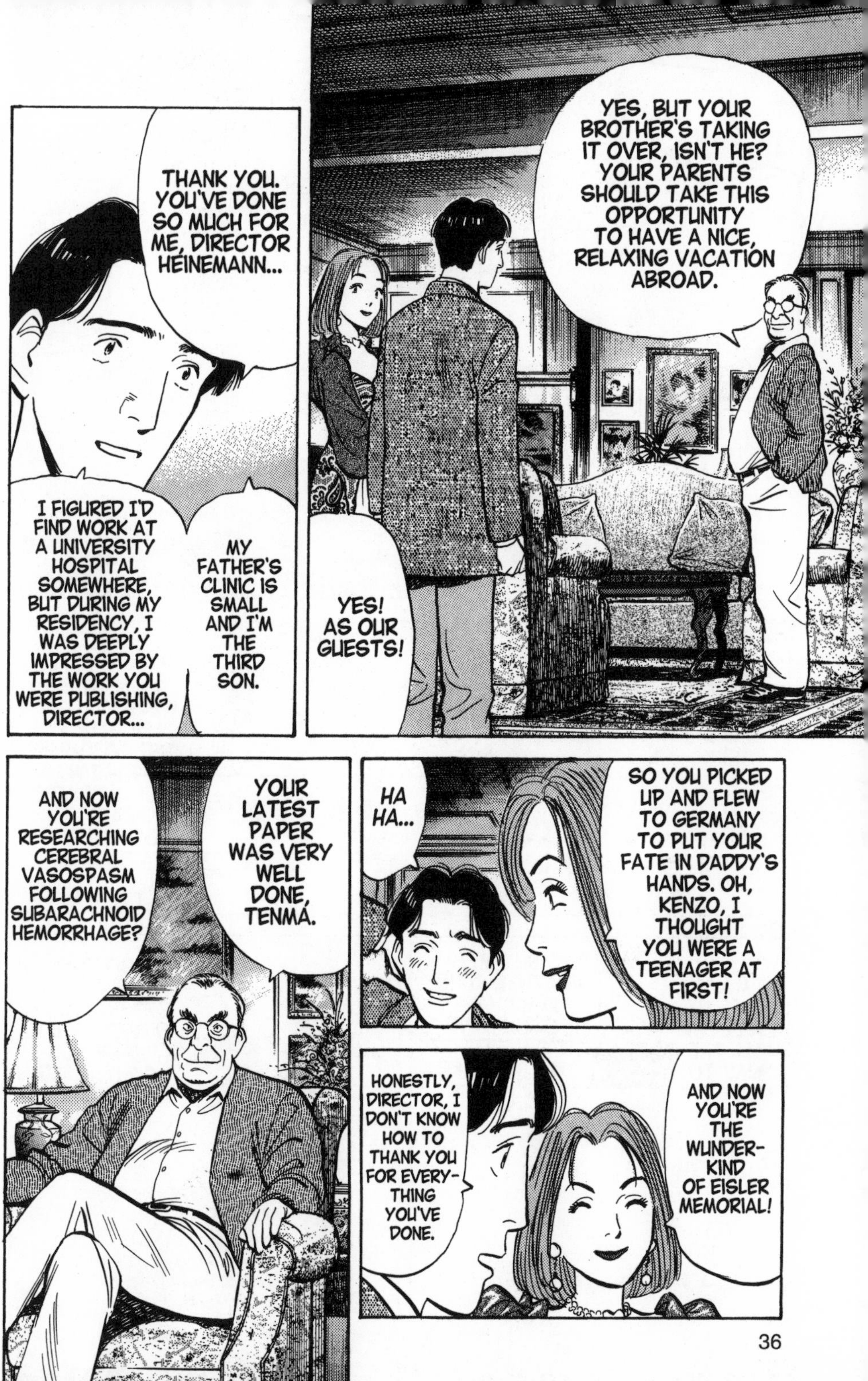
YES, BUT YOUR BROTHER'S TAKING IT OVER, ISN'T HE? YOUR PARENTS SHOULD TAKE THIS OPPORTUNITY TO HAVE A NICE, RELAXING VACATION ABROAD.
YES! AS OUR GUESTS!
THANK YOU. YOU'VE DONE SO MUCH FOR ME, DIRECTOR HEINEMANN...
MY FATHER'S CLINIC IS SMALL AND I'M THE THIRD SON.
I FIGURED I'D FIND WORK AT A UNIVERSITY HOSPITAL SOMEWHERE, BUT DURING MY RESIDENCY, I WAS DEEPLY IMPRESSED BY THE WORK YOU WERE PUBLISHING, DIRECTOR...
SO YOU PICKED UP AND FLEW TO GERMANY TO PUT YOUR FATE IN DADDY'S HANDS. OH, KENZO, I THOUGHT YOU WERE A TEENAGER AT FIRST!
HA HA...
AND NOW YOU'RE THE WUNDER-KIND OF EISLER MEMORIAL!
HONESTLY, DIRECTOR, I DON'T KNOW HOW TO THANK YOU FOR EVERY-THING YOU'VE DONE.
YOUR LATEST PAPER WAS VERY WELL DONE, TENMA.
AND NOW YOU'RE RESEARCHING CEREBRAL VASOSPASM FOLLOWING SUBARACHNOID HEMORRHAGE?

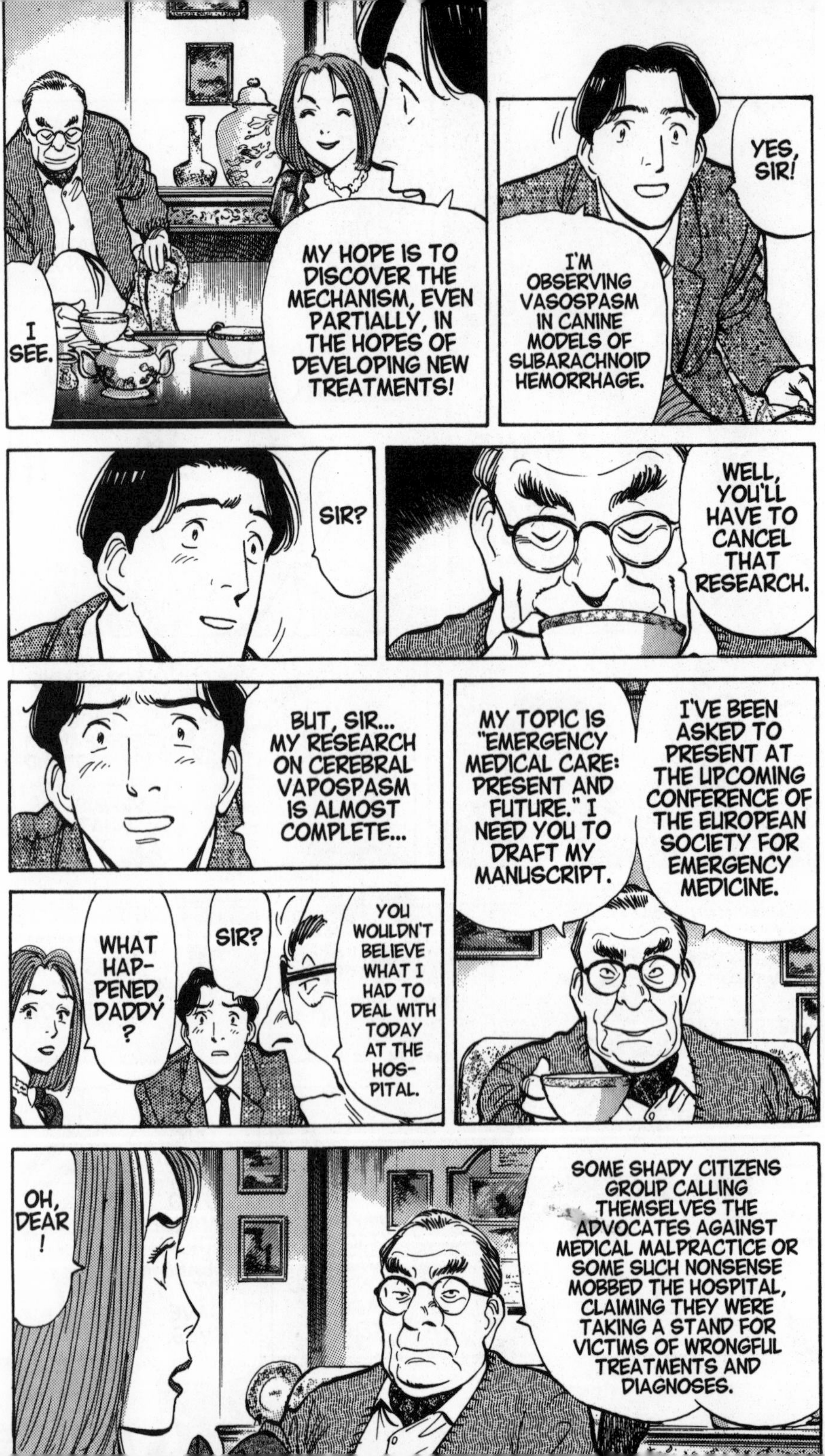
YES, SIR!
I'M OBSERVING VASOSPASM IN CANINE MODELS OF SUBARACHNOID HEMORRHAGE.
MY HOPE IS TO DISCOVER THE MECHANISM, EVEN PARTIALLY, IN THE HOPES OF DEVELOPING NEW TREATMENTS!
I SEE.
WELL, YOU'LL HAVE TO CANCEL THAT RESEARCH.
SIR?
I'VE BEEN ASKED TO PRESENT AT THE UPCOMING CONFERENCE OF THE EUROPEAN SOCIETY FOR EMERGENCY MEDICINE.
MY TOPIC IS "EMERGENCY MEDICAL CARE: PRESENT AND FUTURE." I NEED YOU TO DRAFT MY MANUSCRIPT.
BUT, SIR... MY RESEARCH ON CEREBRAL VAPOSPASM IS ALMOST COMPLETE...
YOU WOULDN'T BELIEVE WHAT I HAD TO DEAL WITH TODAY AT THE HOS-PITAL.
SIR?
WHAT HAP-PENED, DADDY?
SOME SHADY CITIZENS GROUP CALLING THEMSELVES THE ADVOCATES AGAINST MEDICAL MALPRACTICE OR SOME SUCH NONSENSE MOBBED THE HOSPITAL, CLAIMING THEY WERE TAKING A STAND FOR VICTIMS OF WRONGFUL TREATMENTS AND DIAGNOSES.
OH, DEAR!

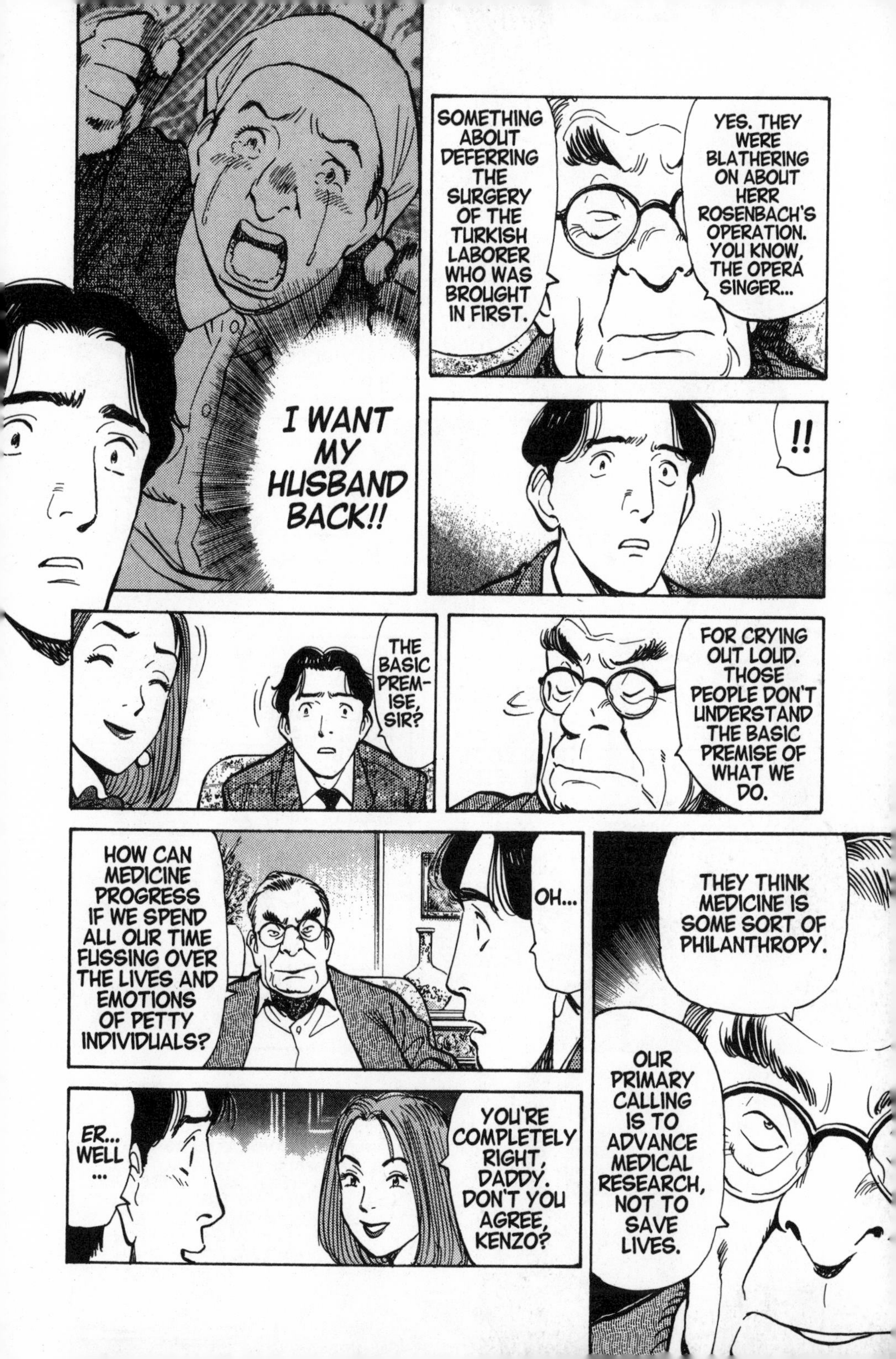
YES. THEY WERE BLATHERING ON ABOUT HERR ROSENBACH'S OPERATION. YOU KNOW, THE OPERA SINGER...
SOMETHING ABOUT DEFERRING THE SURGERY OF THE TURKISH LABORER WHO WAS BROUGHT IN FIRST.
!!
I WANT MY HUSBAND BACK!!
FOR CRYING OUT LOUD. THOSE PEOPLE DON'T UNDERSTAND THE BASIC PREMISE OF WHAT WE DO.
THE BASIC PREM-ISE, SIR?
THEY THINK MEDICINE IS SOME SORT OF PHILANTHROPY.
OUR PRIMARY CALLING IS TO ADVANCE MEDICAL RESEARCH, NOT TO SAVE LIVES.
HOW CAN MEDICINE PROGRESS IF WE SPEND ALL OUR TIME FUSSING OVER THE LIVES AND EMOTIONS OF PETTY INDIVIDUALS?
OH...
YOU'RE COMPLETELY RIGHT, DADDY. DON'T YOU AGREE, KENZO?
ER... WELL ...

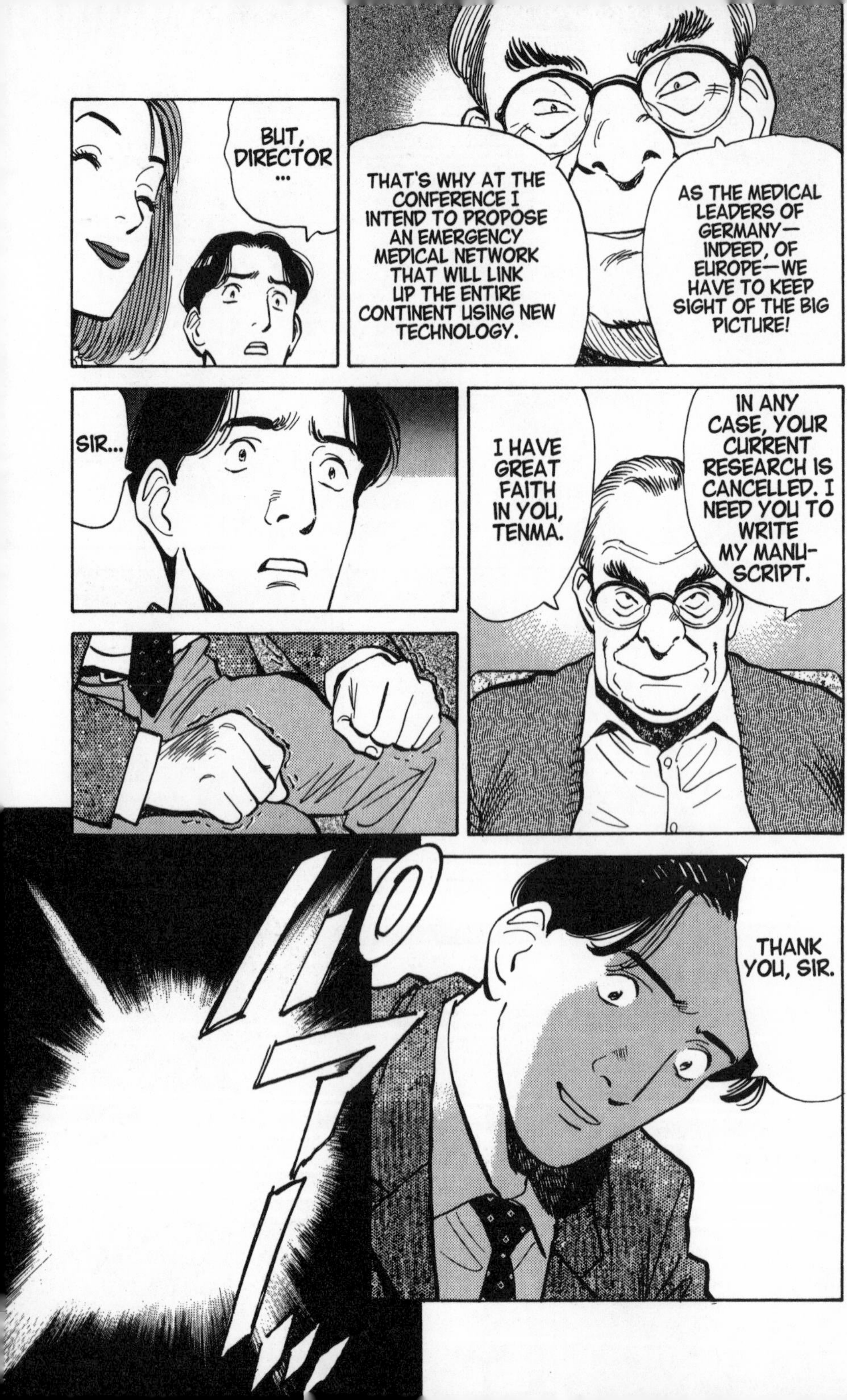
AS THE MEDICAL LEADERS OF GERMANY—INDEED, OF EUROPE—WE HAVE TO KEEP SIGHT OF THE BIG PICTURE!
THAT'S WHY AT THE CONFERENCE I INTEND TO PROPOSE AN EMERGENCY MEDICAL NETWORK THAT WILL LINK UP THE ENTIRE CONTINENT USING NEW TECHNOLOGY.
BUT, DIRECTOR ...
IN ANY CASE, YOUR CURRENT RESEARCH IS CANCELLED. I NEED YOU TO WRITE MY MANU-SCRIPT.
I HAVE GREAT FAITH IN YOU, TENMA.
SIR...
THANK YOU, SIR.

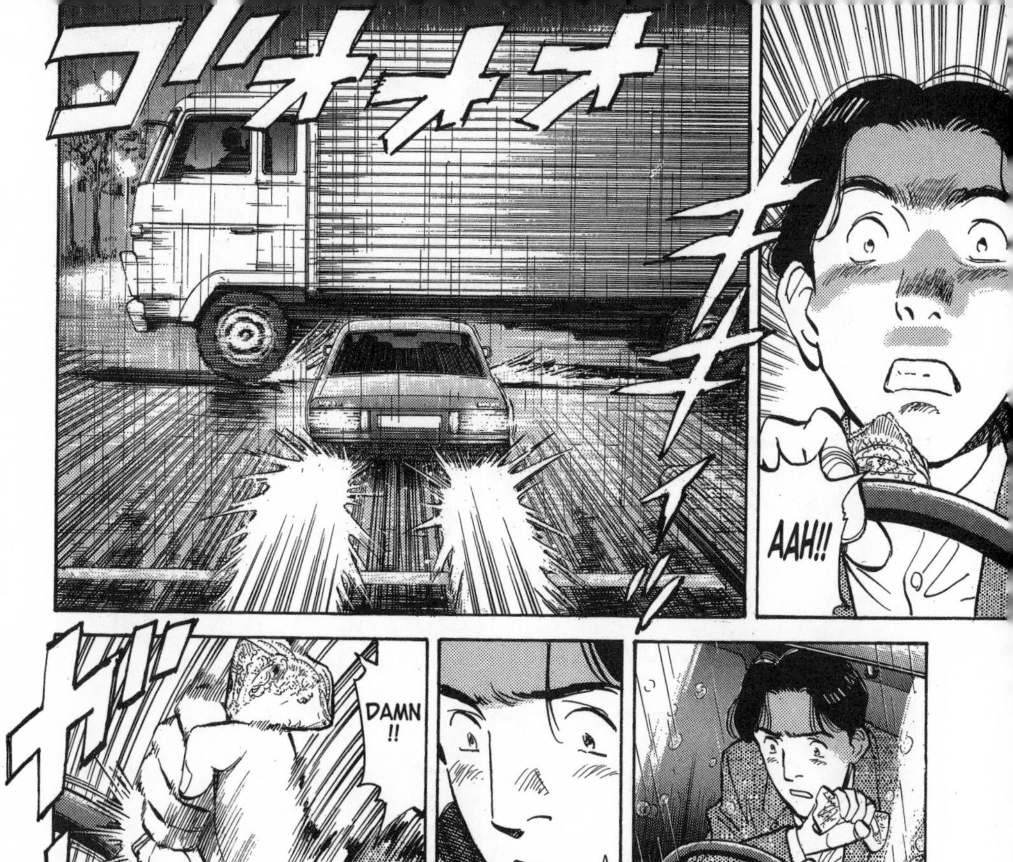
AAH!!
...
DAMN !!

8

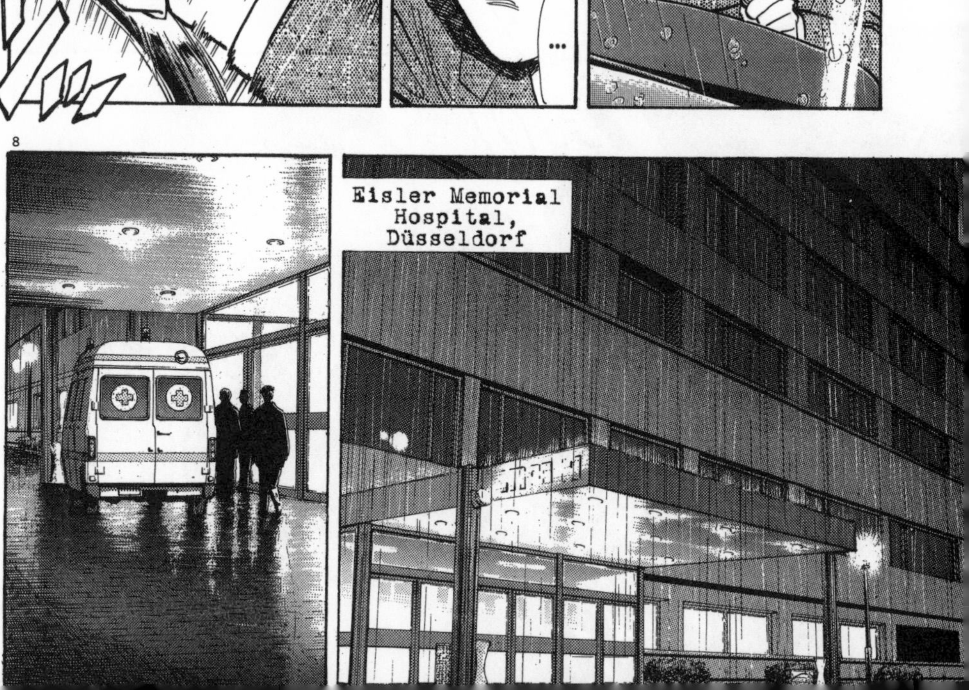
Eisler Memorial Hospital, Düsseldorf

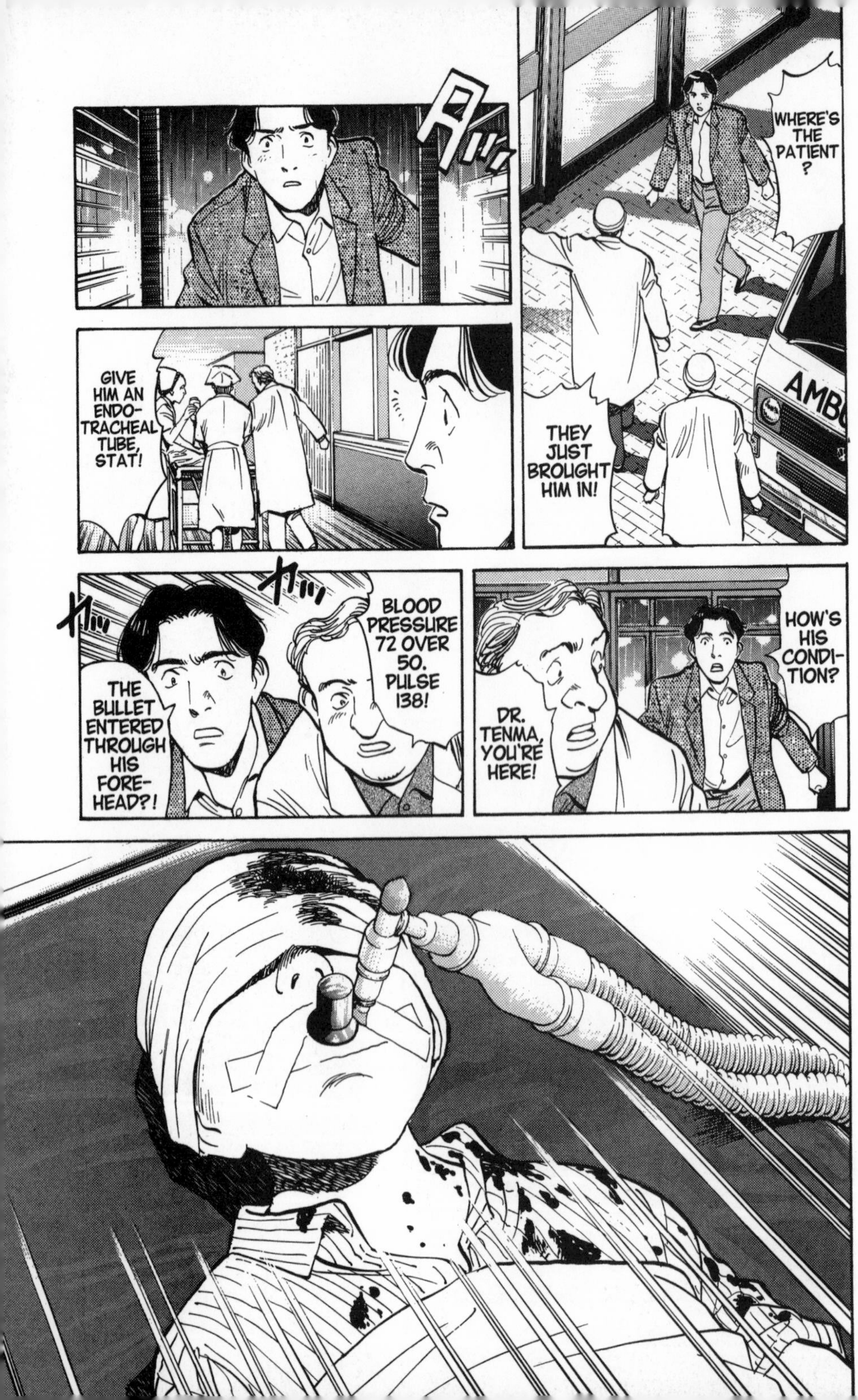
WHERE'S THE PATIENT ?
THEY JUST BROUGHT HIM IN!
GIVE HIM AN ENDO-TRACHEAL TUBE, STAT!
HOW'S HIS CONDITION?
DR. TENMA, YOU'RE HERE!
BLOOD PRESSURE 72 OVER 50. PULSE 138!
THE BULLET ENTERED THROUGH HIS FORE-HEAD?!

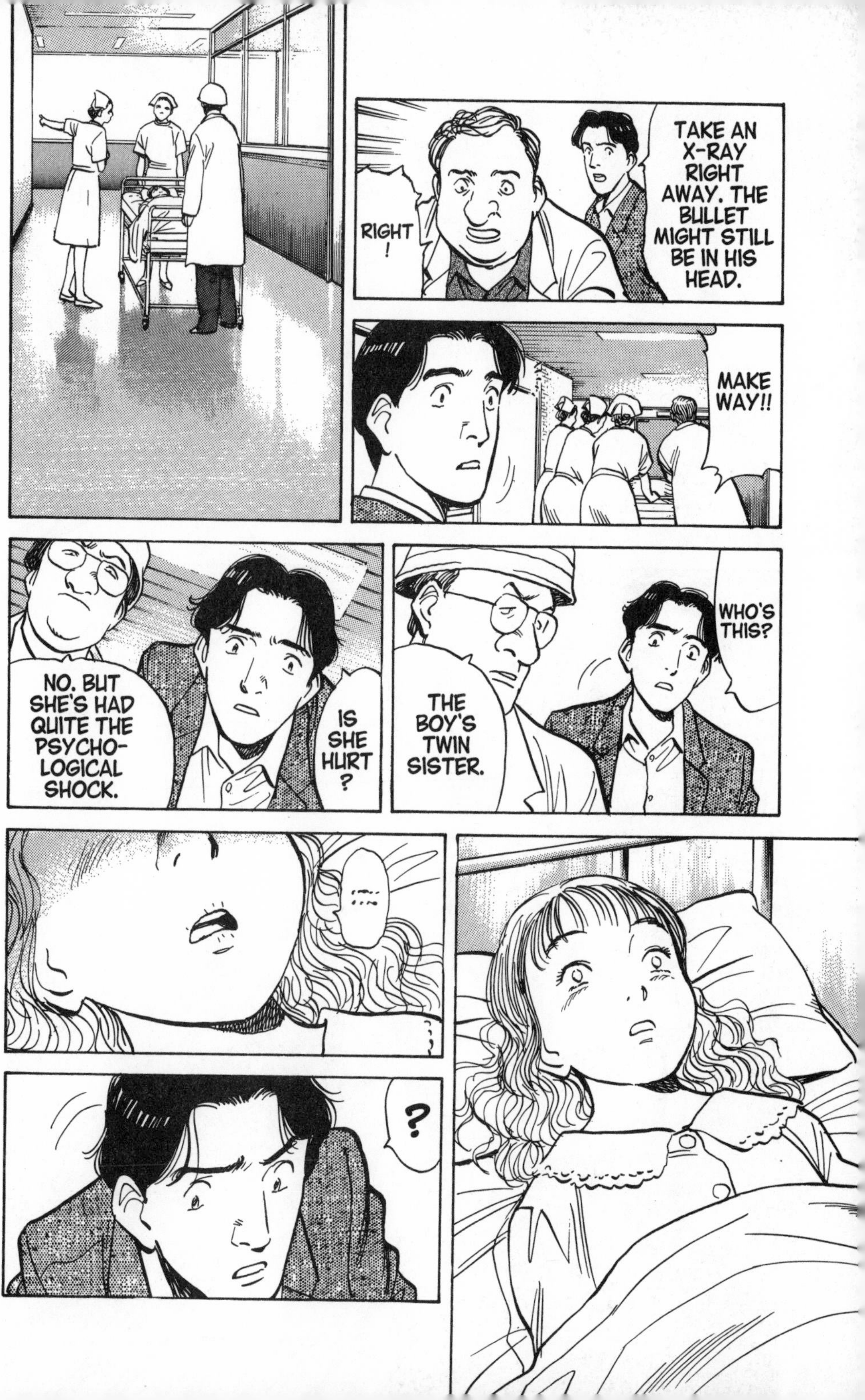
TAKE AN X-RAY RIGHT AWAY. THE BULLET MIGHT STILL BE IN HIS HEAD.
RIGHT!
MAKE WAY!!
WHO'S THIS?
THE BOY'S TWIN SISTER.
IS SHE HURT?
NO. BUT SHE'S HAD QUITE THE PSYCHOLOGICAL SHOCK.
......
?

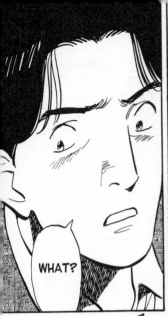

KILL...
WHAT?
DR. TENMA, THE CT SCAN AND X-RAYS ARE READY IN THE VIEWING ROOM.
RIGHT.
OKAY. LET'S HAVE A LOOK.

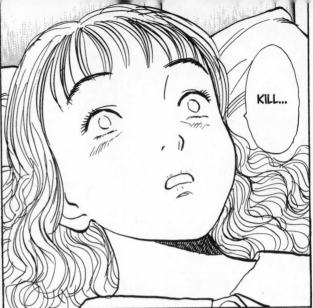

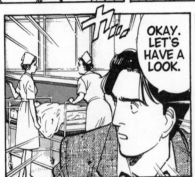

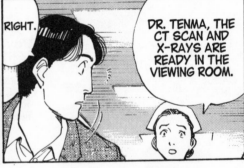

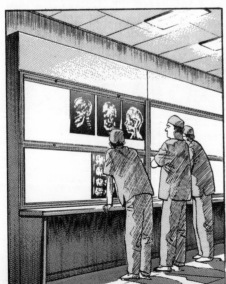

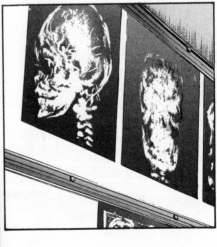

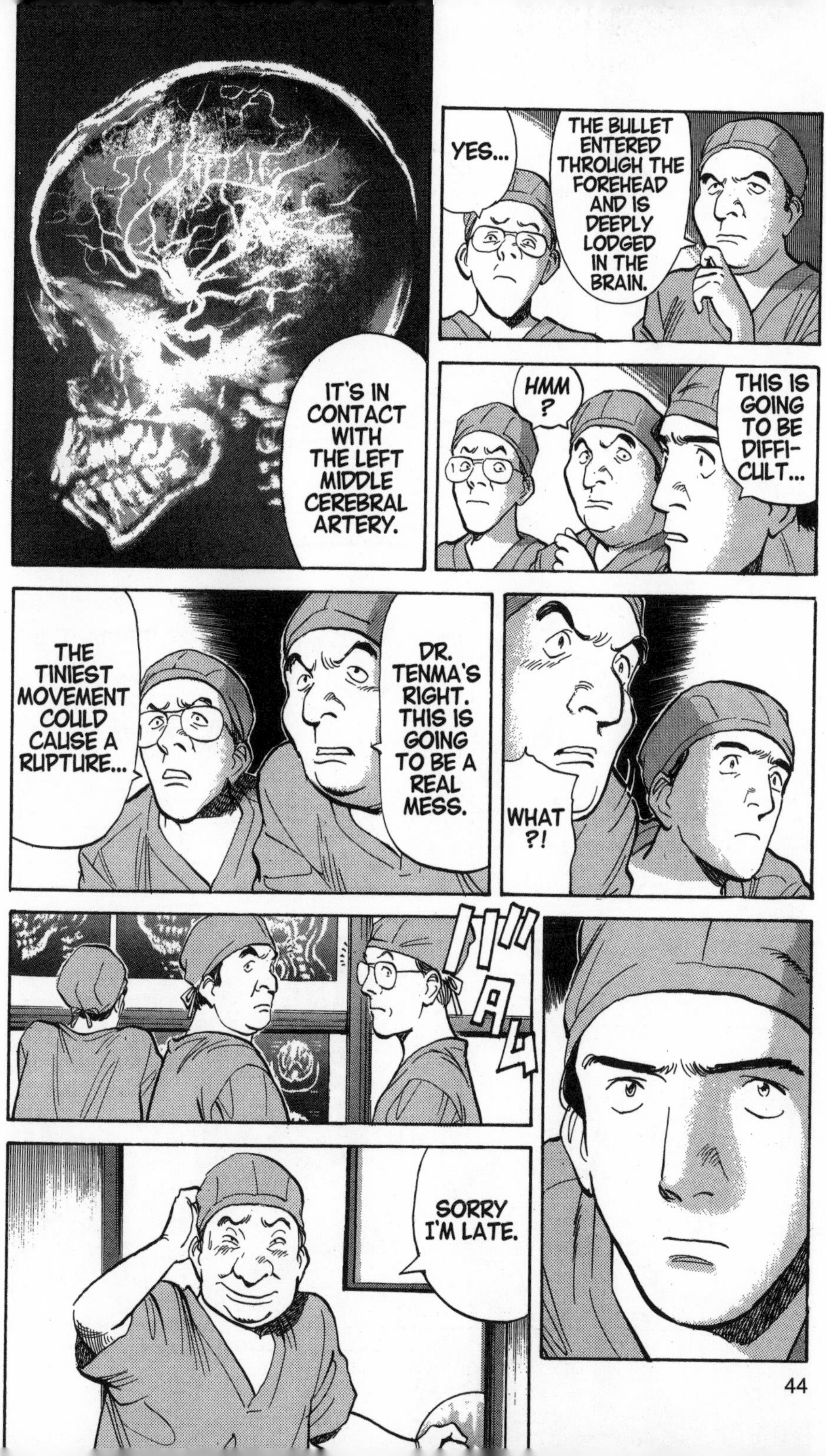
THE BULLET ENTERED THROUGH THE FOREHEAD AND IS DEEPLY LODGED IN THE BRAIN.
YES...
THIS IS GOING TO BE DIFFICULT...
HMM?
IT'S IN CONTACT WITH THE LEFT MIDDLE CEREBRAL ARTERY.
WHAT?!
DR. TENMA'S RIGHT. THIS IS GOING TO BE A REAL MESS.
THE TINIEST MOVEMENT COULD CAUSE A RUPTURE...
SORRY I'M LATE.

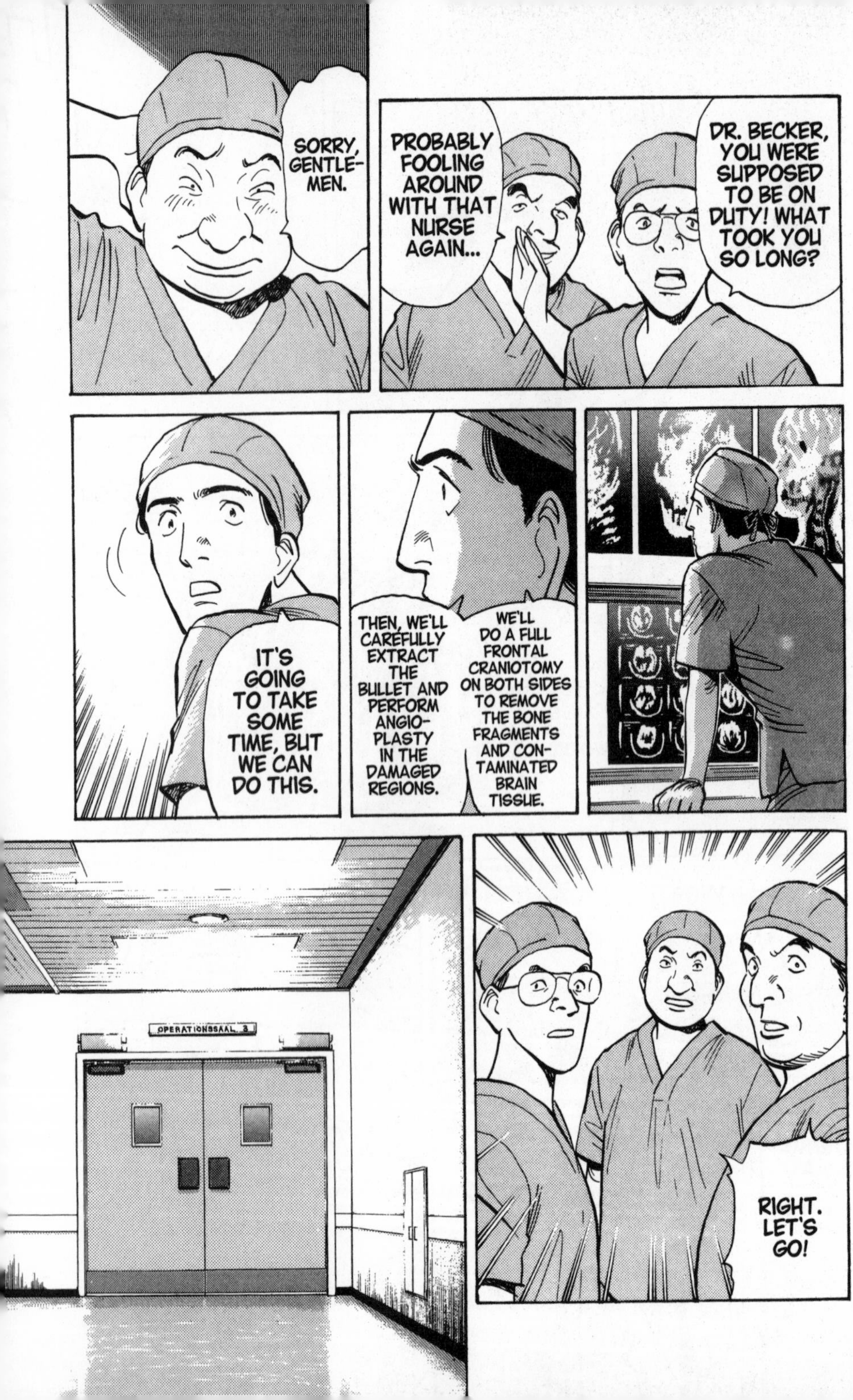
DR. BECKER, YOU WERE SUPPOSED TO BE ON DUTY! WHAT TOOK YOU SO LONG?
PROBABLY FOOLING AROUND WITH THAT NURSE AGAIN...
SORRY, GENTLE-MEN.
WE'LL DO A FULL FRONTAL CRANIOTOMY ON BOTH SIDES TO REMOVE THE BONE FRAGMENTS AND CON-TAMINATED BRAIN TISSUE.
THEN, WE'LL CAREFULLY EXTRACT THE BULLET AND PERFORM ANGIO-PLASTY IN THE DAMAGED REGIONS.
IT'S GOING TO TAKE SOME TIME, BUT WE CAN DO THIS.
RIGHT. LET'S GO!
OPERATIONSSAAL 3

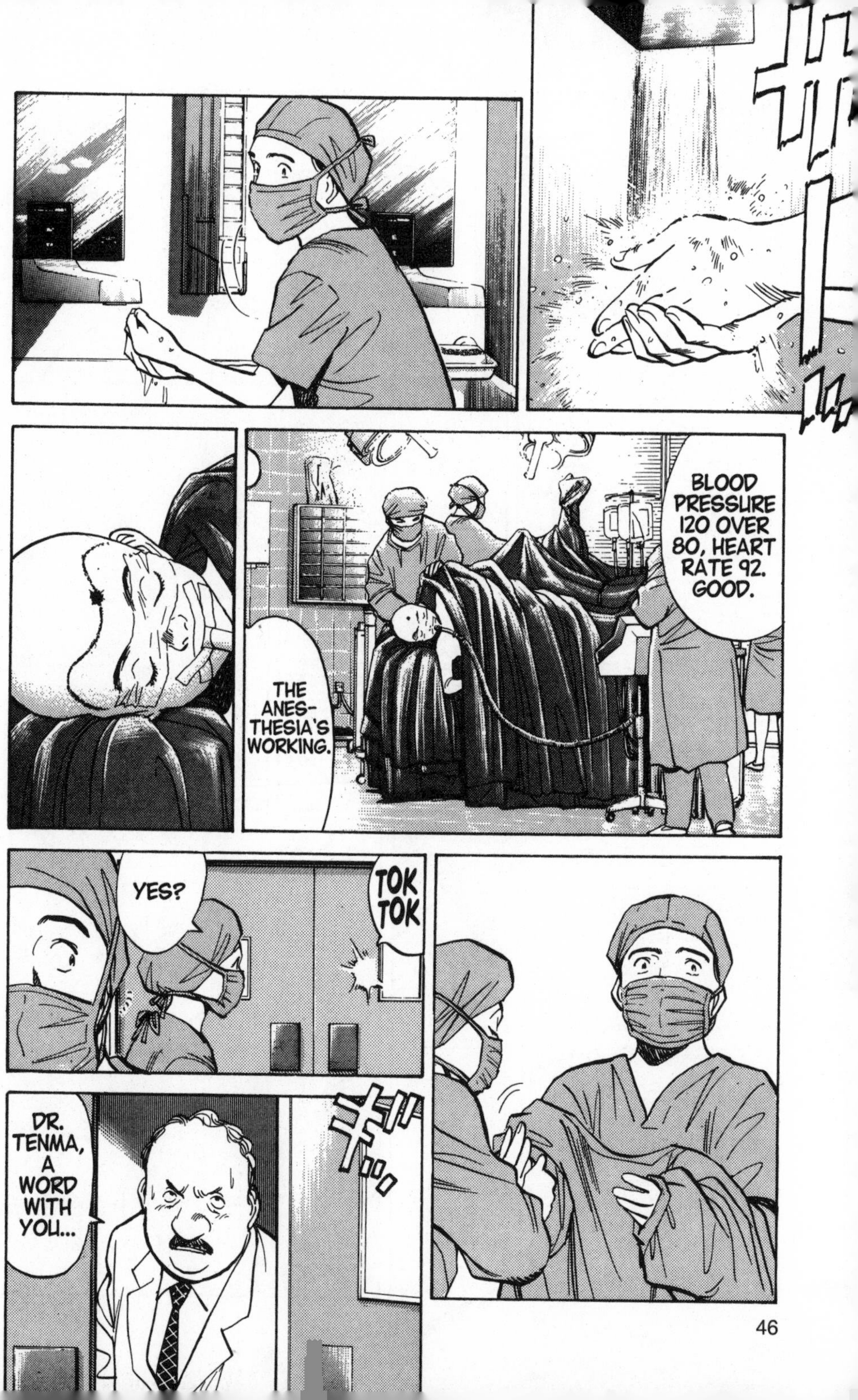
BLOOD PRESSURE 120 OVER 80, HEART RATE 92. GOOD.
THE ANES-THESIA'S WORKING.
TOK TOK
YES?
DR. TENMA, A WORD WITH YOU...

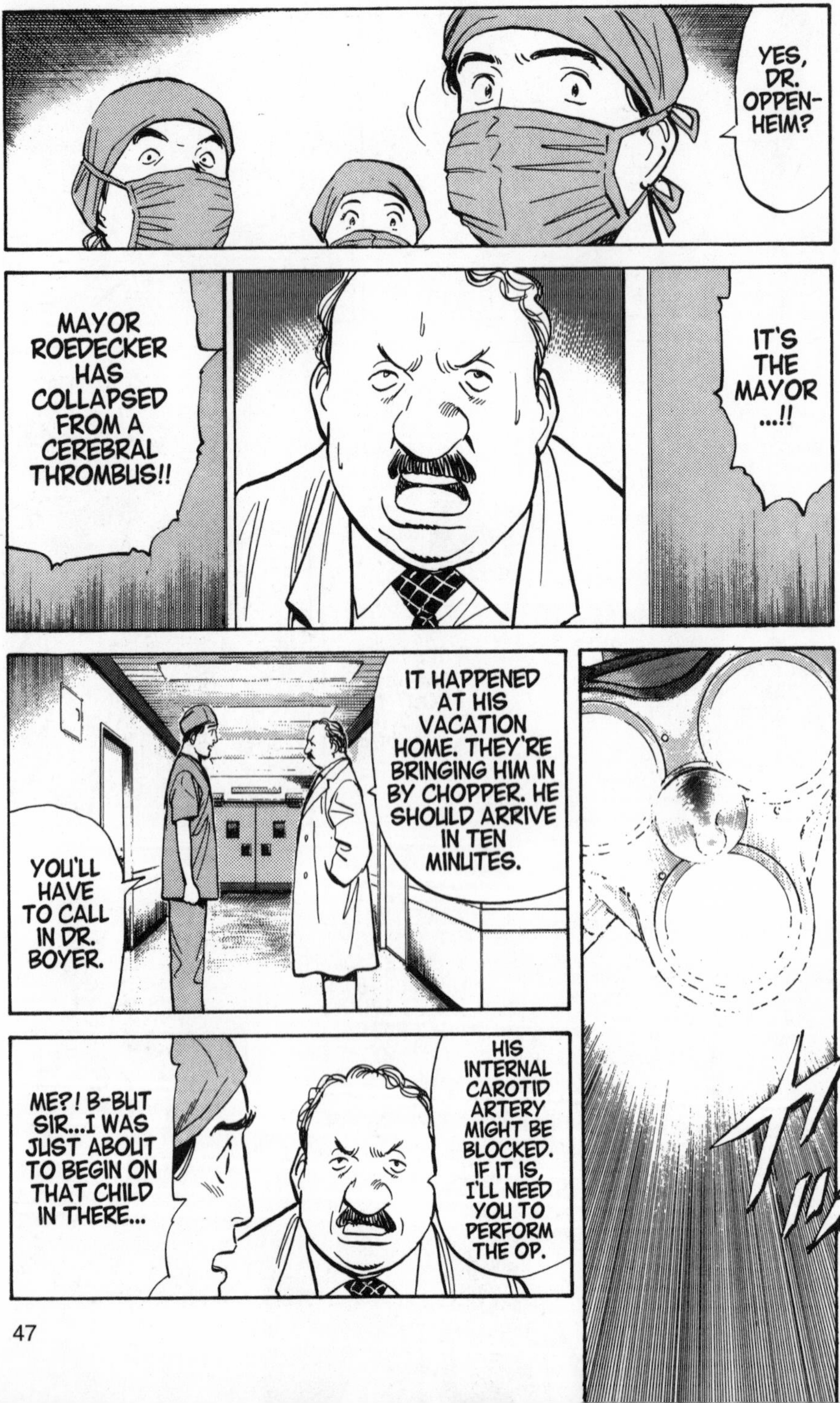
YES, DR. OPPEN-HEIM?
IT'S THE MAYOR ...!!
MAYOR ROEDECKER HAS COLLAPSED FROM A CEREBRAL THROMBUS!!
IT HAPPENED AT HIS VACATION HOME. THEY'RE BRINGING HIM IN BY CHOPPER. HE SHOULD ARRIVE IN TEN MINUTES.
YOU'LL HAVE TO CALL IN DR. BOYER.
HIS INTERNAL CAROTID ARTERY MIGHT BE BLOCKED. IF IT IS, I'LL NEED YOU TO PERFORM THE OP.
ME?! B-BUT SIR...I WAS JUST ABOUT TO BEGIN ON THAT CHILD IN THERE...

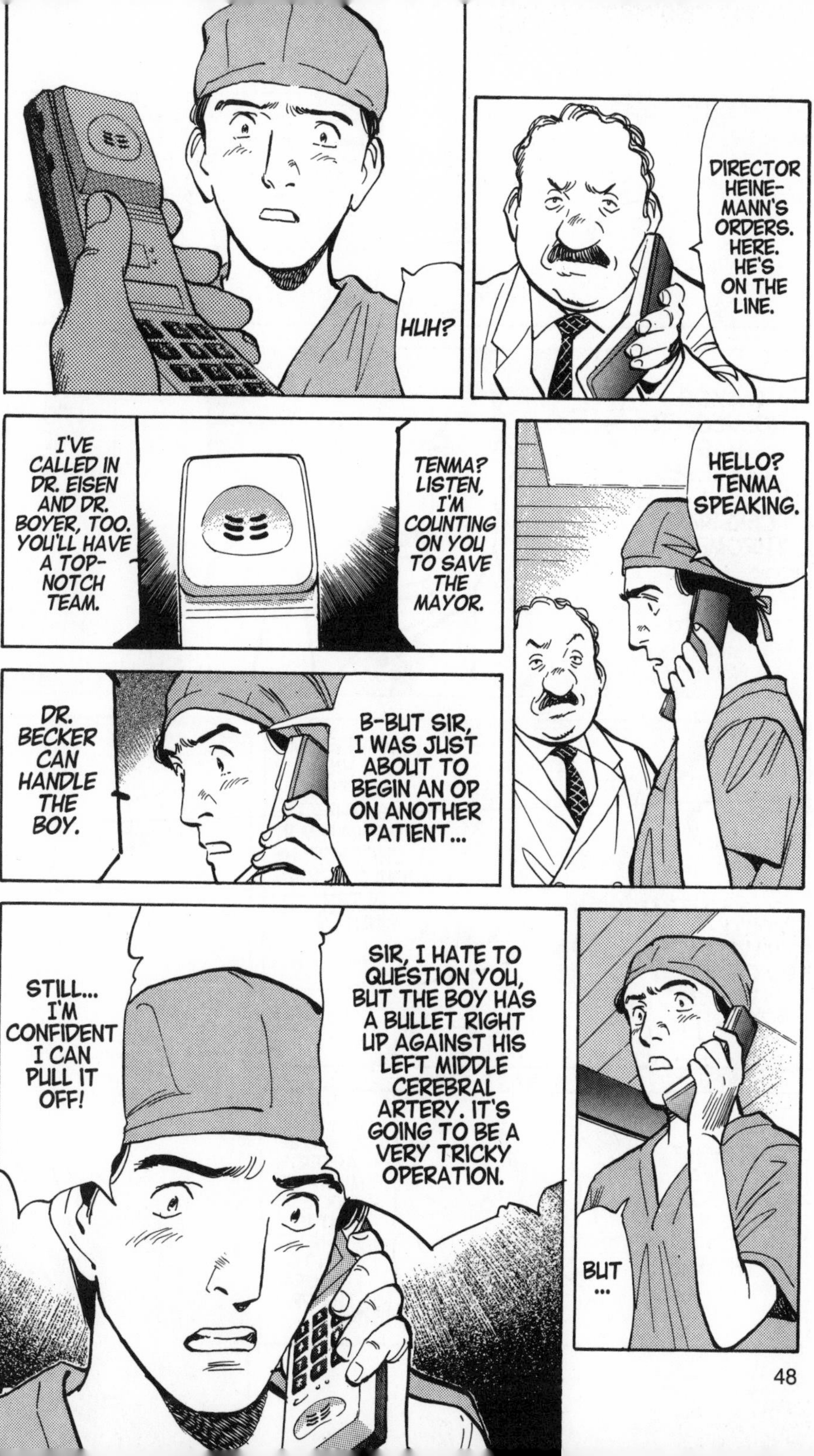
DIRECTOR HEINEMANN'S ORDERS. HERE. HE'S ON THE LINE.
HUH?
HELLO? TENMA SPEAKING.
TENMA? LISTEN, I'M COUNTING ON YOU TO SAVE THE MAYOR.
I'VE CALLED IN DR. EISEN AND DR. BOYER, TOO. YOU'LL HAVE A TOP-NOTCH TEAM.
B-BUT SIR, I WAS JUST ABOUT TO BEGIN AN OP ON ANOTHER PATIENT...
DR. BECKER CAN HANDLE THE BOY.
BUT...
SIR, I HATE TO QUESTION YOU, BUT THE BOY HAS A BULLET RIGHT UP AGAINST HIS LEFT MIDDLE CEREBRAL ARTERY. IT'S GOING TO BE A VERY TRICKY OPERATION.
STILL... I'M CONFIDENT I CAN PULL IT OFF!

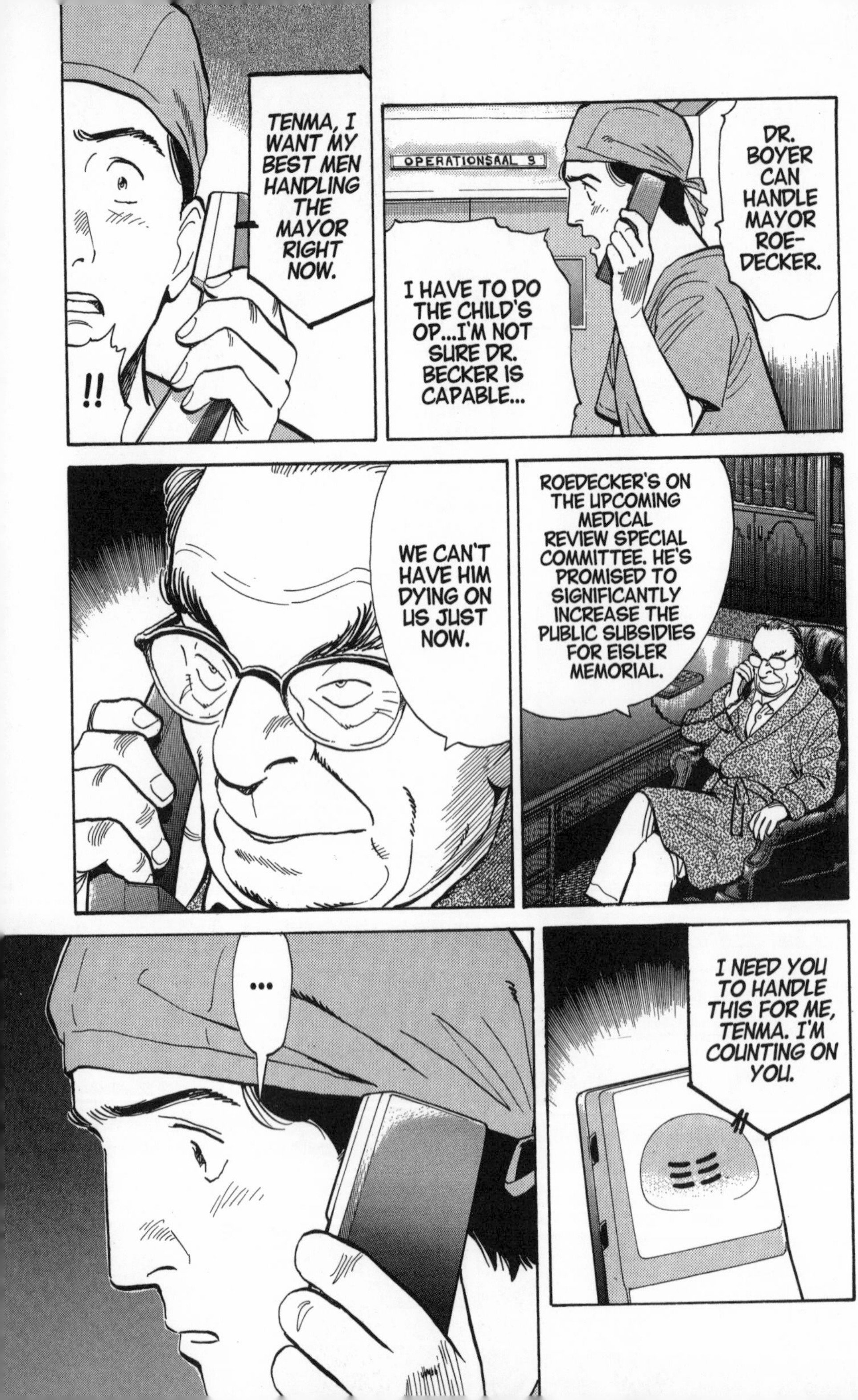
OPERATIONSAAL 9
DR. BOYER CAN HANDLE MAYOR ROE-DECKER.
I HAVE TO DO THE CHILD'S OP...I'M NOT SURE DR. BECKER IS CAPABLE...
TENMA, I WANT MY BEST MEN HANDLING THE MAYOR RIGHT NOW.
!!
ROEDECKER'S ON THE UPCOMING MEDICAL REVIEW SPECIAL COMMITTEE. HE'S PROMISED TO SIGNIFICANTLY INCREASE THE PUBLIC SUBSIDIES FOR EISLER MEMORIAL.
WE CAN'T HAVE HIM DYING ON US JUST NOW.
I NEED YOU TO HANDLE THIS FOR ME, TENMA. I'M COUNTING ON YOU.
...

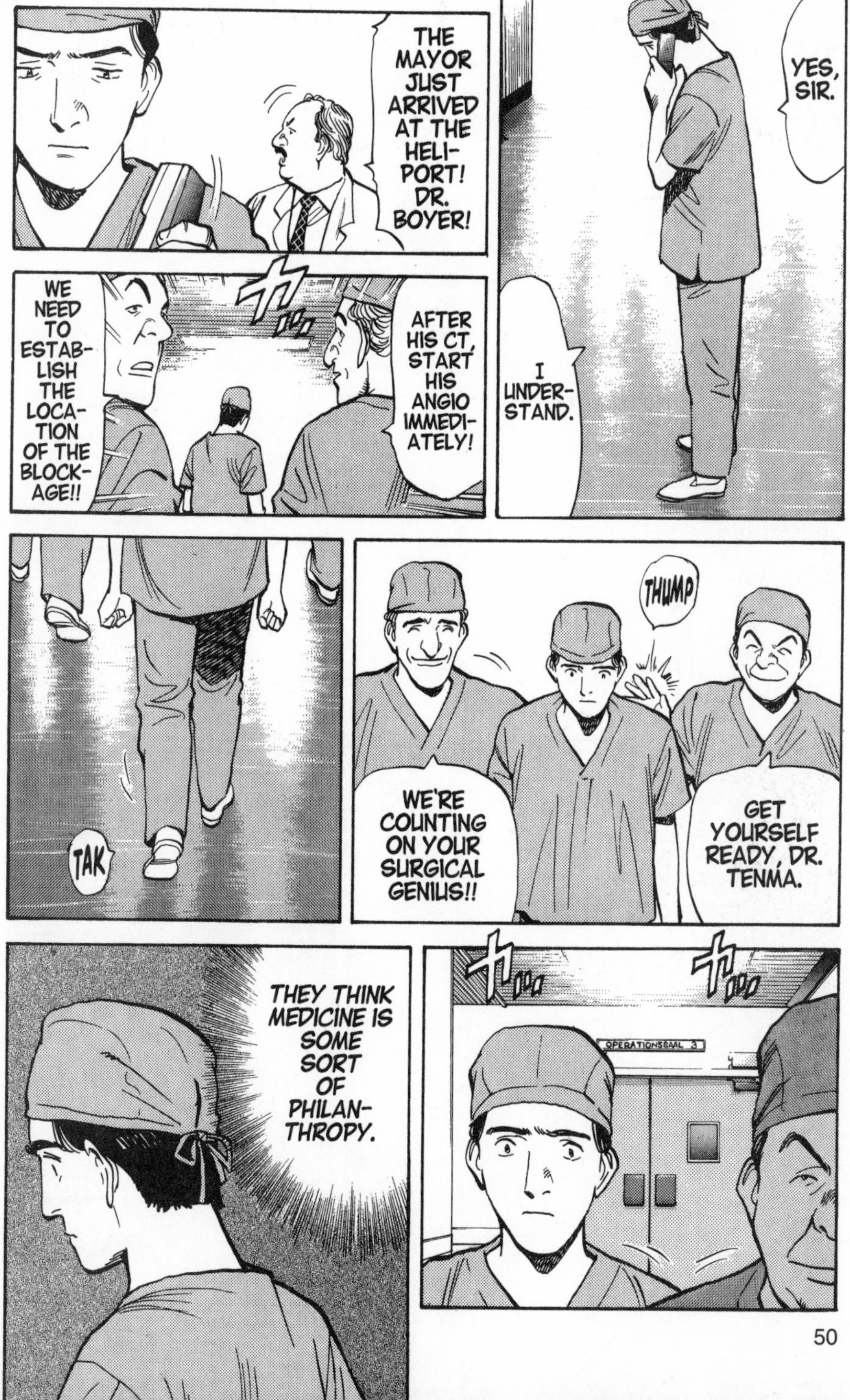
YES, SIR.
I UNDERSTAND.
THE MAYOR JUST ARRIVED AT THE HELIPORT! DR. BOYER!
AFTER HIS CT, START HIS ANGIO IMMEDIATELY!
WE NEED TO ESTABLISH THE LOCATION OF THE BLOCKAGE!!
THUMP
GET YOURSELF READY, DR. TENMA.
WE'RE COUNTING ON YOUR SURGICAL GENIUS!!
TAK
OPERATIONSSAAL 3
THEY THINK MEDICINE IS SOME SORT OF PHILANTHROPY.

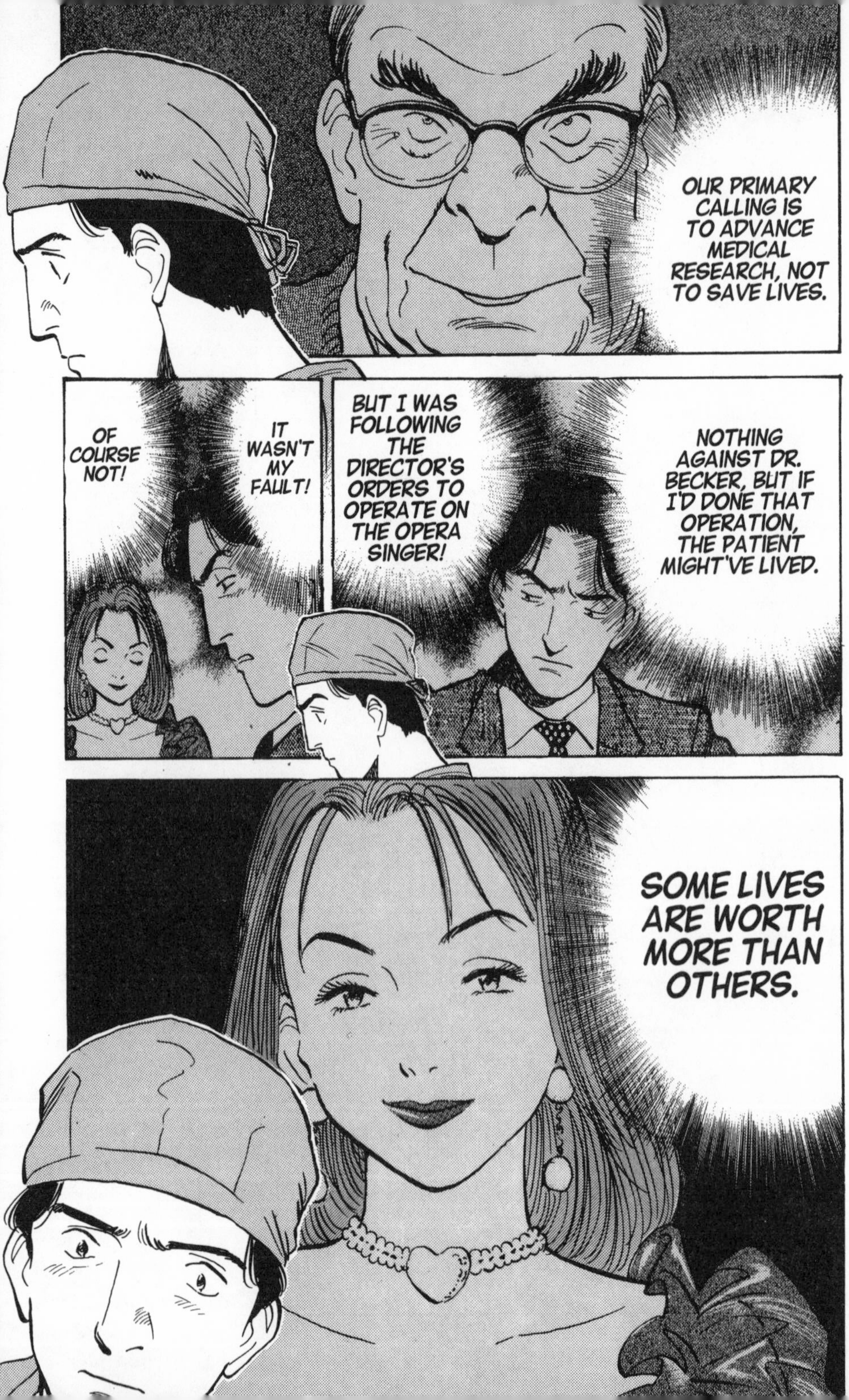
OUR PRIMARY CALLING IS TO ADVANCE MEDICAL RESEARCH, NOT TO SAVE LIVES.
NOTHING AGAINST DR. BECKER, BUT IF I'D DONE THAT OPERATION, THE PATIENT MIGHT'VE LIVED.
BUT I WAS FOLLOWING THE DIRECTOR'S ORDERS TO OPERATE ON THE OPERA SINGER!
IT WASN'T MY FAULT!
OF COURSE NOT!
SOME LIVES ARE WORTH MORE THAN OTHERS.

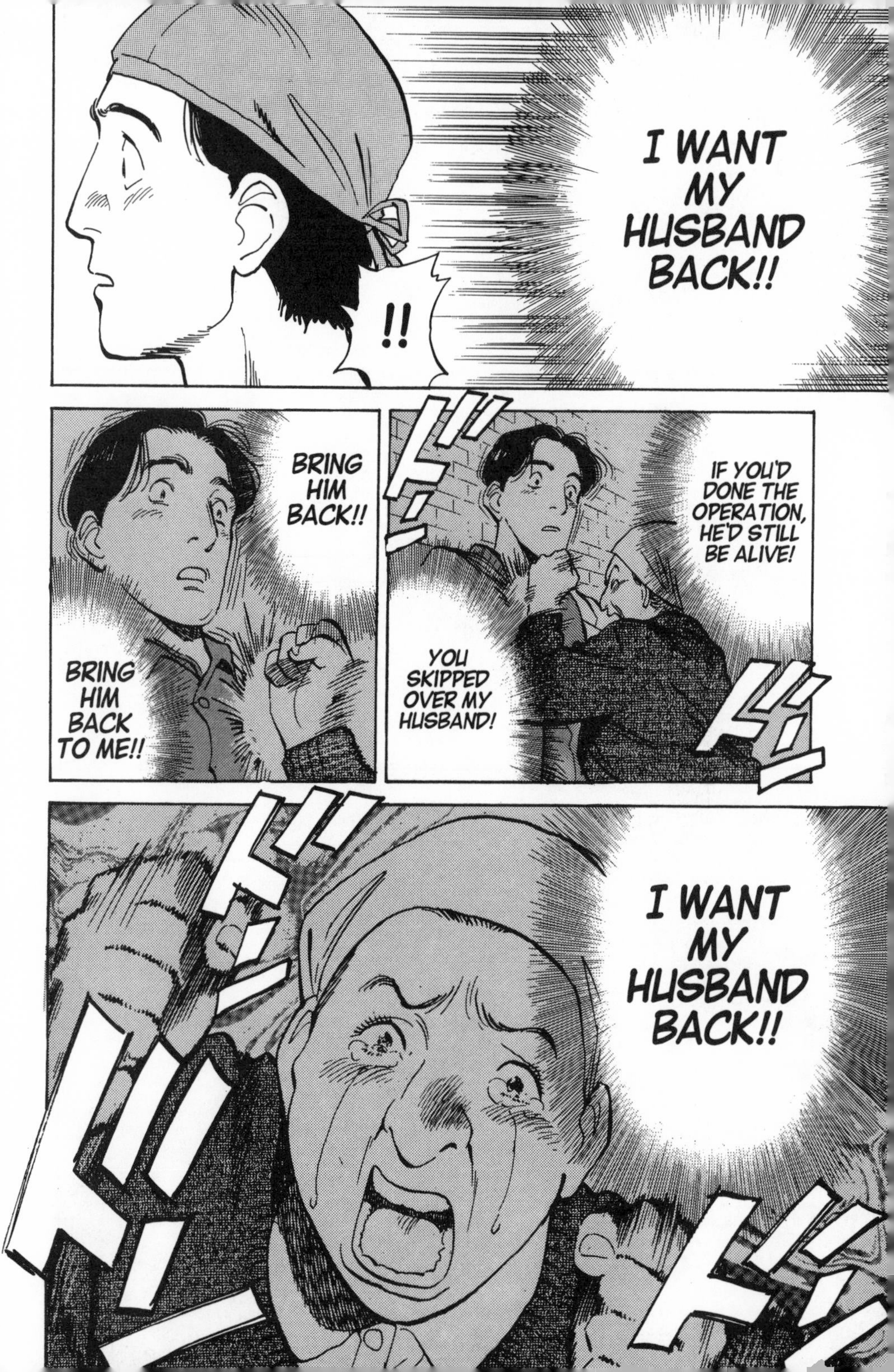
I WANT MY HUSBAND BACK!!
!!
IF YOU'D DONE THE OPERATION, HE'D STILL BE ALIVE!
YOU SKIPPED OVER MY HUSBAND!
BRING HIM BACK!!
BRING HIM BACK TO ME!!
I WANT MY HUSBAND BACK!!

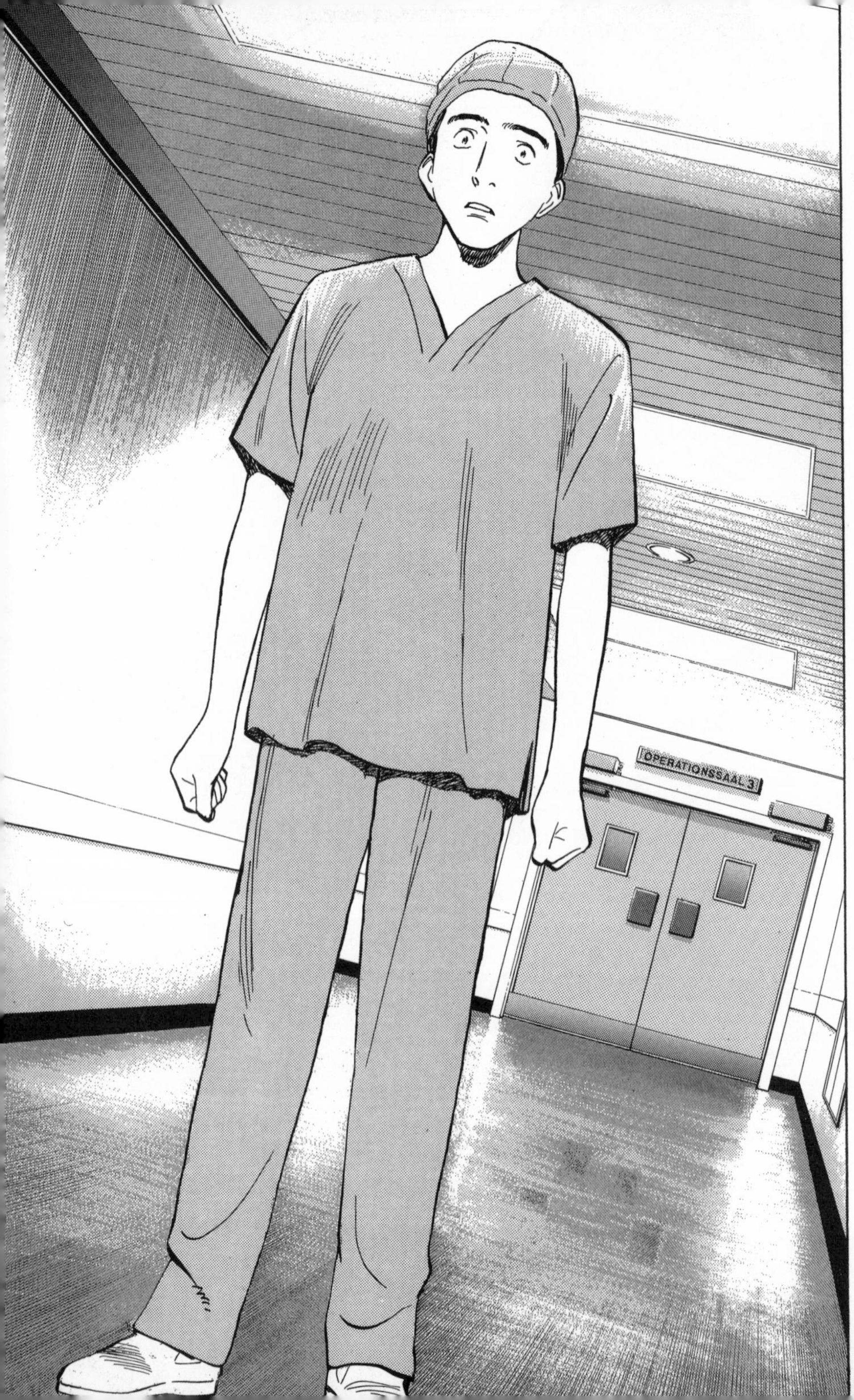
OPERATIONSSAAL 3

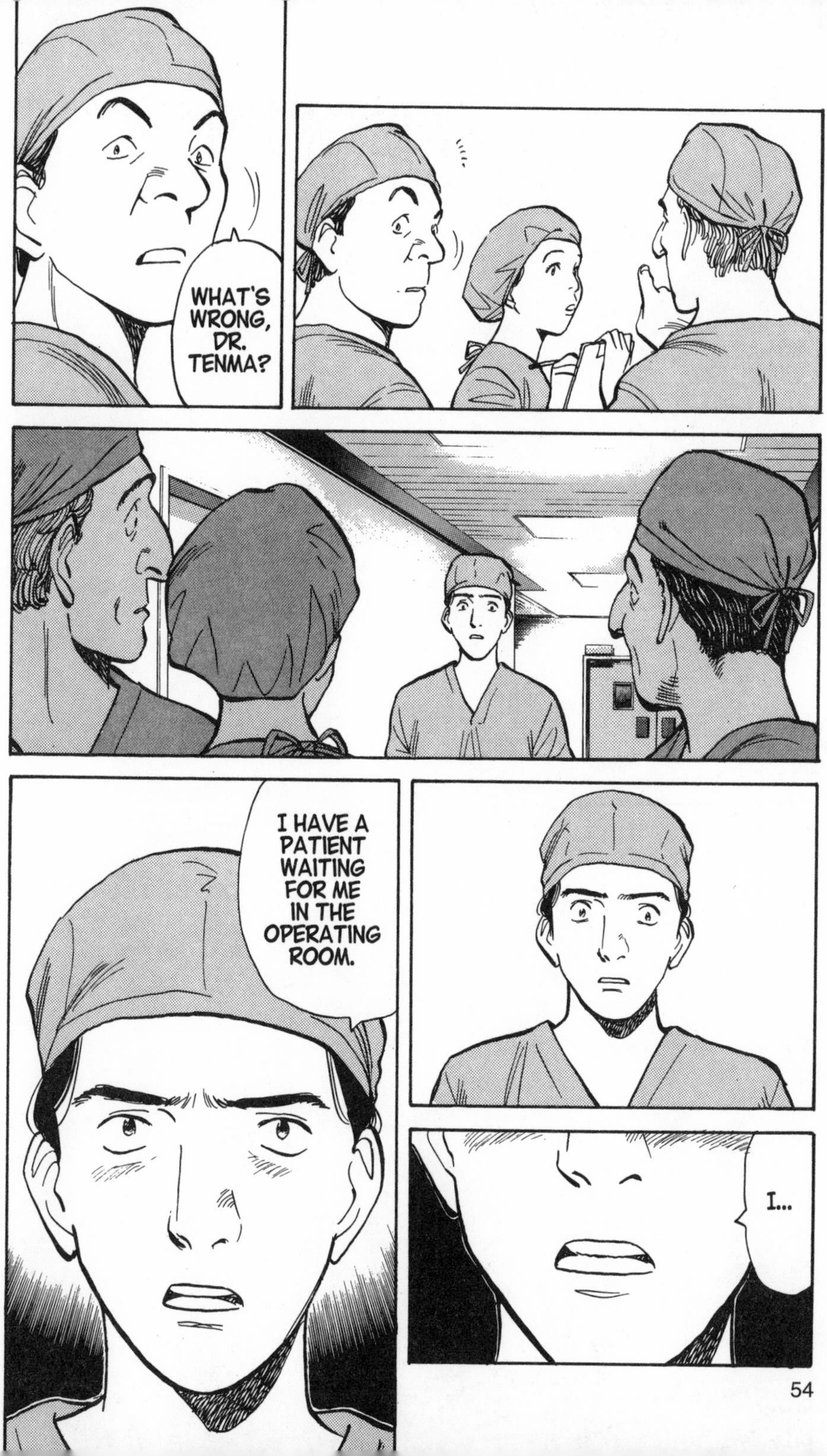
WHAT'S WRONG, DR. TENMA?
I...
I HAVE A PATIENT WAITING FOR ME IN THE OPERATING ROOM.

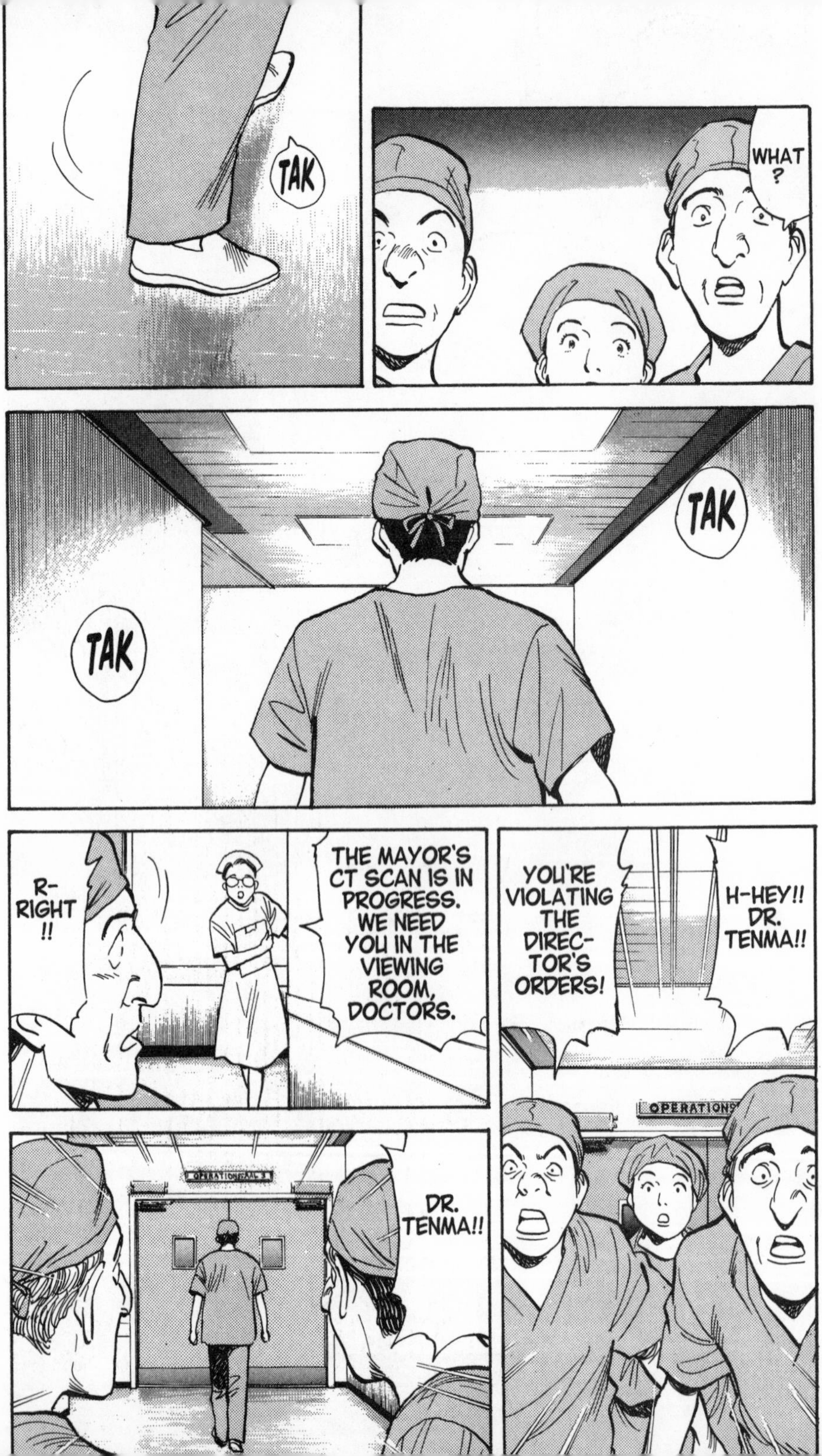
WHAT?
TAK
TAK
TAK
H-HEY!! DR. TENMA!!
YOU'RE VIOLATING THE DIRECTOR'S ORDERS!
THE MAYOR'S CT SCAN IS IN PROGRESS. WE NEED YOU IN THE VIEWING ROOM, DOCTORS.
R-RIGHT!!
DR. TENMA!!

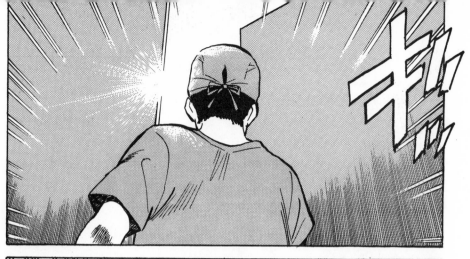

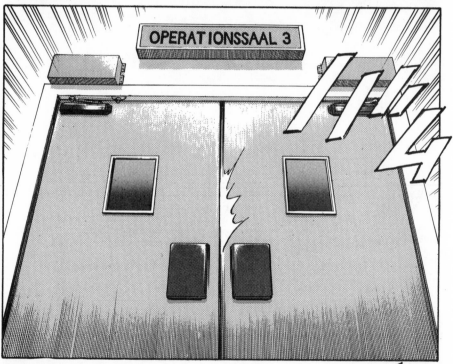

OPERATIONSSAAL 3

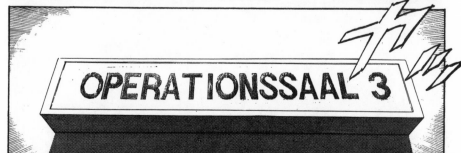

OPERATIONSSAAL 3

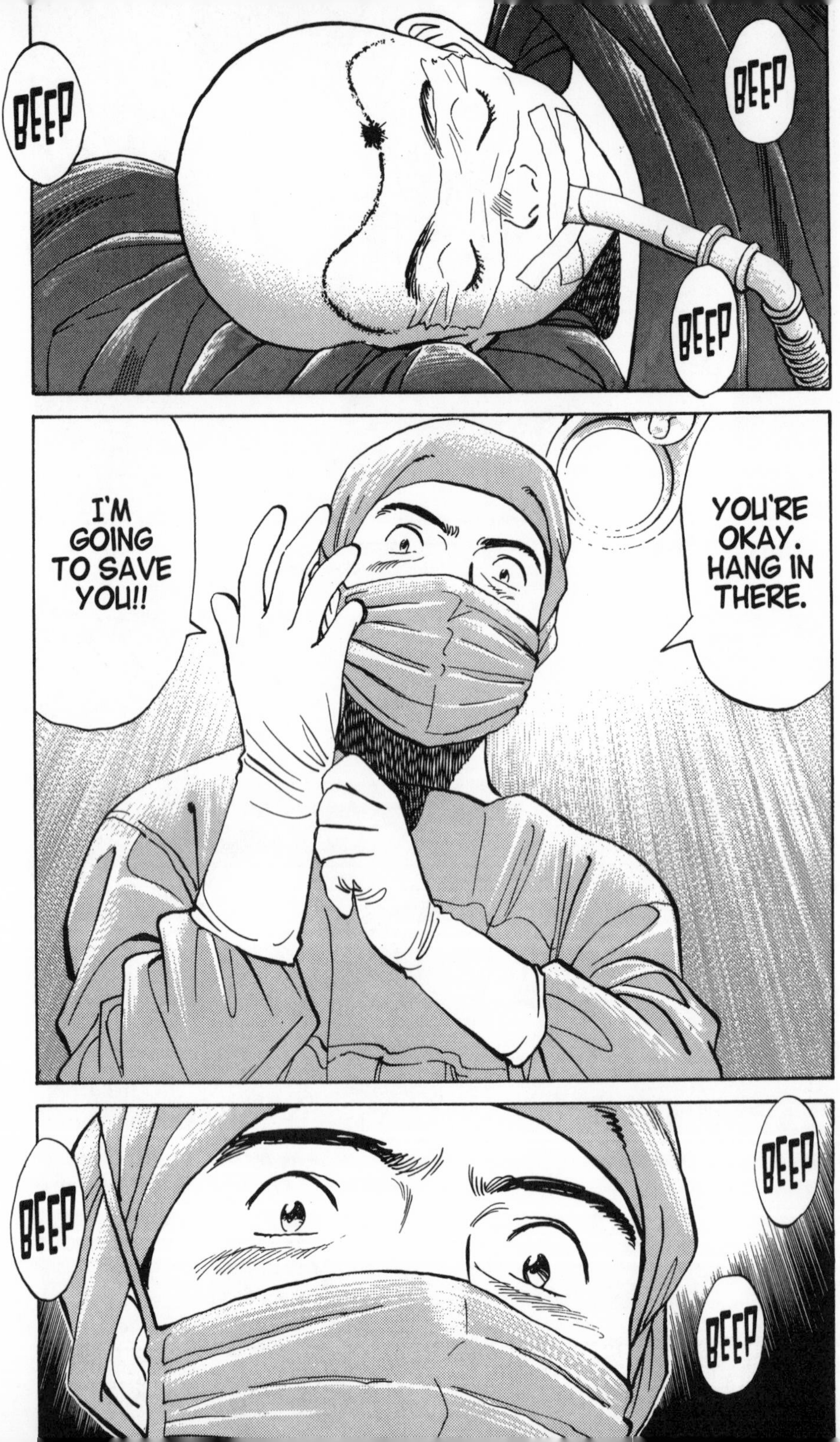
BEEP
BEEP
BEEP
YOU'RE OKAY. HANG IN THERE.
I'M GOING TO SAVE YOU!!
BEEP
BEEP
BEEP

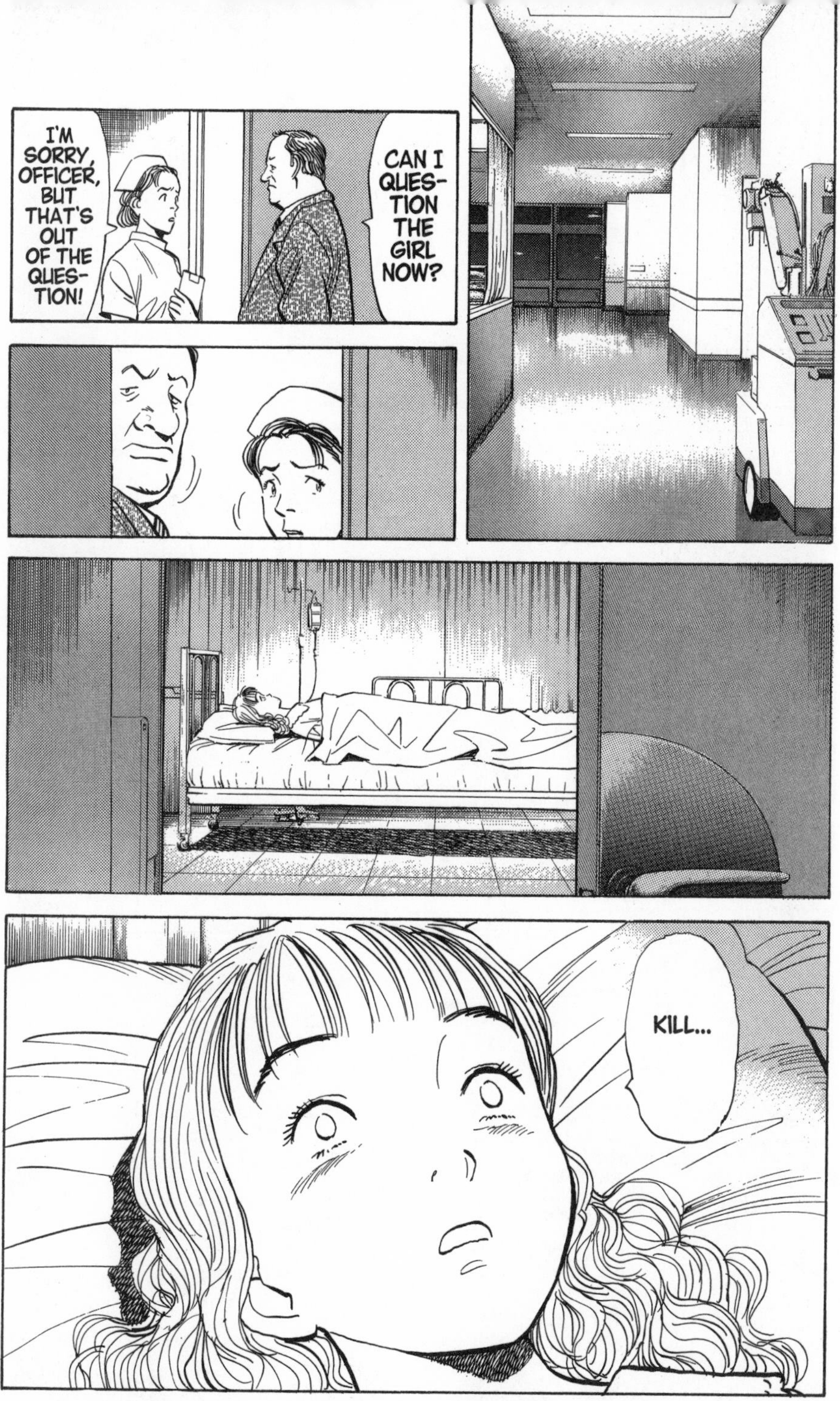
CAN I QUES-TION THE GIRL NOW?
I'M SORRY, OFFICER, BUT THAT'S OUT OF THE QUES-TION!
KILL...

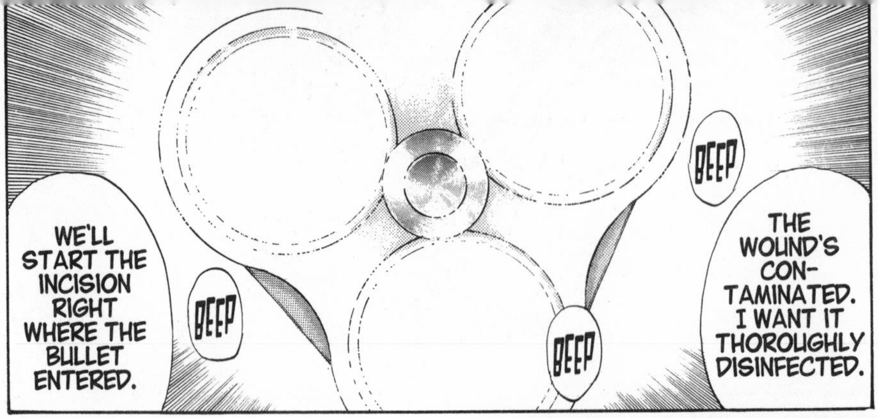
BEEP
THE WOUND'S CON-TAMINATED. I WANT IT THOROUGHLY DISINFECTED.
BEEP
BEEP
WE'LL START THE INCISION RIGHT WHERE THE BULLET ENTERED.

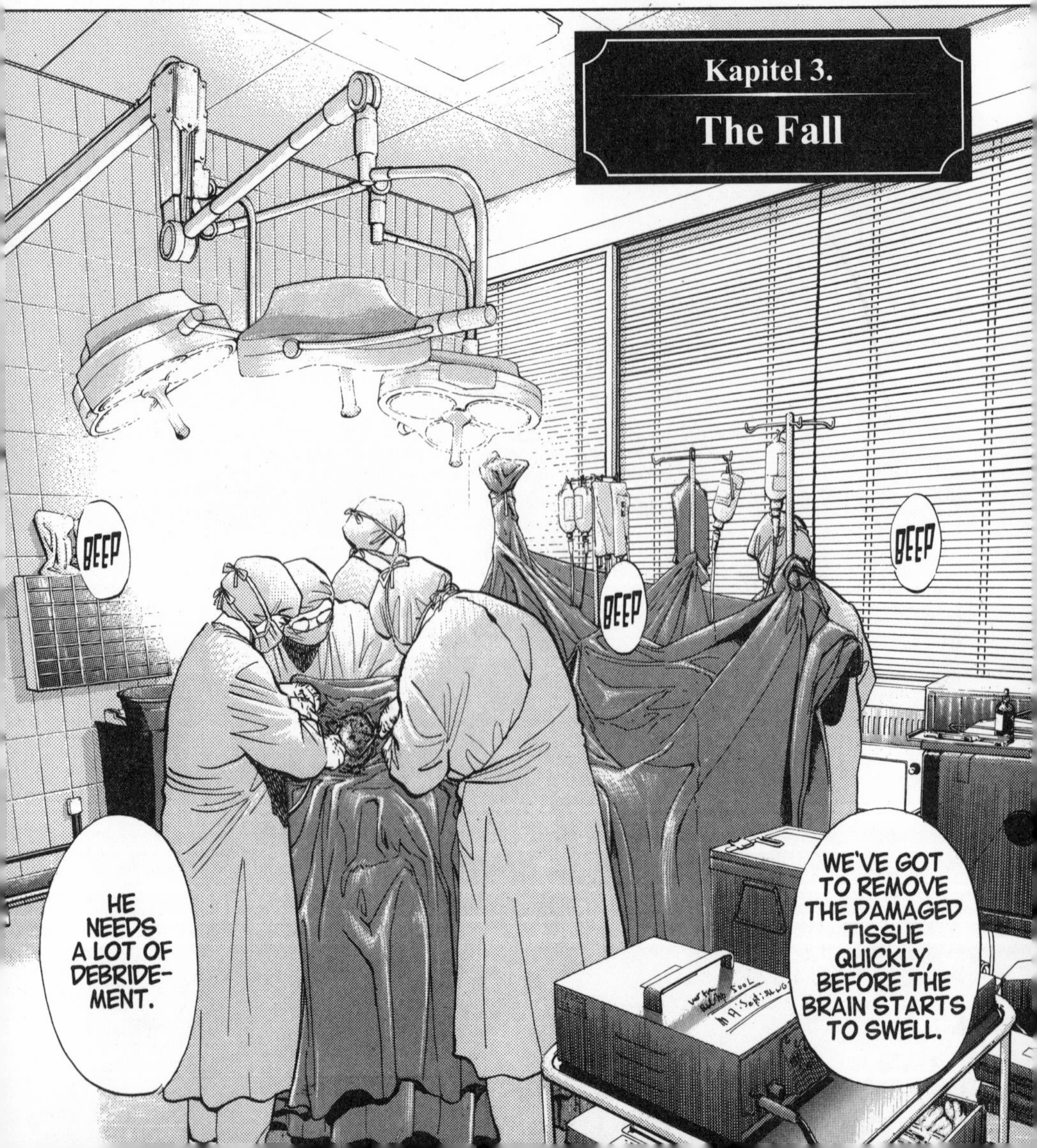
Kapitel 3.
The Fall
BEEP
BEEP
BEEP
WE'VE GOT TO REMOVE THE DAMAGED TISSUE QUICKLY, BEFORE THE BRAIN STARTS TO SWELL.
HE NEEDS A LOT OF DEBRIDE-MENT.

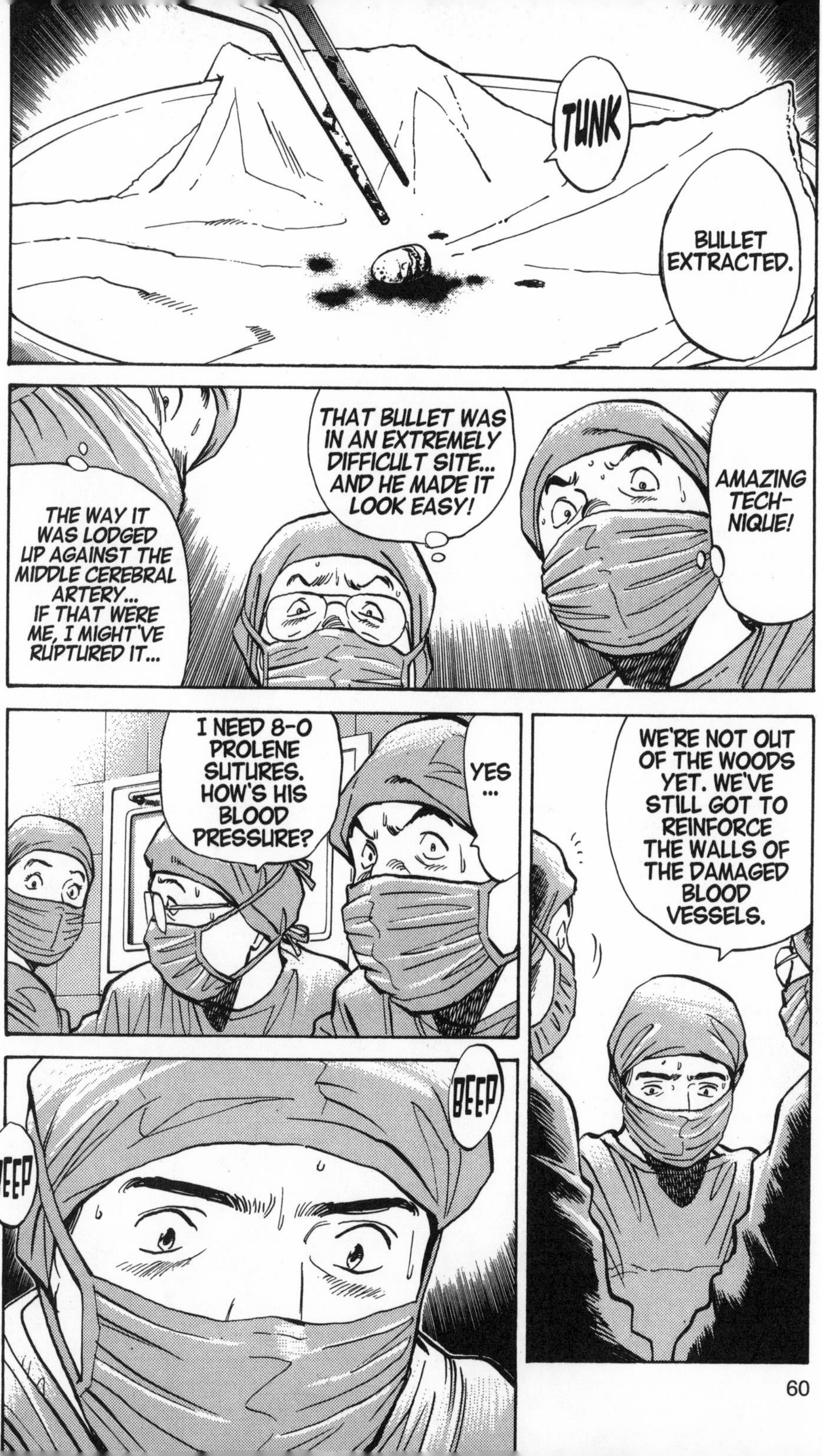
TUNK
BULLET EXTRACTED.
AMAZING TECH-NIQUE!
THAT BULLET WAS IN AN EXTREMELY DIFFICULT SITE... AND HE MADE IT LOOK EASY!
THE WAY IT WAS LODGED UP AGAINST THE MIDDLE CEREBRAL ARTERY... IF THAT WERE ME, I MIGHT'VE RUPTURED IT...
WE'RE NOT OUT OF THE WOODS YET. WE'VE STILL GOT TO REINFORCE THE WALLS OF THE DAMAGED BLOOD VESSELS.
YES ...
I NEED 8-0 PROLENE SUTURES. HOW'S HIS BLOOD PRESSURE?
BEEP
BEEP

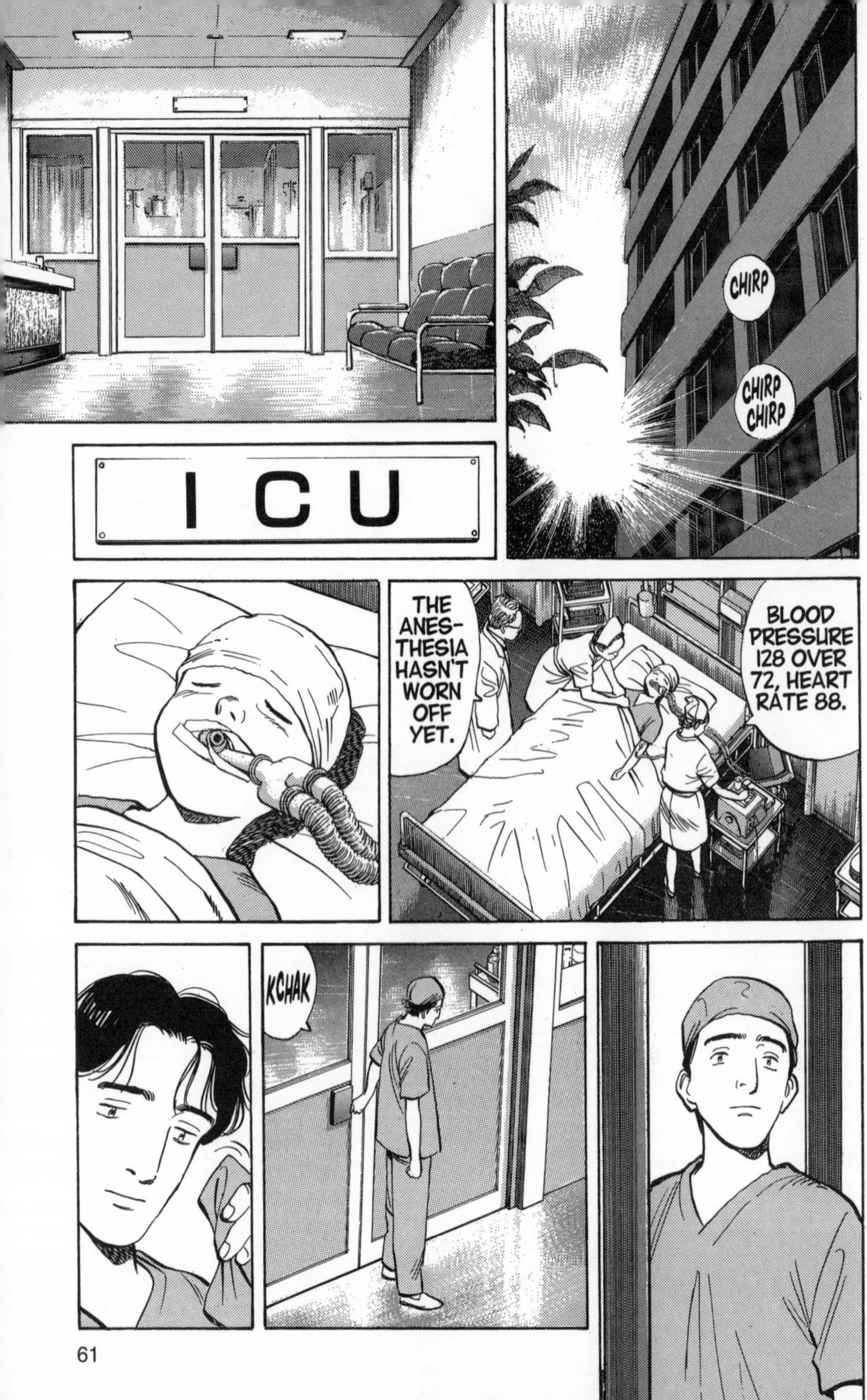
CHIRP
CHIRP CHIRP
ICU
BLOOD PRESSURE 128 OVER 72, HEART RATE 88.
THE ANES-THESIA HASN'T WORN OFF YET.
KCHAK

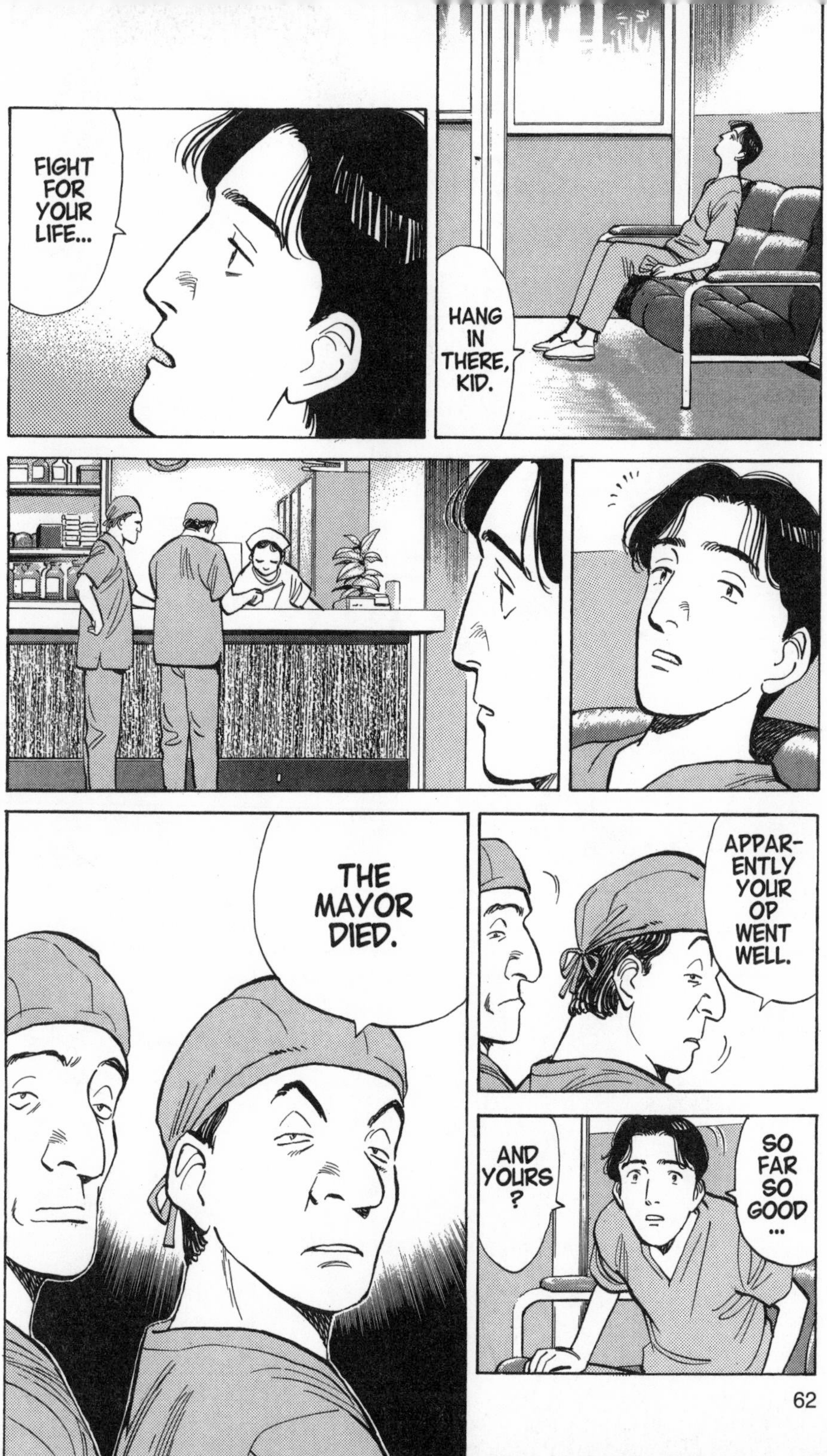
HANG IN THERE, KID.
FIGHT FOR YOUR LIFE...
APPAR-ENTLY YOUR OP WENT WELL.
SO FAR SO GOOD...
AND YOURS?
THE MAYOR DIED.

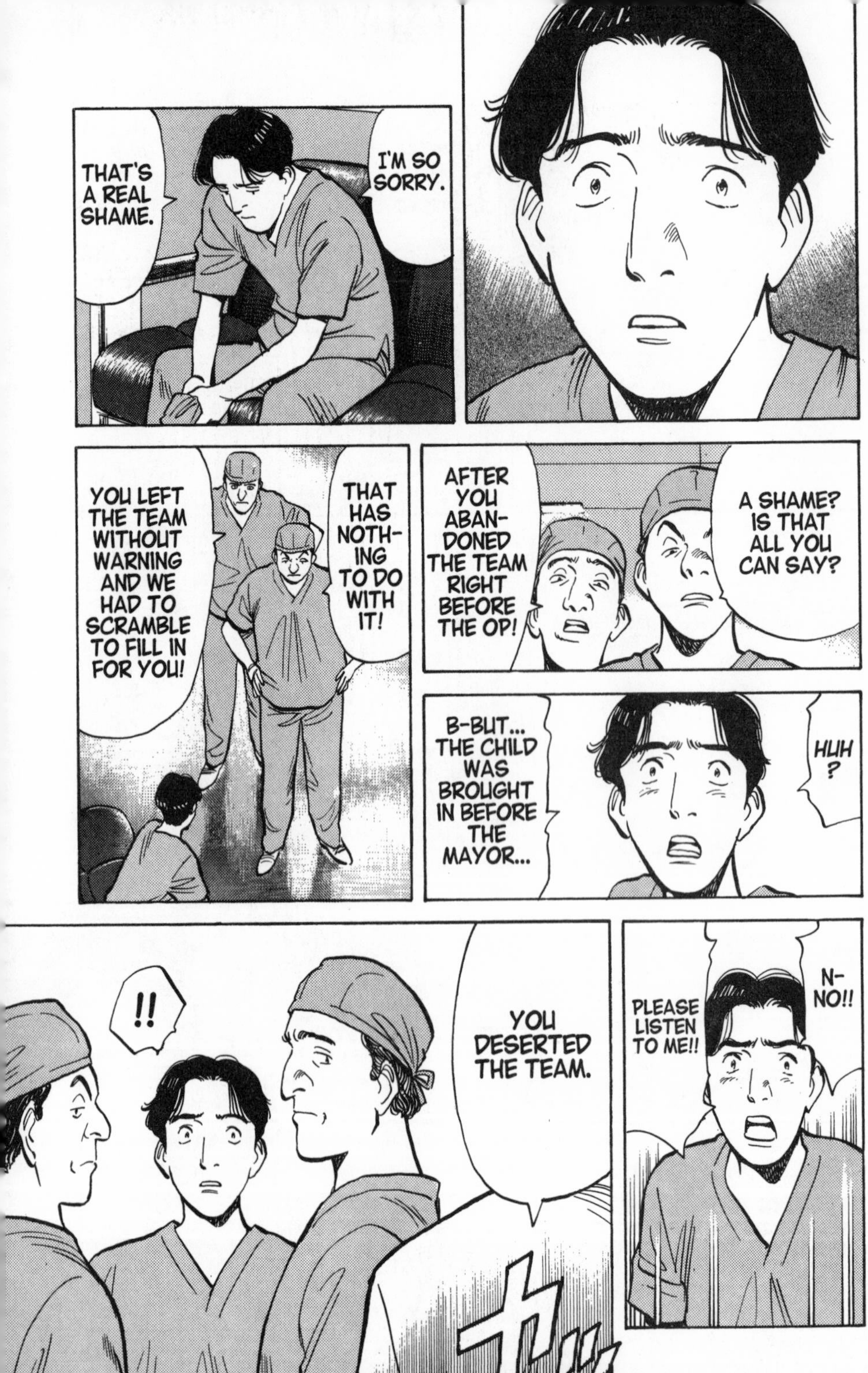
I'M SO SORRY.
THAT'S A REAL SHAME.
A SHAME? IS THAT ALL YOU CAN SAY?
AFTER YOU ABANDONED THE TEAM RIGHT BEFORE THE OP!
HUH?
B-BUT... THE CHILD WAS BROUGHT IN BEFORE THE MAYOR...
THAT HAS NOTHING TO DO WITH IT!
YOU LEFT THE TEAM WITHOUT WARNING AND WE HAD TO SCRAMBLE TO FILL IN FOR YOU!
N-NO!!
PLEASE LISTEN TO ME!!
YOU DESERTED THE TEAM.
!!

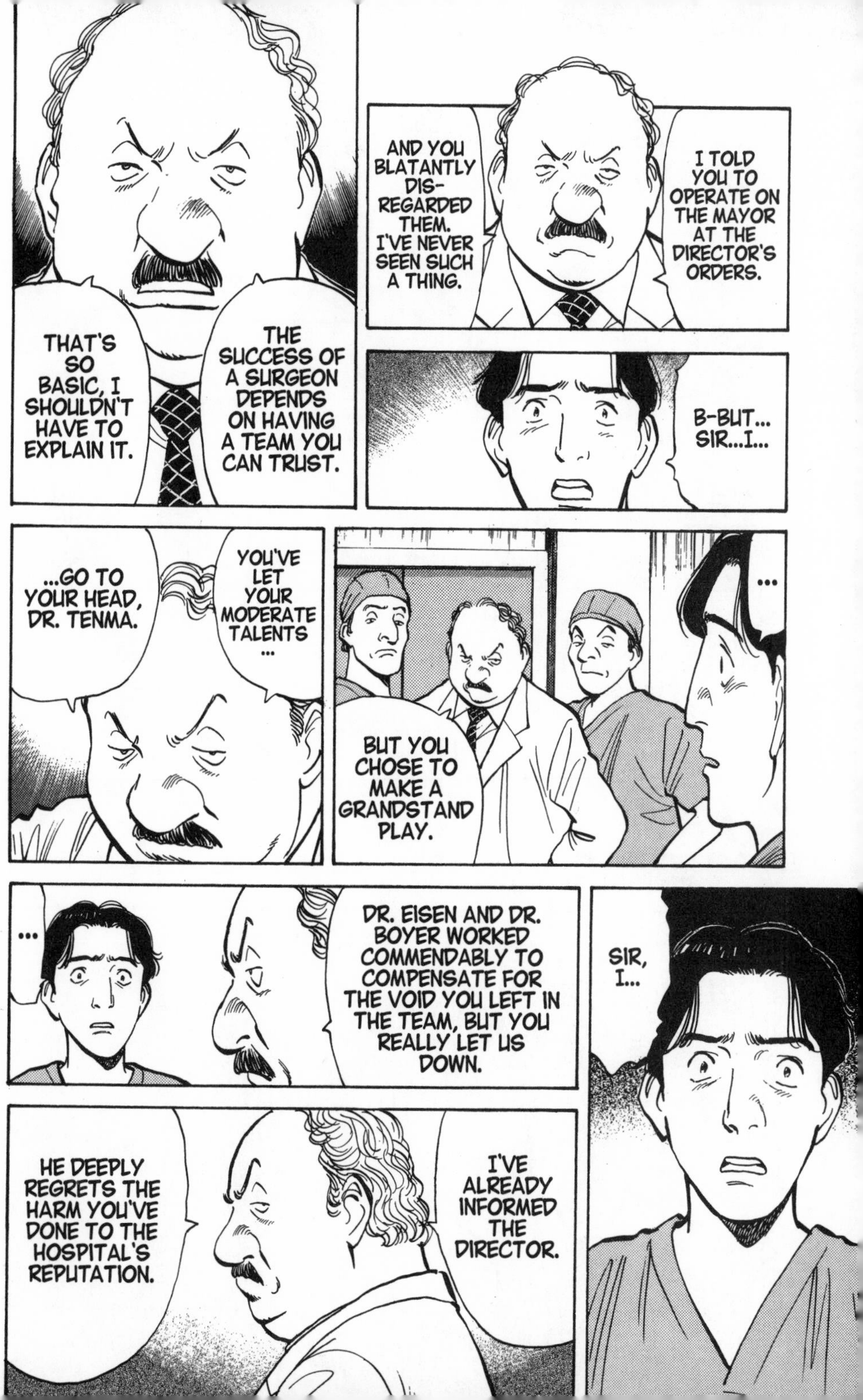
I TOLD YOU TO OPERATE ON THE MAYOR AT THE DIRECTOR'S ORDERS.
AND YOU BLATANTLY DIS-REGARDED THEM. I'VE NEVER SEEN SUCH A THING.
B-BUT... SIR...I...
THE SUCCESS OF A SURGEON DEPENDS ON HAVING A TEAM YOU CAN TRUST.
THAT'S SO BASIC, I SHOULDN'T HAVE TO EXPLAIN IT.
...
BUT YOU CHOSE TO MAKE A GRANDSTAND PLAY.
YOU'VE LET YOUR MODERATE TALENTS ...
...GO TO YOUR HEAD, DR. TENMA.
SIR, I...
DR. EISEN AND DR. BOYER WORKED COMMENDABLY TO COMPENSATE FOR THE VOID YOU LEFT IN THE TEAM, BUT YOU REALLY LET US DOWN.
...
I'VE ALREADY INFORMED THE DIRECTOR.
HE DEEPLY REGRETS THE HARM YOU'VE DONE TO THE HOSPITAL'S REPUTATION.

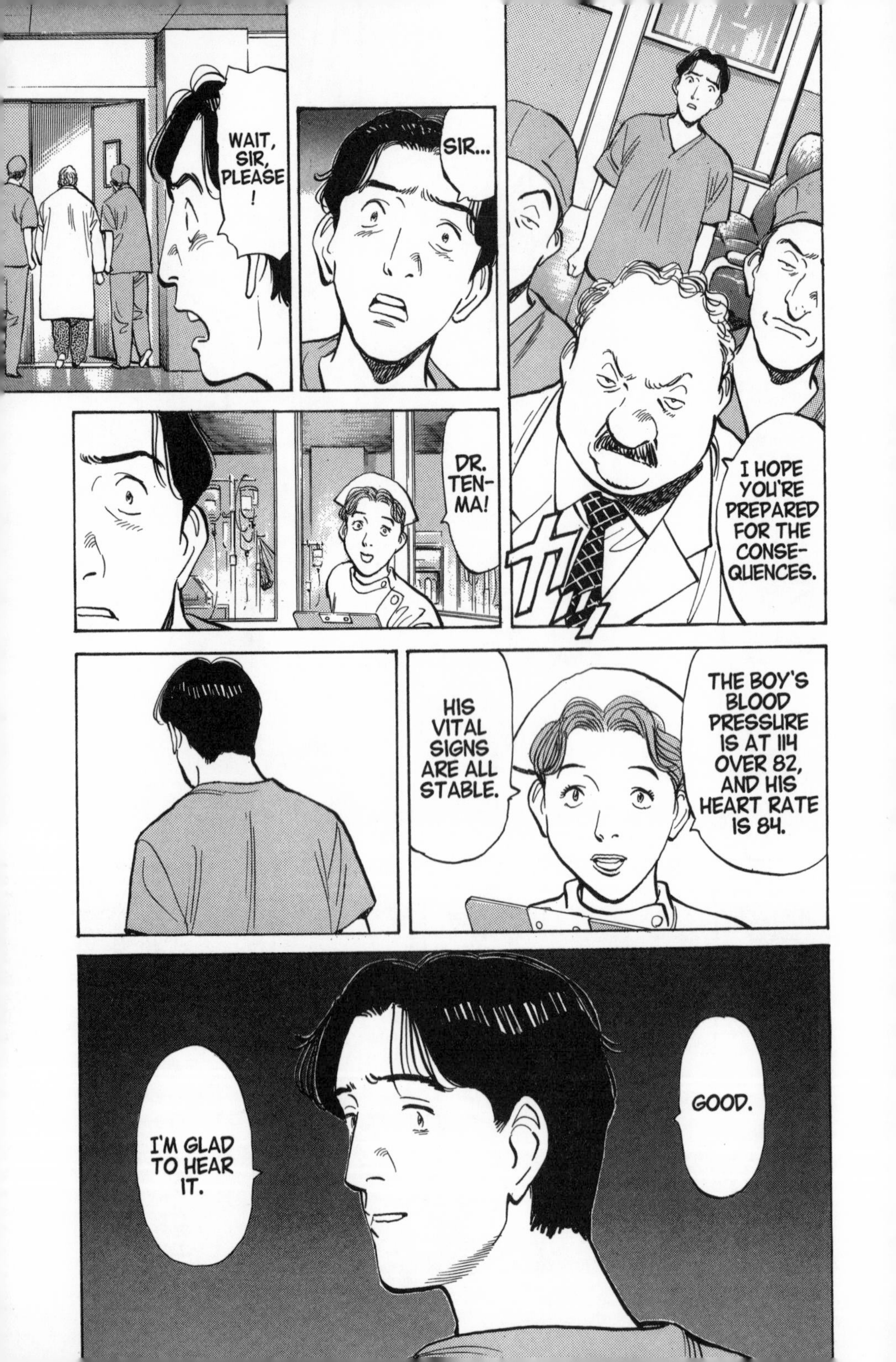

I HOPE YOU'RE PREPARED FOR THE CONSEQUENCES.
カッ
SIR...
WAIT, SIR, PLEASE!
DR. TEN-MA!
THE BOY'S BLOOD PRESSURE IS AT 114 OVER 82, AND HIS HEART RATE IS 84.
HIS VITAL SIGNS ARE ALL STABLE.
GOOD.
I'M GLAD TO HEAR IT.

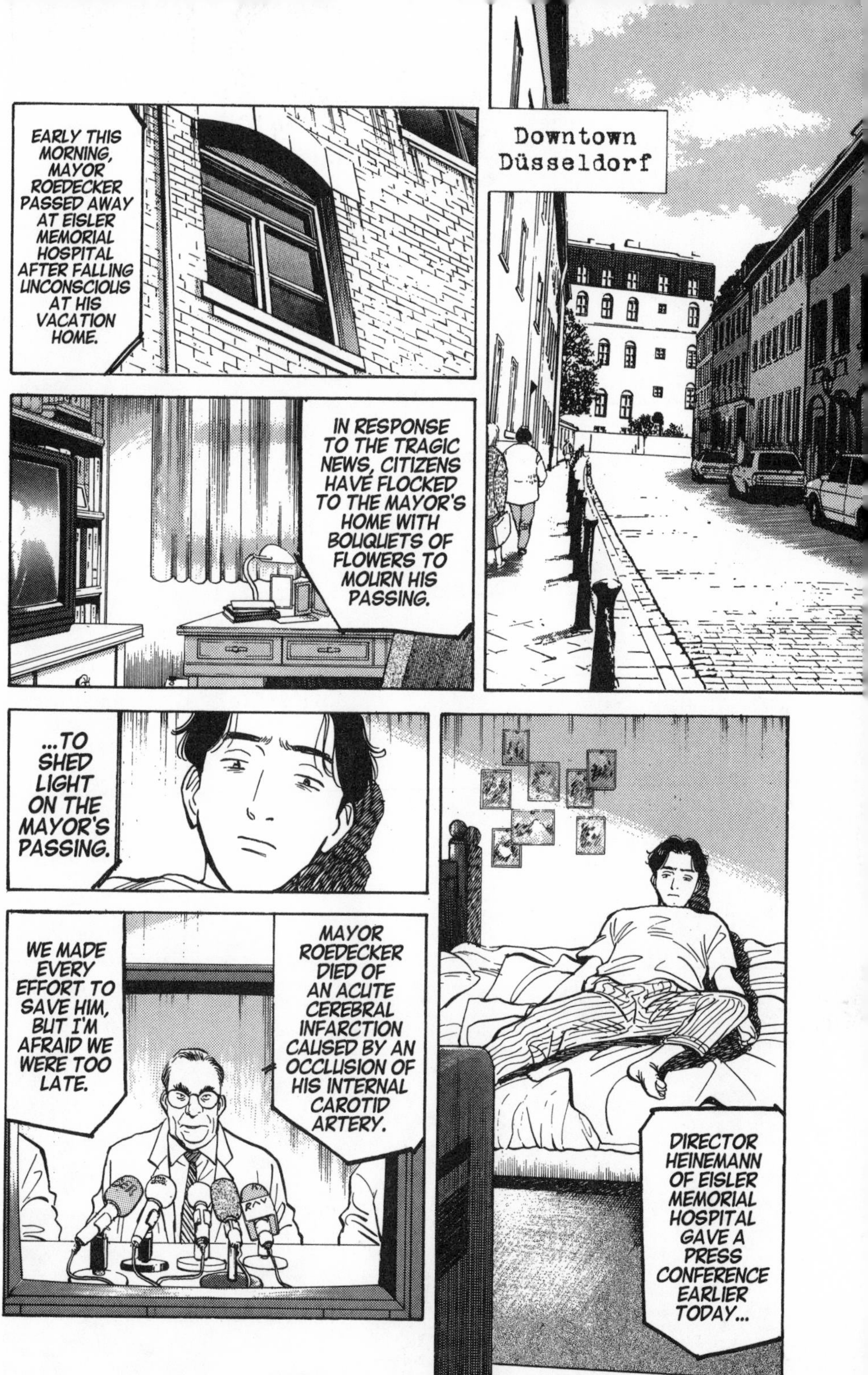
Downtown Düsseldorf
EARLY THIS MORNING, MAYOR ROEDECKER PASSED AWAY AT EISLER MEMORIAL HOSPITAL AFTER FALLING UNCONSCIOUS AT HIS VACATION HOME.
IN RESPONSE TO THE TRAGIC NEWS, CITIZENS HAVE FLOCKED TO THE MAYOR'S HOME WITH BOUQUETS OF FLOWERS TO MOURN HIS PASSING.
DIRECTOR HEINEMANN OF EISLER MEMORIAL HOSPITAL GAVE A PRESS CONFERENCE EARLIER TODAY...
...TO SHED LIGHT ON THE MAYOR'S PASSING.
MAYOR ROEDECKER DIED OF AN ACUTE CEREBRAL INFARCTION CAUSED BY AN OCCLUSION OF HIS INTERNAL CAROTID ARTERY.
WE MADE EVERY EFFORT TO SAVE HIM, BUT I'M AFRAID WE WERE TOO LATE.

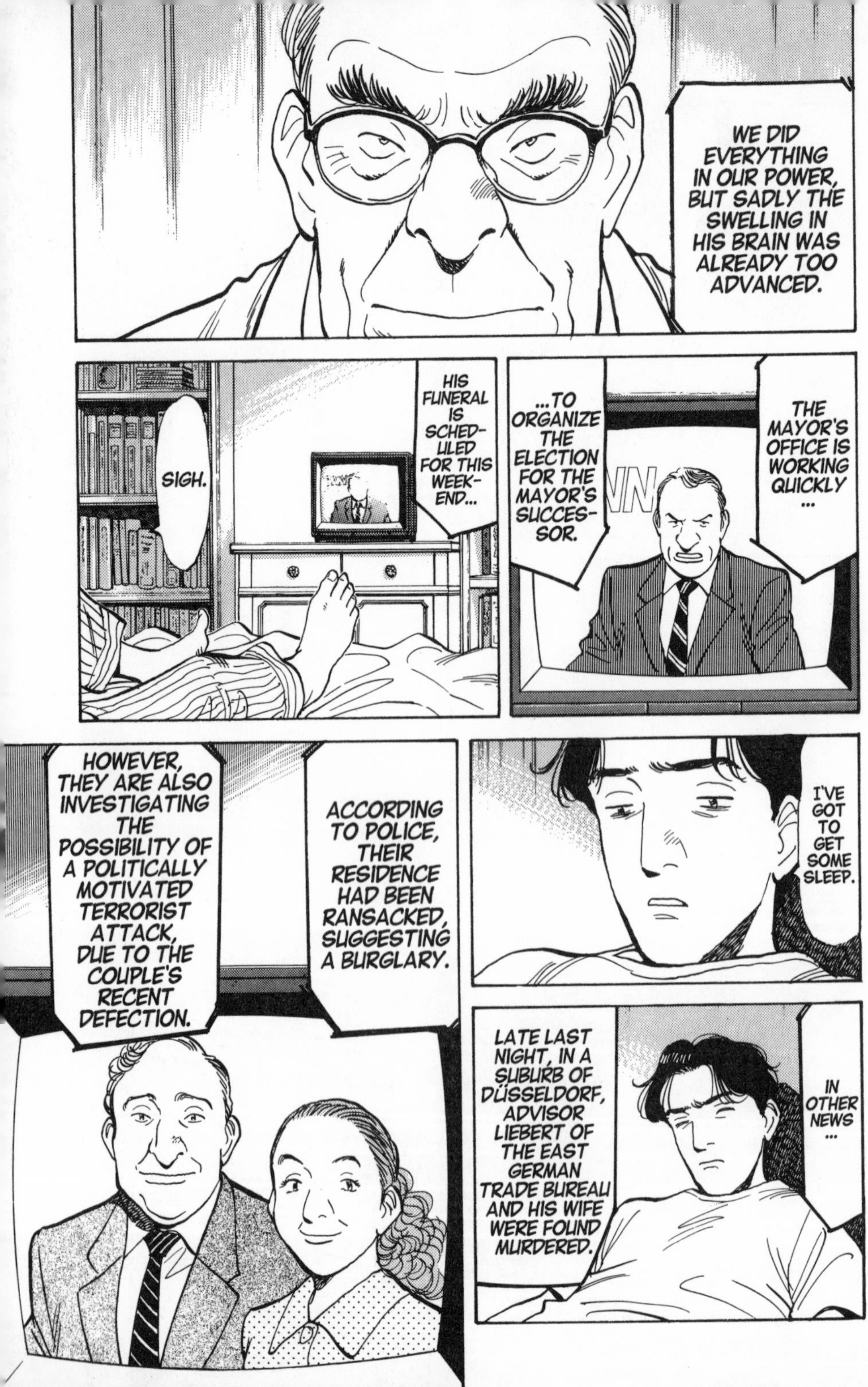

WE DID EVERYTHING IN OUR POWER, BUT SADLY THE SWELLING IN HIS BRAIN WAS ALREADY TOO ADVANCED.
THE MAYOR'S OFFICE IS WORKING QUICKLY...
...TO ORGANIZE THE ELECTION FOR THE MAYOR'S SUCCESSOR.
HIS FUNERAL IS SCHEDULED FOR THIS WEEKEND...
SIGH.
I'VE GOT TO GET SOME SLEEP.
IN OTHER NEWS...
LATE LAST NIGHT, IN A SUBURB OF DÜSSELDORF, ADVISOR LIEBERT OF THE EAST GERMAN TRADE BUREAU AND HIS WIFE WERE FOUND MURDERED.
ACCORDING TO POLICE, THEIR RESIDENCE HAD BEEN RANSACKED, SUGGESTING A BURGLARY.
HOWEVER, THEY ARE ALSO INVESTIGATING THE POSSIBILITY OF A POLITICALLY MOTIVATED TERRORIST ATTACK, DUE TO THE COUPLE'S RECENT DEFECTION.

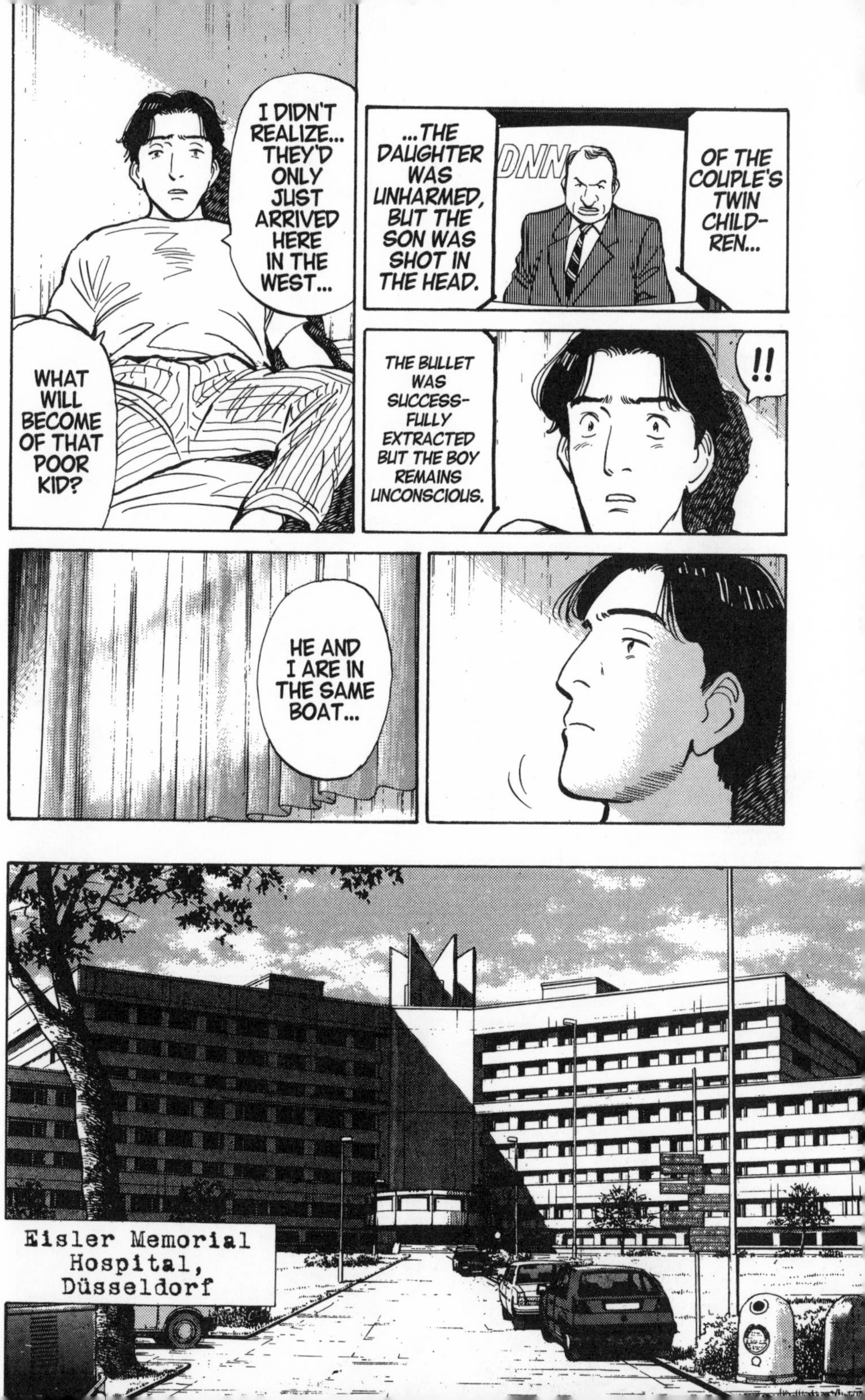
OF THE COUPLE'S TWIN CHILD-REN...
...THE DAUGHTER WAS UNHARMED, BUT THE SON WAS SHOT IN THE HEAD.
DNN
!!
THE BULLET WAS SUCCESS-FULLY EXTRACTED BUT THE BOY REMAINS UNCONSCIOUS.
I DIDN'T REALIZE... THEY'D ONLY JUST ARRIVED HERE IN THE WEST...
WHAT WILL BECOME OF THAT POOR KID?
HE AND I ARE IN THE SAME BOAT...
Eisler Memorial Hospital, Düsseldorf

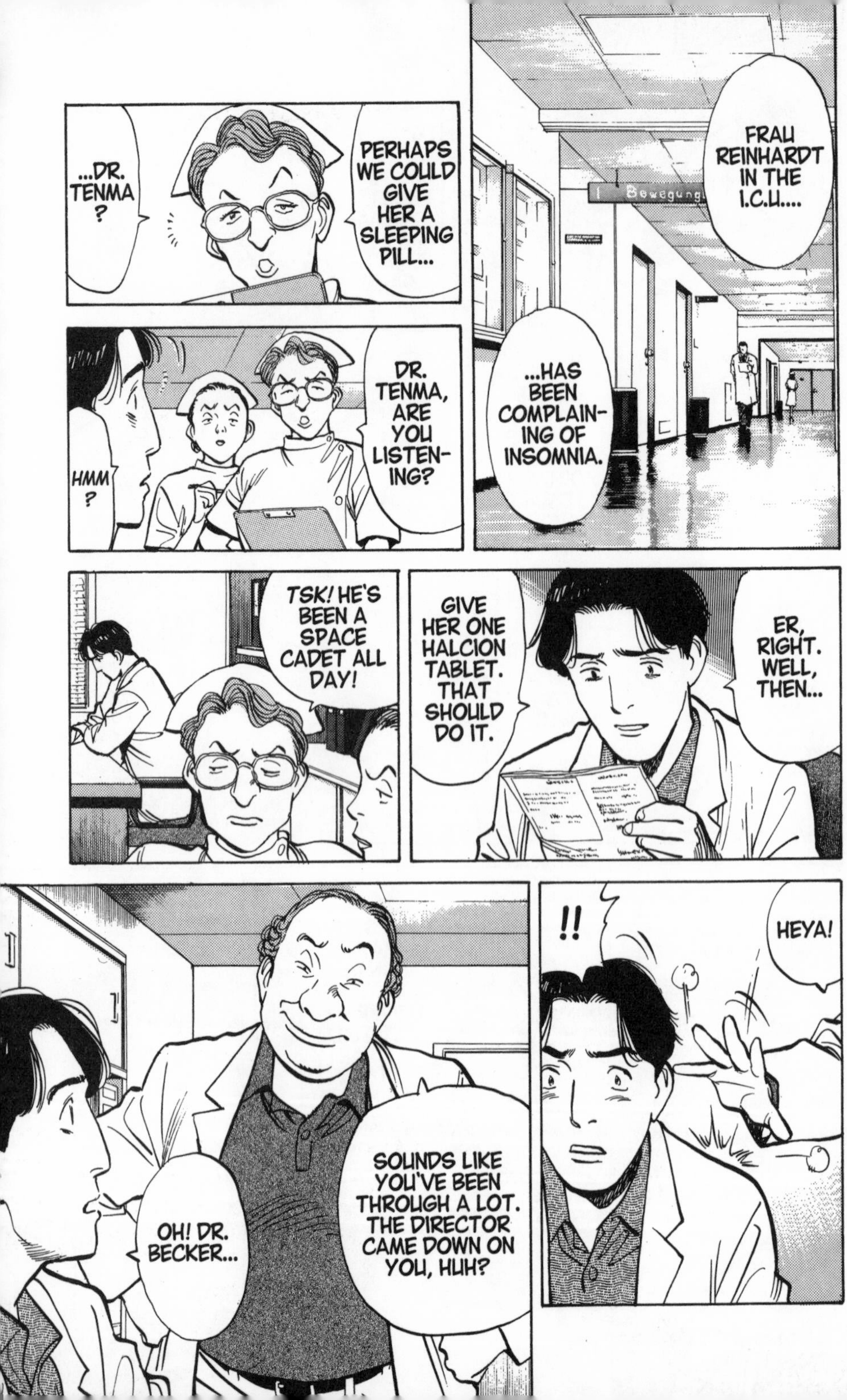
FRAU REINHARDT IN THE I.C.U....
...HAS BEEN COMPLAINING OF INSOMNIA.
PERHAPS WE COULD GIVE HER A SLEEPING PILL...
...DR. TENMA?
DR. TENMA, ARE YOU LISTENING?
HMM?
ER, RIGHT. WELL, THEN...
GIVE HER ONE HALCION TABLET. THAT SHOULD DO IT.
TSK! HE'S BEEN A SPACE CADET ALL DAY!
HEYA!
!!
SOUNDS LIKE YOU'VE BEEN THROUGH A LOT. THE DIRECTOR CAME DOWN ON YOU, HUH?
OH! DR. BECKER...

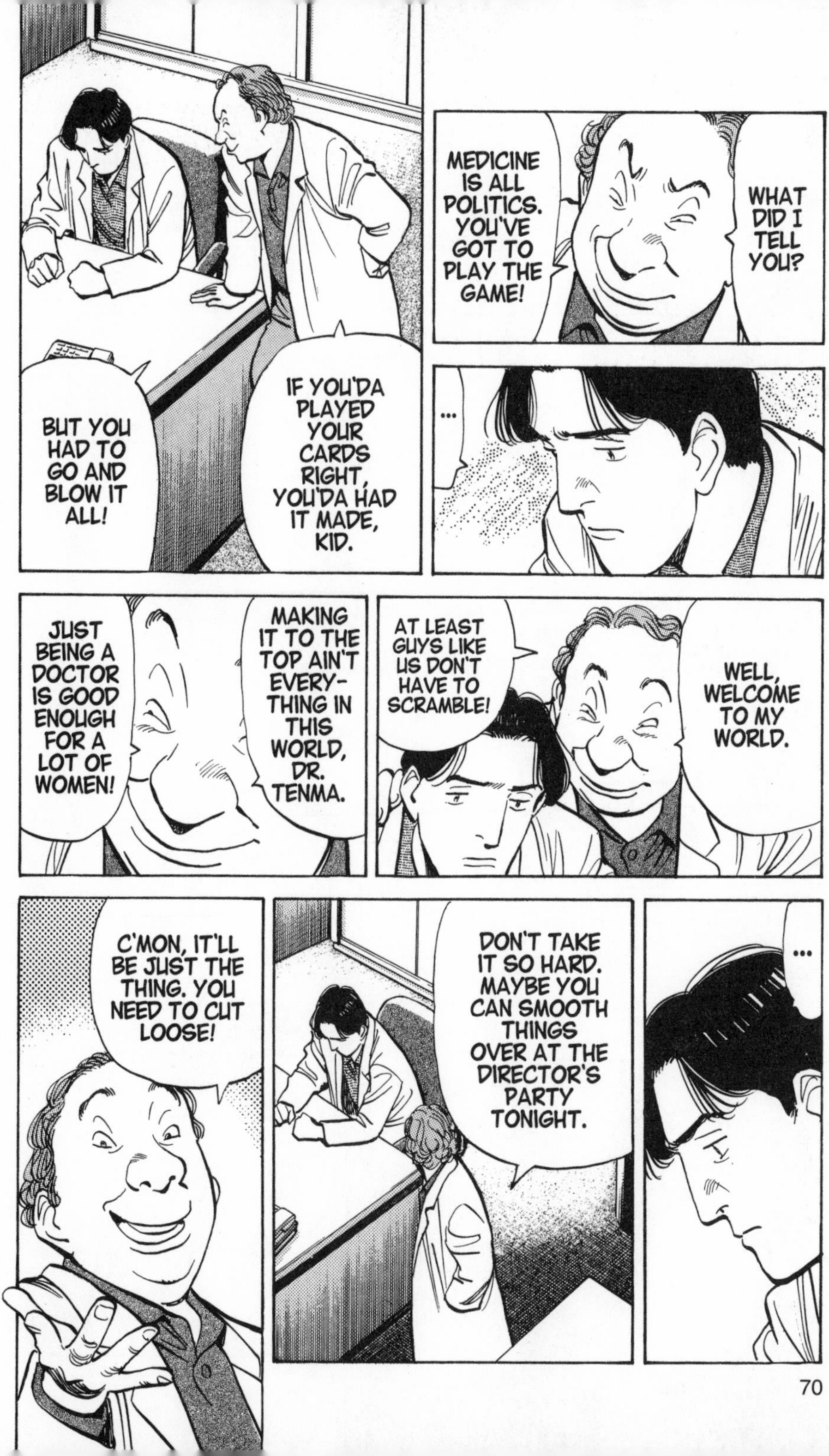
WHAT DID I TELL YOU?
MEDICINE IS ALL POLITICS. YOU'VE GOT TO PLAY THE GAME!
...
IF YOU'DA PLAYED YOUR CARDS RIGHT, YOU'DA HAD IT MADE, KID.
BUT YOU HAD TO GO AND BLOW IT ALL!
WELL, WELCOME TO MY WORLD.
AT LEAST GUYS LIKE US DON'T HAVE TO SCRAMBLE!
MAKING IT TO THE TOP AIN'T EVERY-THING IN THIS WORLD, DR. TENMA.
JUST BEING A DOCTOR IS GOOD ENOUGH FOR A LOT OF WOMEN!
...
DON'T TAKE IT SO HARD. MAYBE YOU CAN SMOOTH THINGS OVER AT THE DIRECTOR'S PARTY TONIGHT.
C'MON, IT'LL BE JUST THE THING. YOU NEED TO CUT LOOSE!

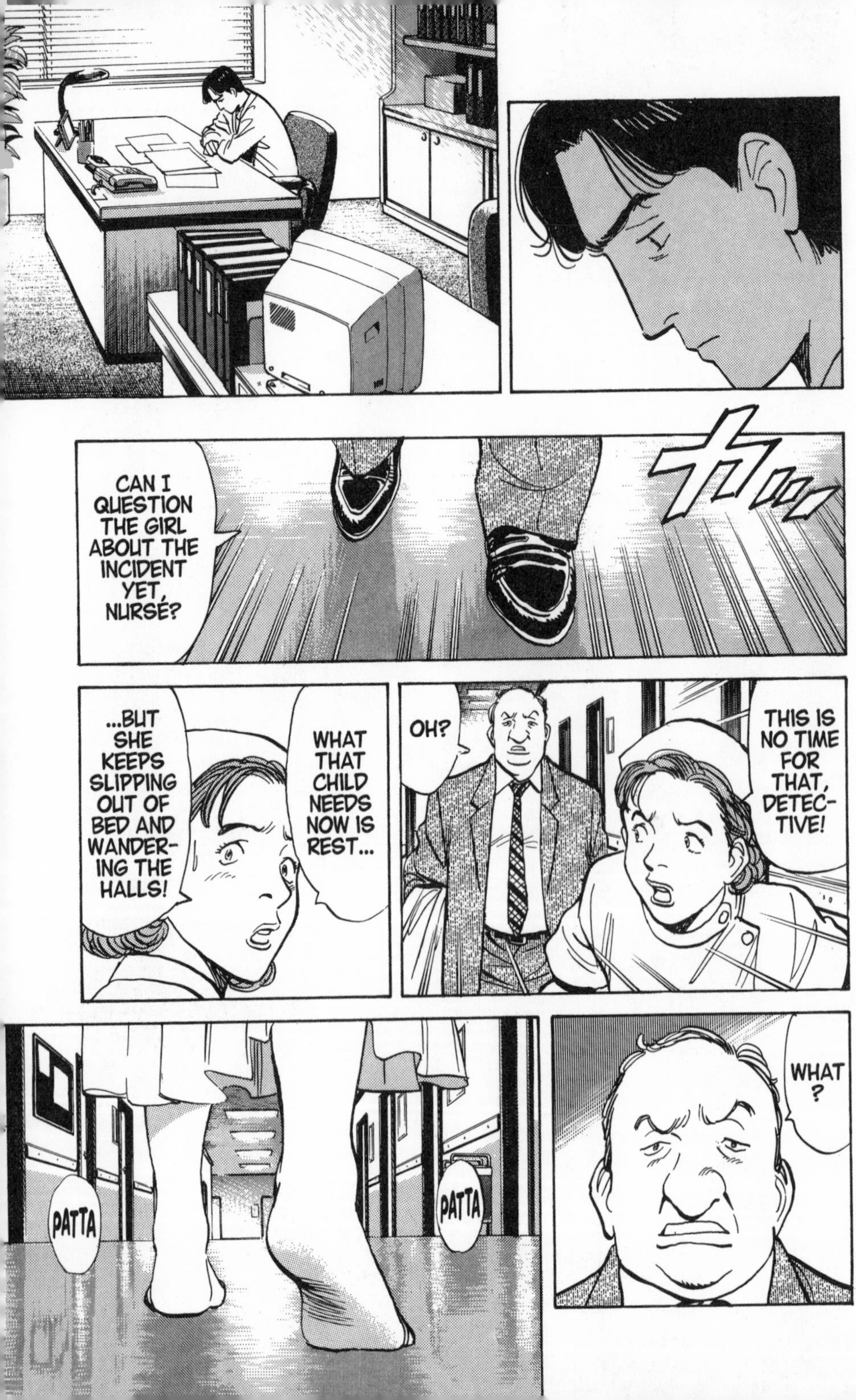
カッ
CAN I QUESTION THE GIRL ABOUT THE INCIDENT YET, NURSE?
THIS IS NO TIME FOR THAT, DETECTIVE!
OH?
WHAT THAT CHILD NEEDS NOW IS REST...
...BUT SHE KEEPS SLIPPING OUT OF BED AND WANDERING THE HALLS!
WHAT?
PATTA
PATTA

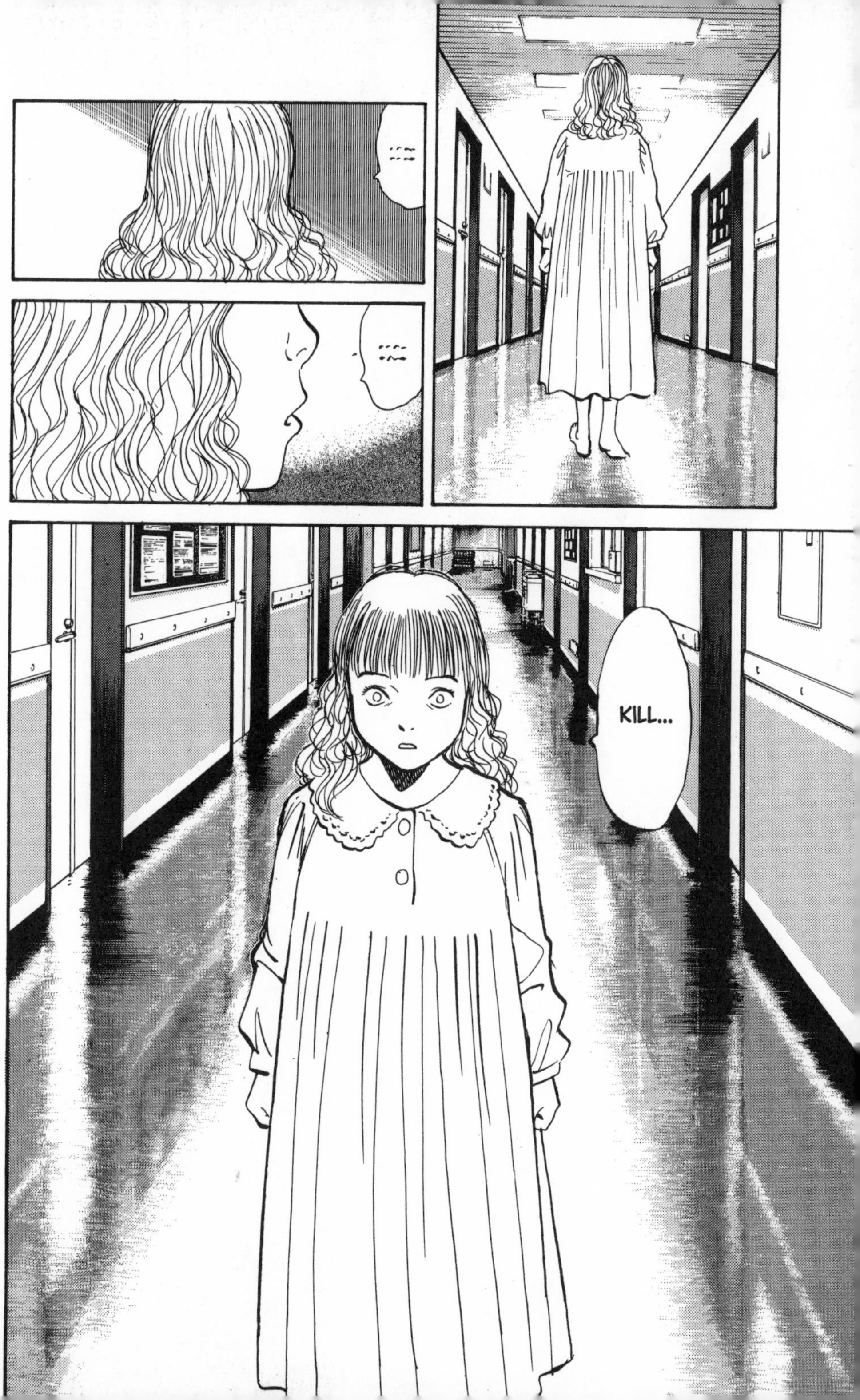
KILL...

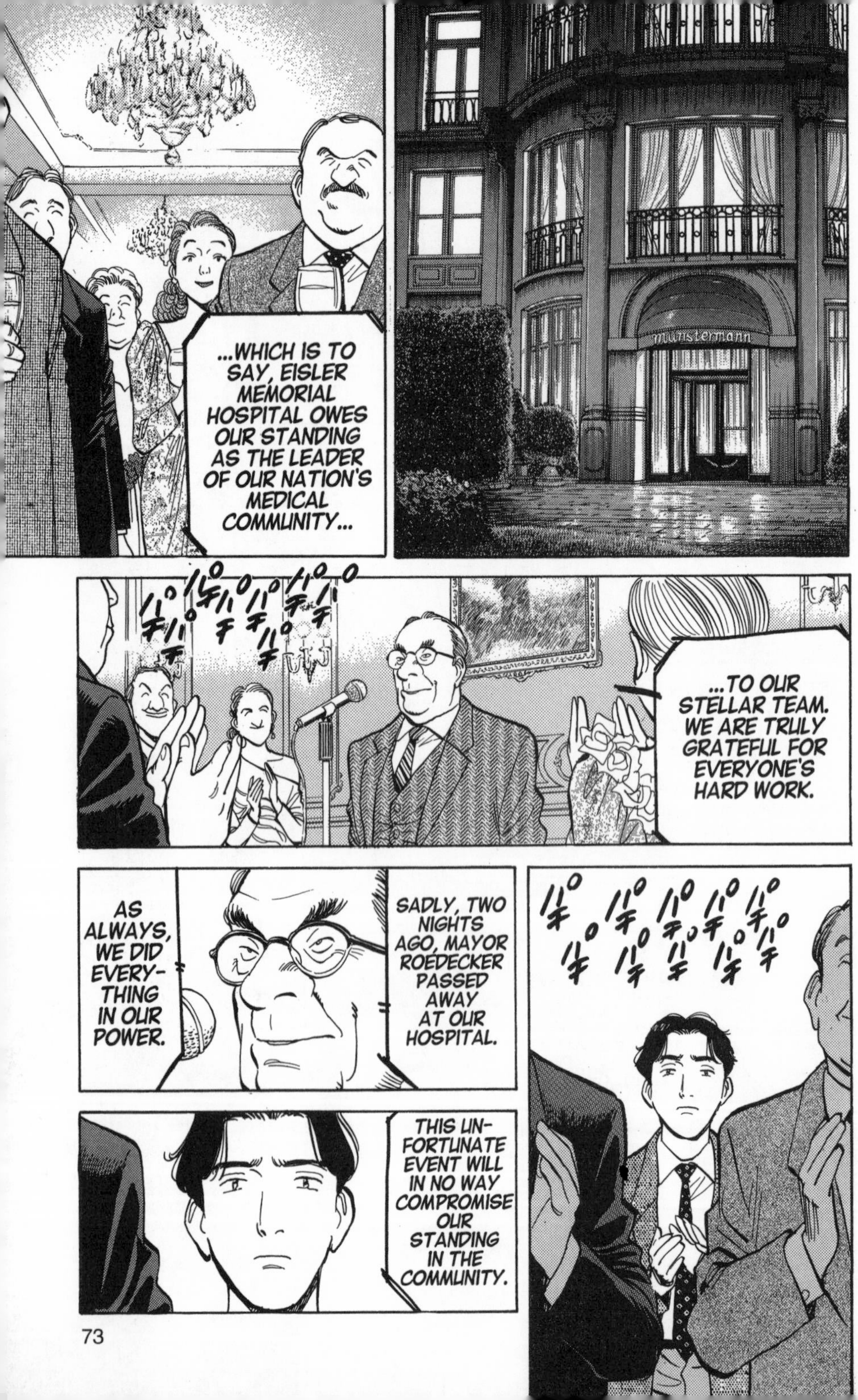
...WHICH IS TO SAY, EISLER MEMORIAL HOSPITAL OWES OUR STANDING AS THE LEADER OF OUR NATION'S MEDICAL COMMUNITY...
パチパチパチパチ
...TO OUR STELLAR TEAM. WE ARE TRULY GRATEFUL FOR EVERYONE'S HARD WORK.
パチパチパチパチ
SADLY, TWO NIGHTS AGO, MAYOR ROEDECKER PASSED AWAY AT OUR HOSPITAL.
AS ALWAYS, WE DID EVERYTHING IN OUR POWER.
THIS UNFORTUNATE EVENT WILL IN NO WAY COMPROMISE OUR STANDING IN THE COMMUNITY.

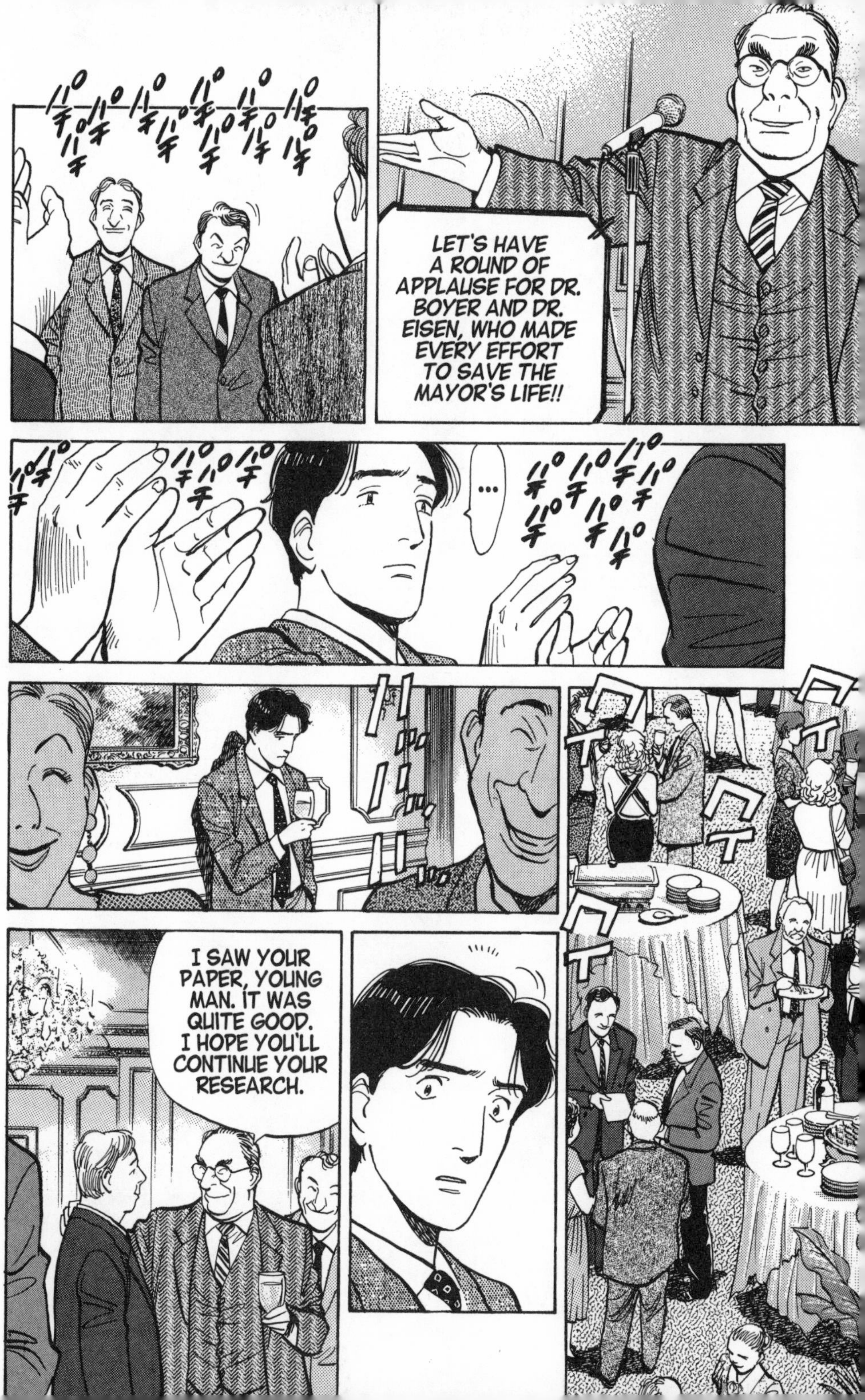

LET'S HAVE A ROUND OF APPLAUSE FOR DR. BOYER AND DR. EISEN, WHO MADE EVERY EFFORT TO SAVE THE MAYOR'S LIFE!!
...
I SAW YOUR PAPER, YOUNG MAN. IT WAS QUITE GOOD. I HOPE YOU'LL CONTINUE YOUR RESEARCH.

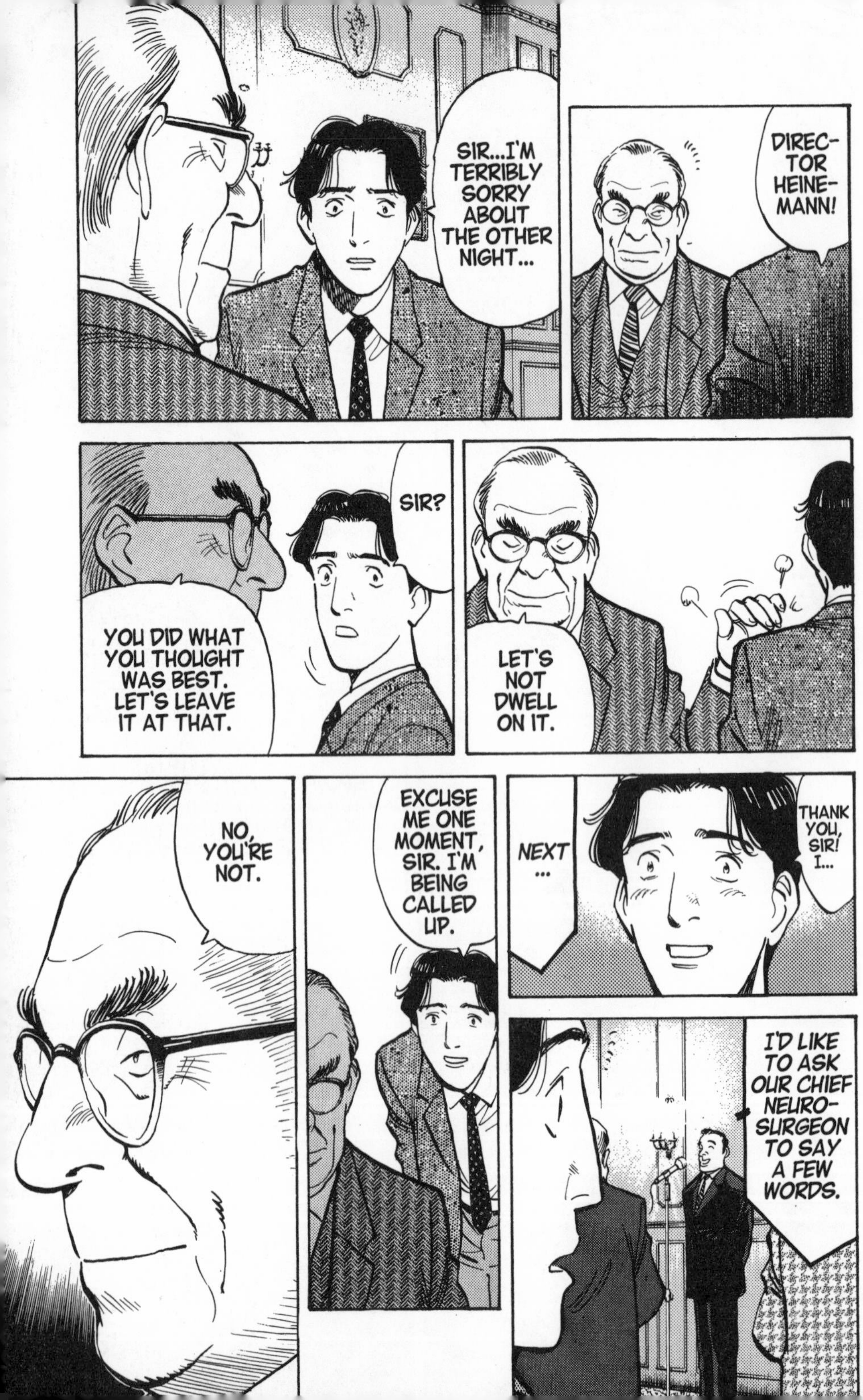
DIREC-
TOR
HEINE-
MANN!
SIR...I'M TERRIBLY SORRY ABOUT THE OTHER NIGHT...
LET'S NOT DWELL ON IT.
SIR?
YOU DID WHAT YOU THOUGHT WAS BEST. LET'S LEAVE IT AT THAT.
THANK YOU, SIR! I...
NEXT...
I'D LIKE TO ASK OUR CHIEF NEURO-
SURGEON TO SAY A FEW WORDS.
EXCUSE ME ONE MOMENT, SIR. I'M BEING CALLED UP.
NO, YOU'RE NOT.

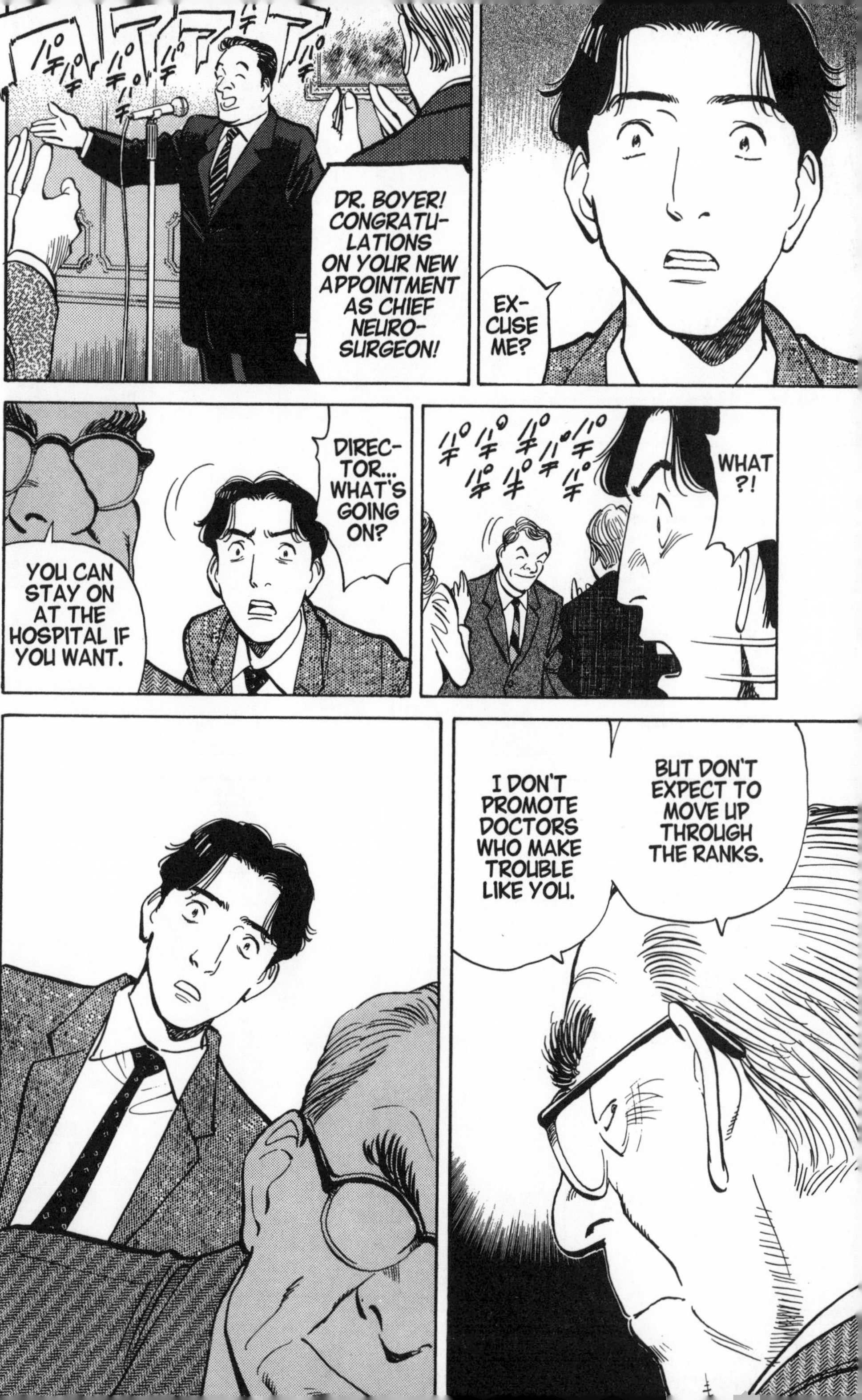

EX-CUSE ME?
DR. BOYER! CONGRATU-LATIONS ON YOUR NEW APPOINTMENT AS CHIEF NEURO-SURGEON!
WHAT ?!
DIREC-TOR... WHAT'S GOING ON?
YOU CAN STAY ON AT THE HOSPITAL IF YOU WANT.
BUT DON'T EXPECT TO MOVE UP THROUGH THE RANKS.
I DON'T PROMOTE DOCTORS WHO MAKE TROUBLE LIKE YOU.

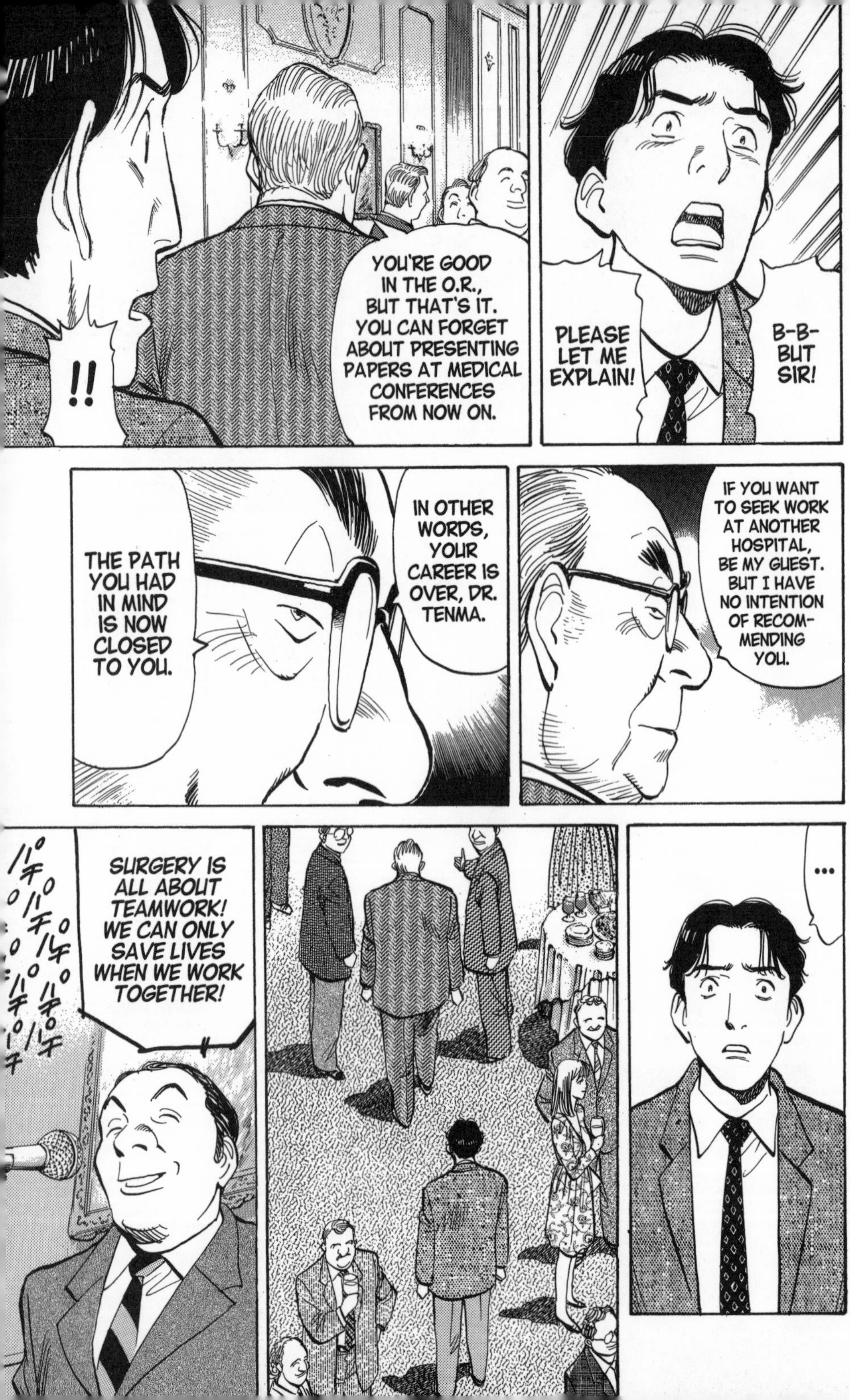

B-B-BUT SIR!
PLEASE LET ME EXPLAIN!
YOU'RE GOOD IN THE O.R., BUT THAT'S IT. YOU CAN FORGET ABOUT PRESENTING PAPERS AT MEDICAL CONFERENCES FROM NOW ON.
!!
IF YOU WANT TO SEEK WORK AT ANOTHER HOSPITAL, BE MY GUEST. BUT I HAVE NO INTENTION OF RECOMMENDING YOU.
IN OTHER WORDS, YOUR CAREER IS OVER, DR. TENMA.
THE PATH YOU HAD IN MIND IS NOW CLOSED TO YOU.
...
SURGERY IS ALL ABOUT TEAMWORK! WE CAN ONLY SAVE LIVES WHEN WE WORK TOGETHER!

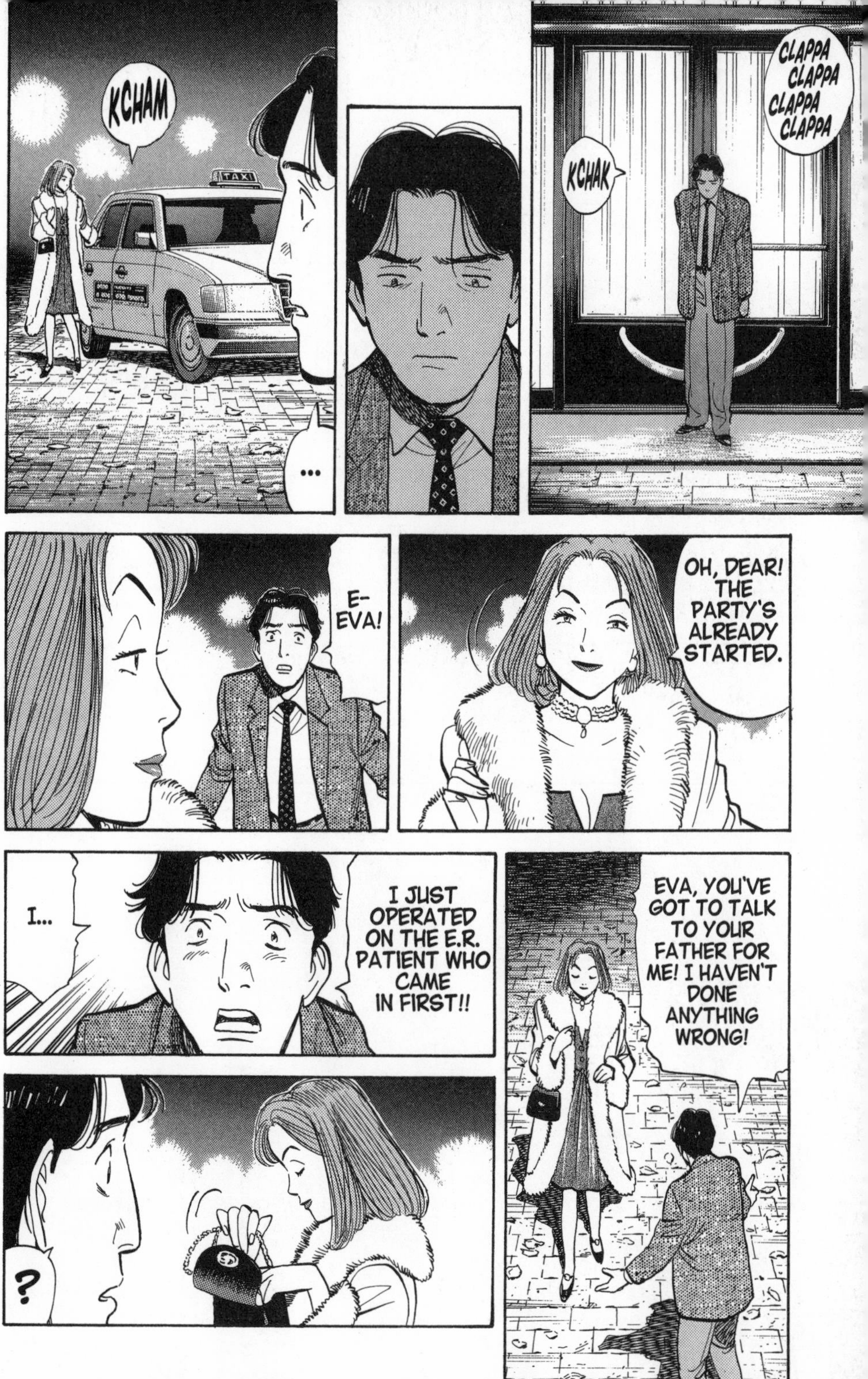
CLAPPA CLAPPA CLAPPA CLAPPA
KCHAK
KCHAM
...
OH, DEAR! THE PARTY'S ALREADY STARTED.
E- EVA!
EVA, YOU'VE GOT TO TALK TO YOUR FATHER FOR ME! I HAVEN'T DONE ANYTHING WRONG!
I JUST OPERATED ON THE E.R. PATIENT WHO CAME IN FIRST!!
I...
?

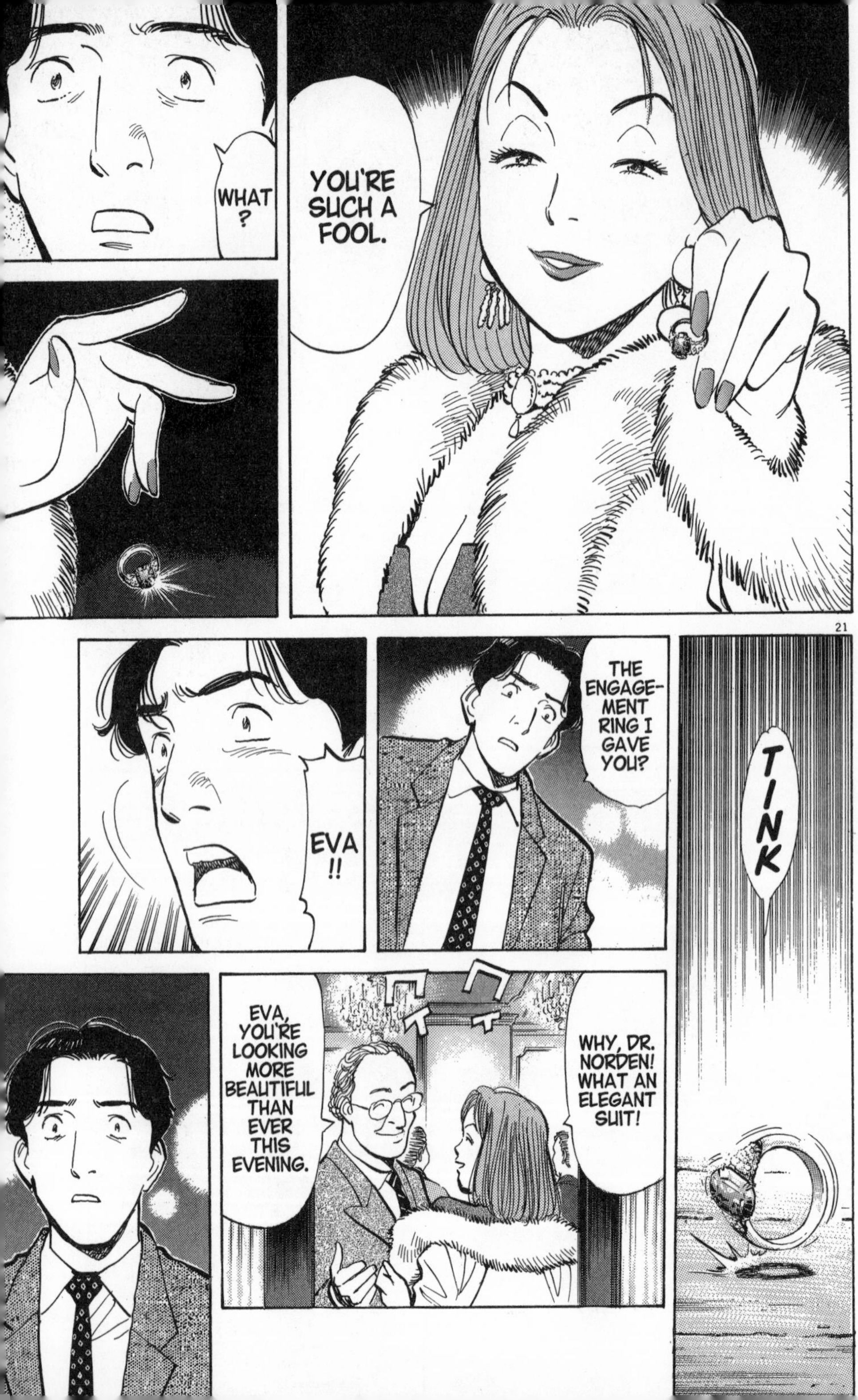
YOU'RE SUCH A FOOL.
WHAT ?
TINK
THE ENGAGE-MENT RING I GAVE YOU?
EVA !!
WHY, DR. NORDEN! WHAT AN ELEGANT SUIT!
EVA, YOU'RE LOOKING MORE BEAUTIFUL THAN EVER THIS EVENING.

ICU
MONITOR

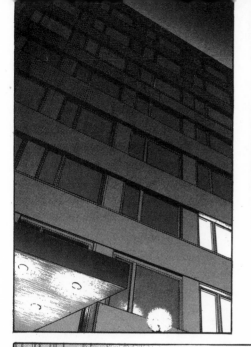

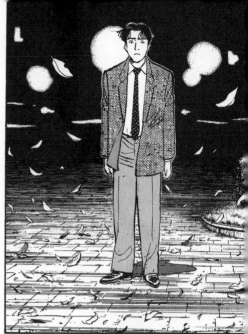

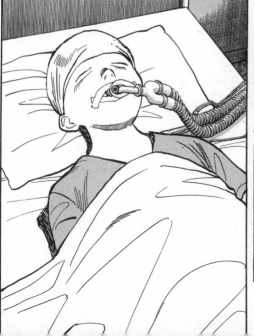

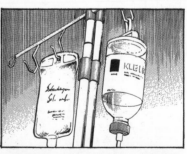

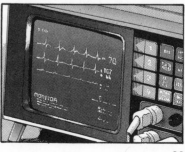

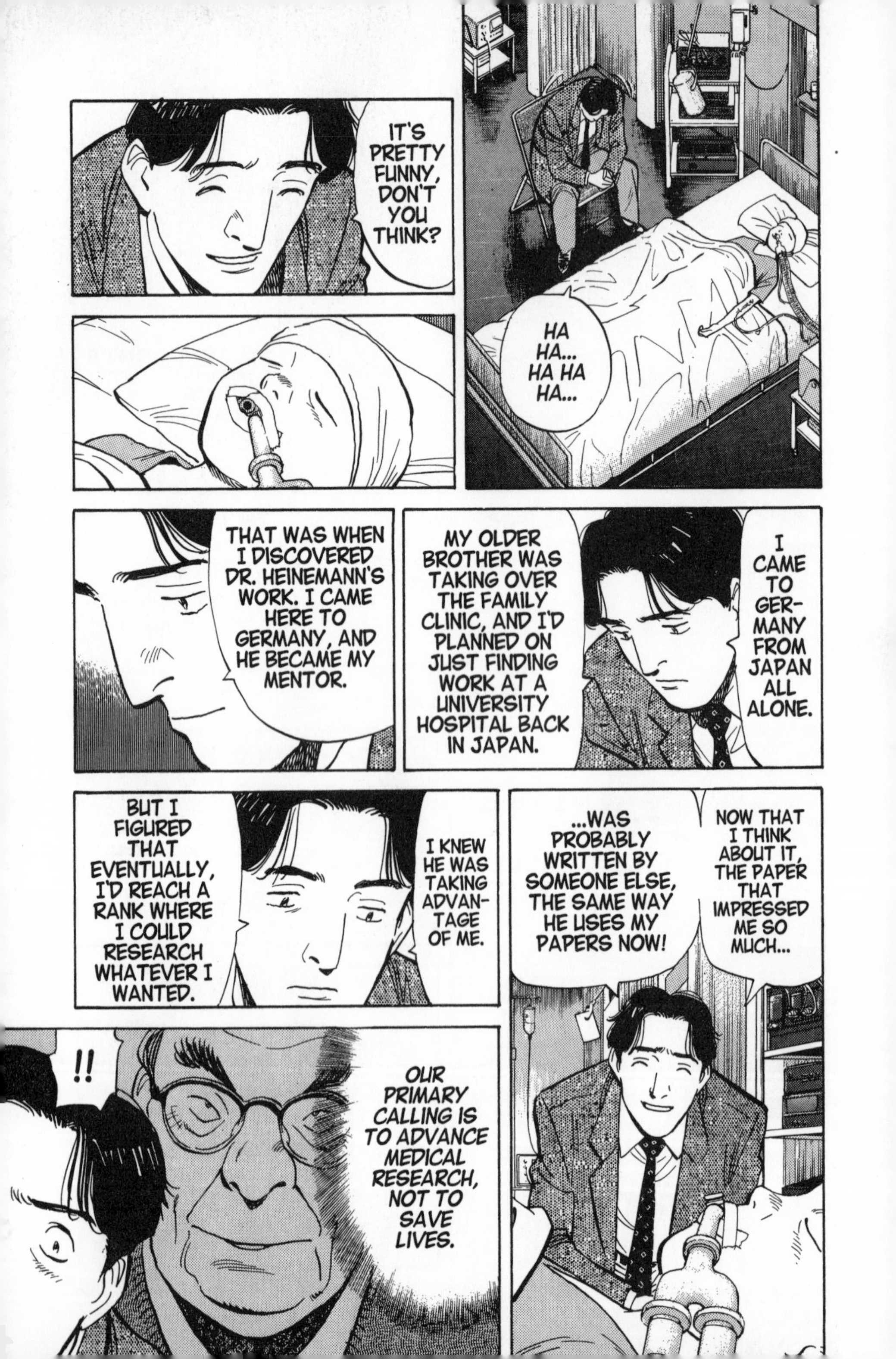
HA HA... HA HA HA...
IT'S PRETTY FUNNY, DON'T YOU THINK?
I CAME TO GERMANY FROM JAPAN ALL ALONE.
MY OLDER BROTHER WAS TAKING OVER THE FAMILY CLINIC, AND I'D PLANNED ON JUST FINDING WORK AT A UNIVERSITY HOSPITAL BACK IN JAPAN.
THAT WAS WHEN I DISCOVERED DR. HEINEMANN'S WORK. I CAME HERE TO GERMANY, AND HE BECAME MY MENTOR.
NOW THAT I THINK ABOUT IT, THE PAPER THAT IMPRESSED ME SO MUCH...
...WAS PROBABLY WRITTEN BY SOMEONE ELSE, THE SAME WAY HE USES MY PAPERS NOW!
I KNEW HE WAS TAKING ADVANTAGE OF ME.
BUT I FIGURED THAT EVENTUALLY, I'D REACH A RANK WHERE I COULD RESEARCH WHATEVER I WANTED.
OUR PRIMARY CALLING IS TO ADVANCE MEDICAL RESEARCH, NOT TO SAVE LIVES.
!!

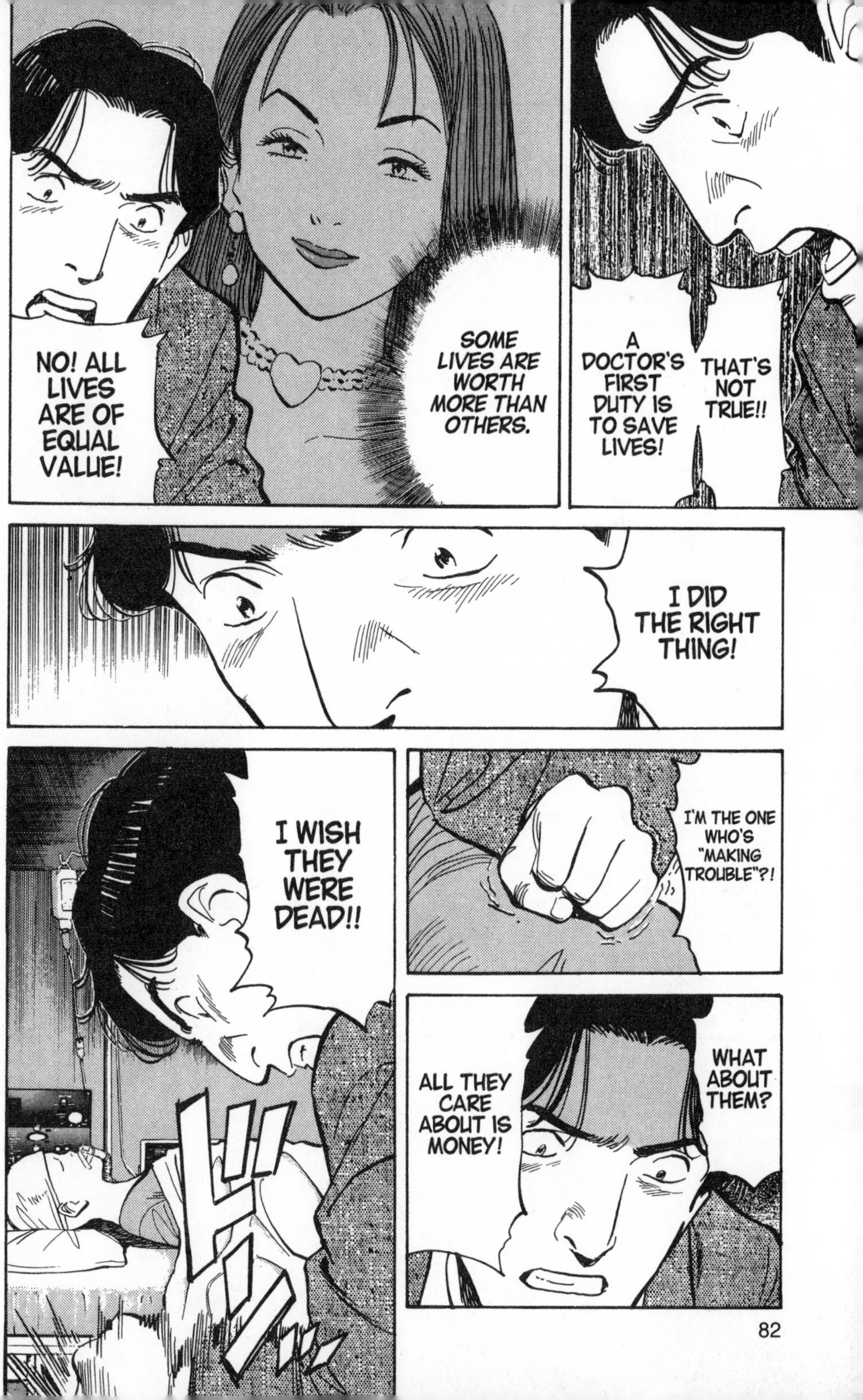
THAT'S NOT TRUE!!
A DOCTOR'S FIRST DUTY IS TO SAVE LIVES!
SOME LIVES ARE WORTH MORE THAN OTHERS.
NO! ALL LIVES ARE OF EQUAL VALUE!
I DID THE RIGHT THING!
I'M THE ONE WHO'S "MAKING TROUBLE"?!
WHAT ABOUT THEM?
ALL THEY CARE ABOUT IS MONEY!
I WISH THEY WERE DEAD!!

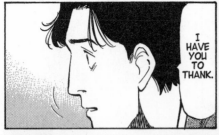

I HAVE YOU TO THANK.
YOU OPENED MY EYES AS A DOCTOR.
HANG IN THERE. FIGHT FOR YOUR LIFE.
I GAVE UP EVERY-THING TO PERFORM YOUR SURGERY.
THAT'S HOW MUCH I WANTED TO SAVE YOUR LIFE.

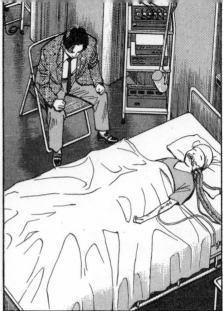

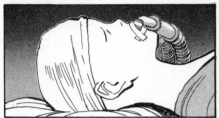

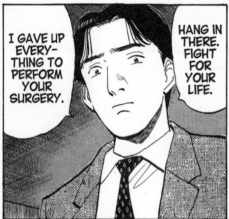

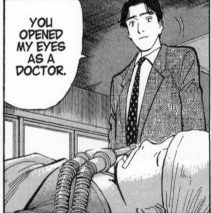

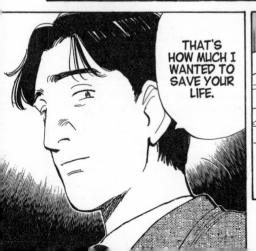

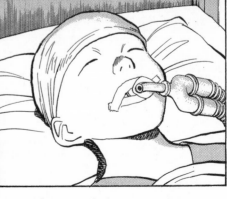

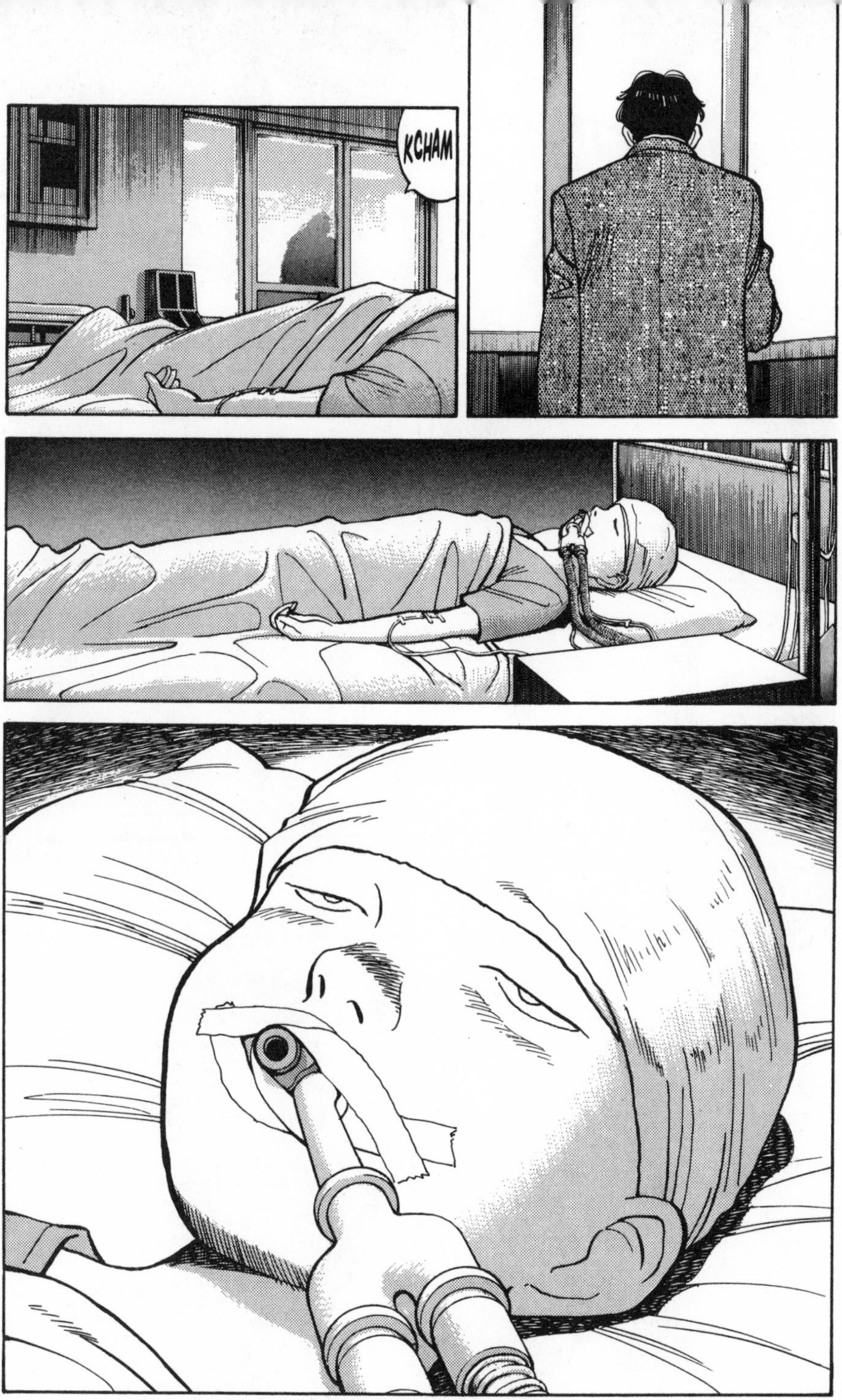
KCHAM

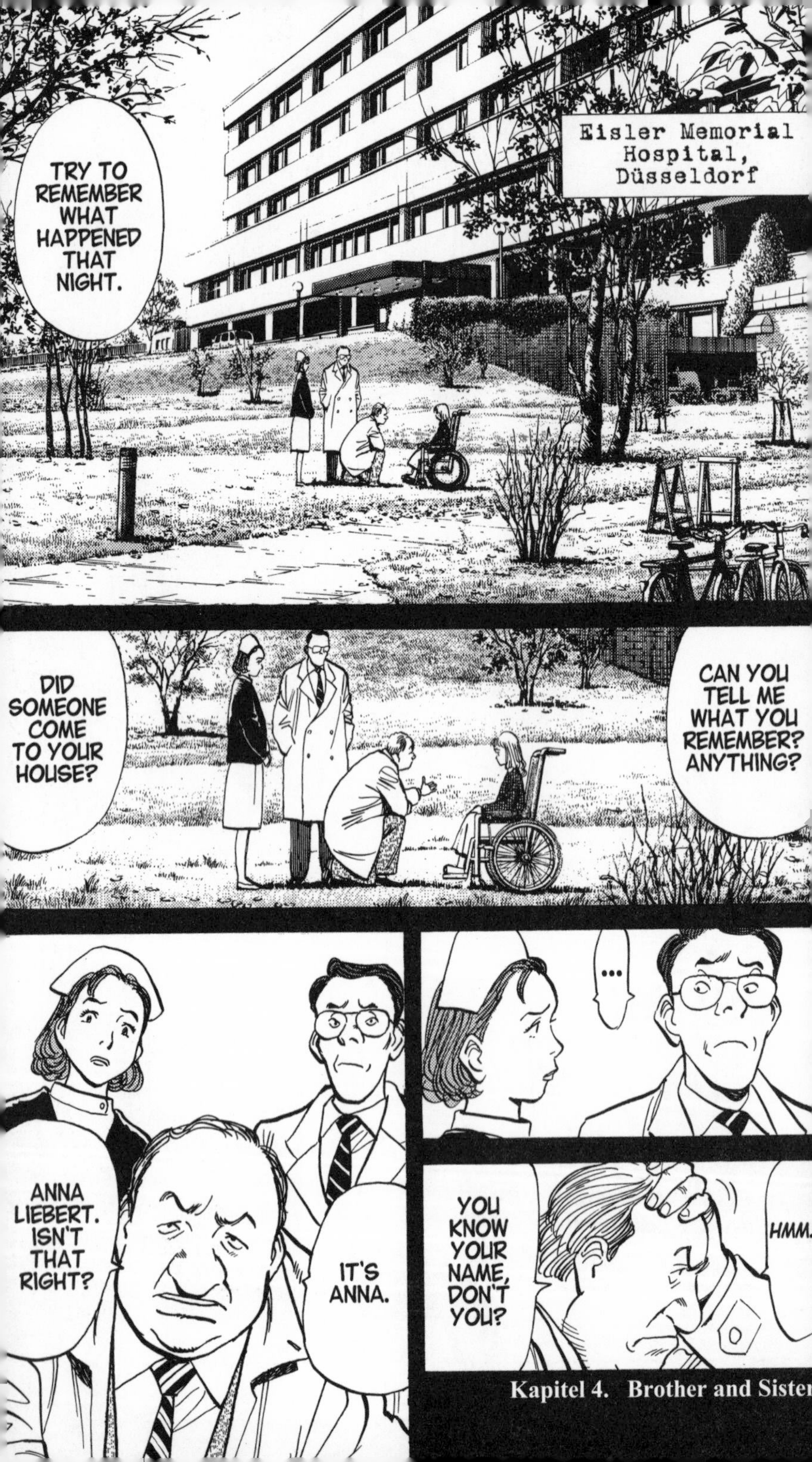

Eisler Memorial Hospital, Düsseldorf
TRY TO REMEMBER WHAT HAPPENED THAT NIGHT.
CAN YOU TELL ME WHAT YOU REMEMBER? ANYTHING?
DID SOMEONE COME TO YOUR HOUSE?
...
HMM.
YOU KNOW YOUR NAME, DON'T YOU?
IT'S ANNA.
ANNA LIEBERT. ISN'T THAT RIGHT?

Kapitel 4. Brother and Sister

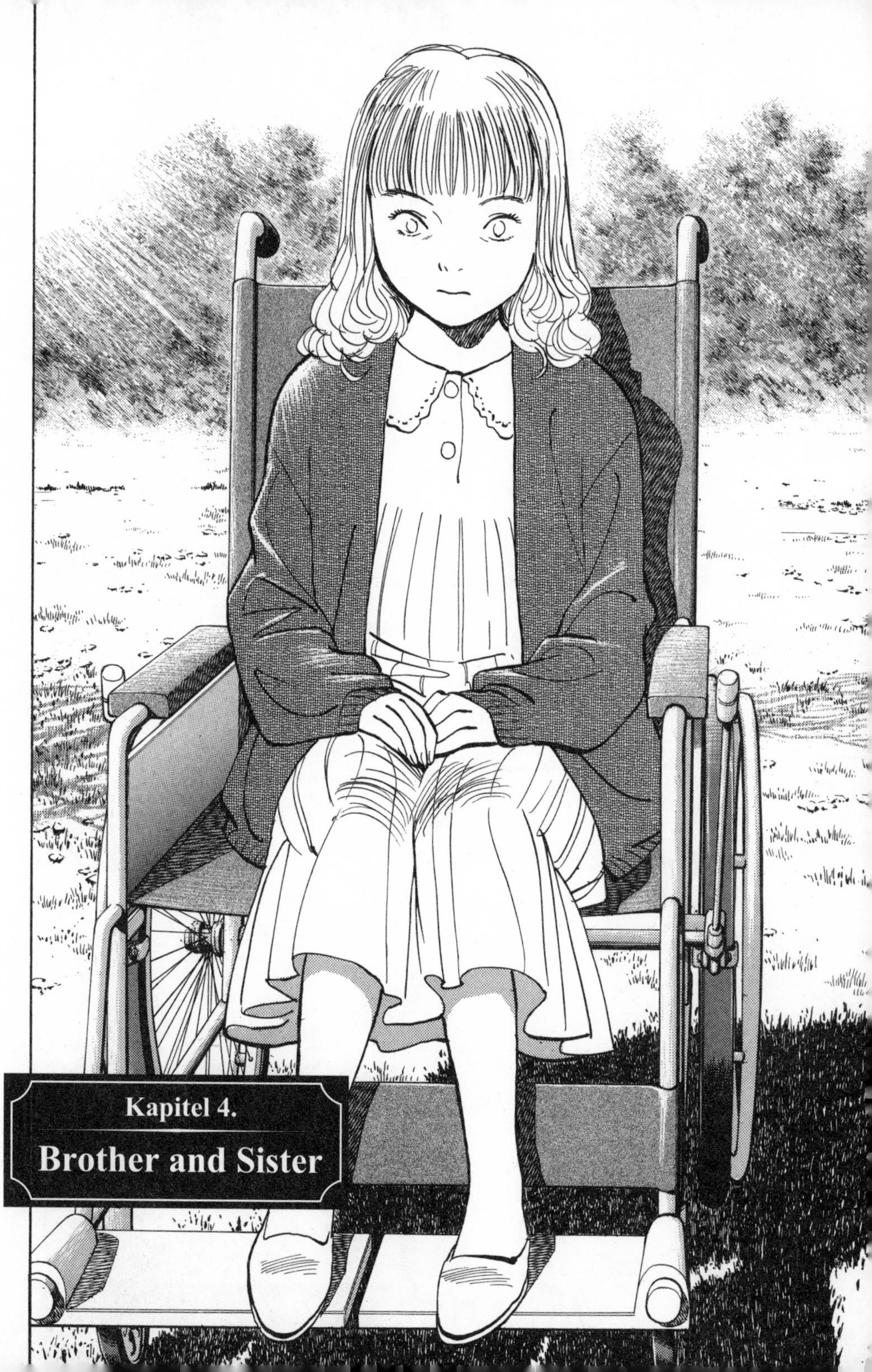
Kapitel 4.
Brother and Sister

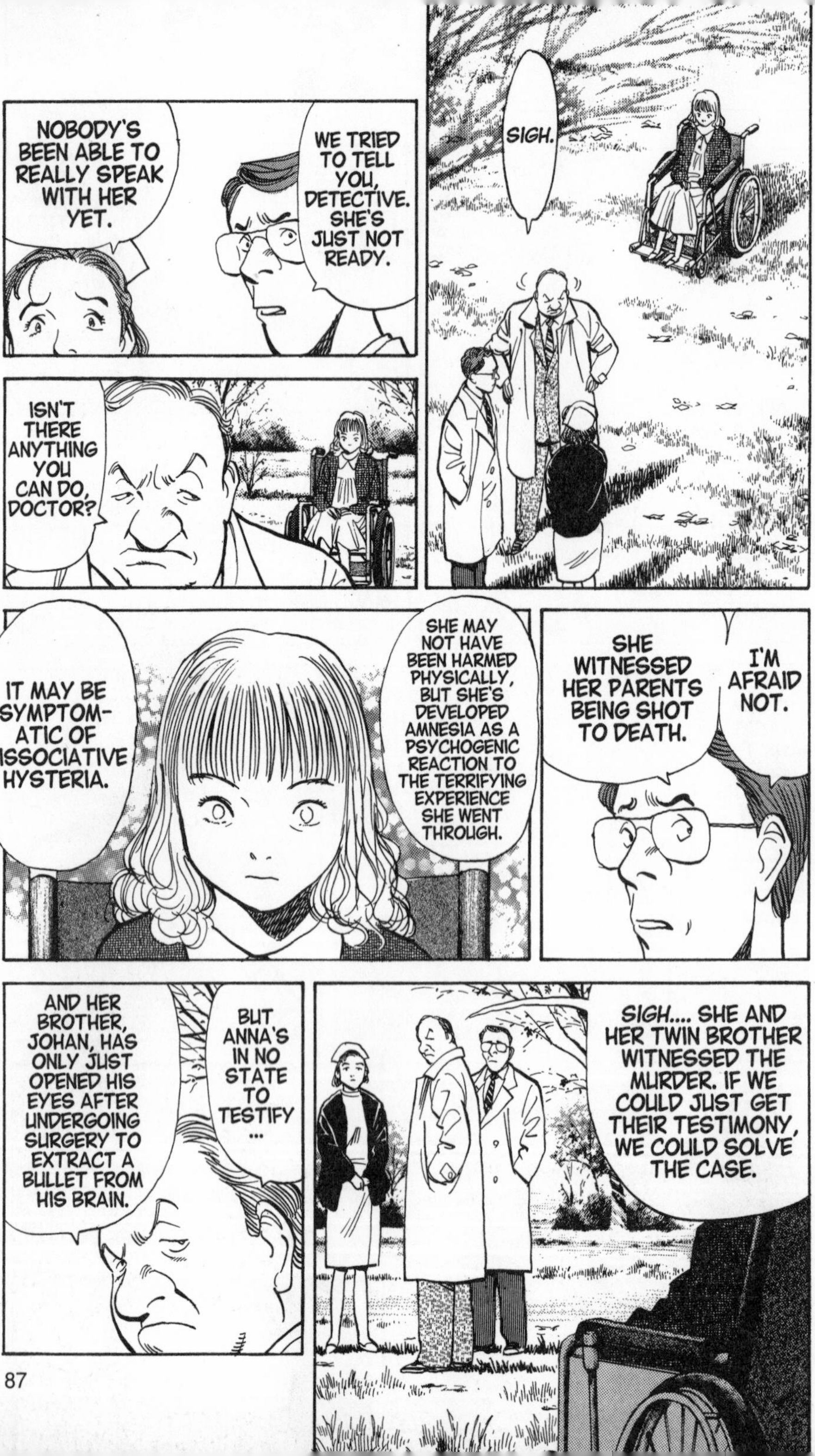

SIGH.
WE TRIED TO TELL YOU, DETECTIVE. SHE'S JUST NOT READY.
NOBODY'S BEEN ABLE TO REALLY SPEAK WITH HER YET.
ISN'T THERE ANYTHING YOU CAN DO, DOCTOR?
I'M AFRAID NOT.
SHE WITNESSED HER PARENTS BEING SHOT TO DEATH.
SHE MAY NOT HAVE BEEN HARMED PHYSICALLY, BUT SHE'S DEVELOPED AMNESIA AS A PSYCHOGENIC REACTION TO THE TERRIFYING EXPERIENCE SHE WENT THROUGH.
IT MAY BE SYMPTOM-ATIC OF DISSOCIATIVE HYSTERIA.
SIGH.... SHE AND HER TWIN BROTHER WITNESSED THE MURDER. IF WE COULD JUST GET THEIR TESTIMONY, WE COULD SOLVE THE CASE.
BUT ANNA'S IN NO STATE TO TESTIFY ...
AND HER BROTHER, JOHAN, HAS ONLY JUST OPENED HIS EYES AFTER UNDERGOING SURGERY TO EXTRACT A BULLET FROM HIS BRAIN.

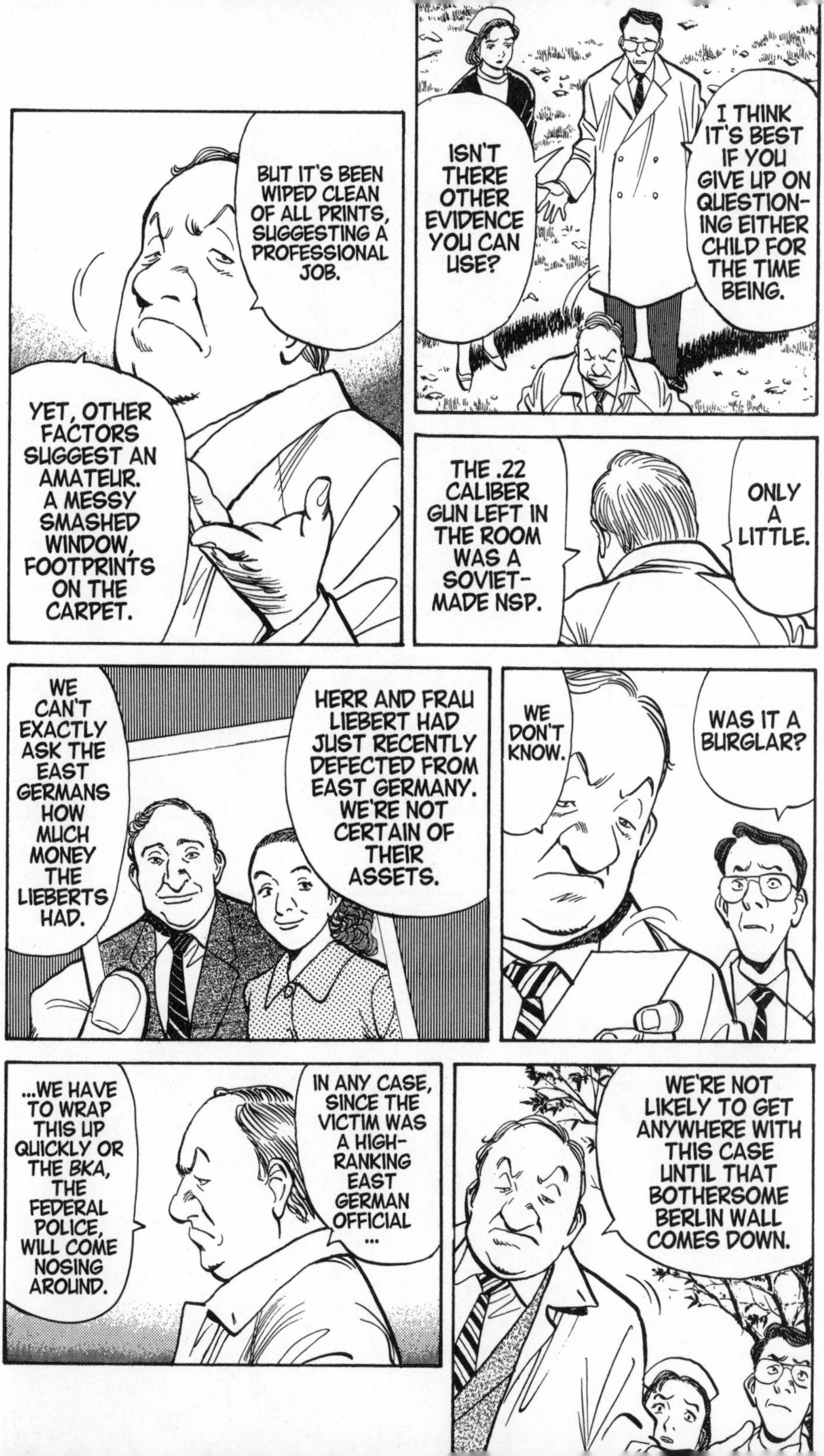
I THINK IT'S BEST IF YOU GIVE UP ON QUESTION-ING EITHER CHILD FOR THE TIME BEING.
ISN'T THERE OTHER EVIDENCE YOU CAN USE?
ONLY A LITTLE.
THE .22 CALIBER GUN LEFT IN THE ROOM WAS A SOVIET-MADE NSP.
BUT IT'S BEEN WIPED CLEAN OF ALL PRINTS, SUGGESTING A PROFESSIONAL JOB.
YET, OTHER FACTORS SUGGEST AN AMATEUR. A MESSY SMASHED WINDOW, FOOTPRINTS ON THE CARPET.
WAS IT A BURGLAR?
WE DON'T KNOW.
HERR AND FRAU LIEBERT HAD JUST RECENTLY DEFECTED FROM EAST GERMANY. WE'RE NOT CERTAIN OF THEIR ASSETS.
WE CAN'T EXACTLY ASK THE EAST GERMANS HOW MUCH MONEY THE LIEBERTS HAD.
WE'RE NOT LIKELY TO GET ANYWHERE WITH THIS CASE UNTIL THAT BOTHERSOME BERLIN WALL COMES DOWN.
IN ANY CASE, SINCE THE VICTIM WAS A HIGH-RANKING EAST GERMAN OFFICIAL ...
...WE HAVE TO WRAP THIS UP QUICKLY OR THE BKA, THE FEDERAL POLICE, WILL COME NOSING AROUND.

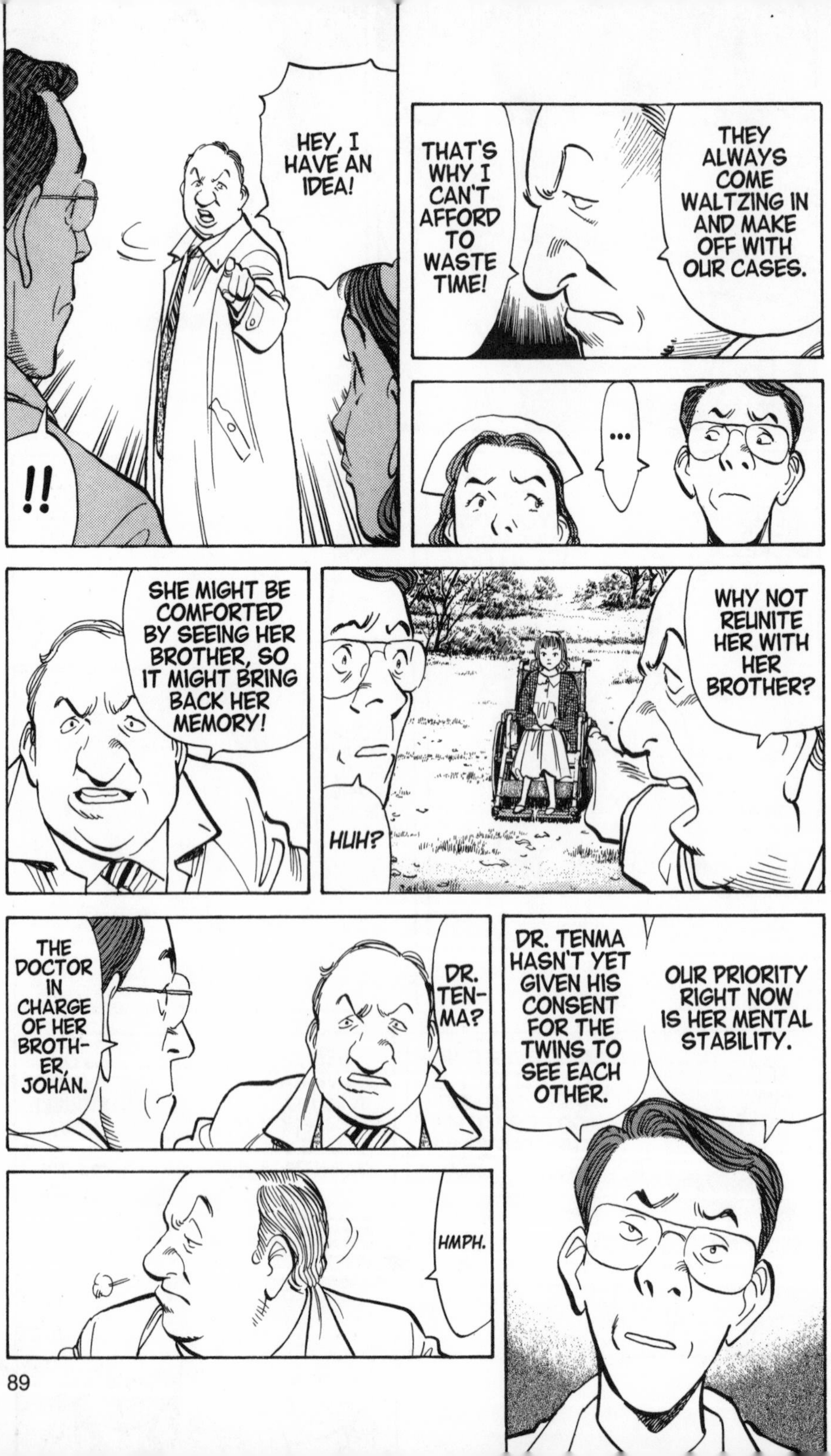
THEY ALWAYS COME WALTZING IN AND MAKE OFF WITH OUR CASES.
THAT'S WHY I CAN'T AFFORD TO WASTE TIME!
...
HEY, I HAVE AN IDEA!
!!
WHY NOT REUNITE HER WITH HER BROTHER?
HUH?
SHE MIGHT BE COMFORTED BY SEEING HER BROTHER, SO IT MIGHT BRING BACK HER MEMORY!
OUR PRIORITY RIGHT NOW IS HER MENTAL STABILITY.
DR. TENMA HASN'T YET GIVEN HIS CONSENT FOR THE TWINS TO SEE EACH OTHER.
DR. TEN-MA?
THE DOCTOR IN CHARGE OF HER BROTH-ER, JOHAN.
HMPH.

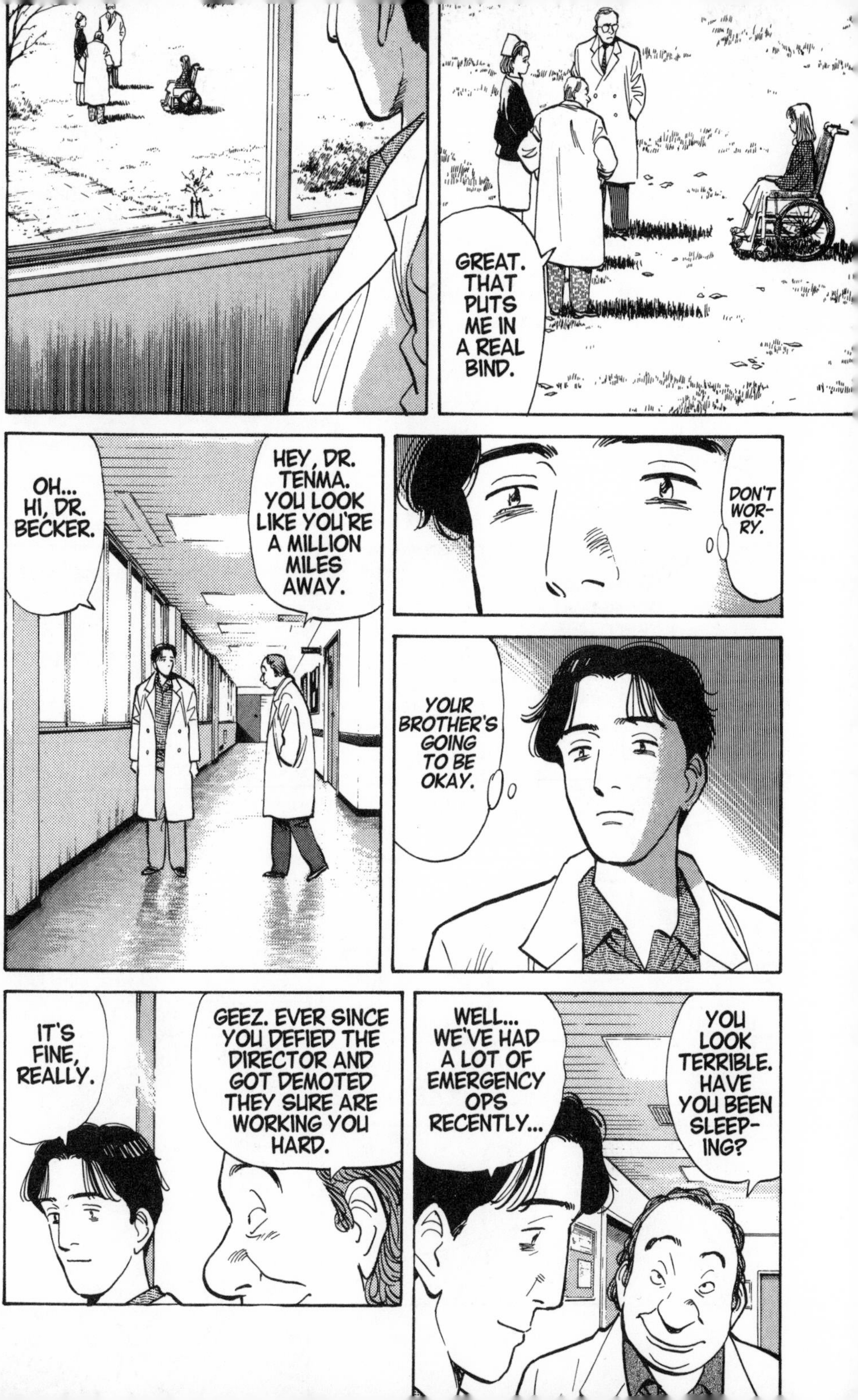
GREAT. THAT PUTS ME IN A REAL BIND.
DON'T WOR-RY.
YOUR BROTHER'S GOING TO BE OKAY.
HEY, DR. TENMA. YOU LOOK LIKE YOU'RE A MILLION MILES AWAY.
OH... HI, DR. BECKER.
YOU LOOK TERRIBLE. HAVE YOU BEEN SLEEP-ING?
WELL... WE'VE HAD A LOT OF EMERGENCY OPS RECENTLY...
GEEZ. EVER SINCE YOU DEFIED THE DIRECTOR AND GOT DEMOTED THEY SURE ARE WORKING YOU HARD.
IT'S FINE, REALLY.

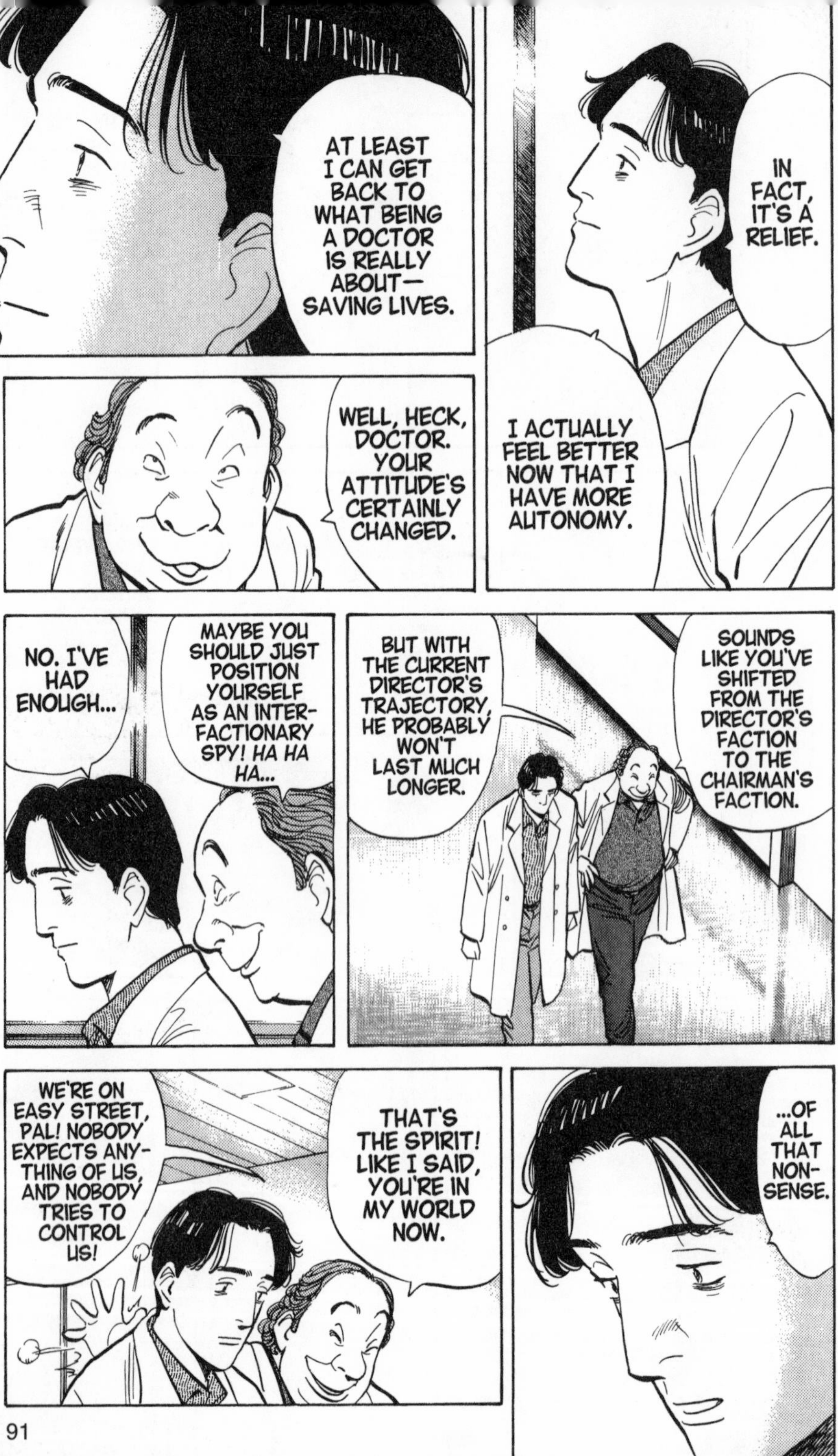
IN FACT, IT'S A RELIEF.
I ACTUALLY FEEL BETTER NOW THAT I HAVE MORE AUTONOMY.
AT LEAST I CAN GET BACK TO WHAT BEING A DOCTOR IS REALLY ABOUT— SAVING LIVES.
WELL, HECK, DOCTOR. YOUR ATTITUDE'S CERTAINLY CHANGED.
SOUNDS LIKE YOU'VE SHIFTED FROM THE DIRECTOR'S FACTION TO THE CHAIRMAN'S FACTION.
BUT WITH THE CURRENT DIRECTOR'S TRAJECTORY, HE PROBABLY WON'T LAST MUCH LONGER.
MAYBE YOU SHOULD JUST POSITION YOURSELF AS AN INTER-FACTIONARY SPY! HA HA HA...
NO. I'VE HAD ENOUGH...
...OF ALL THAT NON-SENSE.
THAT'S THE SPIRIT! LIKE I SAID, YOU'RE IN MY WORLD NOW.
WE'RE ON EASY STREET, PAL! NOBODY EXPECTS ANY-THING OF US, AND NOBODY TRIES TO CONTROL US!

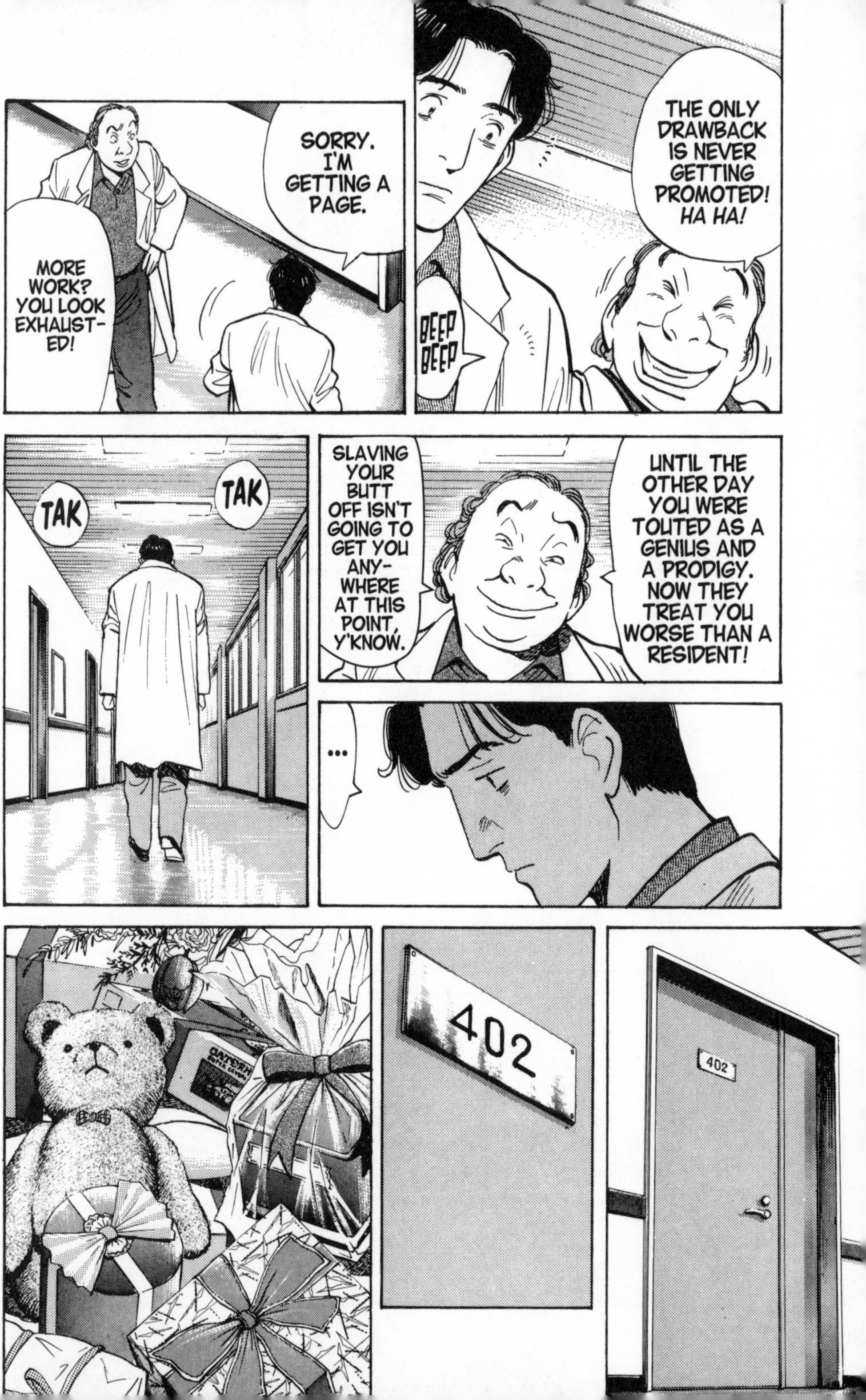
THE ONLY DRAWBACK IS NEVER GETTING PROMOTED! HA HA!
…
BEEP BEEP
SORRY. I'M GETTING A PAGE.
MORE WORK? YOU LOOK EXHAUST-ED!
UNTIL THE OTHER DAY YOU WERE TOUTED AS A GENIUS AND A PRODIGY. NOW THEY TREAT YOU WORSE THAN A RESIDENT!
SLAVING YOUR BUTT OFF ISN'T GOING TO GET YOU ANY-WHERE AT THIS POINT, Y'KNOW.
...
TAK
TAK
402
402

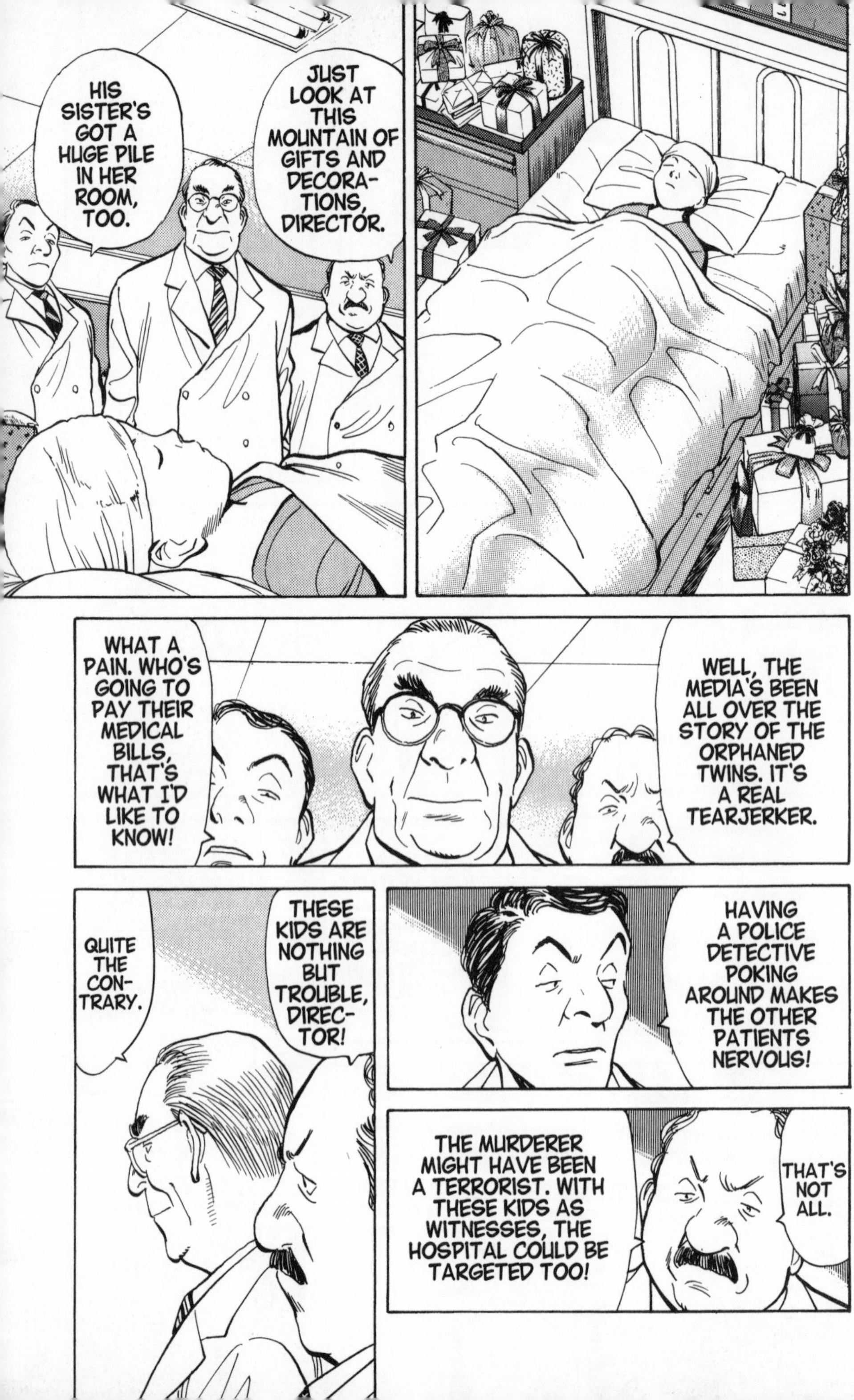

JUST LOOK AT THIS MOUNTAIN OF GIFTS AND DECORATIONS, DIRECTOR.
HIS SISTER'S GOT A HUGE PILE IN HER ROOM, TOO.
WELL, THE MEDIA'S BEEN ALL OVER THE STORY OF THE ORPHANED TWINS. IT'S A REAL TEARJERKER.
WHAT A PAIN. WHO'S GOING TO PAY THEIR MEDICAL BILLS, THAT'S WHAT I'D LIKE TO KNOW!
HAVING A POLICE DETECTIVE POKING AROUND MAKES THE OTHER PATIENTS NERVOUS!
THAT'S NOT ALL.
THE MURDERER MIGHT HAVE BEEN A TERRORIST. WITH THESE KIDS AS WITNESSES, THE HOSPITAL COULD BE TARGETED TOO!
THESE KIDS ARE NOTHING BUT TROUBLE, DIRECTOR!
QUITE THE CONTRARY.

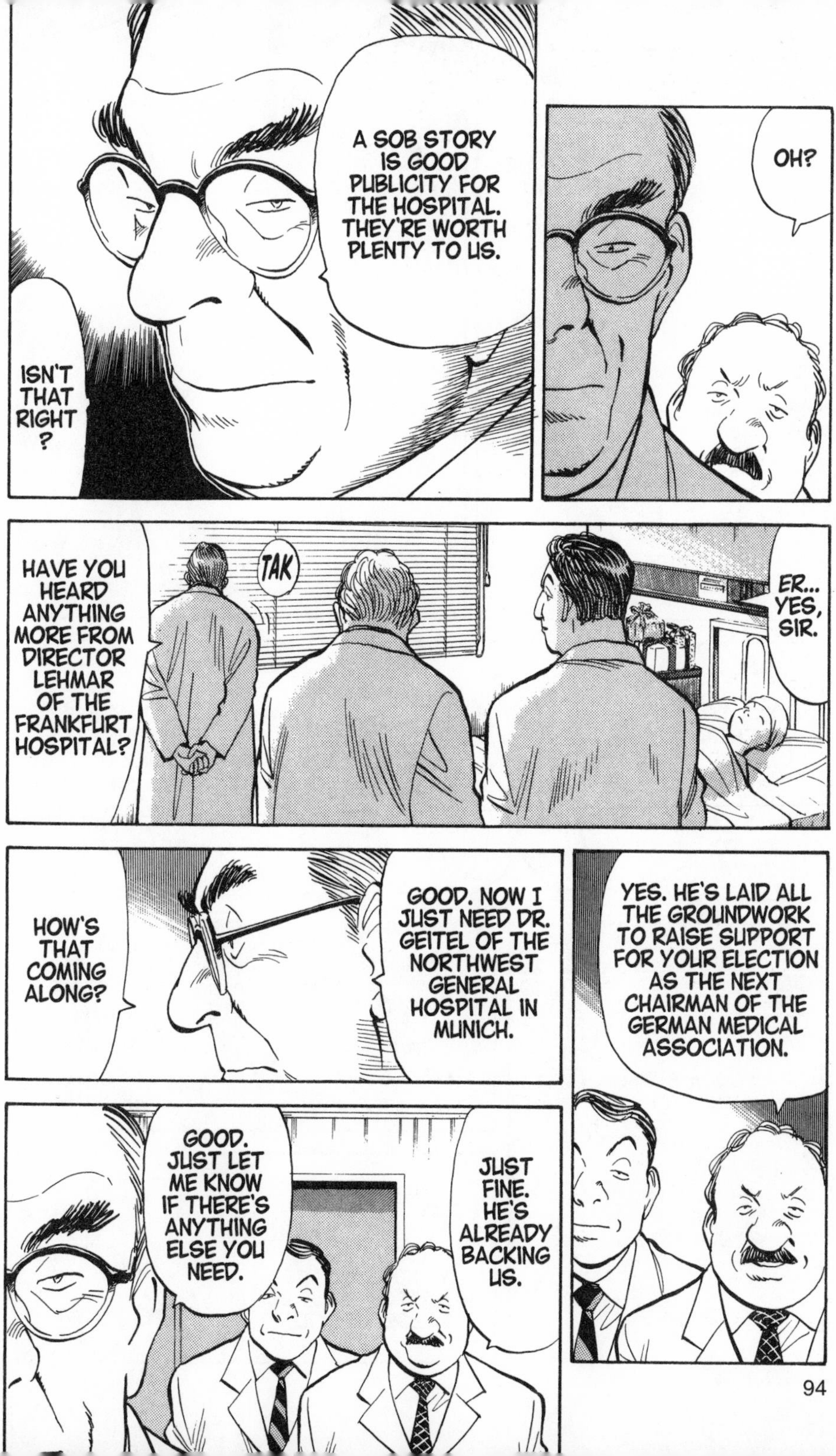
OH?
A SOB STORY IS GOOD PUBLICITY FOR THE HOSPITAL. THEY'RE WORTH PLENTY TO US.
ISN'T THAT RIGHT?
ER... YES, SIR.
TAK
HAVE YOU HEARD ANYTHING MORE FROM DIRECTOR LEHMAR OF THE FRANKFURT HOSPITAL?
YES. HE'S LAID ALL THE GROUNDWORK TO RAISE SUPPORT FOR YOUR ELECTION AS THE NEXT CHAIRMAN OF THE GERMAN MEDICAL ASSOCIATION.
GOOD. NOW I JUST NEED DR. GEITEL OF THE NORTHWEST GENERAL HOSPITAL IN MUNICH.
HOW'S THAT COMING ALONG?
JUST FINE. HE'S ALREADY BACKING US.
GOOD. JUST LET ME KNOW IF THERE'S ANYTHING ELSE YOU NEED.

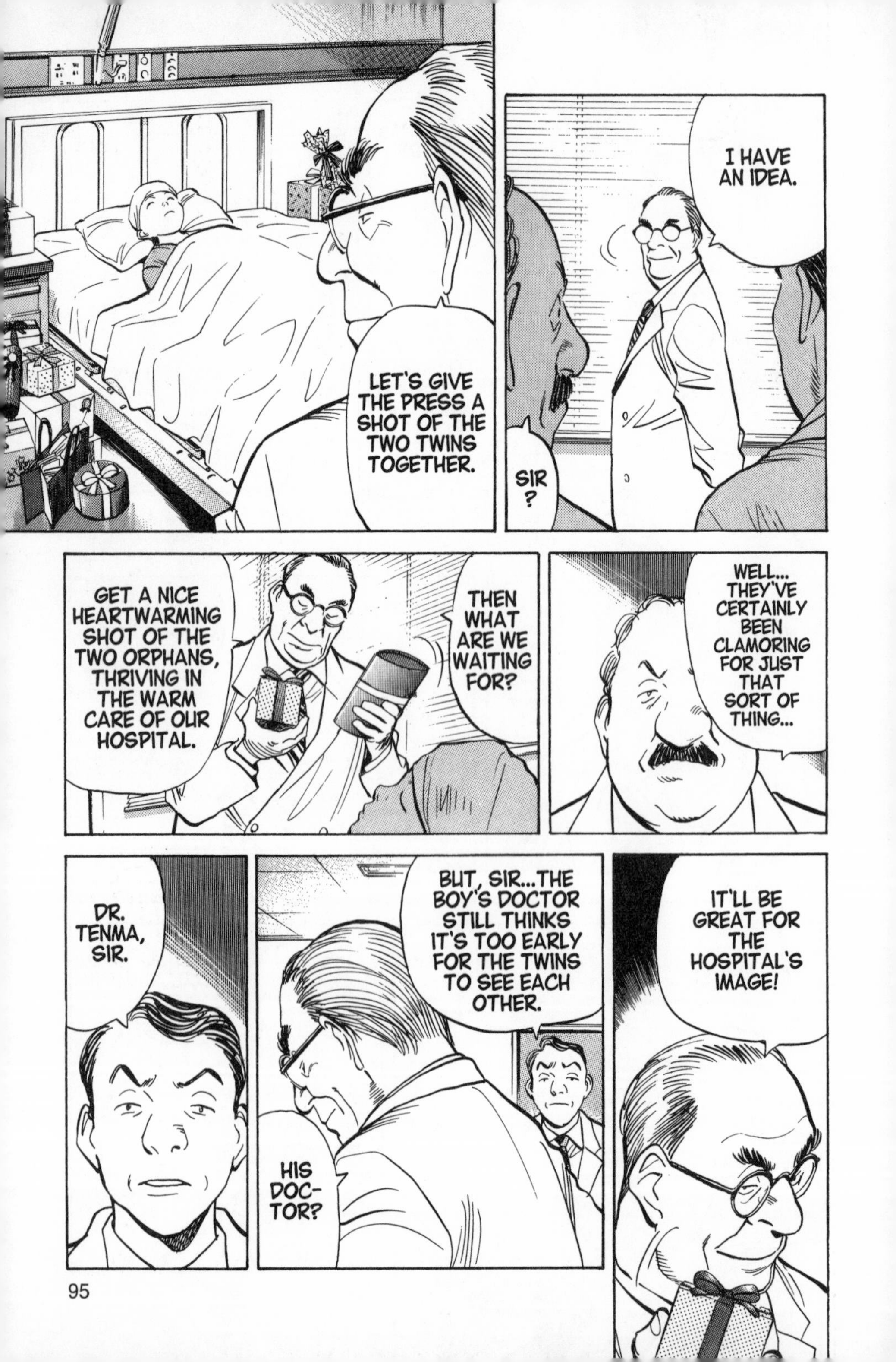
I HAVE AN IDEA.
SIR?
LET'S GIVE THE PRESS A SHOT OF THE TWO TWINS TOGETHER.
WELL... THEY'VE CERTAINLY BEEN CLAMORING FOR JUST THAT SORT OF THING...
THEN WHAT ARE WE WAITING FOR?
GET A NICE HEARTWARMING SHOT OF THE TWO ORPHANS, THRIVING IN THE WARM CARE OF OUR HOSPITAL.
IT'LL BE GREAT FOR THE HOSPITAL'S IMAGE!
BUT, SIR...THE BOY'S DOCTOR STILL THINKS IT'S TOO EARLY FOR THE TWINS TO SEE EACH OTHER.
HIS DOC-TOR?
DR. TENMA, SIR.

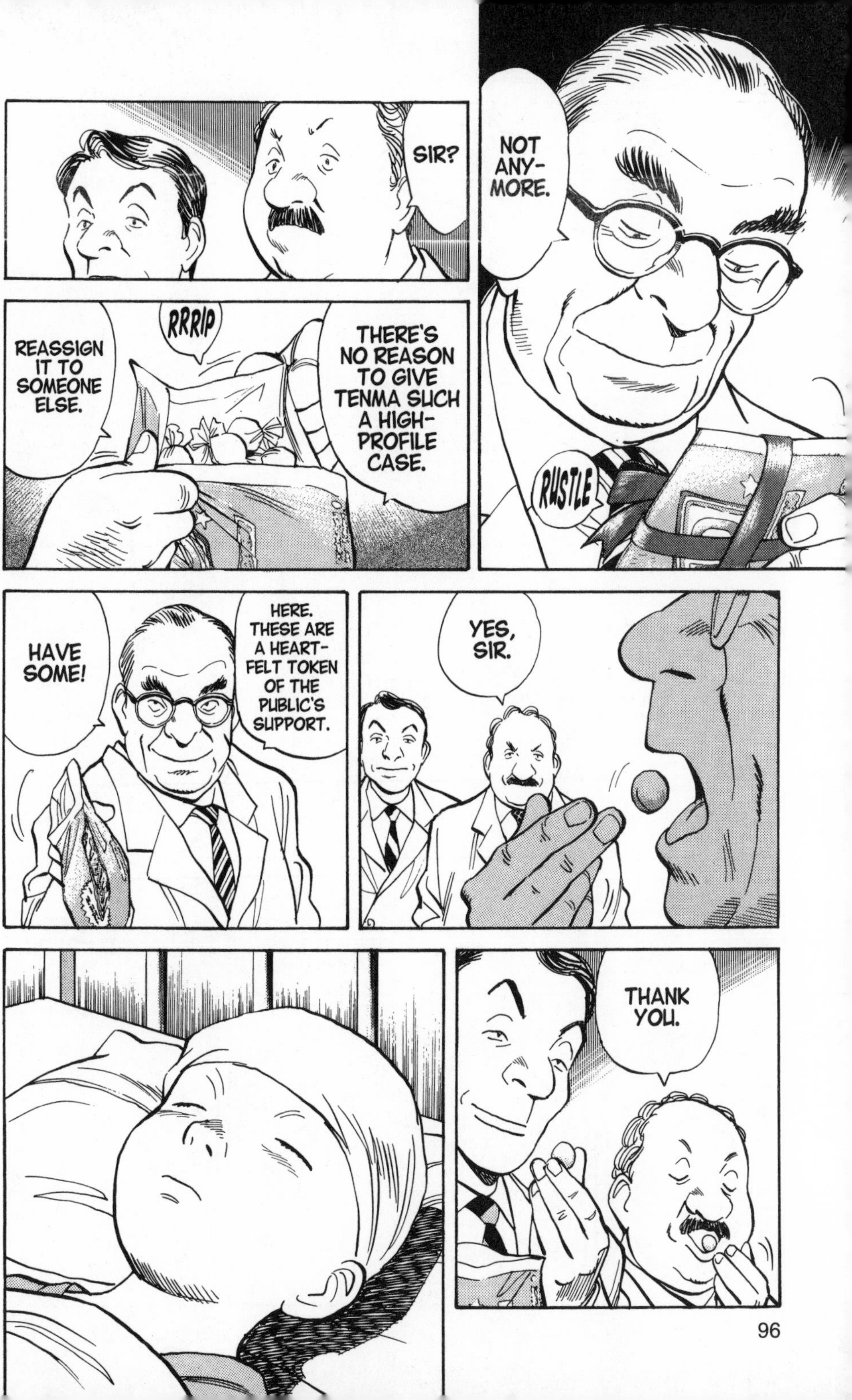
NOT ANYMORE.
RUSTLE
SIR?
THERE'S NO REASON TO GIVE TENMA SUCH A HIGH-PROFILE CASE.
RRRIP
REASSIGN IT TO SOMEONE ELSE.
YES, SIR.
HERE. THESE ARE A HEART-FELT TOKEN OF THE PUBLIC'S SUPPORT.
HAVE SOME!
THANK YOU.

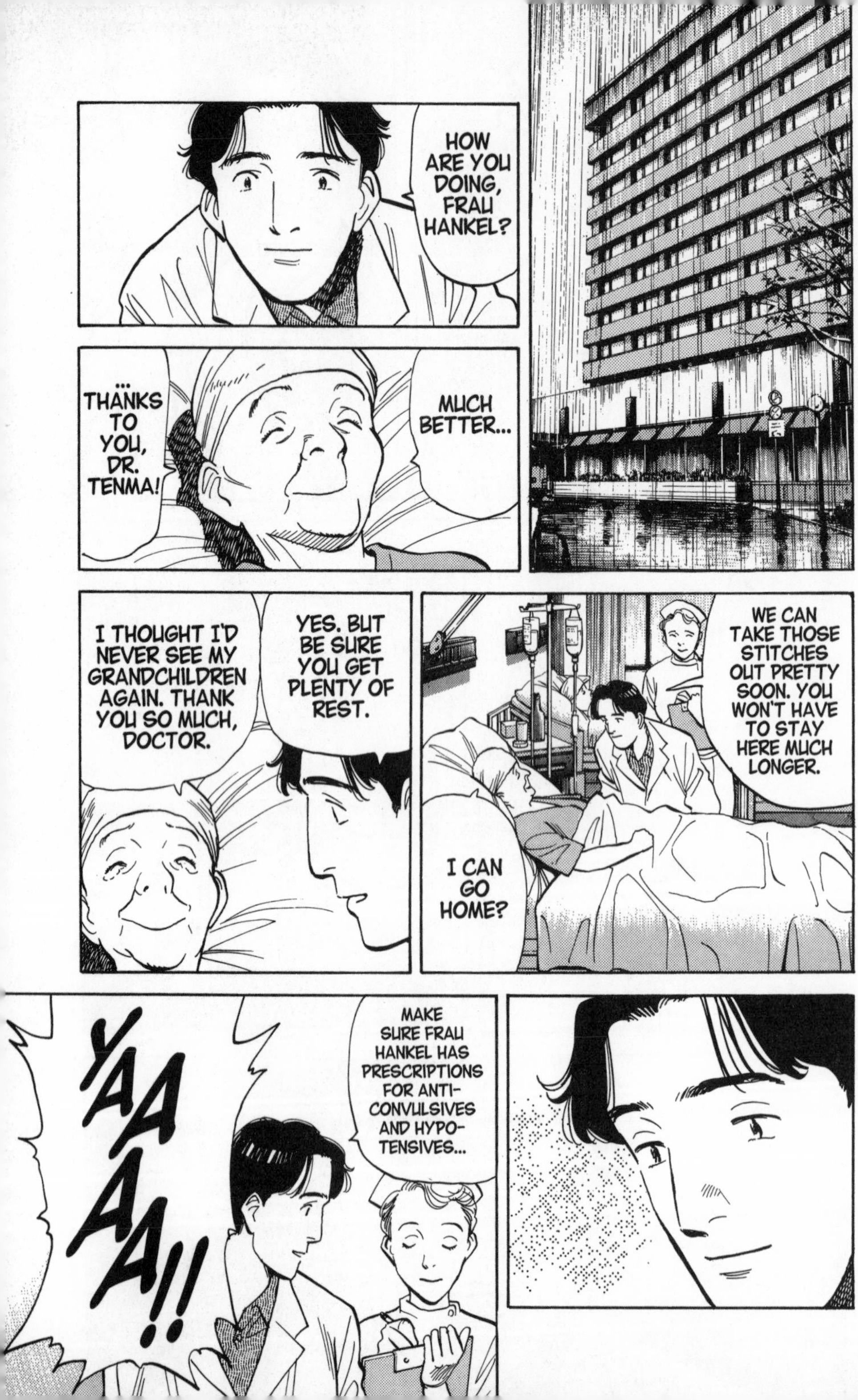
HOW ARE YOU DOING, FRAU HANKEL?
MUCH BETTER...
...THANKS TO YOU, DR. TENMA!
WE CAN TAKE THOSE STITCHES OUT PRETTY SOON. YOU WON'T HAVE TO STAY HERE MUCH LONGER.
I CAN GO HOME?
YES. BUT BE SURE YOU GET PLENTY OF REST.
I THOUGHT I'D NEVER SEE MY GRANDCHILDREN AGAIN. THANK YOU SO MUCH, DOCTOR.
MAKE SURE FRAU HANKEL HAS PRESCRIPTIONS FOR ANTI-CONVULSIVES AND HYPO-TENSIVES...
YAAAAA!!

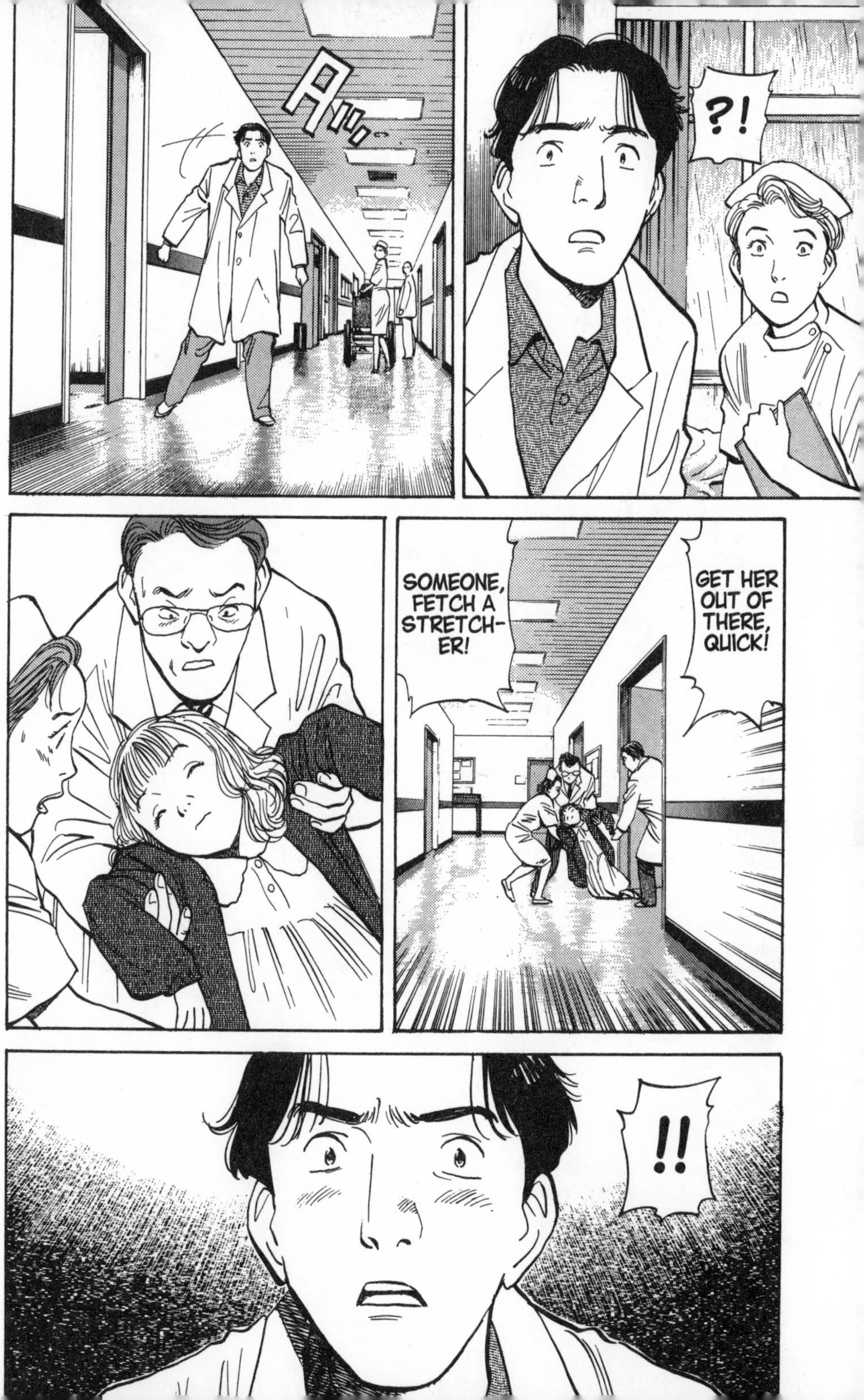
?!
GET HER OUT OF THERE, QUICK!
SOMEONE, FETCH A STRETCH-ER!
!!

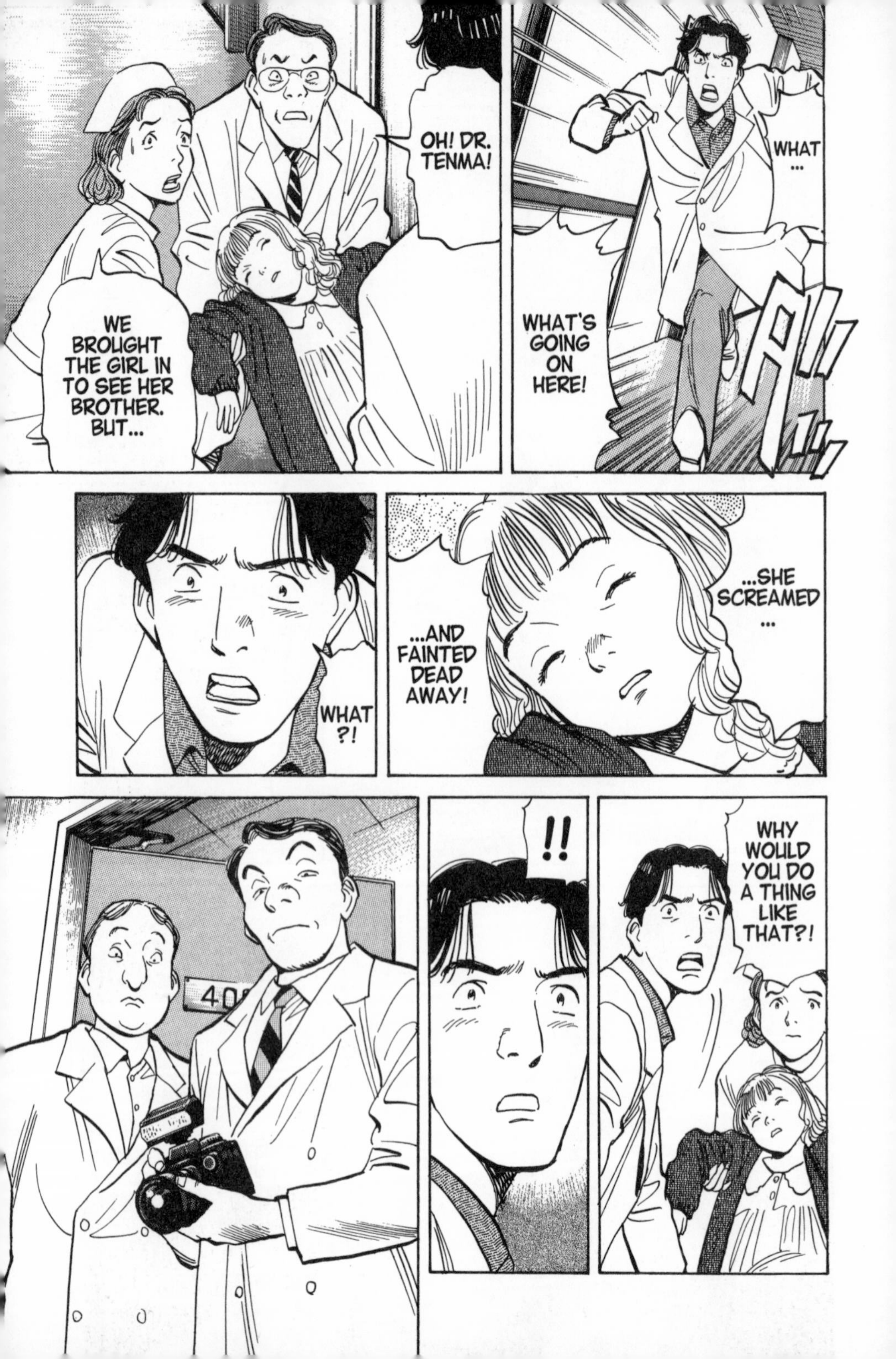
WHAT ...
WHAT'S GOING ON HERE!
OH! DR. TENMA!
WE BROUGHT THE GIRL IN TO SEE HER BROTHER. BUT...
...SHE SCREAMED ...
...AND FAINTED DEAD AWAY!
WHAT ?!
WHY WOULD YOU DO A THING LIKE THAT?!
!!

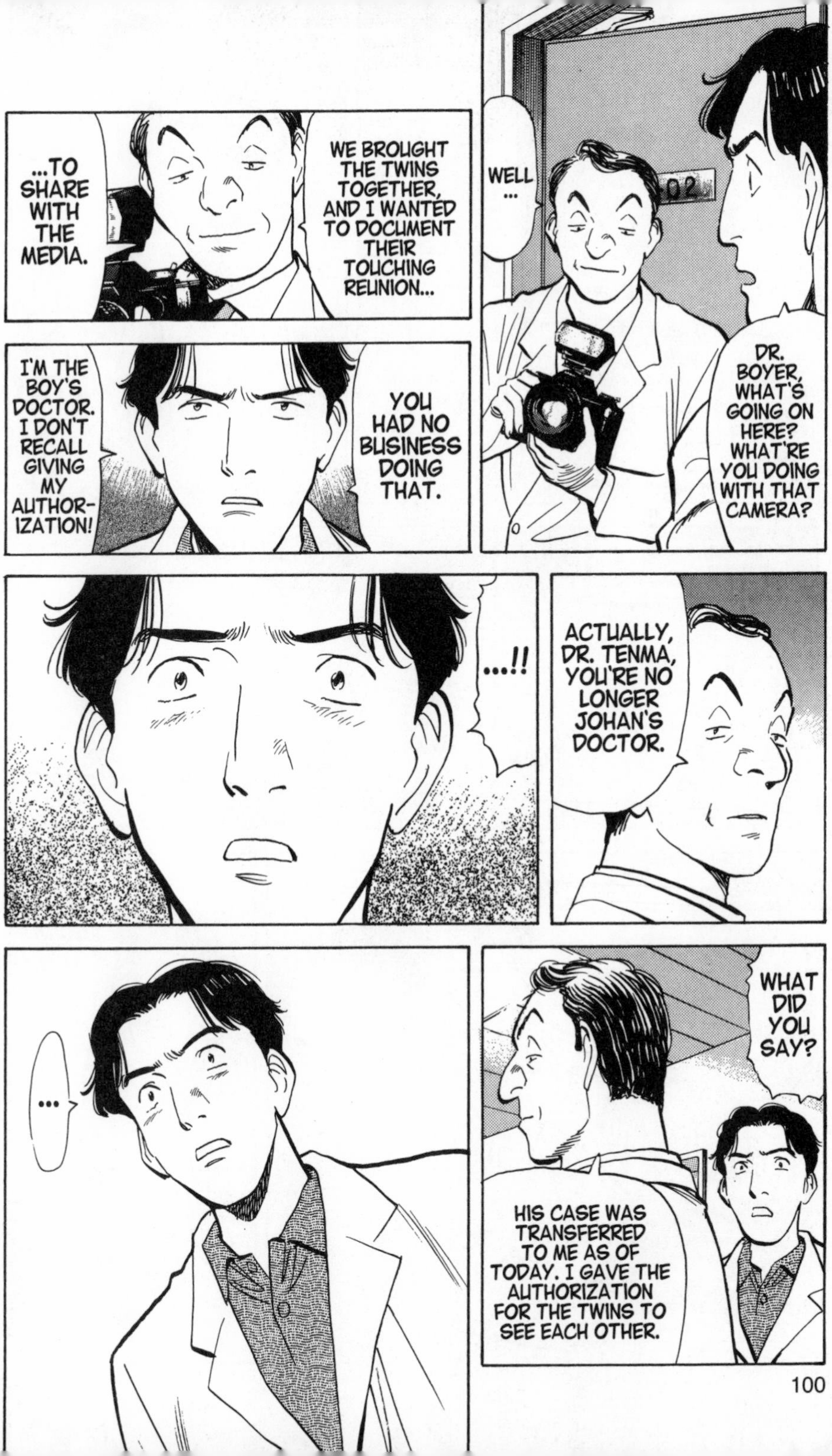
DR. BOYER, WHAT'S GOING ON HERE? WHAT'RE YOU DOING WITH THAT CAMERA?
WELL ...
WE BROUGHT THE TWINS TOGETHER, AND I WANTED TO DOCUMENT THEIR TOUCHING REUNION...
...TO SHARE WITH THE MEDIA.
YOU HAD NO BUSINESS DOING THAT.
I'M THE BOY'S DOCTOR. I DON'T RECALL GIVING MY AUTHORIZATION!
ACTUALLY, DR. TENMA, YOU'RE NO LONGER JOHAN'S DOCTOR.
...!!
WHAT DID YOU SAY?
HIS CASE WAS TRANSFERRED TO ME AS OF TODAY. I GAVE THE AUTHORIZATION FOR THE TWINS TO SEE EACH OTHER.
...

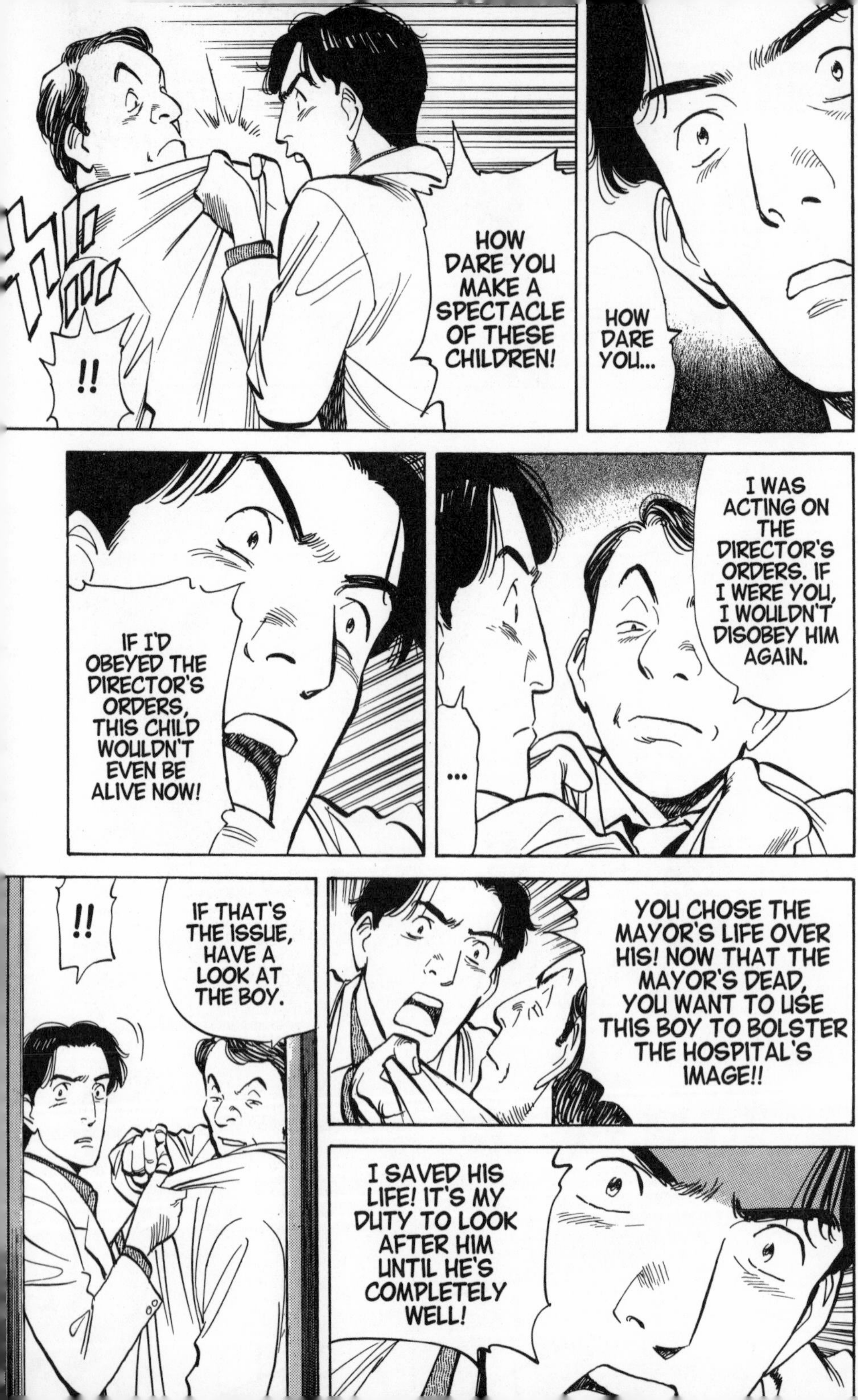

HOW DARE YOU...
HOW DARE YOU MAKE A SPECTACLE OF THESE CHILDREN!
!!
I WAS ACTING ON THE DIRECTOR'S ORDERS. IF I WERE YOU, I WOULDN'T DISOBEY HIM AGAIN.
...
IF I'D OBEYED THE DIRECTOR'S ORDERS, THIS CHILD WOULDN'T EVEN BE ALIVE NOW!
YOU CHOSE THE MAYOR'S LIFE OVER HIS! NOW THAT THE MAYOR'S DEAD, YOU WANT TO USE THIS BOY TO BOLSTER THE HOSPITAL'S IMAGE!!
I SAVED HIS LIFE! IT'S MY DUTY TO LOOK AFTER HIM UNTIL HE'S COMPLETELY WELL!
IF THAT'S THE ISSUE, HAVE A LOOK AT THE BOY.
!!

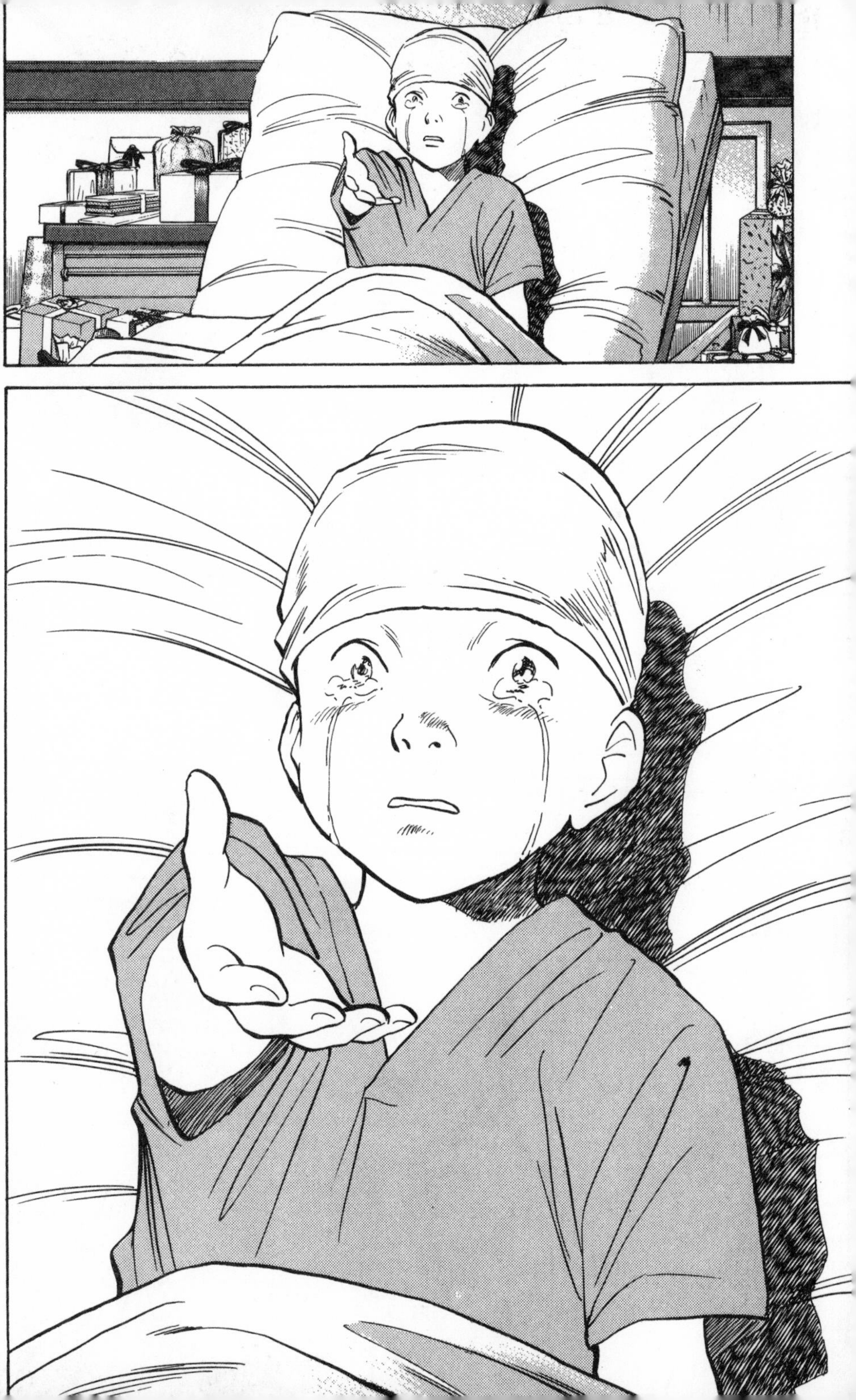

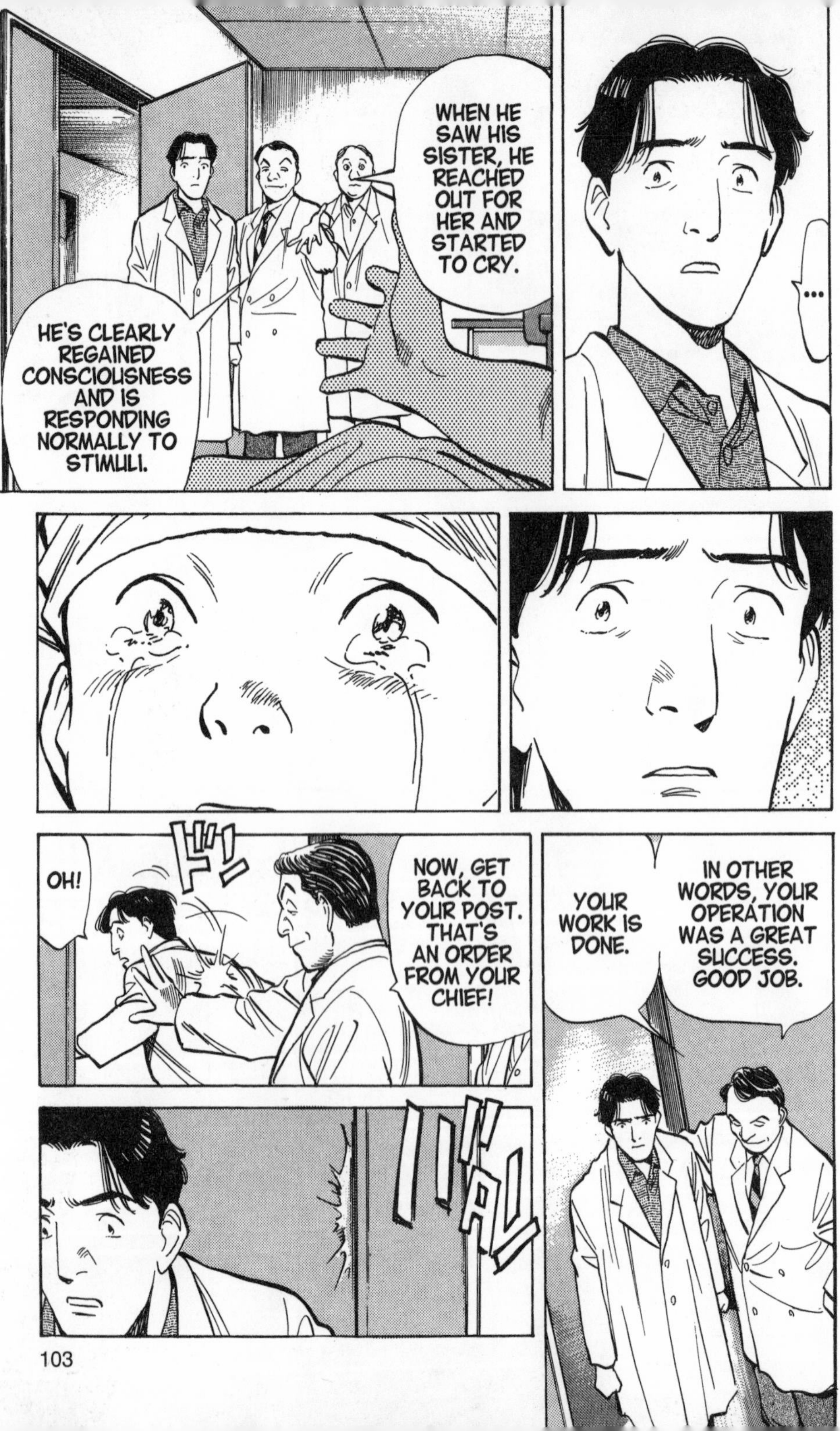
...
WHEN HE SAW HIS SISTER, HE REACHED OUT FOR HER AND STARTED TO CRY.
HE'S CLEARLY REGAINED CONSCIOUSNESS AND IS RESPONDING NORMALLY TO STIMULI.
IN OTHER WORDS, YOUR OPERATION WAS A GREAT SUCCESS. GOOD JOB.
YOUR WORK IS DONE.
NOW, GET BACK TO YOUR POST. THAT'S AN ORDER FROM YOUR CHIEF!
ドン
OH!
バタン

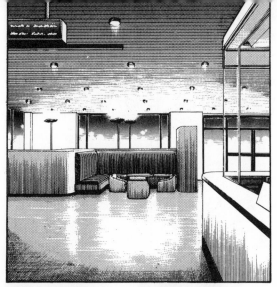

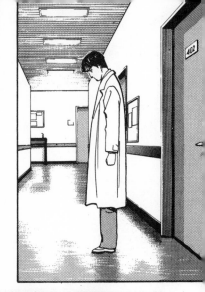

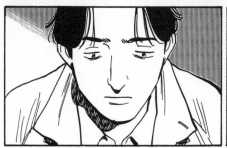

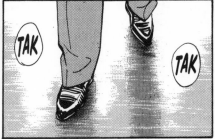

TAK

TAK

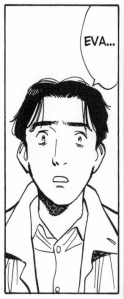

EVA...

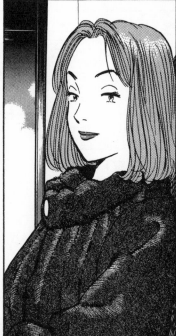

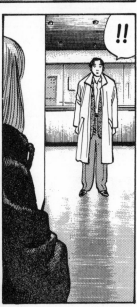

!!

104

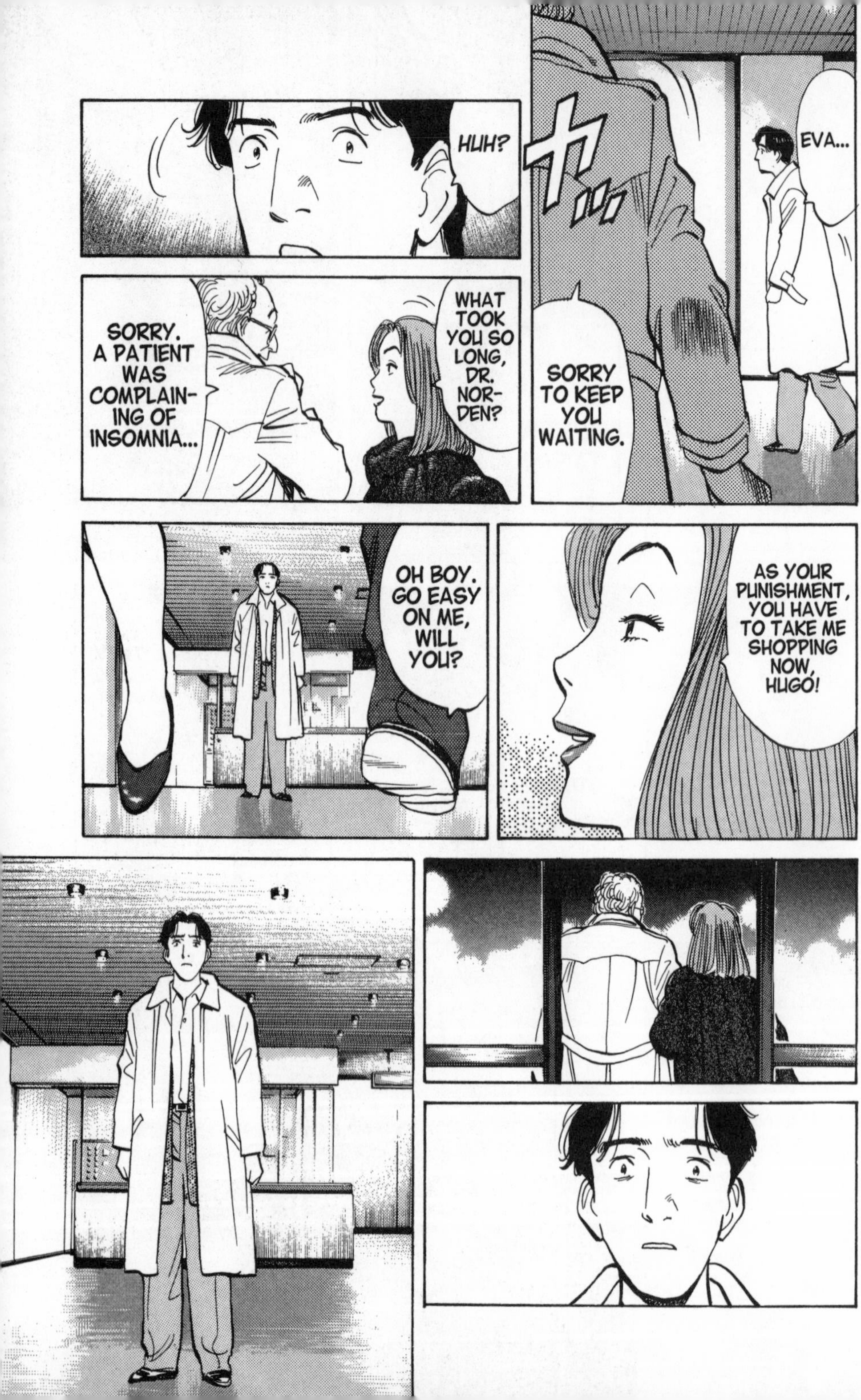
EVA...
SORRY TO KEEP YOU WAITING.
HUH?
WHAT TOOK YOU SO LONG, DR. NORDEN?
SORRY. A PATIENT WAS COMPLAINING OF INSOMNIA...
AS YOUR PUNISHMENT, YOU HAVE TO TAKE ME SHOPPING NOW, HUGO!
OH BOY. GO EASY ON ME, WILL YOU?

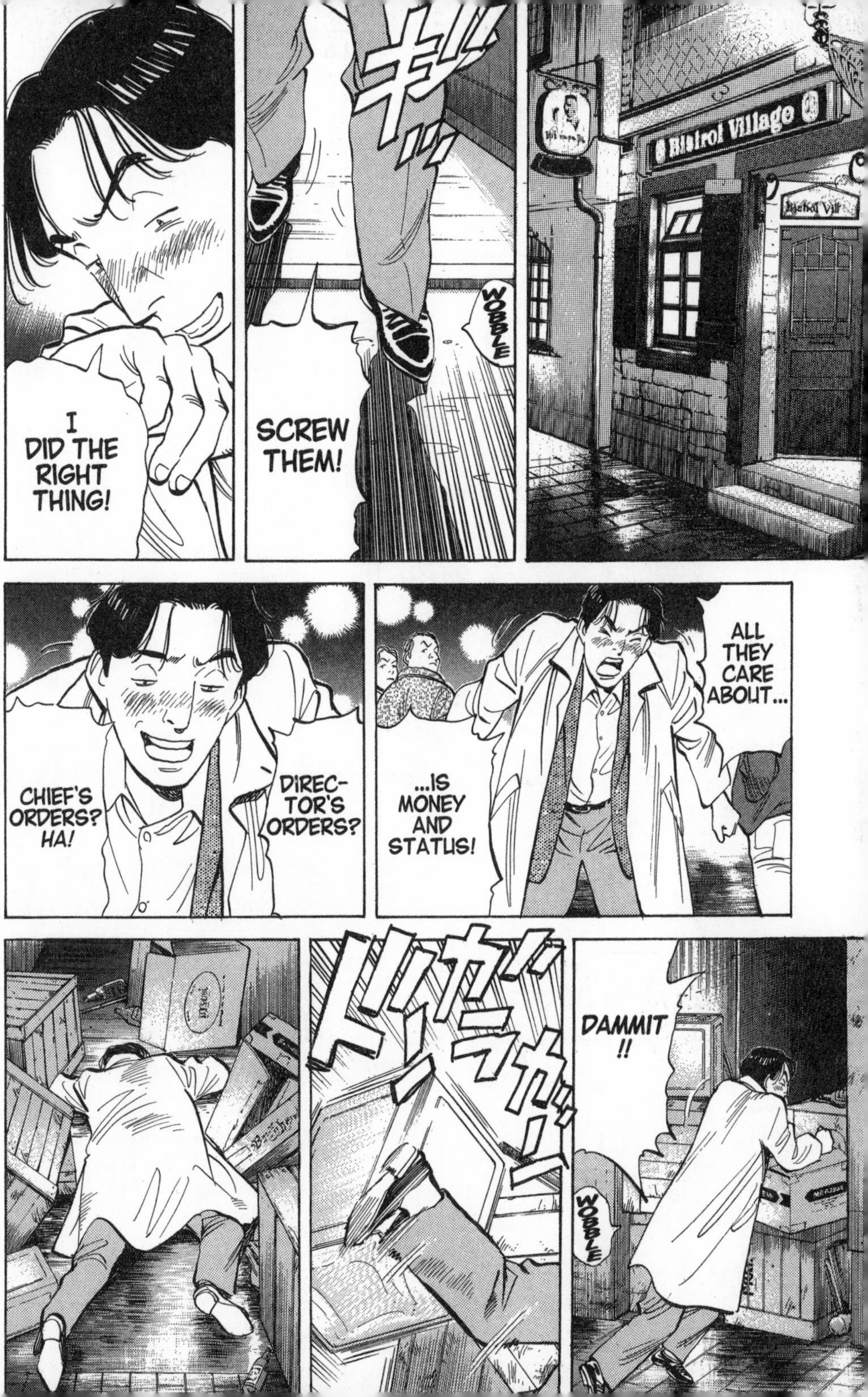
WOBBLE
SCREW THEM!
I DID THE RIGHT THING!
ALL THEY CARE ABOUT...
...IS MONEY AND STATUS!
DIREC-TOR'S ORDERS?
CHIEF'S ORDERS? HA!
DAMMIT!!
WOBBLE

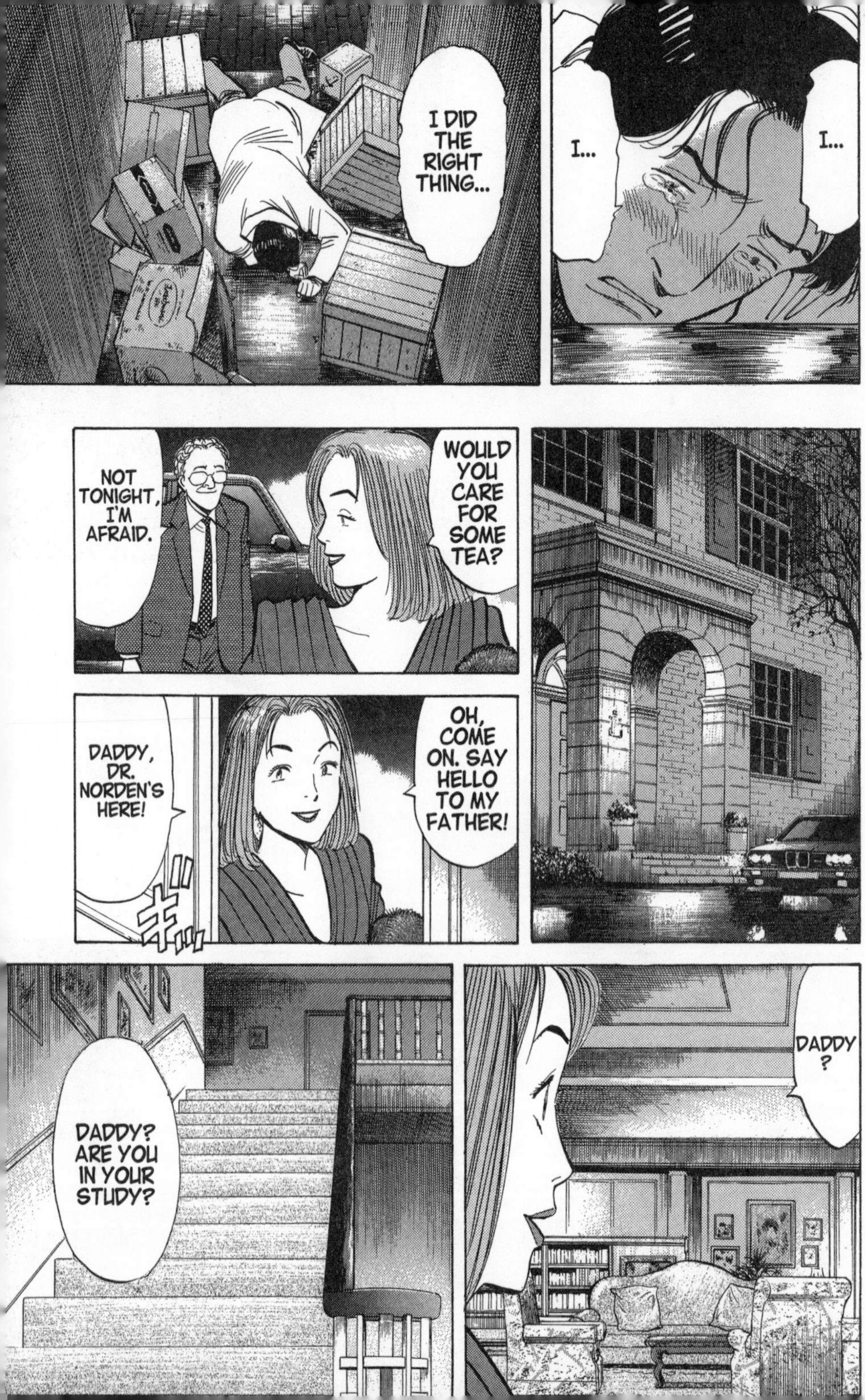
I...
I...
I DID THE RIGHT THING...
WOULD YOU CARE FOR SOME TEA?
NOT TONIGHT, I'M AFRAID.
OH, COME ON. SAY HELLO TO MY FATHER!
DADDY, DR. NORDEN'S HERE!
DADDY?
DADDY? ARE YOU IN YOUR STUDY?

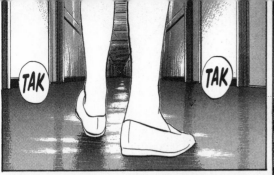
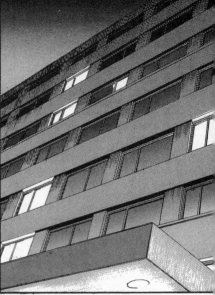

TAK

TAK

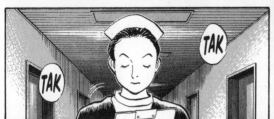

TAK

TAK

DR. OPPEN-HEIM? DR. BOYER?

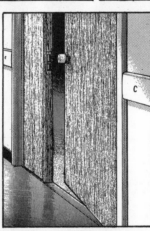

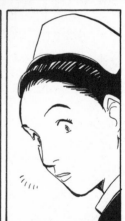

ARE YOU STILL MEETING AT THIS HOUR?

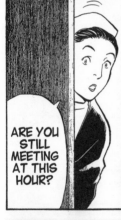

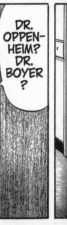

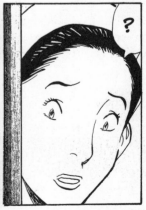

?

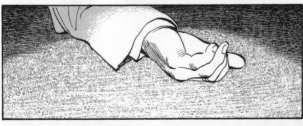

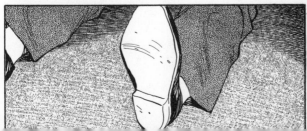

108

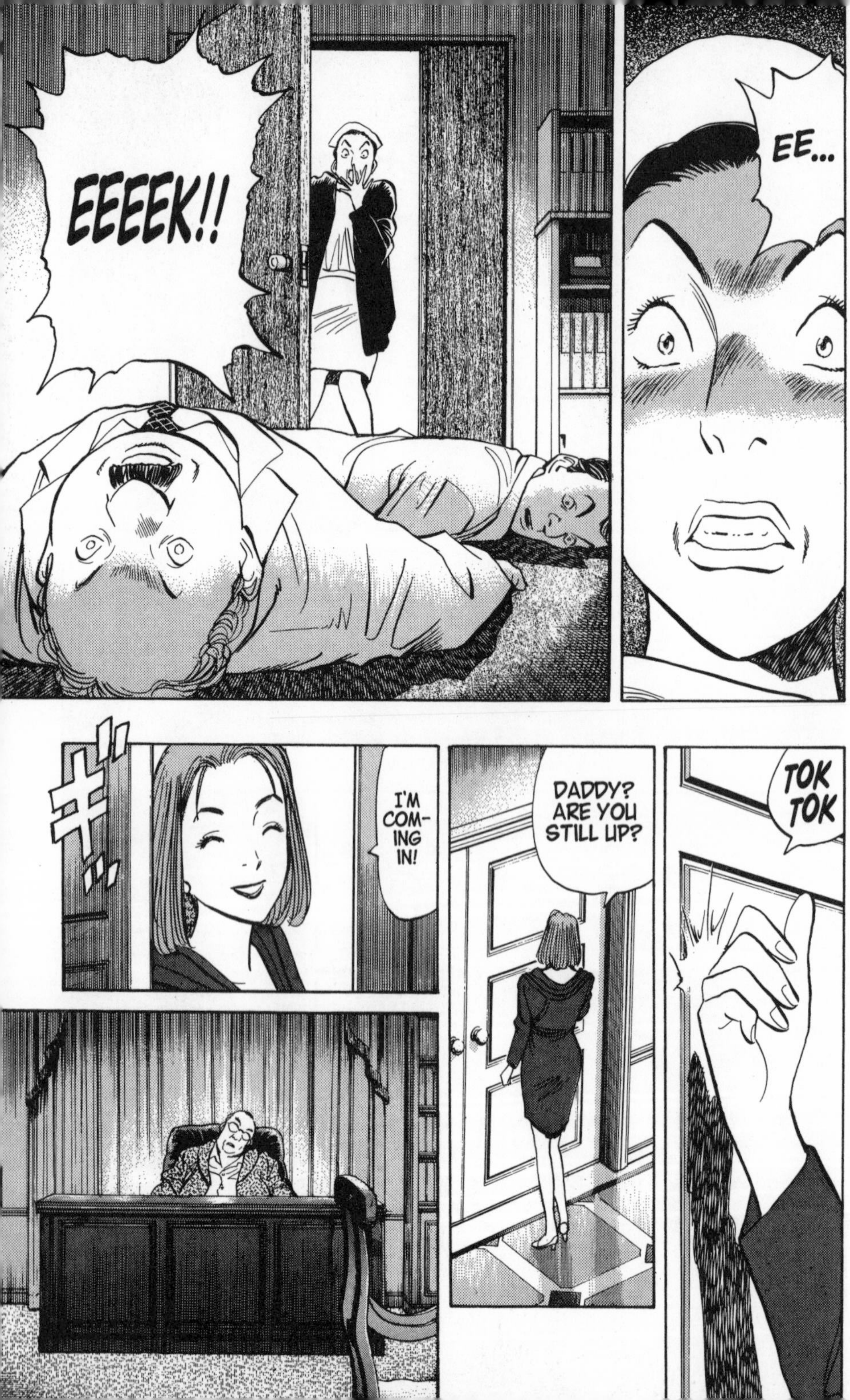
EE...
EEEEK!!
TOK TOK
DADDY? ARE YOU STILL UP?
I'M COM-ING IN!
ギ

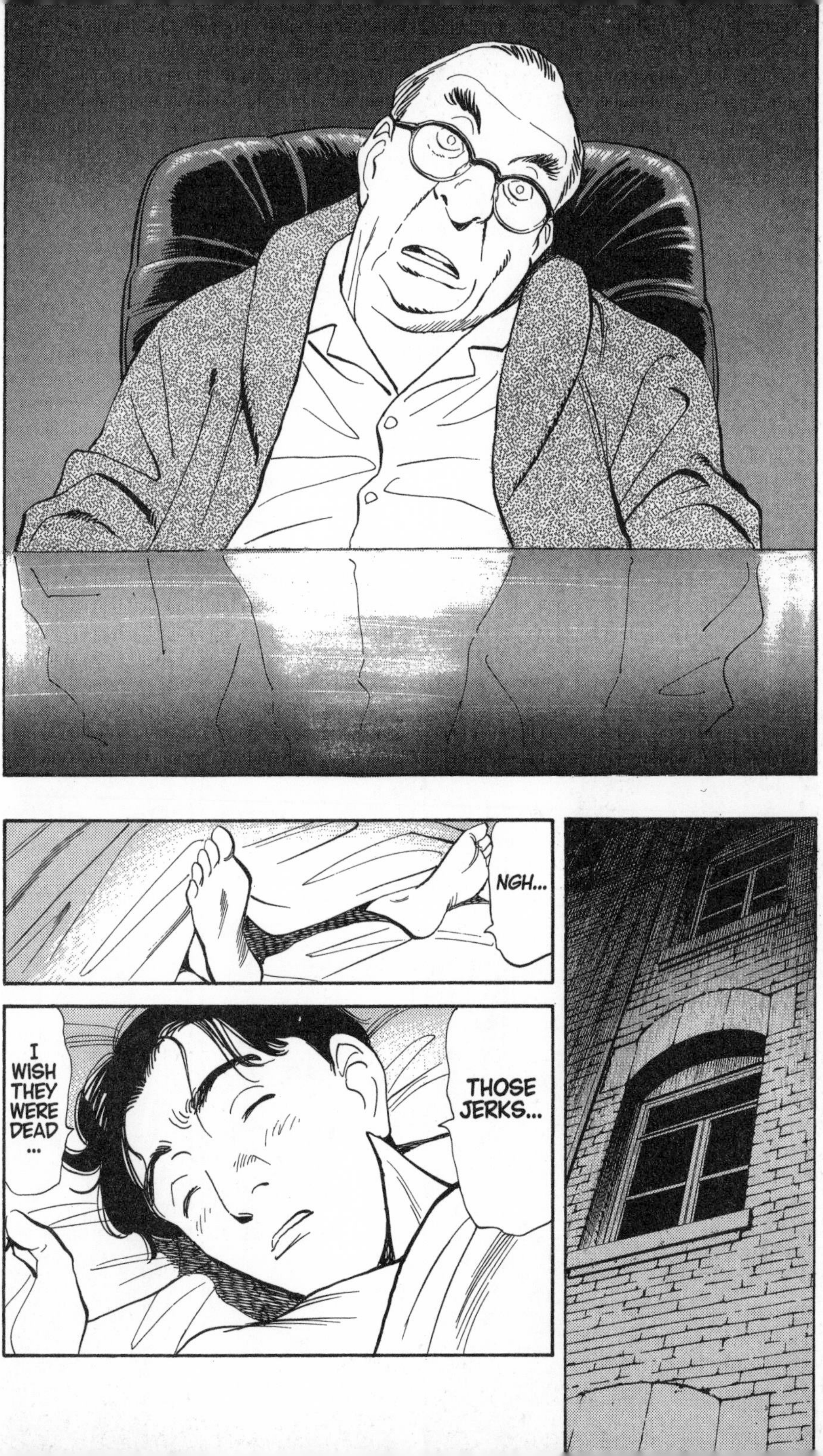
NGH...
THOSE JERKS...
I WISH THEY WERE DEAD ...

Kapitel 5. Murder

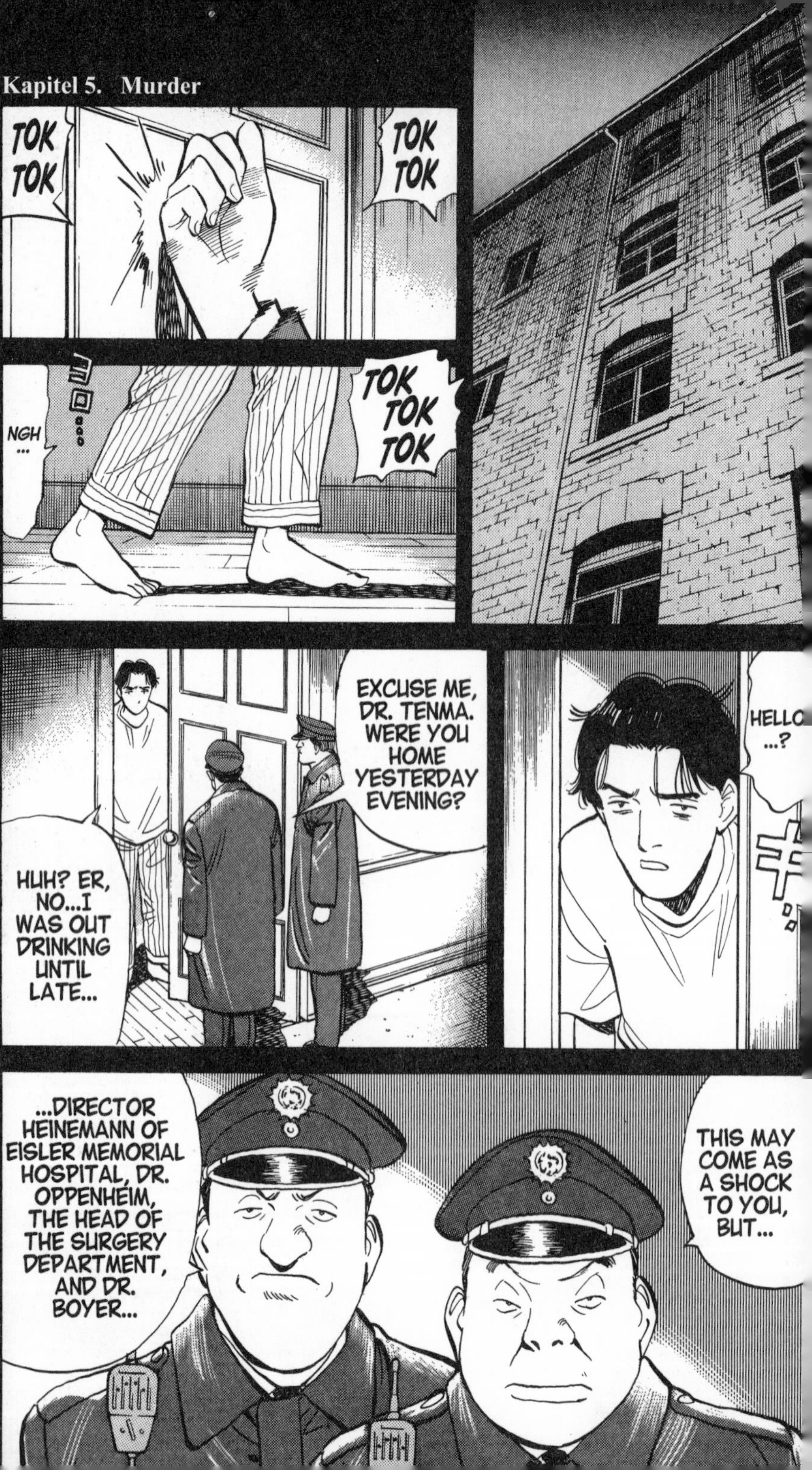
TOK TOK
TOK TOK
TOK TOK TOK
NGH ...
HELLO ...?
EXCUSE ME, DR. TENMA. WERE YOU HOME YESTERDAY EVENING?
HUH? ER, NO...I WAS OUT DRINKING UNTIL LATE...
THIS MAY COME AS A SHOCK TO YOU, BUT...
...DIRECTOR HEINEMANN OF EISLER MEMORIAL HOSPITAL, DR. OPPENHEIM, THE HEAD OF THE SURGERY DEPARTMENT, AND DR. BOYER...

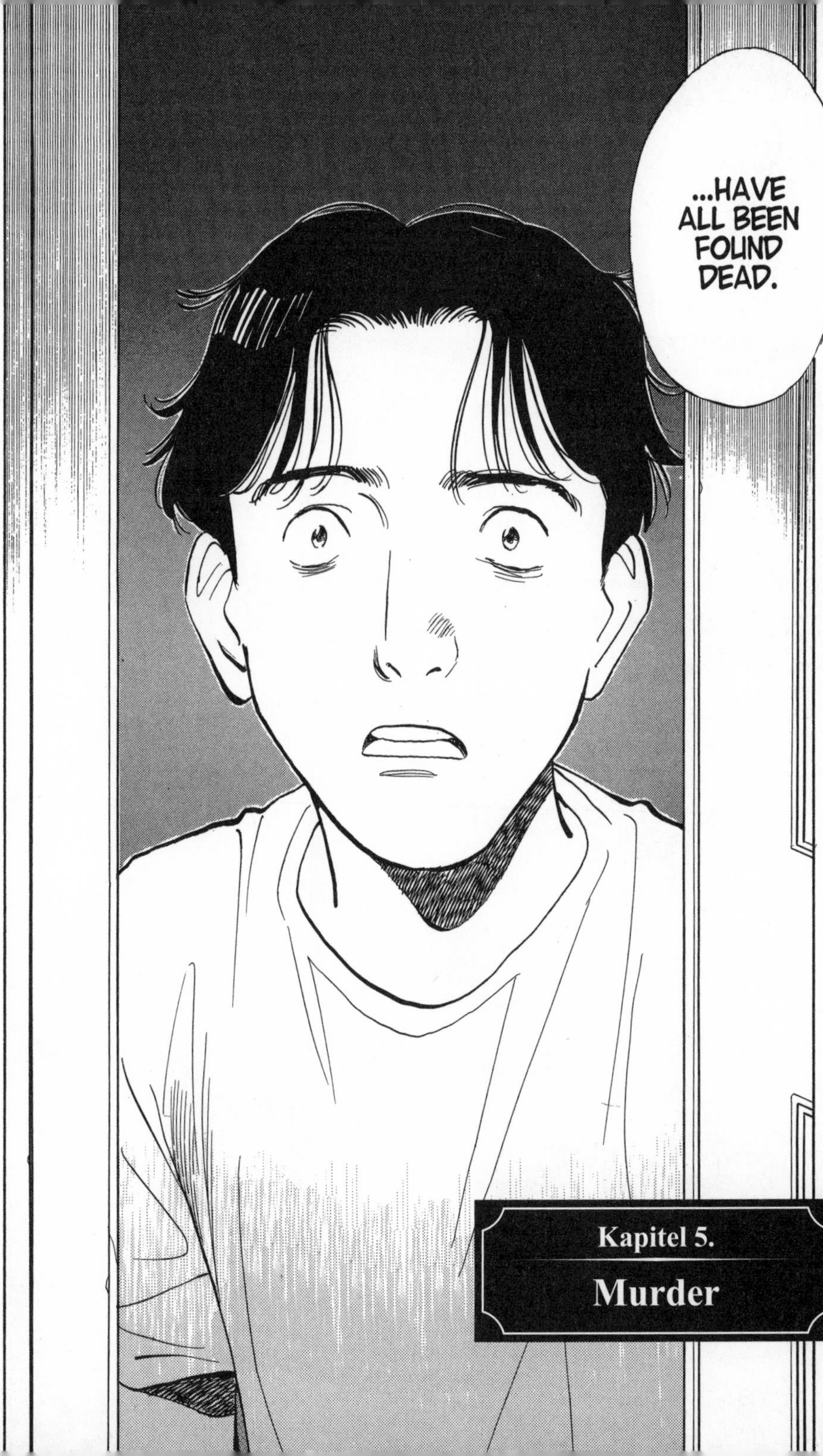
...HAVE ALL BEEN FOUND DEAD.
Kapitel 5.
Murder

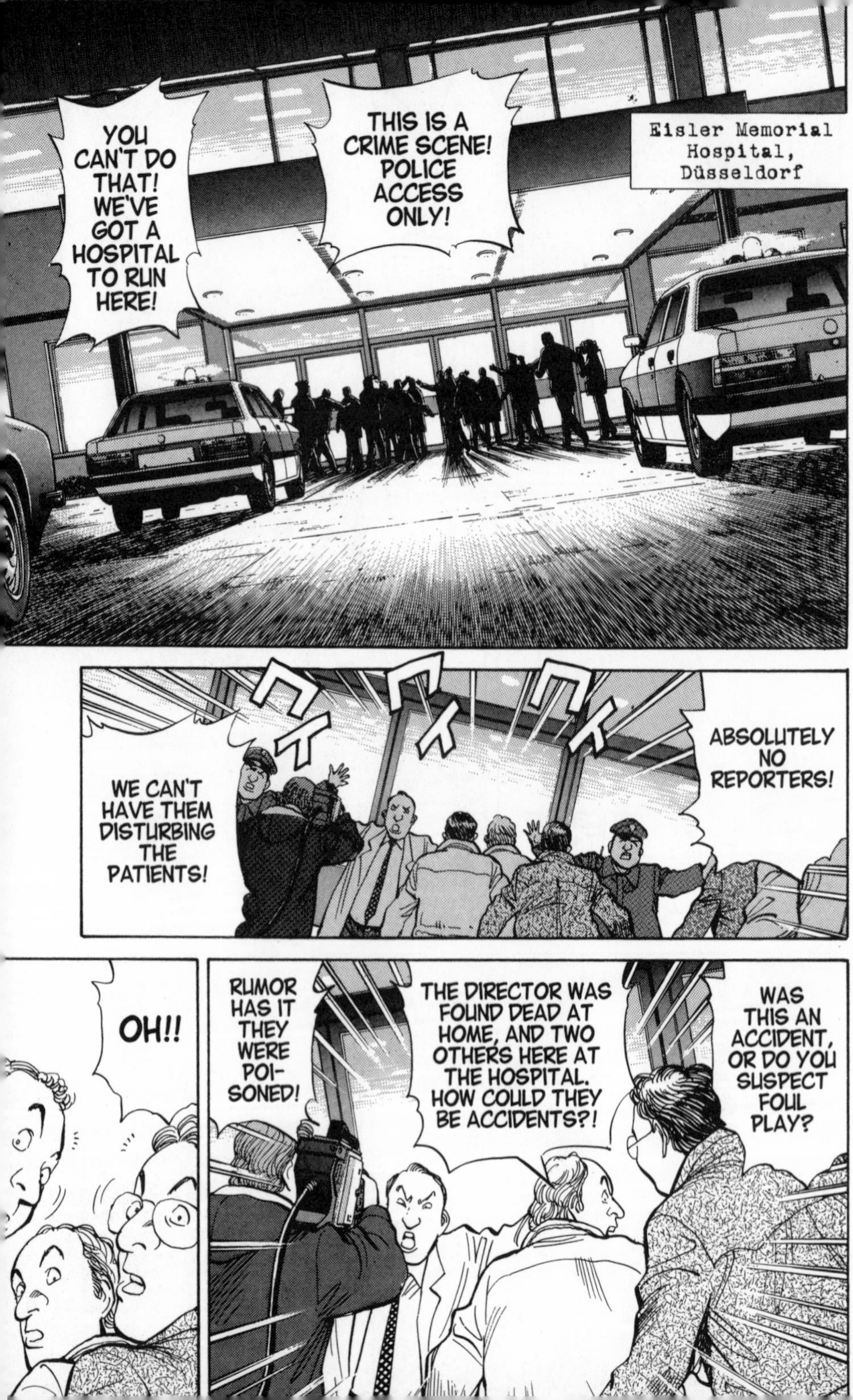
Eisler Memorial Hospital, Düsseldorf
THIS IS A CRIME SCENE! POLICE ACCESS ONLY!
YOU CAN'T DO THAT! WE'VE GOT A HOSPITAL TO RUN HERE!
ABSOLUTELY NO REPORTERS!
WE CAN'T HAVE THEM DISTURBING THE PATIENTS!
WAS THIS AN ACCIDENT, OR DO YOU SUSPECT FOUL PLAY?
THE DIRECTOR WAS FOUND DEAD AT HOME, AND TWO OTHERS HERE AT THE HOSPITAL. HOW COULD THEY BE ACCIDENTS?!
RUMOR HAS IT THEY WERE POI-SONED!
OH!!

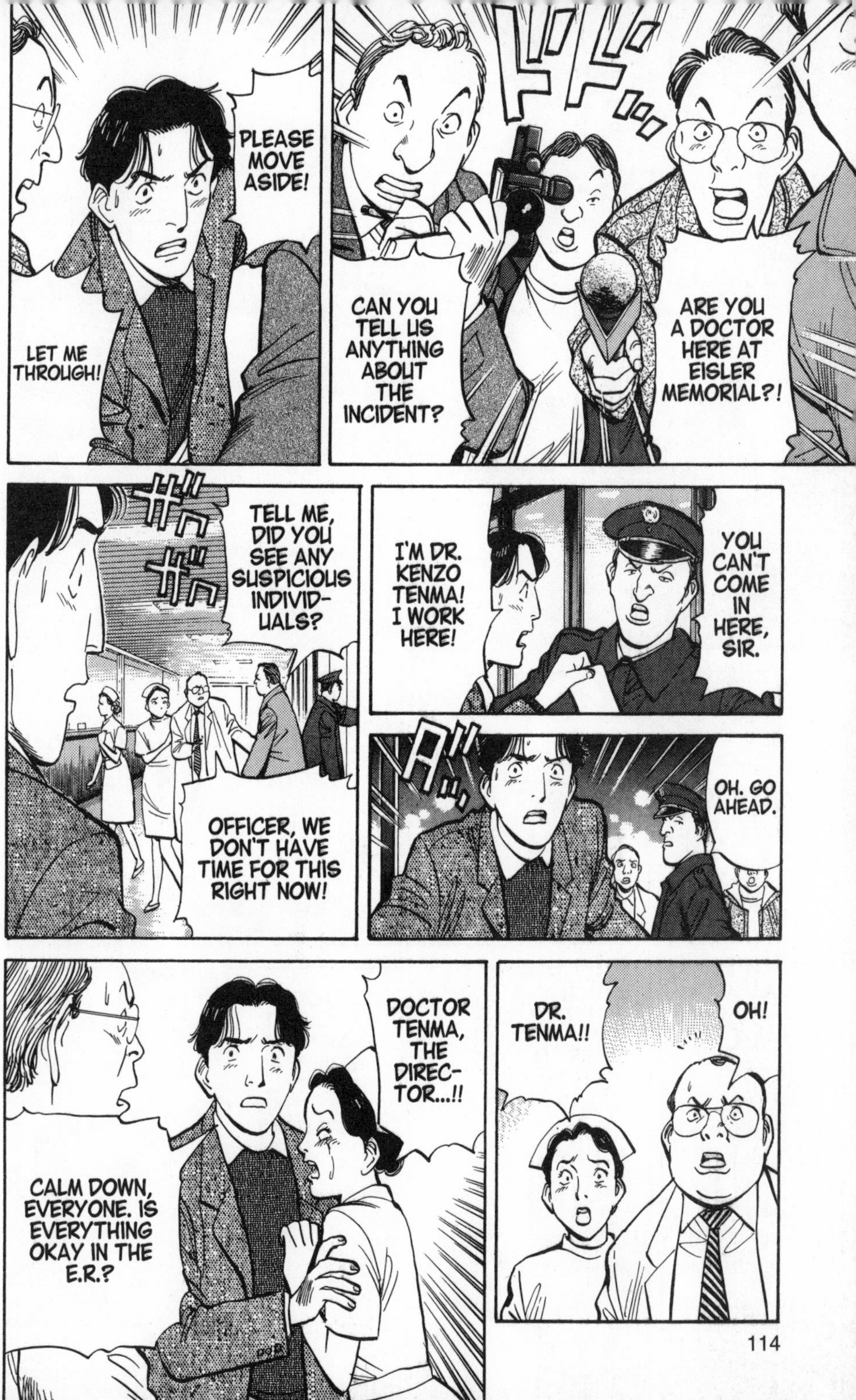
ARE YOU A DOCTOR HERE AT EISLER MEMORIAL?!
CAN YOU TELL US ANYTHING ABOUT THE INCIDENT?
PLEASE MOVE ASIDE!
LET ME THROUGH!
YOU CAN'T COME IN HERE, SIR.
I'M DR. KENZO TENMA! I WORK HERE!
OH. GO AHEAD.
TELL ME, DID YOU SEE ANY SUSPICIOUS INDIVID-UALS?
OFFICER, WE DON'T HAVE TIME FOR THIS RIGHT NOW!
OH!
DR. TENMA!!
DOCTOR TENMA, THE DIREC-TOR...!!
CALM DOWN, EVERYONE. IS EVERYTHING OKAY IN THE E.R.?

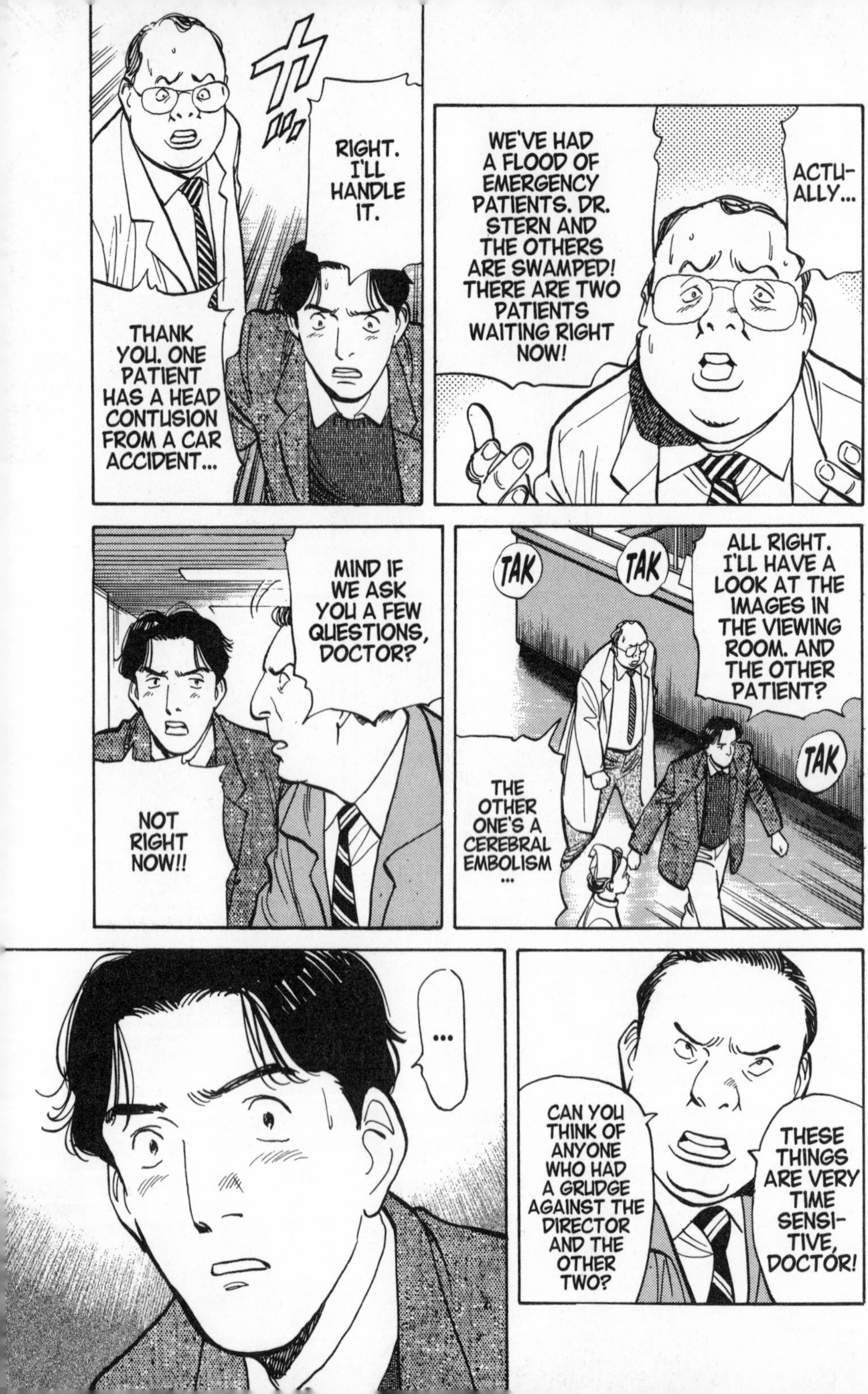
ACTU-ALLY...
WE'VE HAD A FLOOD OF EMERGENCY PATIENTS. DR. STERN AND THE OTHERS ARE SWAMPED! THERE ARE TWO PATIENTS WAITING RIGHT NOW!
カッ
RIGHT. I'LL HANDLE IT.
THANK YOU. ONE PATIENT HAS A HEAD CONTUSION FROM A CAR ACCIDENT...
ALL RIGHT. I'LL HAVE A LOOK AT THE IMAGES IN THE VIEWING ROOM. AND THE OTHER PATIENT?
TAK
TAK
TAK
THE OTHER ONE'S A CEREBRAL EMBOLISM ...
MIND IF WE ASK YOU A FEW QUESTIONS, DOCTOR?
NOT RIGHT NOW!!
THESE THINGS ARE VERY TIME SENSI-TIVE, DOCTOR!
CAN YOU THINK OF ANYONE WHO HAD A GRUDGE AGAINST THE DIRECTOR AND THE OTHER TWO?
...

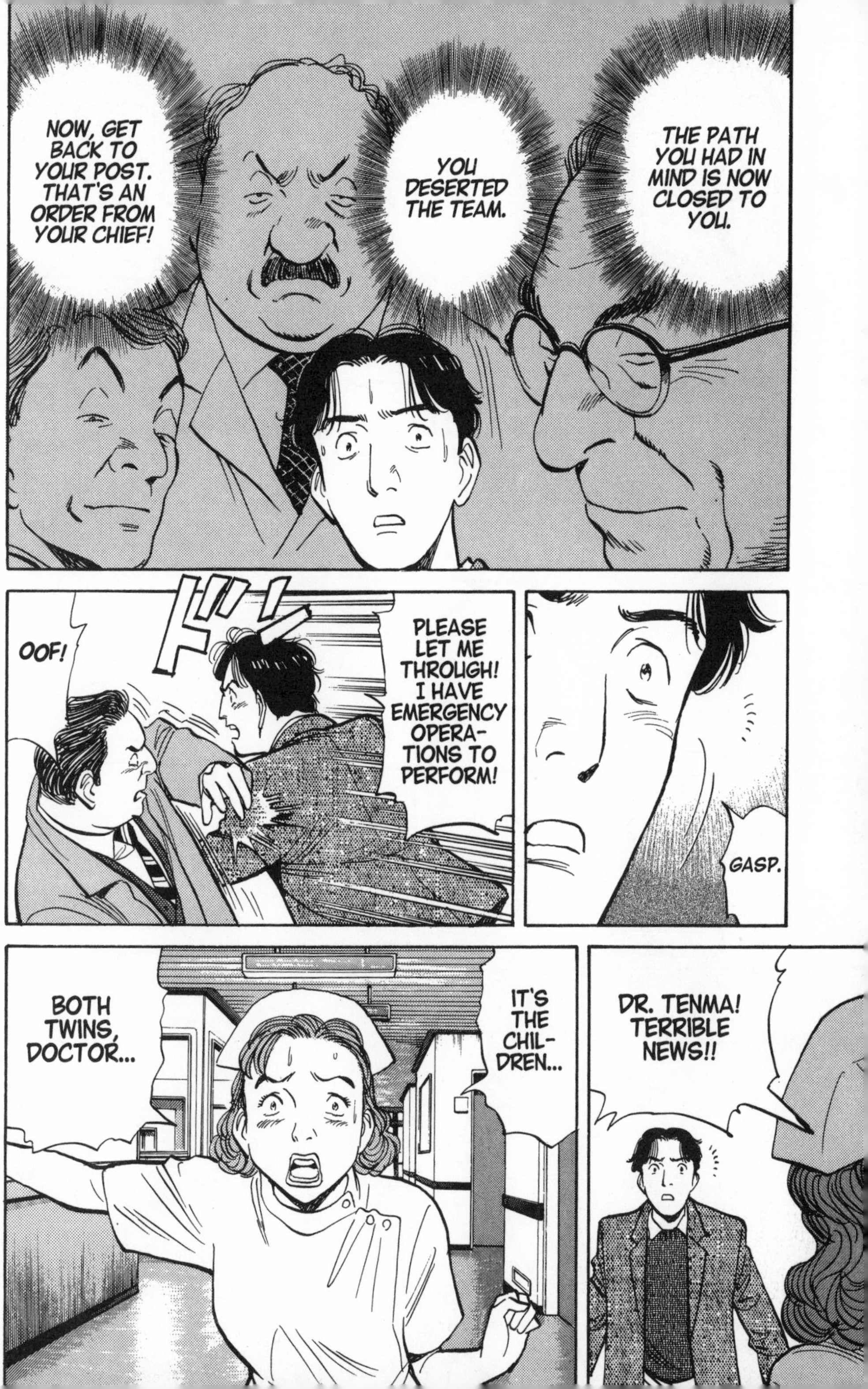
THE PATH YOU HAD IN MIND IS NOW CLOSED TO YOU.
YOU DESERTED THE TEAM.
NOW, GET BACK TO YOUR POST. THAT'S AN ORDER FROM YOUR CHIEF!
GASP.
PLEASE LET ME THROUGH! I HAVE EMERGENCY OPERA-TIONS TO PERFORM!
ドン
OOF!
DR. TENMA! TERRIBLE NEWS!!
IT'S THE CHIL-DREN...
BOTH TWINS, DOCTOR...

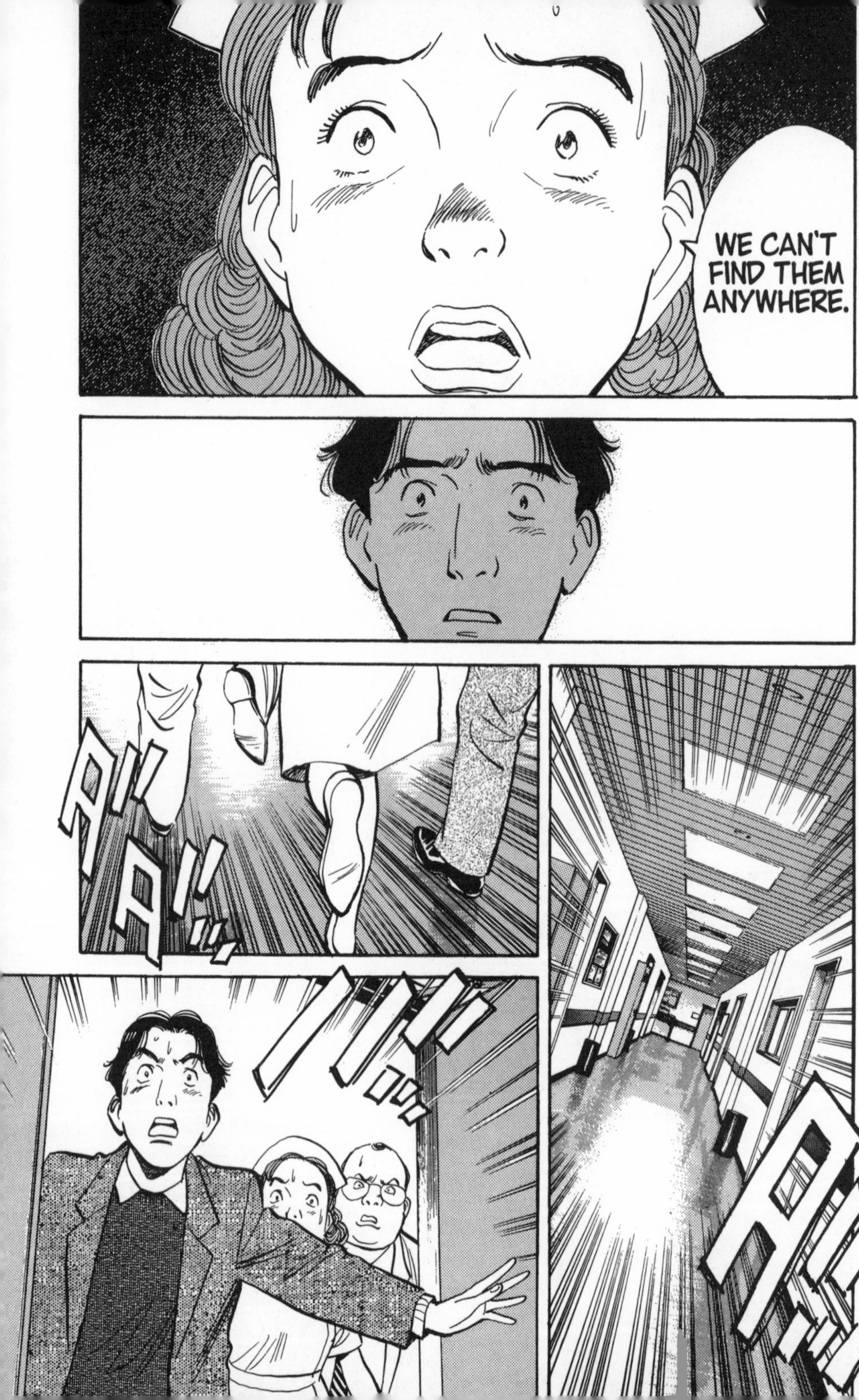
WE CAN'T FIND THEM ANYWHERE.

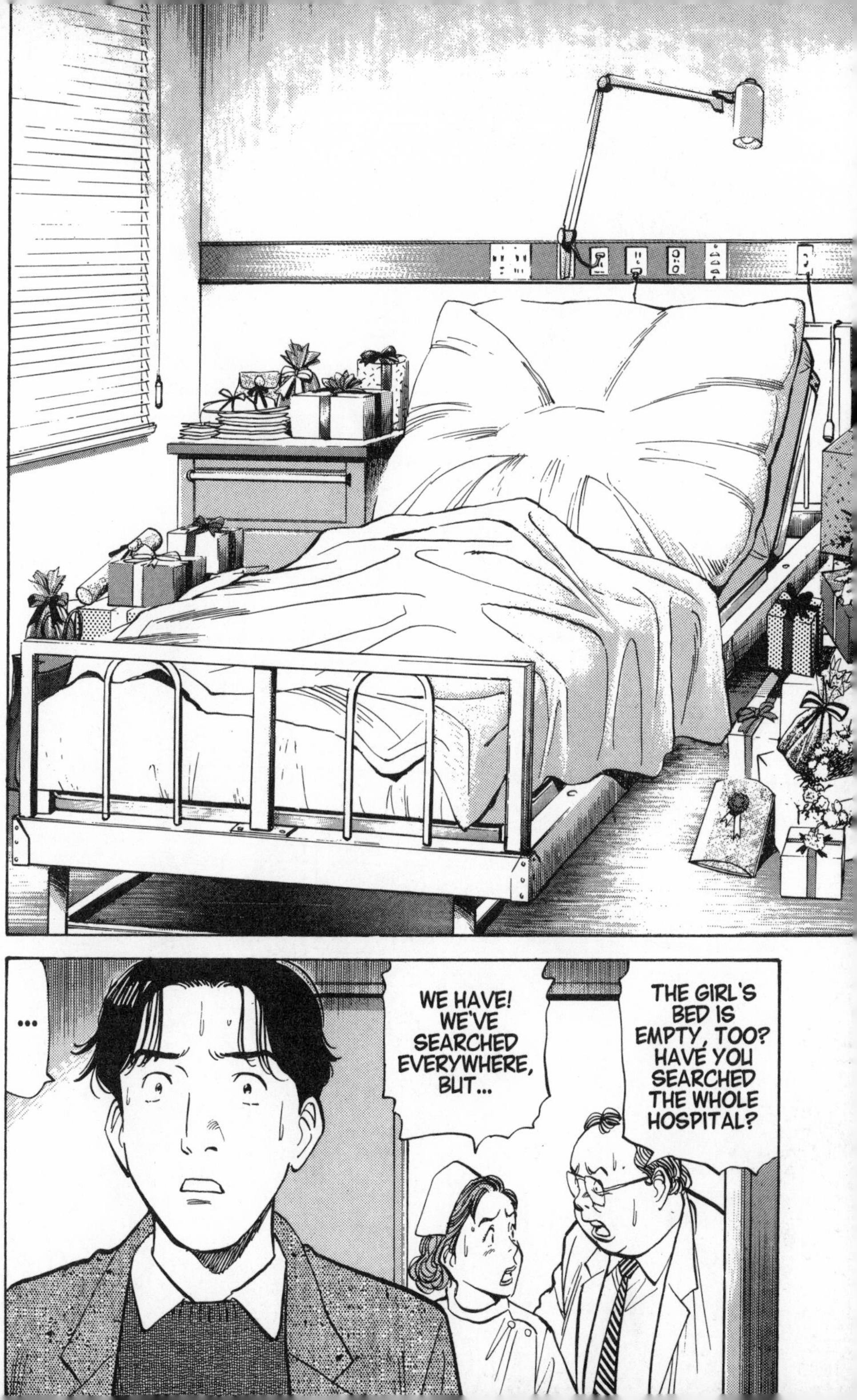
THE GIRL'S BED IS EMPTY, TOO? HAVE YOU SEARCHED THE WHOLE HOSPITAL?
WE HAVE! WE'VE SEARCHED EVERYWHERE, BUT...
...

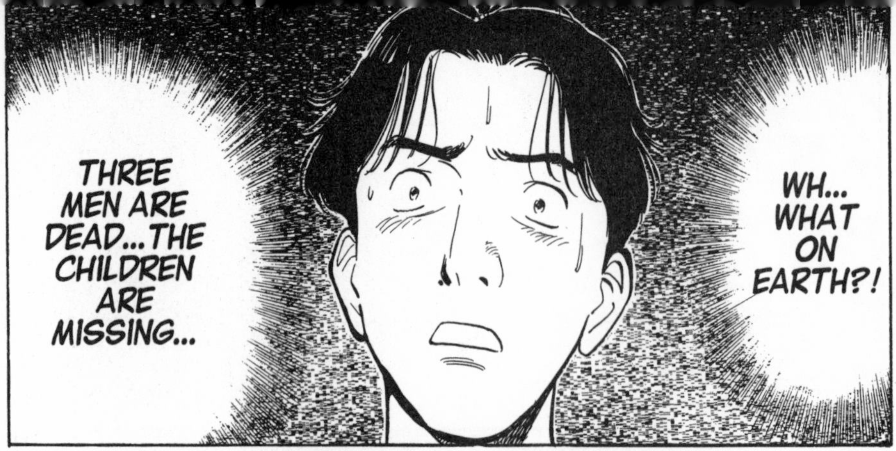
WH... WHAT ON EARTH?!
THREE MEN ARE DEAD...THE CHILDREN ARE MISSING...
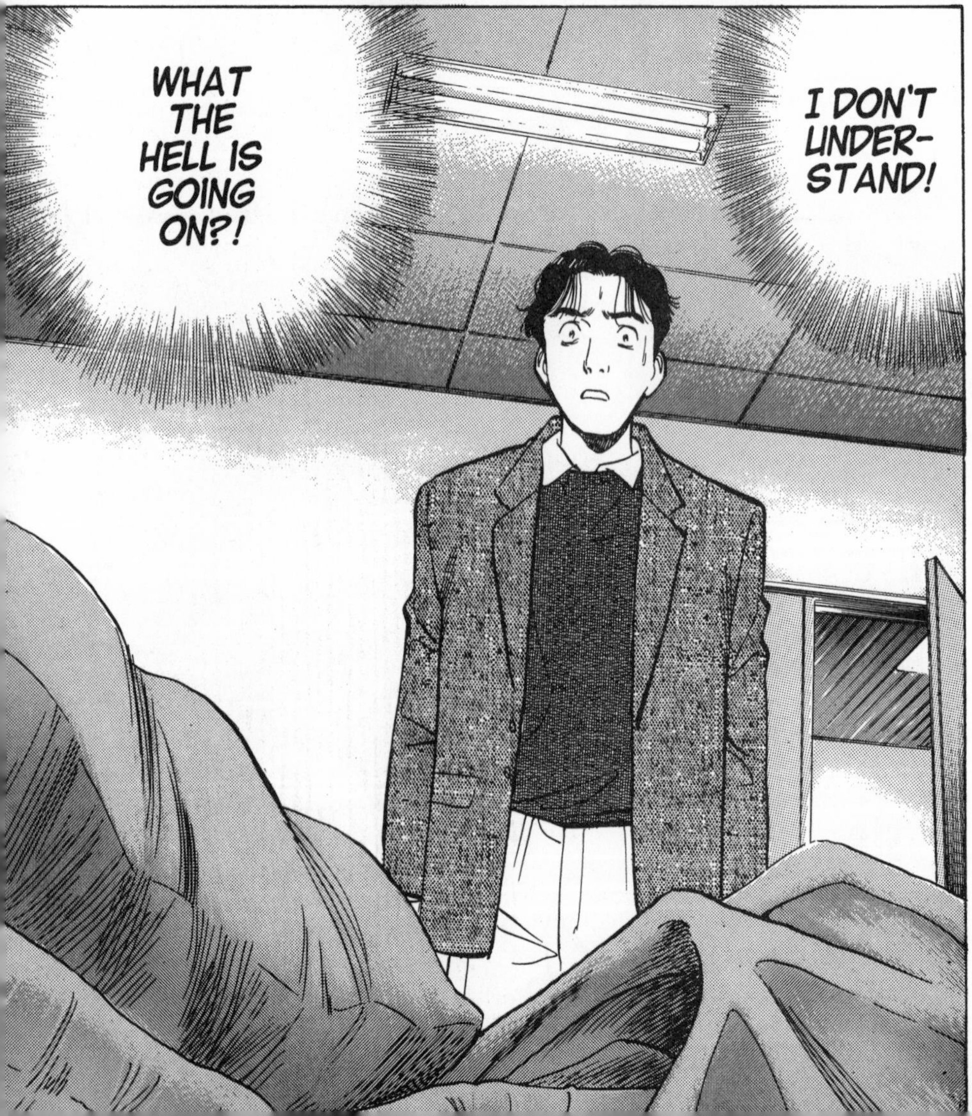
I DON'T UNDER-STAND!
WHAT THE HELL IS GOING ON?!

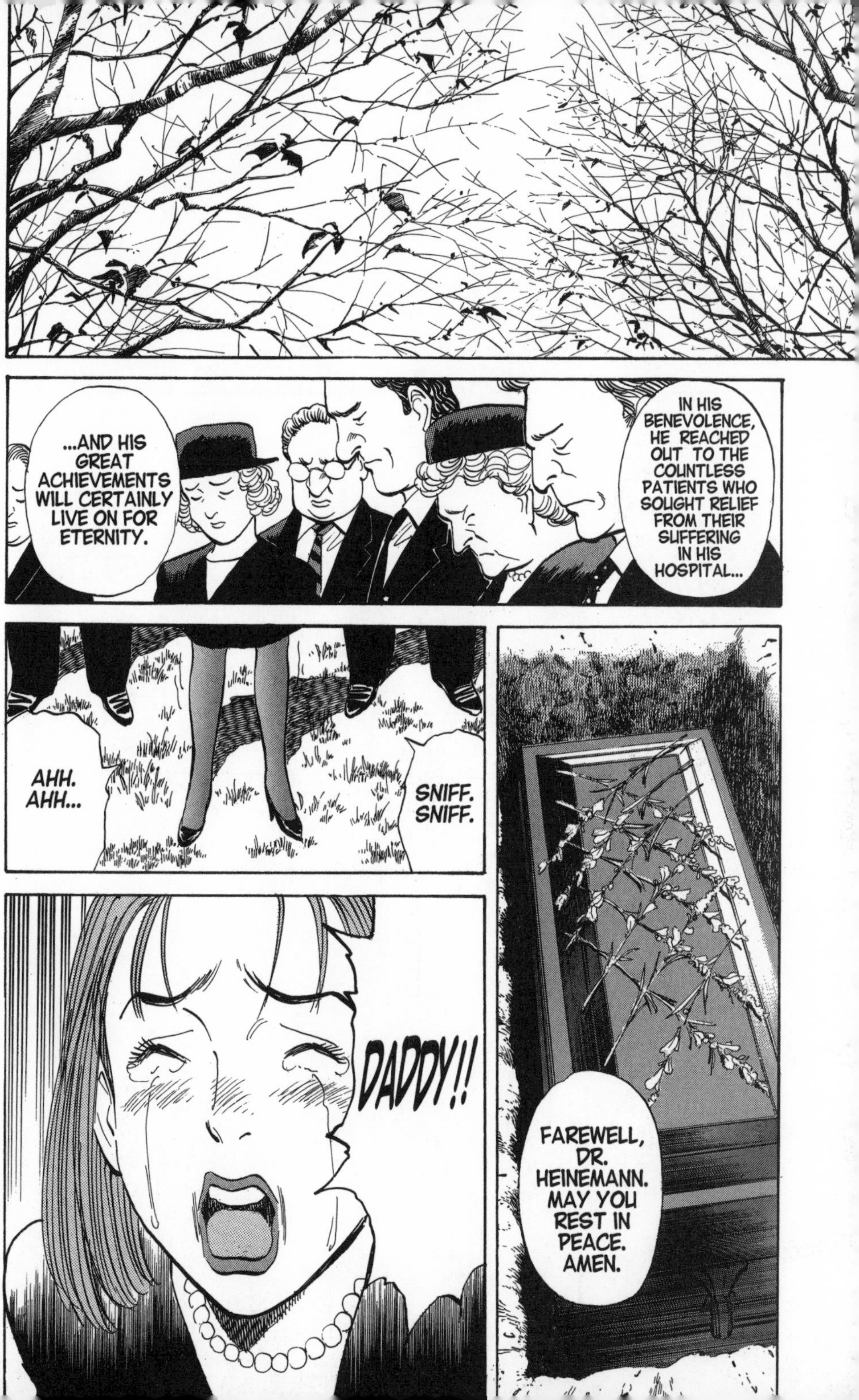
IN HIS BENEVOLENCE, HE REACHED OUT TO THE COUNTLESS PATIENTS WHO SOUGHT RELIEF FROM THEIR SUFFERING IN HIS HOSPITAL...
...AND HIS GREAT ACHIEVEMENTS WILL CERTAINLY LIVE ON FOR ETERNITY.
FAREWELL, DR. HEINEMANN. MAY YOU REST IN PEACE. AMEN.
SNIFF. SNIFF.
AHH. AHH...
DADDY!!

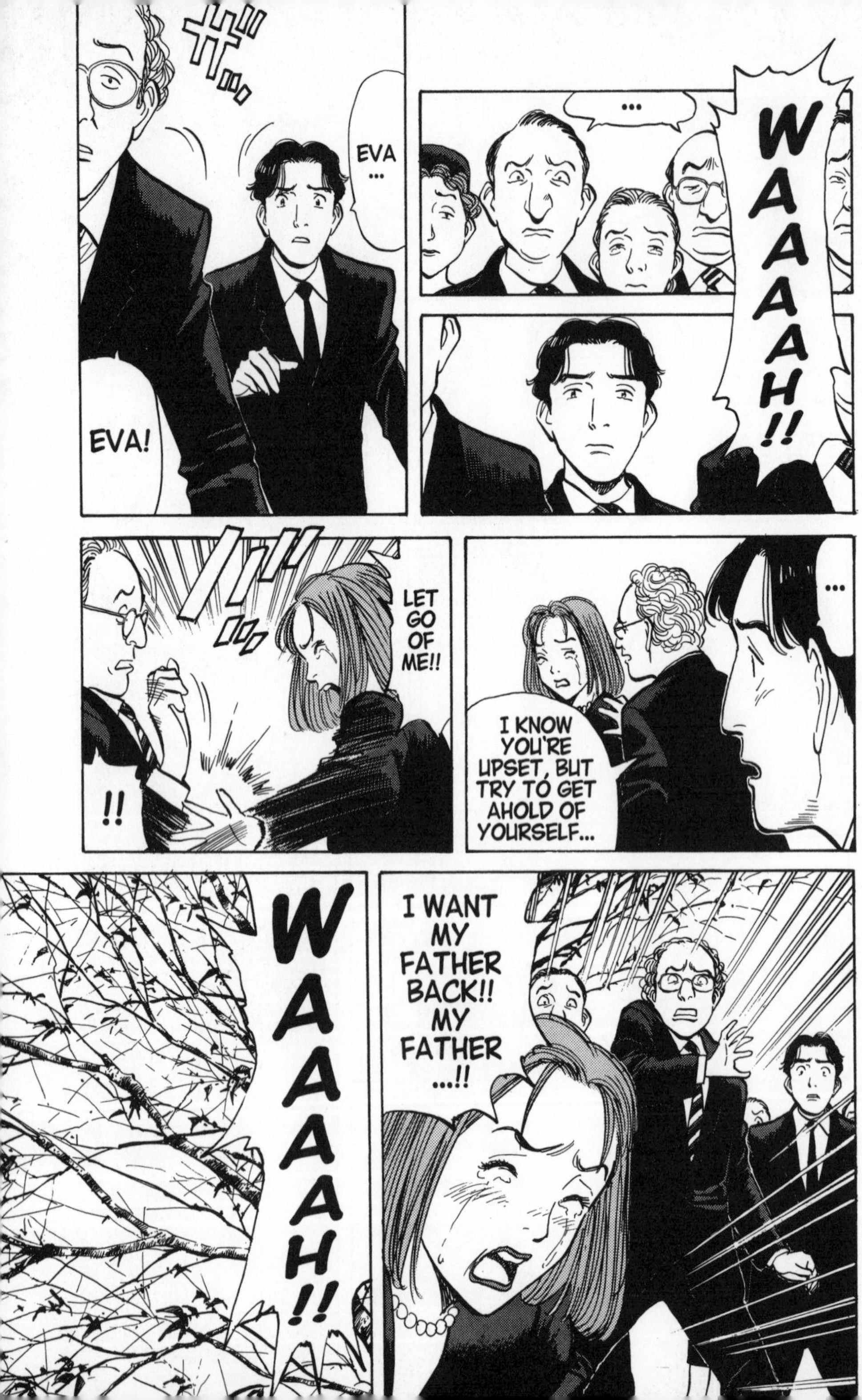
WAAAAAH!!
...
EVA ...
EVA!
...
I KNOW YOU'RE UPSET, BUT TRY TO GET AHOLD OF YOURSELF...
LET GO OF ME!!
!!
I WANT MY FATHER BACK!! MY FATHER ...!!
WAAAAAH!!

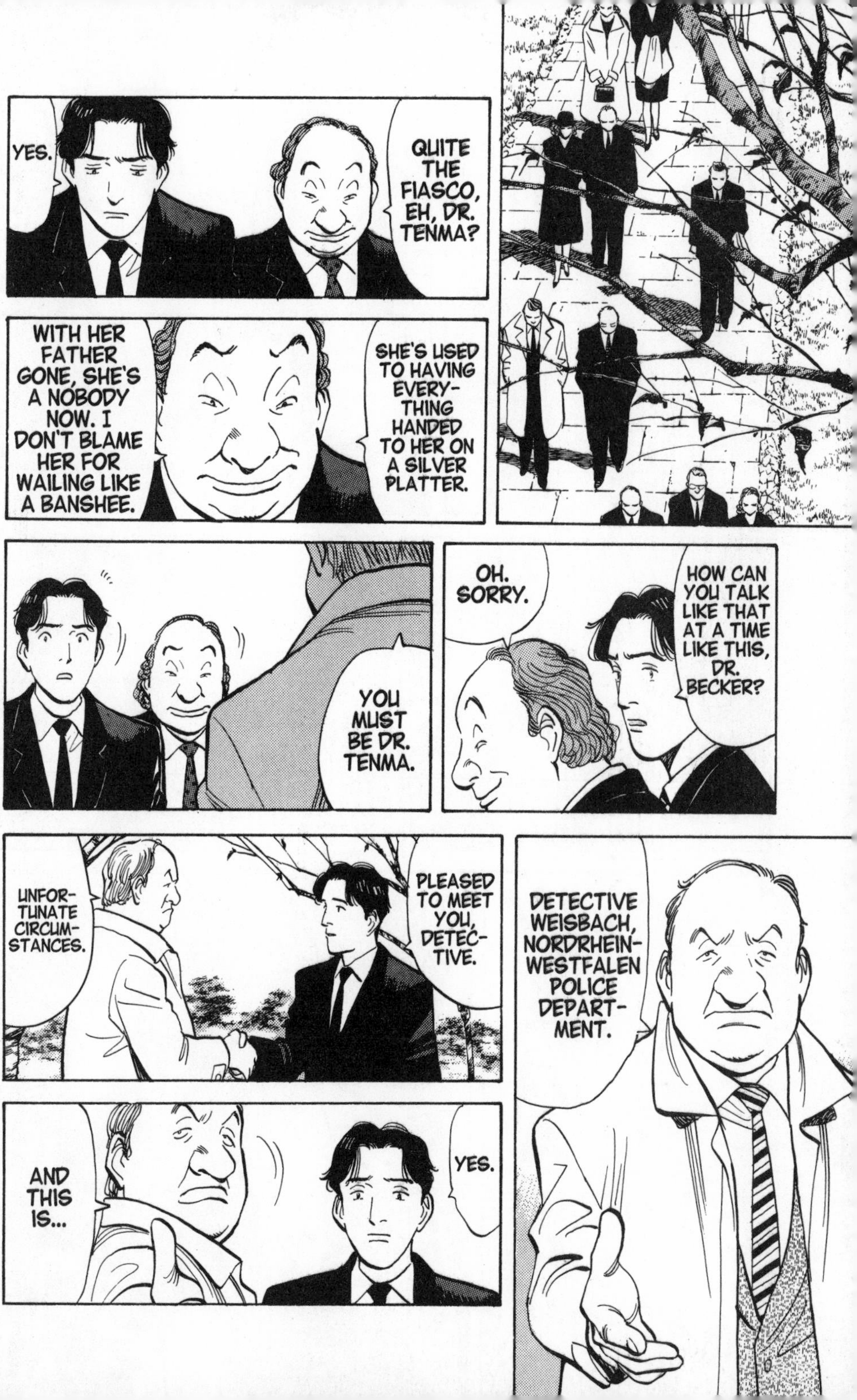
QUITE THE FIASCO, EH, DR. TENMA?
YES.
SHE'S USED TO HAVING EVERY-THING HANDED TO HER ON A SILVER PLATTER.
WITH HER FATHER GONE, SHE'S A NOBODY NOW. I DON'T BLAME HER FOR WAILING LIKE A BANSHEE.
HOW CAN YOU TALK LIKE THAT AT A TIME LIKE THIS, DR. BECKER?
OH. SORRY.
YOU MUST BE DR. TENMA.
DETECTIVE WEISBACH, NORDRHEIN-WESTFALEN POLICE DEPART-MENT.
PLEASED TO MEET YOU, DETEC-TIVE.
UNFOR-TUNATE CIRCUM-STANCES.
YES.
AND THIS IS...

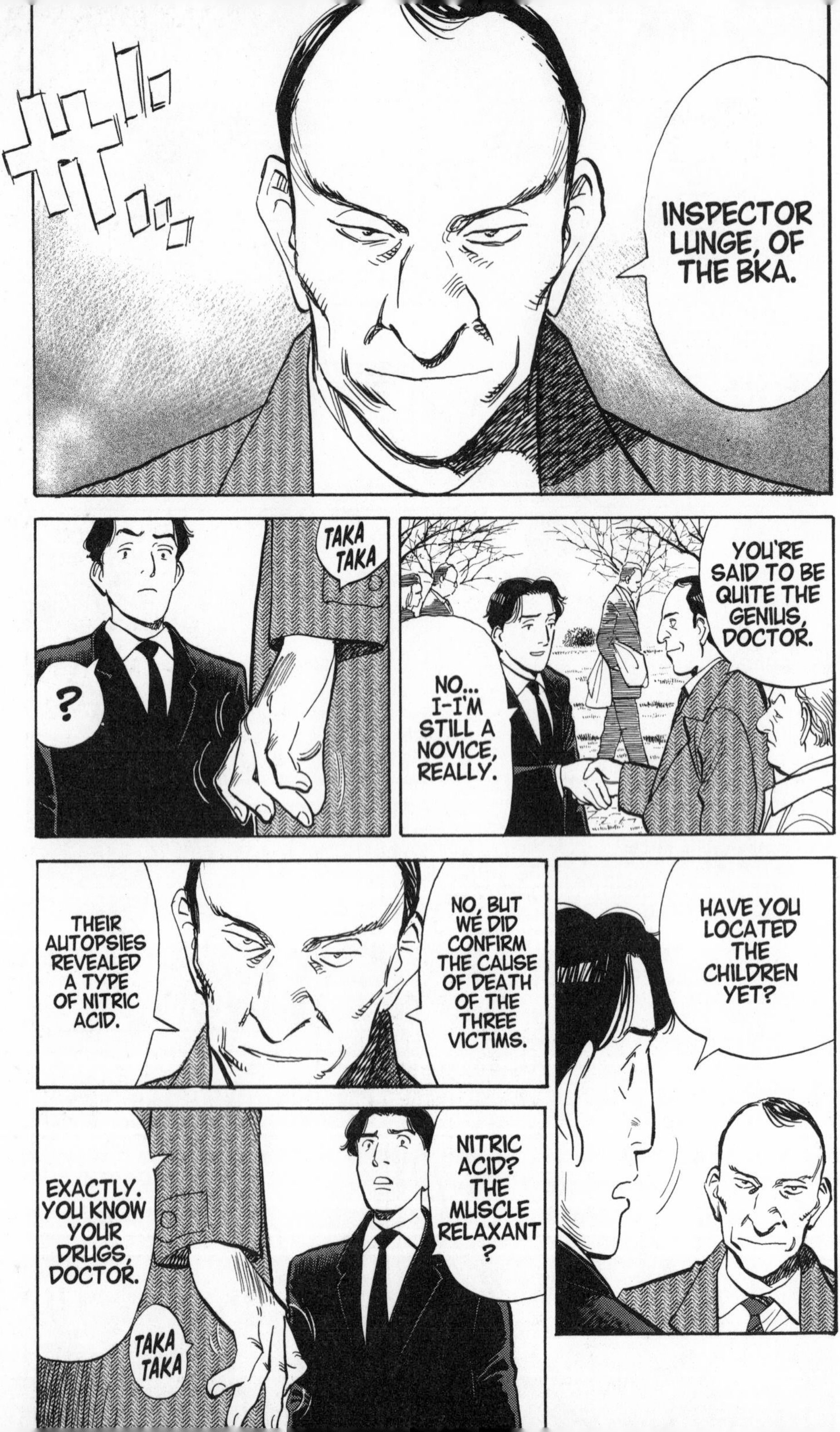
INSPECTOR LUNGE, OF THE BKA.
YOU'RE SAID TO BE QUITE THE GENIUS, DOCTOR.
NO... I-I'M STILL A NOVICE, REALLY.
TAKA TAKA
?
HAVE YOU LOCATED THE CHILDREN YET?
NO, BUT WE DID CONFIRM THE CAUSE OF DEATH OF THE THREE VICTIMS.
THEIR AUTOPSIES REVEALED A TYPE OF NITRIC ACID.
NITRIC ACID? THE MUSCLE RELAXANT?
EXACTLY. YOU KNOW YOUR DRUGS, DOCTOR.
TAKA TAKA

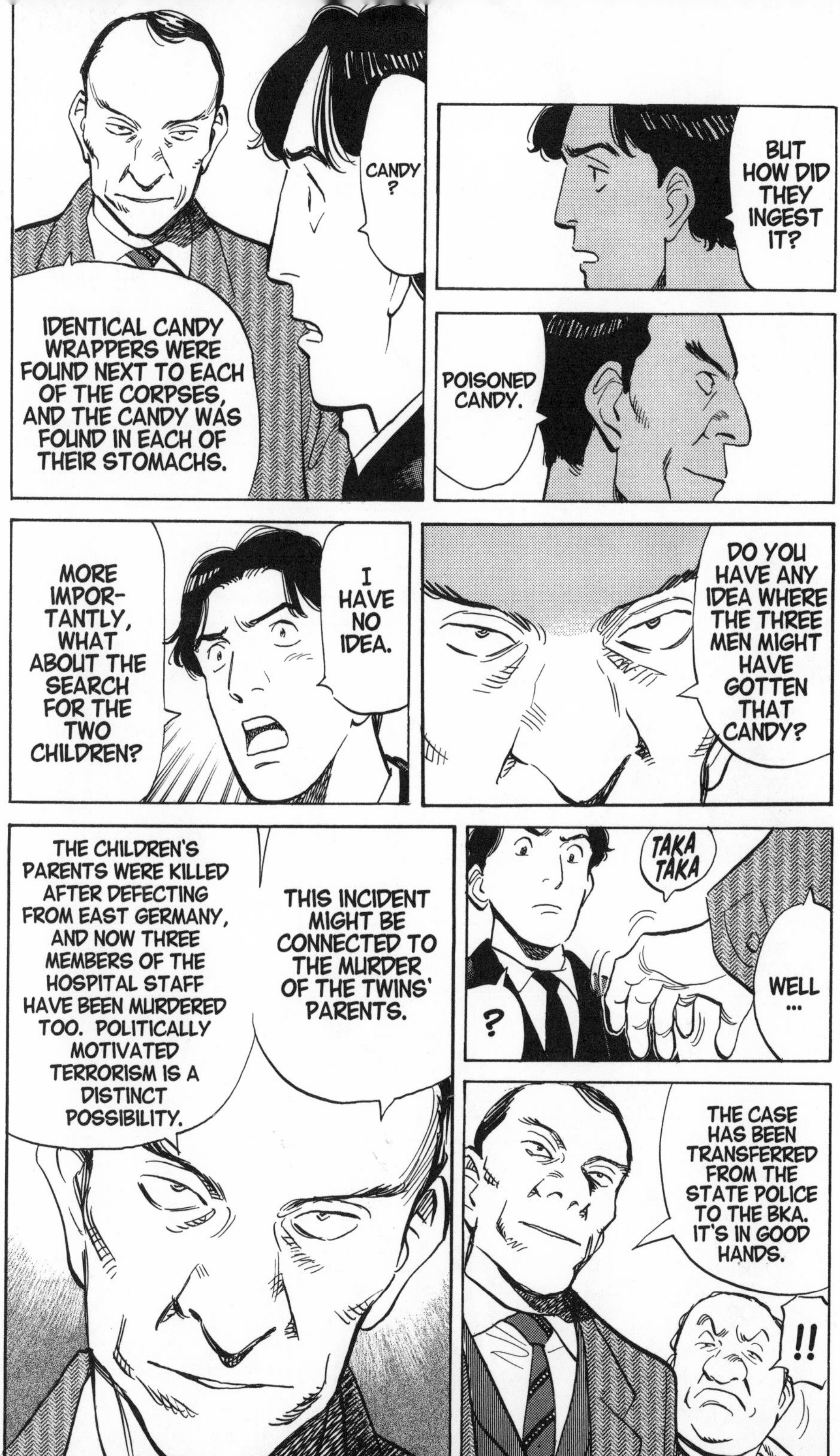
BUT HOW DID THEY INGEST IT?
POISONED CANDY.
CANDY?
IDENTICAL CANDY WRAPPERS WERE FOUND NEXT TO EACH OF THE CORPSES, AND THE CANDY WAS FOUND IN EACH OF THEIR STOMACHS.
DO YOU HAVE ANY IDEA WHERE THE THREE MEN MIGHT HAVE GOTTEN THAT CANDY?
I HAVE NO IDEA.
MORE IMPOR-TANTLY, WHAT ABOUT THE SEARCH FOR THE TWO CHILDREN?
WELL ...
TAKA TAKA
?
THE CASE HAS BEEN TRANSFERRED FROM THE STATE POLICE TO THE BKA. IT'S IN GOOD HANDS.
!!
THIS INCIDENT MIGHT BE CONNECTED TO THE MURDER OF THE TWINS' PARENTS.
THE CHILDREN'S PARENTS WERE KILLED AFTER DEFECTING FROM EAST GERMANY, AND NOW THREE MEMBERS OF THE HOSPITAL STAFF HAVE BEEN MURDERED TOO. POLITICALLY MOTIVATED TERRORISM IS A DISTINCT POSSIBILITY.

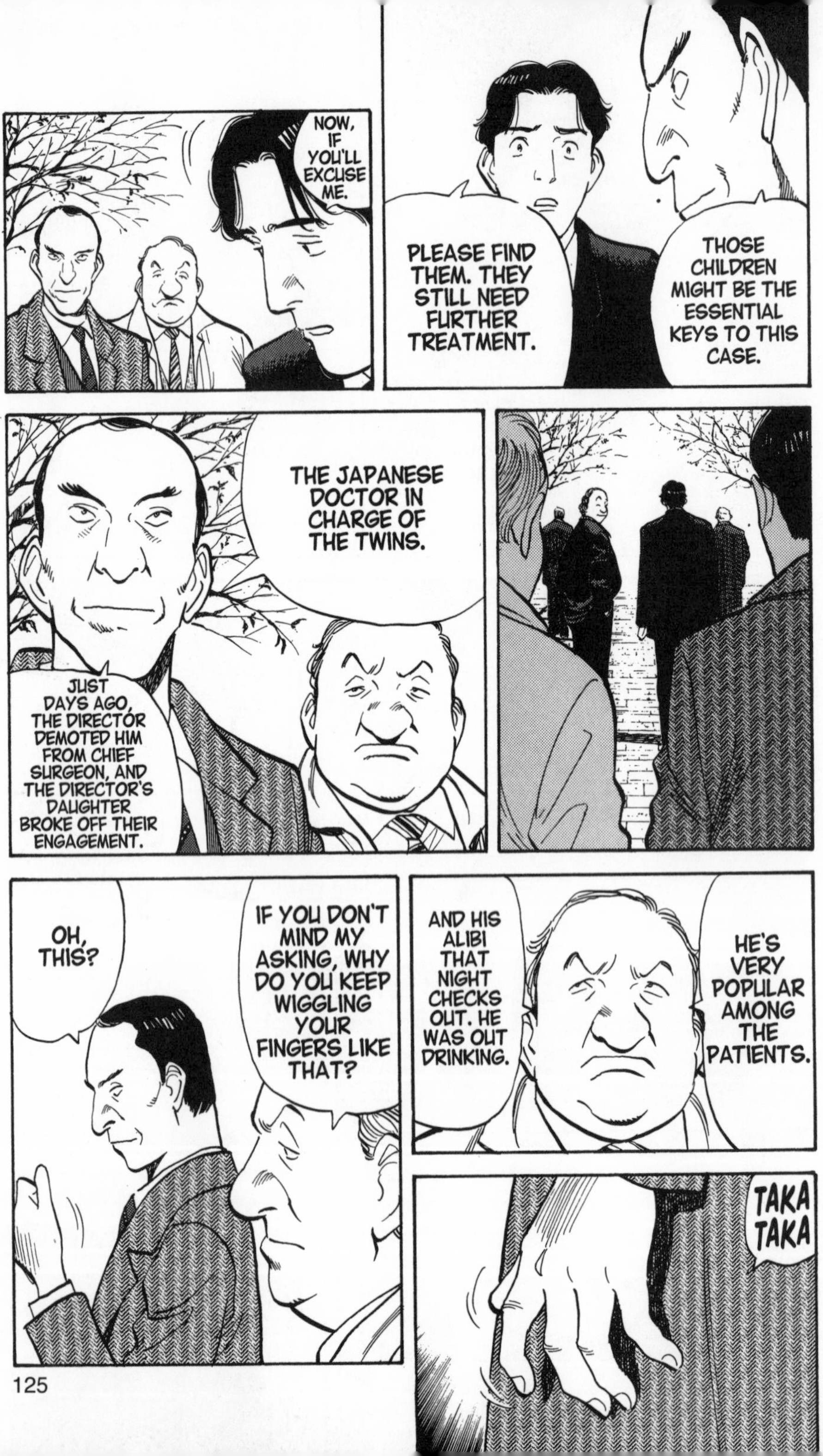
THOSE CHILDREN MIGHT BE THE ESSENTIAL KEYS TO THIS CASE.
PLEASE FIND THEM. THEY STILL NEED FURTHER TREATMENT.
NOW, IF YOU'LL EXCUSE ME.
THE JAPANESE DOCTOR IN CHARGE OF THE TWINS.
JUST DAYS AGO, THE DIRECTOR DEMOTED HIM FROM CHIEF SURGEON, AND THE DIRECTOR'S DAUGHTER BROKE OFF THEIR ENGAGEMENT.
HE'S VERY POPULAR AMONG THE PATIENTS.
AND HIS ALIBI THAT NIGHT CHECKS OUT. HE WAS OUT DRINKING.
TAKA TAKA
IF YOU DON'T MIND MY ASKING, WHY DO YOU KEEP WIGGLING YOUR FINGERS LIKE THAT?
OH, THIS?

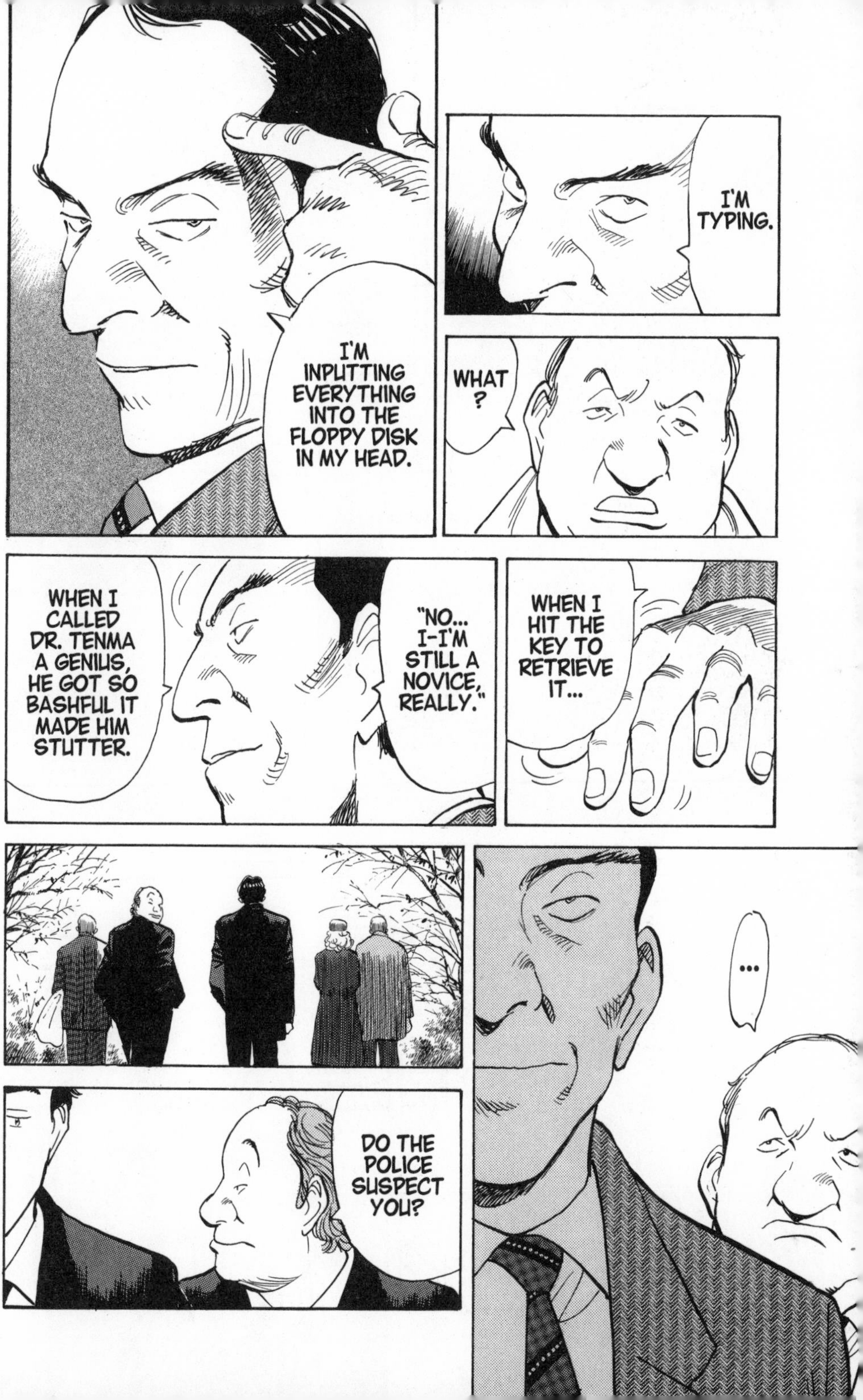
I'M TYPING.
WHAT?
I'M INPUTTING EVERYTHING INTO THE FLOPPY DISK IN MY HEAD.
WHEN I HIT THE KEY TO RETRIEVE IT...
"NO... I-I'M STILL A NOVICE, REALLY."
WHEN I CALLED DR. TENMA A GENIUS, HE GOT SO BASHFUL IT MADE HIM STUTTER.
...
DO THE POLICE SUSPECT YOU?

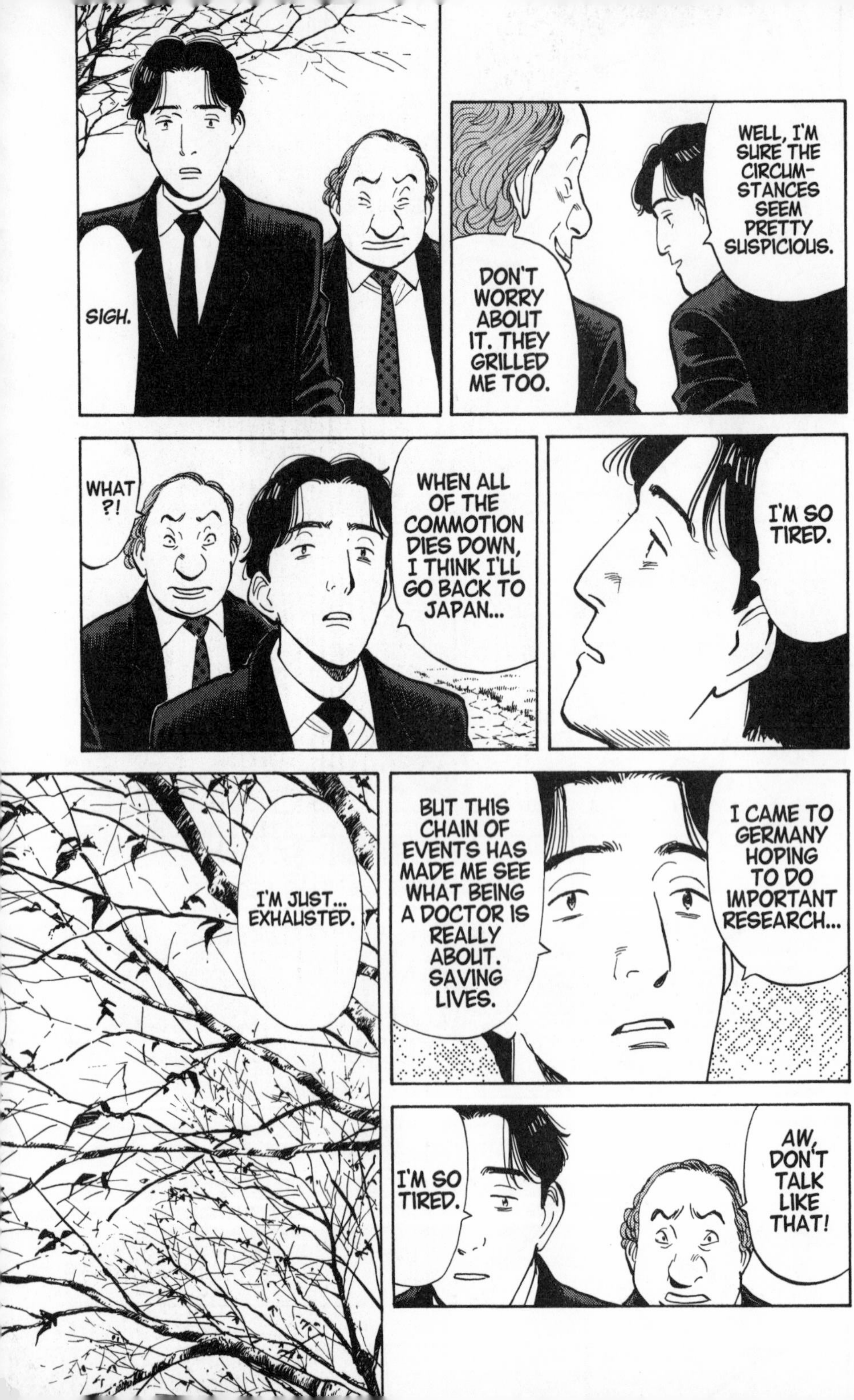
WELL, I'M SURE THE CIRCUM-STANCES SEEM PRETTY SUSPICIOUS.
DON'T WORRY ABOUT IT. THEY GRILLED ME TOO.
SIGH.
I'M SO TIRED.
WHEN ALL OF THE COMMOTION DIES DOWN, I THINK I'LL GO BACK TO JAPAN...
WHAT ?!
I CAME TO GERMANY HOPING TO DO IMPORTANT RESEARCH...
BUT THIS CHAIN OF EVENTS HAS MADE ME SEE WHAT BEING A DOCTOR IS REALLY ABOUT. SAVING LIVES.
AW, DON'T TALK LIKE THAT!
I'M SO TIRED.
I'M JUST... EXHAUSTED.

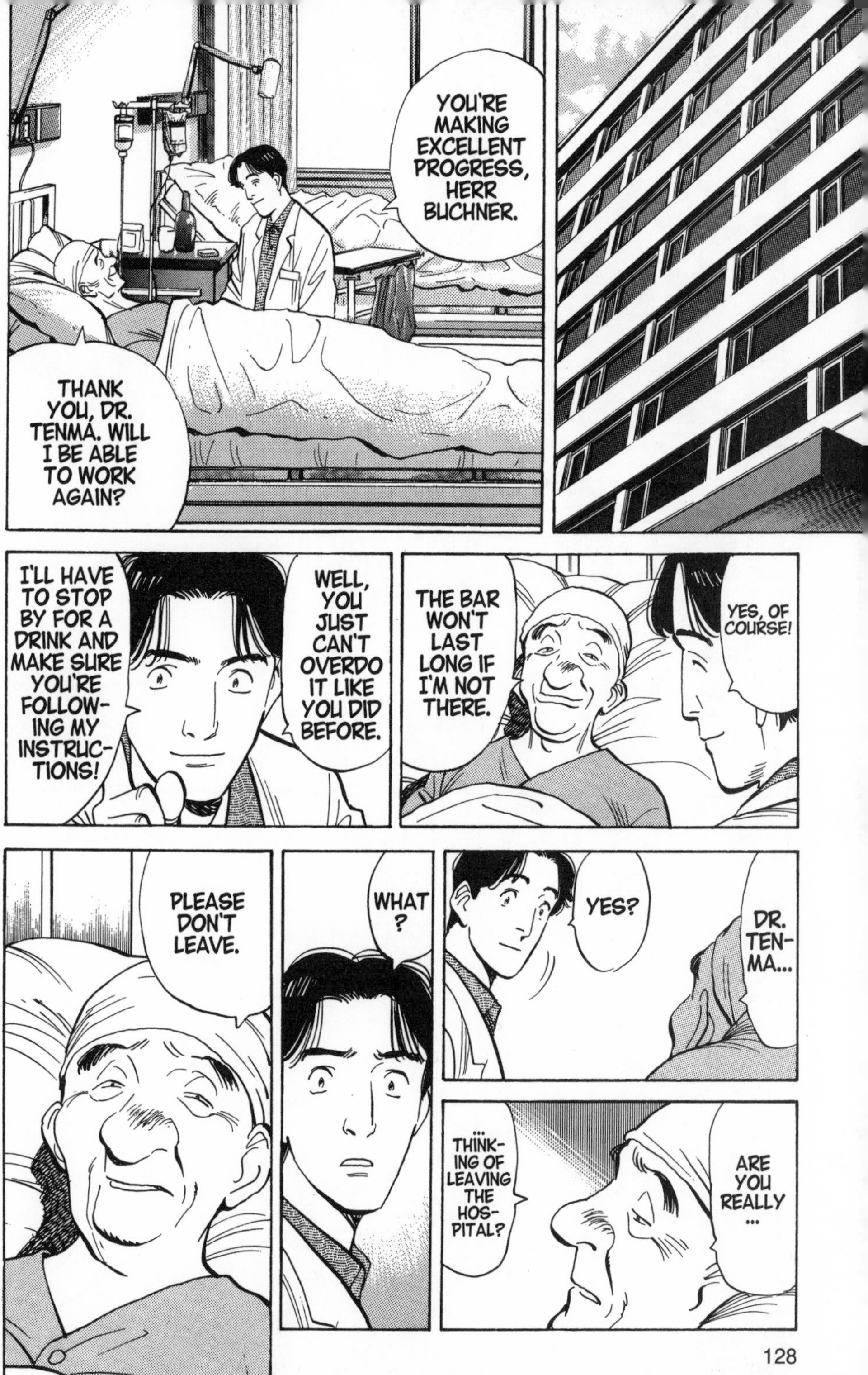
YOU'RE MAKING EXCELLENT PROGRESS, HERR BUCHNER.
THANK YOU, DR. TENMA. WILL I BE ABLE TO WORK AGAIN?
YES, OF COURSE!
THE BAR WON'T LAST LONG IF I'M NOT THERE.
WELL, YOU JUST CAN'T OVERDO IT LIKE YOU DID BEFORE.
I'LL HAVE TO STOP BY FOR A DRINK AND MAKE SURE YOU'RE FOLLOW-ING MY INSTRUC-TIONS!
DR. TEN-MA...
YES?
ARE YOU REALLY...
...THINK-ING OF LEAVING THE HOS-PITAL?
WHAT?
PLEASE DON'T LEAVE.

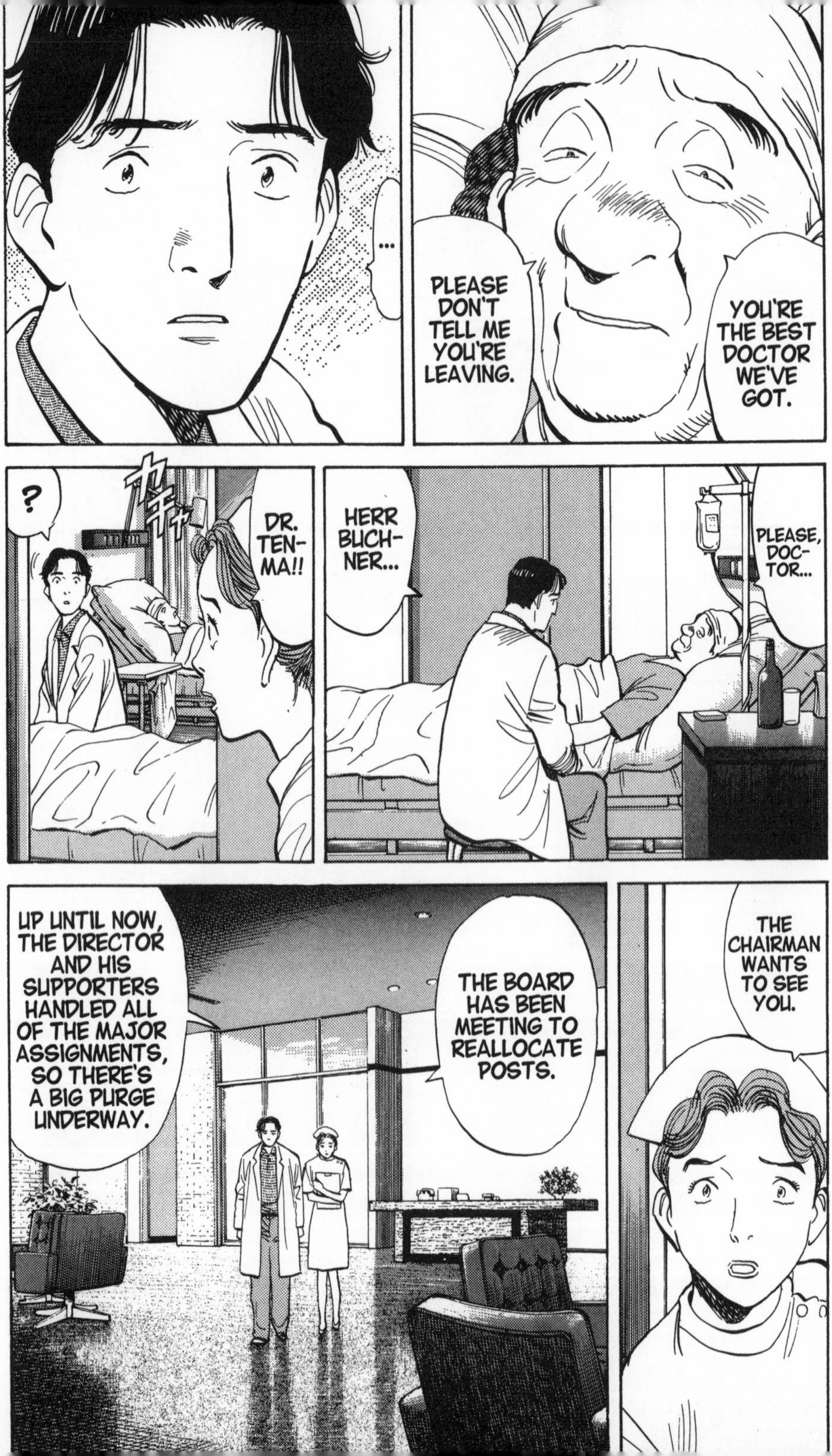
YOU'RE THE BEST DOCTOR WE'VE GOT.
PLEASE DON'T TELL ME YOU'RE LEAVING.
...
PLEASE, DOCTOR...
HERR BUCHNER...
DR. TENMA!!
カチャ
?
THE CHAIRMAN WANTS TO SEE YOU.
THE BOARD HAS BEEN MEETING TO REALLOCATE POSTS.
UP UNTIL NOW, THE DIRECTOR AND HIS SUPPORTERS HANDLED ALL OF THE MAJOR ASSIGNMENTS, SO THERE'S A BIG PURGE UNDERWAY.

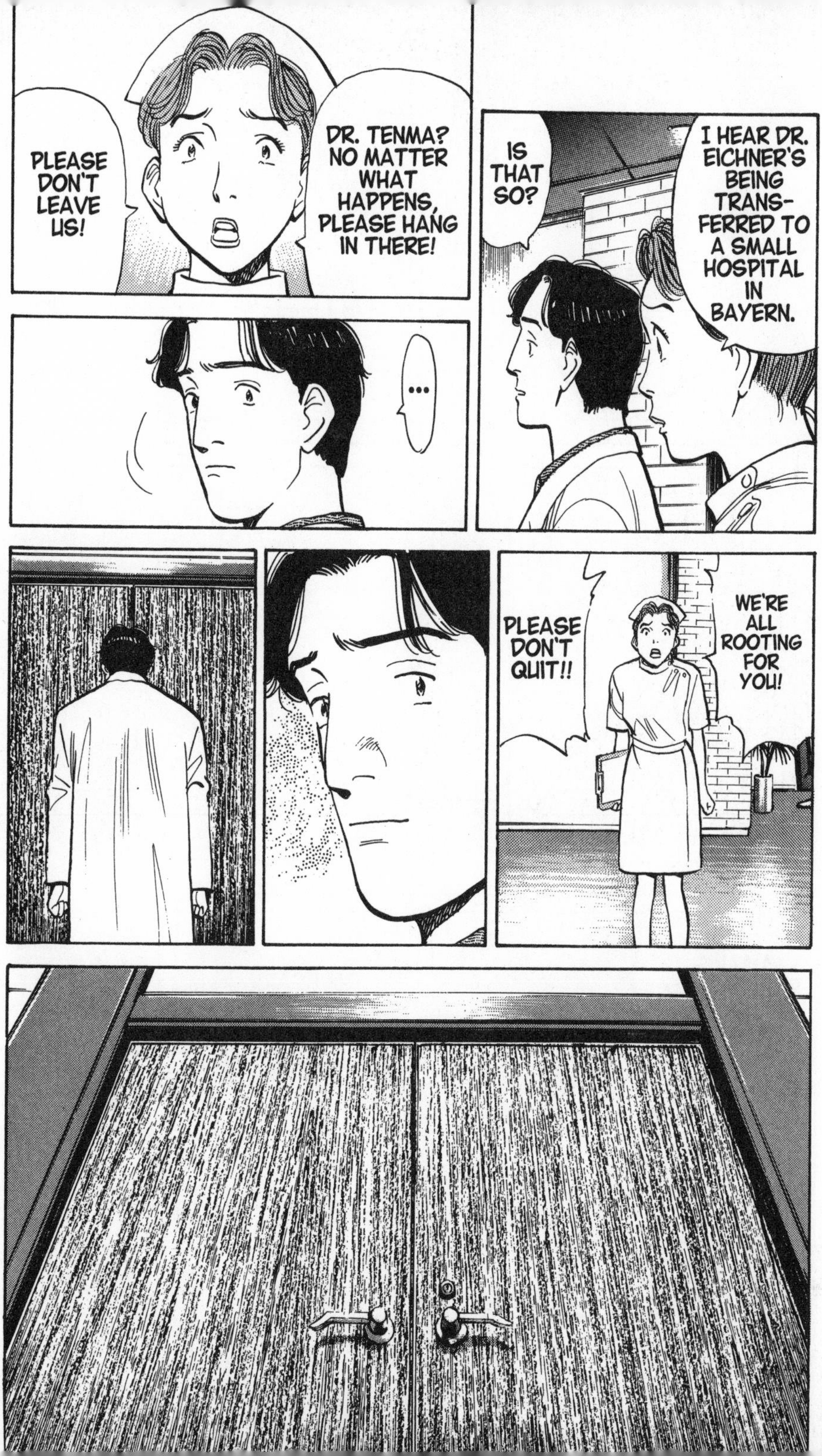
I HEAR DR. EICHNER'S BEING TRANS-FERRED TO A SMALL HOSPITAL IN BAYERN.
IS THAT SO?
DR. TENMA? NO MATTER WHAT HAPPENS, PLEASE HANG IN THERE!
PLEASE DON'T LEAVE US!
...
WE'RE ALL ROOTING FOR YOU!
PLEASE DON'T QUIT!!

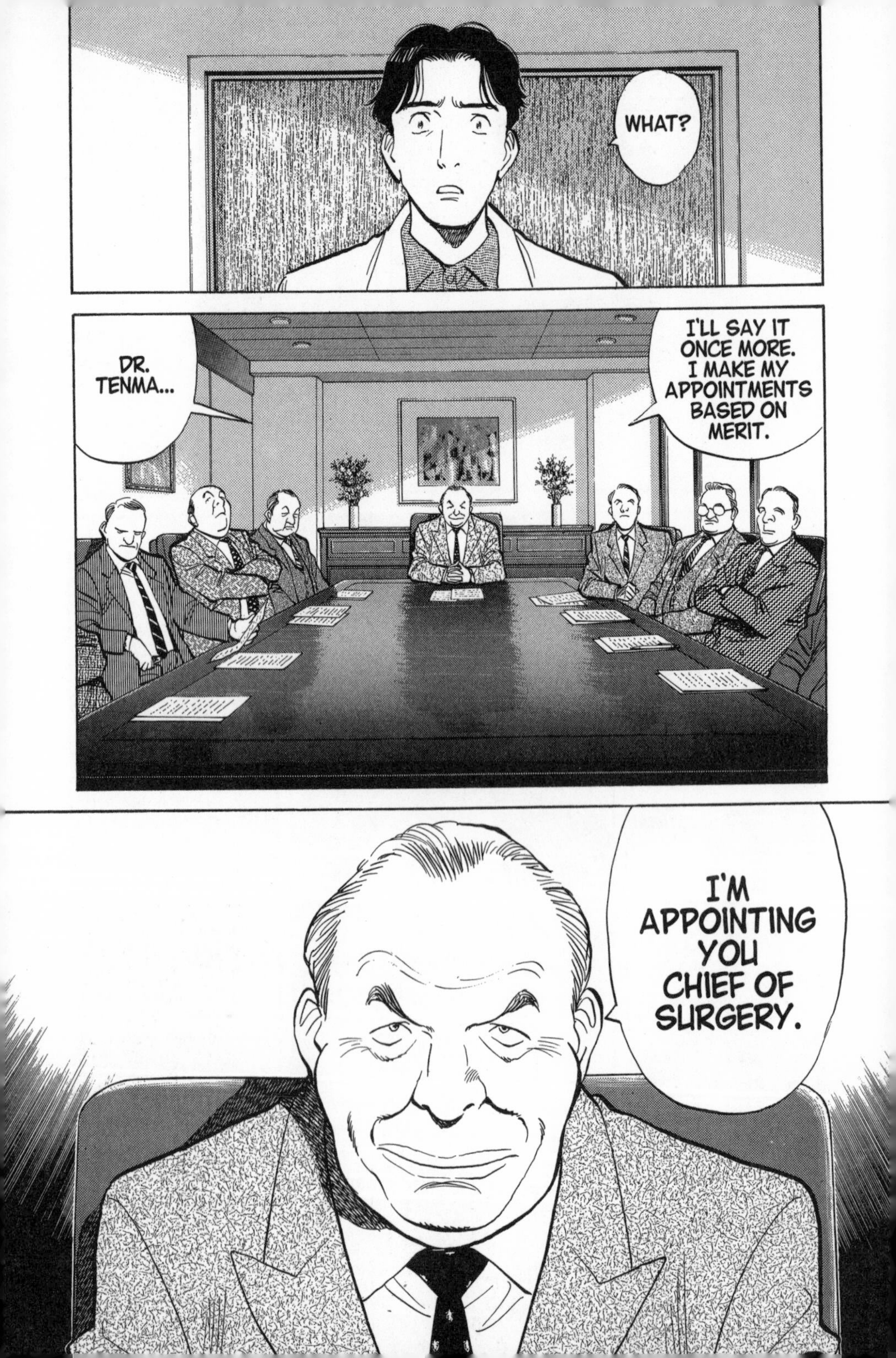
WHAT?
I'LL SAY IT ONCE MORE. I MAKE MY APPOINTMENTS BASED ON MERIT.
DR. TENMA...
I'M APPOINTING YOU CHIEF OF SURGERY.

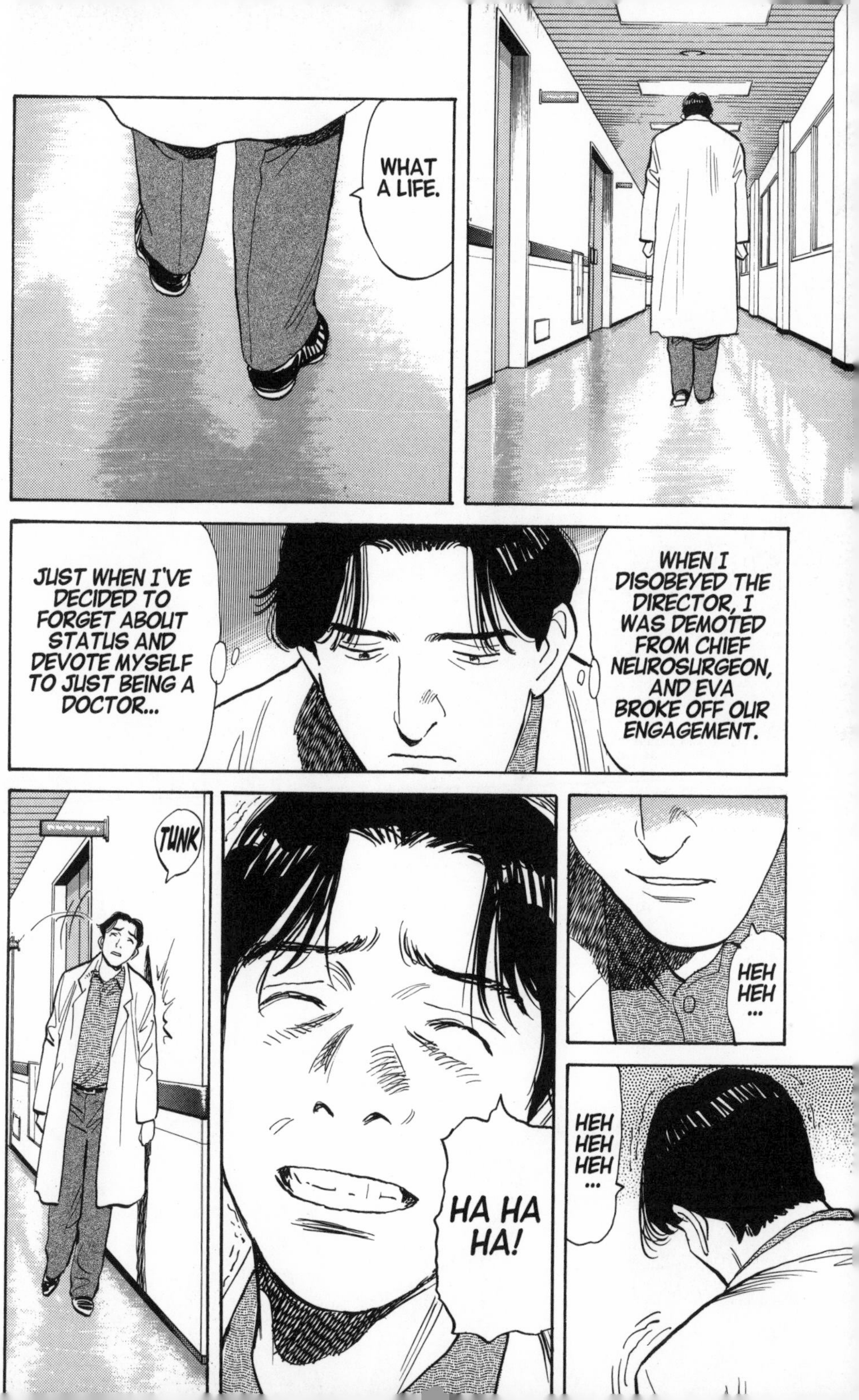
WHAT A LIFE.
WHEN I DISOBEYED THE DIRECTOR, I WAS DEMOTED FROM CHIEF NEUROSURGEON, AND EVA BROKE OFF OUR ENGAGEMENT.
JUST WHEN I'VE DECIDED TO FORGET ABOUT STATUS AND DEVOTE MYSELF TO JUST BEING A DOCTOR...
HEH HEH ...
HEH HEH HEH ...
HA HA HA!
TUNK

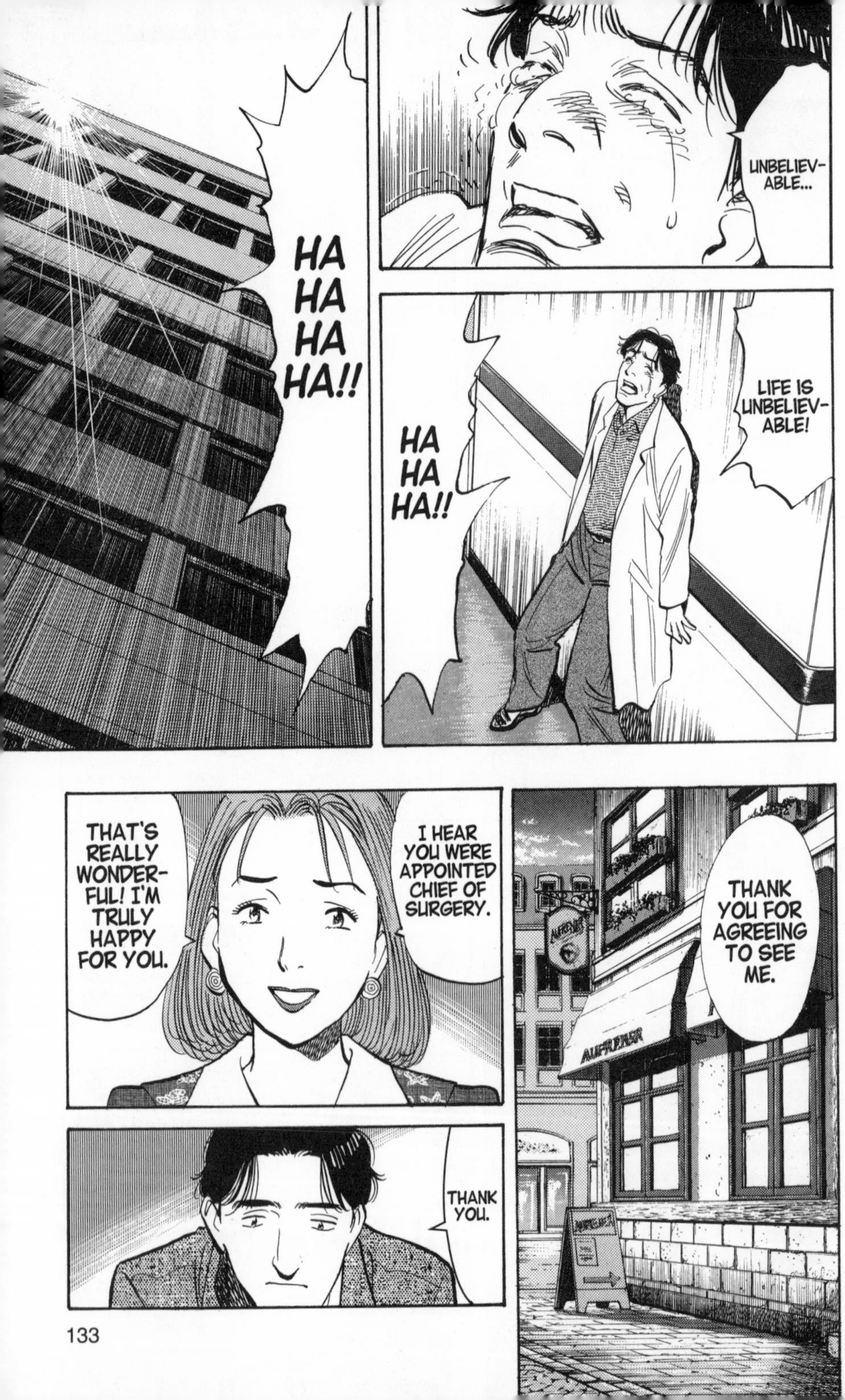
UNBELIEVABLE...
LIFE IS UNBELIEVABLE!
HA HA HA!!
HA HA HA HA!!
THANK YOU FOR AGREEING TO SEE ME.
I HEAR YOU WERE APPOINTED CHIEF OF SURGERY.
THAT'S REALLY WONDERFUL! I'M TRULY HAPPY FOR YOU.
THANK YOU.

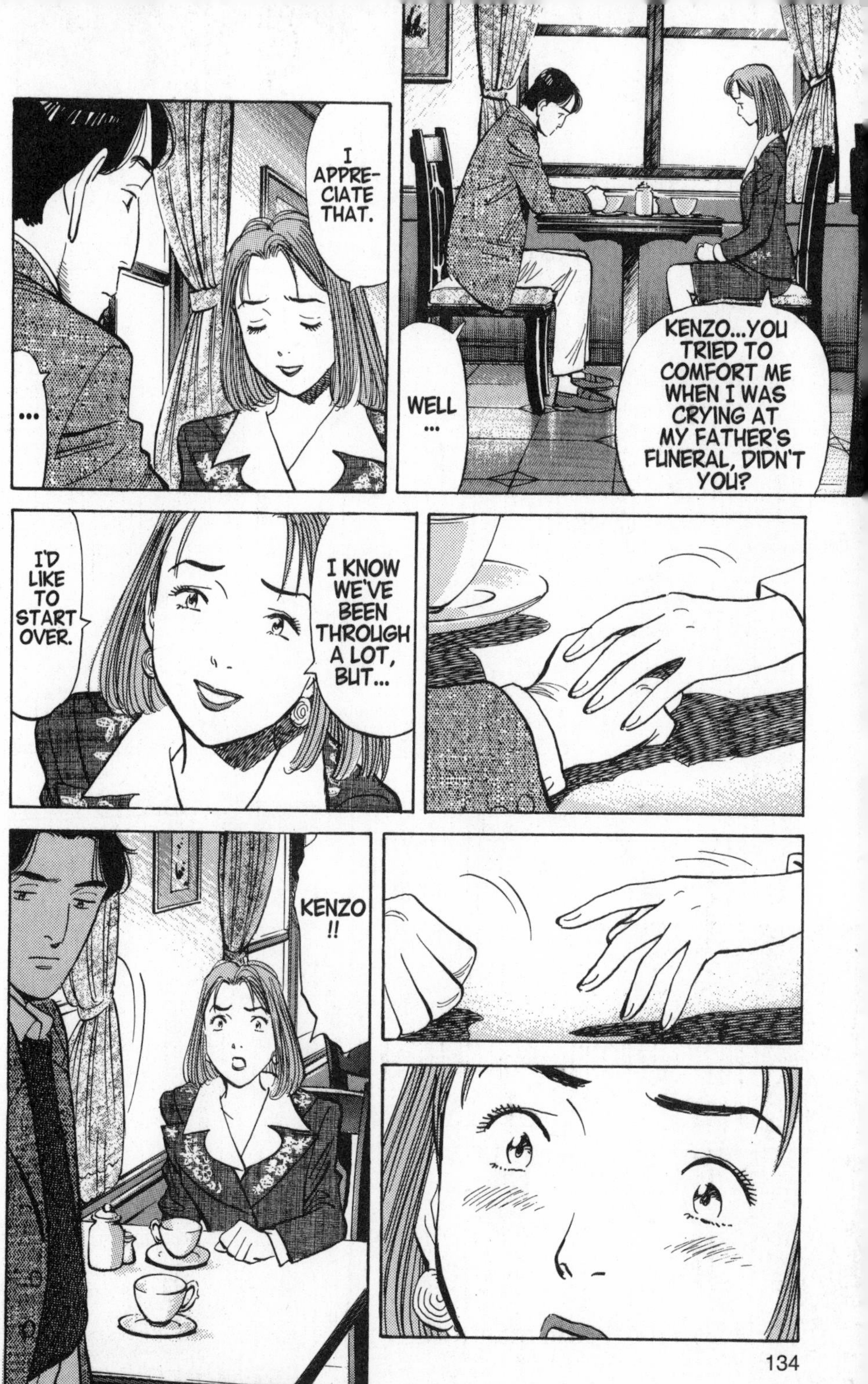
KENZO...YOU TRIED TO COMFORT ME WHEN I WAS CRYING AT MY FATHER'S FUNERAL, DIDN'T YOU?
WELL ...
I APPRECIATE THAT.
...
I KNOW WE'VE BEEN THROUGH A LOT, BUT...
I'D LIKE TO START OVER.
KENZO !!

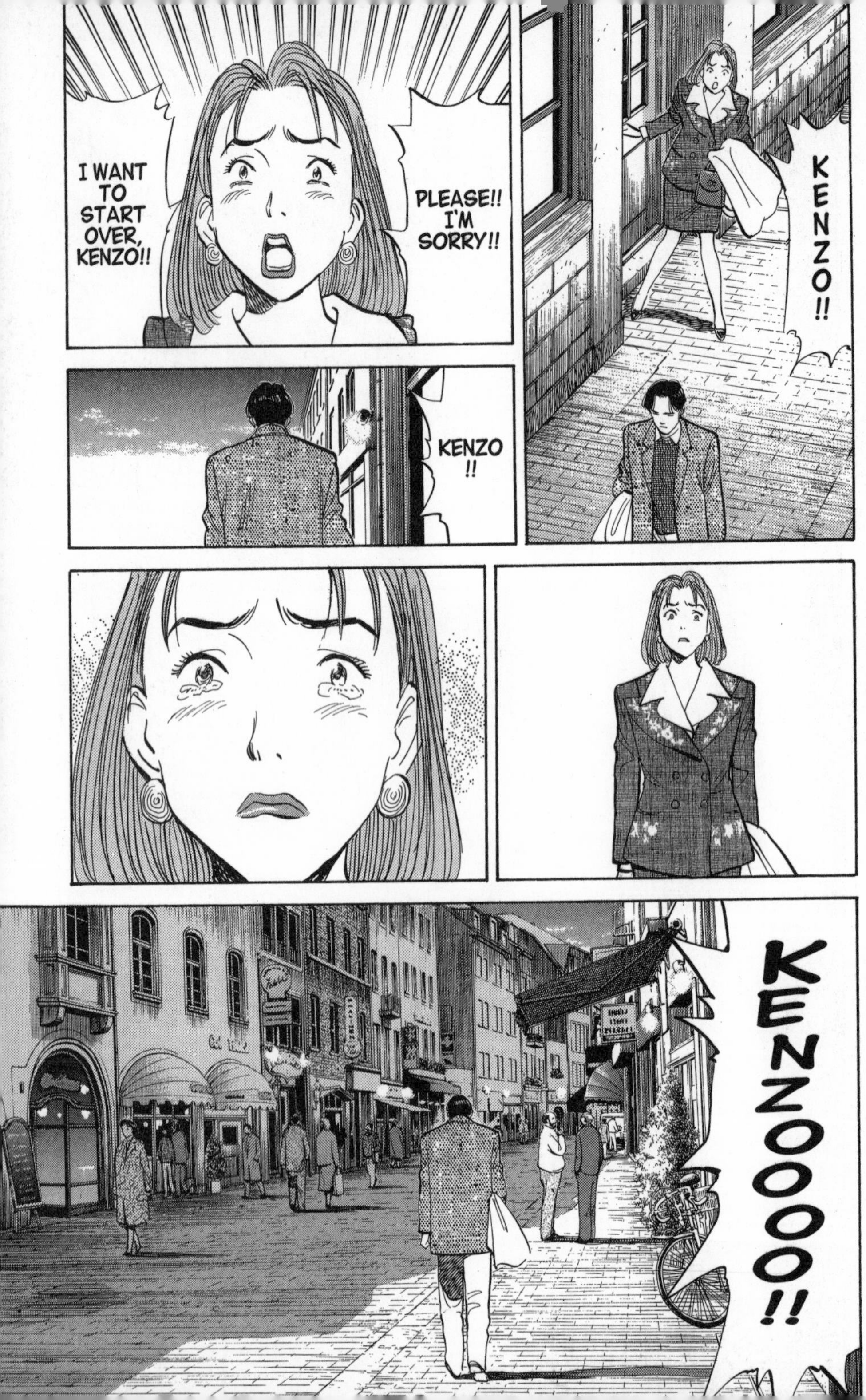
KENZO!!
PLEASE!! I'M SORRY!!
I WANT TO START OVER, KENZO!!
KENZO !!
KENZOOOOO!!

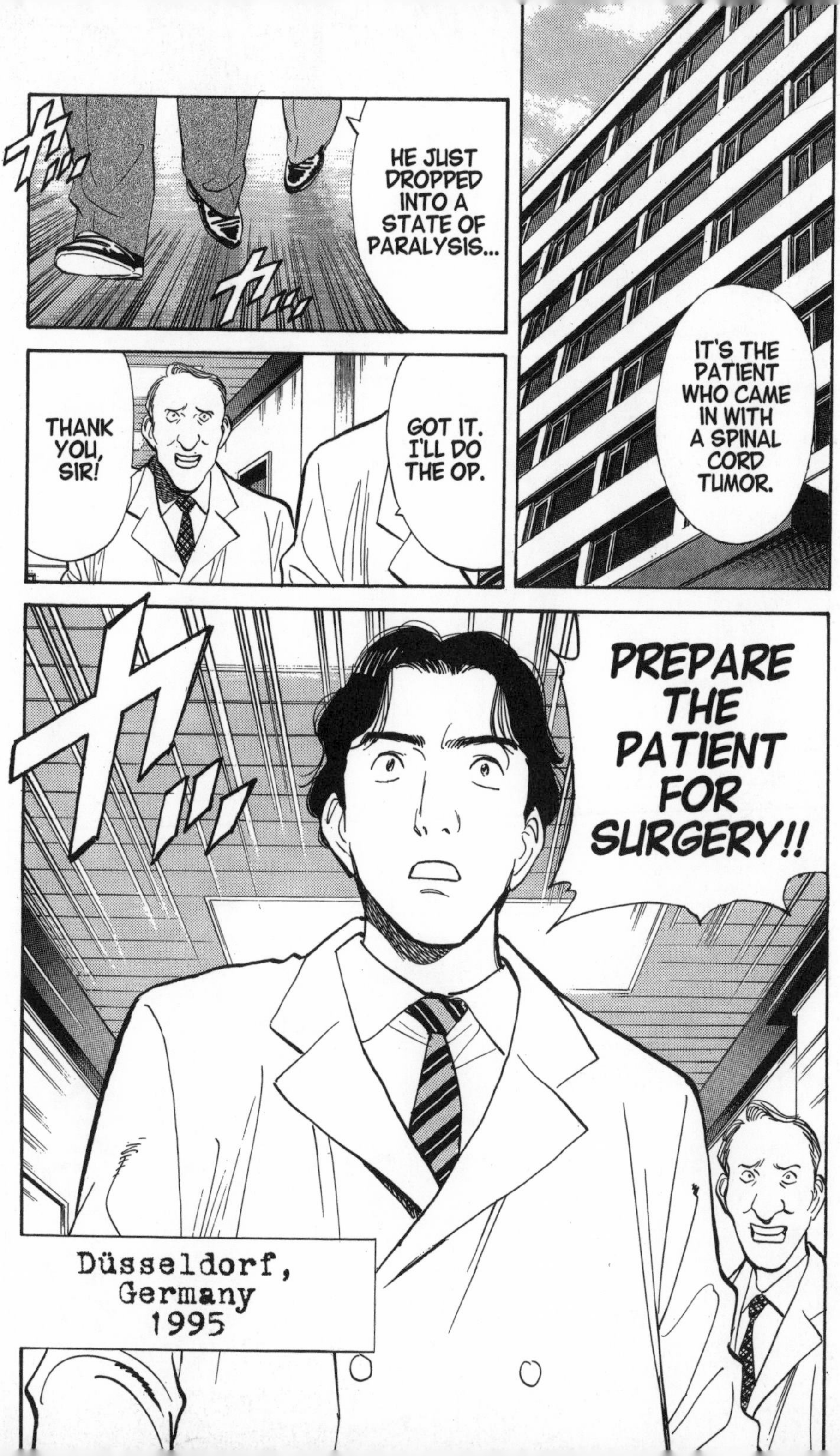
IT'S THE PATIENT WHO CAME IN WITH A SPINAL CORD TUMOR.
HE JUST DROPPED INTO A STATE OF PARALYSIS...
GOT IT. I'LL DO THE OP.
THANK YOU, SIR!
PREPARE THE PATIENT FOR SURGERY!!
Düsseldorf, Germany 1995

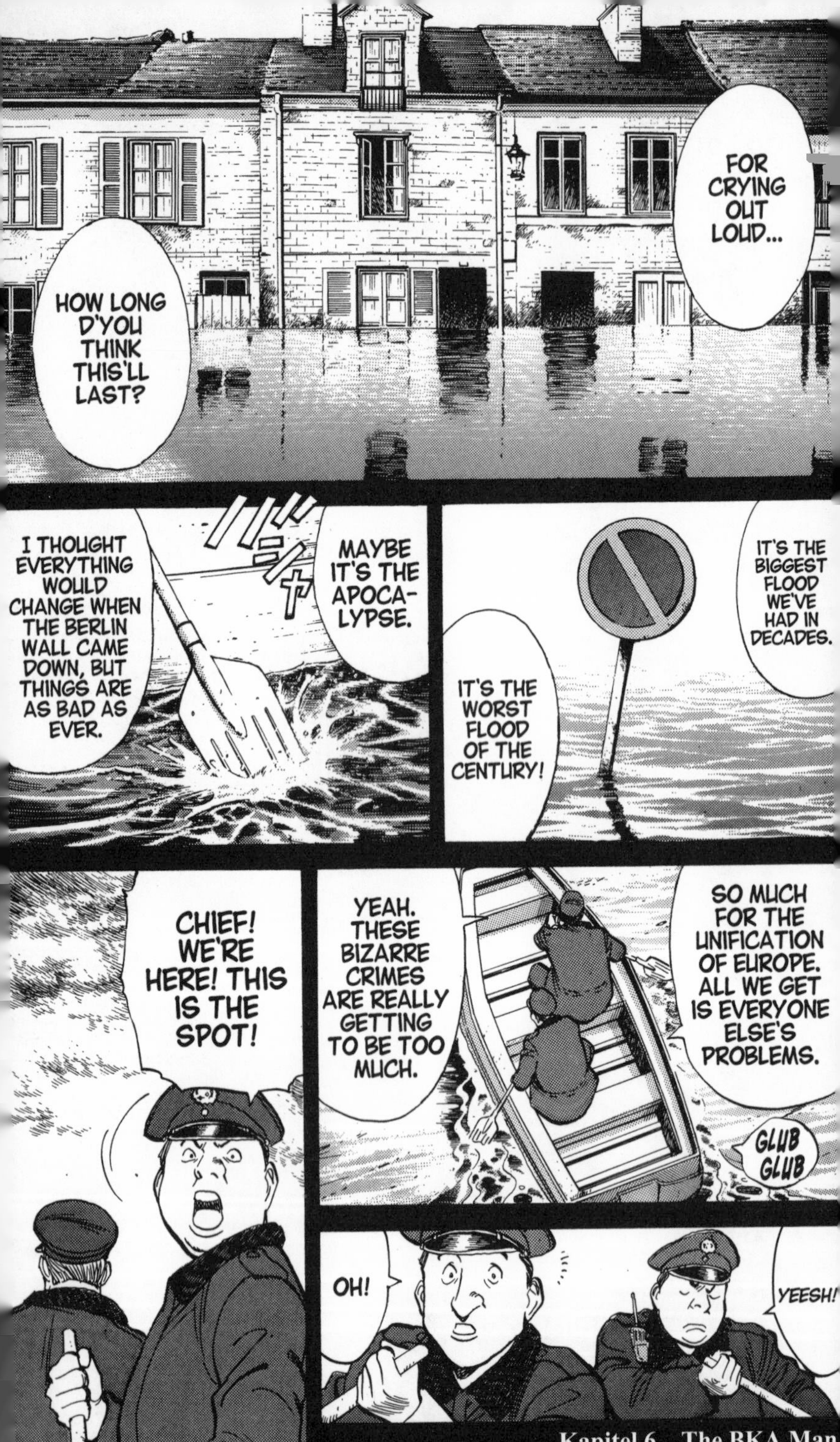
FOR CRYING OUT LOUD...
HOW LONG D'YOU THINK THIS'LL LAST?
IT'S THE BIGGEST FLOOD WE'VE HAD IN DECADES.
IT'S THE WORST FLOOD OF THE CENTURY!
MAYBE IT'S THE APOCA-LYPSE.
I THOUGHT EVERYTHING WOULD CHANGE WHEN THE BERLIN WALL CAME DOWN, BUT THINGS ARE AS BAD AS EVER.
SO MUCH FOR THE UNIFICATION OF EUROPE. ALL WE GET IS EVERYONE ELSE'S PROBLEMS.
GLUB GLUB
YEAH. THESE BIZARRE CRIMES ARE REALLY GETTING TO BE TOO MUCH.
YEESH!
OH!
CHIEF! WE'RE HERE! THIS IS THE SPOT!

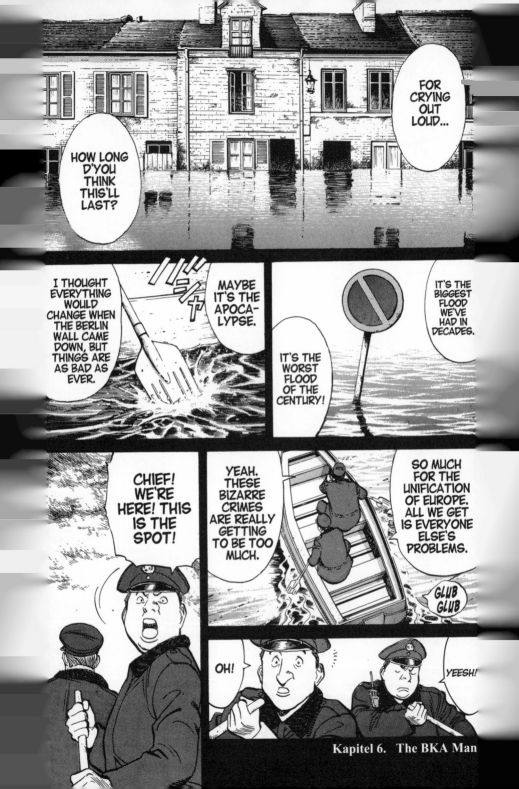

Kapitel 6. The BKA Man

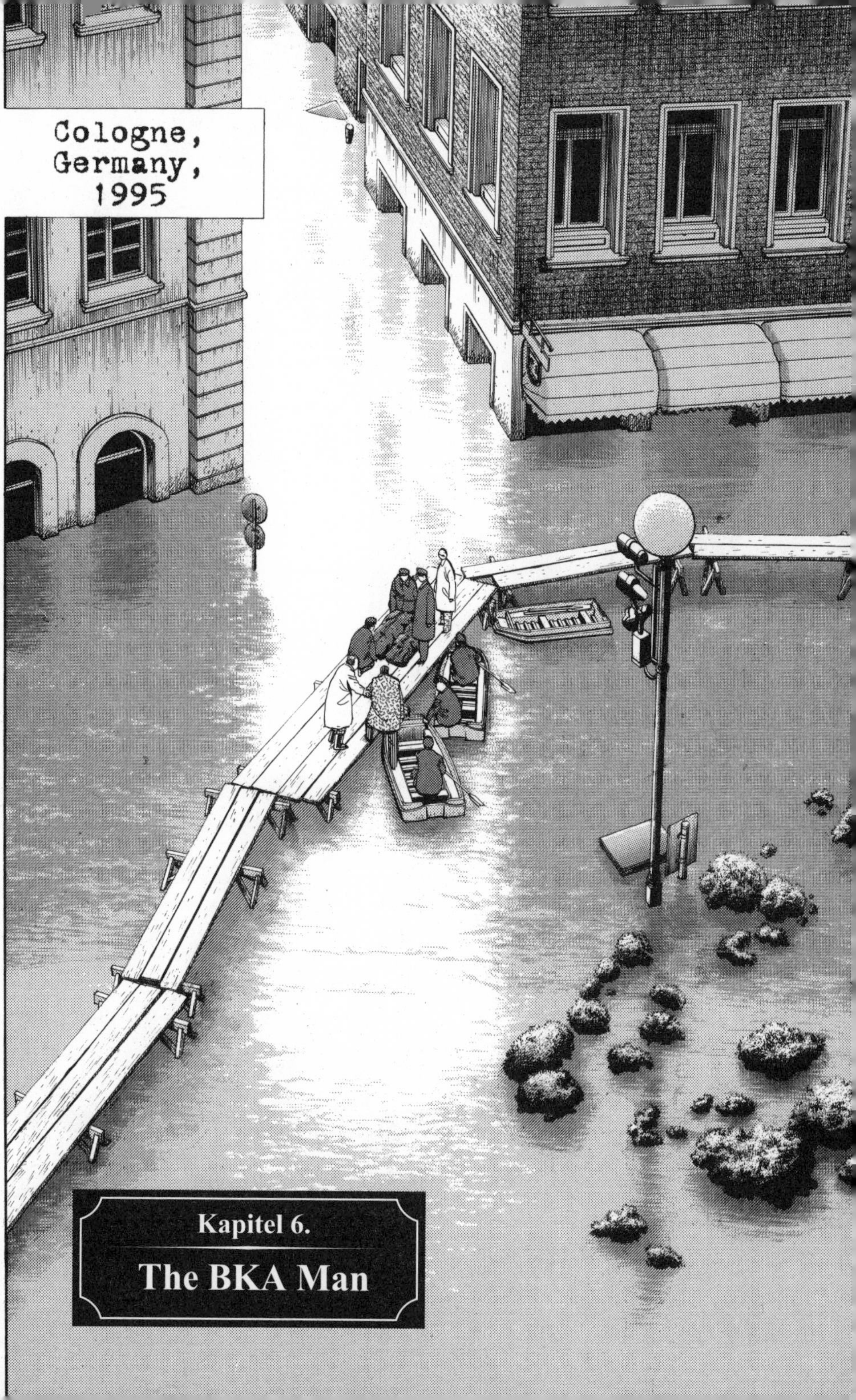

Cologne, Germany, 1995
Kapitel 6.
The BKA Man

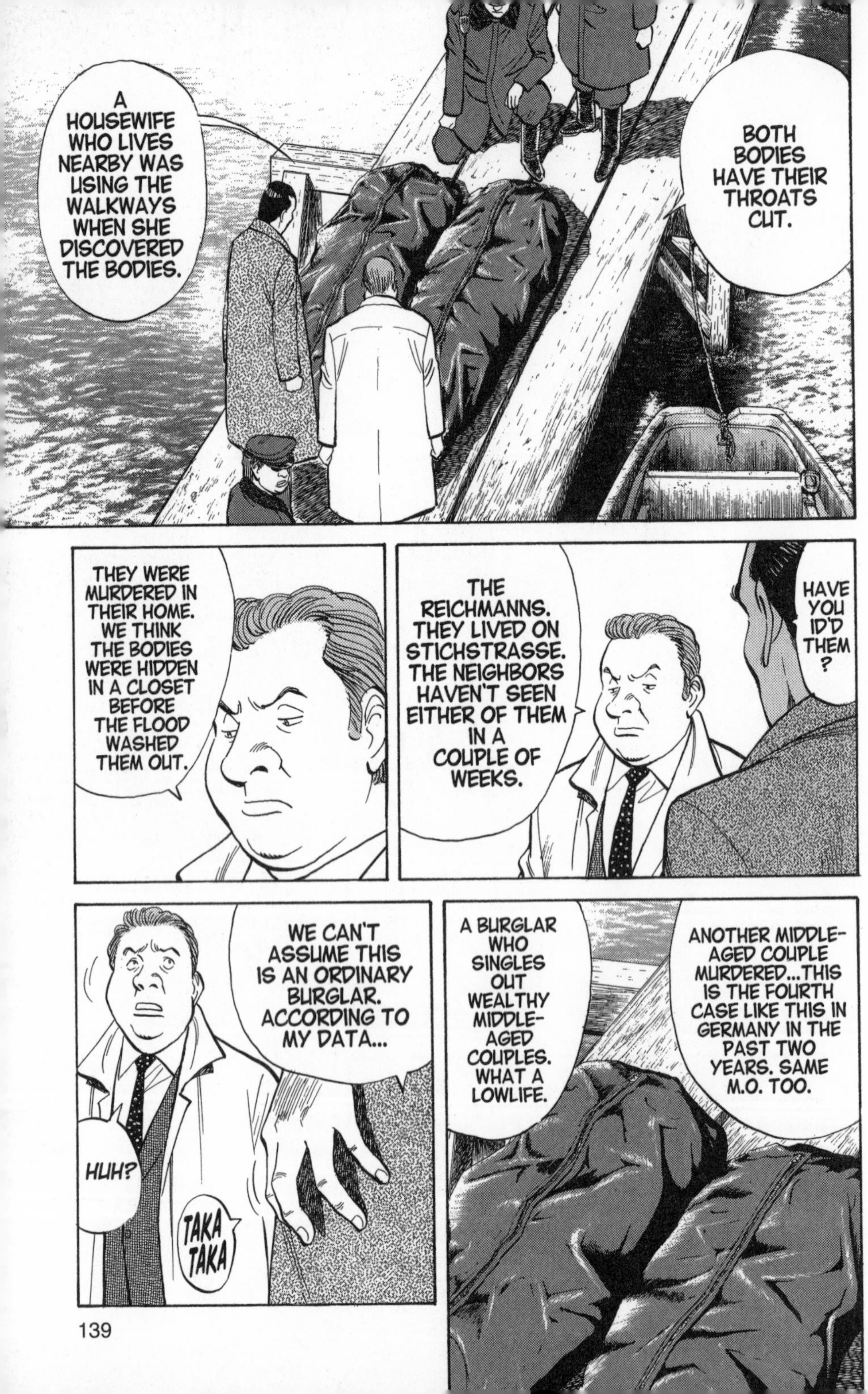

BOTH BODIES HAVE THEIR THROATS CUT.
A HOUSEWIFE WHO LIVES NEARBY WAS USING THE WALKWAYS WHEN SHE DISCOVERED THE BODIES.
HAVE YOU ID'D THEM?
THE REICHMANNS. THEY LIVED ON STICHSTRASSE. THE NEIGHBORS HAVEN'T SEEN EITHER OF THEM IN A COUPLE OF WEEKS.
THEY WERE MURDERED IN THEIR HOME. WE THINK THE BODIES WERE HIDDEN IN A CLOSET BEFORE THE FLOOD WASHED THEM OUT.
ANOTHER MIDDLE-AGED COUPLE MURDERED...THIS IS THE FOURTH CASE LIKE THIS IN GERMANY IN THE PAST TWO YEARS. SAME M.O. TOO.
A BURGLAR WHO SINGLES OUT WEALTHY MIDDLE-AGED COUPLES. WHAT A LOWLIFE.
WE CAN'T ASSUME THIS IS AN ORDINARY BURGLAR. ACCORDING TO MY DATA...
HUH?
TAKA TAKA

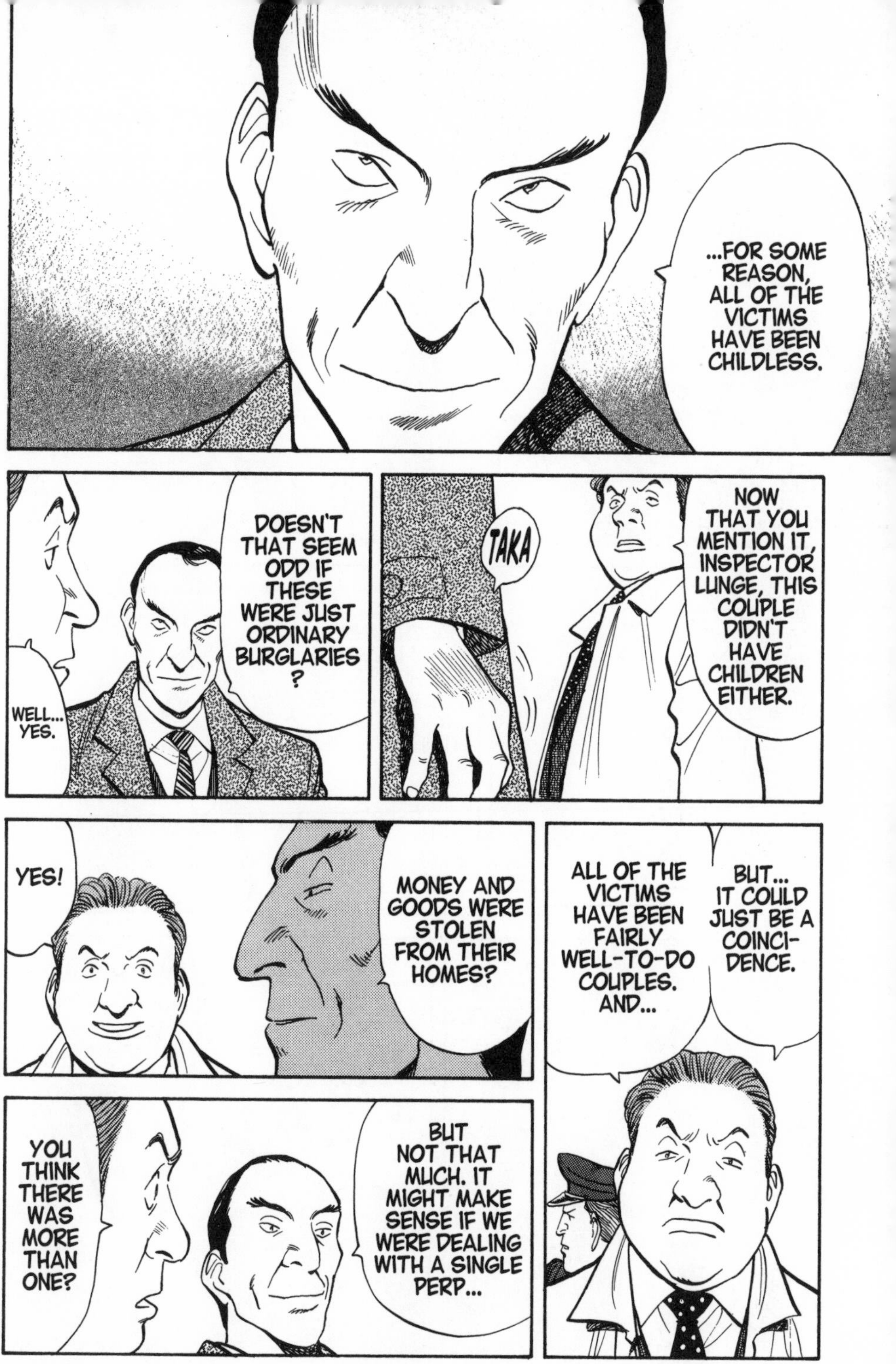
...FOR SOME REASON, ALL OF THE VICTIMS HAVE BEEN CHILDLESS.
NOW THAT YOU MENTION IT, INSPECTOR LUNGE, THIS COUPLE DIDN'T HAVE CHILDREN EITHER.
TAKA
DOESN'T THAT SEEM ODD IF THESE WERE JUST ORDINARY BURGLARIES?
WELL... YES.
BUT... IT COULD JUST BE A COINCIDENCE.
ALL OF THE VICTIMS HAVE BEEN FAIRLY WELL-TO-DO COUPLES. AND...
MONEY AND GOODS WERE STOLEN FROM THEIR HOMES?
YES!
BUT NOT THAT MUCH. IT MIGHT MAKE SENSE IF WE WERE DEALING WITH A SINGLE PERP...
YOU THINK THERE WAS MORE THAN ONE?

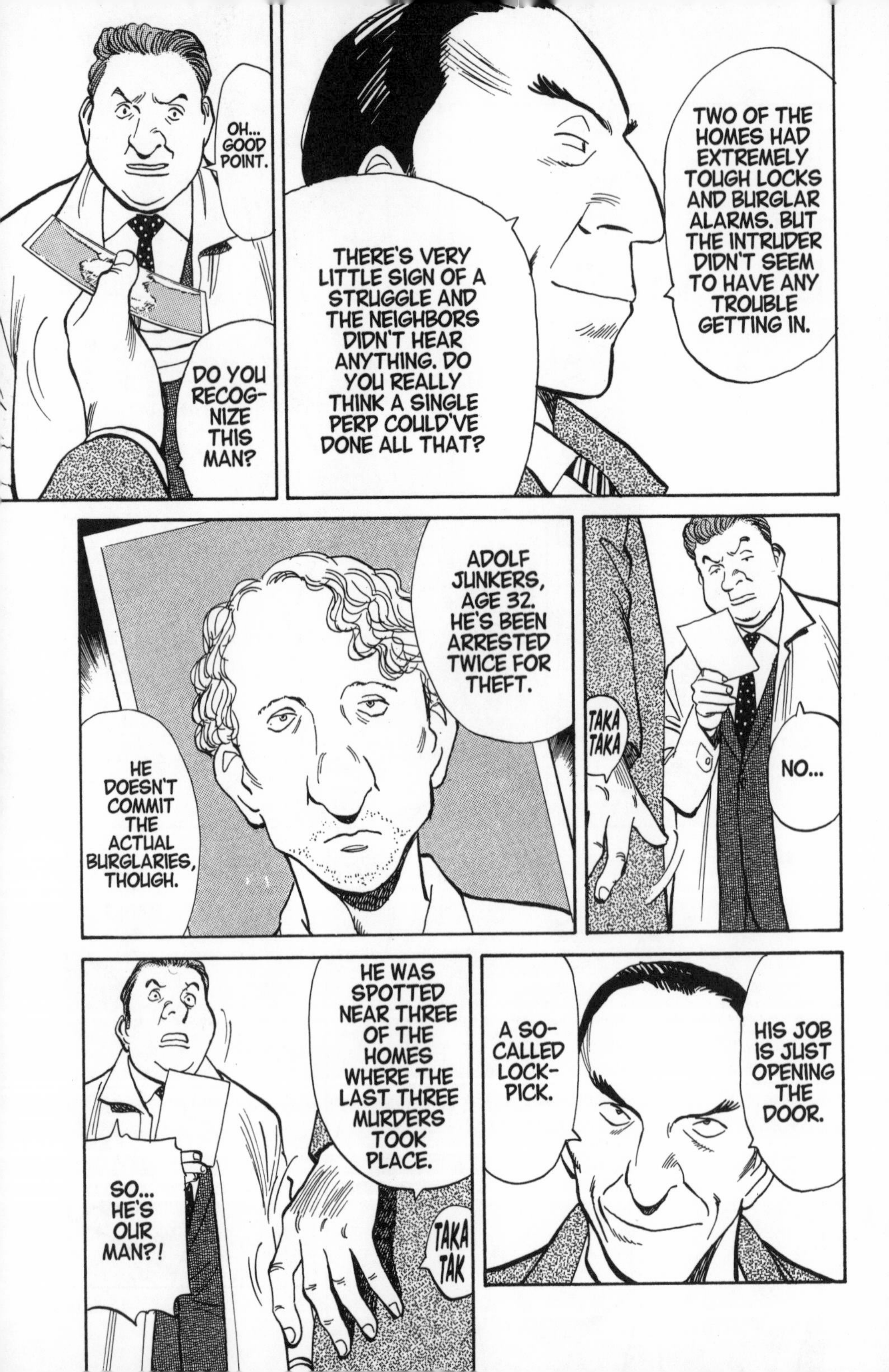
TWO OF THE HOMES HAD EXTREMELY TOUGH LOCKS AND BURGLAR ALARMS. BUT THE INTRUDER DIDN'T SEEM TO HAVE ANY TROUBLE GETTING IN.
THERE'S VERY LITTLE SIGN OF A STRUGGLE AND THE NEIGHBORS DIDN'T HEAR ANYTHING. DO YOU REALLY THINK A SINGLE PERP COULD'VE DONE ALL THAT?
OH... GOOD POINT.
DO YOU RECOG-NIZE THIS MAN?
TAKA TAKA
NO...
ADOLF JUNKERS, AGE 32. HE'S BEEN ARRESTED TWICE FOR THEFT.
HE DOESN'T COMMIT THE ACTUAL BURGLARIES, THOUGH.
HIS JOB IS JUST OPENING THE DOOR.
A SO-CALLED LOCK-PICK.
HE WAS SPOTTED NEAR THREE OF THE HOMES WHERE THE LAST THREE MURDERS TOOK PLACE.
TAKA TAK
SO... HE'S OUR MAN?!

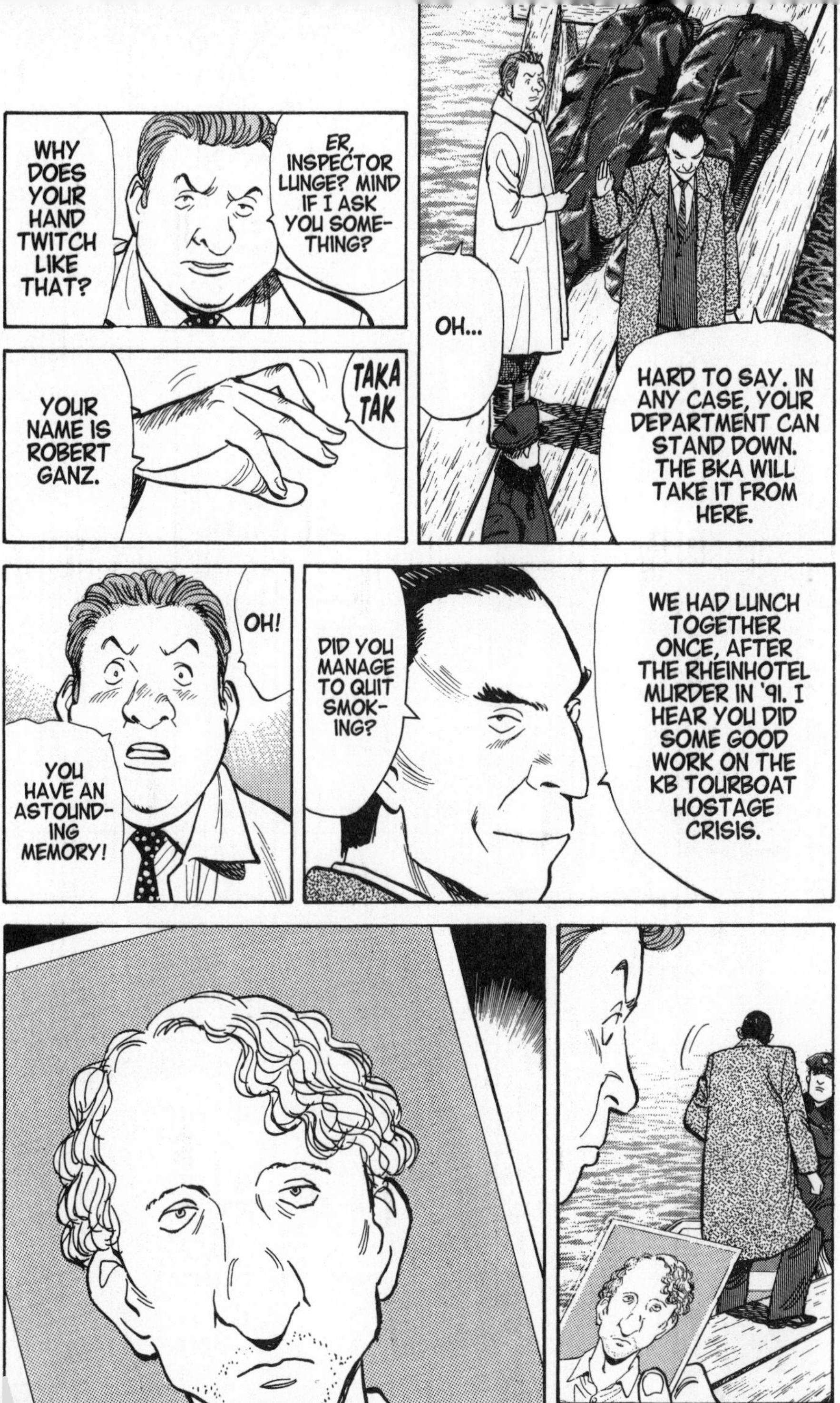
HARD TO SAY. IN ANY CASE, YOUR DEPARTMENT CAN STAND DOWN. THE BKA WILL TAKE IT FROM HERE.
OH...
ER, INSPECTOR LUNGE? MIND IF I ASK YOU SOMETHING?
WHY DOES YOUR HAND TWITCH LIKE THAT?
TAKA TAK
YOUR NAME IS ROBERT GANZ.
WE HAD LUNCH TOGETHER ONCE, AFTER THE RHEINHOTEL MURDER IN '91. I HEAR YOU DID SOME GOOD WORK ON THE KB TOURBOAT HOSTAGE CRISIS.
DID YOU MANAGE TO QUIT SMOKING?
OH!
YOU HAVE AN ASTOUNDING MEMORY!

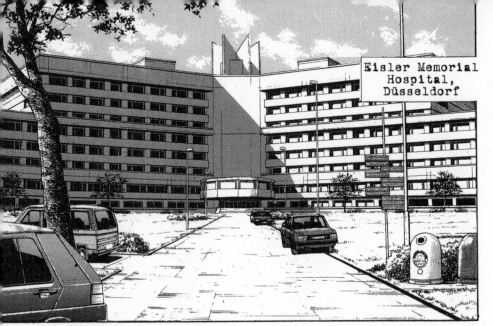

Eisler Memorial Hospital, Düsseldorf

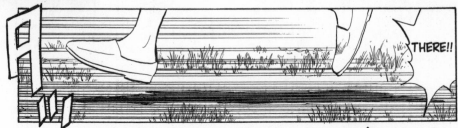

THERE!!

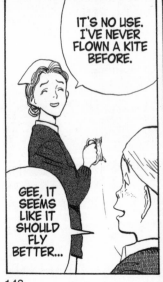

IT'S NO USE. I'VE NEVER FLOWN A KITE BEFORE.

GEE, IT SEEMS LIKE IT SHOULD FLY BETTER...

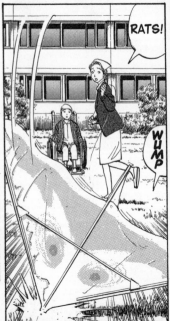

RATS!

WUMP

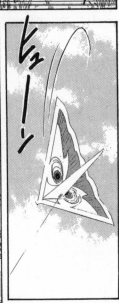

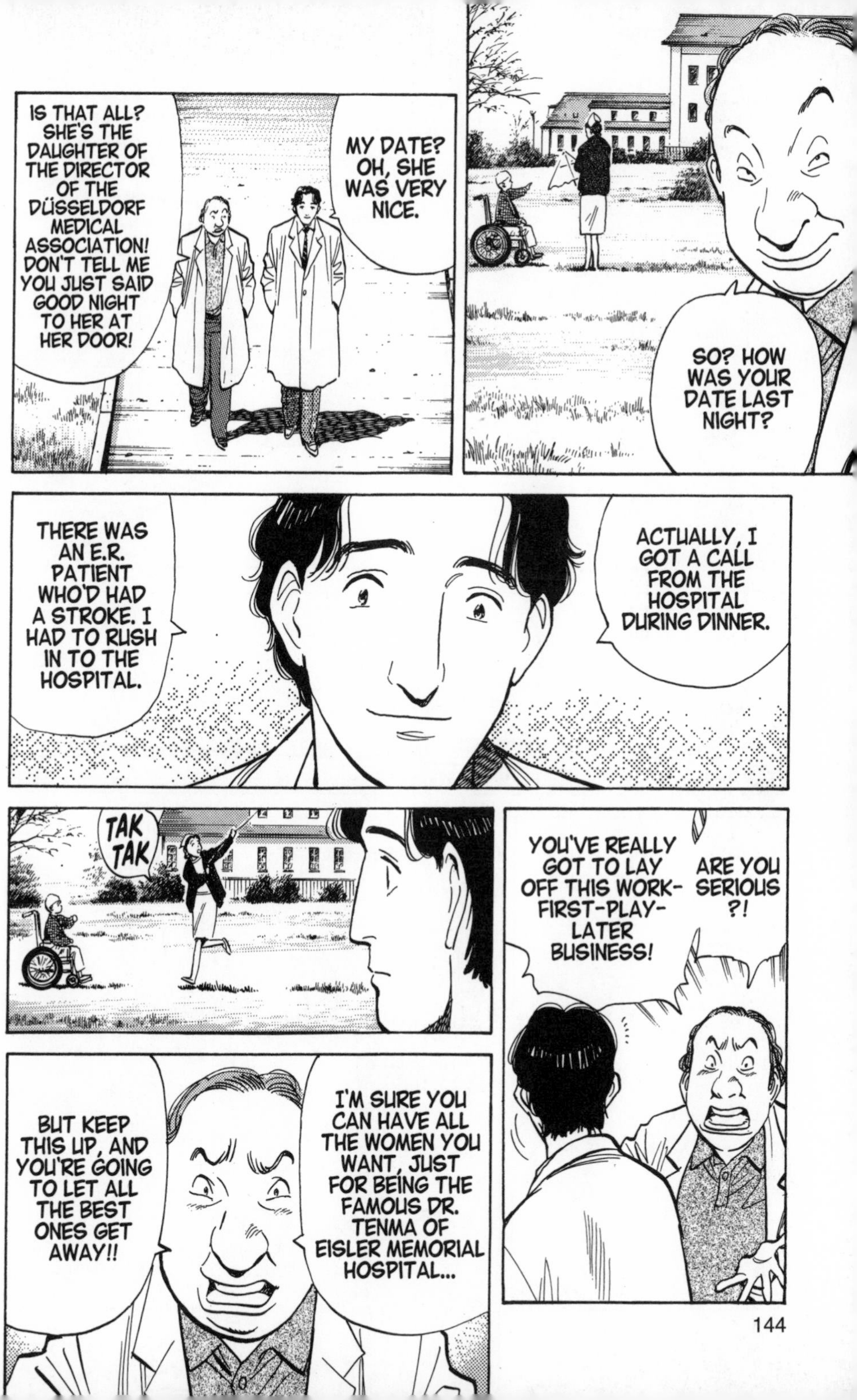
SO? HOW WAS YOUR DATE LAST NIGHT?
MY DATE? OH, SHE WAS VERY NICE.
IS THAT ALL? SHE'S THE DAUGHTER OF THE DIRECTOR OF THE DÜSSELDORF MEDICAL ASSOCIATION! DON'T TELL ME YOU JUST SAID GOOD NIGHT TO HER AT HER DOOR!
ACTUALLY, I GOT A CALL FROM THE HOSPITAL DURING DINNER.
THERE WAS AN E.R. PATIENT WHO'D HAD A STROKE. I HAD TO RUSH IN TO THE HOSPITAL.
ARE YOU SERIOUS?!
YOU'VE REALLY GOT TO LAY OFF THIS WORK-FIRST-PLAY-LATER BUSINESS!
TAK TAK
I'M SURE YOU CAN HAVE ALL THE WOMEN YOU WANT, JUST FOR BEING THE FAMOUS DR. TENMA OF EISLER MEMORIAL HOSPITAL...
BUT KEEP THIS UP, AND YOU'RE GOING TO LET ALL THE BEST ONES GET AWAY!!

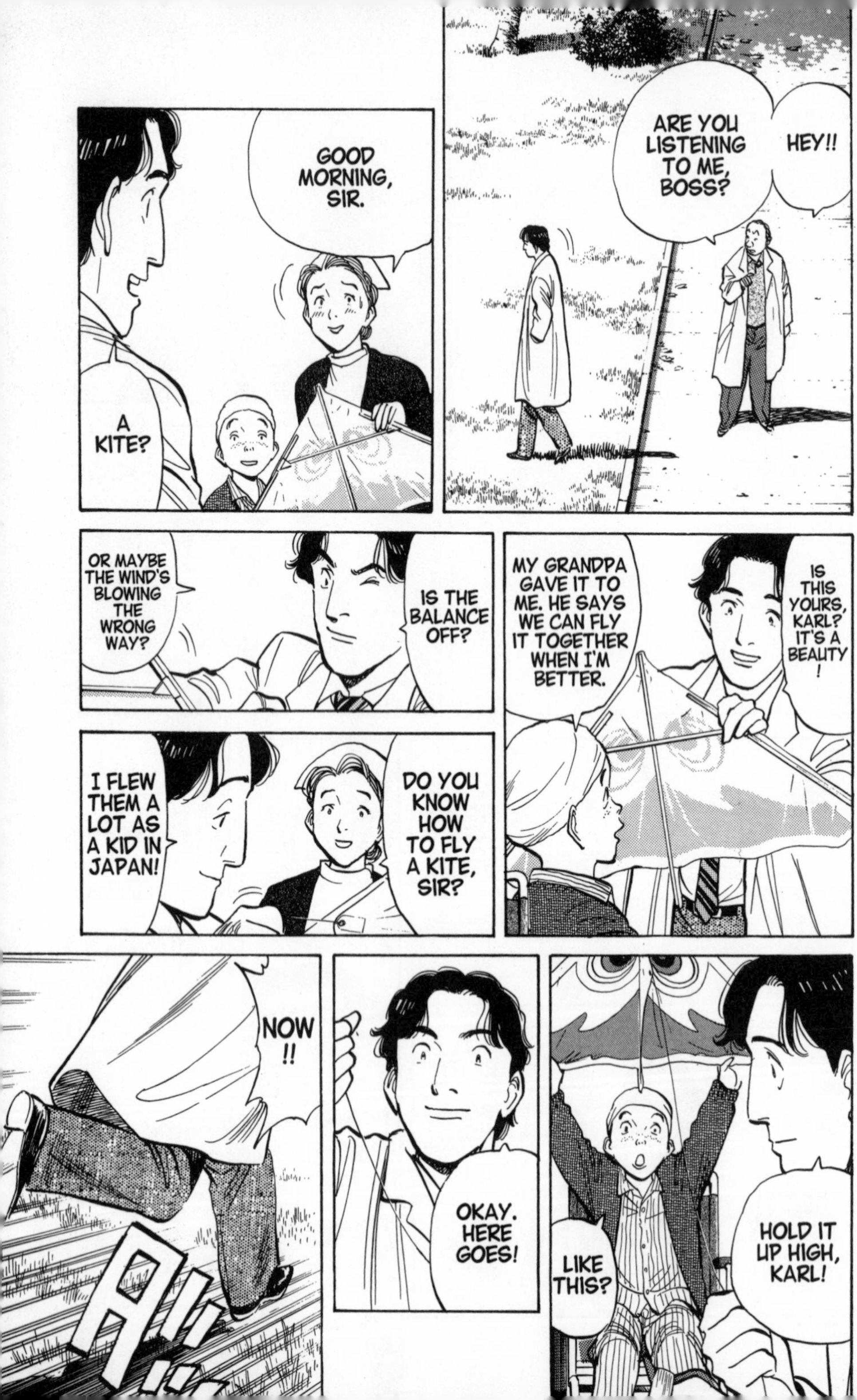
HEY!!
ARE YOU LISTENING TO ME, BOSS?
GOOD MORNING, SIR.
A KITE?
IS THIS YOURS, KARL? IT'S A BEAUTY!
MY GRANDPA GAVE IT TO ME. HE SAYS WE CAN FLY IT TOGETHER WHEN I'M BETTER.
IS THE BALANCE OFF?
OR MAYBE THE WIND'S BLOWING THE WRONG WAY?
DO YOU KNOW HOW TO FLY A KITE, SIR?
I FLEW THEM A LOT AS A KID IN JAPAN!
HOLD IT UP HIGH, KARL!
LIKE THIS?
OKAY. HERE GOES!
NOW!!

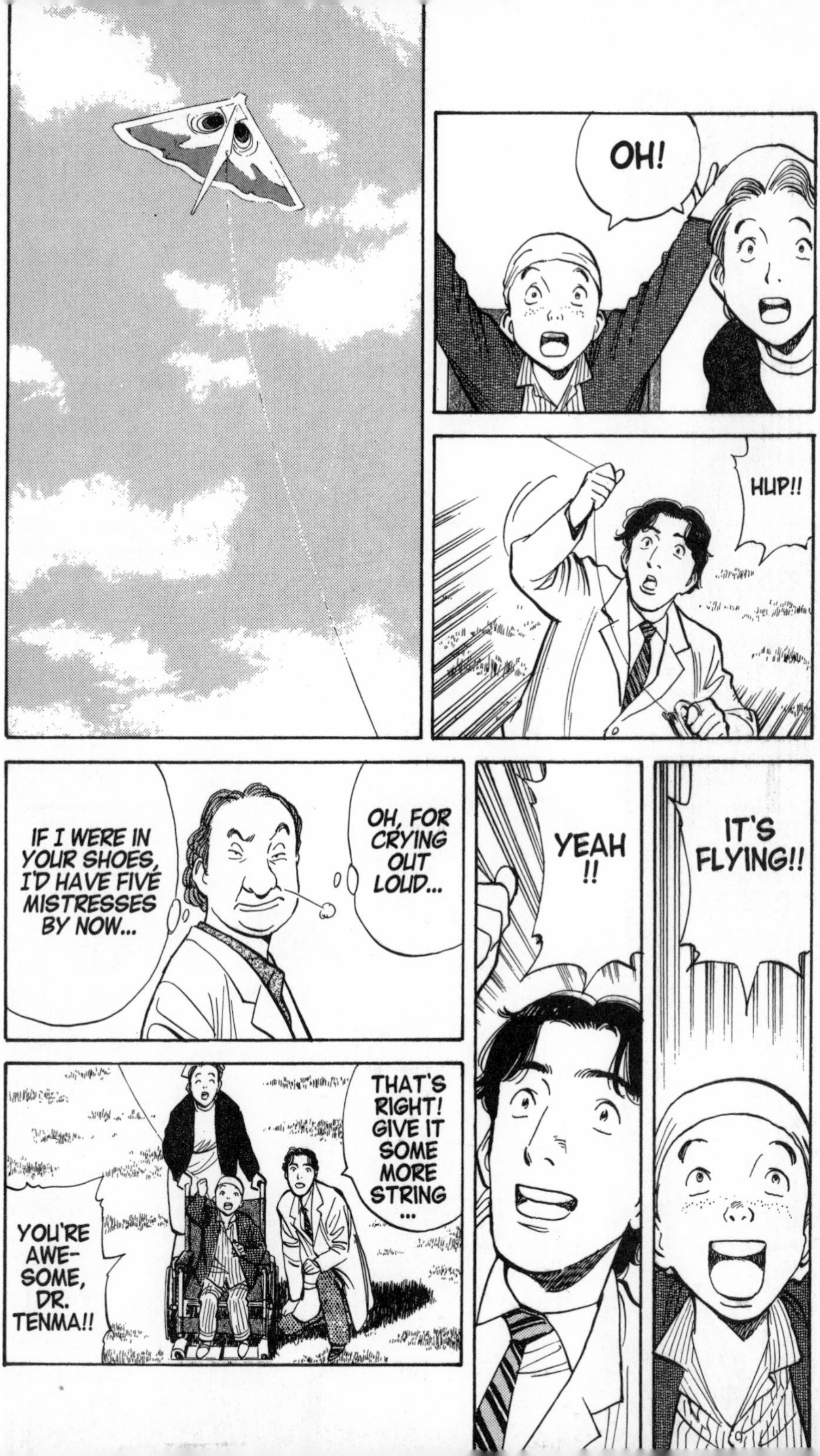
OH!
HUP!!
IT'S FLYING!!
YEAH !!
OH, FOR CRYING OUT LOUD...
IF I WERE IN YOUR SHOES, I'D HAVE FIVE MISTRESSES BY NOW...
THAT'S RIGHT! GIVE IT SOME MORE STRING ...
YOU'RE AWE-SOME, DR. TENMA!!

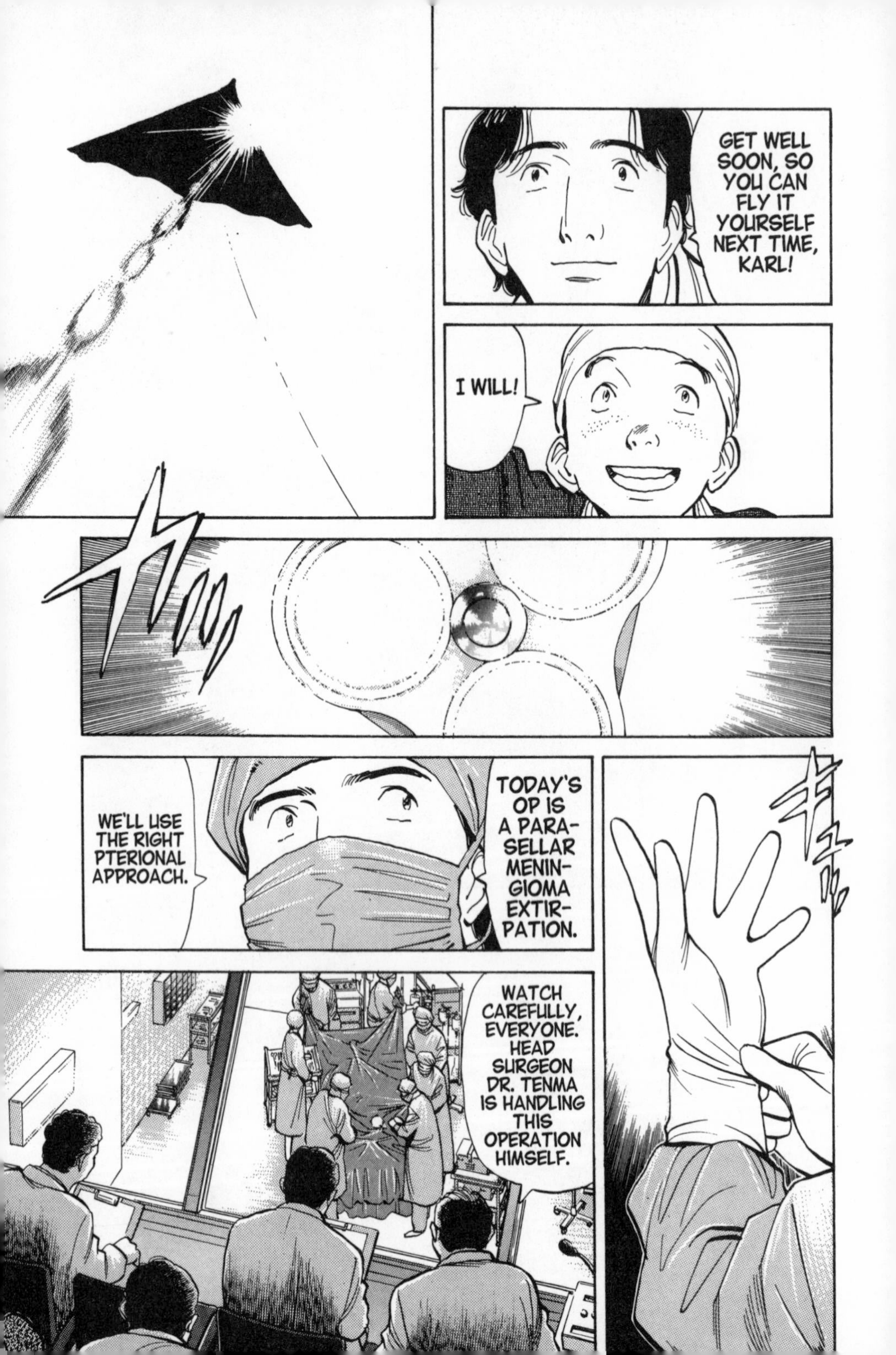
GET WELL SOON, SO YOU CAN FLY IT YOURSELF NEXT TIME, KARL!
I WILL!
TODAY'S OP IS A PARA-SELLAR MENIN-GIOMA EXTIR-PATION.
WE'LL USE THE RIGHT PTERIONAL APPROACH.
WATCH CAREFULLY, EVERYONE. HEAD SURGEON DR. TENMA IS HANDLING THIS OPERATION HIMSELF.

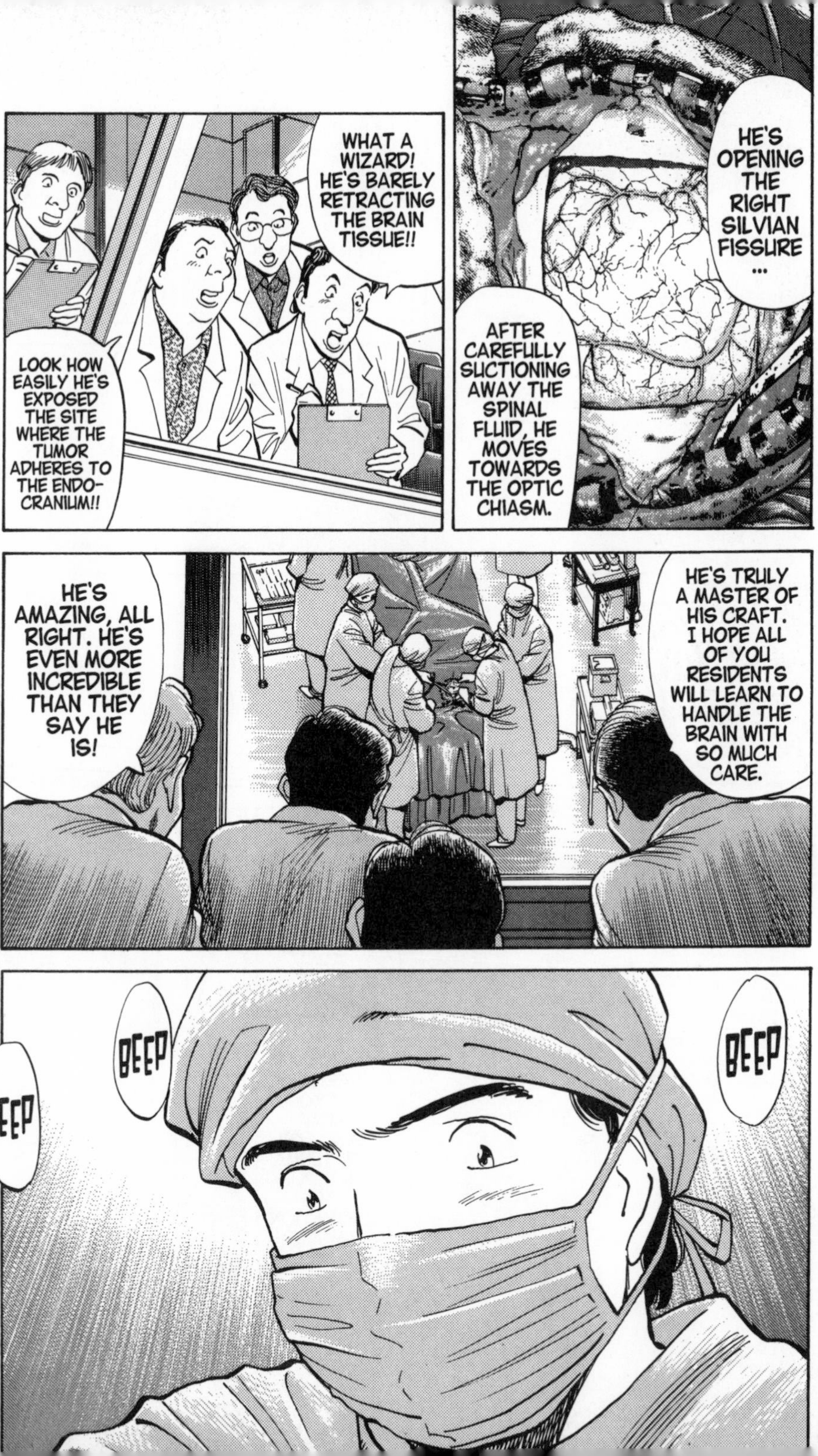
HE'S OPENING THE RIGHT SILVIAN FISSURE ...
AFTER CAREFULLY SUCTIONING AWAY THE SPINAL FLUID, HE MOVES TOWARDS THE OPTIC CHIASM.
WHAT A WIZARD! HE'S BARELY RETRACTING THE BRAIN TISSUE!!
LOOK HOW EASILY HE'S EXPOSED THE SITE WHERE THE TUMOR ADHERES TO THE ENDO-CRANIUM!!
HE'S TRULY A MASTER OF HIS CRAFT. I HOPE ALL OF YOU RESIDENTS WILL LEARN TO HANDLE THE BRAIN WITH SO MUCH CARE.
HE'S AMAZING, ALL RIGHT. HE'S EVEN MORE INCREDIBLE THAN THEY SAY HE IS!
BEEP
BEEP
BEEP

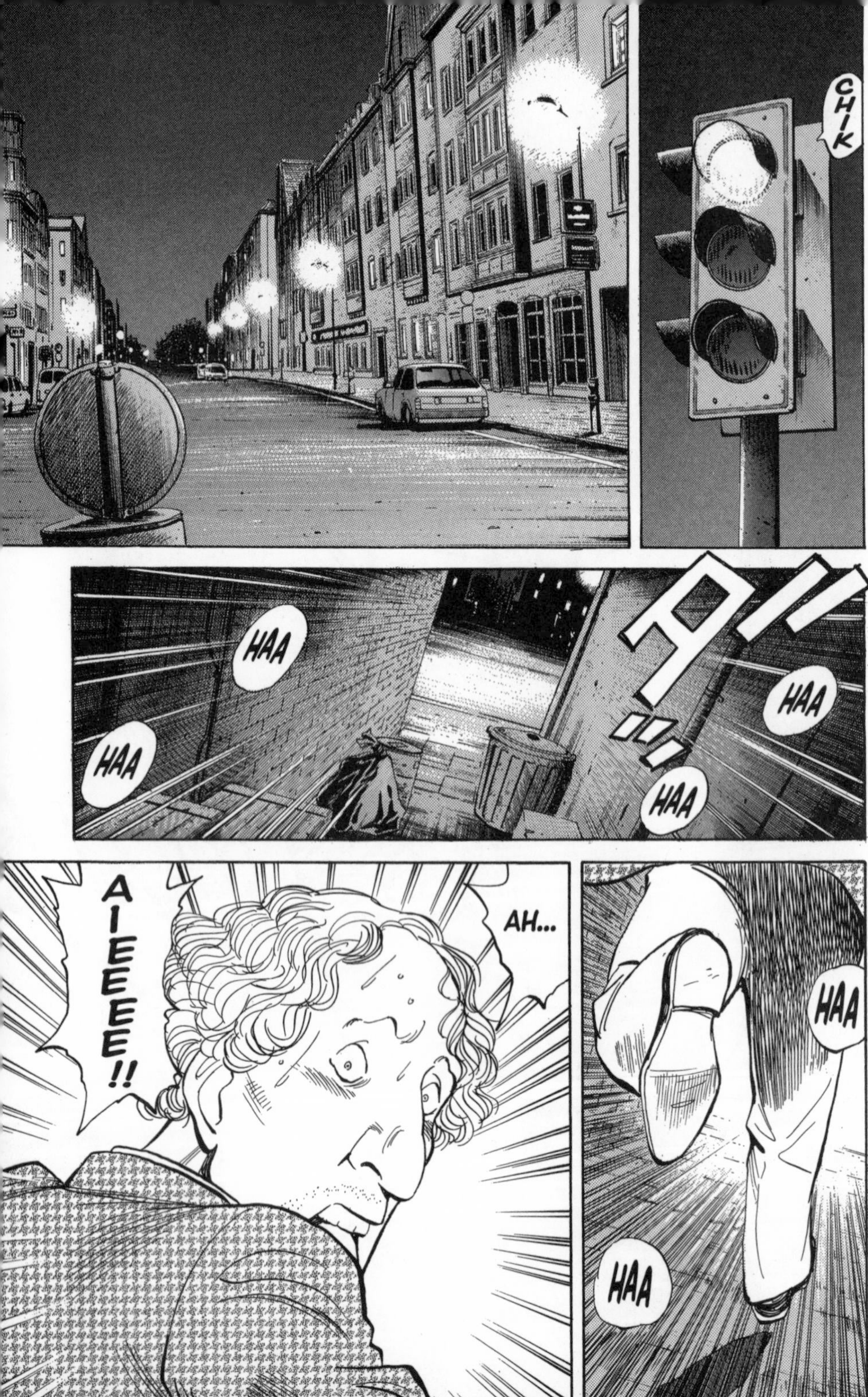
CHIK
HAA
HAA
HAA
HAA
HAA
HAA
AH...
AIEEEEE!!

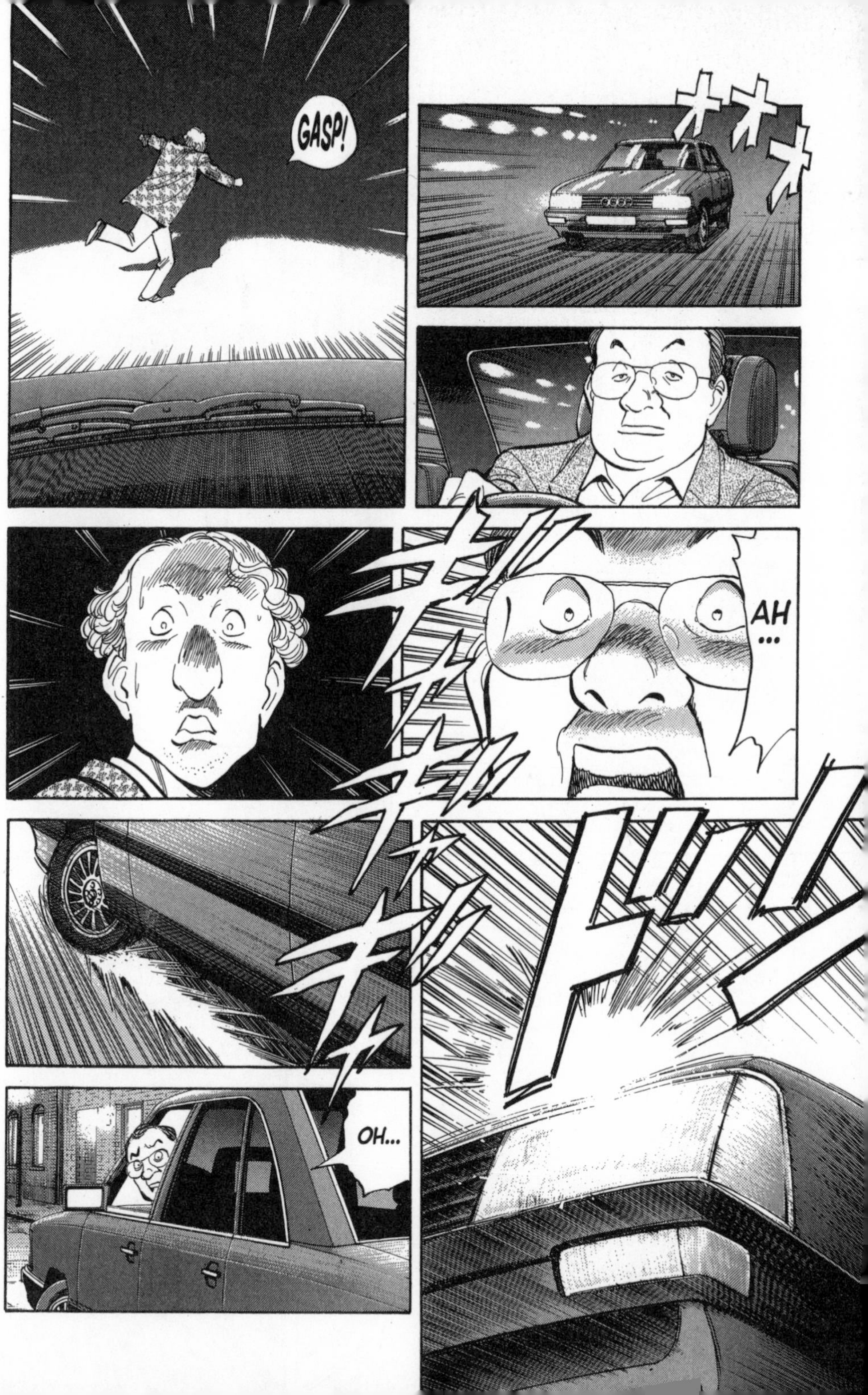

オオオ
GASP!
AH...
OH...

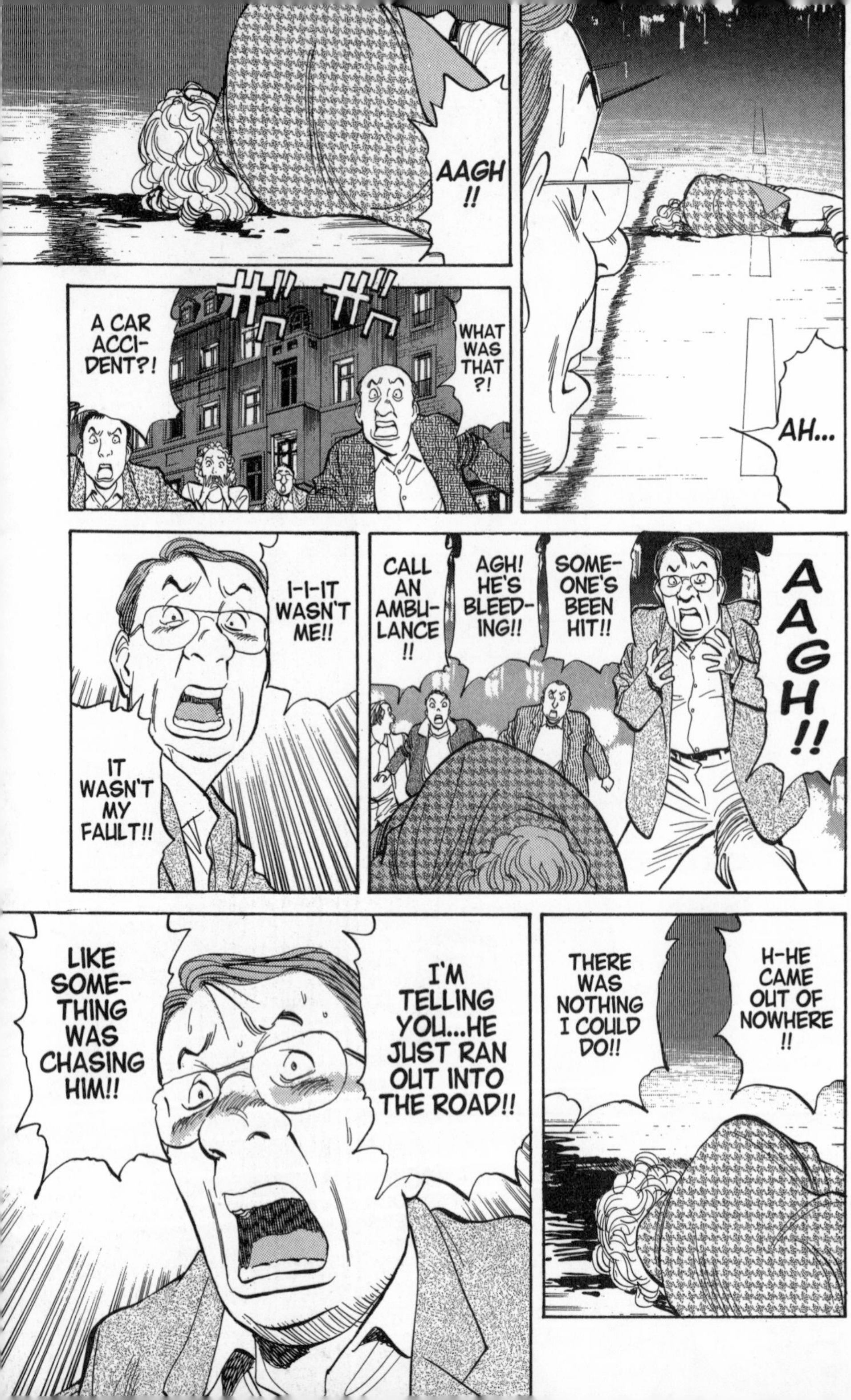
AH...
AAGH!!
ザワ ザワ
WHAT WAS THAT?!
A CAR ACCI-DENT?!
AAGH!!
SOME-ONE'S BEEN HIT!!
AGH! HE'S BLEED-ING!!
CALL AN AMBU-LANCE!!
I-I-IT WASN'T ME!!
IT WASN'T MY FAULT!!
H-HE CAME OUT OF NOWHERE!!
THERE WAS NOTHING I COULD DO!!
I'M TELLING YOU...HE JUST RAN OUT INTO THE ROAD!!
LIKE SOME-THING WAS CHASING HIM!!

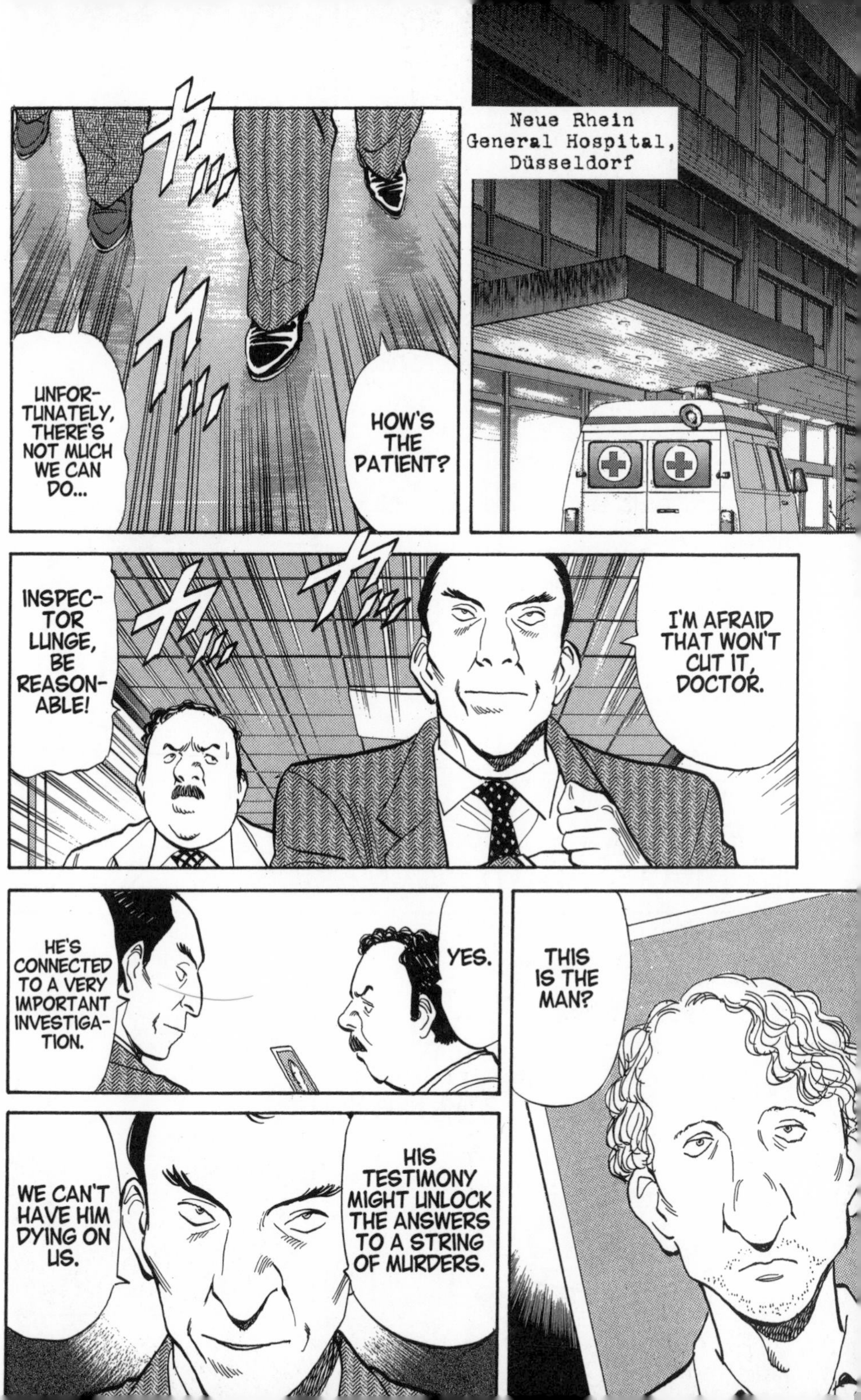
Neue Rhein General Hospital, Düsseldorf
HOW'S THE PATIENT?
UNFORTUNATELY, THERE'S NOT MUCH WE CAN DO...
I'M AFRAID THAT WON'T CUT IT, DOCTOR.
INSPECTOR LUNGE, BE REASONABLE!
THIS IS THE MAN?
YES.
HE'S CONNECTED TO A VERY IMPORTANT INVESTIGATION.
HIS TESTIMONY MIGHT UNLOCK THE ANSWERS TO A STRING OF MURDERS.
WE CAN'T HAVE HIM DYING ON US.

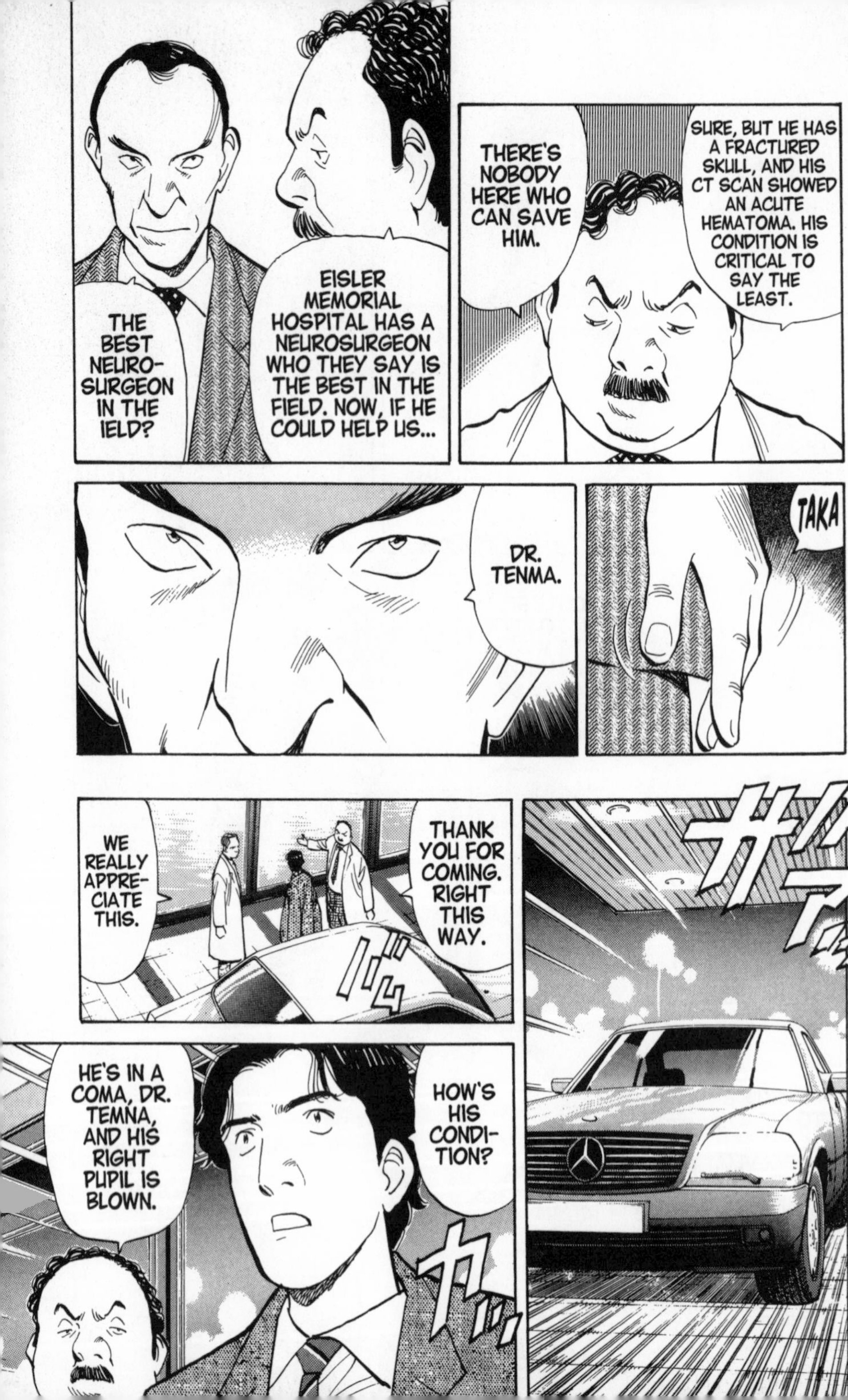
SURE, BUT HE HAS A FRACTURED SKULL, AND HIS CT SCAN SHOWED AN ACUTE HEMATOMA. HIS CONDITION IS CRITICAL TO SAY THE LEAST.
THERE'S NOBODY HERE WHO CAN SAVE HIM.
EISLER MEMORIAL HOSPITAL HAS A NEUROSURGEON WHO THEY SAY IS THE BEST IN THE FIELD. NOW, IF HE COULD HELP US...
THE BEST NEURO-SURGEON IN THE IELD?
TAKA
DR. TENMA.
THANK YOU FOR COMING. RIGHT THIS WAY.
WE REALLY APPRE-CIATE THIS.
HOW'S HIS CONDI-TION?
HE'S IN A COMA, DR. TEMNA, AND HIS RIGHT PUPIL IS BLOWN.

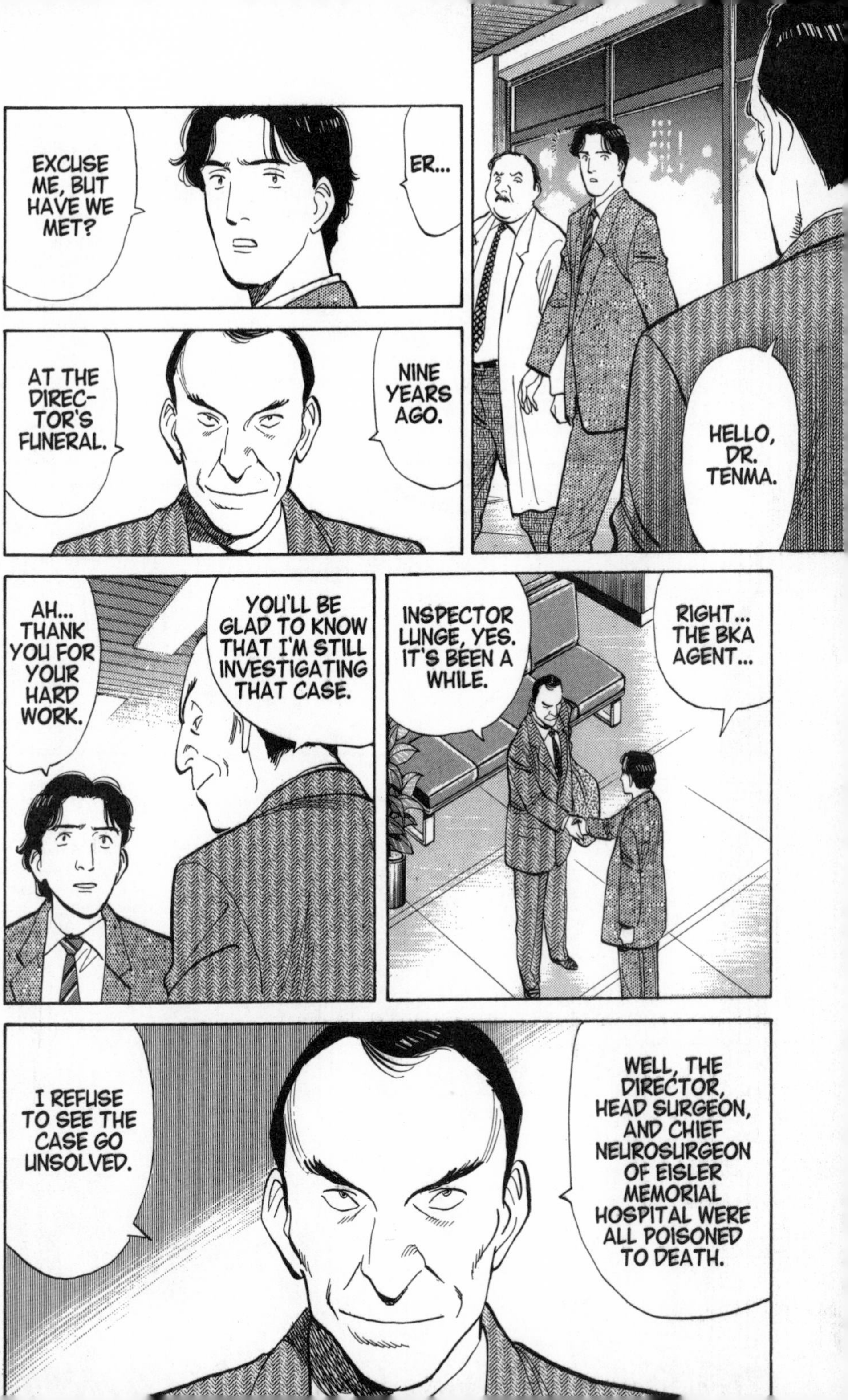
HELLO, DR. TENMA.
ER...
EXCUSE ME, BUT HAVE WE MET?
NINE YEARS AGO.
AT THE DIRECTOR'S FUNERAL.
RIGHT... THE BKA AGENT...
INSPECTOR LUNGE, YES. IT'S BEEN A WHILE.
YOU'LL BE GLAD TO KNOW THAT I'M STILL INVESTIGATING THAT CASE.
AH... THANK YOU FOR YOUR HARD WORK.
WELL, THE DIRECTOR, HEAD SURGEON, AND CHIEF NEUROSURGEON OF EISLER MEMORIAL HOSPITAL WERE ALL POISONED TO DEATH.
I REFUSE TO SEE THE CASE GO UNSOLVED.

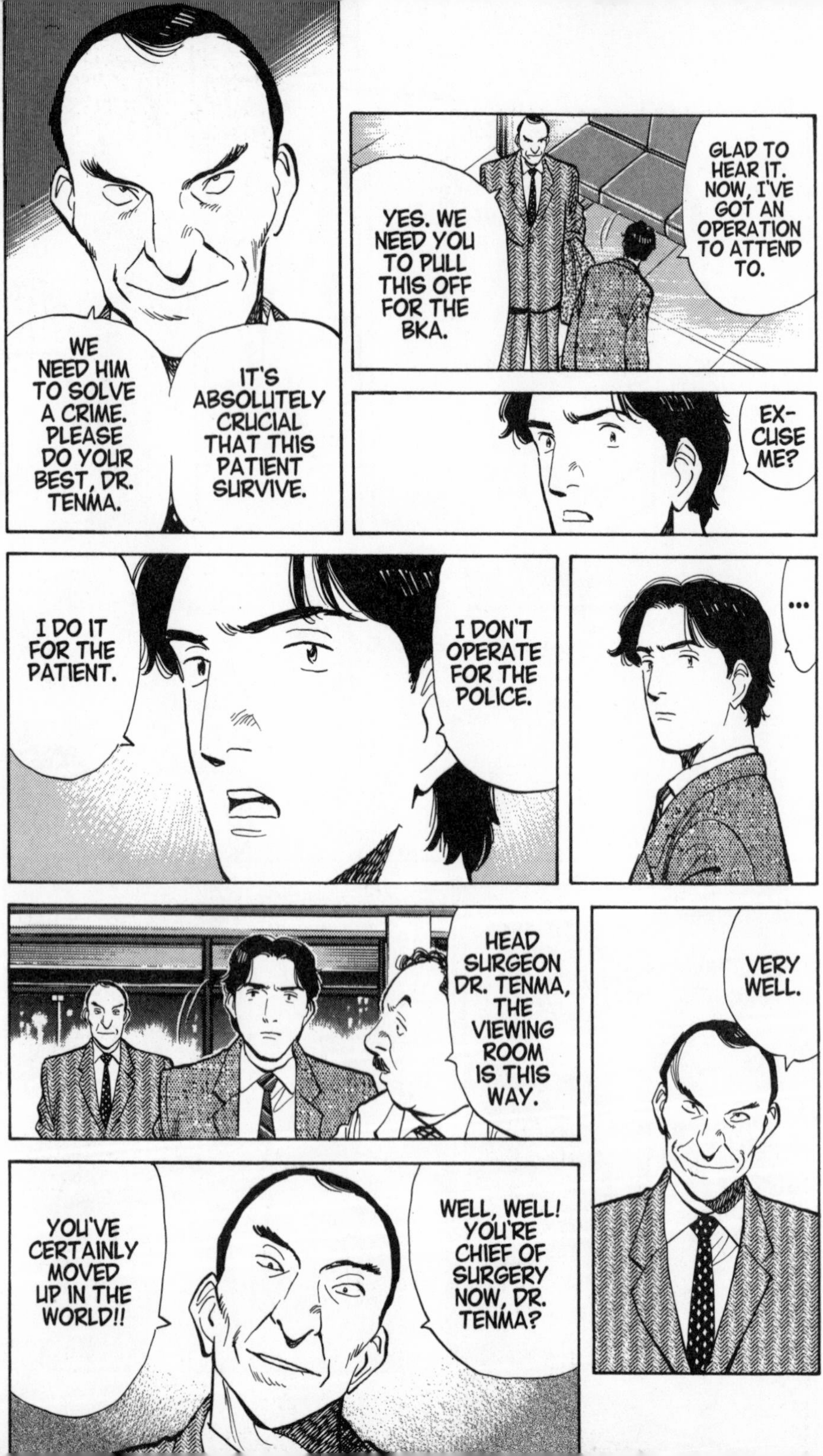
GLAD TO HEAR IT. NOW, I'VE GOT AN OPERATION TO ATTEND TO.
YES. WE NEED YOU TO PULL THIS OFF FOR THE BKA.
EX-CUSE ME?
IT'S ABSOLUTELY CRUCIAL THAT THIS PATIENT SURVIVE.
WE NEED HIM TO SOLVE A CRIME. PLEASE DO YOUR BEST, DR. TENMA.
...
I DON'T OPERATE FOR THE POLICE.
I DO IT FOR THE PATIENT.
VERY WELL.
HEAD SURGEON DR. TENMA, THE VIEWING ROOM IS THIS WAY.
WELL, WELL! YOU'RE CHIEF OF SURGERY NOW, DR. TENMA?
YOU'VE CERTAINLY MOVED UP IN THE WORLD!!

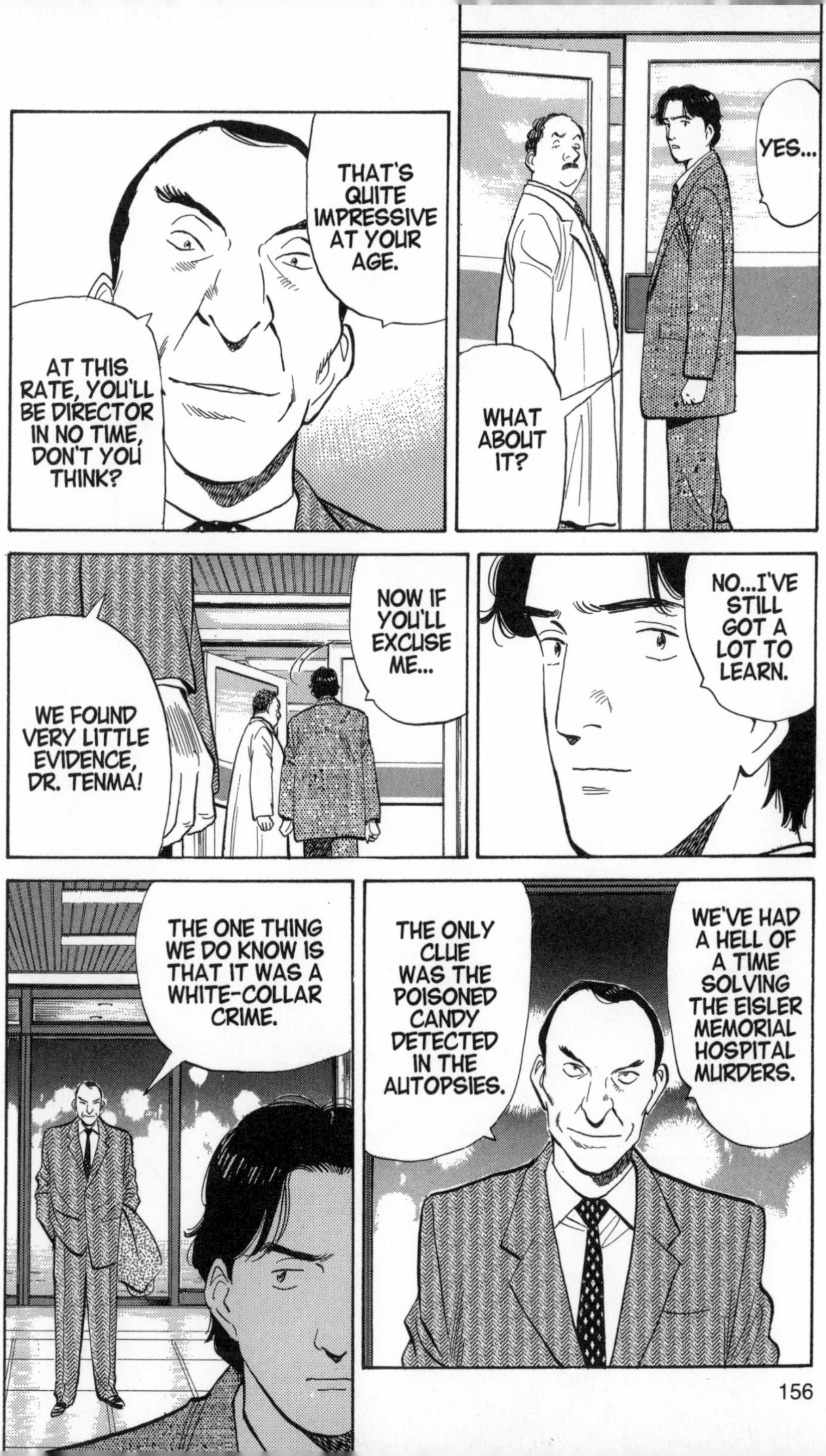
YES...
WHAT ABOUT IT?
THAT'S QUITE IMPRESSIVE AT YOUR AGE.
AT THIS RATE, YOU'LL BE DIRECTOR IN NO TIME, DON'T YOU THINK?
NO...I'VE STILL GOT A LOT TO LEARN.
NOW IF YOU'LL EXCUSE ME...
WE FOUND VERY LITTLE EVIDENCE, DR. TENMA!
WE'VE HAD A HELL OF A TIME SOLVING THE EISLER MEMORIAL HOSPITAL MURDERS.
THE ONLY CLUE WAS THE POISONED CANDY DETECTED IN THE AUTOPSIES.
THE ONE THING WE DO KNOW IS THAT IT WAS A WHITE-COLLAR CRIME.

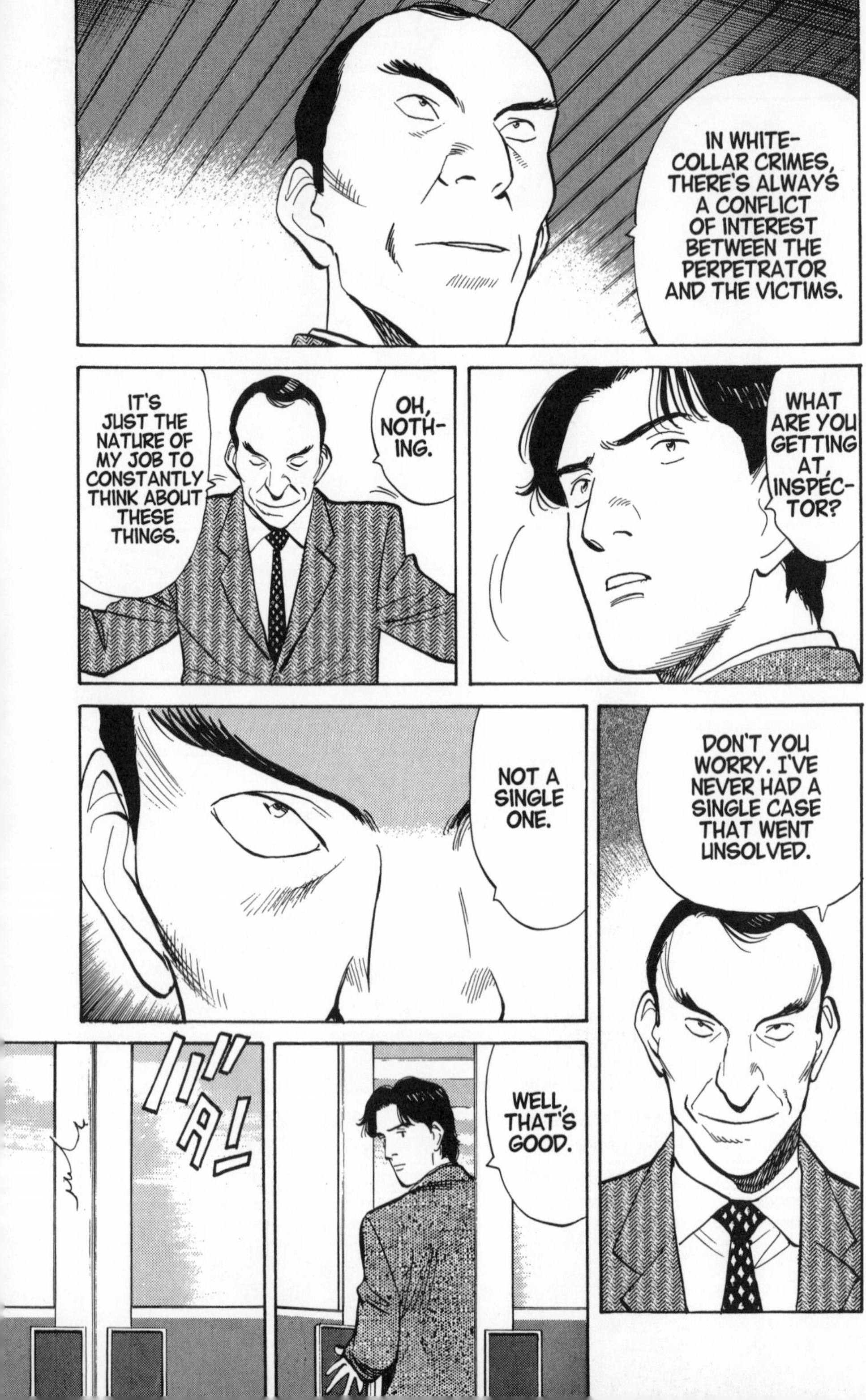
IN WHITE-COLLAR CRIMES, THERE'S ALWAYS A CONFLICT OF INTEREST BETWEEN THE PERPETRATOR AND THE VICTIMS.
WHAT ARE YOU GETTING AT, INSPECTOR?
OH, NOTHING.
IT'S JUST THE NATURE OF MY JOB TO CONSTANTLY THINK ABOUT THESE THINGS.
DON'T YOU WORRY. I'VE NEVER HAD A SINGLE CASE THAT WENT UNSOLVED.
NOT A SINGLE ONE.
WELL, THAT'S GOOD.

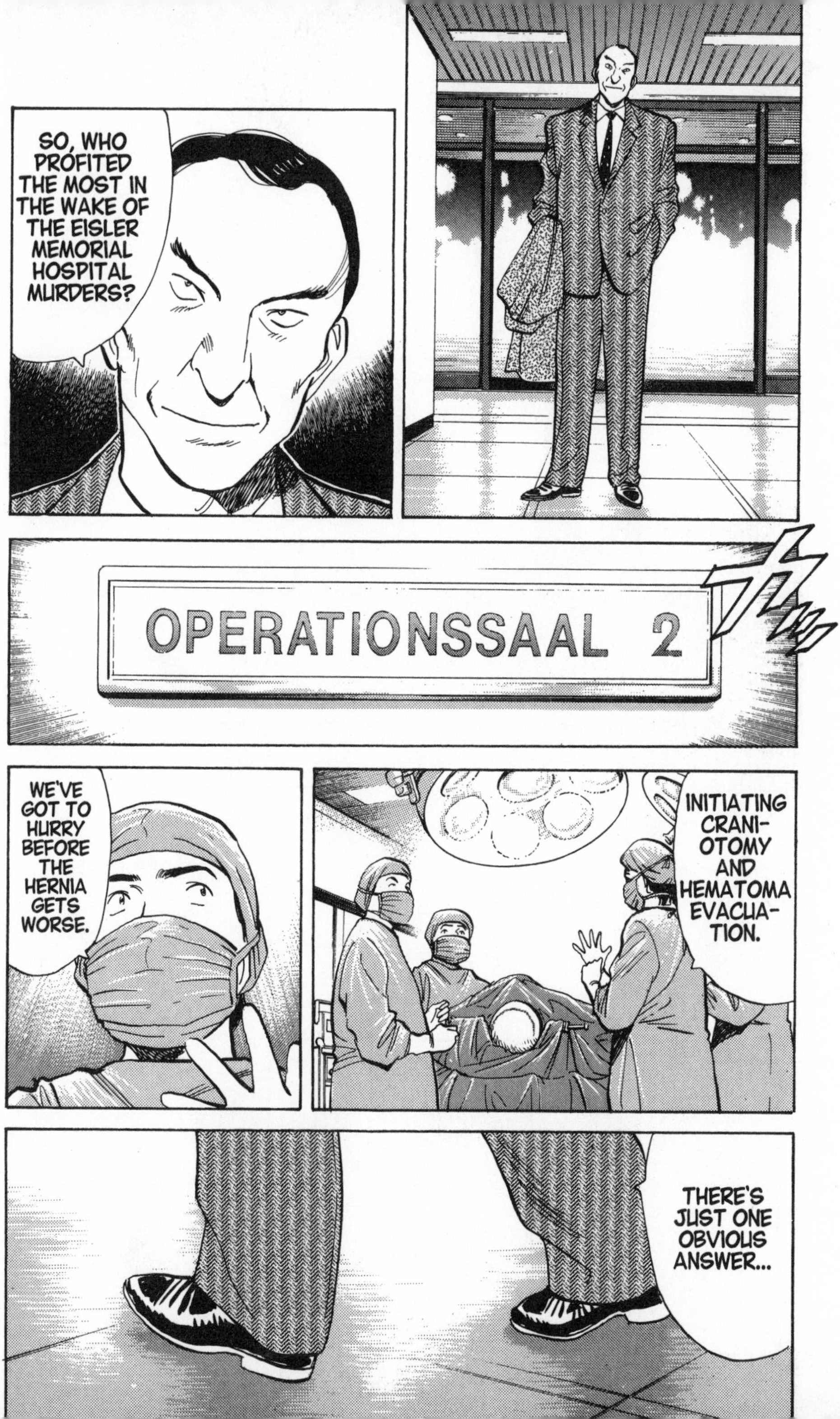
SO, WHO PROFITED THE MOST IN THE WAKE OF THE EISLER MEMORIAL HOSPITAL MURDERS?
OPERATIONSSAAL 2
INITIATING CRANI-OTOMY AND HEMATOMA EVACUA-TION.
WE'VE GOT TO HURRY BEFORE THE HERNIA GETS WORSE.
THERE'S JUST ONE OBVIOUS ANSWER...

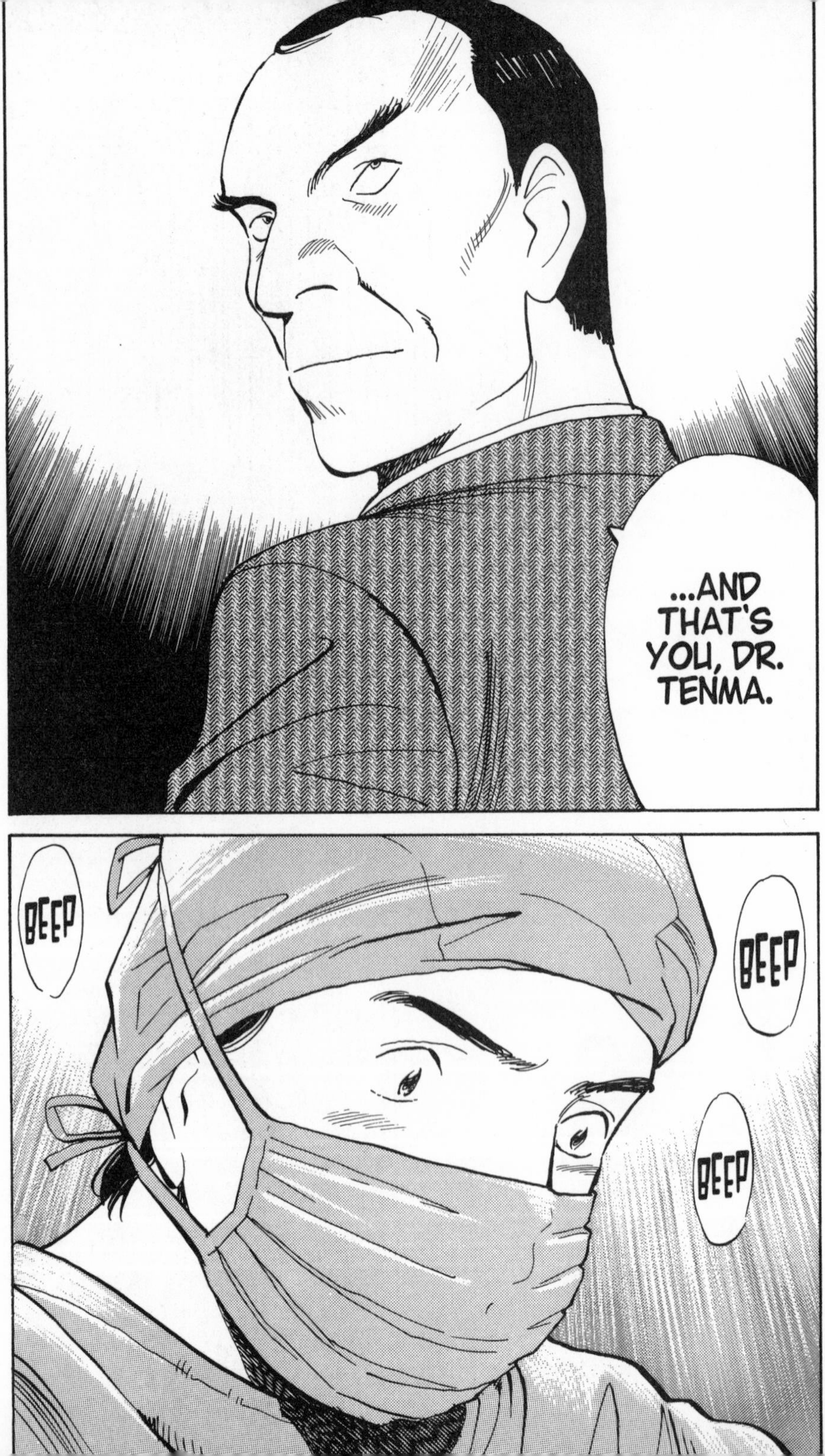
...AND THAT'S YOU, DR. TENMA.
BEEP
BEEP
BEEP

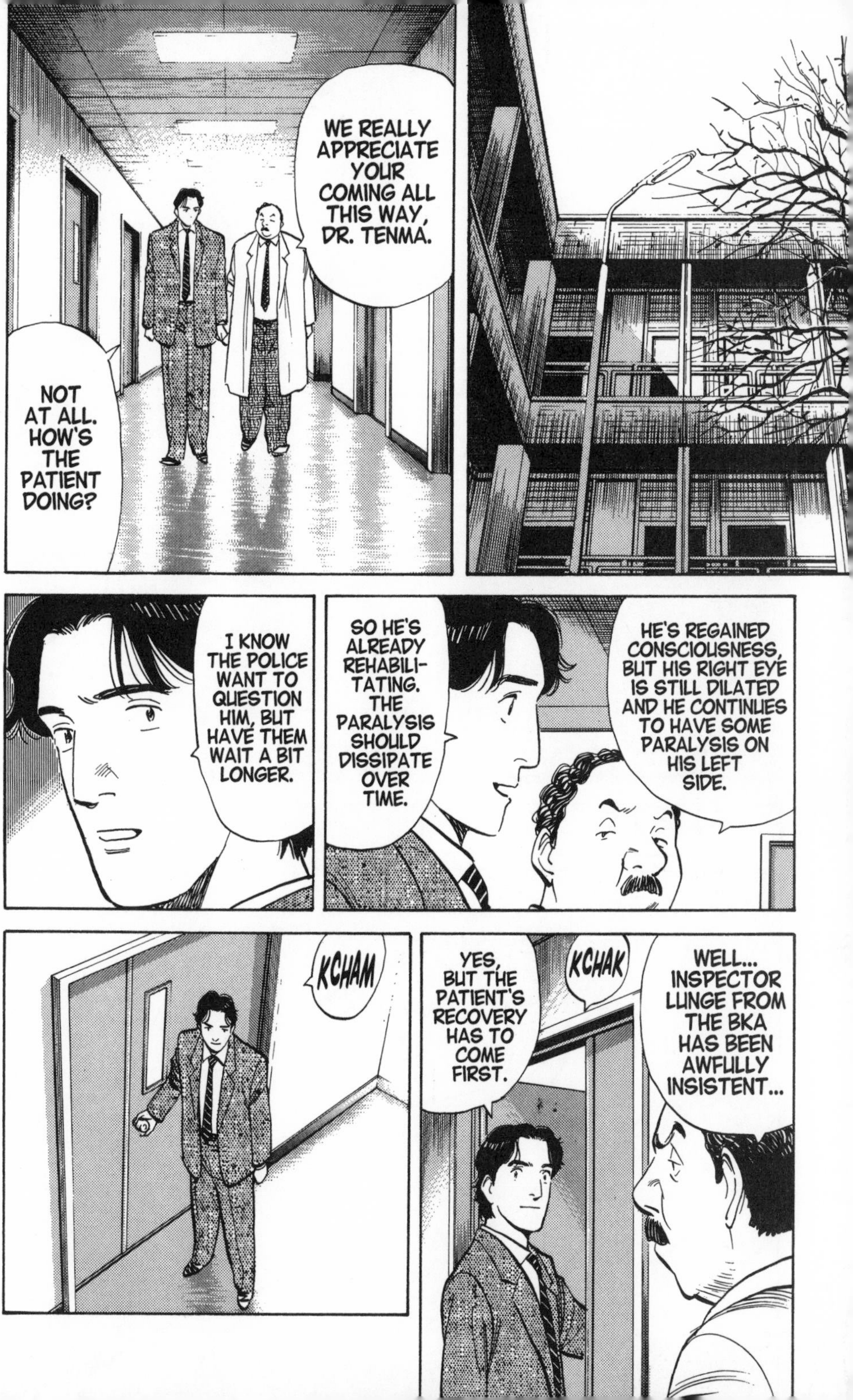
WE REALLY APPRECIATE YOUR COMING ALL THIS WAY, DR. TENMA.
NOT AT ALL. HOW'S THE PATIENT DOING?
HE'S REGAINED CONSCIOUSNESS, BUT HIS RIGHT EYE IS STILL DILATED AND HE CONTINUES TO HAVE SOME PARALYSIS ON HIS LEFT SIDE.
SO HE'S ALREADY REHABILI-TATING. THE PARALYSIS SHOULD DISSIPATE OVER TIME.
I KNOW THE POLICE WANT TO QUESTION HIM, BUT HAVE THEM WAIT A BIT LONGER.
WELL... INSPECTOR LUNGE FROM THE BKA HAS BEEN AWFULLY INSISTENT...
KCHAK
YES, BUT THE PATIENT'S RECOVERY HAS TO COME FIRST.
KCHAM

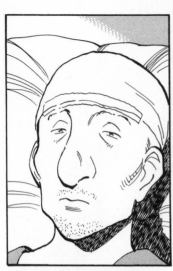

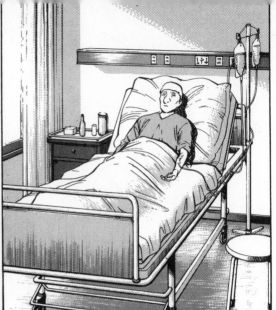

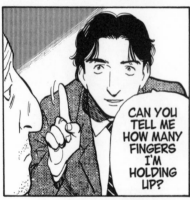

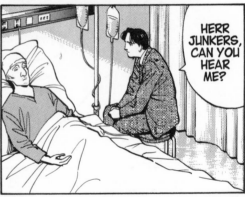

HERR JUNKERS, CAN YOU HEAR ME?
CAN YOU TELL ME HOW MANY FINGERS I'M HOLDING UP?
PAR-DON ME?
HE'S COM-ING...

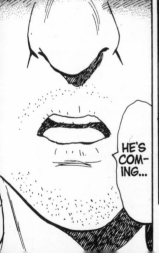

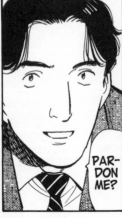

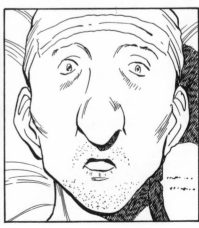

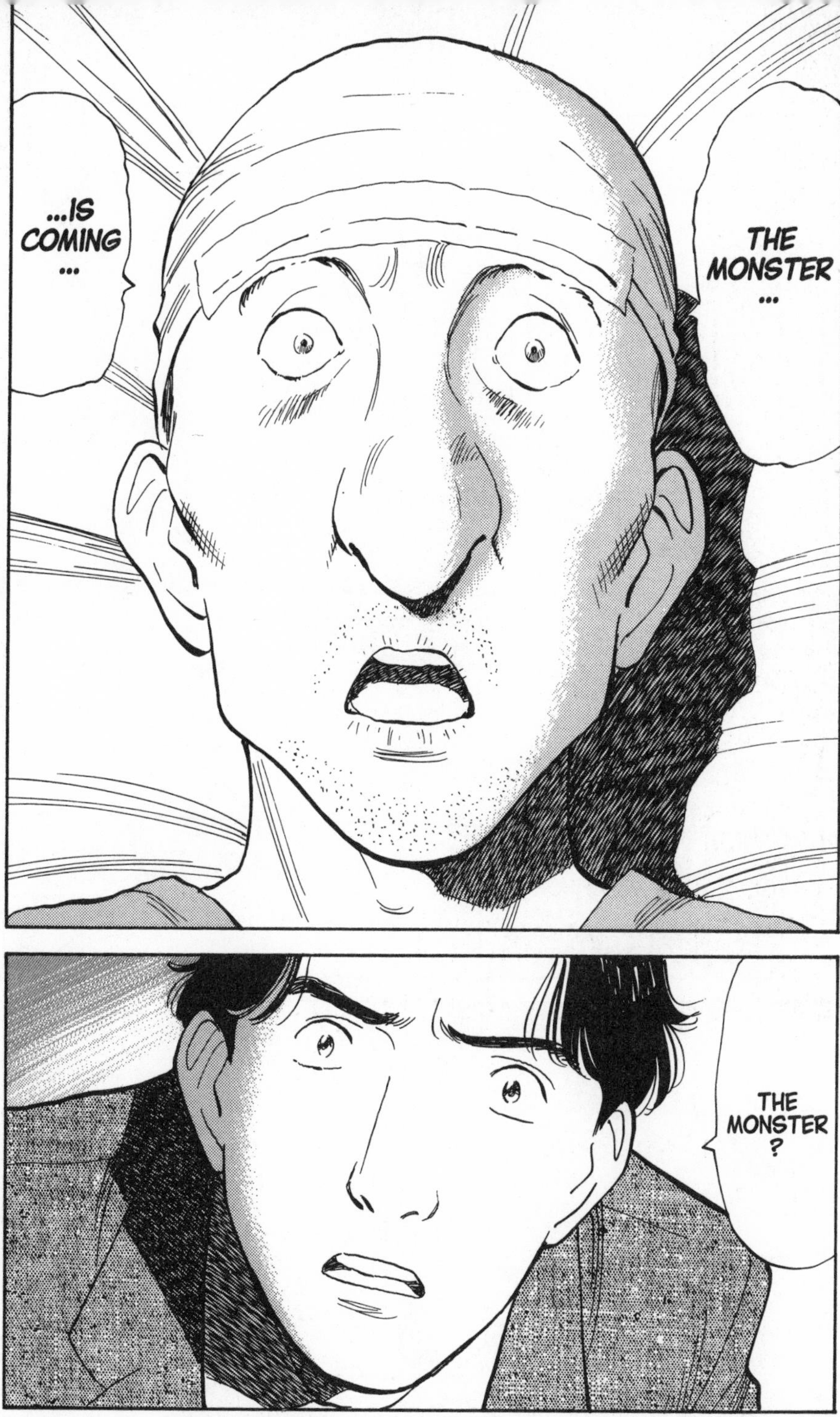
THE MONSTER ...
...IS COMING ...
THE MONSTER ?

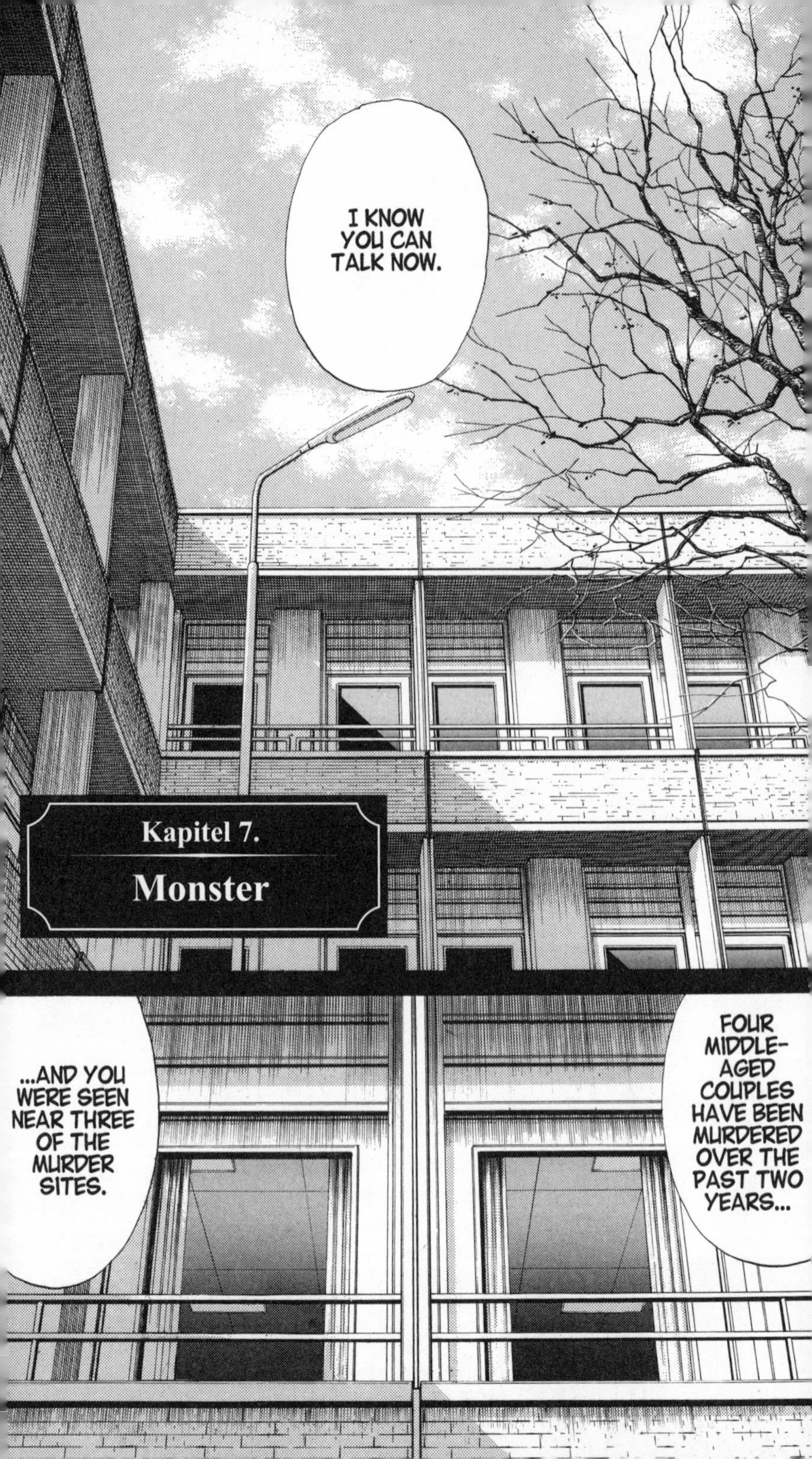
I KNOW YOU CAN TALK NOW.
Kapitel 7.
Monster
FOUR MIDDLE-AGED COUPLES HAVE BEEN MURDERED OVER THE PAST TWO YEARS...
...AND YOU WERE SEEN NEAR THREE OF THE MURDER SITES.

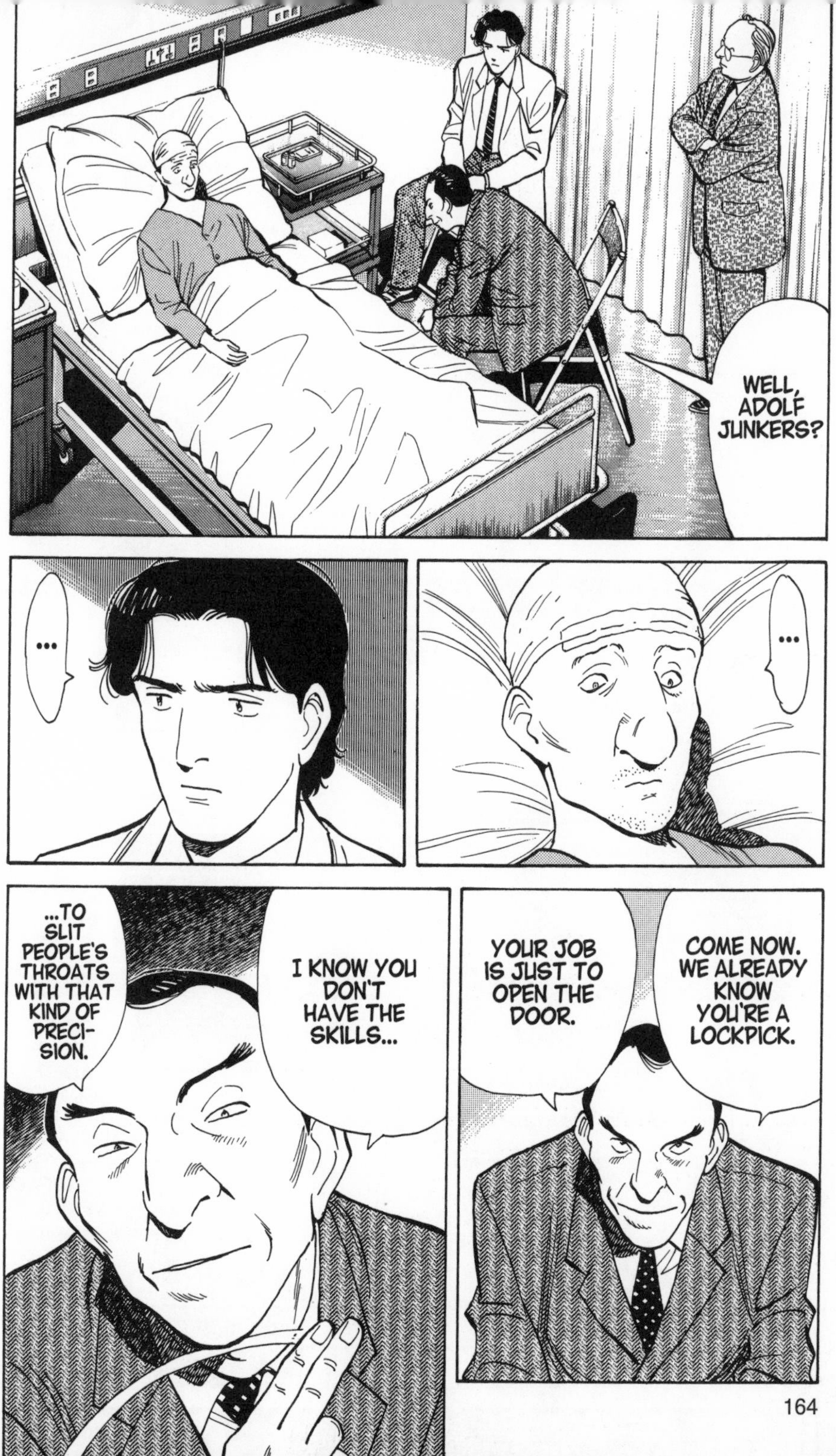
WELL, ADOLF JUNKERS?
...
...
COME NOW. WE ALREADY KNOW YOU'RE A LOCKPICK.
YOUR JOB IS JUST TO OPEN THE DOOR.
I KNOW YOU DON'T HAVE THE SKILLS...
...TO SLIT PEOPLE'S THROATS WITH THAT KIND OF PRECISION.

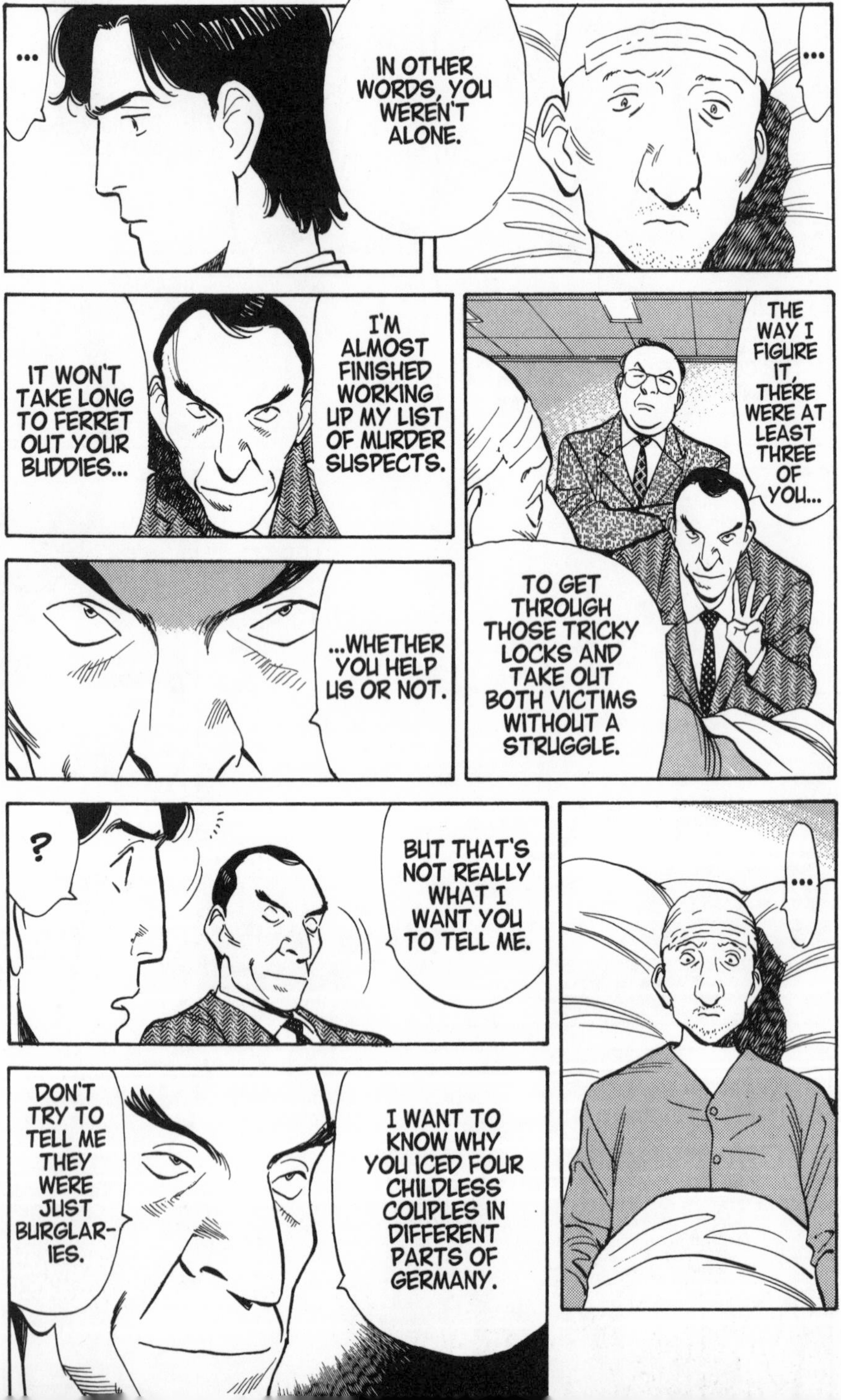
...
IN OTHER WORDS, YOU WEREN'T ALONE.
...
THE WAY I FIGURE IT, THERE WERE AT LEAST THREE OF YOU...
TO GET THROUGH THOSE TRICKY LOCKS AND TAKE OUT BOTH VICTIMS WITHOUT A STRUGGLE.
I'M ALMOST FINISHED WORKING UP MY LIST OF MURDER SUSPECTS.
IT WON'T TAKE LONG TO FERRET OUT YOUR BUDDIES...
...WHETHER YOU HELP US OR NOT.
...
BUT THAT'S NOT REALLY WHAT I WANT YOU TO TELL ME.
?
I WANT TO KNOW WHY YOU ICED FOUR CHILDLESS COUPLES IN DIFFERENT PARTS OF GERMANY.
DON'T TRY TO TELL ME THEY WERE JUST BURGLAR-IES.

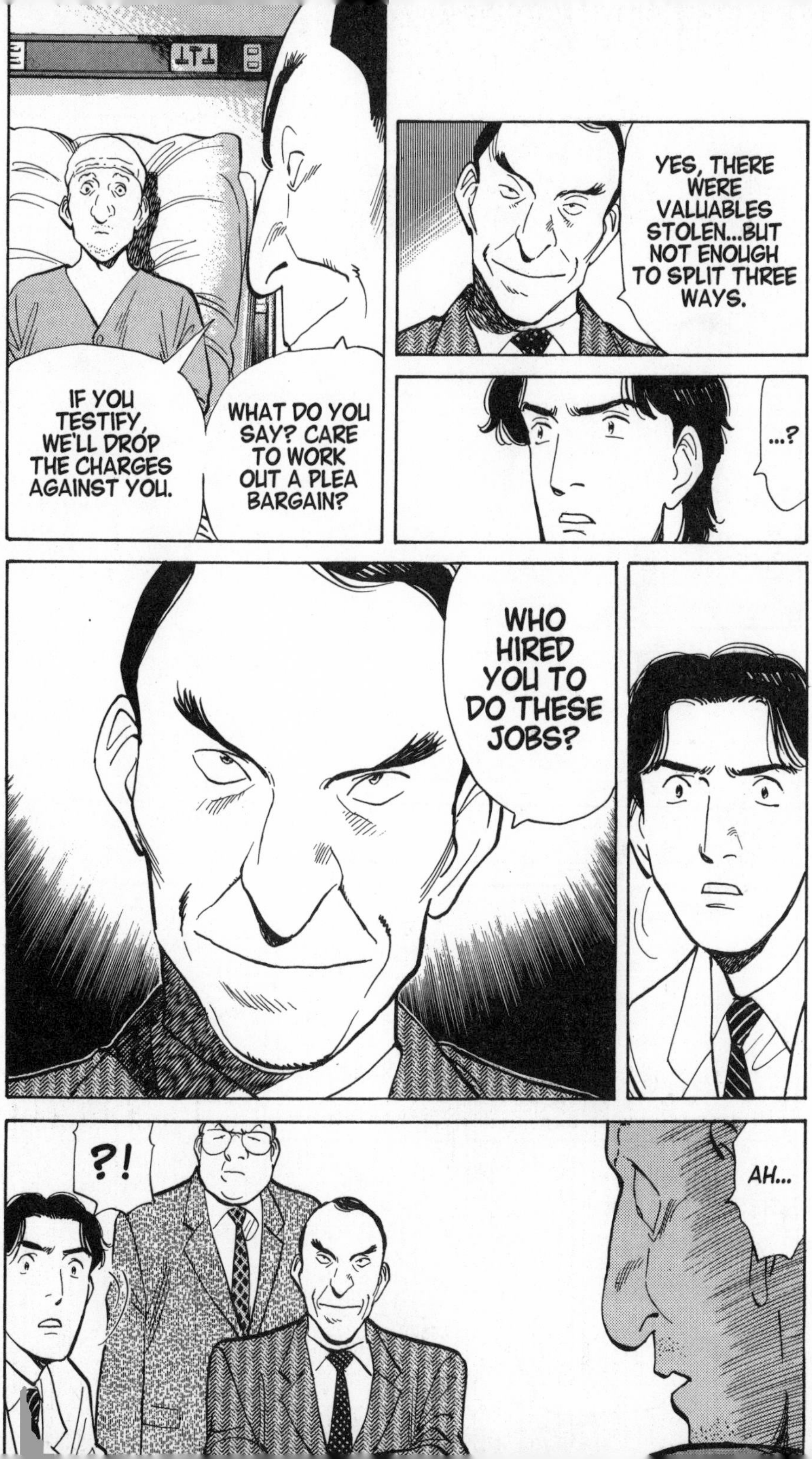
YES, THERE WERE VALUABLES STOLEN...BUT NOT ENOUGH TO SPLIT THREE WAYS.
...?
WHAT DO YOU SAY? CARE TO WORK OUT A PLEA BARGAIN?
IF YOU TESTIFY, WE'LL DROP THE CHARGES AGAINST YOU.
WHO HIRED YOU TO DO THESE JOBS?
AH...
?!

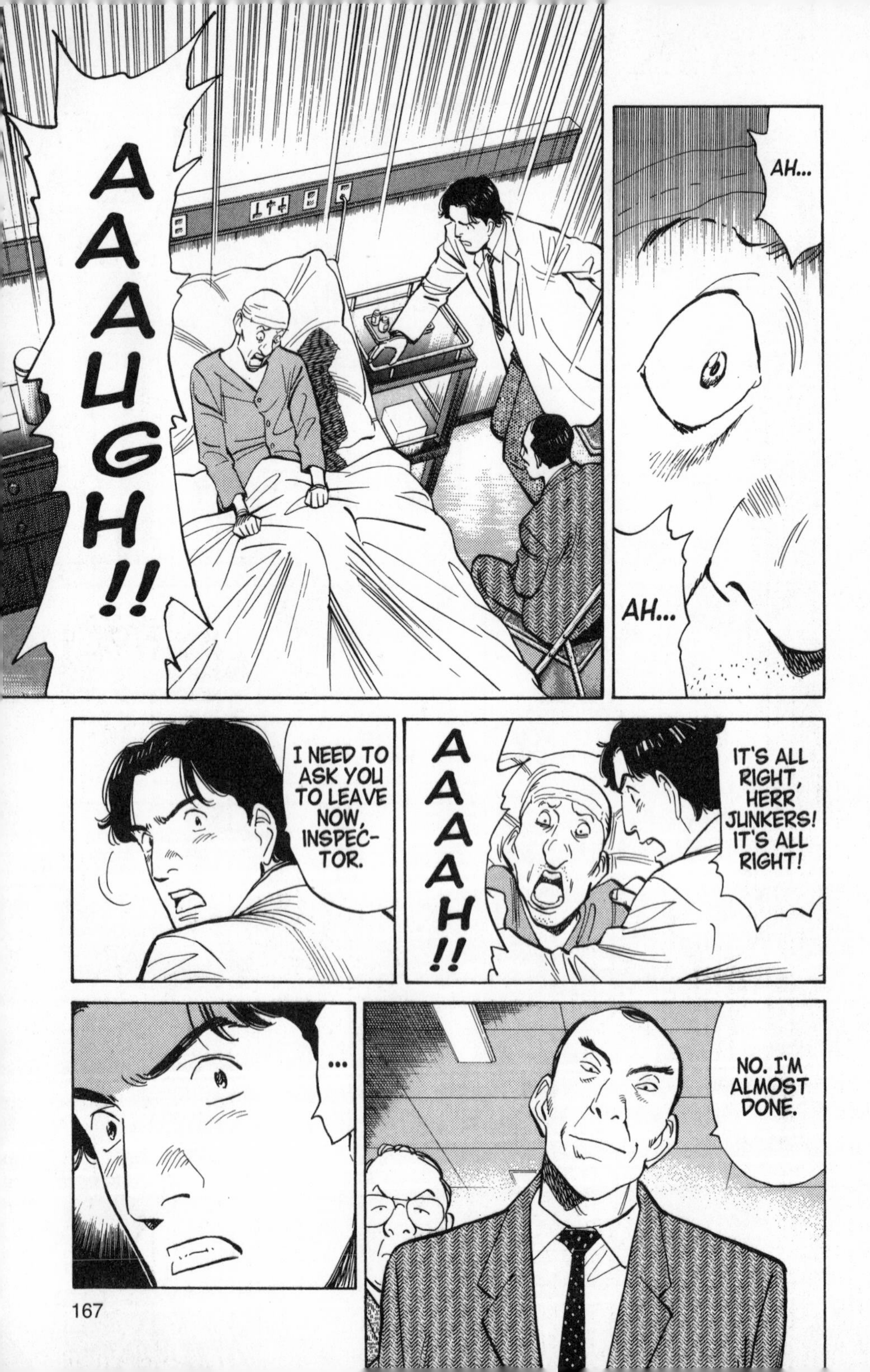
AH...
AH...
AAAUGH!!
IT'S ALL RIGHT, HERR JUNKERS! IT'S ALL RIGHT!
AAAAH!!
I NEED TO ASK YOU TO LEAVE NOW, INSPECTOR.
NO. I'M ALMOST DONE.
...

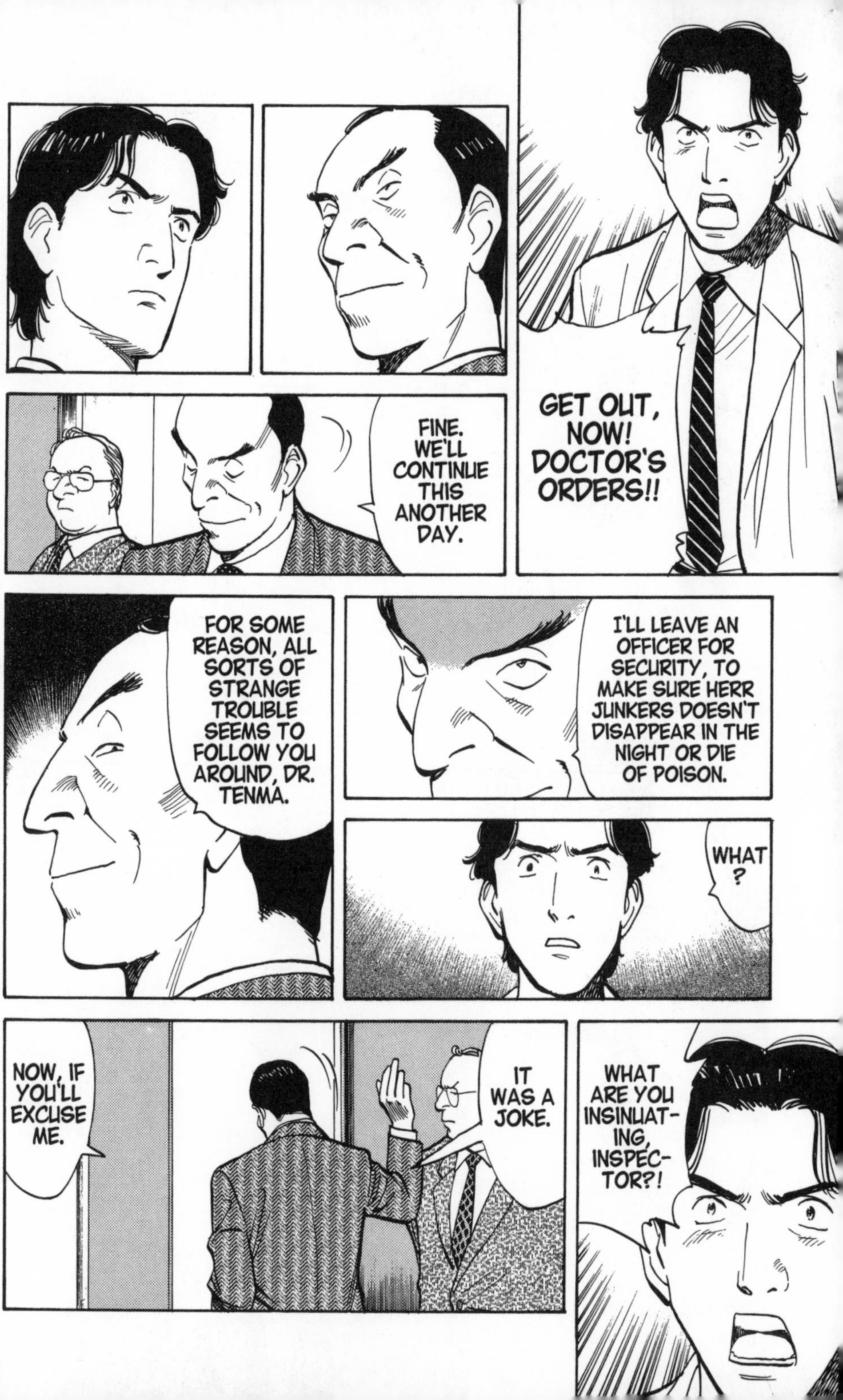
GET OUT, NOW! DOCTOR'S ORDERS!!
FINE. WE'LL CONTINUE THIS ANOTHER DAY.
I'LL LEAVE AN OFFICER FOR SECURITY, TO MAKE SURE HERR JUNKERS DOESN'T DISAPPEAR IN THE NIGHT OR DIE OF POISON.
WHAT?
FOR SOME REASON, ALL SORTS OF STRANGE TROUBLE SEEMS TO FOLLOW YOU AROUND, DR. TENMA.
WHAT ARE YOU INSINUAT-ING, INSPEC-TOR?!
IT WAS A JOKE.
NOW, IF YOU'LL EXCUSE ME.

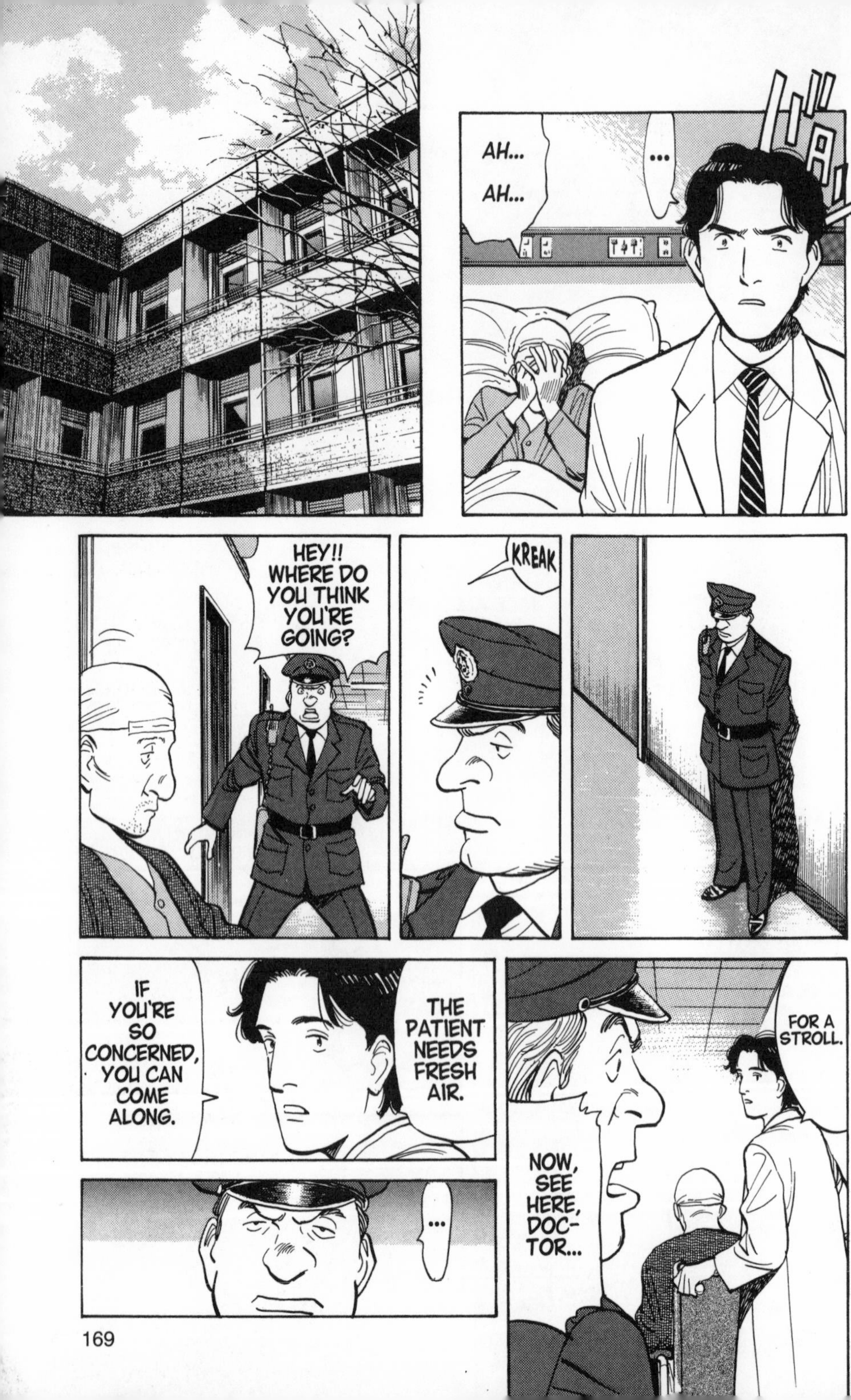

...
AH...
AH...
KREAK
HEY!! WHERE DO YOU THINK YOU'RE GOING?
FOR A STROLL.
NOW, SEE HERE, DOCTOR...
THE PATIENT NEEDS FRESH AIR.
IF YOU'RE SO CONCERNED, YOU CAN COME ALONG.
...

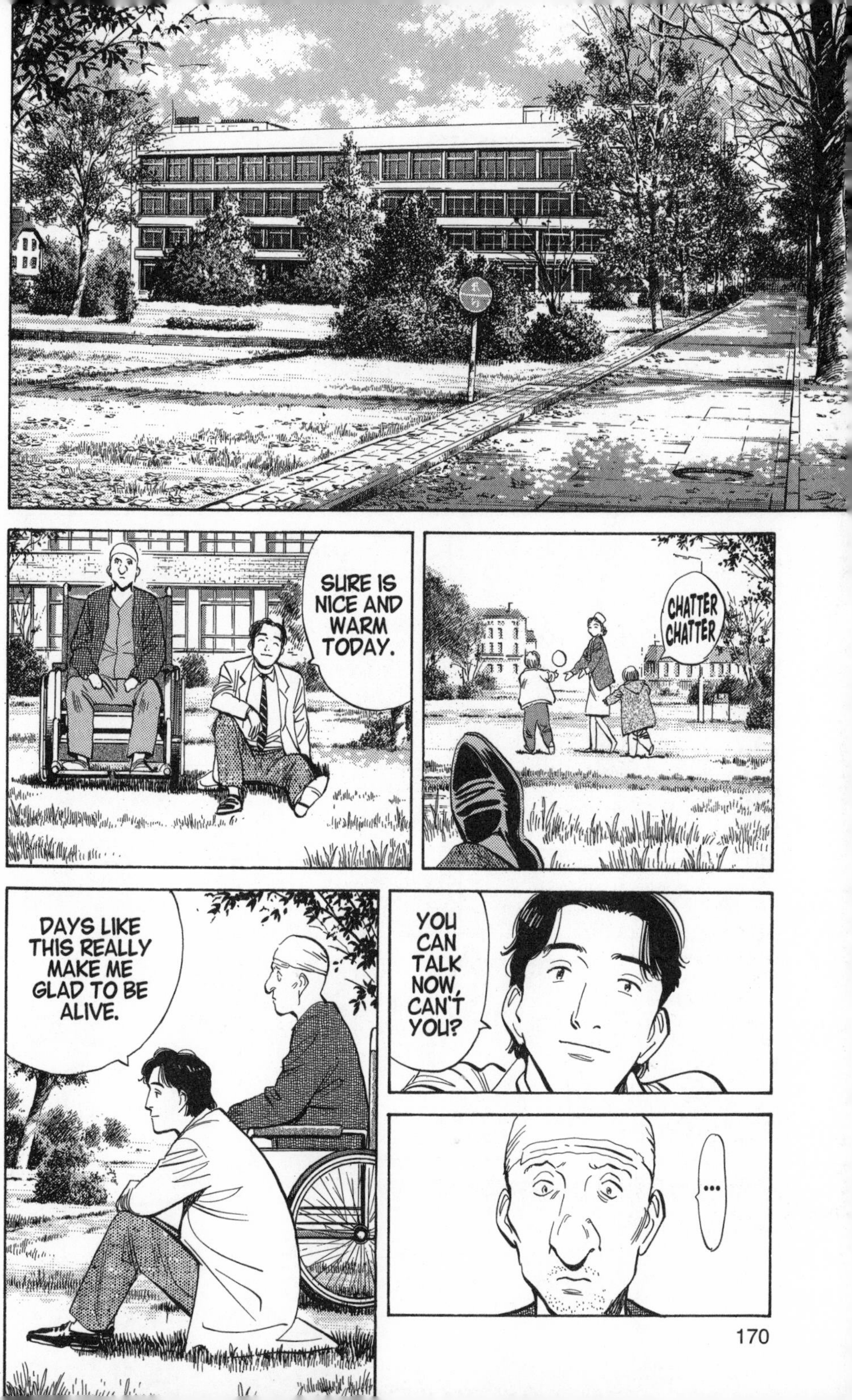

CHATTER CHATTER
SURE IS NICE AND WARM TODAY.
YOU CAN TALK NOW, CAN'T YOU?
...
DAYS LIKE THIS REALLY MAKE ME GLAD TO BE ALIVE.

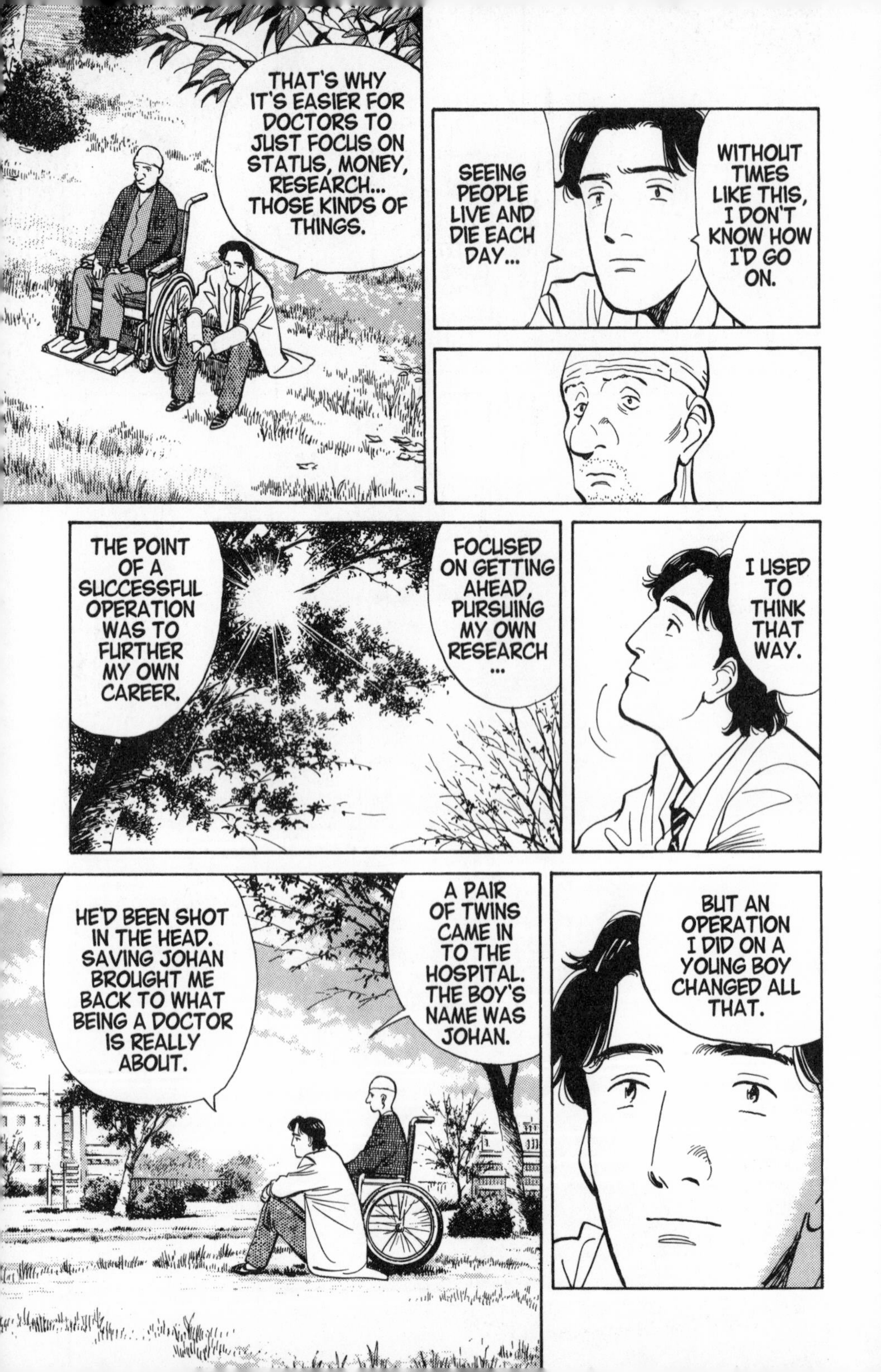
WITHOUT TIMES LIKE THIS, I DON'T KNOW HOW I'D GO ON.
SEEING PEOPLE LIVE AND DIE EACH DAY...
THAT'S WHY IT'S EASIER FOR DOCTORS TO JUST FOCUS ON STATUS, MONEY, RESEARCH... THOSE KINDS OF THINGS.
I USED TO THINK THAT WAY.
FOCUSED ON GETTING AHEAD, PURSUING MY OWN RESEARCH...
THE POINT OF A SUCCESSFUL OPERATION WAS TO FURTHER MY OWN CAREER.
BUT AN OPERATION I DID ON A YOUNG BOY CHANGED ALL THAT.
A PAIR OF TWINS CAME IN TO THE HOSPITAL. THE BOY'S NAME WAS JOHAN.
HE'D BEEN SHOT IN THE HEAD. SAVING JOHAN BROUGHT ME BACK TO WHAT BEING A DOCTOR IS REALLY ABOUT.

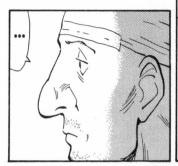

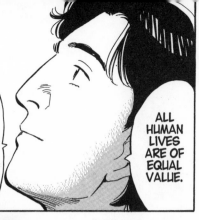

ALL HUMAN LIVES ARE OF EQUAL VALUE.
OUR JOB AS DOCTORS IS TO SAVE THOSE LIVES.
...
YOU CAN ALWAYS START OVER.
IT'S NEVER TOO LATE.
DOC...
YOU AND I ARE PROBABLY ABOUT THE SAME AGE.
BUT YOU SEEM MORE LIKE MY DAD.

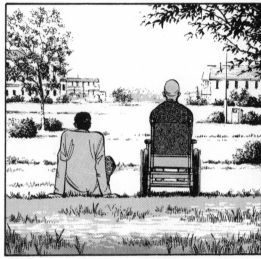

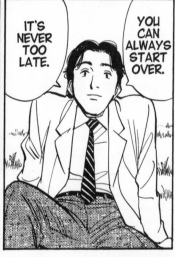

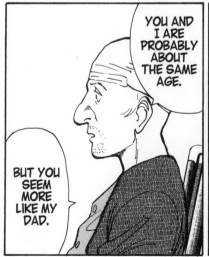

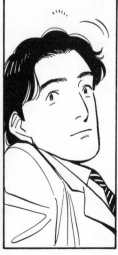

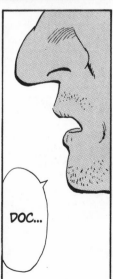

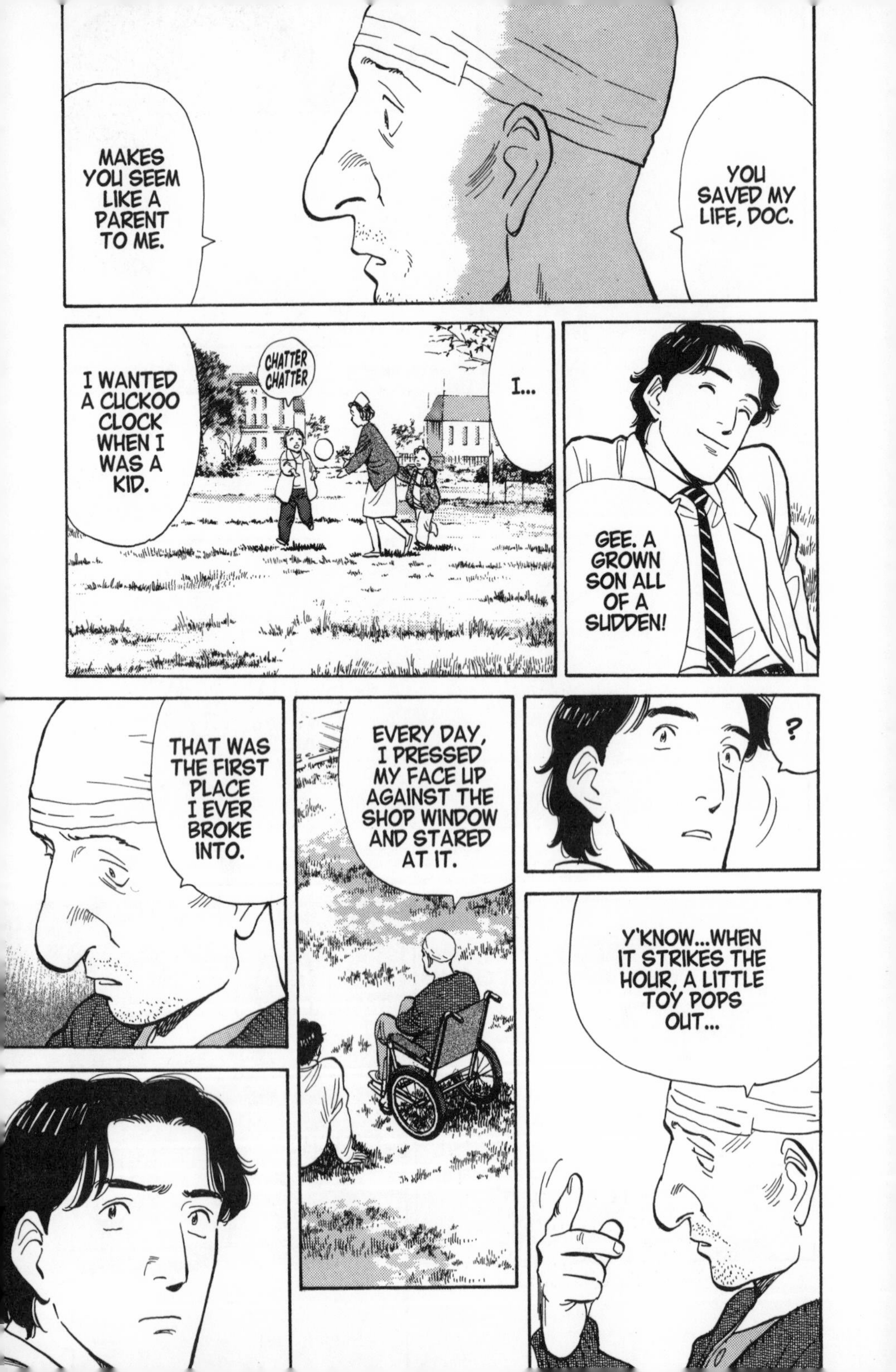
YOU SAVED MY LIFE, DOC.
MAKES YOU SEEM LIKE A PARENT TO ME.
GEE. A GROWN SON ALL OF A SUDDEN!
I...
CHATTER CHATTER
I WANTED A CUCKOO CLOCK WHEN I WAS A KID.
?
Y'KNOW...WHEN IT STRIKES THE HOUR, A LITTLE TOY POPS OUT...
EVERY DAY, I PRESSED MY FACE UP AGAINST THE SHOP WINDOW AND STARED AT IT.
THAT WAS THE FIRST PLACE I EVER BROKE INTO.

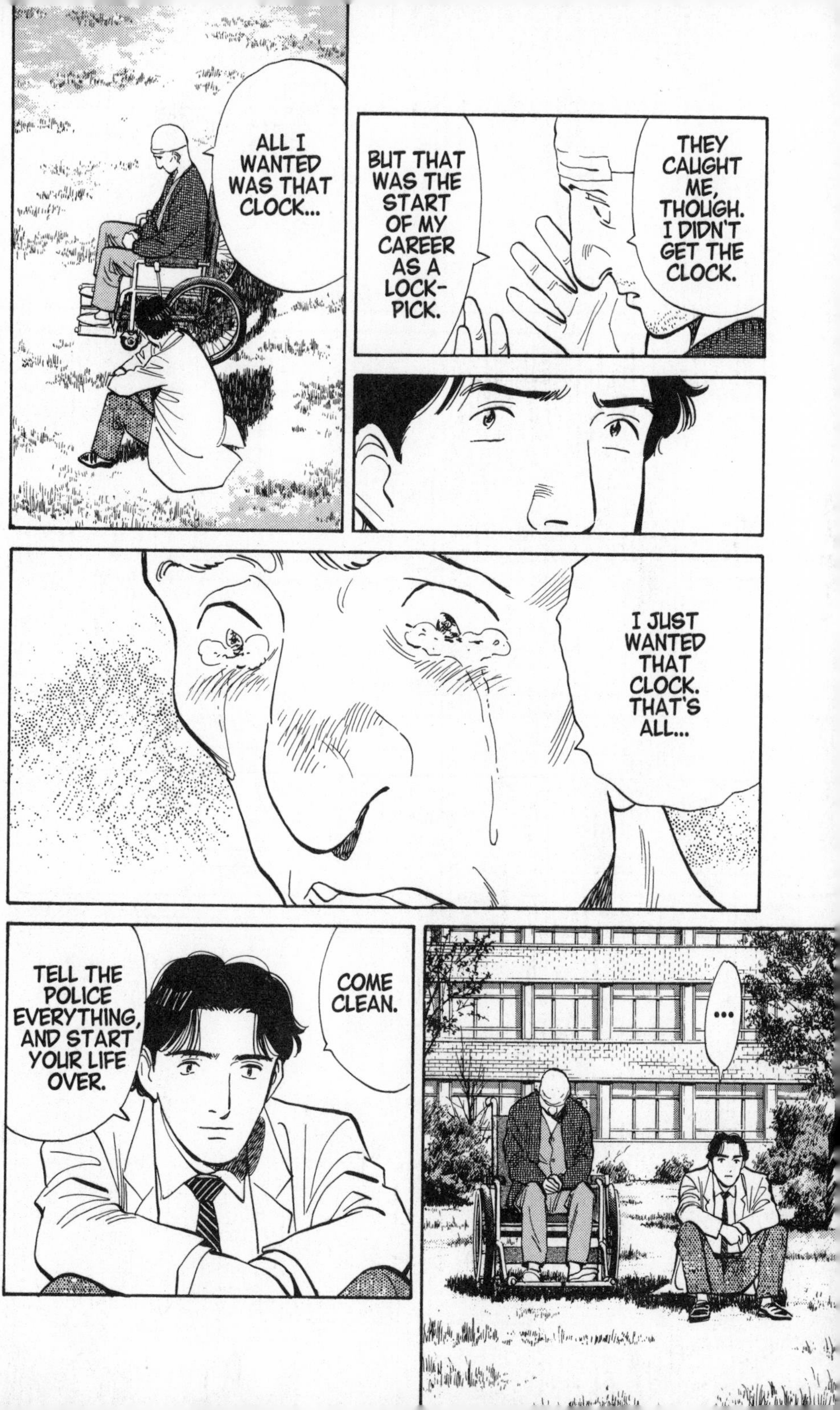
THEY CAUGHT ME, THOUGH. I DIDN'T GET THE CLOCK.
BUT THAT WAS THE START OF MY CAREER AS A LOCK-PICK.
ALL I WANTED WAS THAT CLOCK...
I JUST WANTED THAT CLOCK. THAT'S ALL...
...
COME CLEAN.
TELL THE POLICE EVERYTHING, AND START YOUR LIFE OVER.

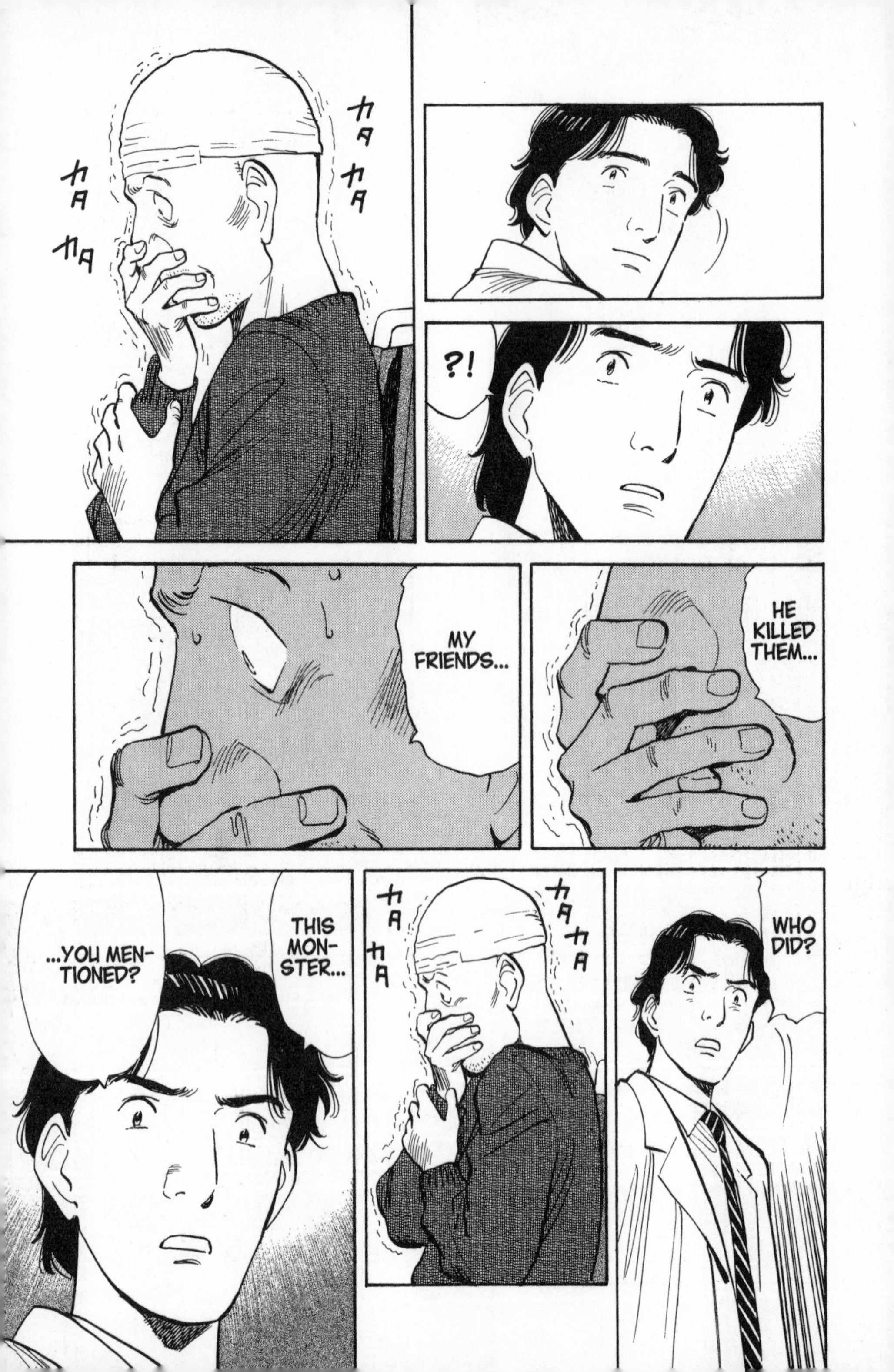

?!
カタ
カタ
カタ
カタ
HE KILLED THEM...
MY FRIENDS...
WHO DID?
カタ
カタ
カタ
カタ
THIS MON-STER...
...YOU MEN-TIONED?

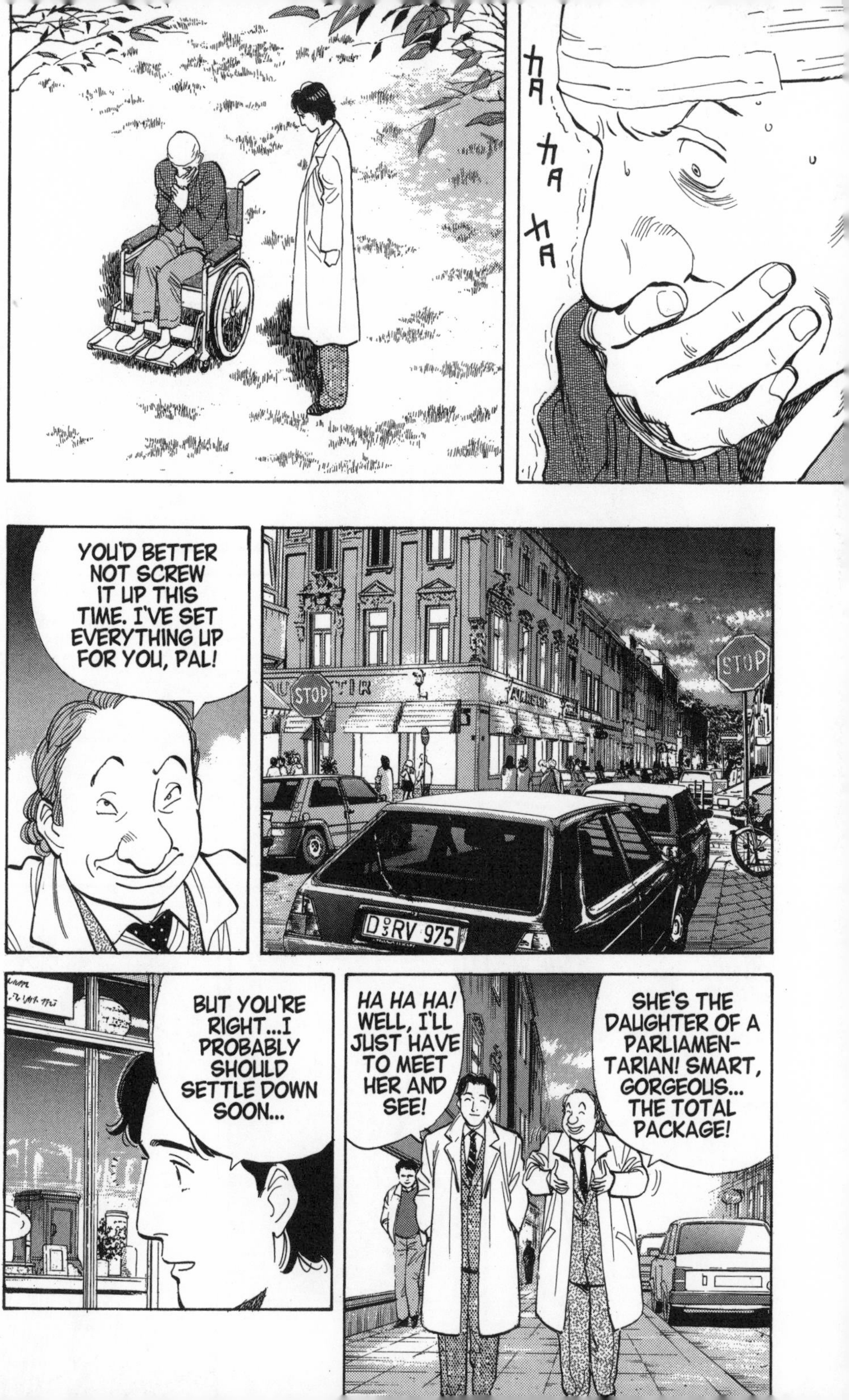
STOP
STOP
D RV 975
YOU'D BETTER NOT SCREW IT UP THIS TIME. I'VE SET EVERYTHING UP FOR YOU, PAL!
SHE'S THE DAUGHTER OF A PARLIAMEN-TARIAN! SMART, GORGEOUS... THE TOTAL PACKAGE!
HA HA HA! WELL, I'LL JUST HAVE TO MEET HER AND SEE!
BUT YOU'RE RIGHT...I PROBABLY SHOULD SETTLE DOWN SOON...

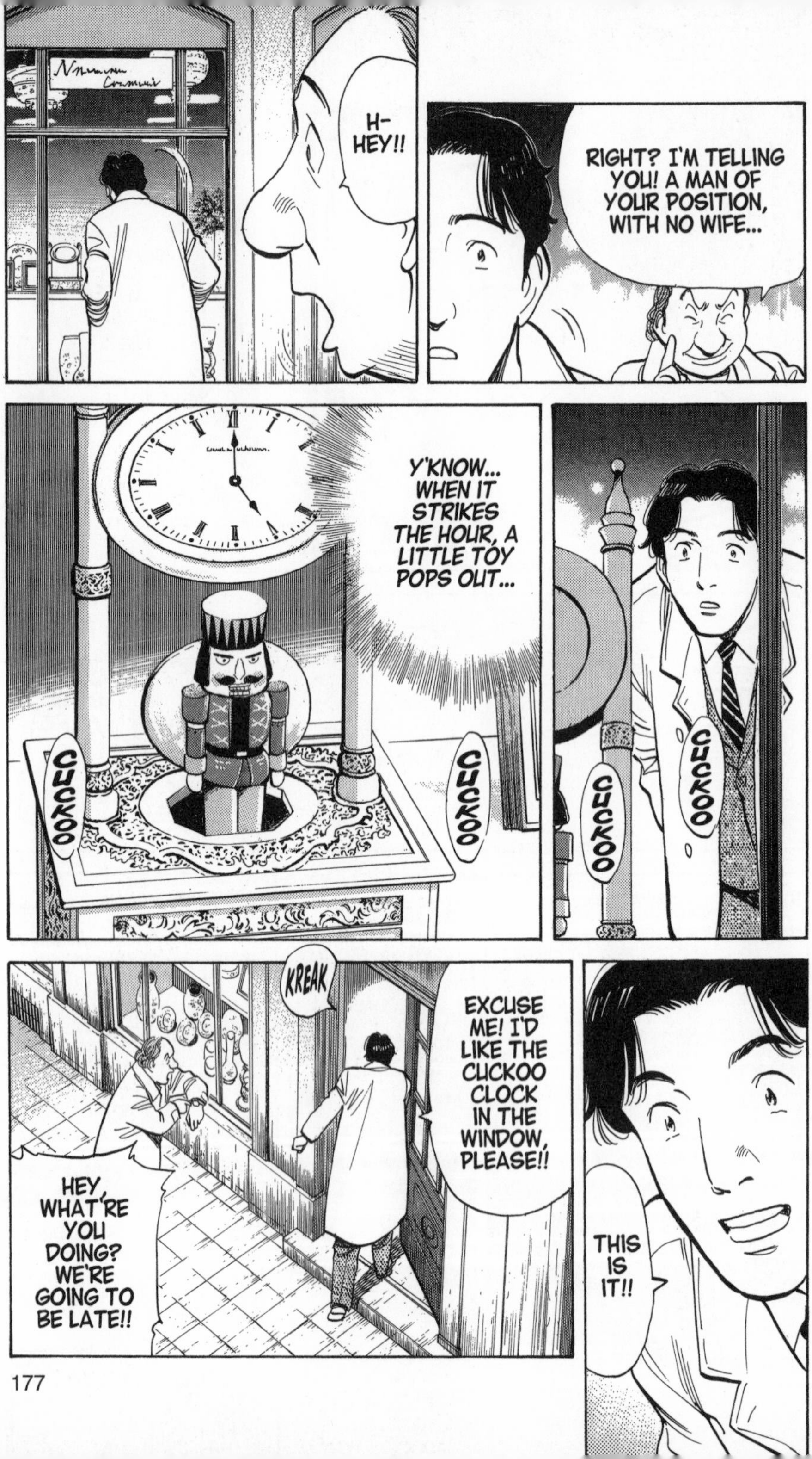
RIGHT? I'M TELLING YOU! A MAN OF YOUR POSITION, WITH NO WIFE...
H-HEY!!
CUCKOO
CUCKOO
Y'KNOW... WHEN IT STRIKES THE HOUR, A LITTLE TOY POPS OUT...
CUCKOO
CUCKOO
THIS IS IT!!
KREAK
EXCUSE ME! I'D LIKE THE CUCKOO CLOCK IN THE WINDOW, PLEASE!!
HEY, WHAT'RE YOU DOING? WE'RE GOING TO BE LATE!!

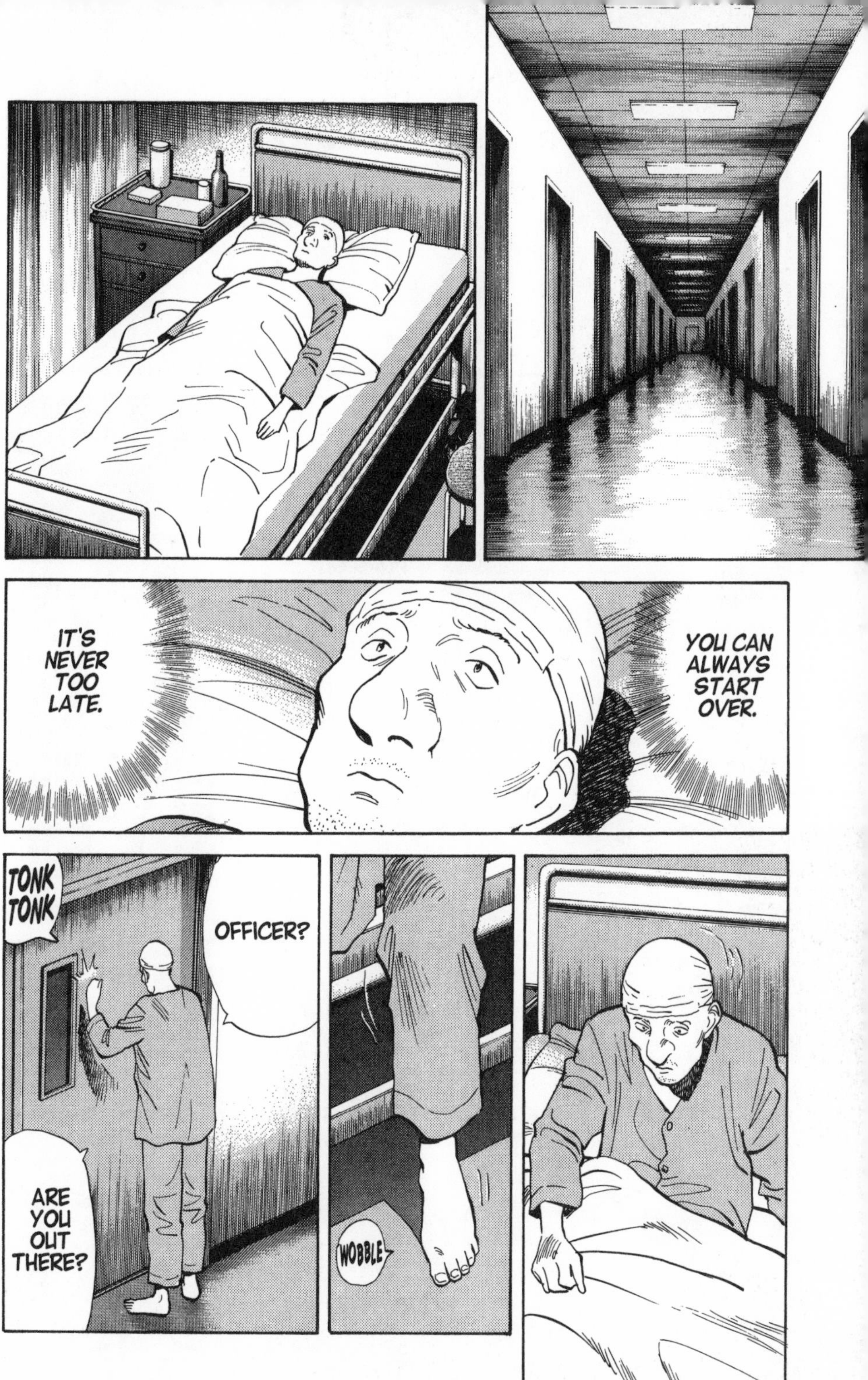
YOU CAN ALWAYS START OVER.
IT'S NEVER TOO LATE.
WOBBLE
TONK TONK
OFFICER?
ARE YOU OUT THERE?

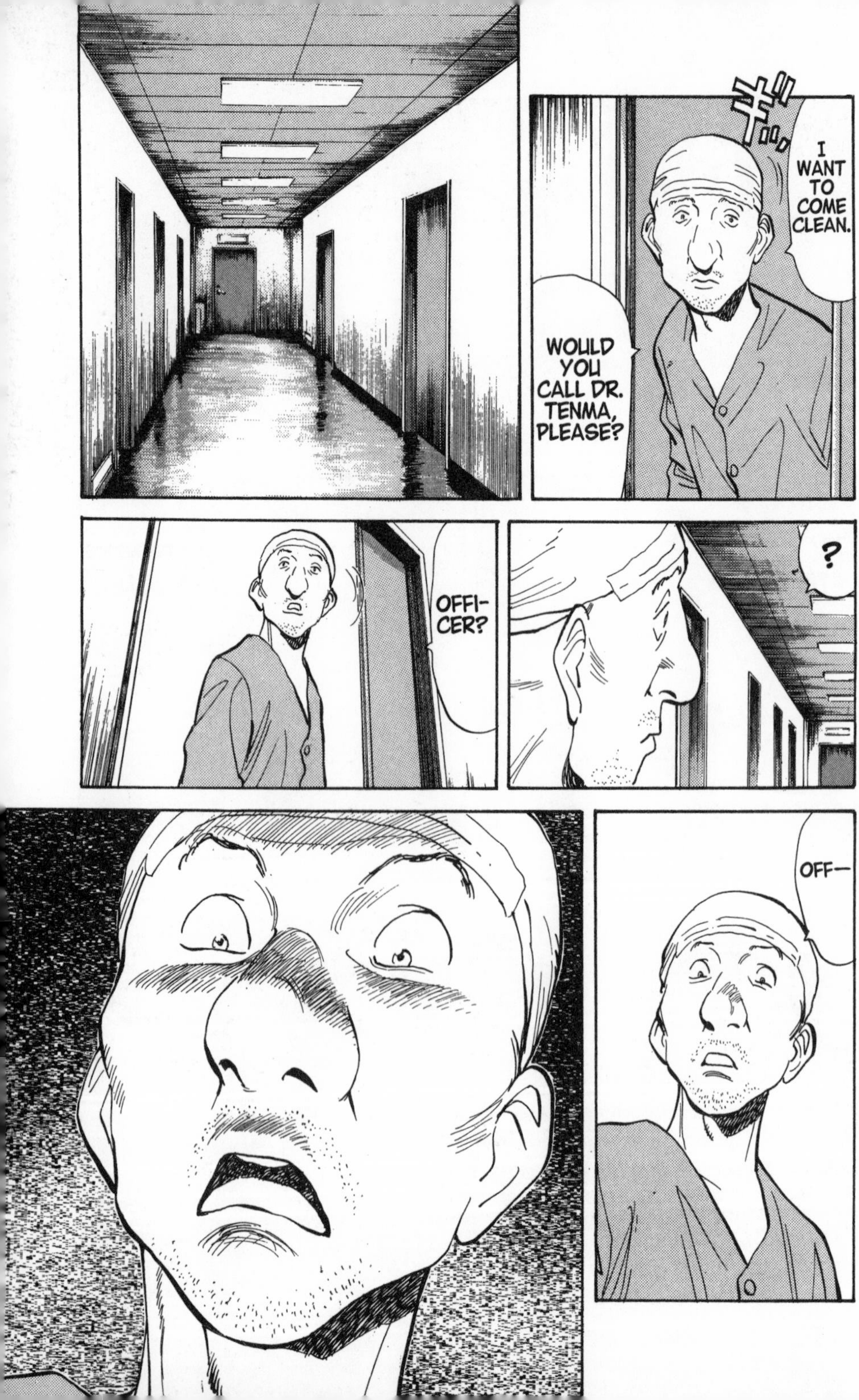
I WANT TO COME CLEAN.
WOULD YOU CALL DR. TENMA, PLEASE?
?
OFFI-CER?
OFF—

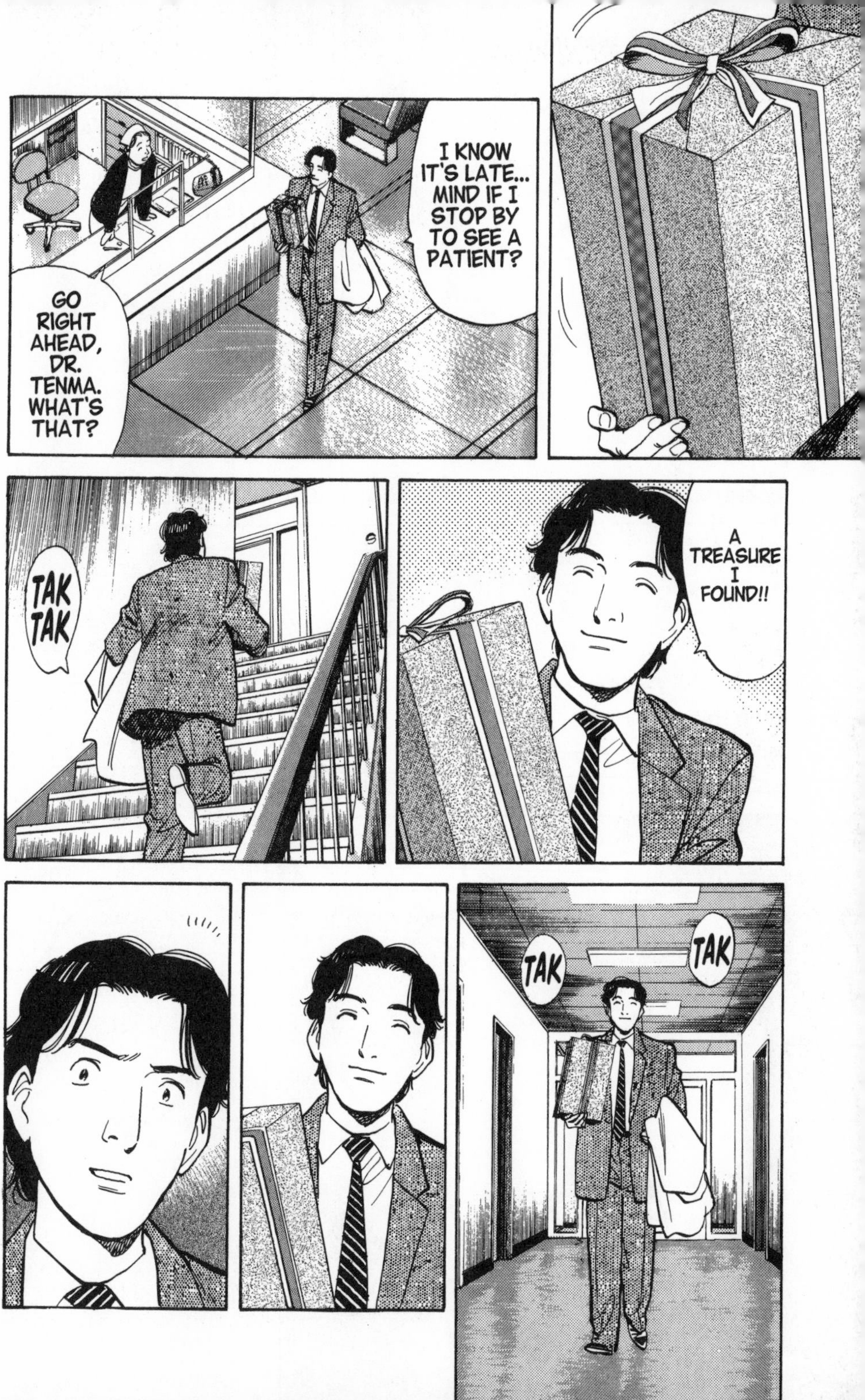
I KNOW IT'S LATE... MIND IF I STOP BY TO SEE A PATIENT?
GO RIGHT AHEAD, DR. TENMA. WHAT'S THAT?
A TREASURE I FOUND!!
TAK TAK
TAK
TAK

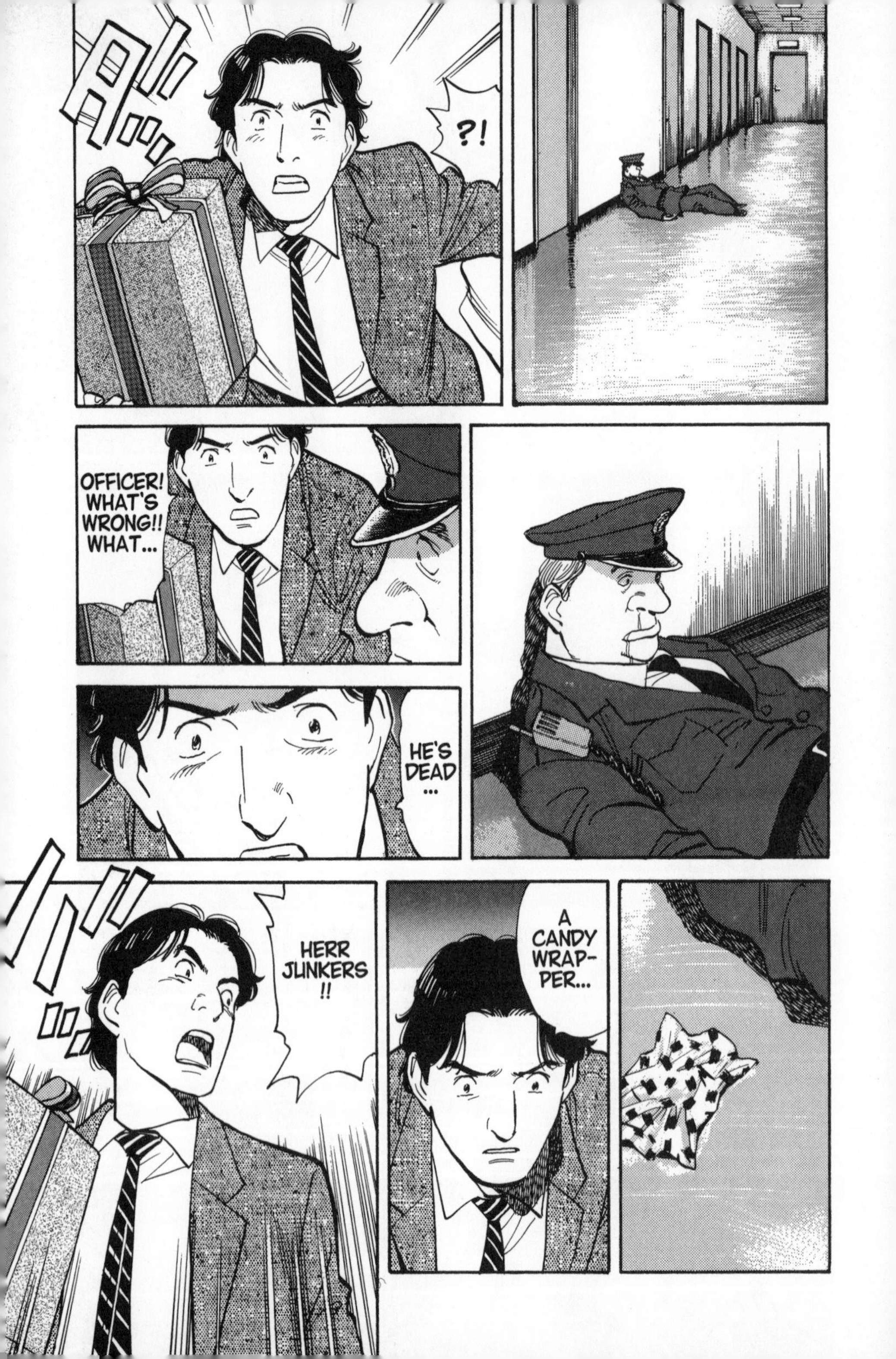
?!
OFFICER! WHAT'S WRONG!! WHAT...
HE'S DEAD ...
A CANDY WRAP-PER...
HERR JUNKERS !!

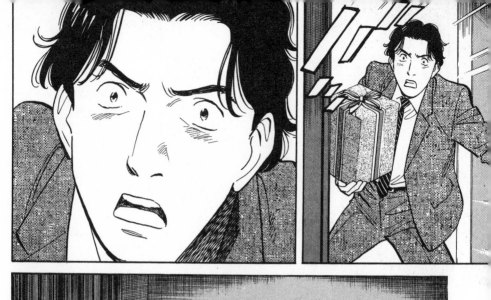

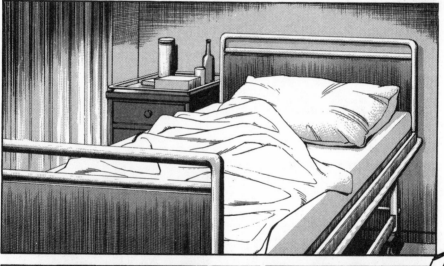

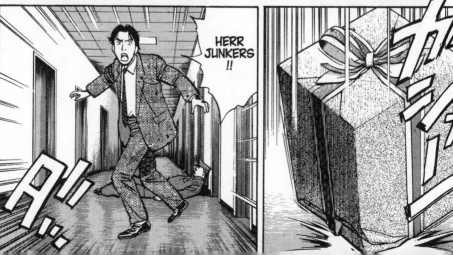

HERR
JUNKERS
!!

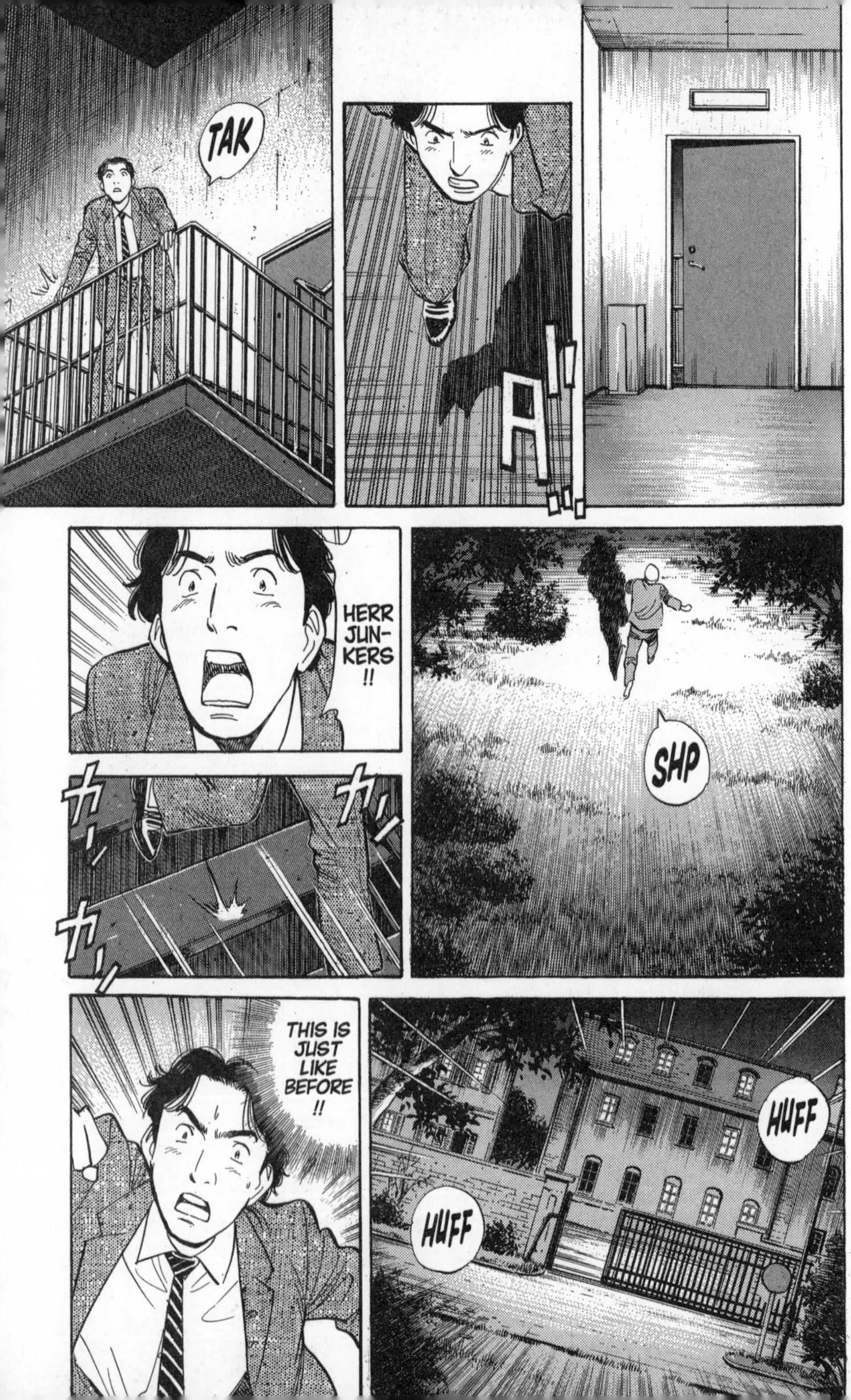
A!!
TAK
SHP
HERR JUNKERS!!
カッ
カッ
カッ
HUFF
HUFF
THIS IS JUST LIKE BEFORE!!

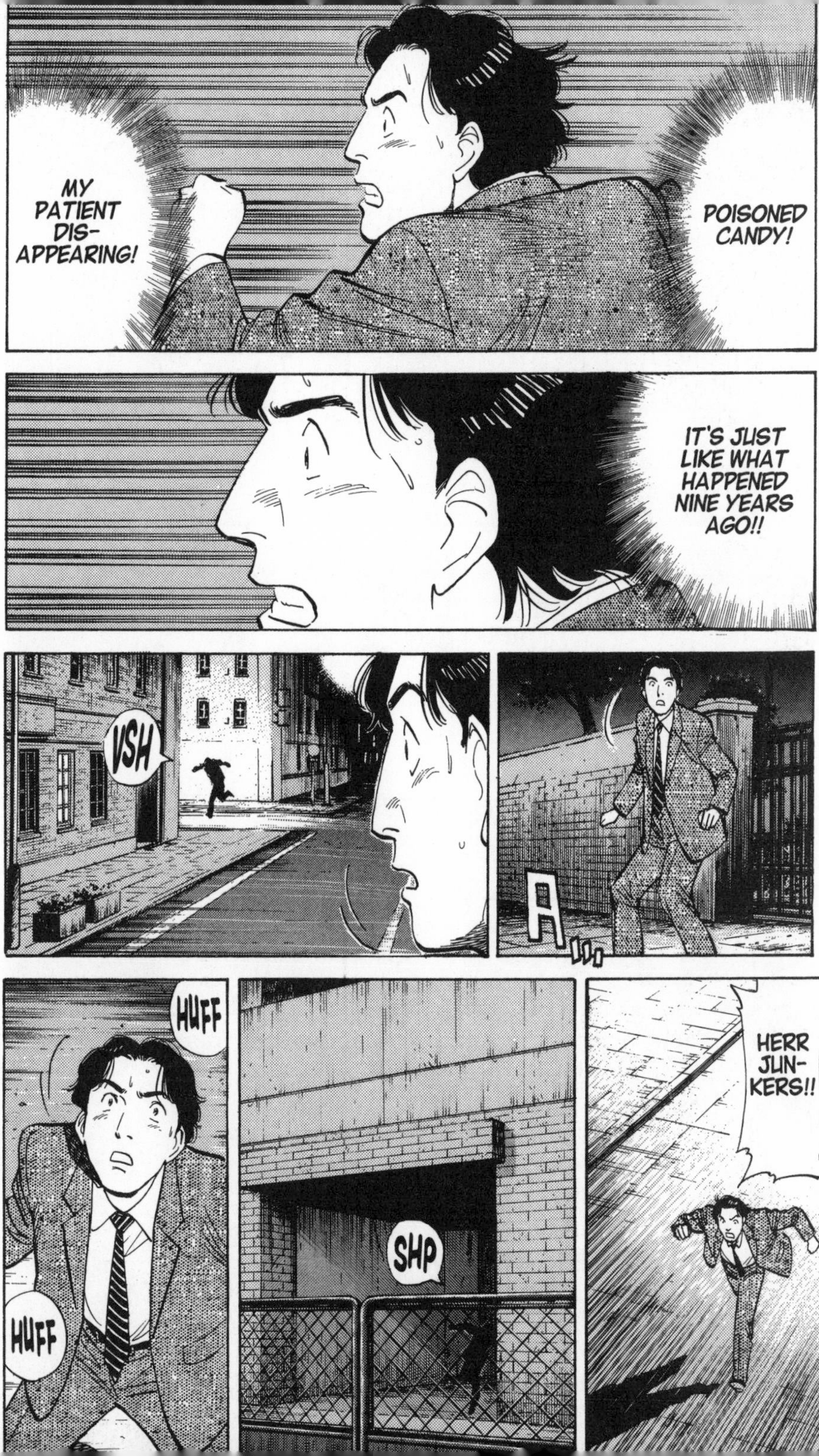
POISONED CANDY!
MY PATIENT DIS-APPEARING!
IT'S JUST LIKE WHAT HAPPENED NINE YEARS AGO!!
A...
VSH
HERR JUN-KERS!!
SHP
HUFF
HUFF

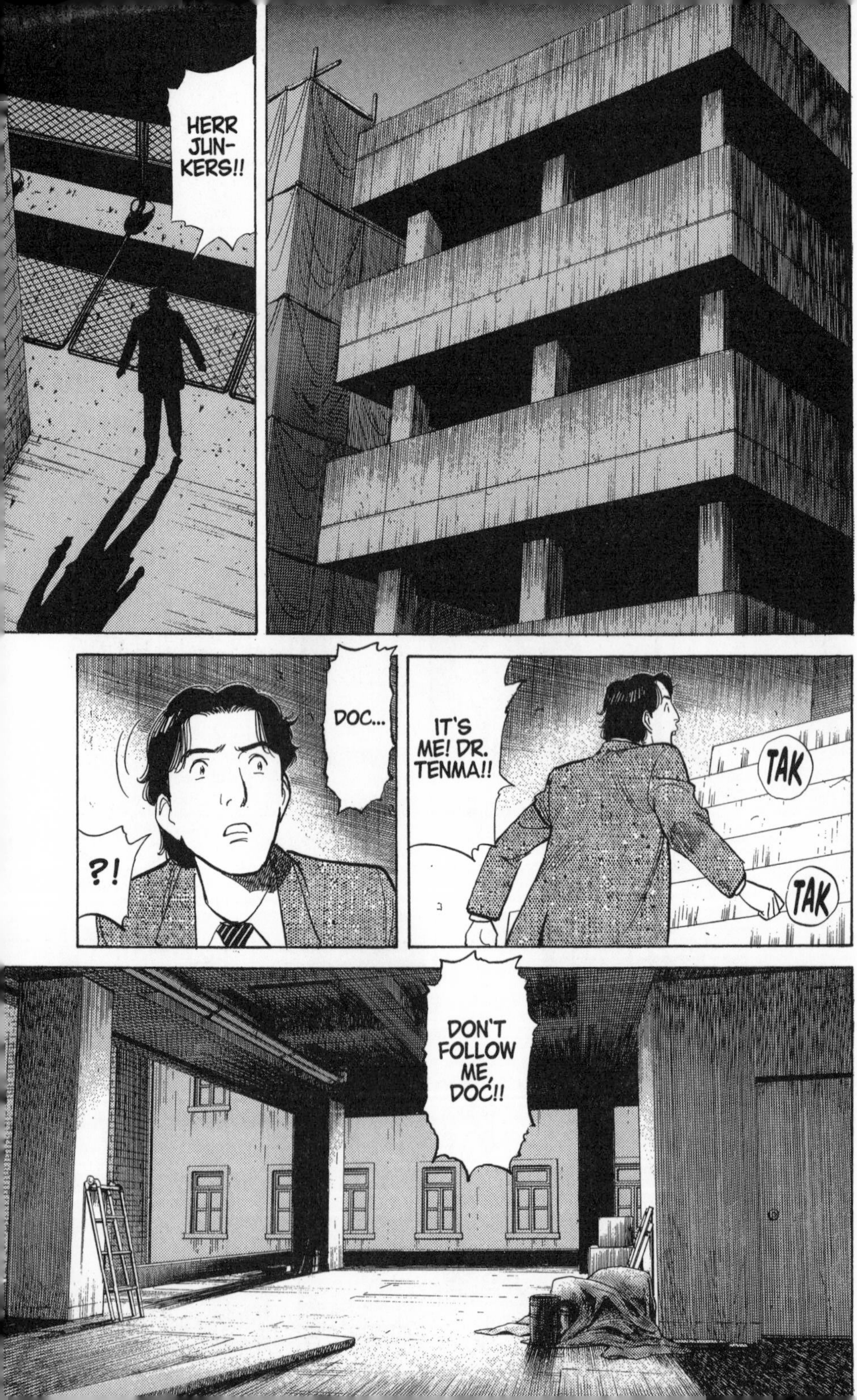
HERR JUNKERS!!
IT'S ME! DR. TENMA!!
TAK
TAK
DOC...
?!
DON'T FOLLOW ME, DOC!!

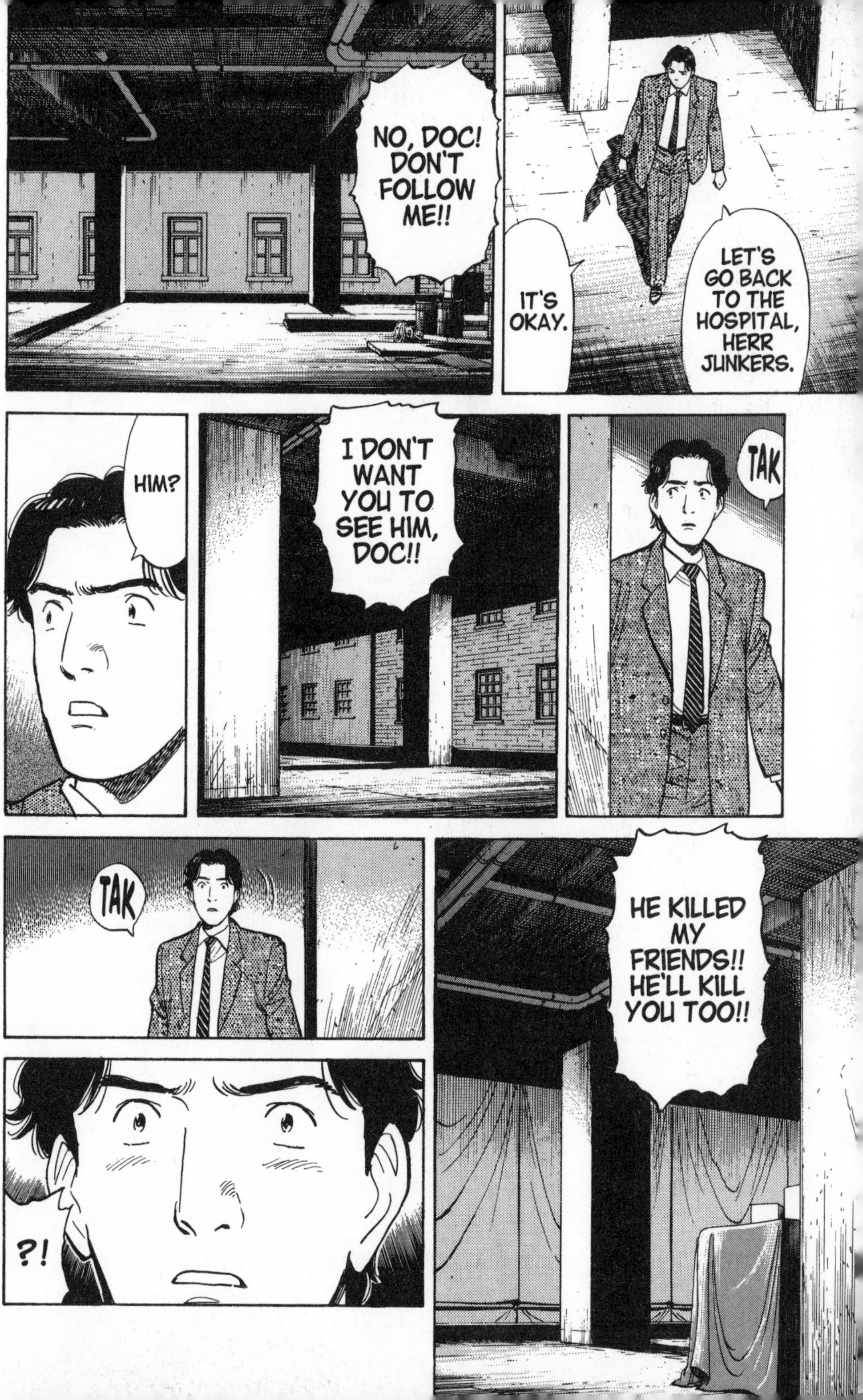
LET'S GO BACK TO THE HOSPITAL, HERR JUNKERS.
IT'S OKAY.
NO, DOC! DON'T FOLLOW ME!!
TAK
I DON'T WANT YOU TO SEE HIM, DOC!!
HIM?
HE KILLED MY FRIENDS!! HE'LL KILL YOU TOO!!
TAK
?!

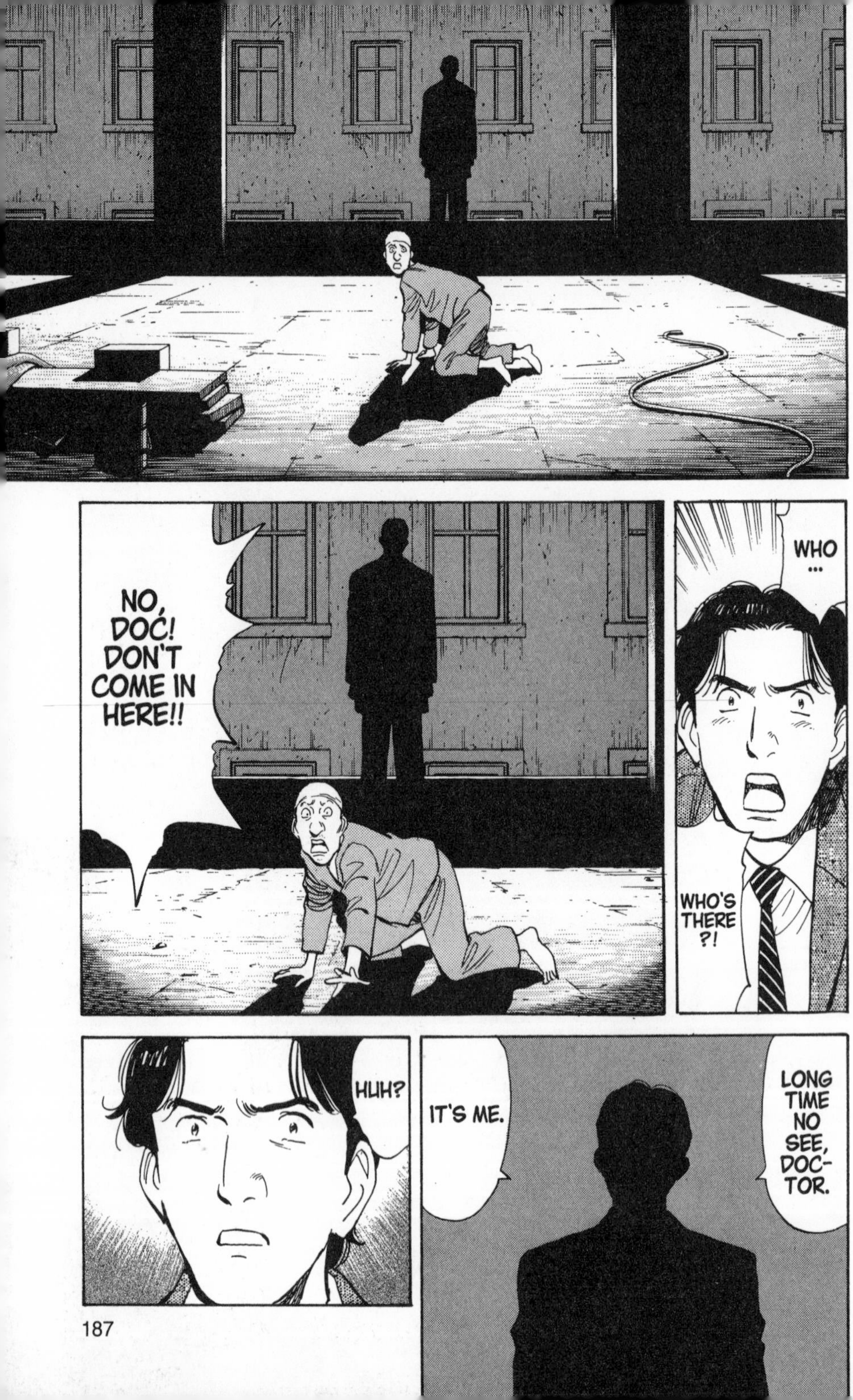
WHO ...
WHO'S THERE ?!
NO, DOC! DON'T COME IN HERE!!
LONG TIME NO SEE, DOC-TOR.
IT'S ME.
HUH?

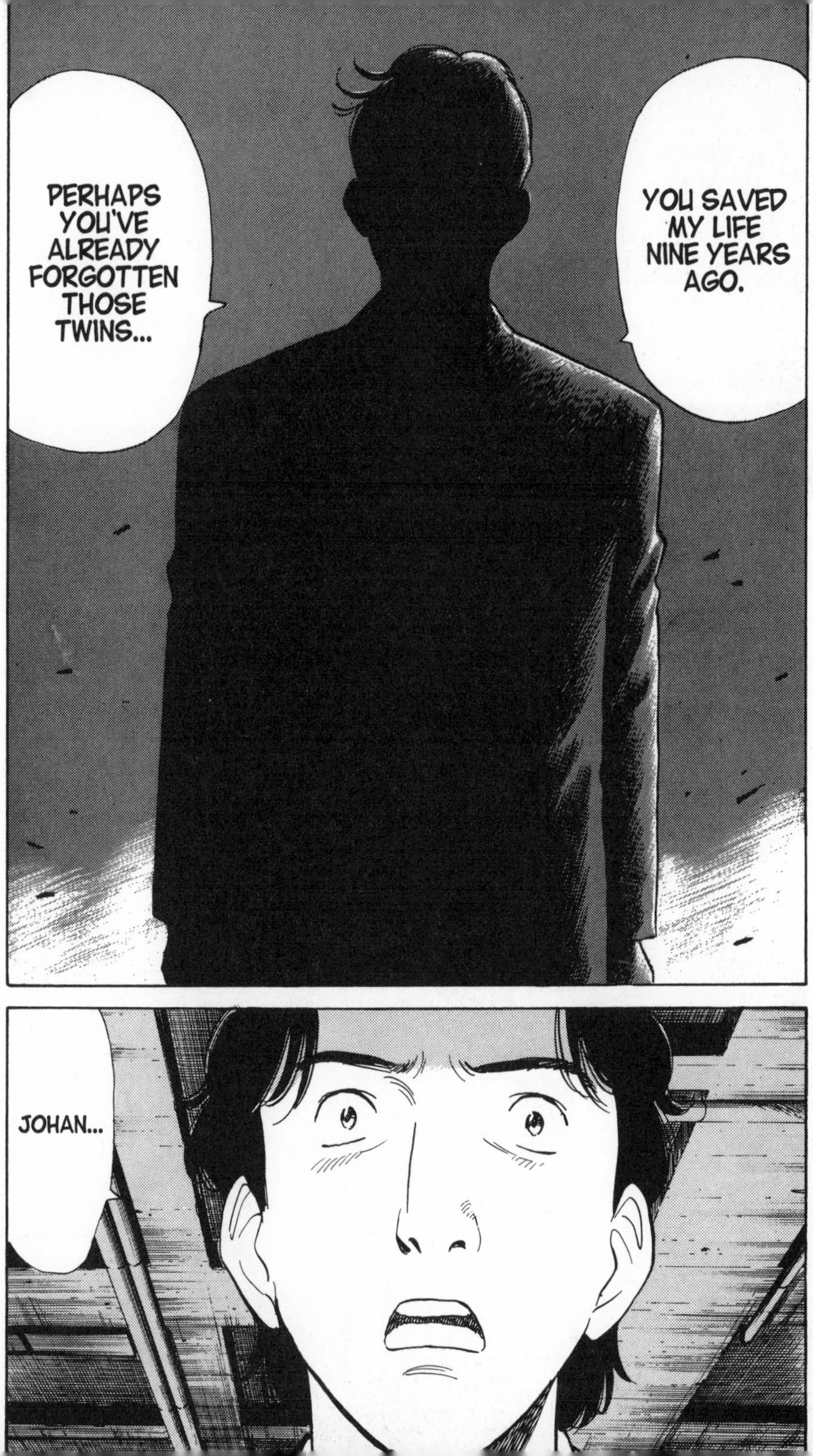
YOU SAVED MY LIFE NINE YEARS AGO.
PERHAPS YOU'VE ALREADY FORGOTTEN THOSE TWINS...
JOHAN...

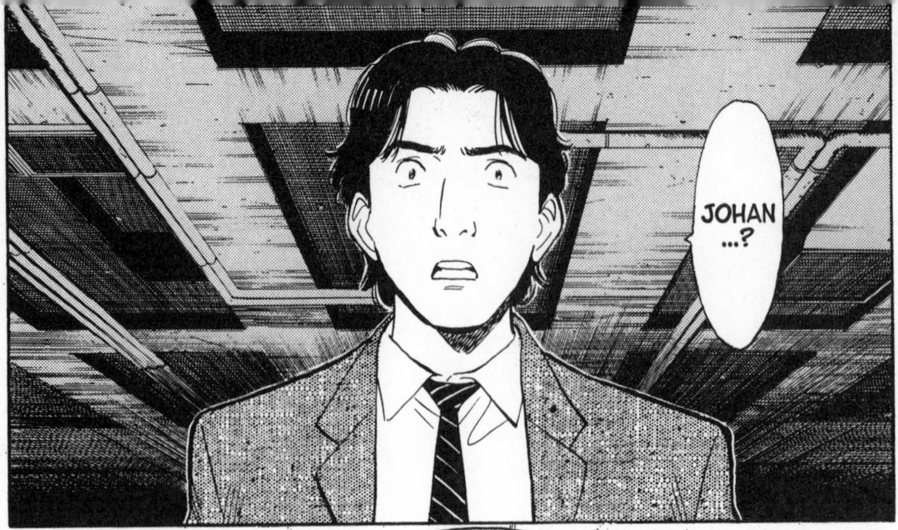
JOHAN ...?

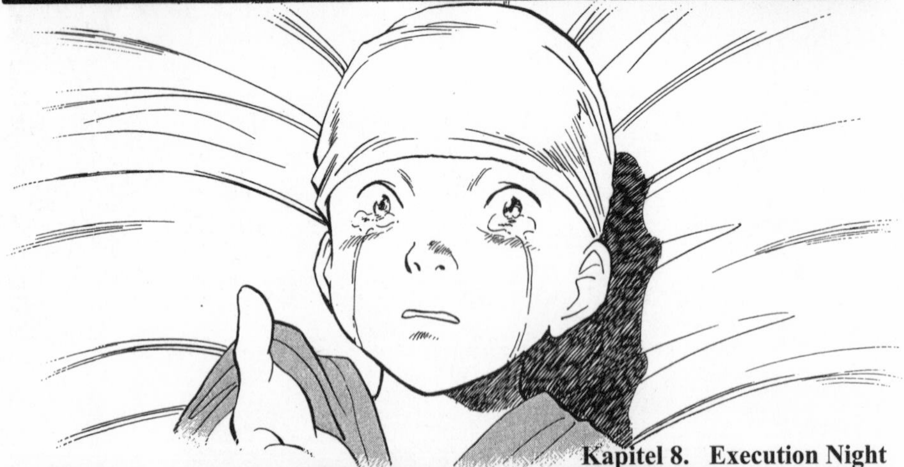

Kapitel 8. Execution Night

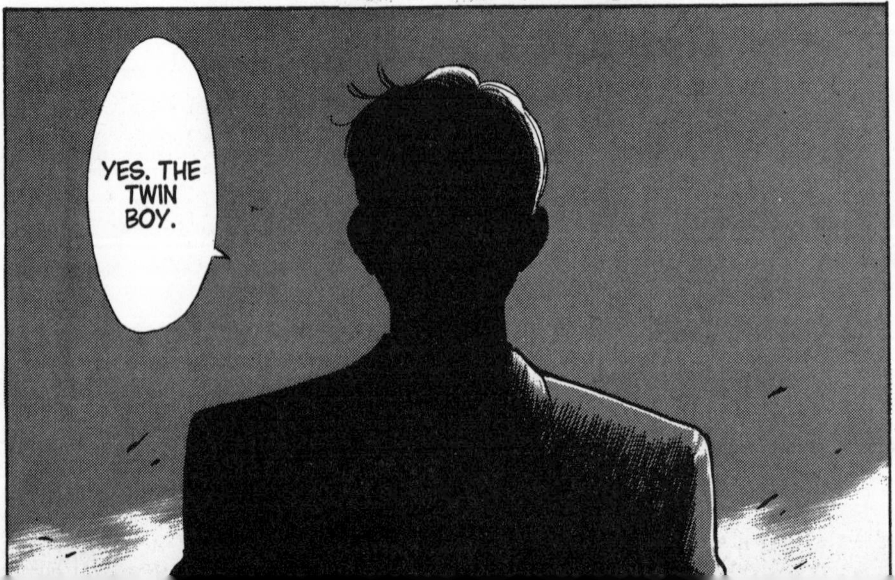
YES. THE TWIN BOY.

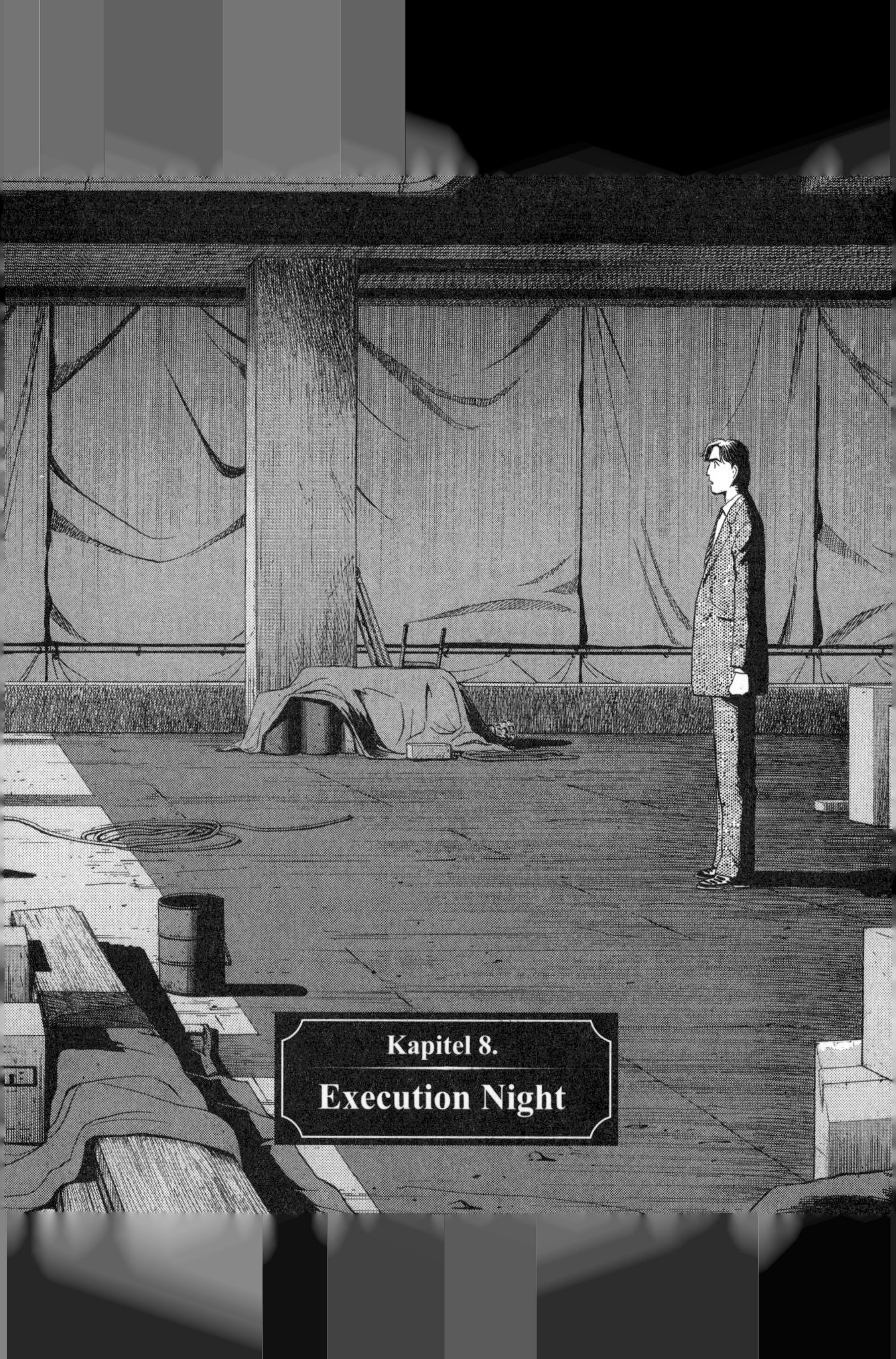
Kapitel 8.
Execution Night

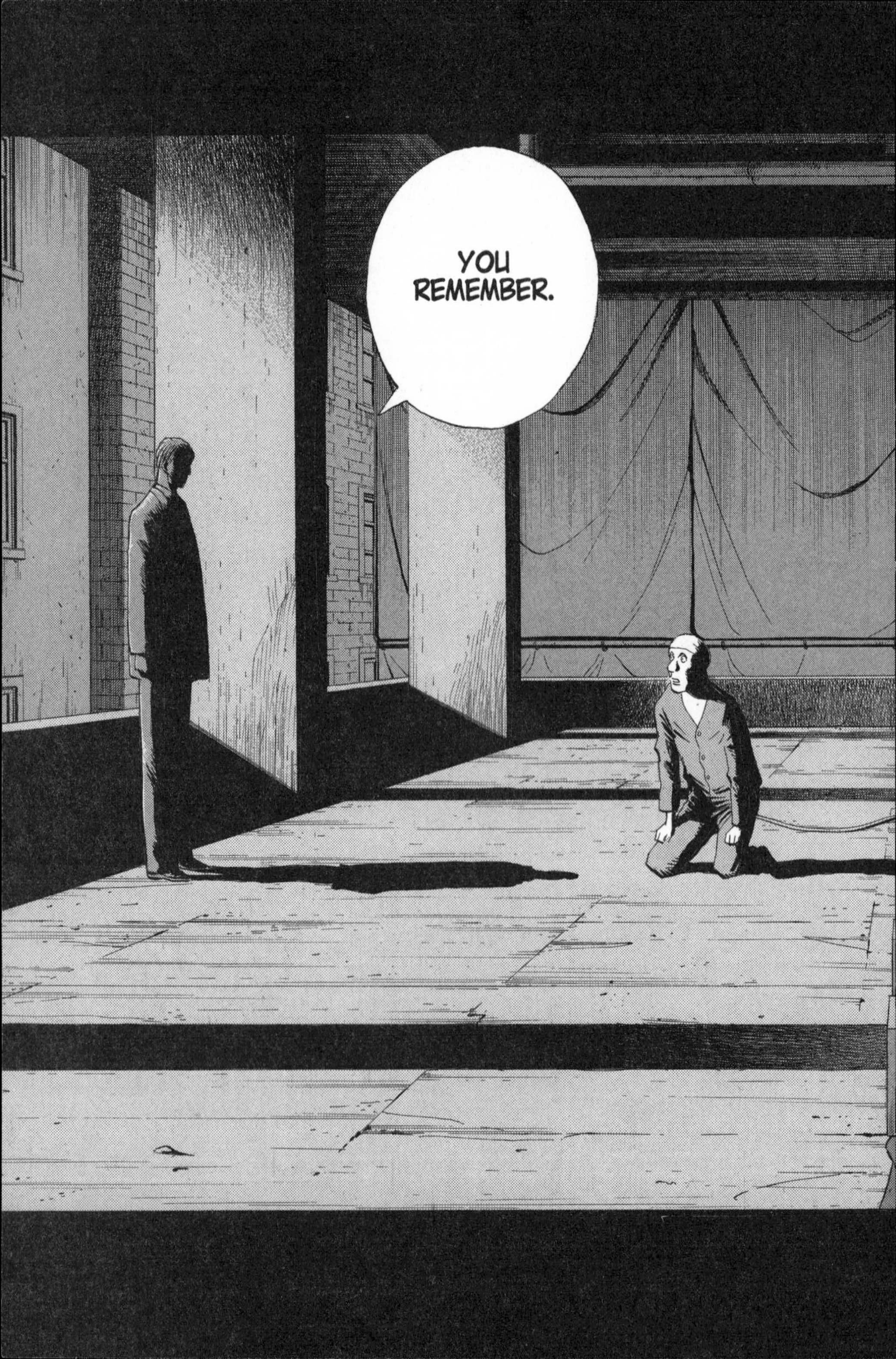
YOU REMEMBER.

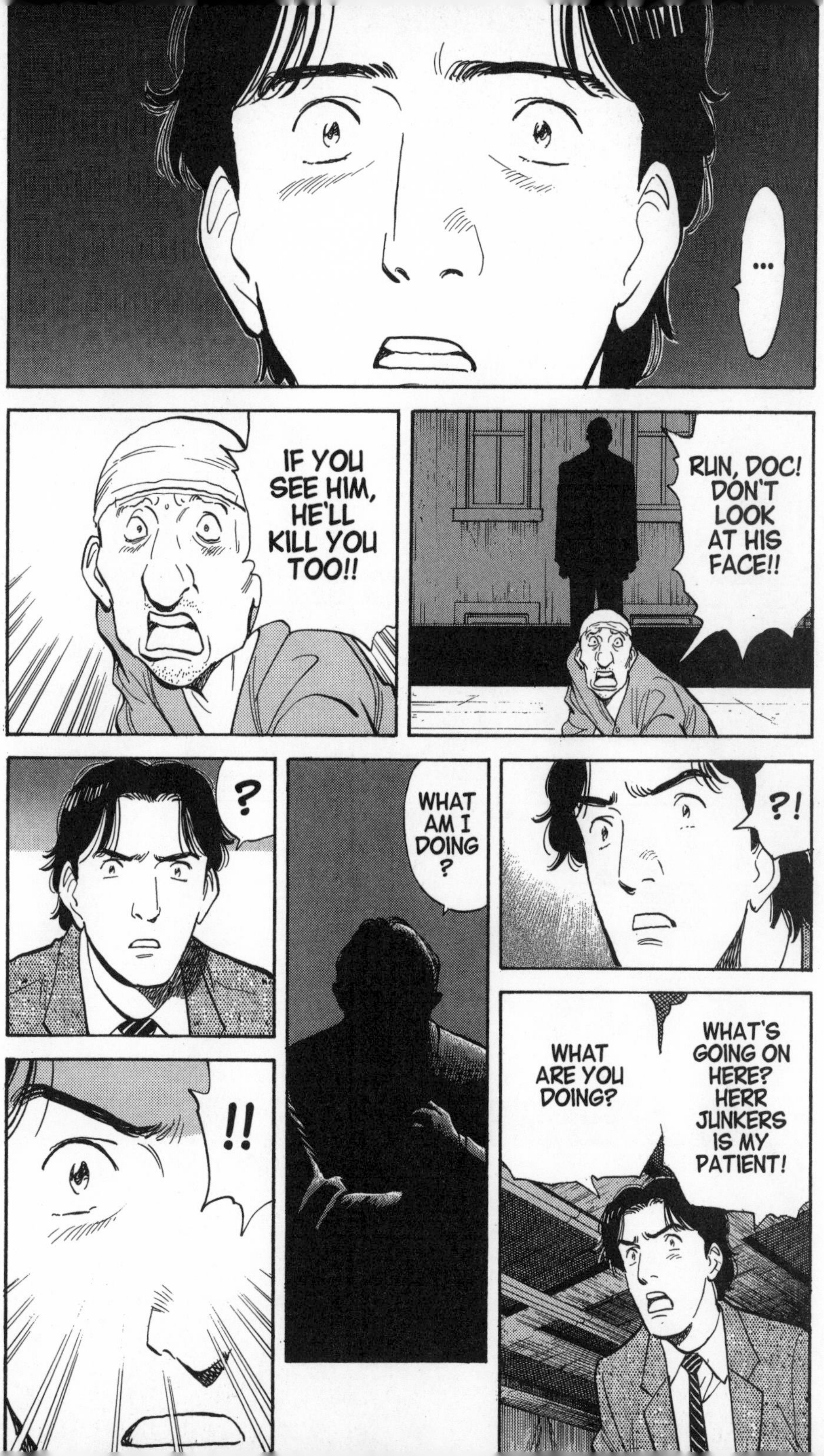
...
RUN, DOC! DON'T LOOK AT HIS FACE!!
IF YOU SEE HIM, HE'LL KILL YOU TOO!!
?!
WHAT'S GOING ON HERE? HERR JUNKERS IS MY PATIENT!
WHAT ARE YOU DOING?
WHAT AM I DOING?
?
!!

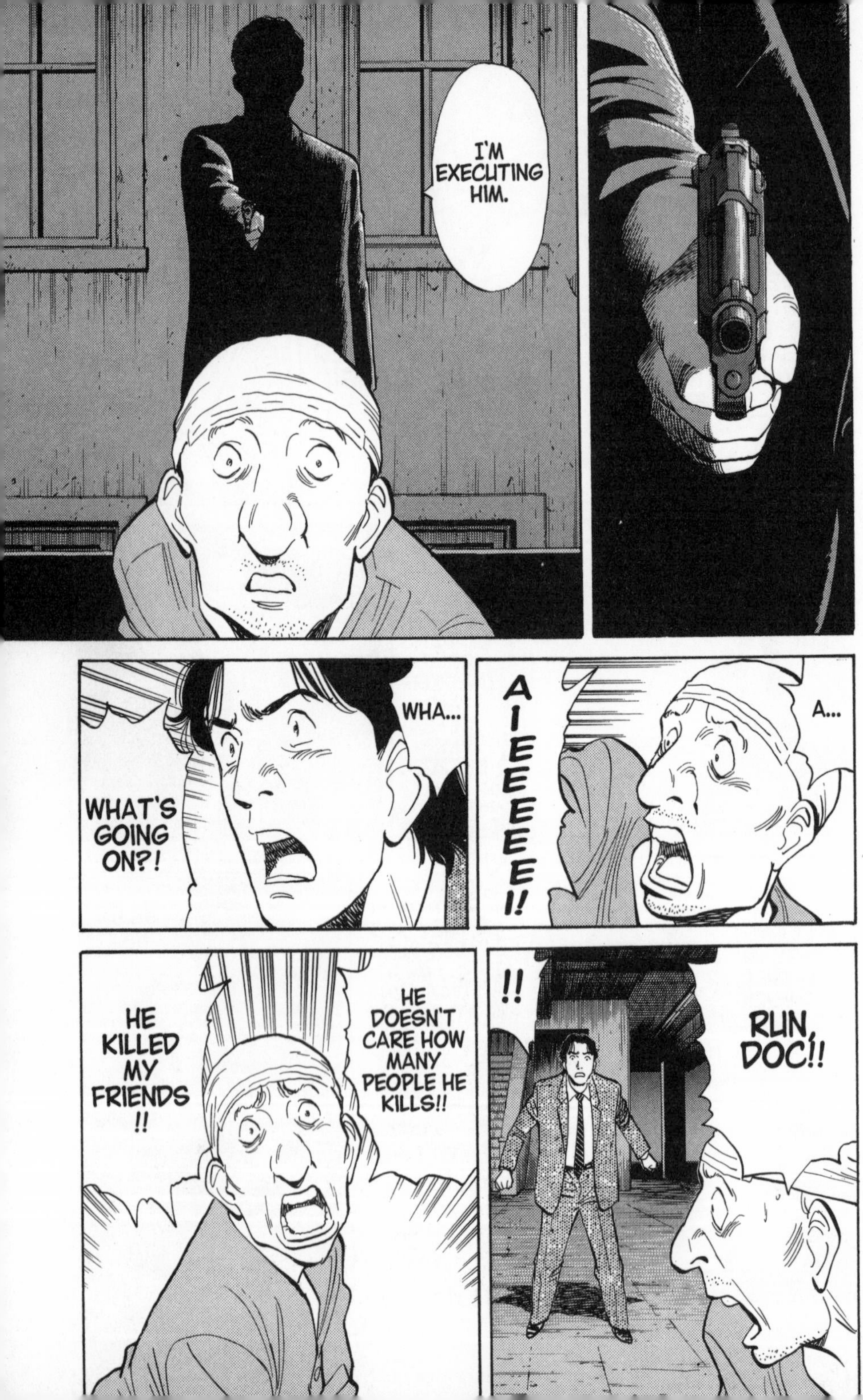
I'M EXECUTING HIM.
A...
AIEEEEE!!
WHA...
WHAT'S GOING ON?!
RUN, DOC!!
!!
HE DOESN'T CARE HOW MANY PEOPLE HE KILLS!!
HE KILLED MY FRIENDS!!

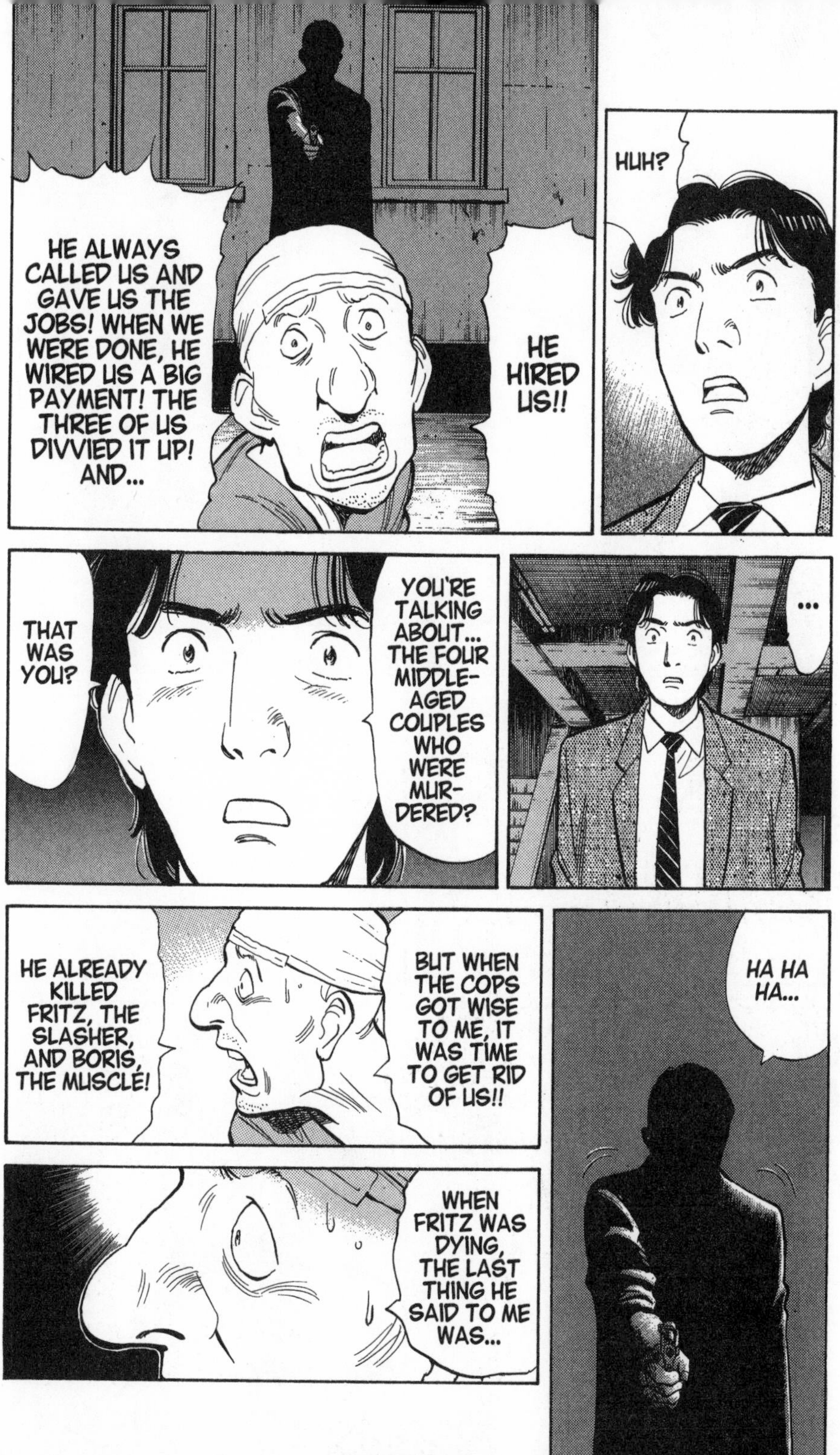
HUH?
HE HIRED US!!
HE ALWAYS CALLED US AND GAVE US THE JOBS! WHEN WE WERE DONE, HE WIRED US A BIG PAYMENT! THE THREE OF US DIVVIED IT UP! AND...
...
YOU'RE TALKING ABOUT... THE FOUR MIDDLE-AGED COUPLES WHO WERE MUR-DERED?
THAT WAS YOU?
HA HA HA...
BUT WHEN THE COPS GOT WISE TO ME, IT WAS TIME TO GET RID OF US!!
HE ALREADY KILLED FRITZ, THE SLASHER, AND BORIS, THE MUSCLE!
WHEN FRITZ WAS DYING, THE LAST THING HE SAID TO ME WAS...

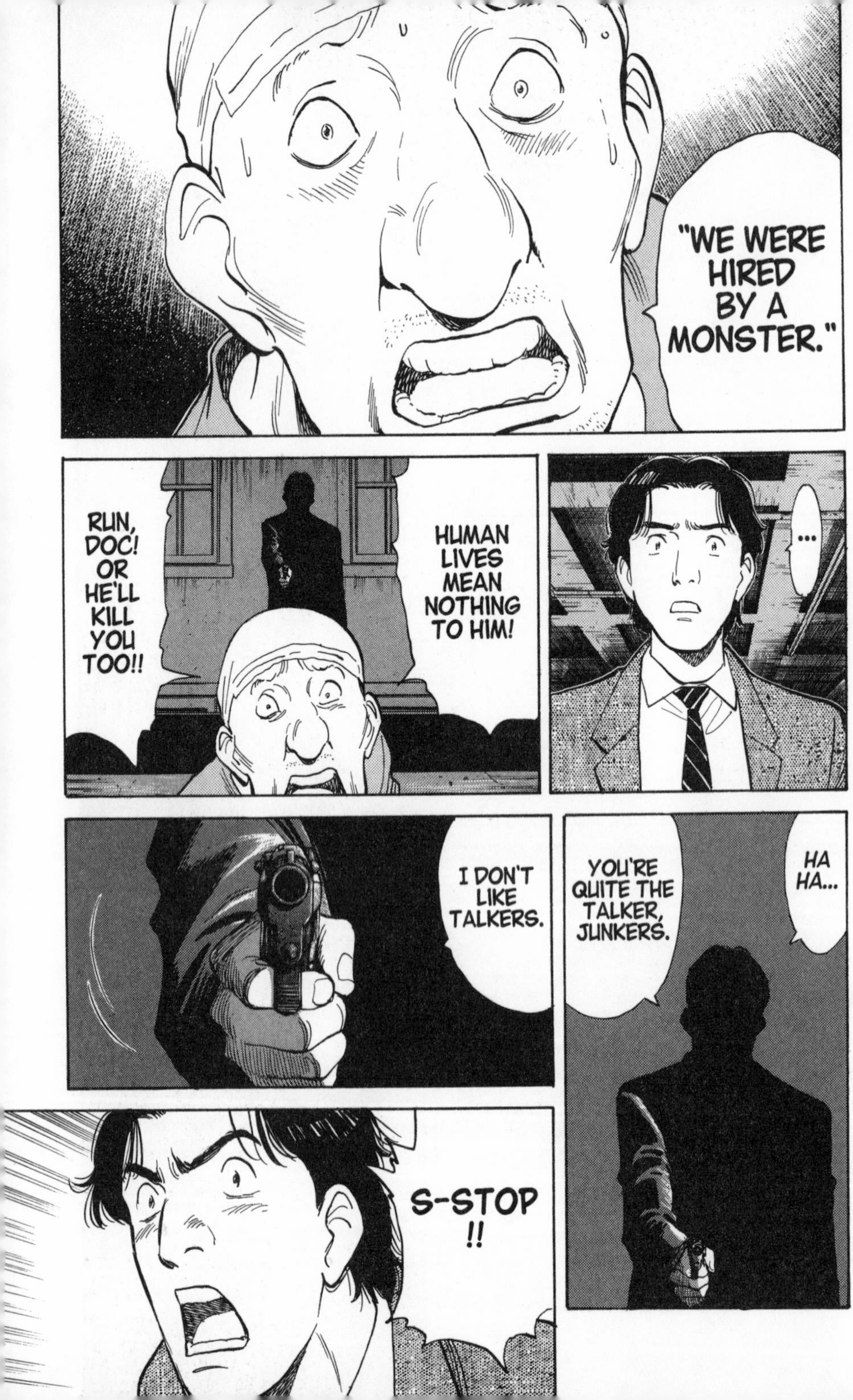
"WE WERE HIRED BY A MONSTER."
...
HUMAN LIVES MEAN NOTHING TO HIM!
RUN, DOC! OR HE'LL KILL YOU TOO!!
HA HA...
YOU'RE QUITE THE TALKER, JUNKERS.
I DON'T LIKE TALKERS.
S-STOP !!

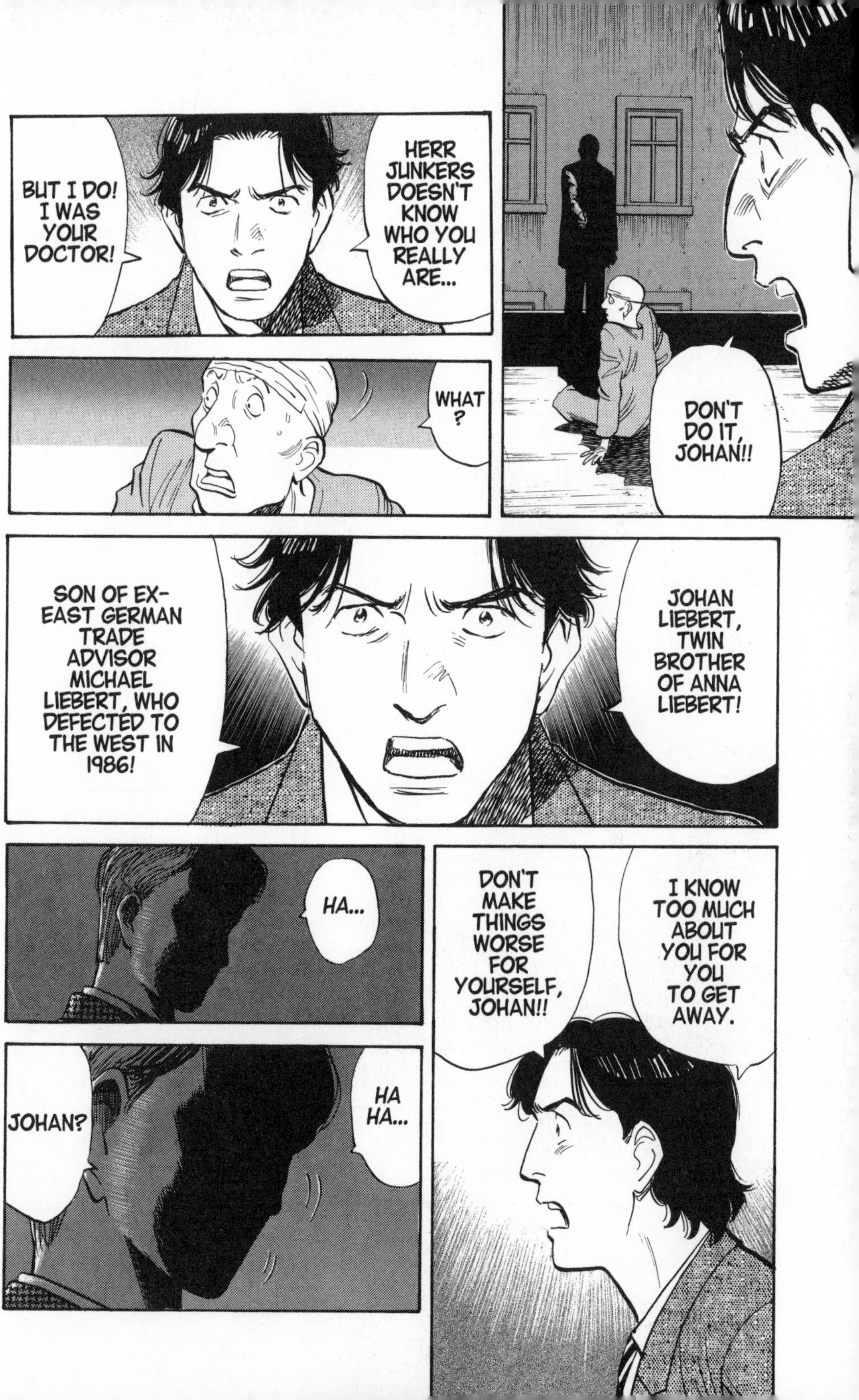
DON'T DO IT, JOHAN!!
HERR JUNKERS DOESN'T KNOW WHO YOU REALLY ARE...
BUT I DO! I WAS YOUR DOCTOR!
WHAT?
JOHAN LIEBERT, TWIN BROTHER OF ANNA LIEBERT!
SON OF EX-EAST GERMAN TRADE ADVISOR MICHAEL LIEBERT, WHO DEFECTED TO THE WEST IN 1986!
I KNOW TOO MUCH ABOUT YOU FOR YOU TO GET AWAY.
DON'T MAKE THINGS WORSE FOR YOURSELF, JOHAN!!
HA...
HA HA...
JOHAN?

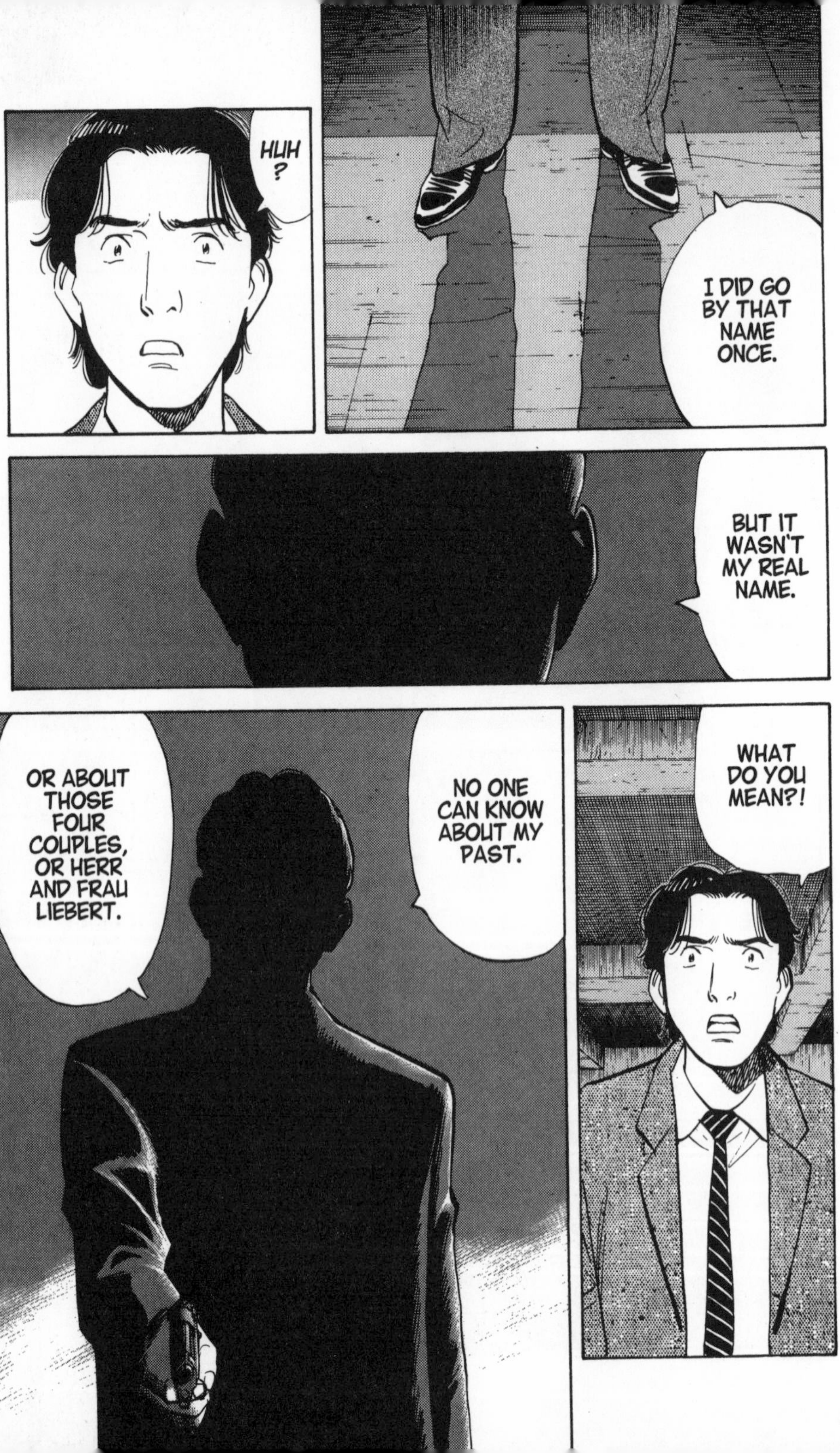
I DID GO BY THAT NAME ONCE.
HUH?
BUT IT WASN'T MY REAL NAME.
WHAT DO YOU MEAN?!
NO ONE CAN KNOW ABOUT MY PAST.
OR ABOUT THOSE FOUR COUPLES, OR HERR AND FRAU LIEBERT.

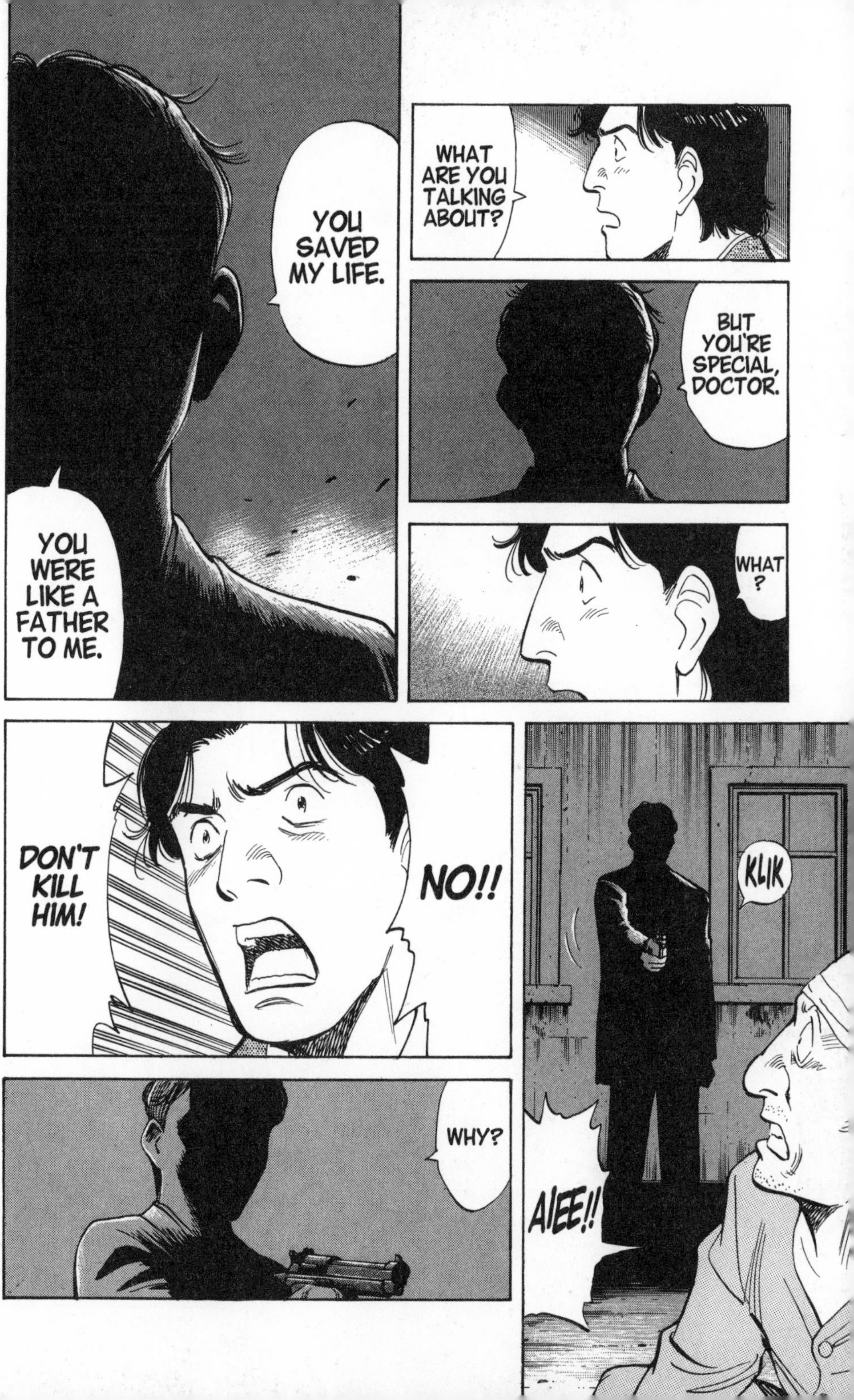

WHAT ARE YOU TALKING ABOUT?
BUT YOU'RE SPECIAL, DOCTOR.
WHAT?
YOU SAVED MY LIFE.
YOU WERE LIKE A FATHER TO ME.
KLIK
AIEE!!
NO!!
DON'T KILL HIM!
WHY?

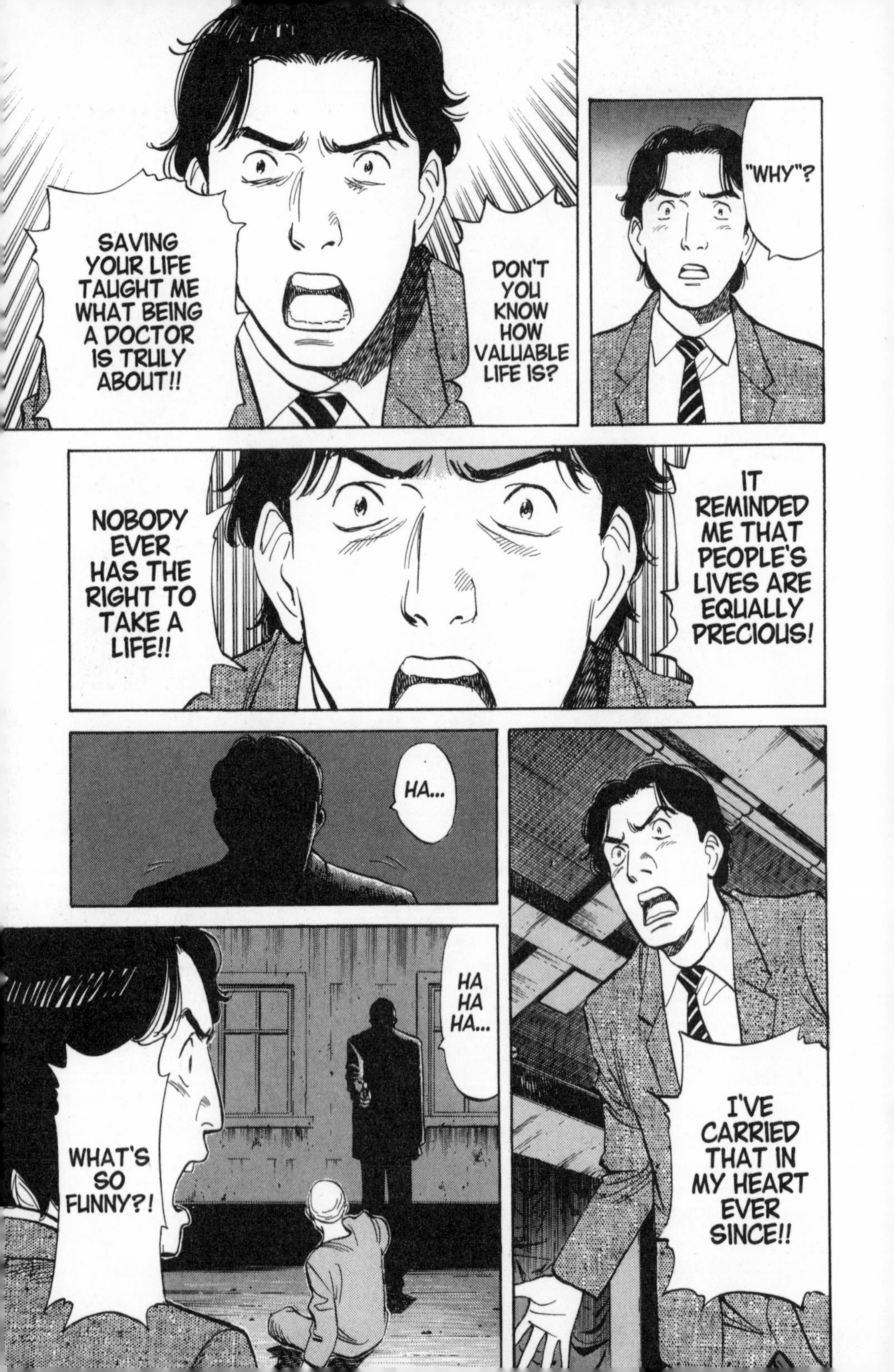
"WHY"?
DON'T YOU KNOW HOW VALUABLE LIFE IS?
SAVING YOUR LIFE TAUGHT ME WHAT BEING A DOCTOR IS TRULY ABOUT!!
IT REMINDED ME THAT PEOPLE'S LIVES ARE EQUALLY PRECIOUS!
NOBODY EVER HAS THE RIGHT TO TAKE A LIFE!!
I'VE CARRIED THAT IN MY HEART EVER SINCE!!
HA...
HA HA HA...
WHAT'S SO FUNNY?!

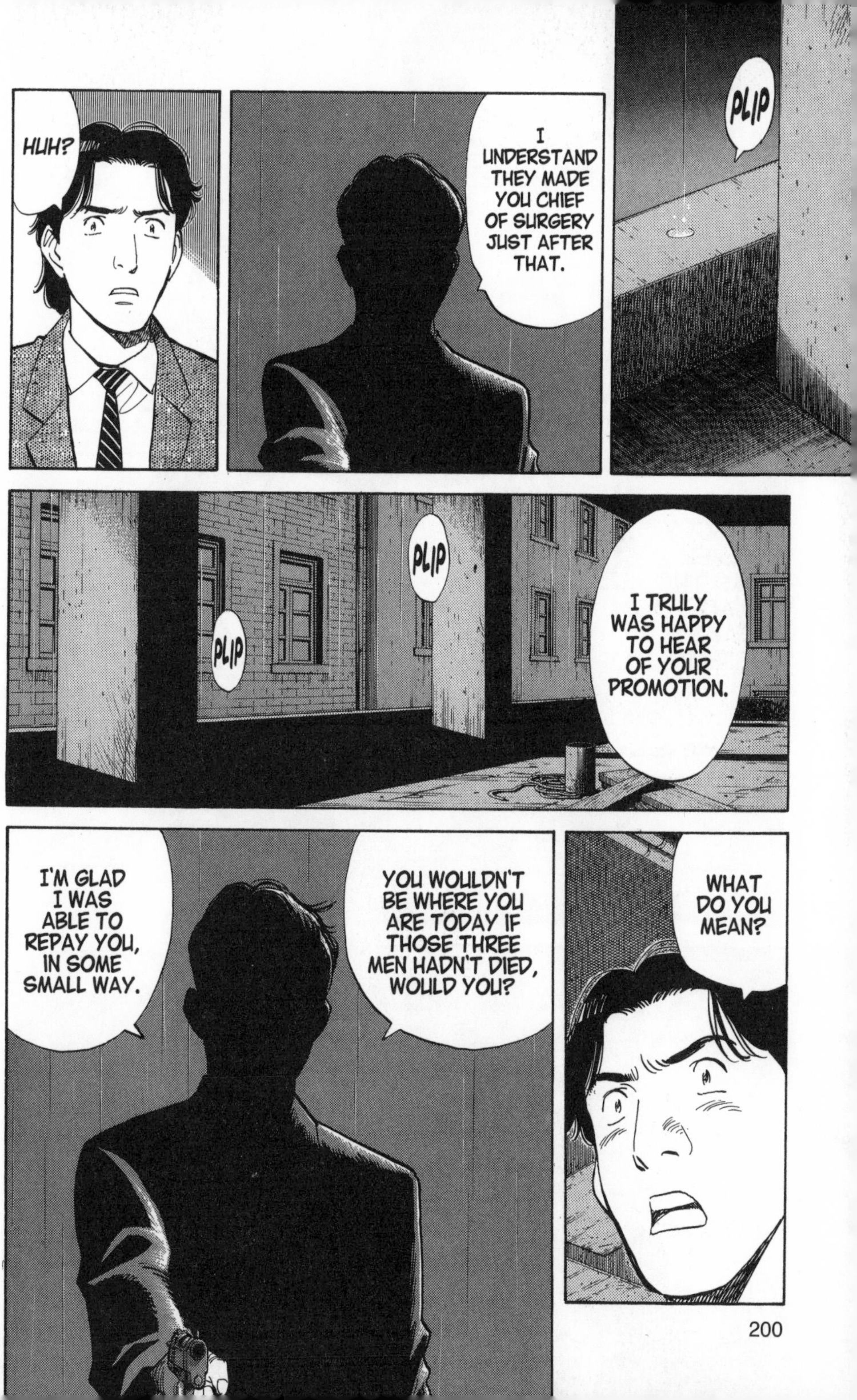
PLIP
I UNDERSTAND THEY MADE YOU CHIEF OF SURGERY JUST AFTER THAT.
HUH?
I TRULY WAS HAPPY TO HEAR OF YOUR PROMOTION.
PLIP
PLIP
WHAT DO YOU MEAN?
YOU WOULDN'T BE WHERE YOU ARE TODAY IF THOSE THREE MEN HADN'T DIED, WOULD YOU?
I'M GLAD I WAS ABLE TO REPAY YOU, IN SOME SMALL WAY.

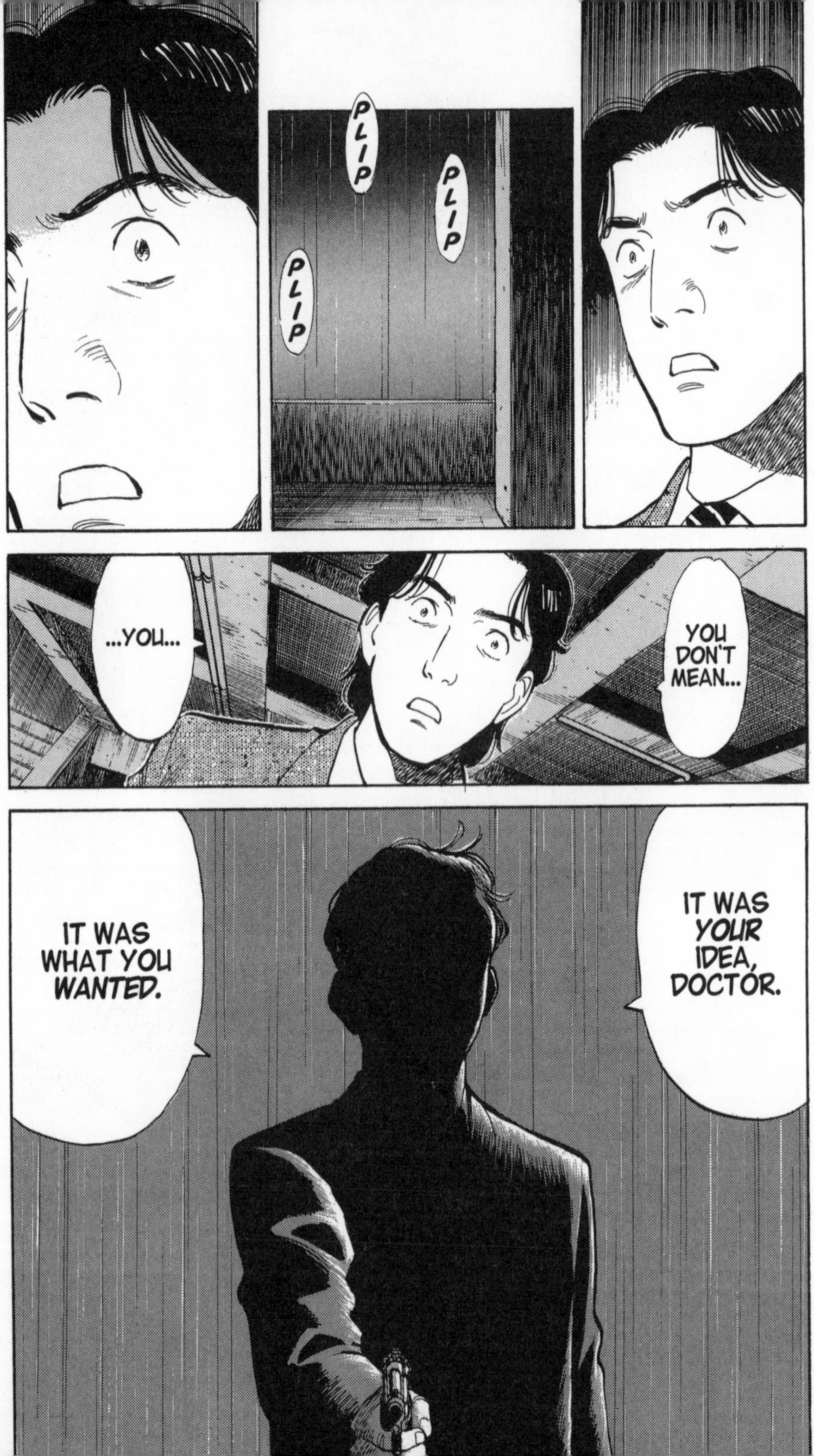
PLIP
PLIP
PLIP
YOU DON'T MEAN...
...YOU...
IT WAS YOUR IDEA, DOCTOR.
IT WAS WHAT YOU WANTED.

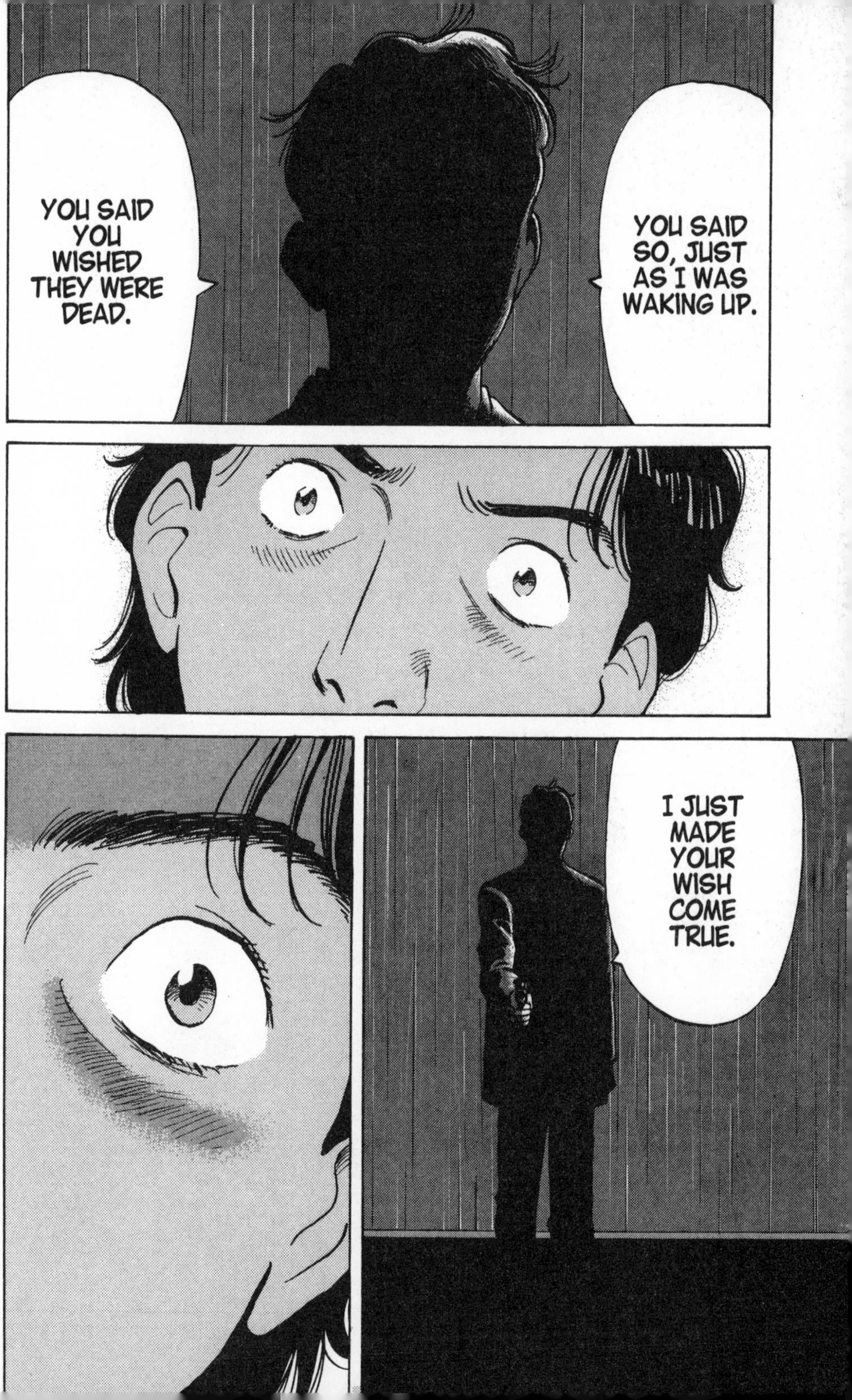
YOU SAID SO, JUST AS I WAS WAKING UP.
YOU SAID YOU WISHED THEY WERE DEAD.
I JUST MADE YOUR WISH COME TRUE.

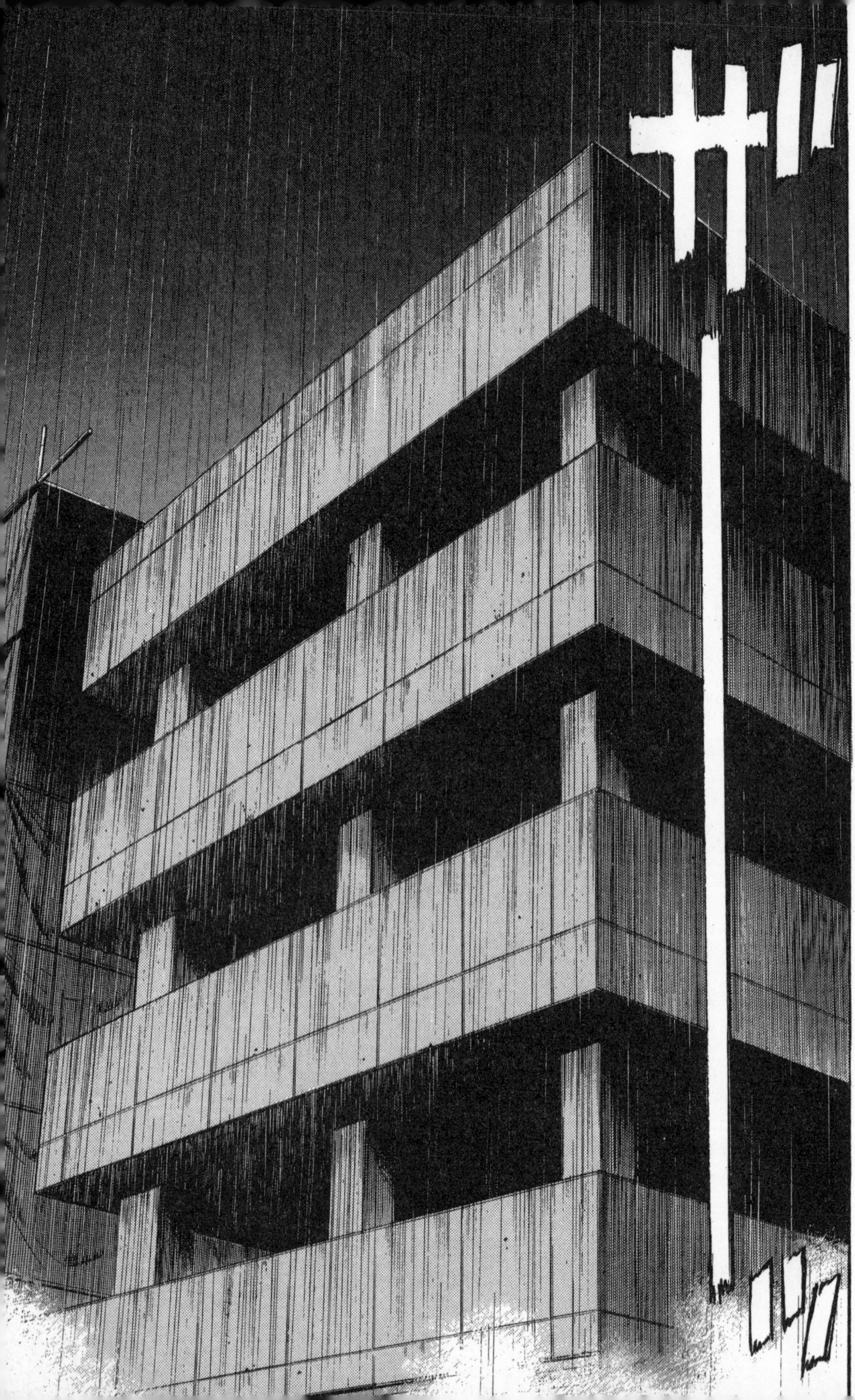
ザーッ

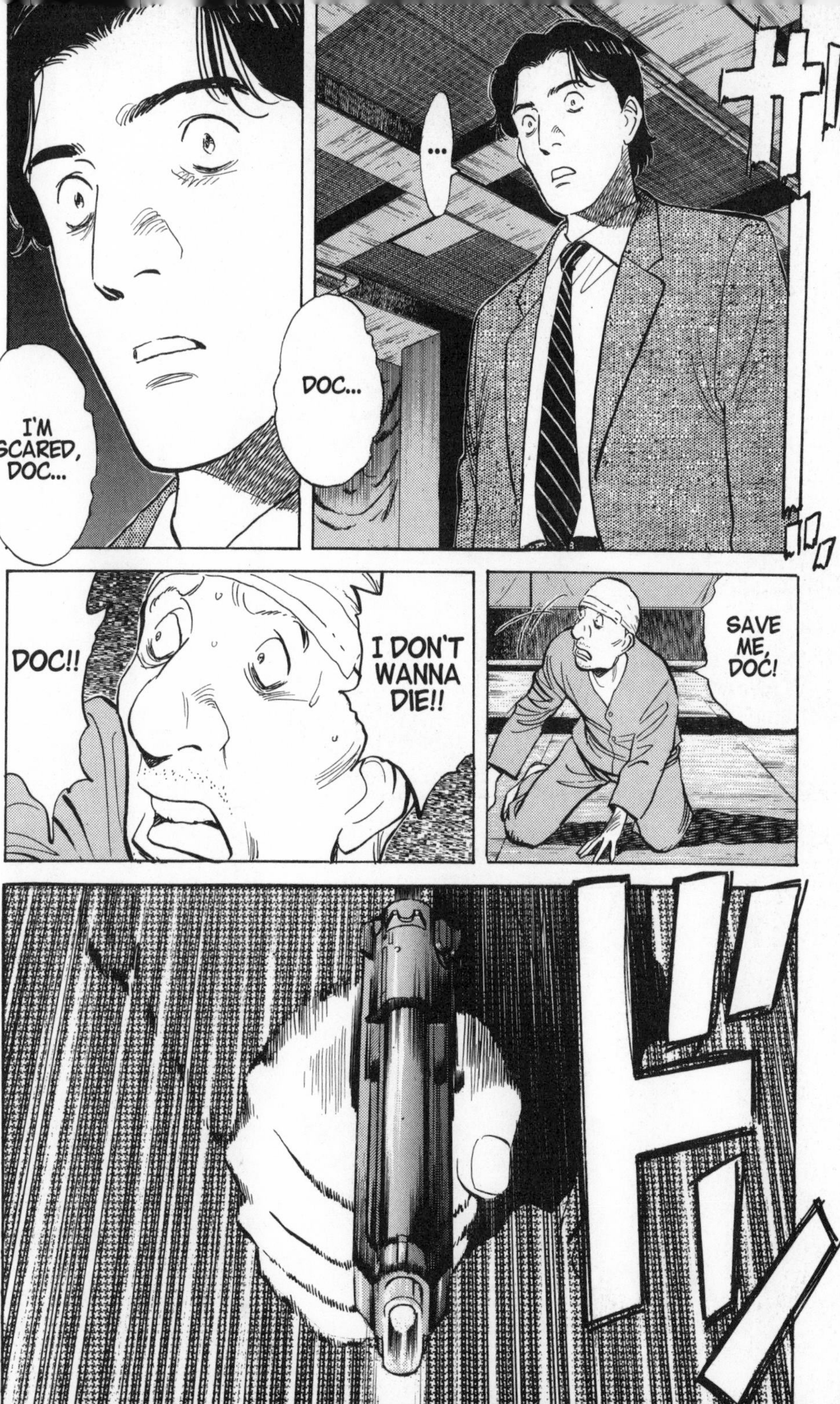
...
DOC...
I'M SCARED, DOC...
SAVE ME, DOC!
I DON'T WANNA DIE!!
DOC!!

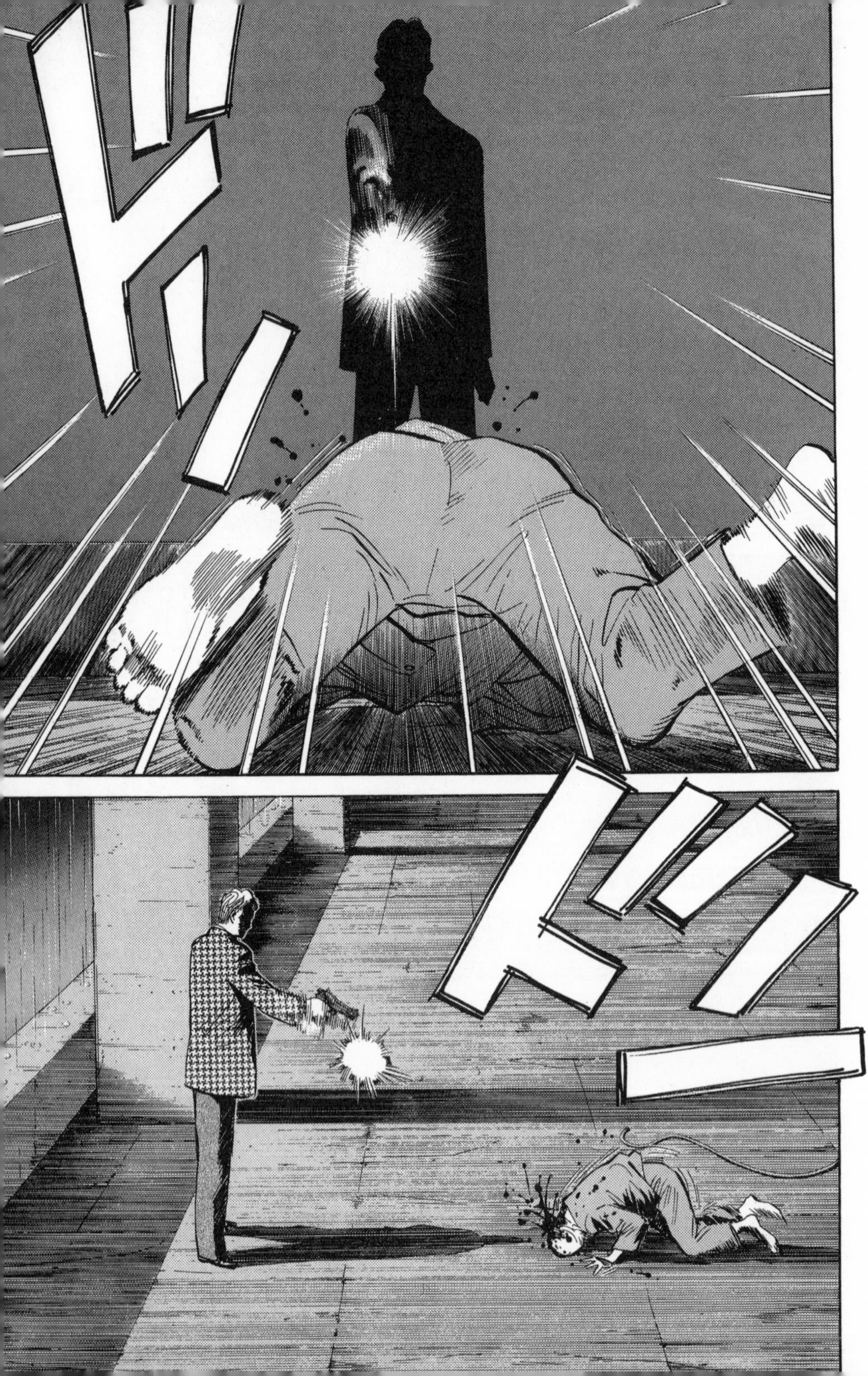
ドン
ドン

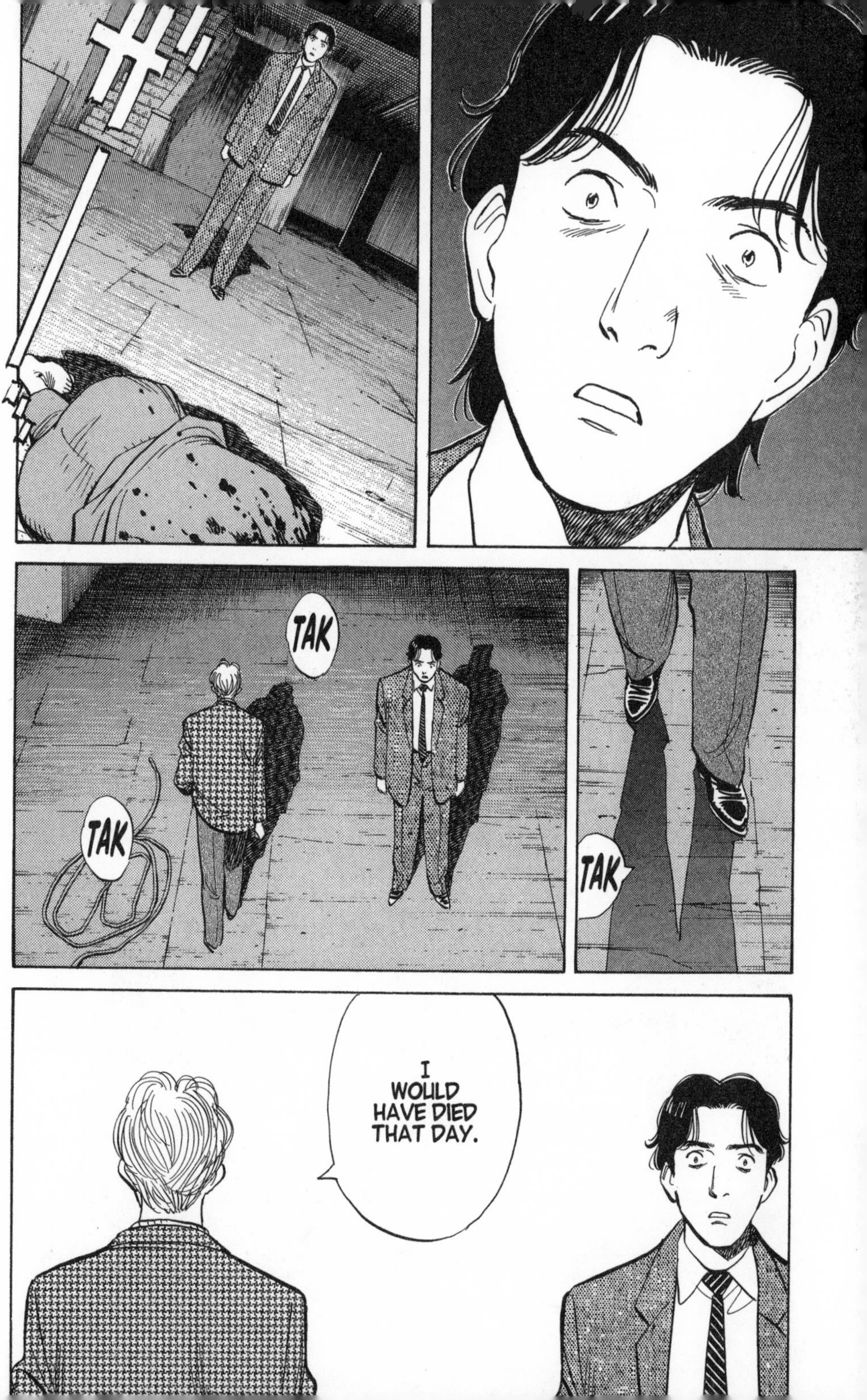
TAK
TAK
TAK
I WOULD HAVE DIED THAT DAY.

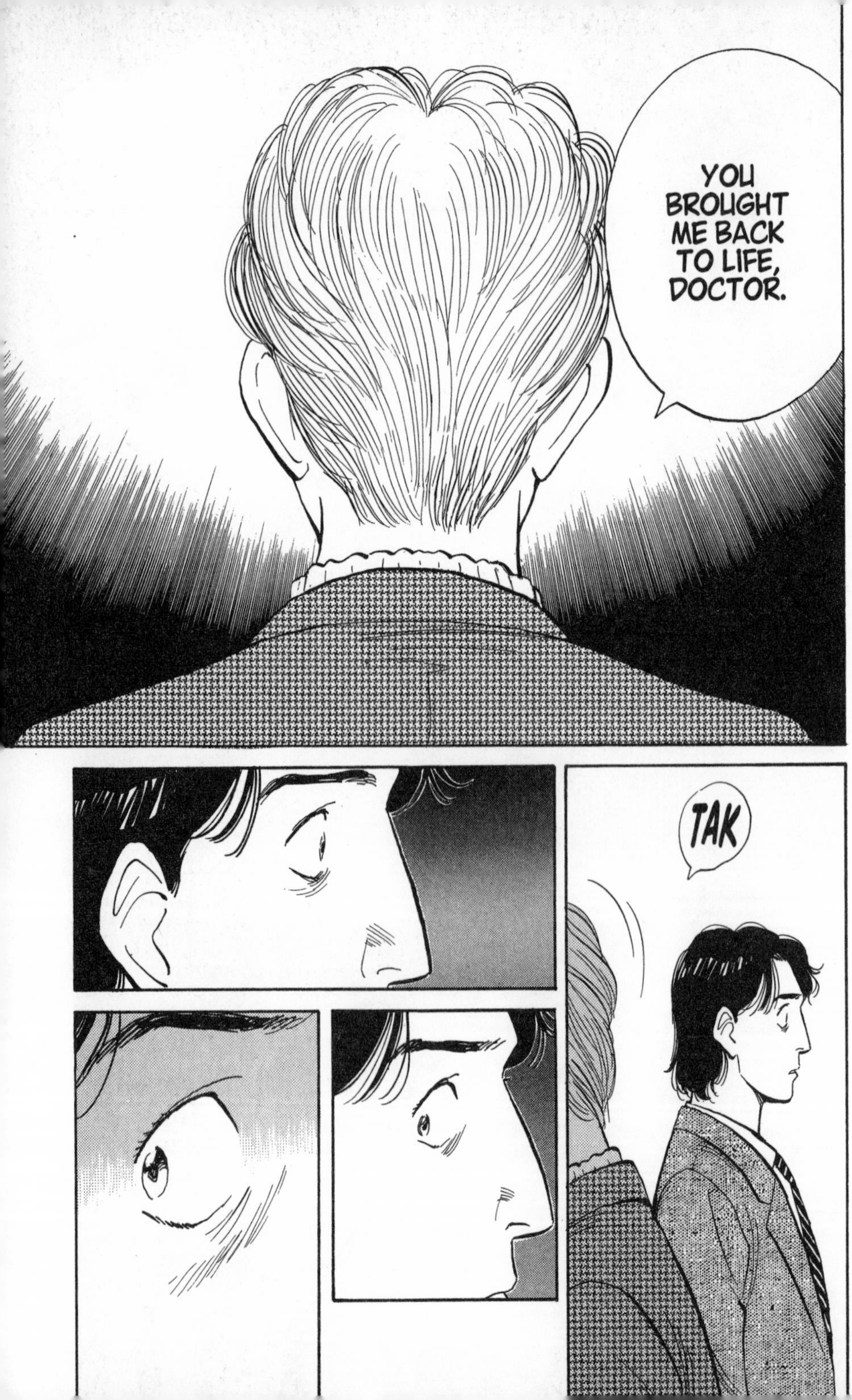
YOU BROUGHT ME BACK TO LIFE, DOCTOR.
TAK

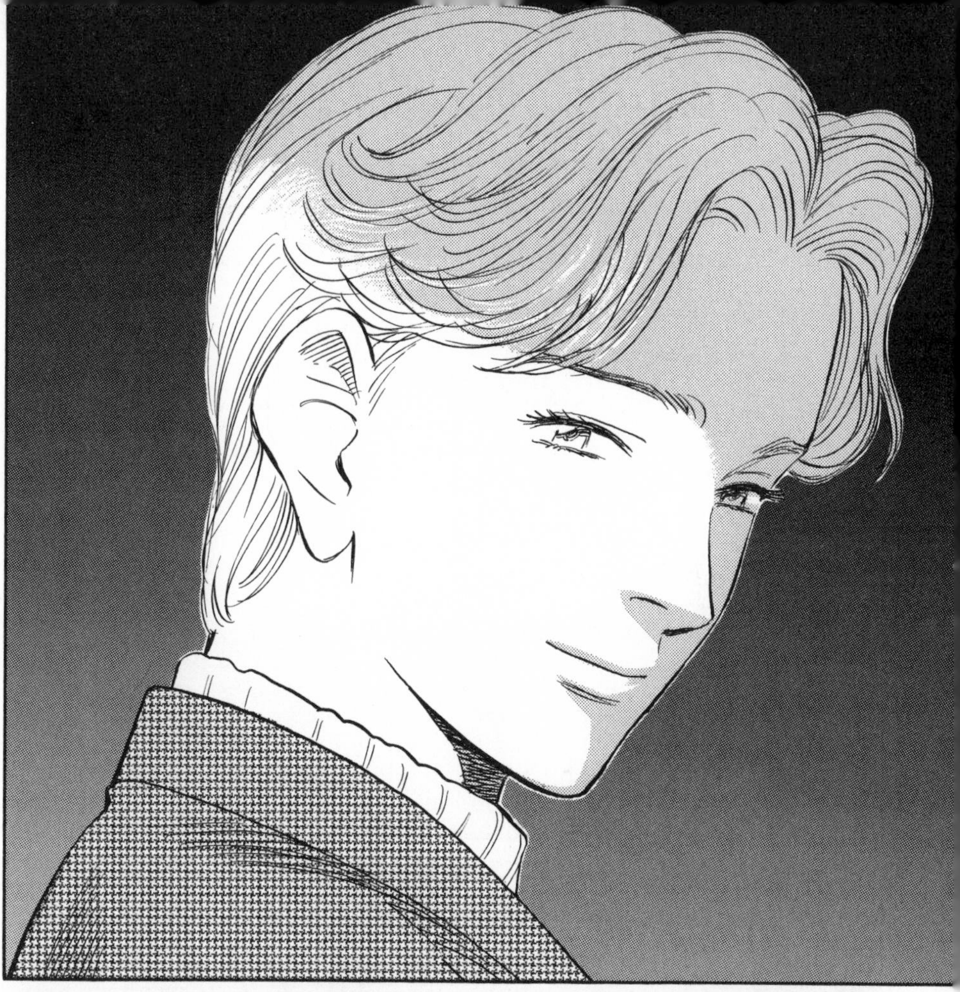
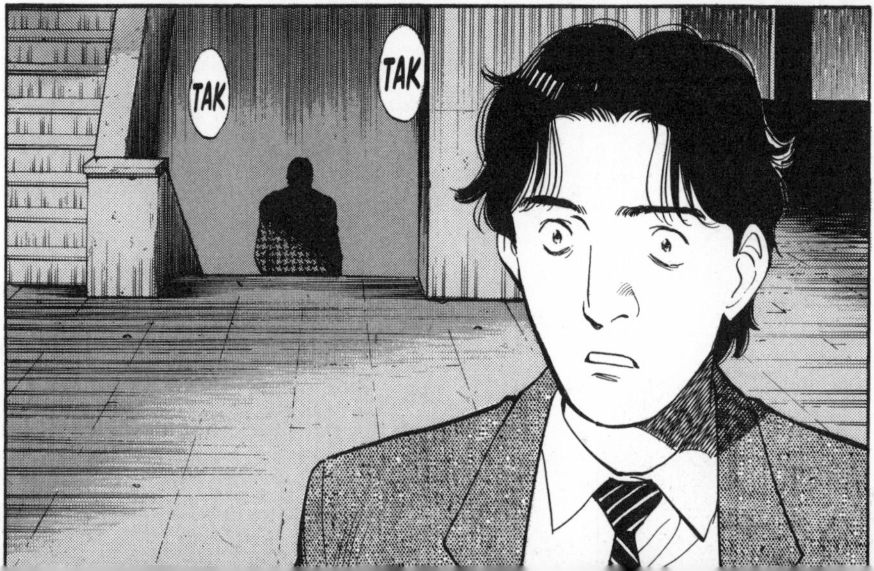
TAK
TAK

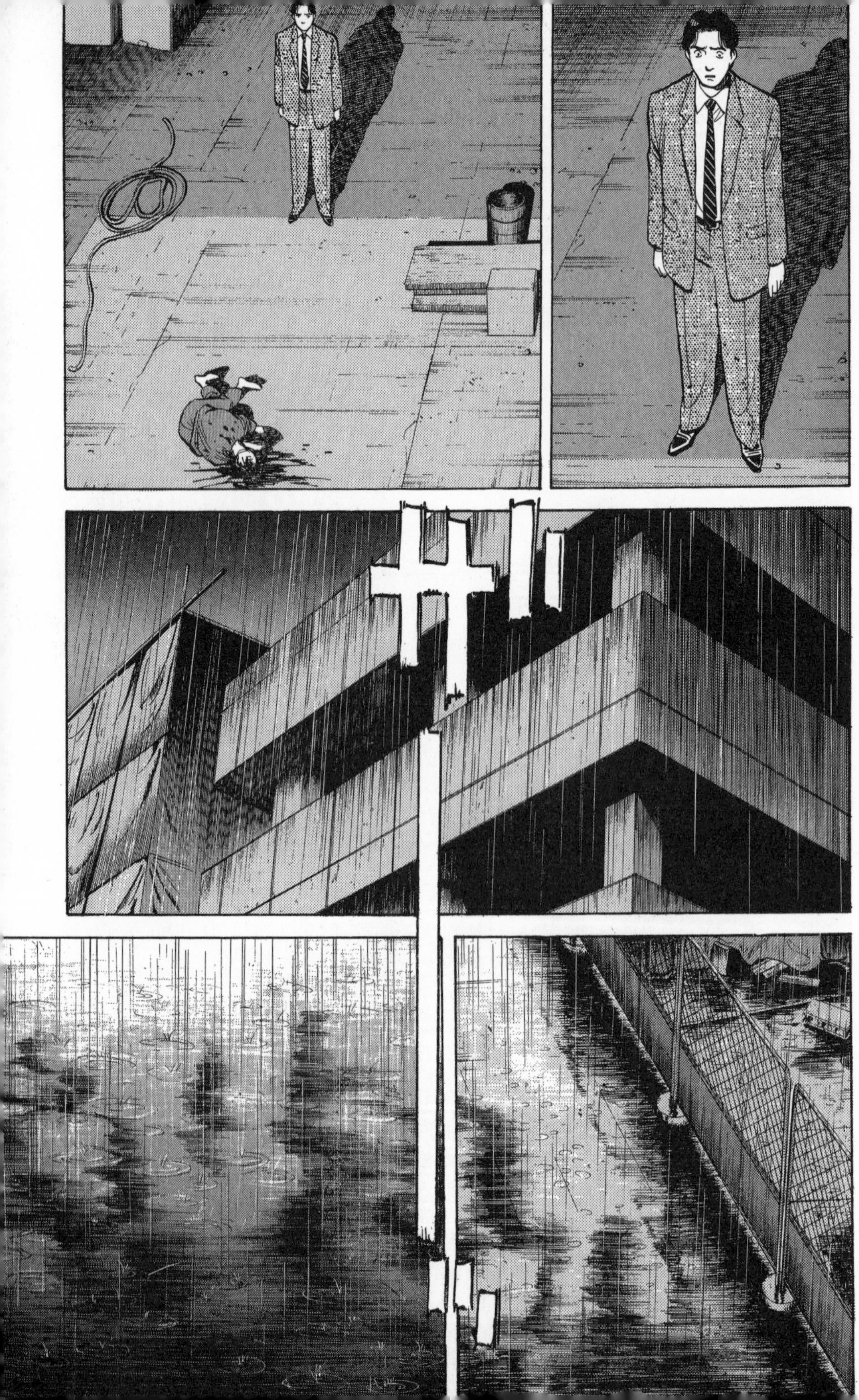
ザー

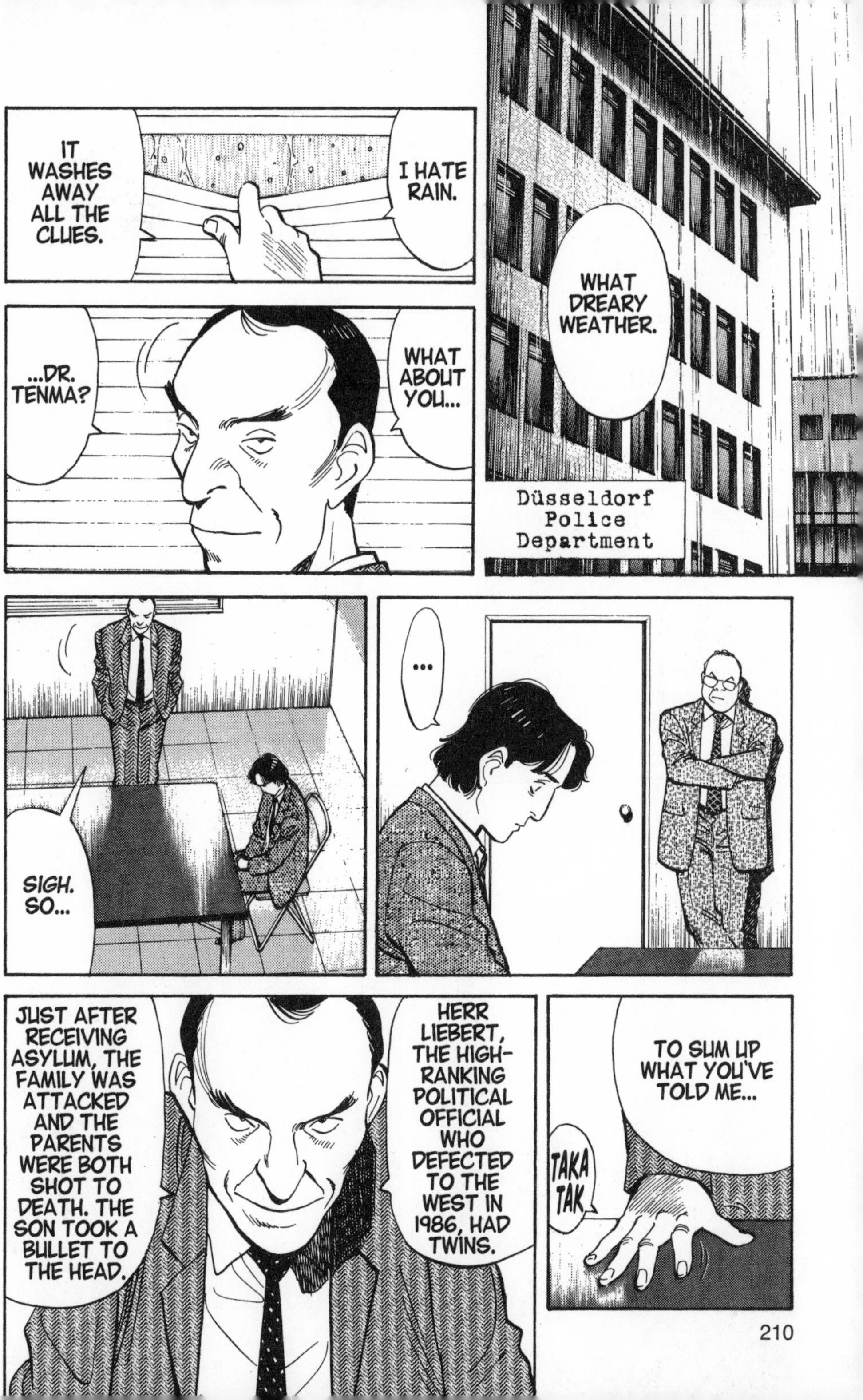
WHAT DREARY WEATHER.
Düsseldorf Police Department
I HATE RAIN.
IT WASHES AWAY ALL THE CLUES.
WHAT ABOUT YOU...
...DR. TENMA?
...
SIGH. SO...
TO SUM UP WHAT YOU'VE TOLD ME...
TAKA TAK
HERR LIEBERT, THE HIGH-RANKING POLITICAL OFFICIAL WHO DEFECTED TO THE WEST IN 1986, HAD TWINS.
JUST AFTER RECEIVING ASYLUM, THE FAMILY WAS ATTACKED AND THE PARENTS WERE BOTH SHOT TO DEATH. THE SON TOOK A BULLET TO THE HEAD.

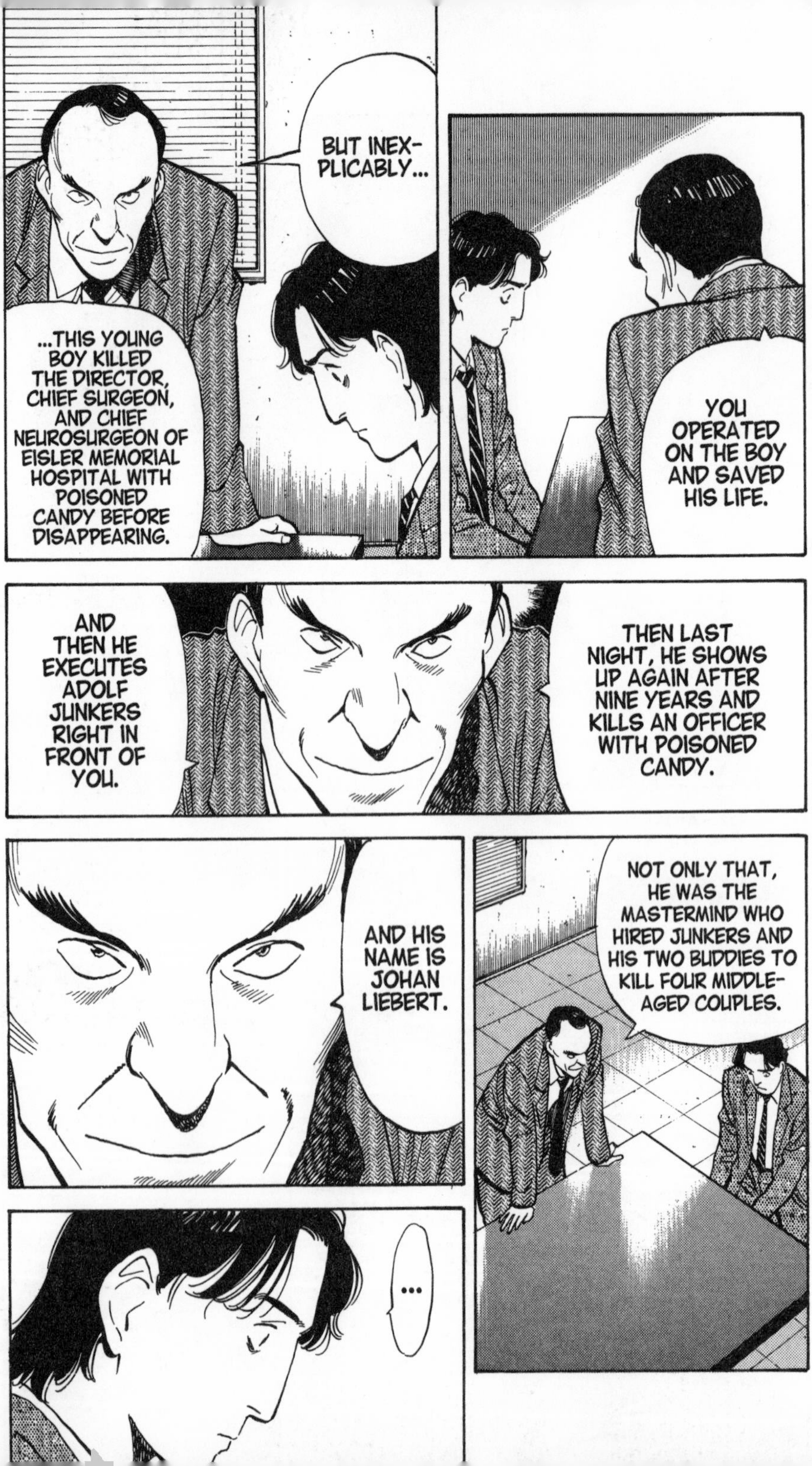
YOU OPERATED ON THE BOY AND SAVED HIS LIFE.
BUT INEX-PLICABLY...
...THIS YOUNG BOY KILLED THE DIRECTOR, CHIEF SURGEON, AND CHIEF NEUROSURGEON OF EISLER MEMORIAL HOSPITAL WITH POISONED CANDY BEFORE DISAPPEARING.
THEN LAST NIGHT, HE SHOWS UP AGAIN AFTER NINE YEARS AND KILLS AN OFFICER WITH POISONED CANDY.
AND THEN HE EXECUTES ADOLF JUNKERS RIGHT IN FRONT OF YOU.
NOT ONLY THAT, HE WAS THE MASTERMIND WHO HIRED JUNKERS AND HIS TWO BUDDIES TO KILL FOUR MIDDLE-AGED COUPLES.
AND HIS NAME IS JOHAN LIEBERT.
...

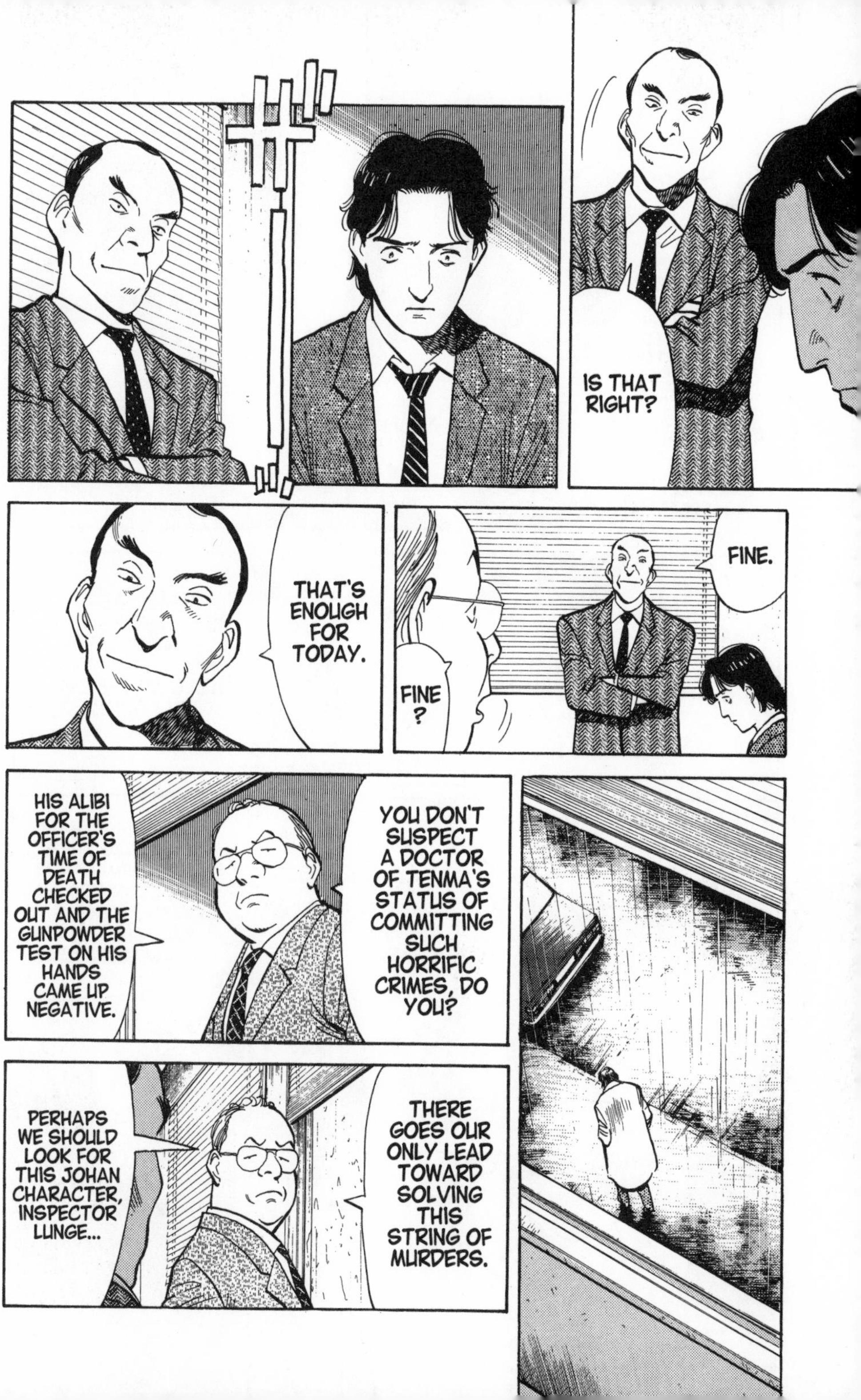
IS THAT RIGHT?
FINE.
FINE ?
THAT'S ENOUGH FOR TODAY.
YOU DON'T SUSPECT A DOCTOR OF TENMA'S STATUS OF COMMITTING SUCH HORRIFIC CRIMES, DO YOU?
HIS ALIBI FOR THE OFFICER'S TIME OF DEATH CHECKED OUT AND THE GUNPOWDER TEST ON HIS HANDS CAME UP NEGATIVE.
THERE GOES OUR ONLY LEAD TOWARD SOLVING THIS STRING OF MURDERS.
PERHAPS WE SHOULD LOOK FOR THIS JOHAN CHARACTER, INSPECTOR LUNGE...

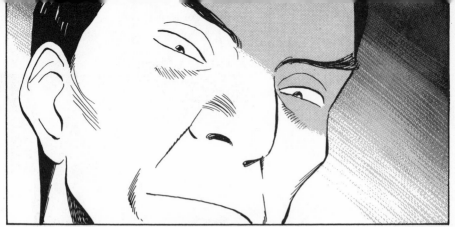

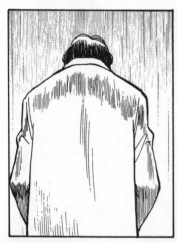

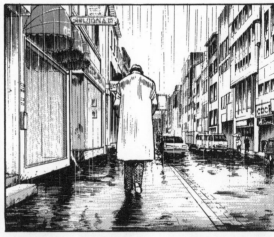

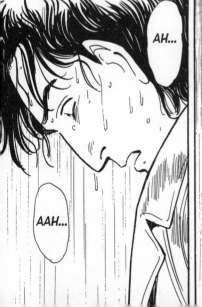

AH...

AAH...

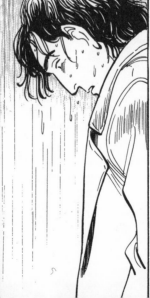

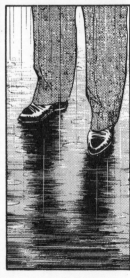

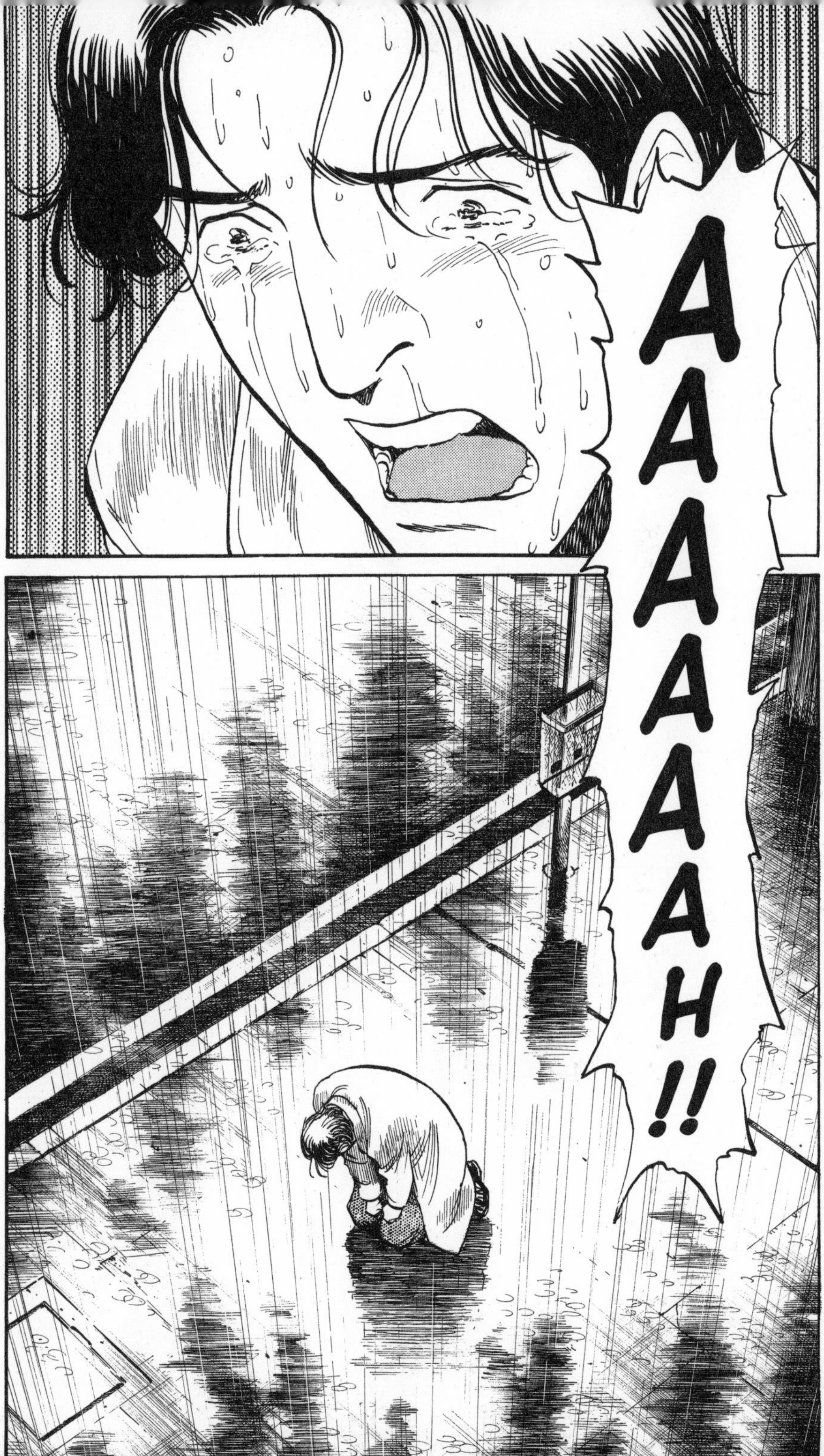
AAAAAAH!!

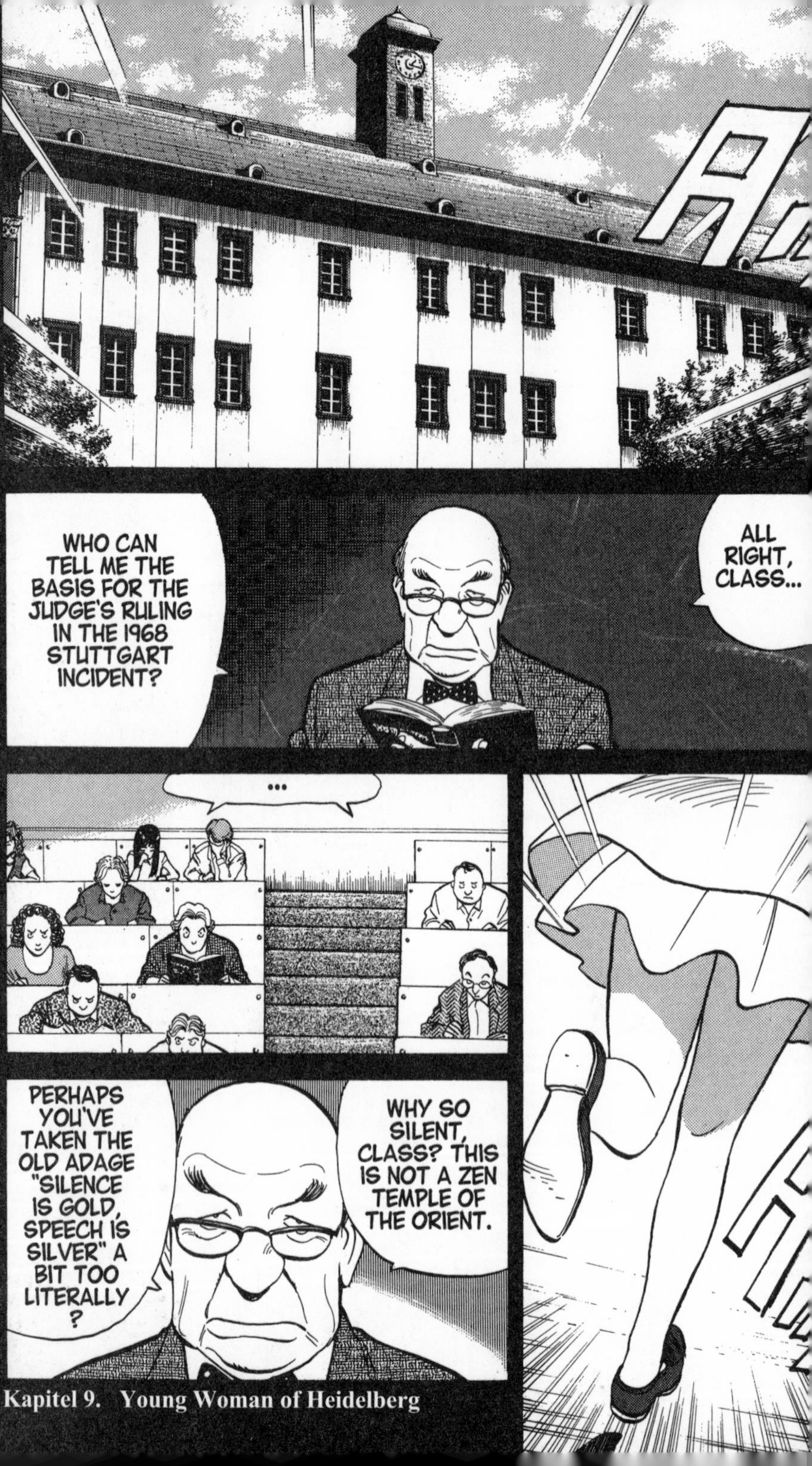
ALL RIGHT, CLASS...
WHO CAN TELL ME THE BASIS FOR THE JUDGE'S RULING IN THE 1968 STUTTGART INCIDENT?
...
WHY SO SILENT, CLASS? THIS IS NOT A ZEN TEMPLE OF THE ORIENT.
PERHAPS YOU'VE TAKEN THE OLD ADAGE "SILENCE IS GOLD, SPEECH IS SILVER" A BIT TOO LITERALLY?

Kapitel 9. Young Woman of Heidelberg

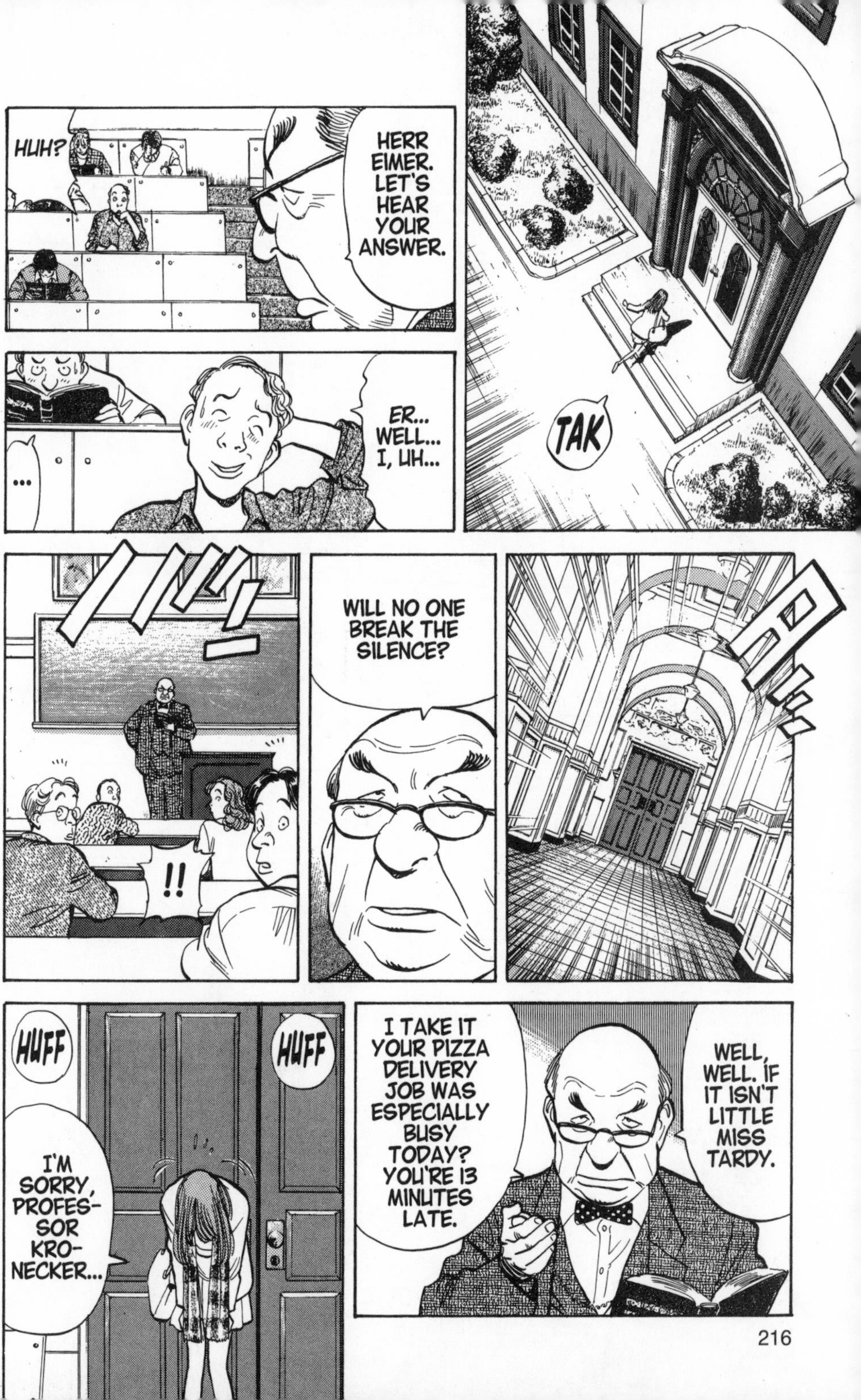
TAK
HERR EIMER. LET'S HEAR YOUR ANSWER.
HUH?
ER... WELL... I, UH...
...
WILL NO ONE BREAK THE SILENCE?
!!
WELL, WELL. IF IT ISN'T LITTLE MISS TARDY.
I TAKE IT YOUR PIZZA DELIVERY JOB WAS ESPECIALLY BUSY TODAY? YOU'RE 13 MINUTES LATE.
HUFF
HUFF
I'M SORRY, PROFES-SOR KRO-NECKER...

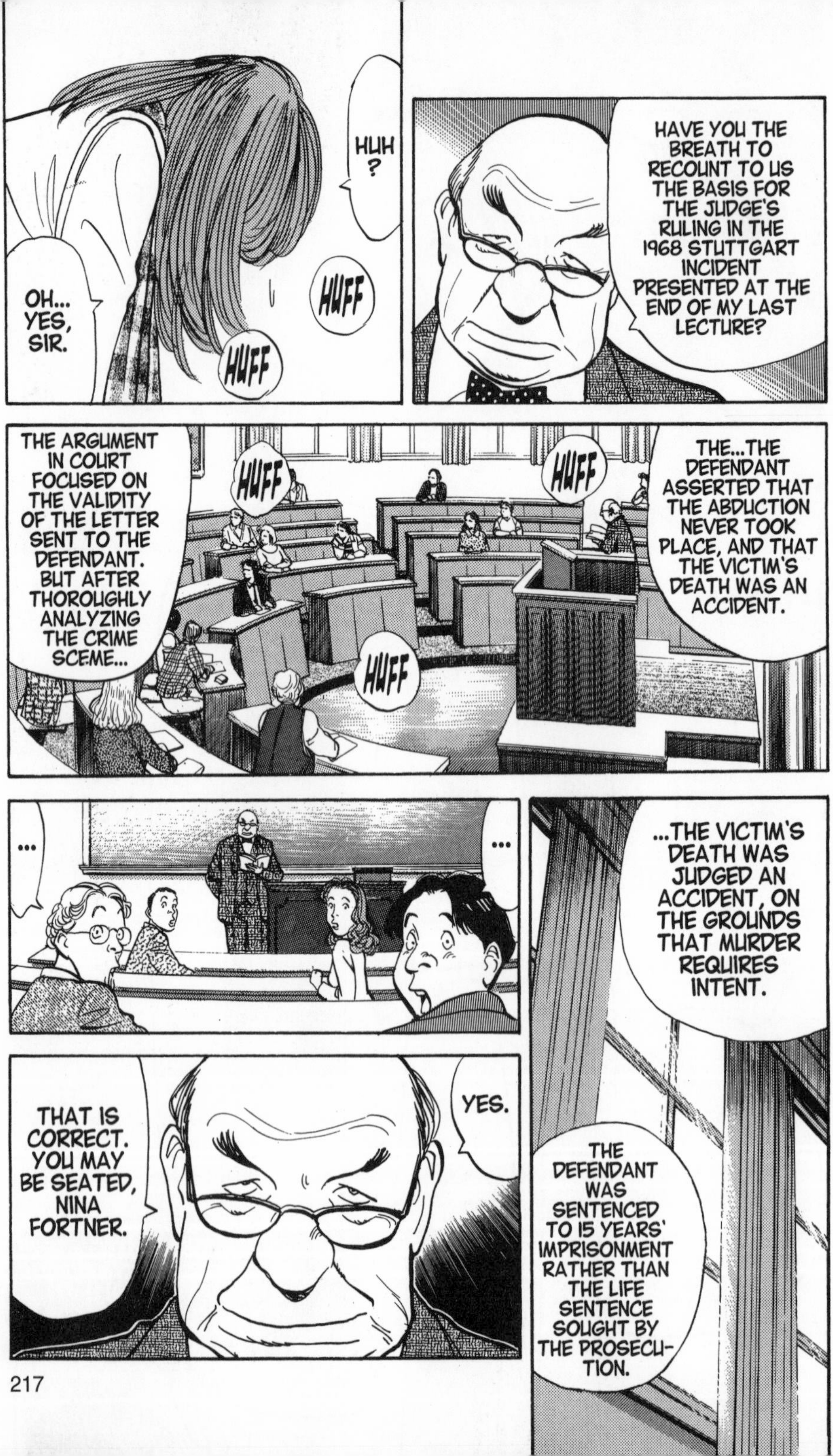
HAVE YOU THE BREATH TO RECOUNT TO US THE BASIS FOR THE JUDGE'S RULING IN THE 1968 STUTTGART INCIDENT PRESENTED AT THE END OF MY LAST LECTURE?
HUH?
HUFF
OH... YES, SIR.
HUFF
THE...THE DEFENDANT ASSERTED THAT THE ABDUCTION NEVER TOOK PLACE, AND THAT THE VICTIM'S DEATH WAS AN ACCIDENT.
HUFF
HUFF
THE ARGUMENT IN COURT FOCUSED ON THE VALIDITY OF THE LETTER SENT TO THE DEFENDANT. BUT AFTER THOROUGHLY ANALYZING THE CRIME SCEME...
HUFF
...THE VICTIM'S DEATH WAS JUDGED AN ACCIDENT, ON THE GROUNDS THAT MURDER REQUIRES INTENT.
THE DEFENDANT WAS SENTENCED TO 15 YEARS' IMPRISONMENT RATHER THAN THE LIFE SENTENCE SOUGHT BY THE PROSECU- TION.
...
...
YES.
THAT IS CORRECT. YOU MAY BE SEATED, NINA FORTNER.

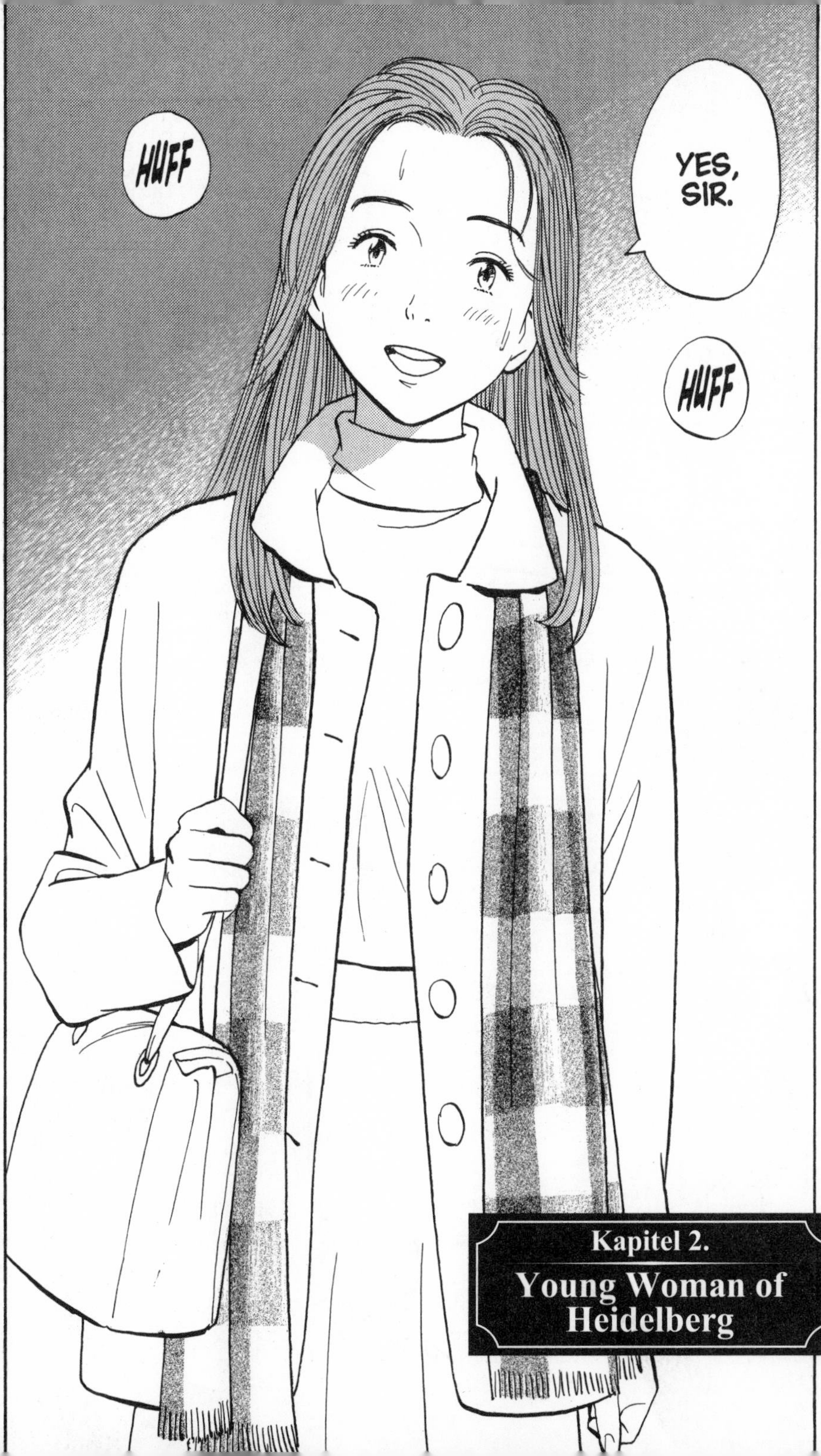
YES, SIR.
HUFF
HUFF
Kapitel 2.
Young Woman of Heidelberg

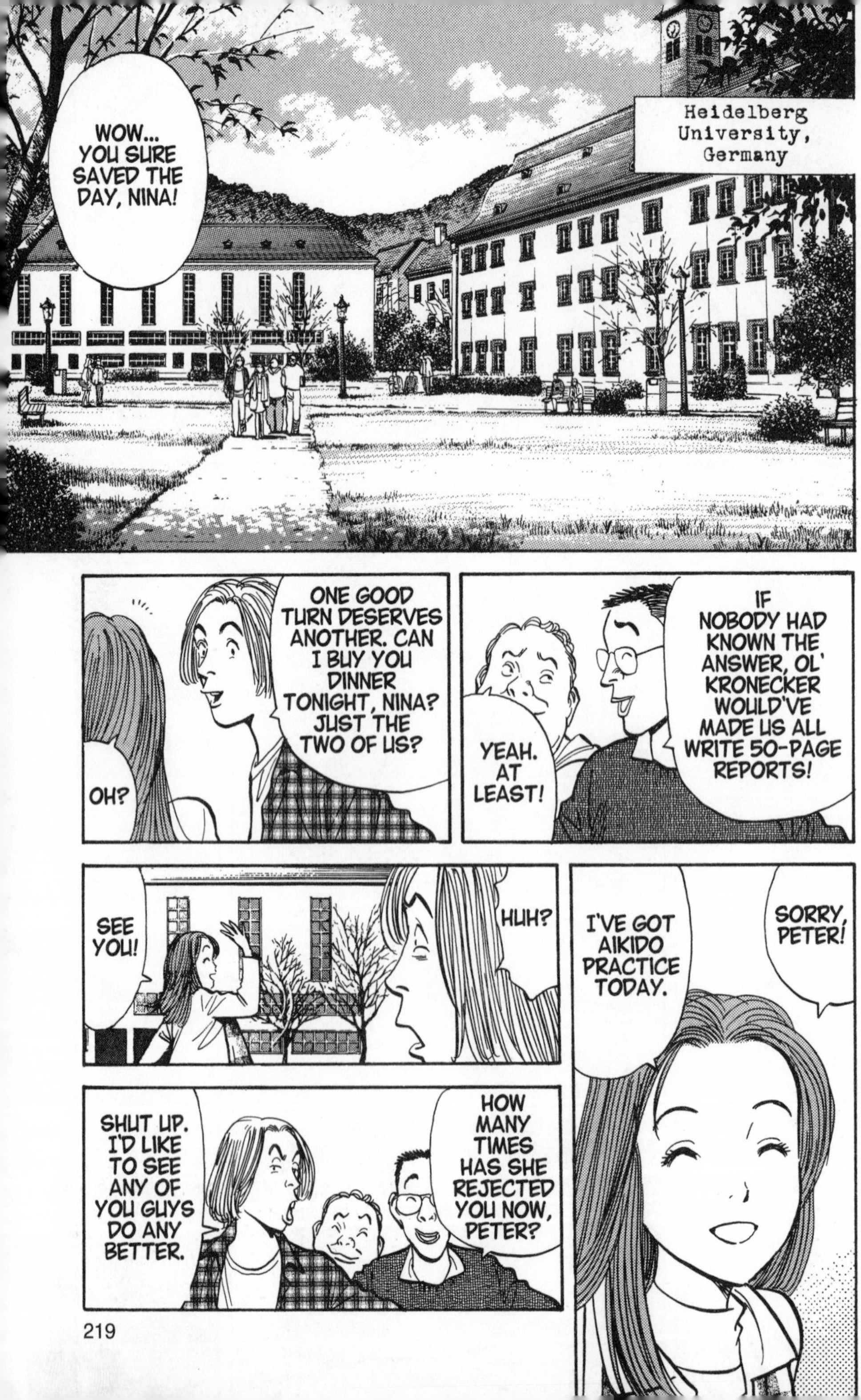

Heidelberg University, Germany
WOW... YOU SURE SAVED THE DAY, NINA!
IF NOBODY HAD KNOWN THE ANSWER, OL' KRONECKER WOULD'VE MADE US ALL WRITE 50-PAGE REPORTS!
YEAH. AT LEAST!
ONE GOOD TURN DESERVES ANOTHER. CAN I BUY YOU DINNER TONIGHT, NINA? JUST THE TWO OF US?
OH?
SORRY, PETER!
I'VE GOT AIKIDO PRACTICE TODAY.
HUH?
SEE YOU!
HOW MANY TIMES HAS SHE REJECTED YOU NOW, PETER?
SHUT UP. I'D LIKE TO SEE ANY OF YOU GUYS DO ANY BETTER.

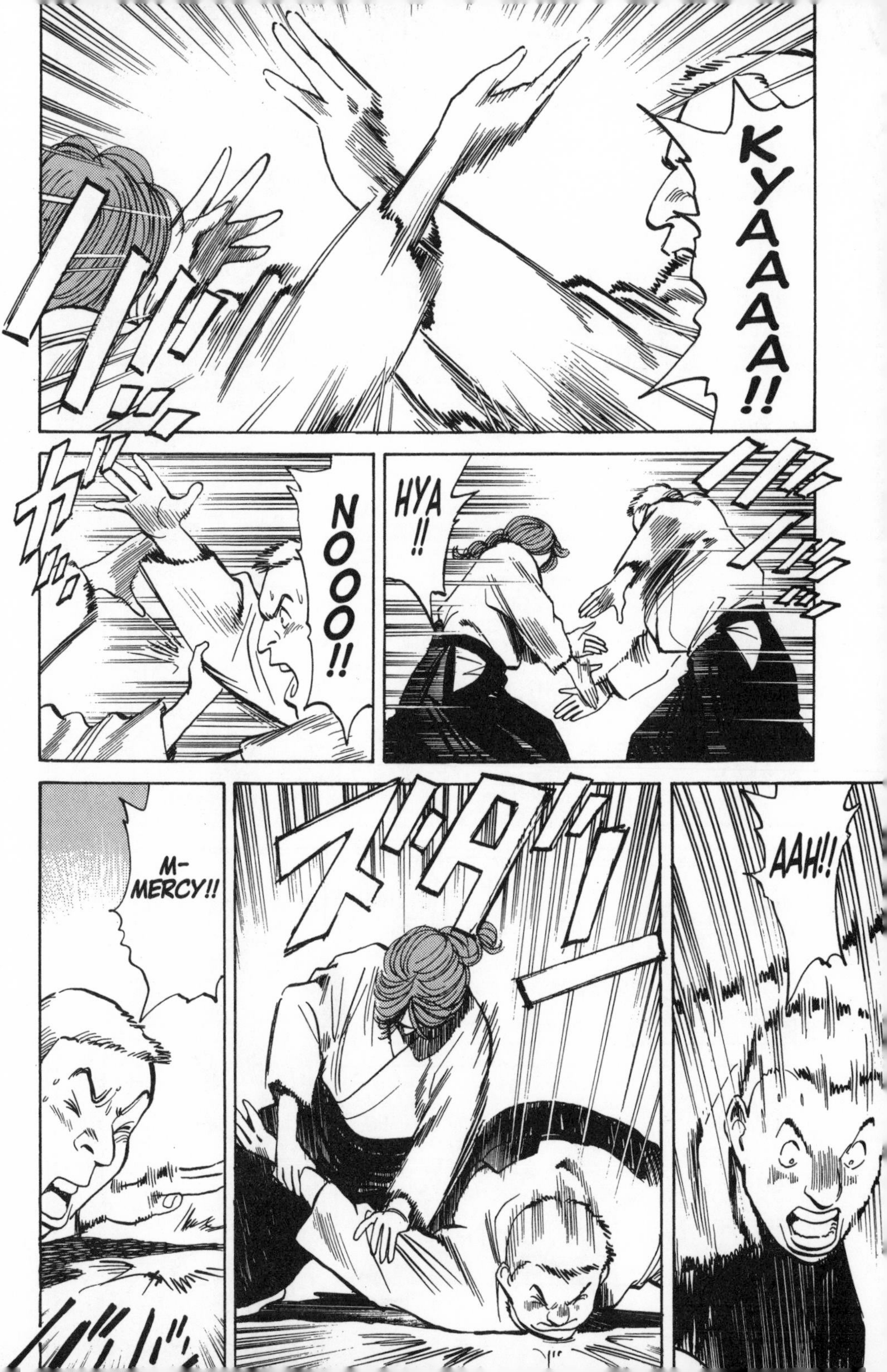
KYAAAA!!
HYA!!
NOOOO!!
AAH!!
M-MERCY!!

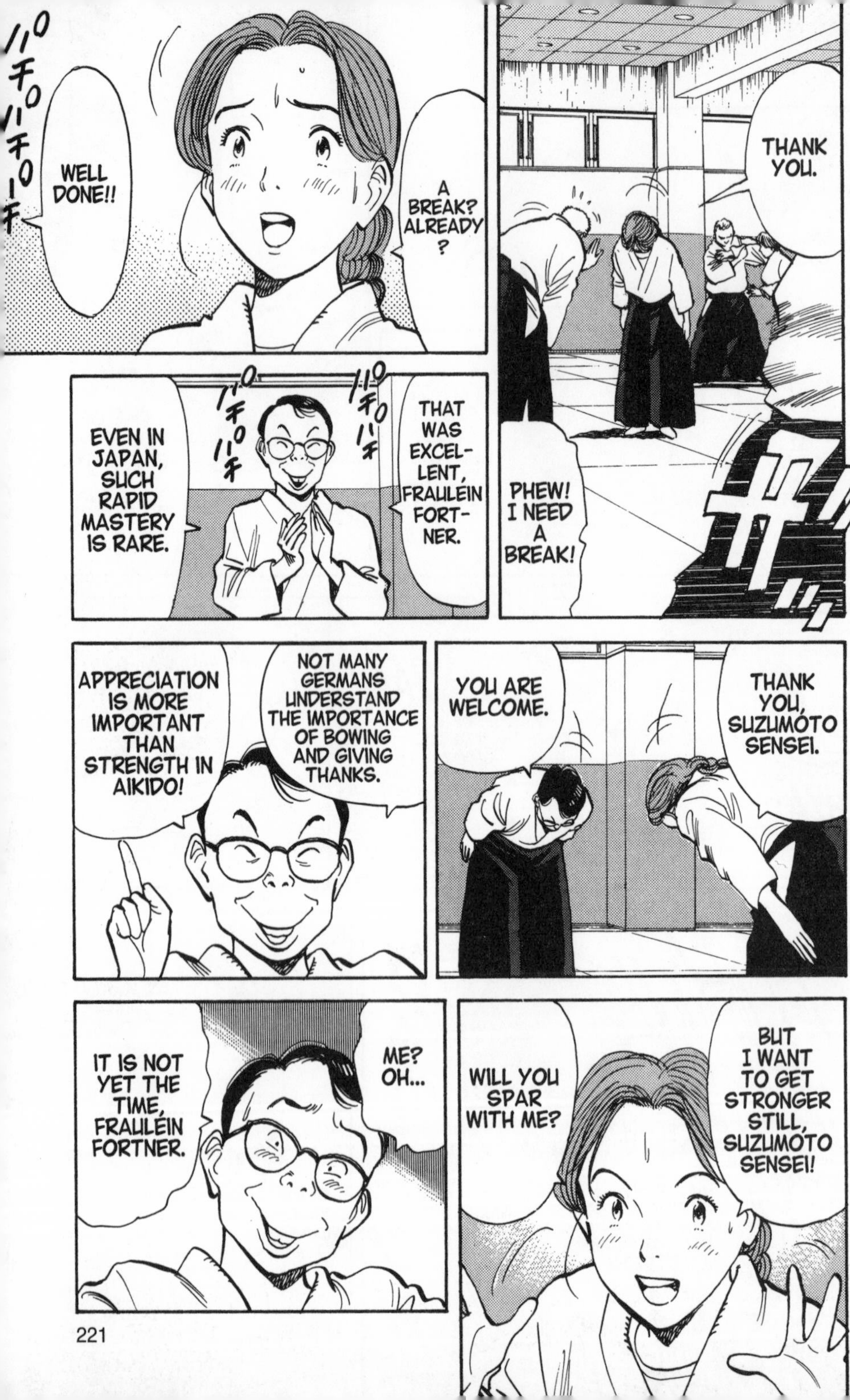
THANK YOU.
PHEW! I NEED A BREAK!
ザッ
A BREAK? ALREADY?
WELL DONE!!
パチパチパチ
THAT WAS EXCELLENT, FRAULEIN FORTNER.
EVEN IN JAPAN, SUCH RAPID MASTERY IS RARE.
パチパチ
THANK YOU, SUZUMOTO SENSEI.
YOU ARE WELCOME.
NOT MANY GERMANS UNDERSTAND THE IMPORTANCE OF BOWING AND GIVING THANKS.
APPRECIATION IS MORE IMPORTANT THAN STRENGTH IN AIKIDO!
BUT I WANT TO GET STRONGER STILL, SUZUMOTO SENSEI!
WILL YOU SPAR WITH ME?
ME? OH...
IT IS NOT YET THE TIME, FRAULEIN FORTNER.

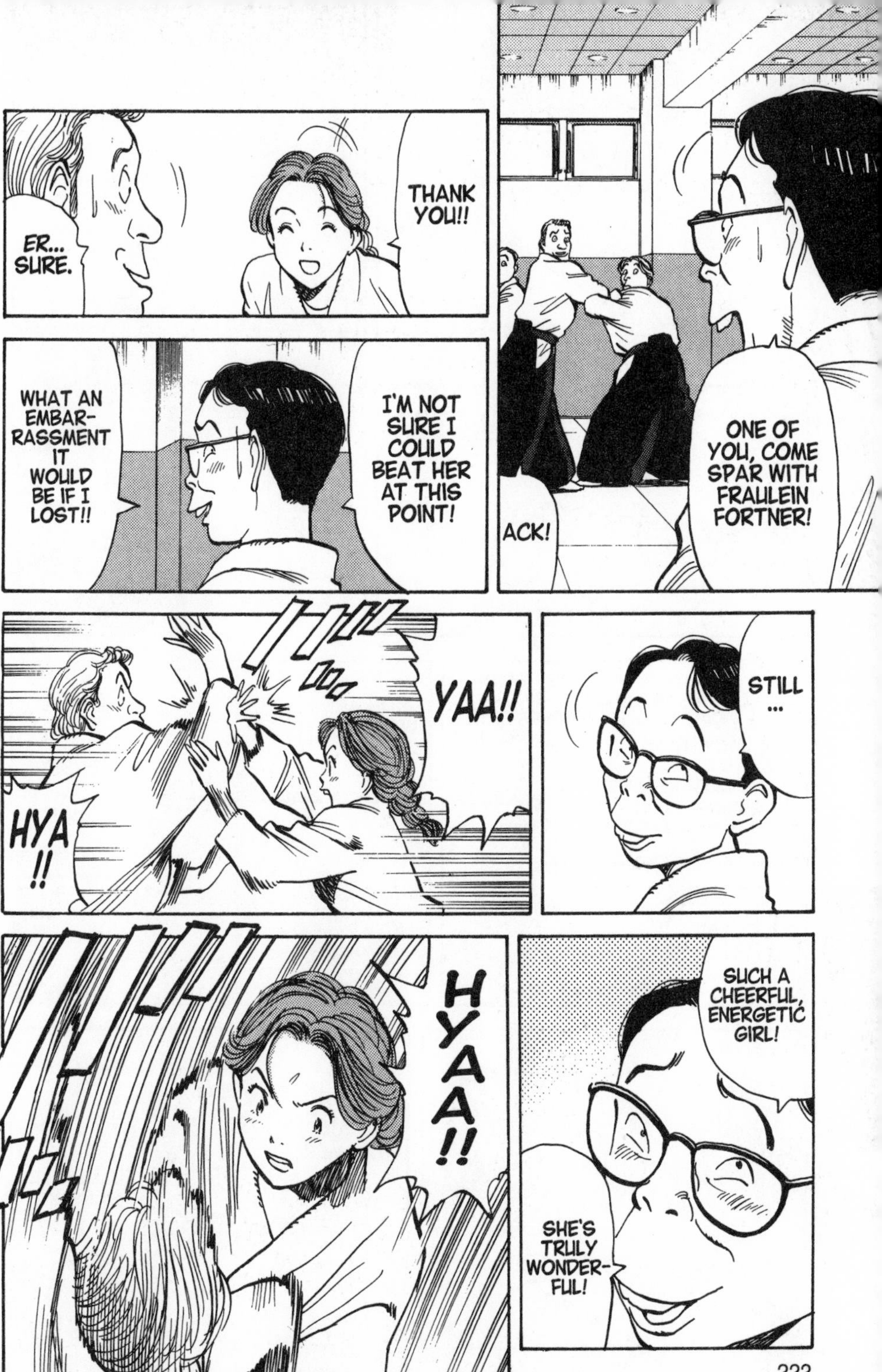
ONE OF YOU, COME SPAR WITH FRAULEIN FORTNER!
ACK!
THANK YOU!!
ER... SURE.
I'M NOT SURE I COULD BEAT HER AT THIS POINT!
WHAT AN EMBAR-RASSMENT IT WOULD BE IF I LOST!!
STILL ...
YAA!!
HYA !!
SUCH A CHEERFUL, ENERGETIC GIRL!
SHE'S TRULY WONDER-FUL!
HYAA!!

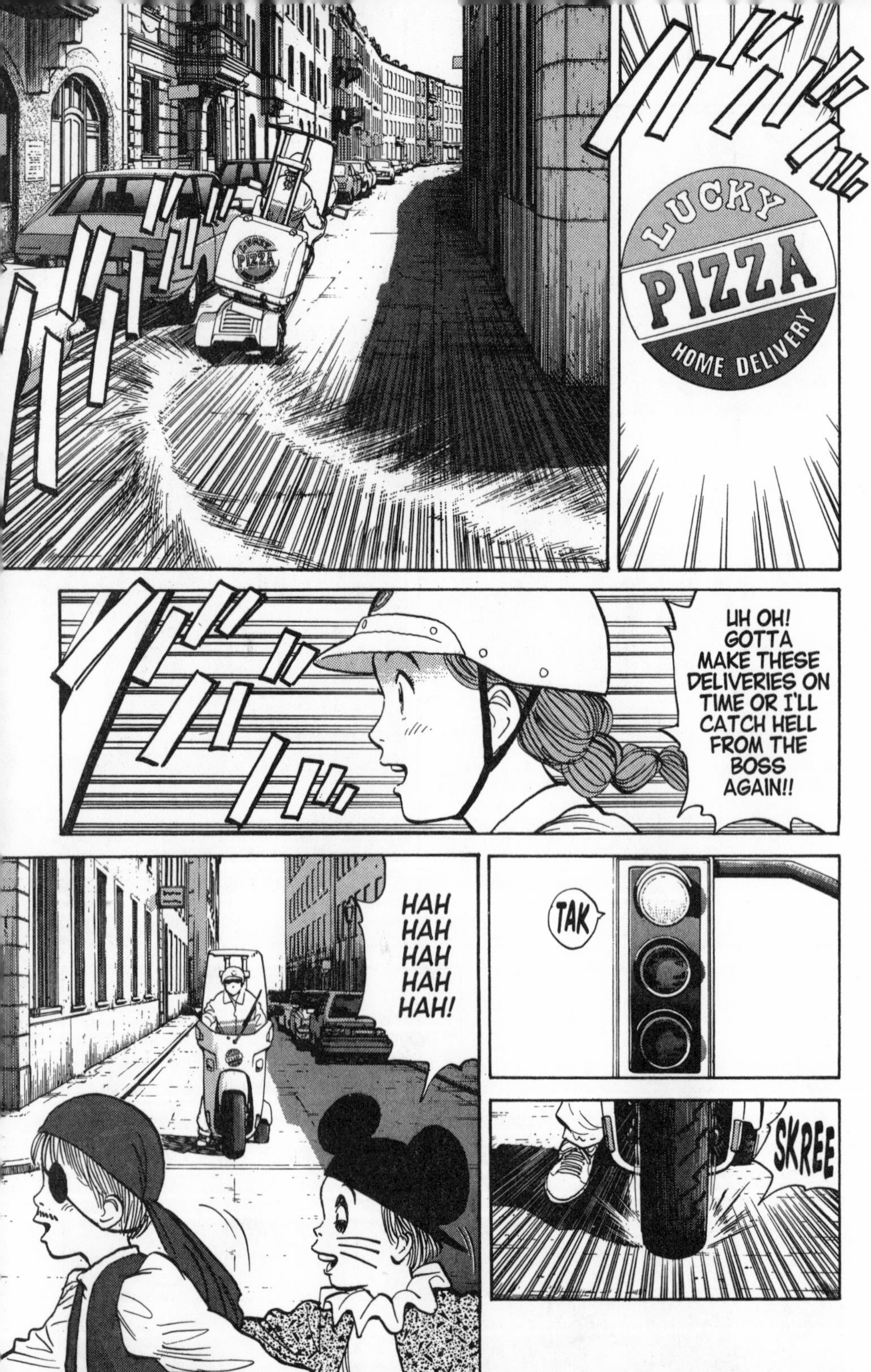
LUCKY
PIZZA
HOME DELIVERY
UH OH! GOTTA MAKE THESE DELIVERIES ON TIME OR I'LL CATCH HELL FROM THE BOSS AGAIN!!
TAK
SKREE
HAH HAH HAH HAH HAH!

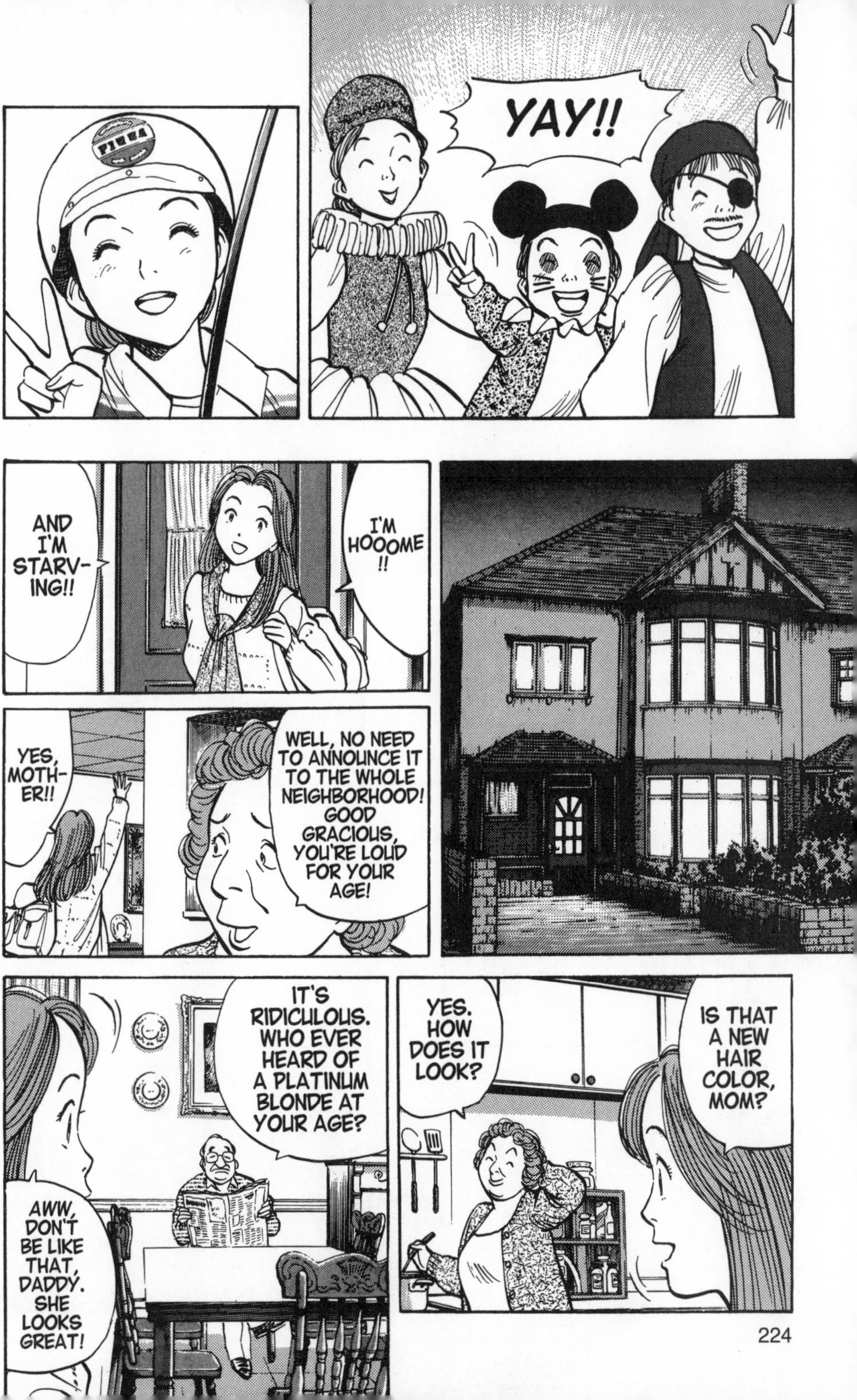
YAY!!
I'M HOOOME!!
AND I'M STARV-ING!!
WELL, NO NEED TO ANNOUNCE IT TO THE WHOLE NEIGHBORHOOD! GOOD GRACIOUS, YOU'RE LOUD FOR YOUR AGE!
YES, MOTH-ER!!
IS THAT A NEW HAIR COLOR, MOM?
YES. HOW DOES IT LOOK?
IT'S RIDICULOUS. WHO EVER HEARD OF A PLATINUM BLONDE AT YOUR AGE?
AWW, DON'T BE LIKE THAT, DADDY. SHE LOOKS GREAT!

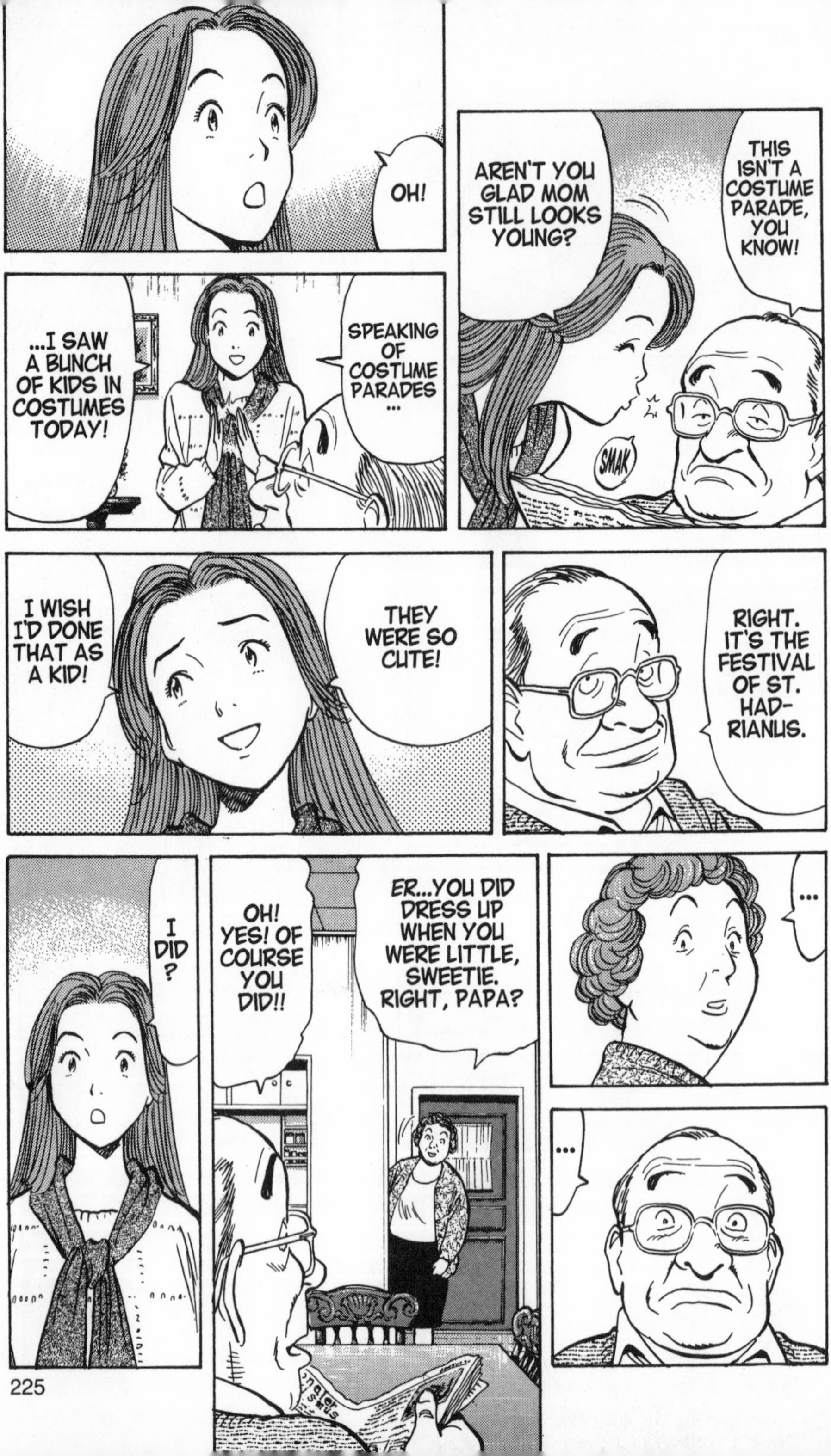
THIS ISN'T A COSTUME PARADE, YOU KNOW!
AREN'T YOU GLAD MOM STILL LOOKS YOUNG?
SMAK
OH!
SPEAKING OF COSTUME PARADES...
...I SAW A BUNCH OF KIDS IN COSTUMES TODAY!
RIGHT. IT'S THE FESTIVAL OF ST. HAD-RIANUS.
THEY WERE SO CUTE!
I WISH I'D DONE THAT AS A KID!
...
...
ER...YOU DID DRESS UP WHEN YOU WERE LITTLE, SWEETIE. RIGHT, PAPA?
OH! YES! OF COURSE YOU DID!!
I DID?

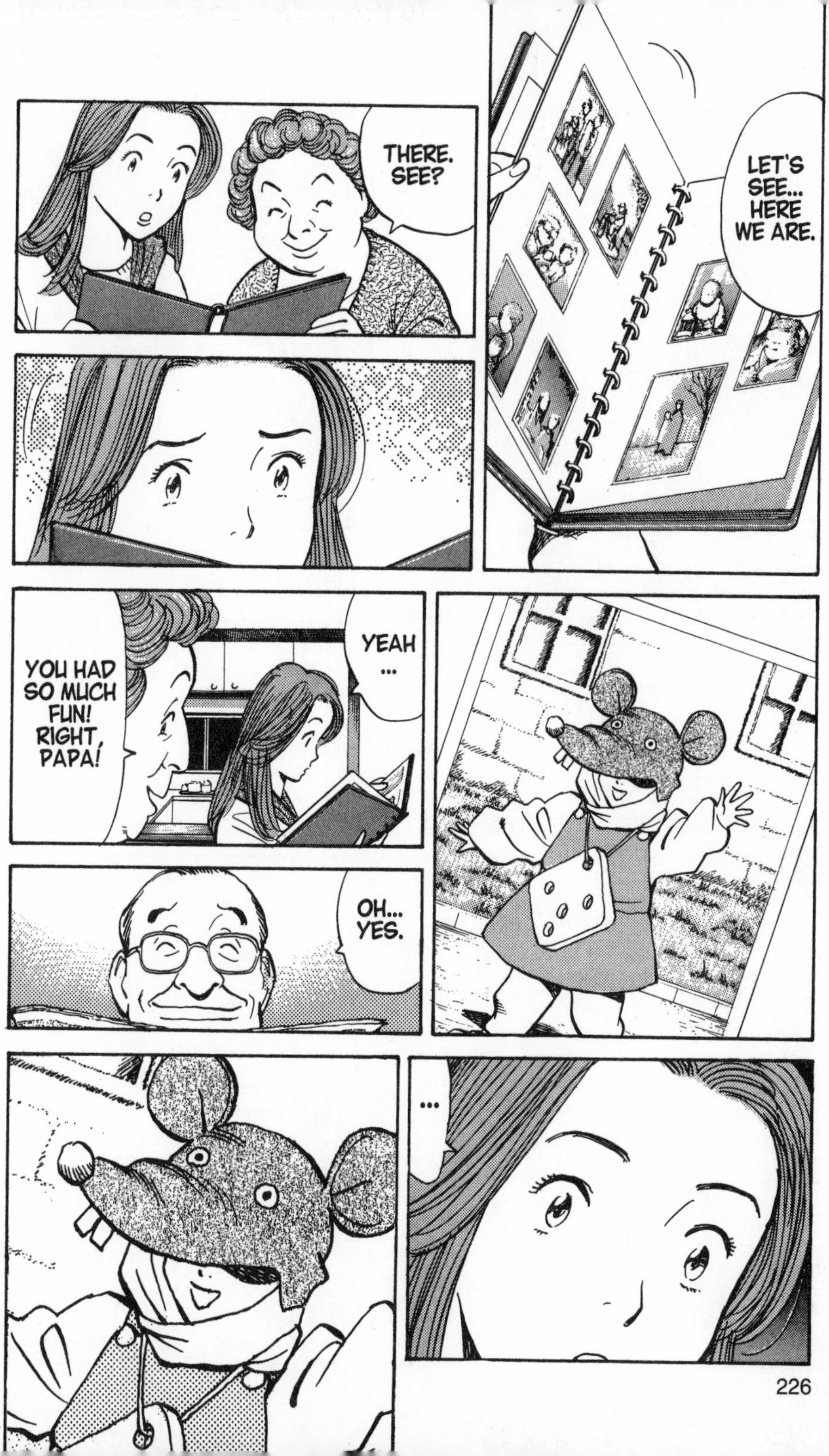
LET'S SEE... HERE WE ARE.
THERE. SEE?
YEAH ...
YOU HAD SO MUCH FUN! RIGHT, PAPA!
OH... YES.
...

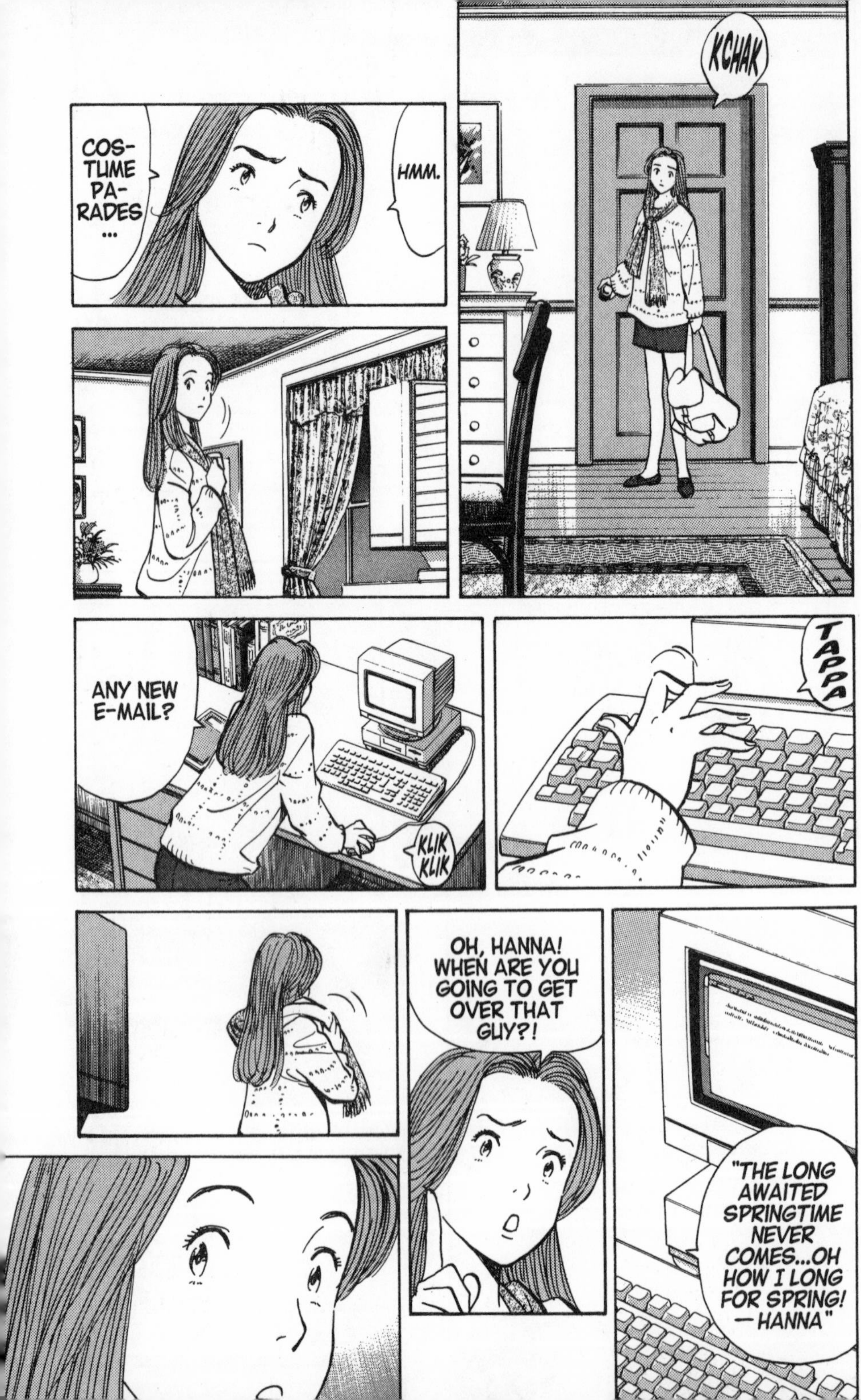
KCHAK
HMM.
COS-TUME PA-RADES...
TAPPA
ANY NEW E-MAIL?
KLIK KLIK
"THE LONG AWAITED SPRINGTIME NEVER COMES...OH HOW I LONG FOR SPRING! —HANNA"
OH, HANNA! WHEN ARE YOU GOING TO GET OVER THAT GUY?!

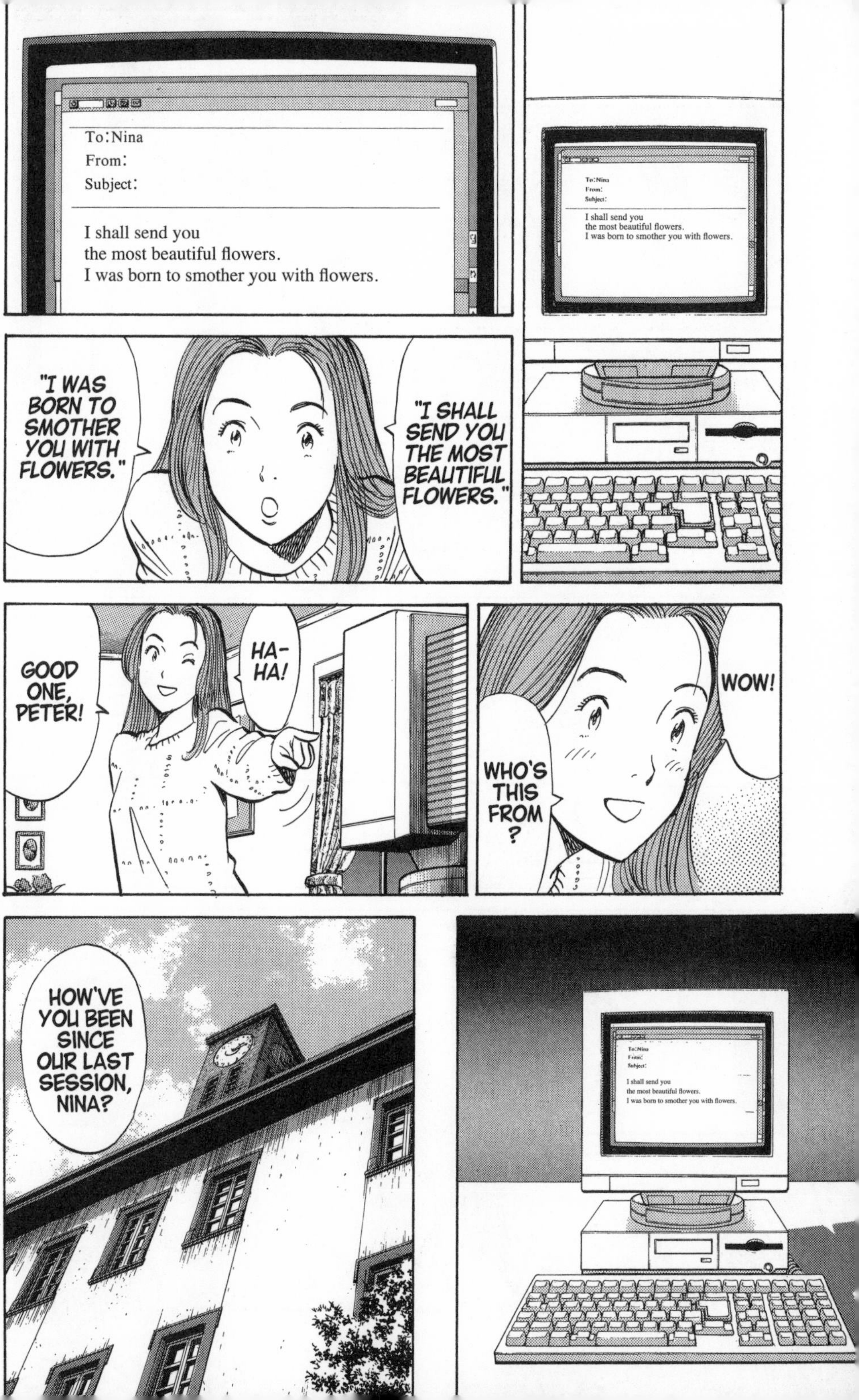
To:Nina
From:
Subject:
I shall send you
the most beautiful flowers.
I was born to smother you with flowers.
To:Nina
From:
Subject:
I shall send you
the most beautiful flowers.
I was born to smother you with flowers.
"I SHALL SEND YOU THE MOST BEAUTIFUL FLOWERS."
"I WAS BORN TO SMOTHER YOU WITH FLOWERS."
WOW!
WHO'S THIS FROM?
HA-HA!
GOOD ONE, PETER!
To:Nina
From:
Subject:
I shall send you
the most beautiful flowers.
I was born to smother you with flowers.
HOW'VE YOU BEEN SINCE OUR LAST SESSION, NINA?

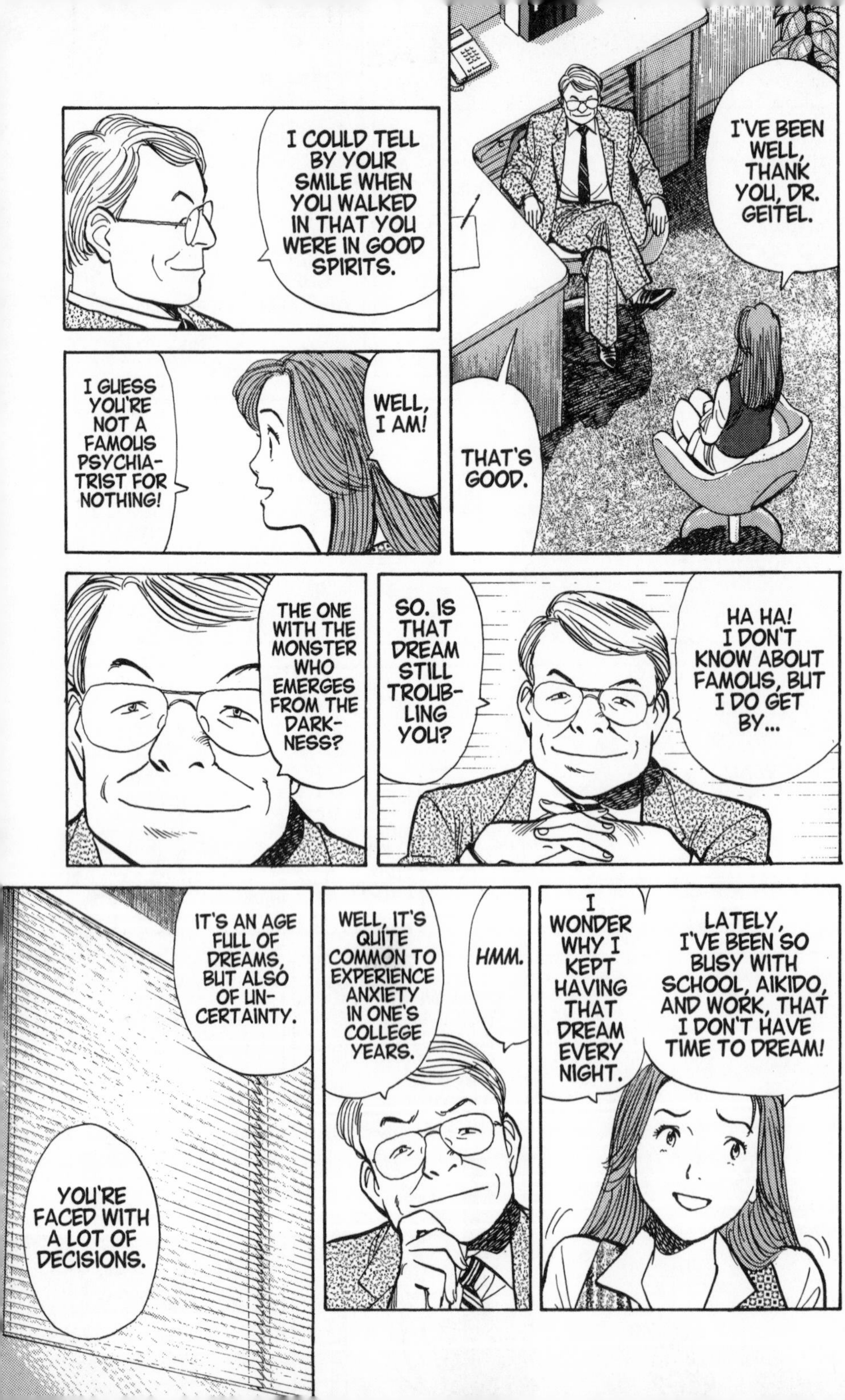
I'VE BEEN WELL, THANK YOU, DR. GEITEL.
THAT'S GOOD.
I COULD TELL BY YOUR SMILE WHEN YOU WALKED IN THAT YOU WERE IN GOOD SPIRITS.
WELL, I AM!
I GUESS YOU'RE NOT A FAMOUS PSYCHIATRIST FOR NOTHING!
HA HA! I DON'T KNOW ABOUT FAMOUS, BUT I DO GET BY...
SO. IS THAT DREAM STILL TROUBLING YOU?
THE ONE WITH THE MONSTER WHO EMERGES FROM THE DARKNESS?
LATELY, I'VE BEEN SO BUSY WITH SCHOOL, AIKIDO, AND WORK, THAT I DON'T HAVE TIME TO DREAM!
I WONDER WHY I KEPT HAVING THAT DREAM EVERY NIGHT.
HMM.
WELL, IT'S QUITE COMMON TO EXPERIENCE ANXIETY IN ONE'S COLLEGE YEARS.
IT'S AN AGE FULL OF DREAMS, BUT ALSO OF UNCERTAINTY.
YOU'RE FACED WITH A LOT OF DECISIONS.

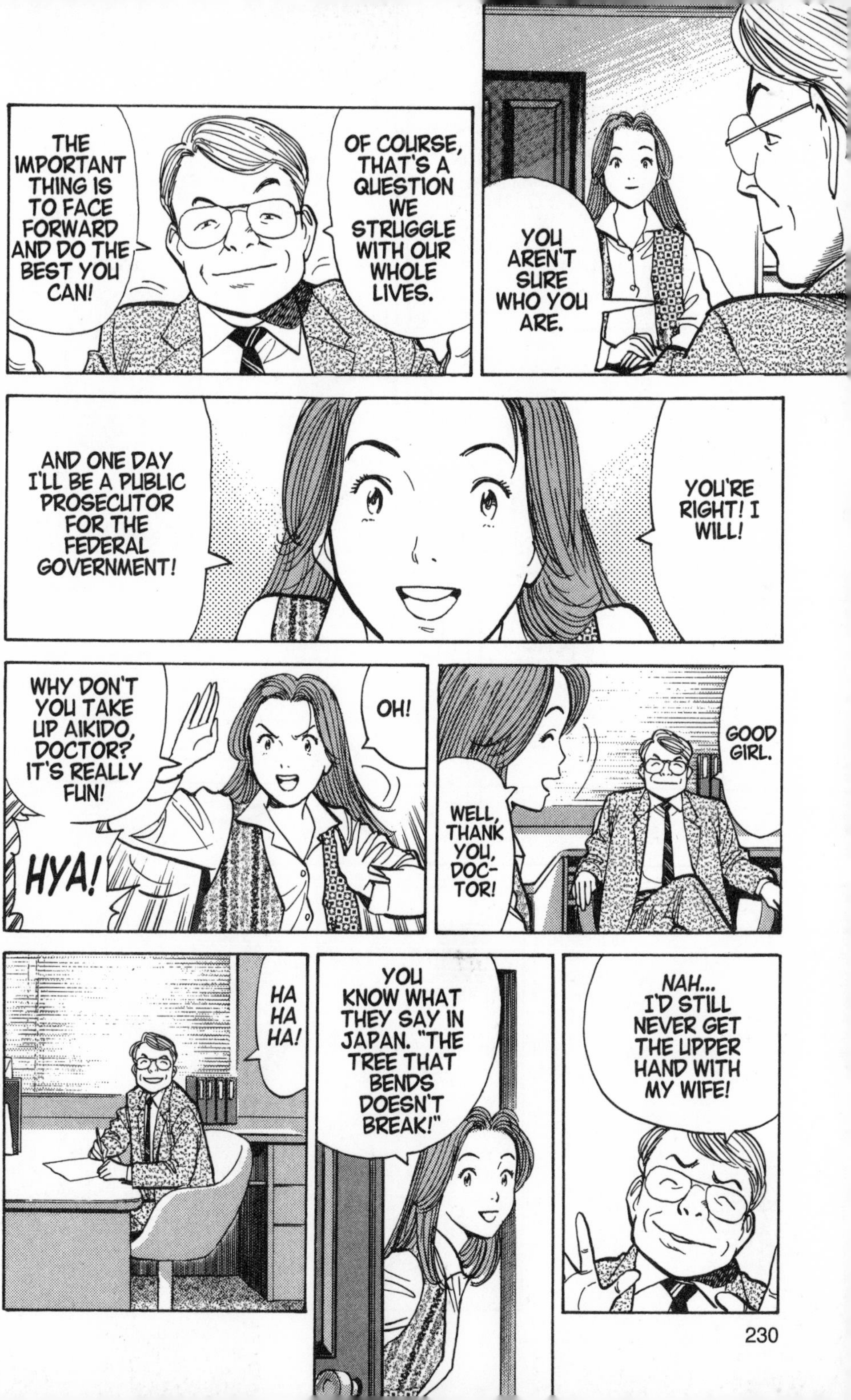
YOU AREN'T SURE WHO YOU ARE.
OF COURSE, THAT'S A QUESTION WE STRUGGLE WITH OUR WHOLE LIVES.
THE IMPORTANT THING IS TO FACE FORWARD AND DO THE BEST YOU CAN!
YOU'RE RIGHT! I WILL!
AND ONE DAY I'LL BE A PUBLIC PROSECUTOR FOR THE FEDERAL GOVERNMENT!
GOOD GIRL.
WELL, THANK YOU, DOC-TOR!
OH!
WHY DON'T YOU TAKE UP AIKIDO, DOCTOR? IT'S REALLY FUN!
HYA!
NAH... I'D STILL NEVER GET THE UPPER HAND WITH MY WIFE!
YOU KNOW WHAT THEY SAY IN JAPAN. "THE TREE THAT BENDS DOESN'T BREAK!"
HA HA HA!

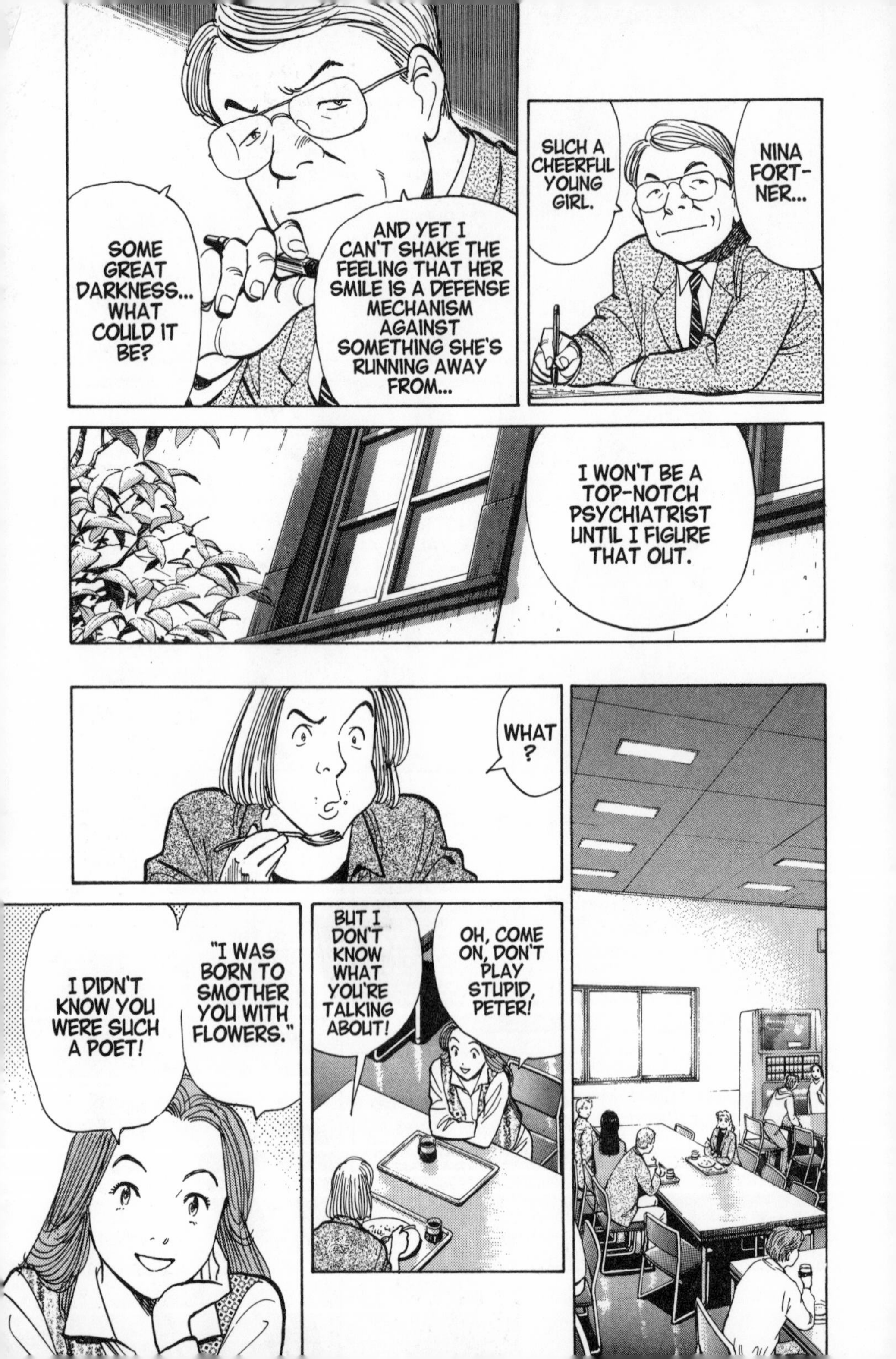
NINA FORT-NER...
SUCH A CHEERFUL YOUNG GIRL.
AND YET I CAN'T SHAKE THE FEELING THAT HER SMILE IS A DEFENSE MECHANISM AGAINST SOMETHING SHE'S RUNNING AWAY FROM...
SOME GREAT DARKNESS... WHAT COULD IT BE?
I WON'T BE A TOP-NOTCH PSYCHIATRIST UNTIL I FIGURE THAT OUT.
WHAT?
OH, COME ON, DON'T PLAY STUPID, PETER!
BUT I DON'T KNOW WHAT YOU'RE TALKING ABOUT!
"I WAS BORN TO SMOTHER YOU WITH FLOWERS."
I DIDN'T KNOW YOU WERE SUCH A POET!

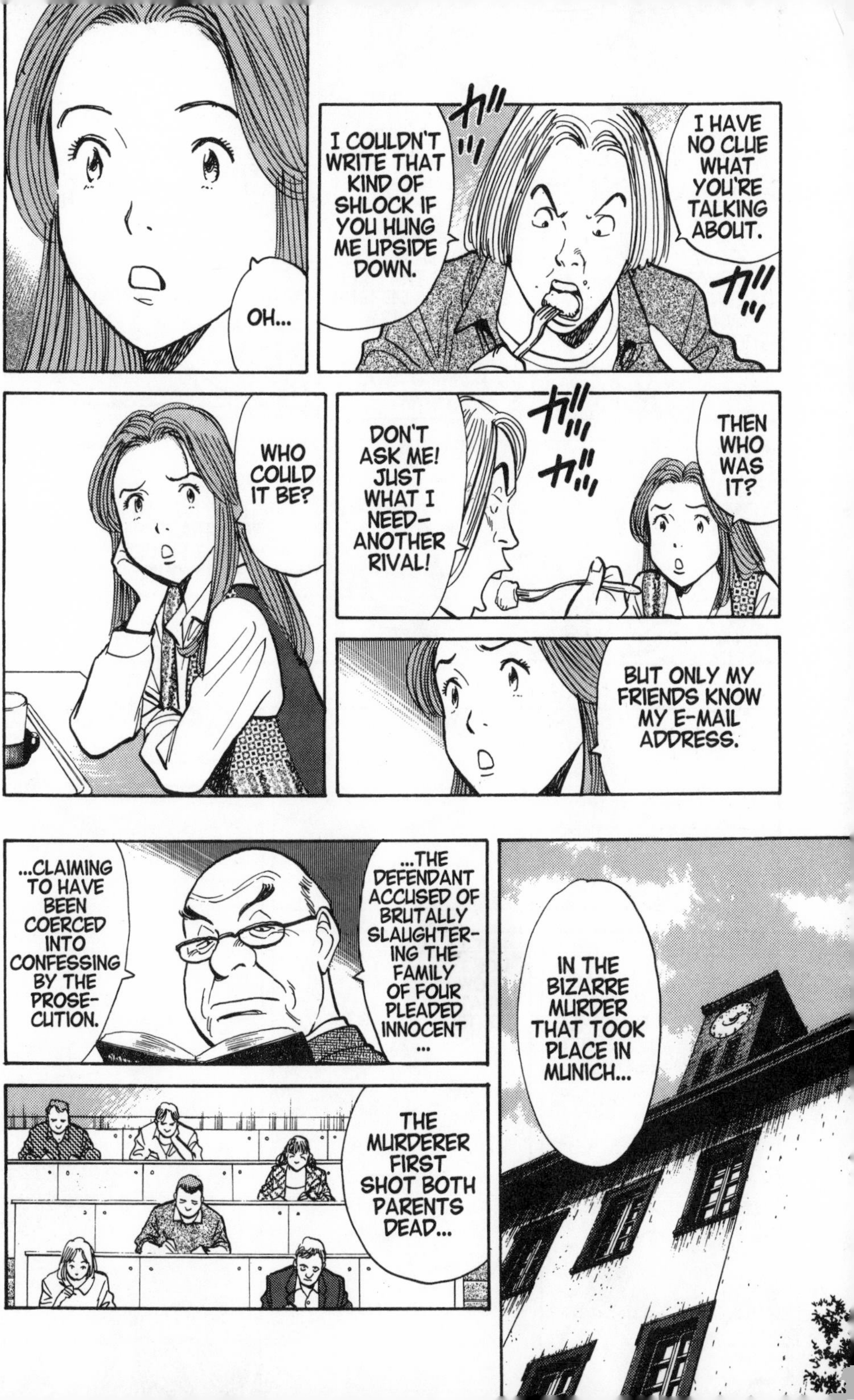
I HAVE NO CLUE WHAT YOU'RE TALKING ABOUT.
I COULDN'T WRITE THAT KIND OF SHLOCK IF YOU HUNG ME UPSIDE DOWN.
OH...
THEN WHO WAS IT?
DON'T ASK ME! JUST WHAT I NEED-ANOTHER RIVAL!
BUT ONLY MY FRIENDS KNOW MY E-MAIL ADDRESS.
WHO COULD IT BE?
IN THE BIZARRE MURDER THAT TOOK PLACE IN MUNICH...
...THE DEFENDANT ACCUSED OF BRUTALLY SLAUGHTER-ING THE FAMILY OF FOUR PLEADED INNOCENT ...
...CLAIMING TO HAVE BEEN COERCED INTO CONFESSING BY THE PROSE-CUTION.
THE MURDERER FIRST SHOT BOTH PARENTS DEAD...

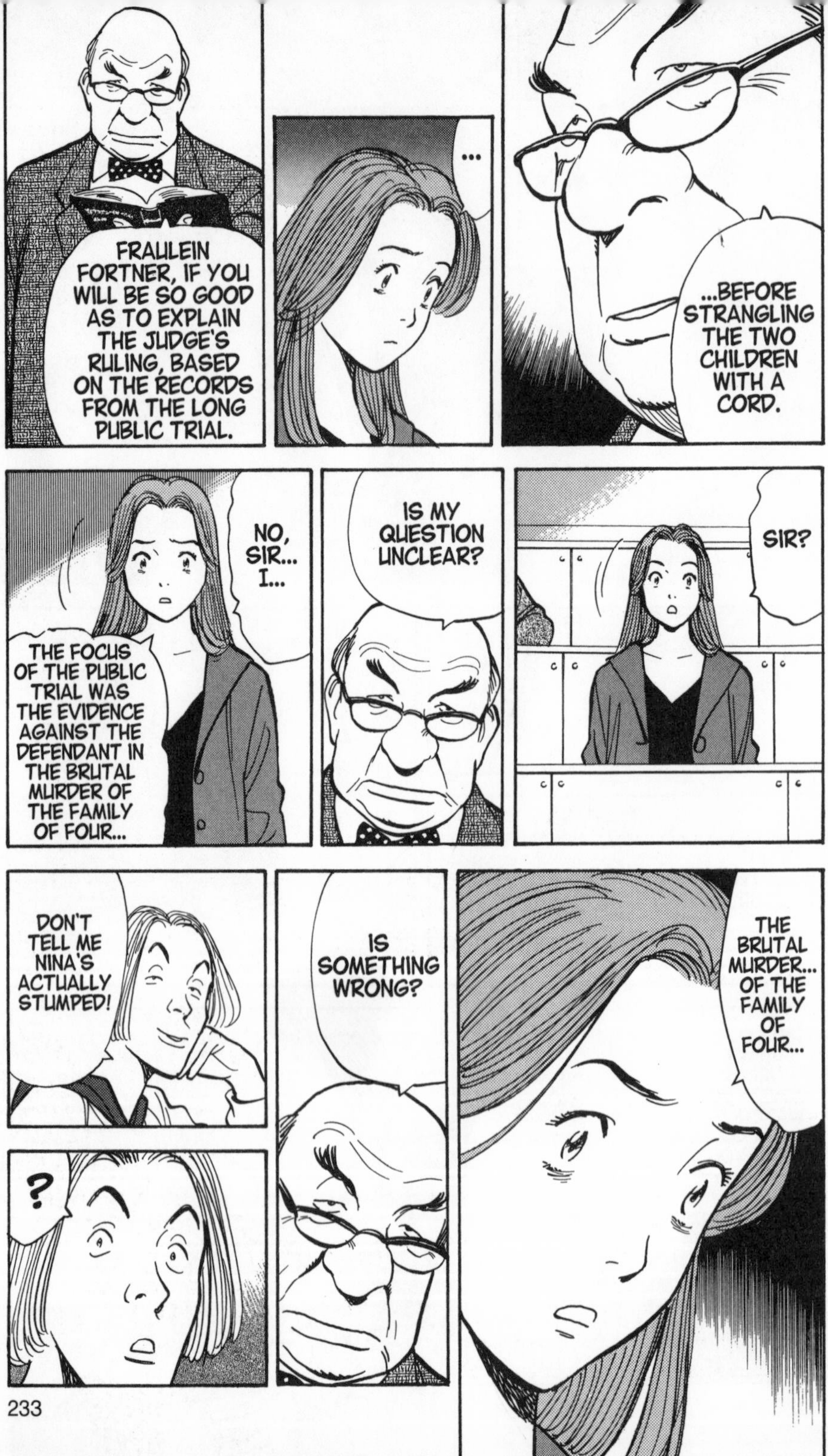
...BEFORE STRANGLING THE TWO CHILDREN WITH A CORD.
...
FRAULEIN FORTNER, IF YOU WILL BE SO GOOD AS TO EXPLAIN THE JUDGE'S RULING, BASED ON THE RECORDS FROM THE LONG PUBLIC TRIAL.
SIR?
IS MY QUESTION UNCLEAR?
NO, SIR... I...
THE FOCUS OF THE PUBLIC TRIAL WAS THE EVIDENCE AGAINST THE DEFENDANT IN THE BRUTAL MURDER OF THE FAMILY OF FOUR...
THE BRUTAL MURDER... OF THE FAMILY OF FOUR...
IS SOMETHING WRONG?
DON'T TELL ME NINA'S ACTUALLY STUMPED!
?

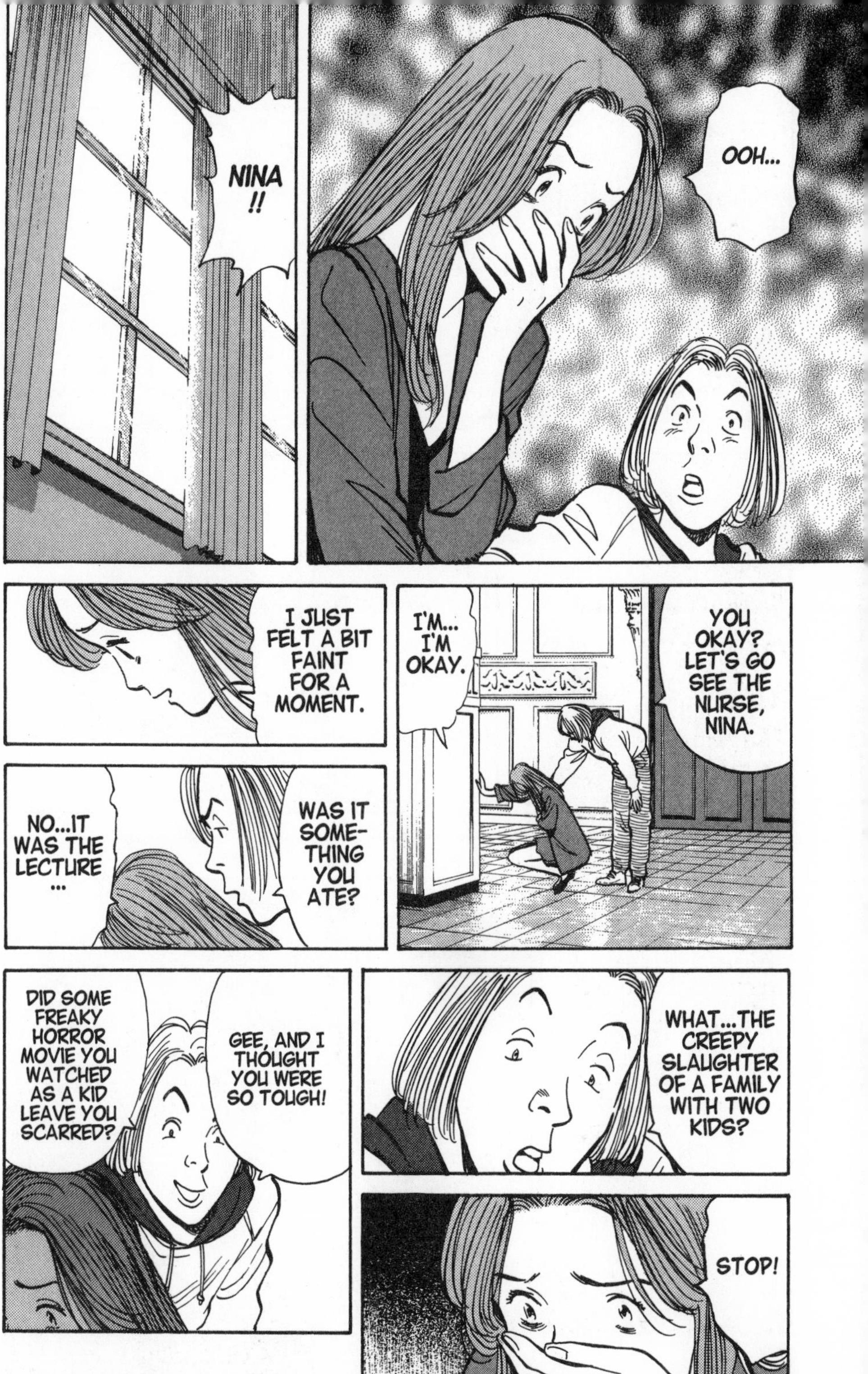
OOH...
NINA !!
YOU OKAY? LET'S GO SEE THE NURSE, NINA.
I'M... I'M OKAY.
I JUST FELT A BIT FAINT FOR A MOMENT.
WAS IT SOME-THING YOU ATE?
NO...IT WAS THE LECTURE ...
WHAT...THE CREEPY SLAUGHTER OF A FAMILY WITH TWO KIDS?
STOP!
GEE, AND I THOUGHT YOU WERE SO TOUGH!
DID SOME FREAKY HORROR MOVIE YOU WATCHED AS A KID LEAVE YOU SCARRED?

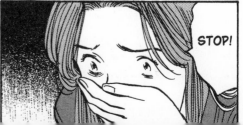

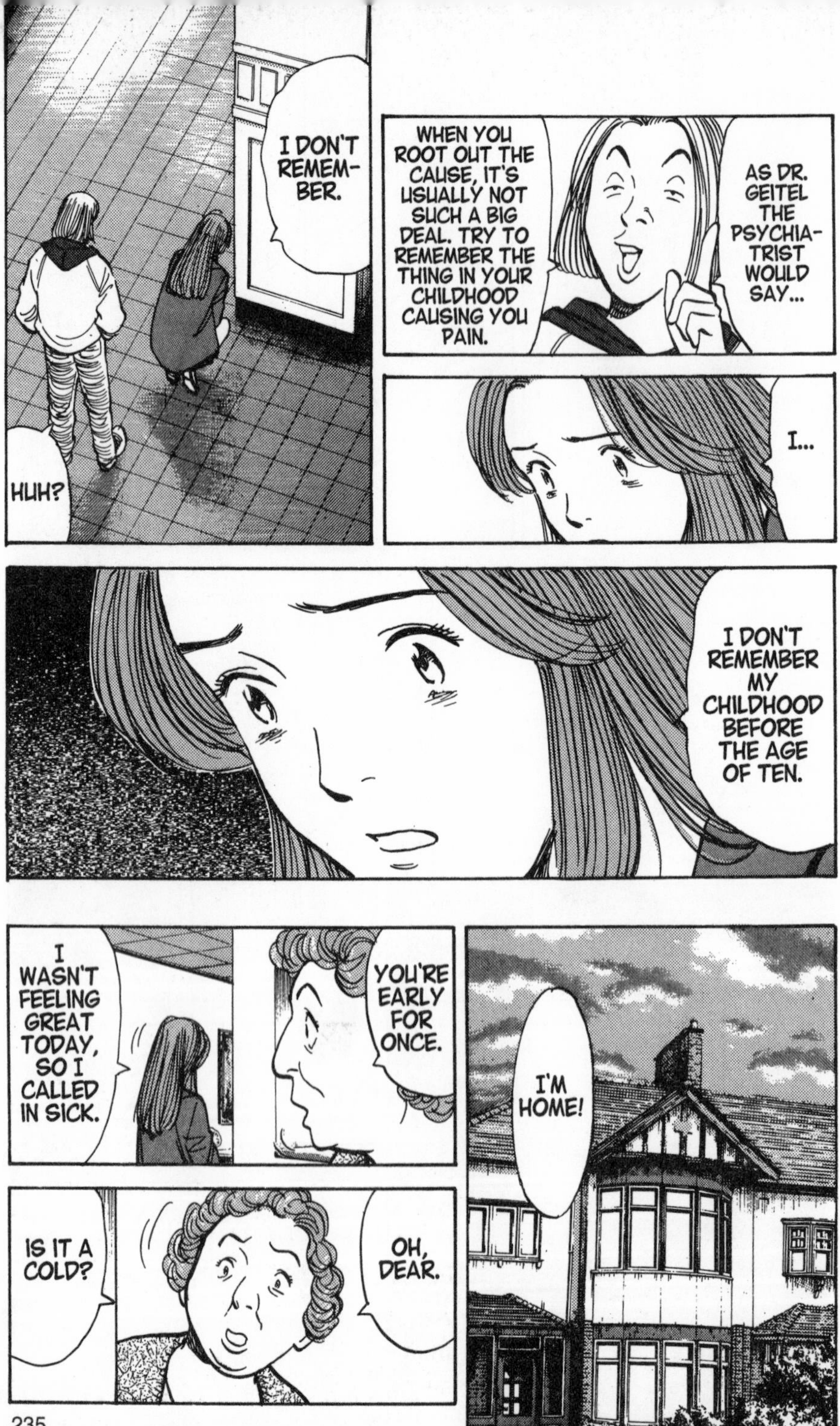
AS DR. GEITEL THE PSYCHIA-TRIST WOULD SAY...
WHEN YOU ROOT OUT THE CAUSE, IT'S USUALLY NOT SUCH A BIG DEAL. TRY TO REMEMBER THE THING IN YOUR CHILDHOOD CAUSING YOU PAIN.
I...
I DON'T REMEM-BER.
HUH?
I DON'T REMEMBER MY CHILDHOOD BEFORE THE AGE OF TEN.
I'M HOME!
YOU'RE EARLY FOR ONCE.
I WASN'T FEELING GREAT TODAY, SO I CALLED IN SICK.
OH, DEAR.
IS IT A COLD?

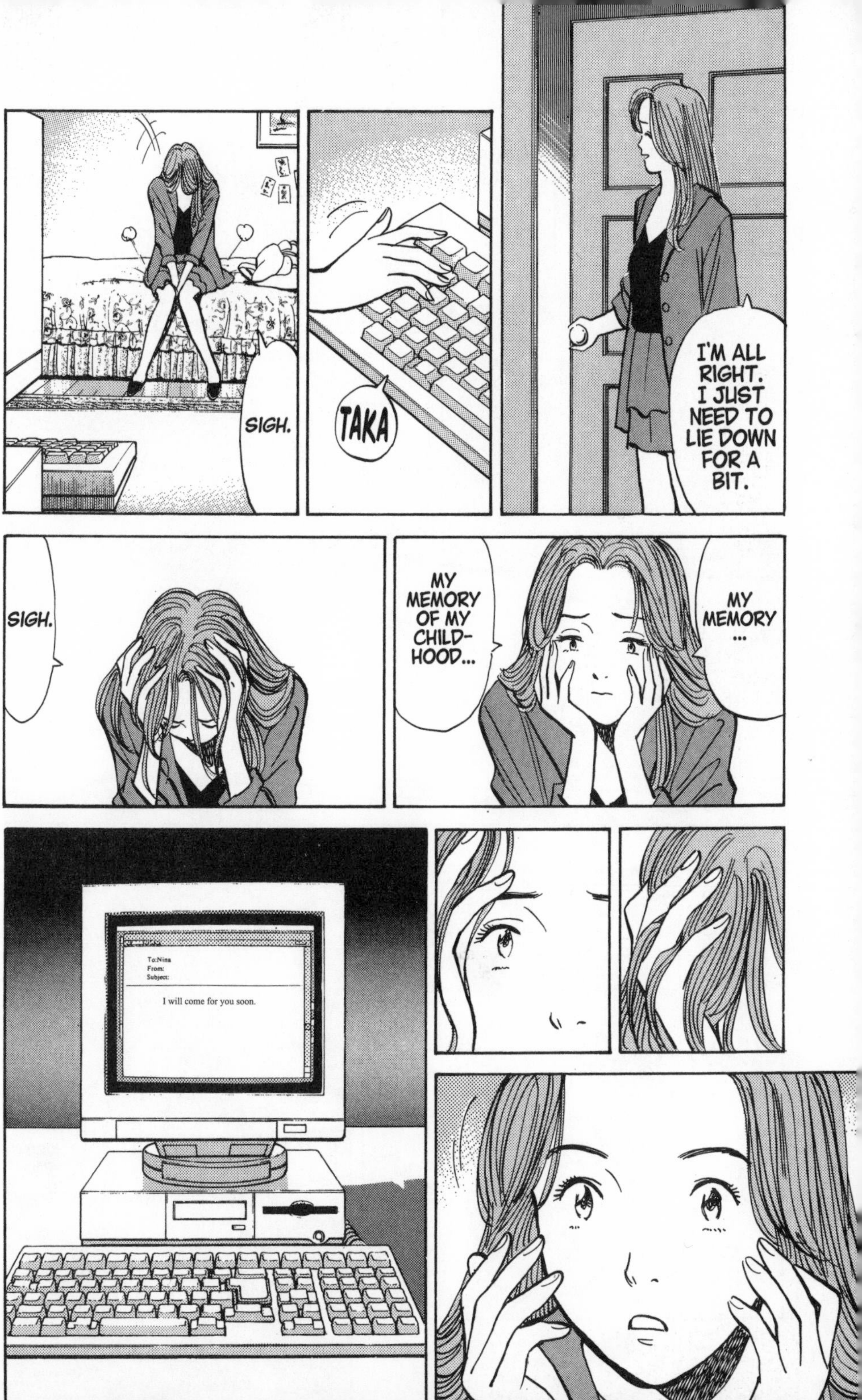
I'M ALL RIGHT. I JUST NEED TO LIE DOWN FOR A BIT.
TAKA
SIGH.
MY MEMORY ...
MY MEMORY OF MY CHILDHOOD...
SIGH.
To:Nina
From:
Subject:
I will come for you soon.

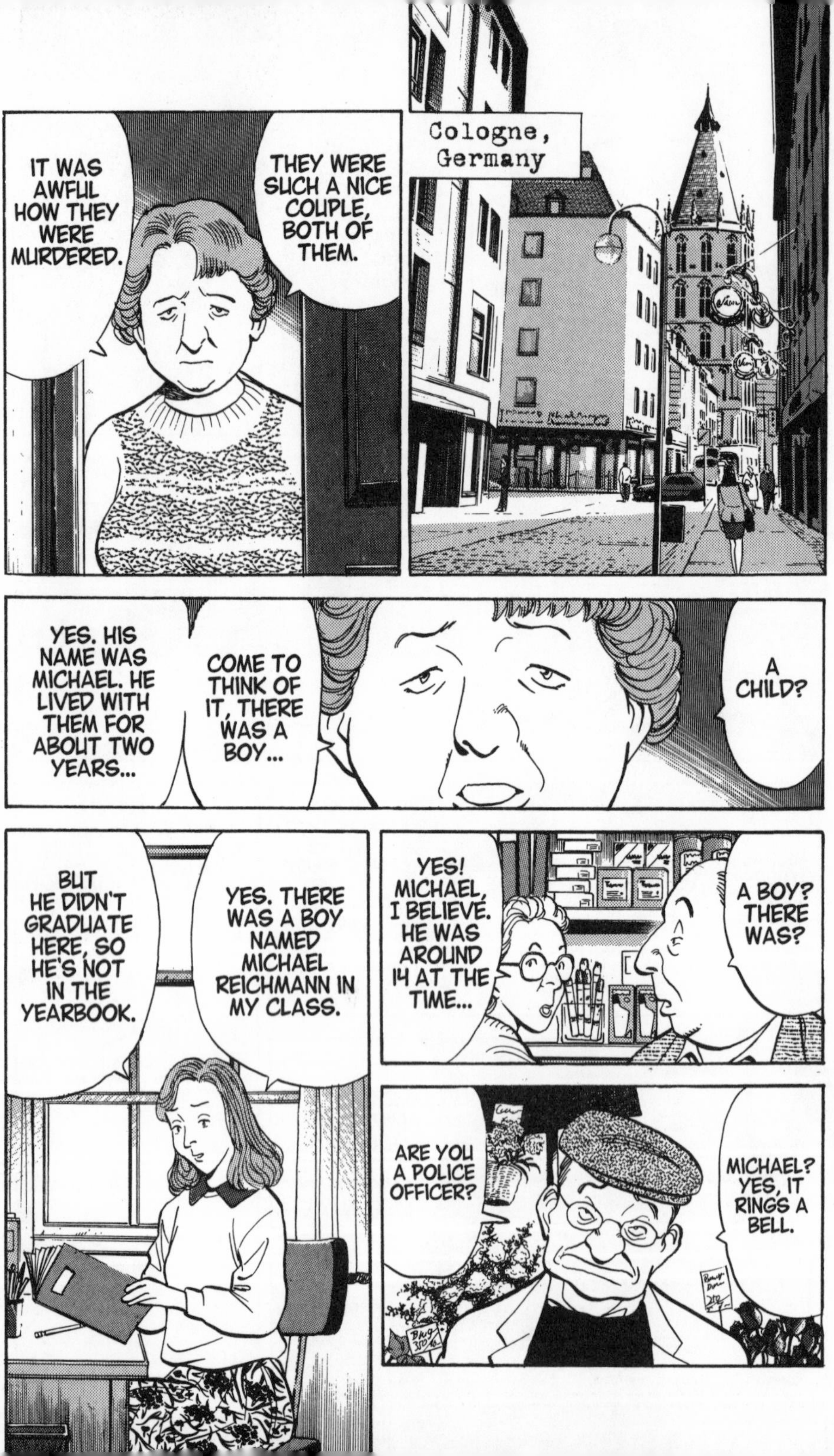
Cologne, Germany
THEY WERE SUCH A NICE COUPLE, BOTH OF THEM.
IT WAS AWFUL HOW THEY WERE MURDERED.
A CHILD?
COME TO THINK OF IT, THERE WAS A BOY...
YES. HIS NAME WAS MICHAEL. HE LIVED WITH THEM FOR ABOUT TWO YEARS...
A BOY? THERE WAS?
YES! MICHAEL, I BELIEVE. HE WAS AROUND 14 AT THE TIME...
MICHAEL? YES, IT RINGS A BELL.
ARE YOU A POLICE OFFICER?
YES. THERE WAS A BOY NAMED MICHAEL REICHMANN IN MY CLASS.
BUT HE DIDN'T GRADUATE HERE, SO HE'S NOT IN THE YEARBOOK.

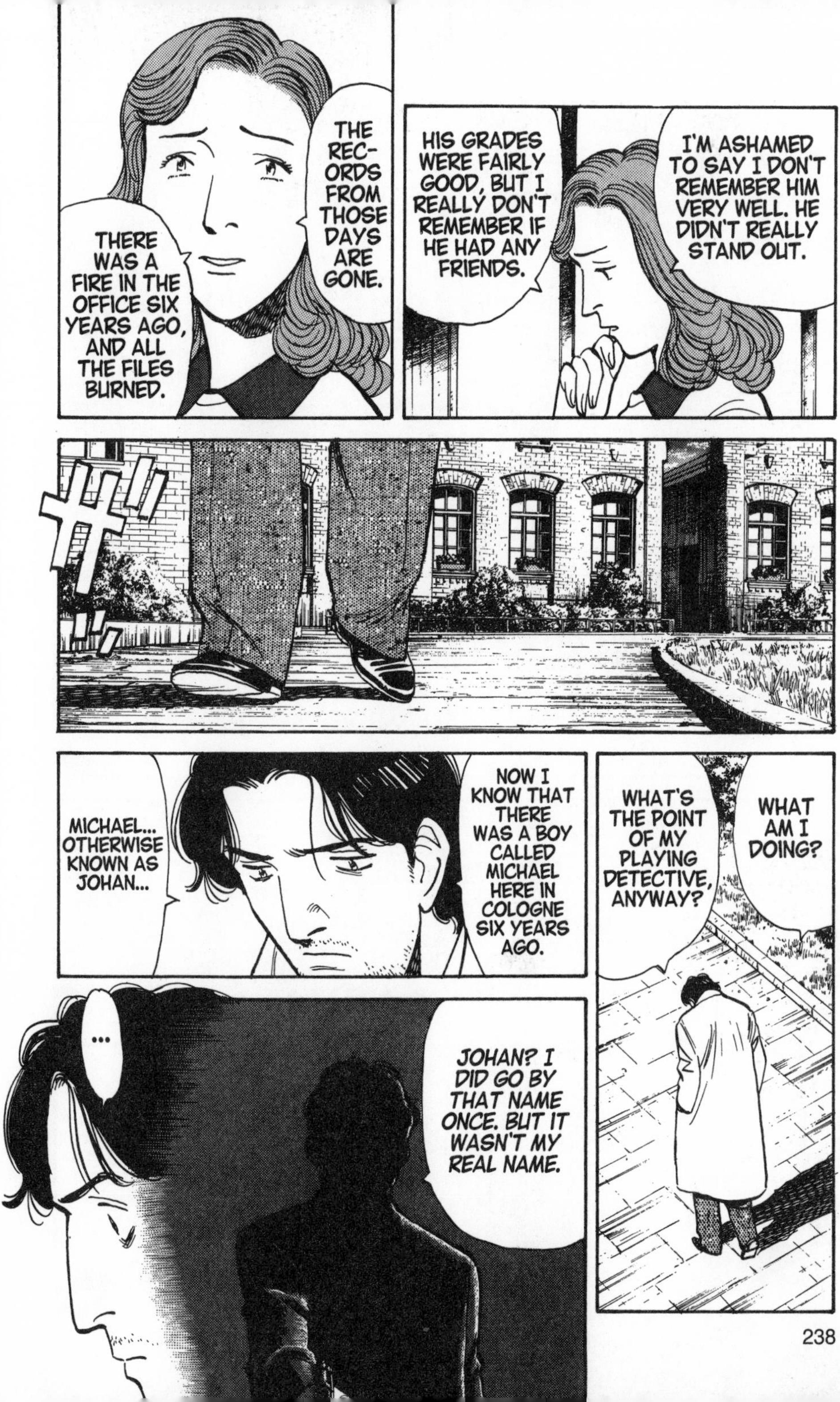
I'M ASHAMED TO SAY I DON'T REMEMBER HIM VERY WELL. HE DIDN'T REALLY STAND OUT.
HIS GRADES WERE FAIRLY GOOD, BUT I REALLY DON'T REMEMBER IF HE HAD ANY FRIENDS.
THE REC-ORDS FROM THOSE DAYS ARE GONE.
THERE WAS A FIRE IN THE OFFICE SIX YEARS AGO, AND ALL THE FILES BURNED.
WHAT AM I DOING?
WHAT'S THE POINT OF MY PLAYING DETECTIVE, ANYWAY?
NOW I KNOW THAT THERE WAS A BOY CALLED MICHAEL HERE IN COLOGNE SIX YEARS AGO.
MICHAEL... OTHERWISE KNOWN AS JOHAN...
JOHAN? I DID GO BY THAT NAME ONCE. BUT IT WASN'T MY REAL NAME.
...

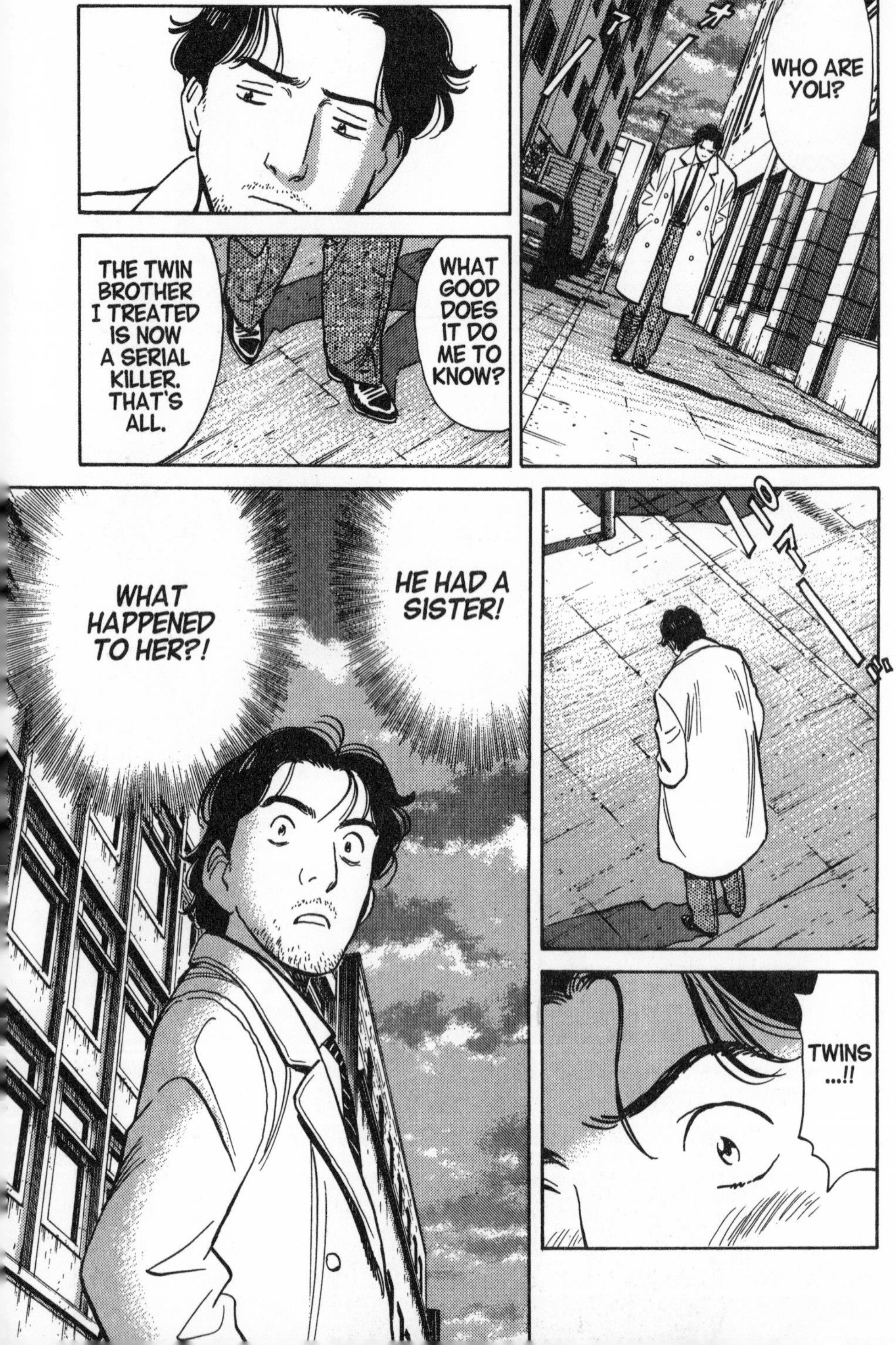
WHO ARE YOU?
WHAT GOOD DOES IT DO ME TO KNOW?
THE TWIN BROTHER I TREATED IS NOW A SERIAL KILLER. THAT'S ALL.
TWINS ...!!
HE HAD A SISTER!
WHAT HAPPENED TO HER?!

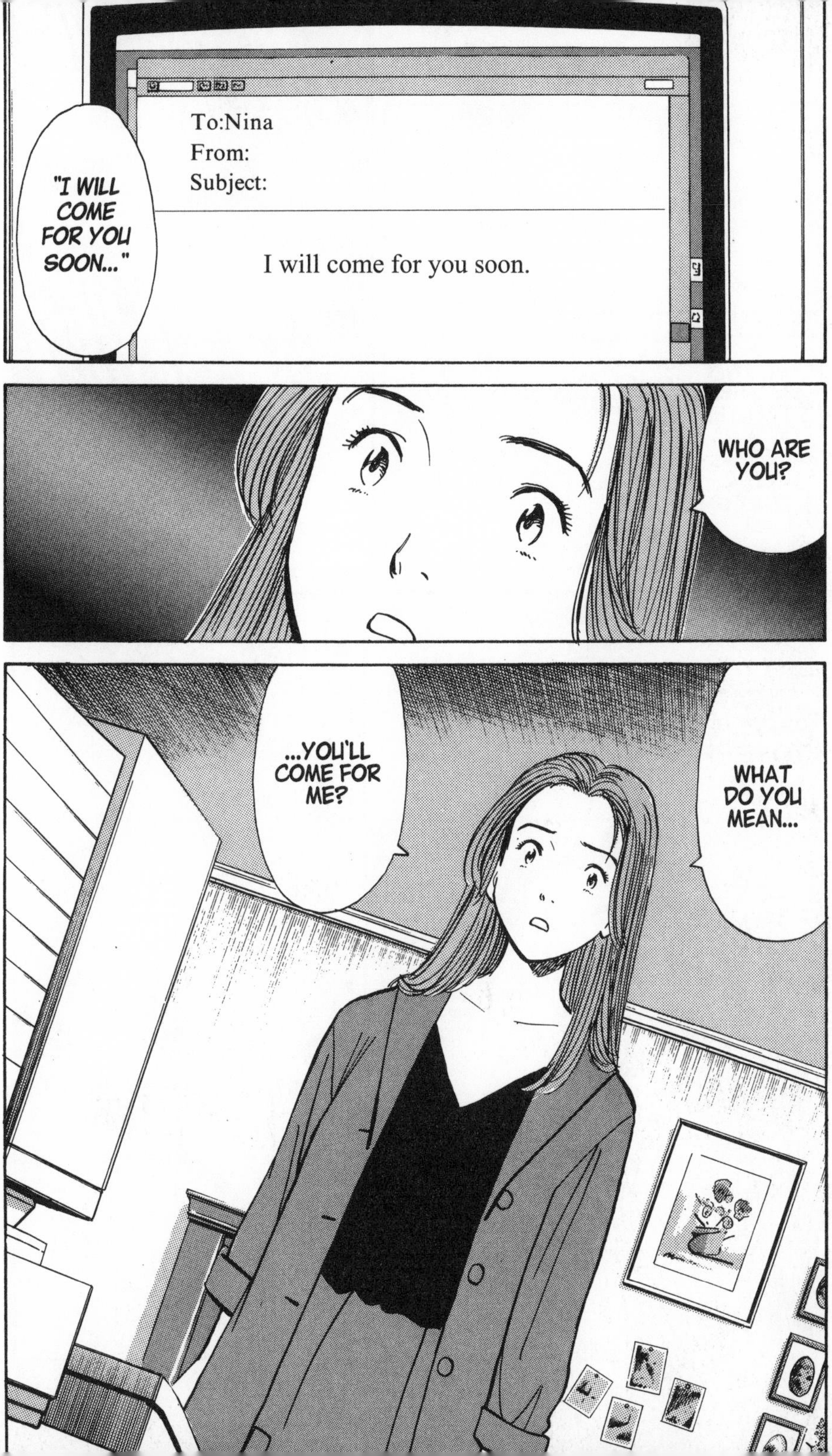
To:Nina
From:
Subject:
I will come for you soon.
"I WILL COME FOR YOU SOON..."
WHO ARE YOU?
WHAT DO YOU MEAN...
...YOU'LL COME FOR ME?

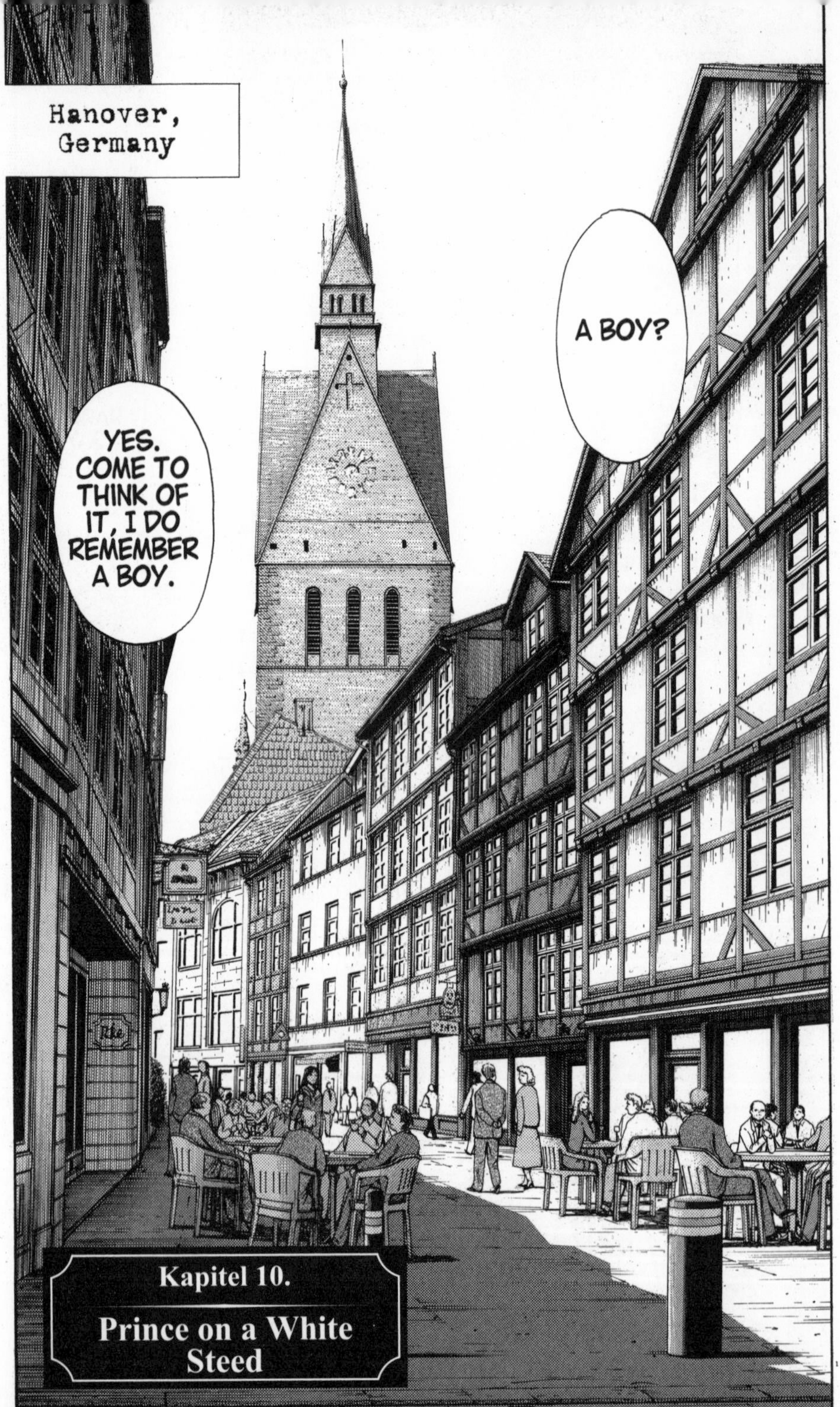
Hanover, Germany
A BOY?
YES. COME TO THINK OF IT, I DO REMEMBER A BOY.
Kapitel 10.
Prince on a White Steed

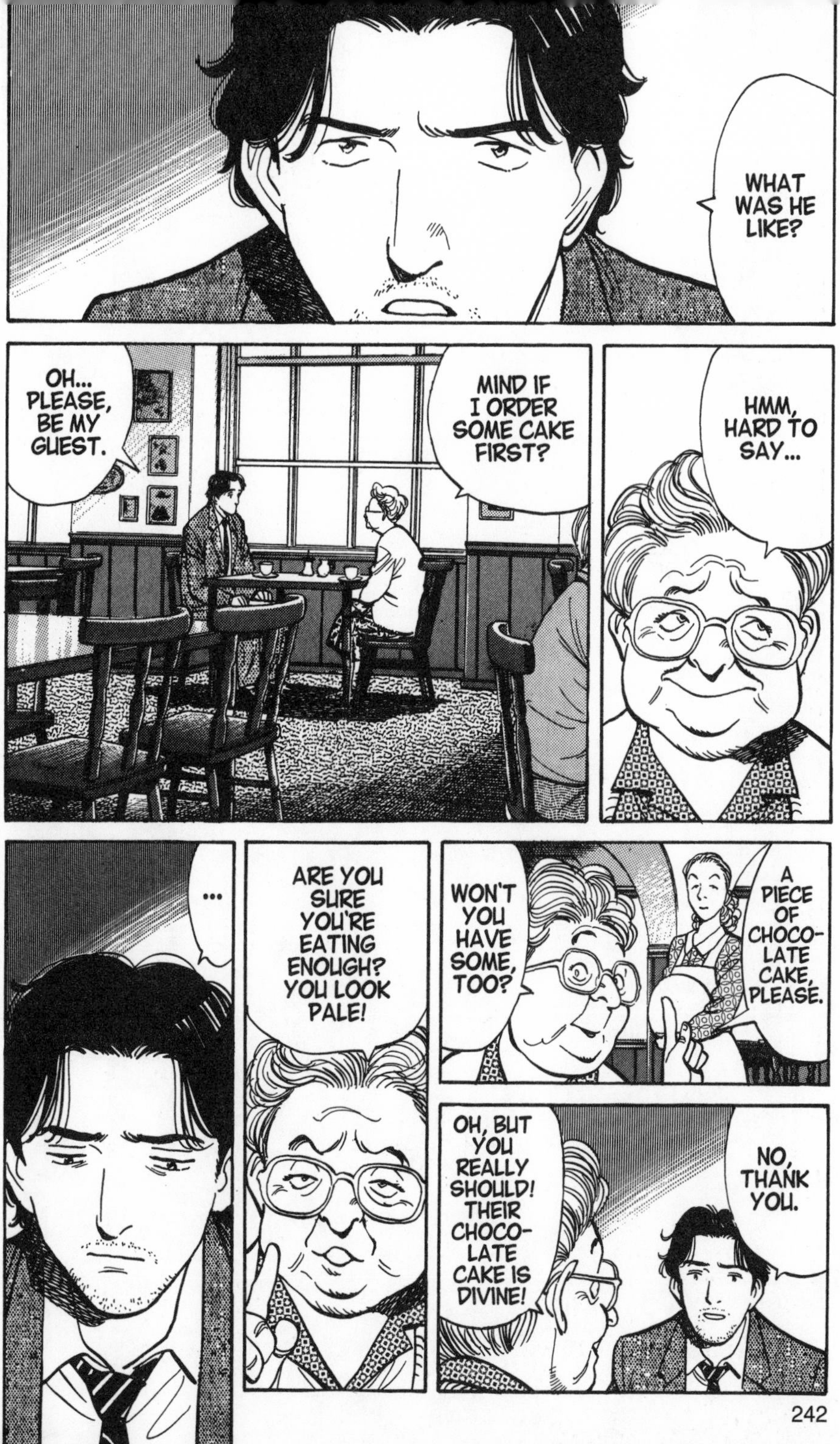
WHAT WAS HE LIKE?
HMM, HARD TO SAY...
MIND IF I ORDER SOME CAKE FIRST?
OH... PLEASE, BE MY GUEST.
A PIECE OF CHOCO-LATE CAKE, PLEASE.
WON'T YOU HAVE SOME, TOO?
NO, THANK YOU.
OH, BUT YOU REALLY SHOULD! THEIR CHOCO-LATE CAKE IS DIVINE!
ARE YOU SURE YOU'RE EATING ENOUGH? YOU LOOK PALE!
...

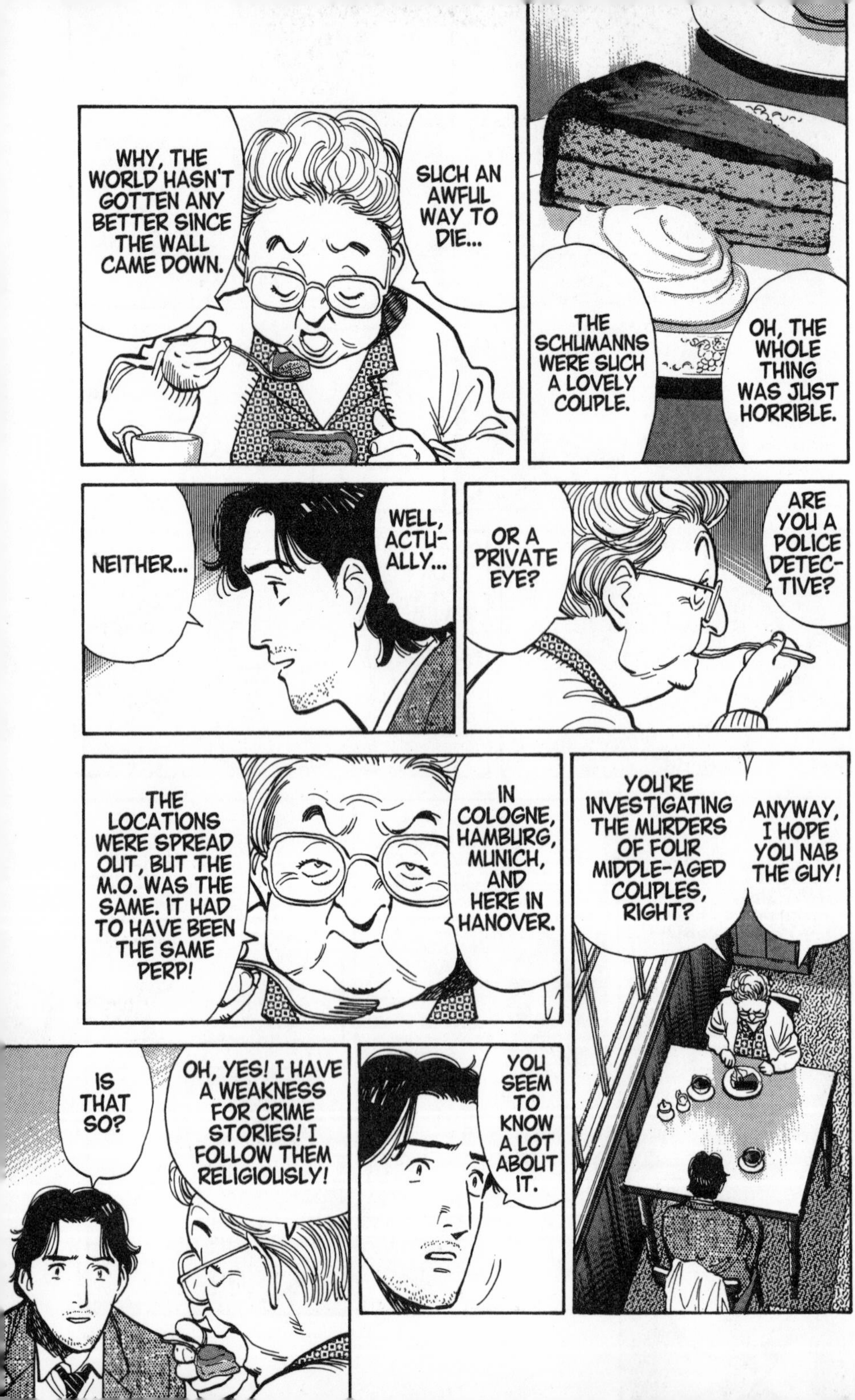
OH, THE WHOLE THING WAS JUST HORRIBLE.
THE SCHUMANNS WERE SUCH A LOVELY COUPLE.
SUCH AN AWFUL WAY TO DIE...
WHY, THE WORLD HASN'T GOTTEN ANY BETTER SINCE THE WALL CAME DOWN.
ARE YOU A POLICE DETEC-TIVE?
OR A PRIVATE EYE?
WELL, ACTU-ALLY...
NEITHER...
ANYWAY, I HOPE YOU NAB THE GUY!
YOU'RE INVESTIGATING THE MURDERS OF FOUR MIDDLE-AGED COUPLES, RIGHT?
IN COLOGNE, HAMBURG, MUNICH, AND HERE IN HANOVER.
THE LOCATIONS WERE SPREAD OUT, BUT THE M.O. WAS THE SAME. IT HAD TO HAVE BEEN THE SAME PERP!
YOU SEEM TO KNOW A LOT ABOUT IT.
OH, YES! I HAVE A WEAKNESS FOR CRIME STORIES! I FOLLOW THEM RELIGIOUSLY!
IS THAT SO?

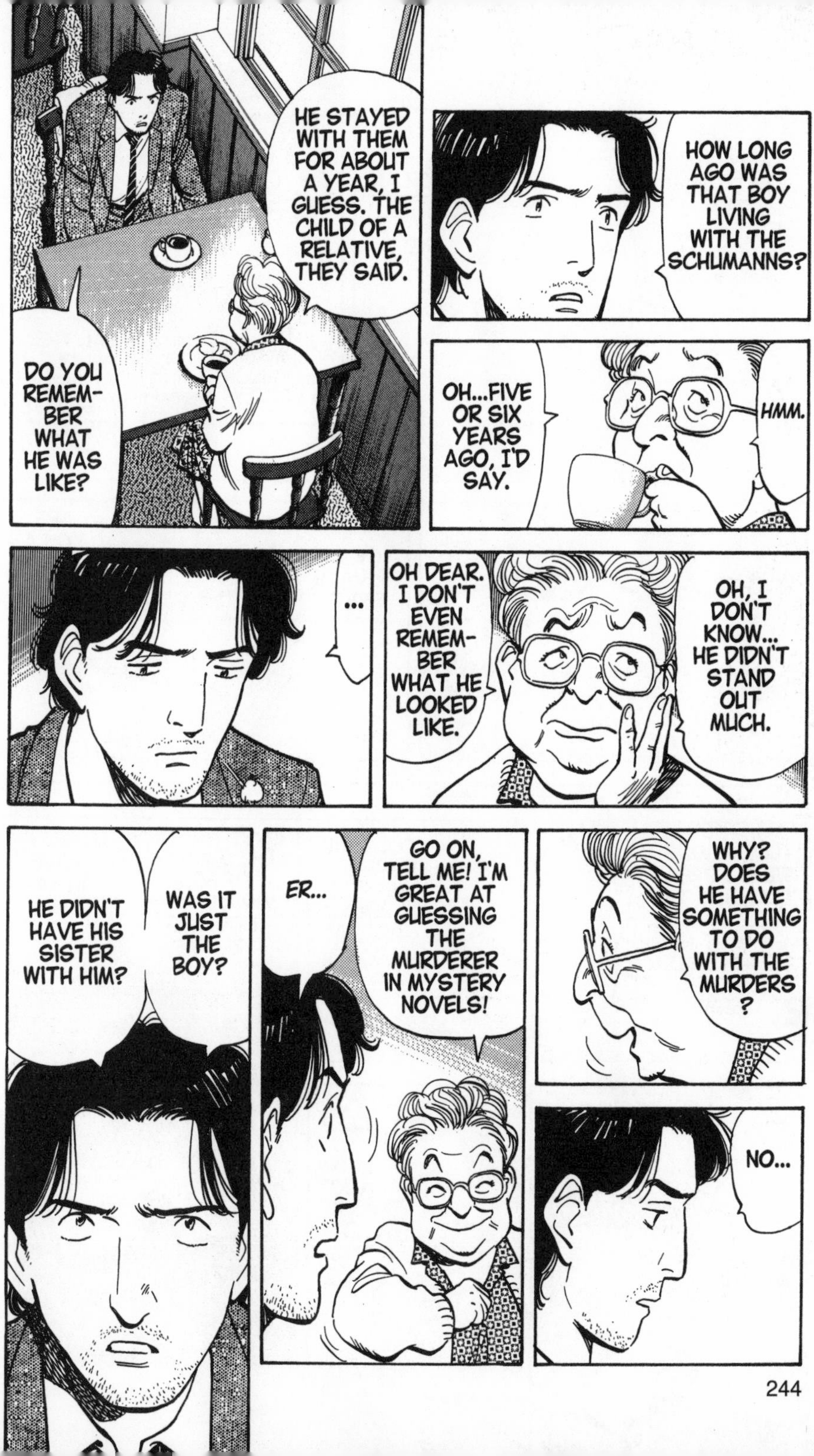
HOW LONG AGO WAS THAT BOY LIVING WITH THE SCHUMANNS?
HMM.
OH...FIVE OR SIX YEARS AGO, I'D SAY.
HE STAYED WITH THEM FOR ABOUT A YEAR, I GUESS. THE CHILD OF A RELATIVE, THEY SAID.
DO YOU REMEMBER WHAT HE WAS LIKE?
OH, I DON'T KNOW... HE DIDN'T STAND OUT MUCH.
OH DEAR. I DON'T EVEN REMEMBER WHAT HE LOOKED LIKE.
...
WHY? DOES HE HAVE SOMETHING TO DO WITH THE MURDERS?
NO...
GO ON, TELL ME! I'M GREAT AT GUESSING THE MURDERER IN MYSTERY NOVELS!
ER...
WAS IT JUST THE BOY?
HE DIDN'T HAVE HIS SISTER WITH HIM?

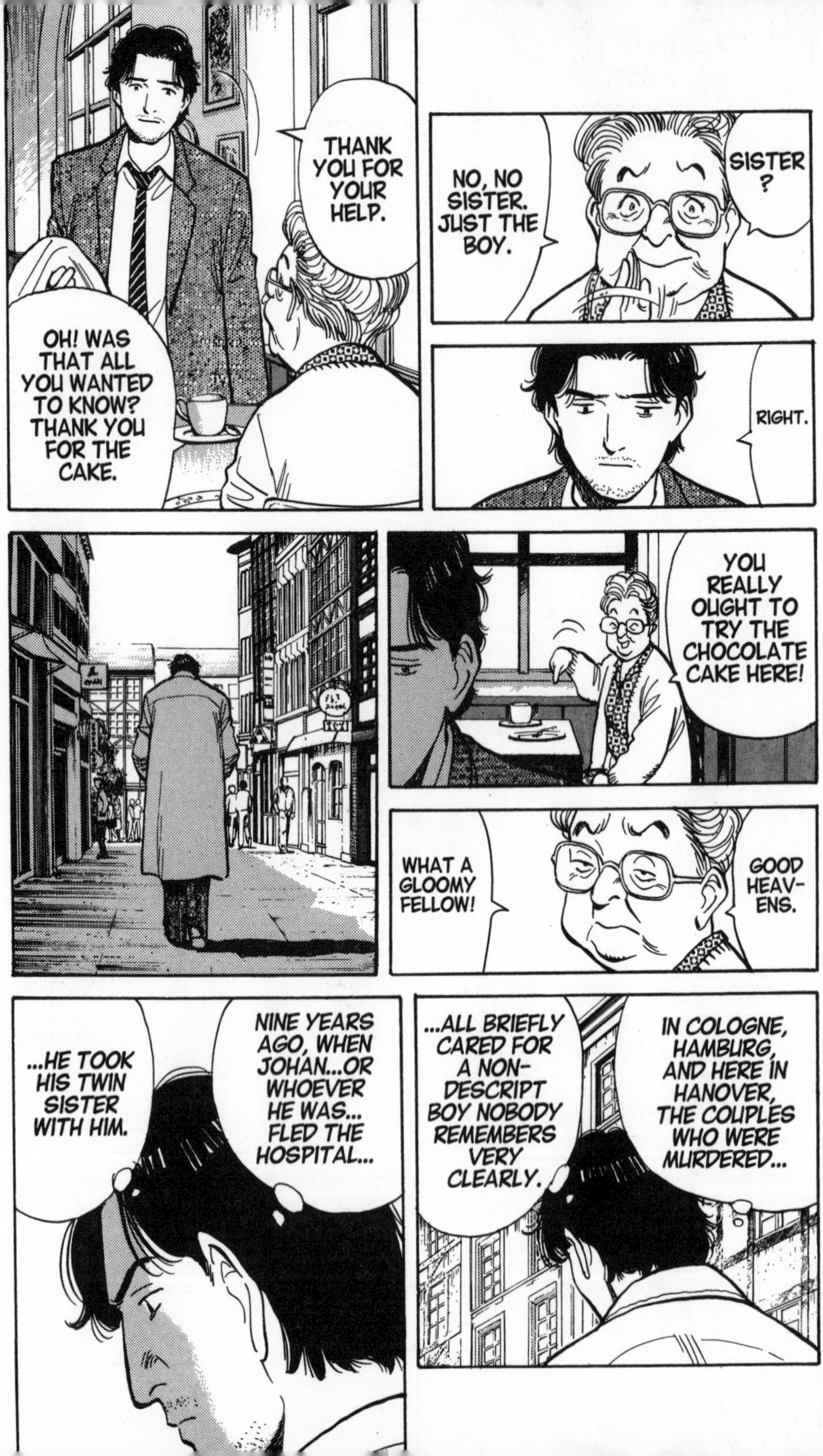
SISTER?
NO, NO SISTER. JUST THE BOY.
RIGHT.
THANK YOU FOR YOUR HELP.
OH! WAS THAT ALL YOU WANTED TO KNOW? THANK YOU FOR THE CAKE.
YOU REALLY OUGHT TO TRY THE CHOCOLATE CAKE HERE!
GOOD HEAVENS.
WHAT A GLOOMY FELLOW!
IN COLOGNE, HAMBURG, AND HERE IN HANOVER, THE COUPLES WHO WERE MURDERED...
...ALL BRIEFLY CARED FOR A NON-DESCRIPT BOY NOBODY REMEMBERS VERY CLEARLY.
NINE YEARS AGO, WHEN JOHAN...OR WHOEVER HE WAS... FLED THE HOSPITAL...
...HE TOOK HIS TWIN SISTER WITH HIM.

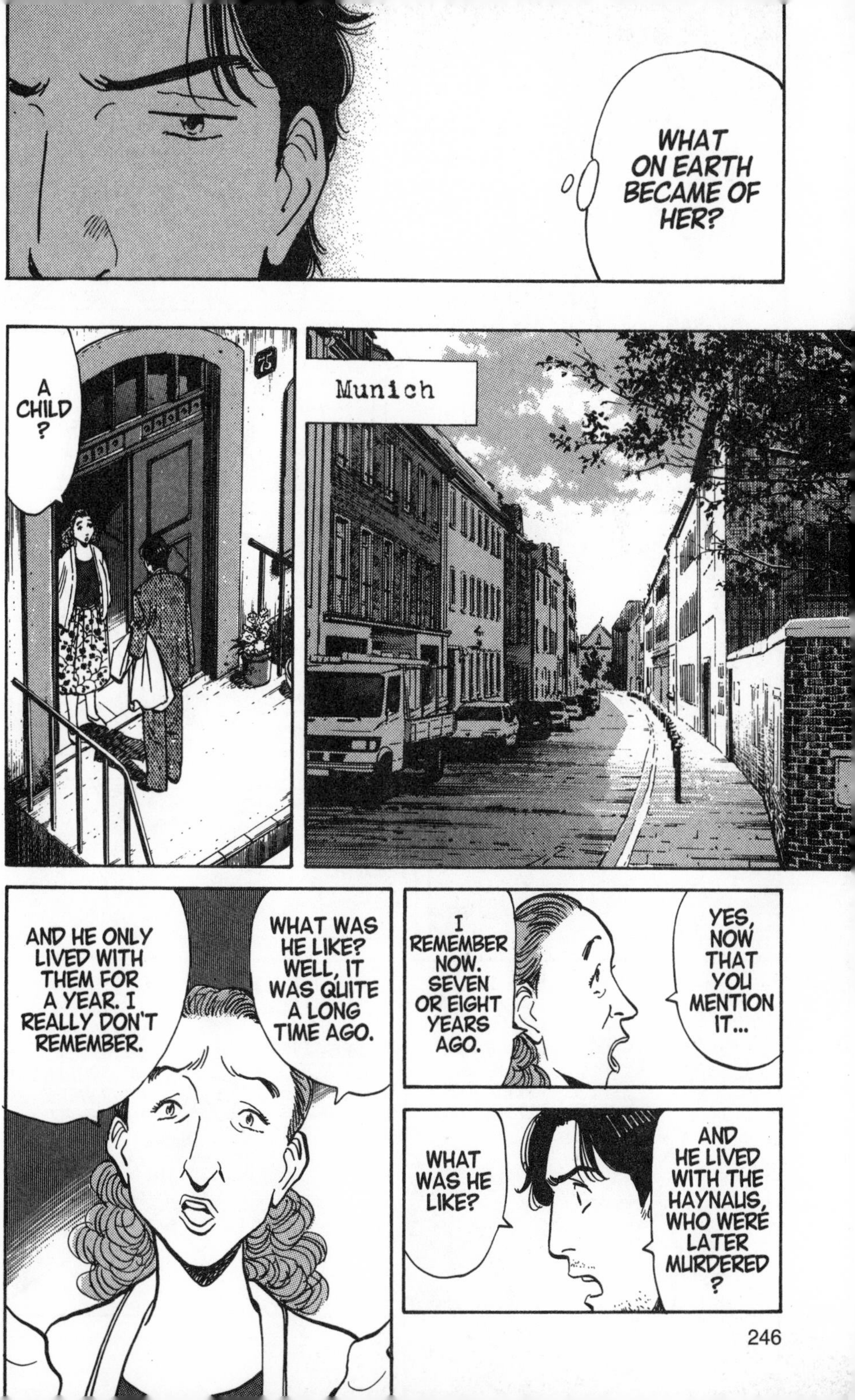
WHAT ON EARTH BECAME OF HER?
Munich
A CHILD ?
YES, NOW THAT YOU MENTION IT...
I REMEMBER NOW. SEVEN OR EIGHT YEARS AGO.
AND HE LIVED WITH THE HAYNAUS, WHO WERE LATER MURDERED ?
WHAT WAS HE LIKE?
WHAT WAS HE LIKE? WELL, IT WAS QUITE A LONG TIME AGO.
AND HE ONLY LIVED WITH THEM FOR A YEAR. I REALLY DON'T REMEMBER.

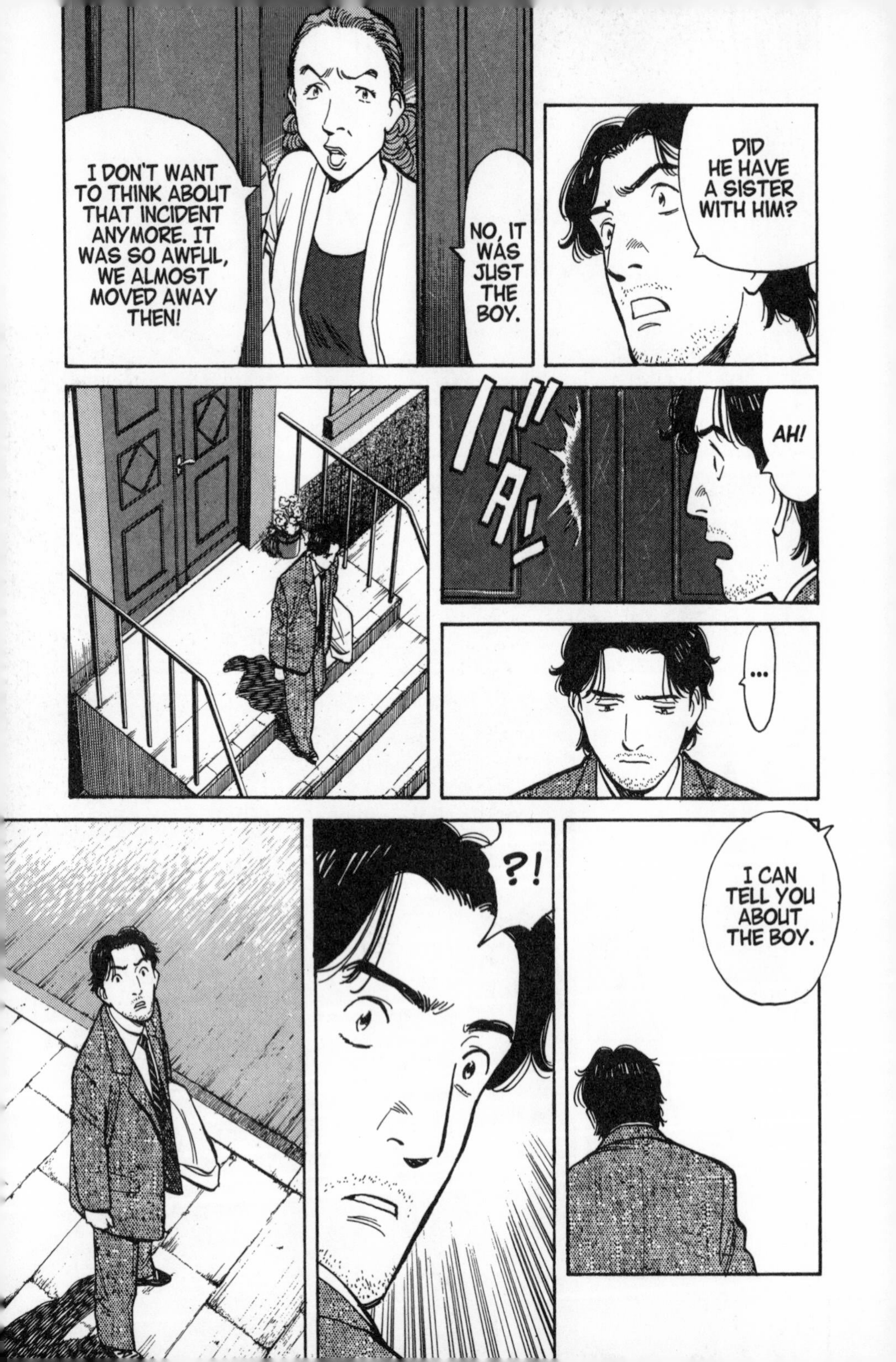
DID HE HAVE A SISTER WITH HIM?
NO, IT WAS JUST THE BOY.
I DON'T WANT TO THINK ABOUT THAT INCIDENT ANYMORE. IT WAS SO AWFUL, WE ALMOST MOVED AWAY THEN!
AH!
...
I CAN TELL YOU ABOUT THE BOY.
?!

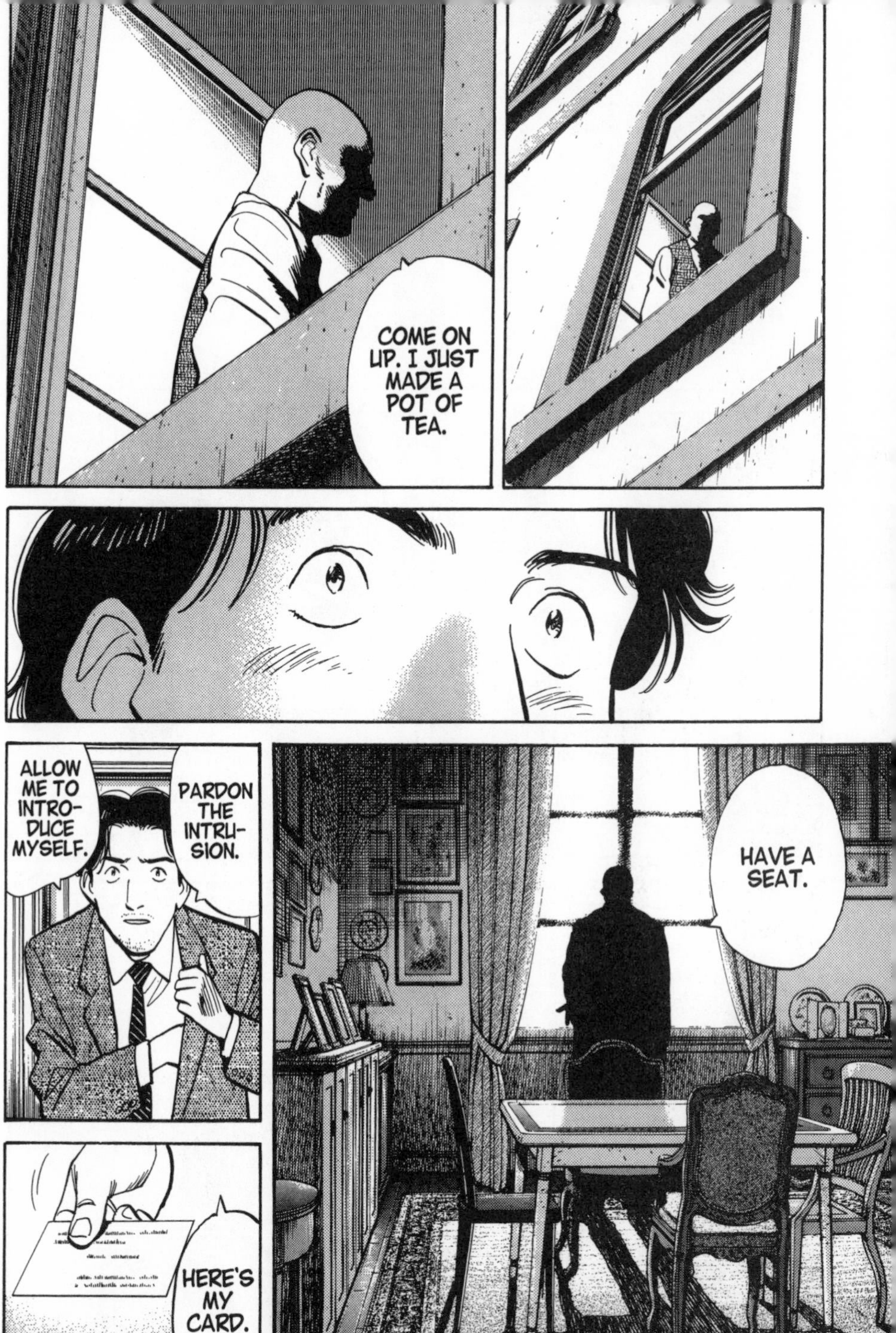
COME ON UP. I JUST MADE A POT OF TEA.
HAVE A SEAT.
PARDON THE INTRUSION.
ALLOW ME TO INTRODUCE MYSELF.
HERE'S MY CARD.

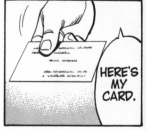

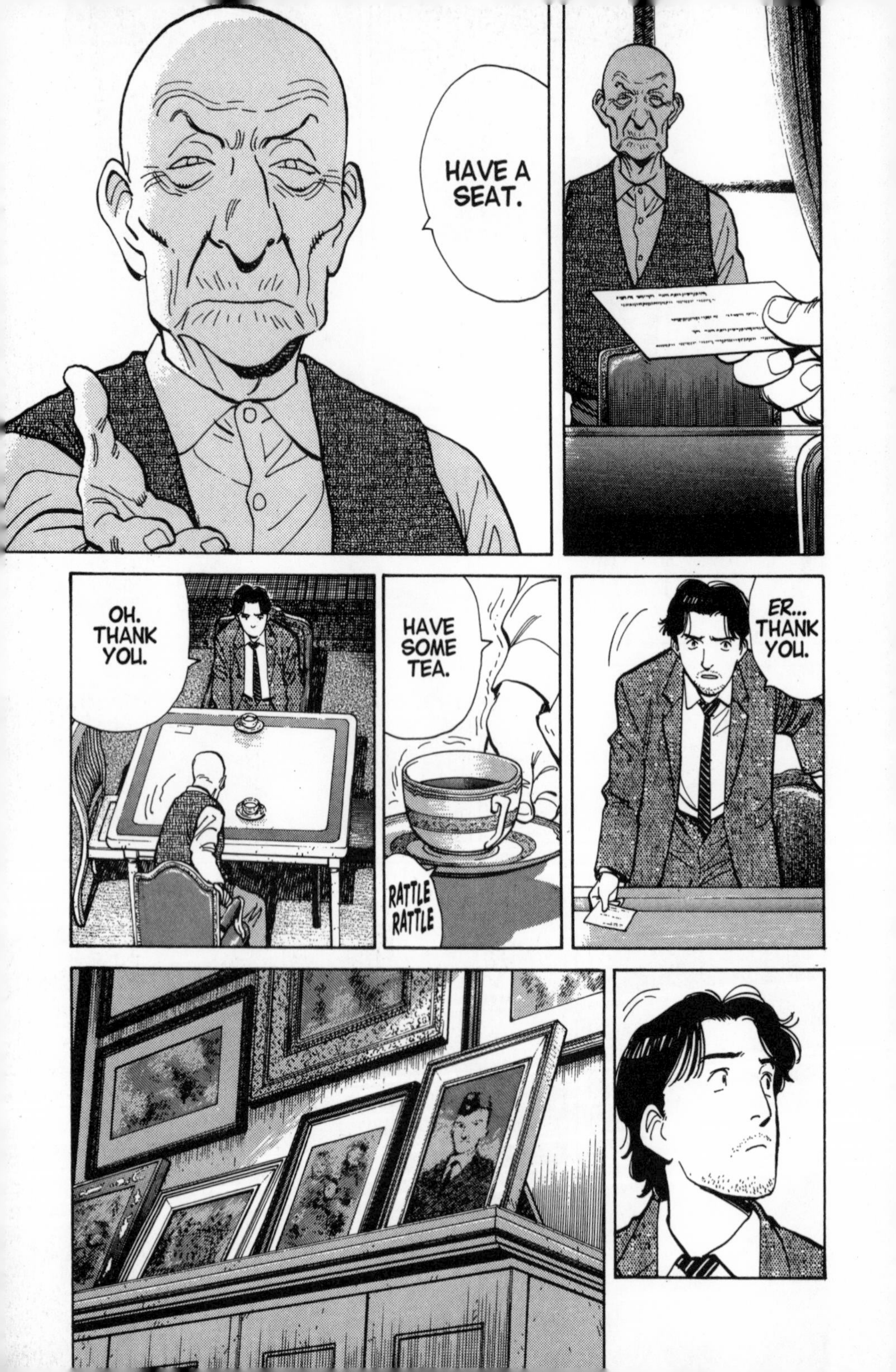
HAVE A SEAT.
ER... THANK YOU.
HAVE SOME TEA.
RATTLE RATTLE
OH. THANK YOU.

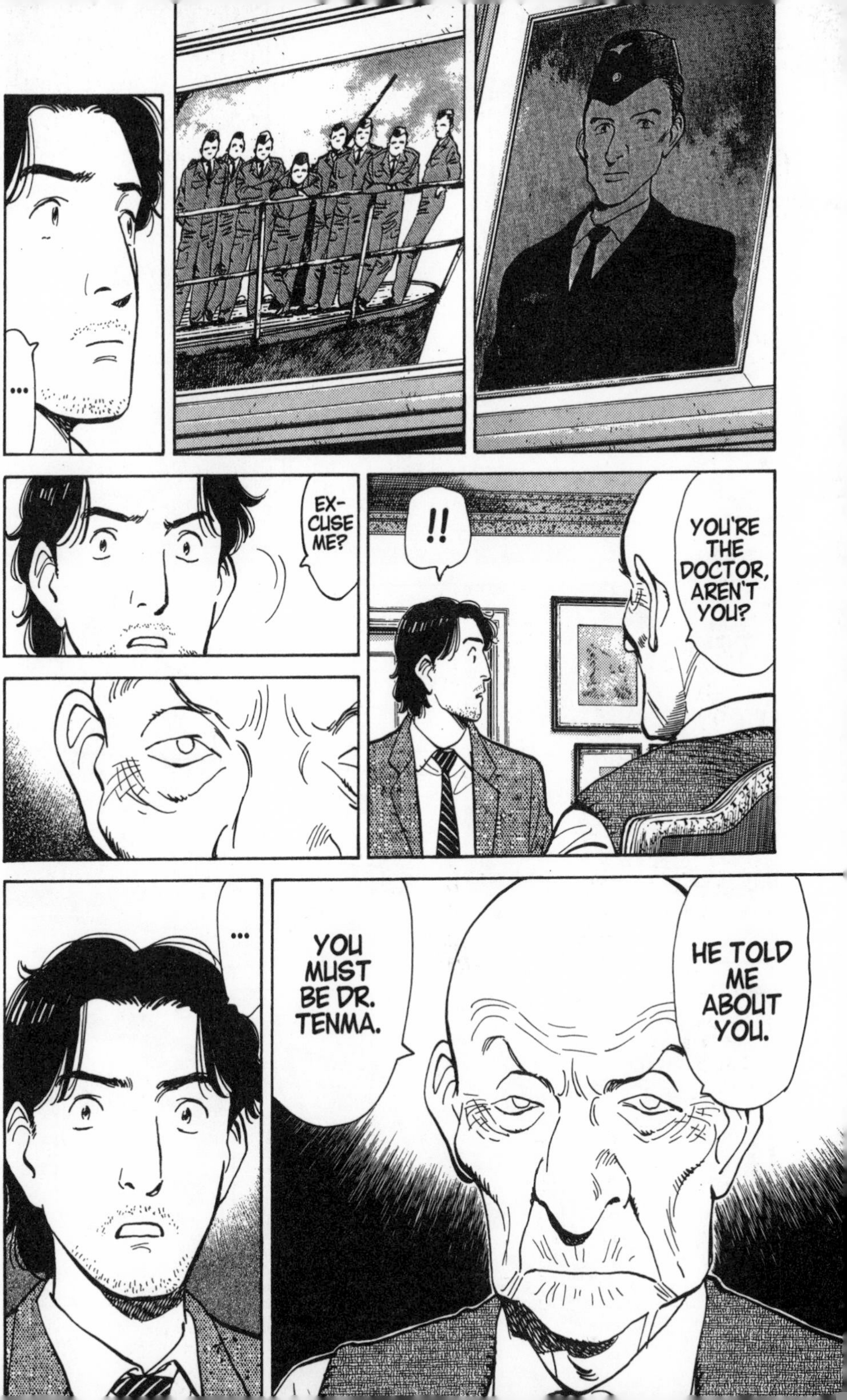

...
YOU'RE THE DOCTOR, AREN'T YOU?
!!
EX-CUSE ME?
HE TOLD ME ABOUT YOU.
YOU MUST BE DR. TENMA.
...

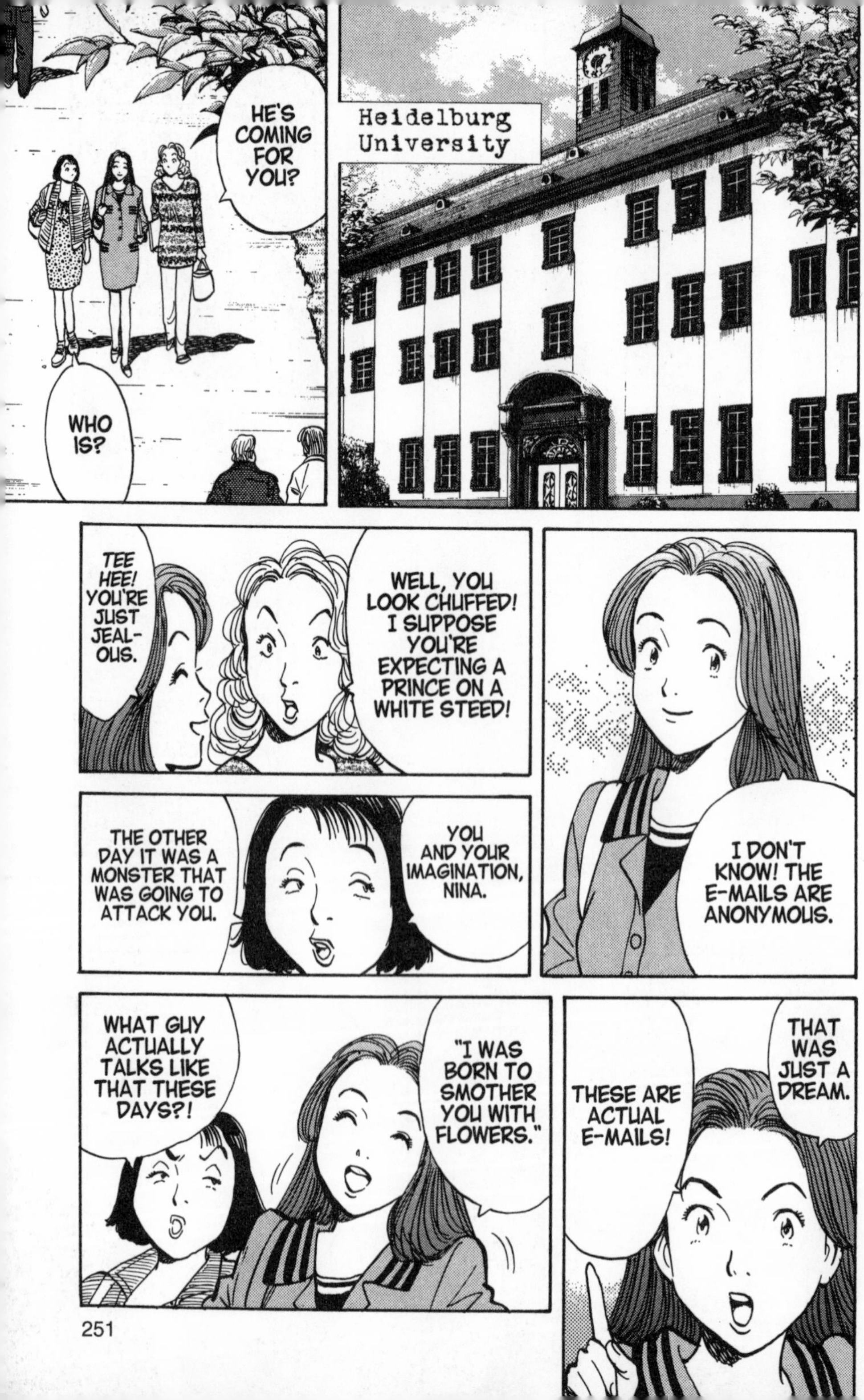
Heidelburg University
HE'S COMING FOR YOU?
WHO IS?
I DON'T KNOW! THE E-MAILS ARE ANONYMOUS.
WELL, YOU LOOK CHUFFED! I SUPPOSE YOU'RE EXPECTING A PRINCE ON A WHITE STEED!
TEE HEE! YOU'RE JUST JEAL-OUS.
YOU AND YOUR IMAGINATION, NINA.
THE OTHER DAY IT WAS A MONSTER THAT WAS GOING TO ATTACK YOU.
THAT WAS JUST A DREAM.
THESE ARE ACTUAL E-MAILS!
"I WAS BORN TO SMOTHER YOU WITH FLOWERS."
WHAT GUY ACTUALLY TALKS LIKE THAT THESE DAYS?!

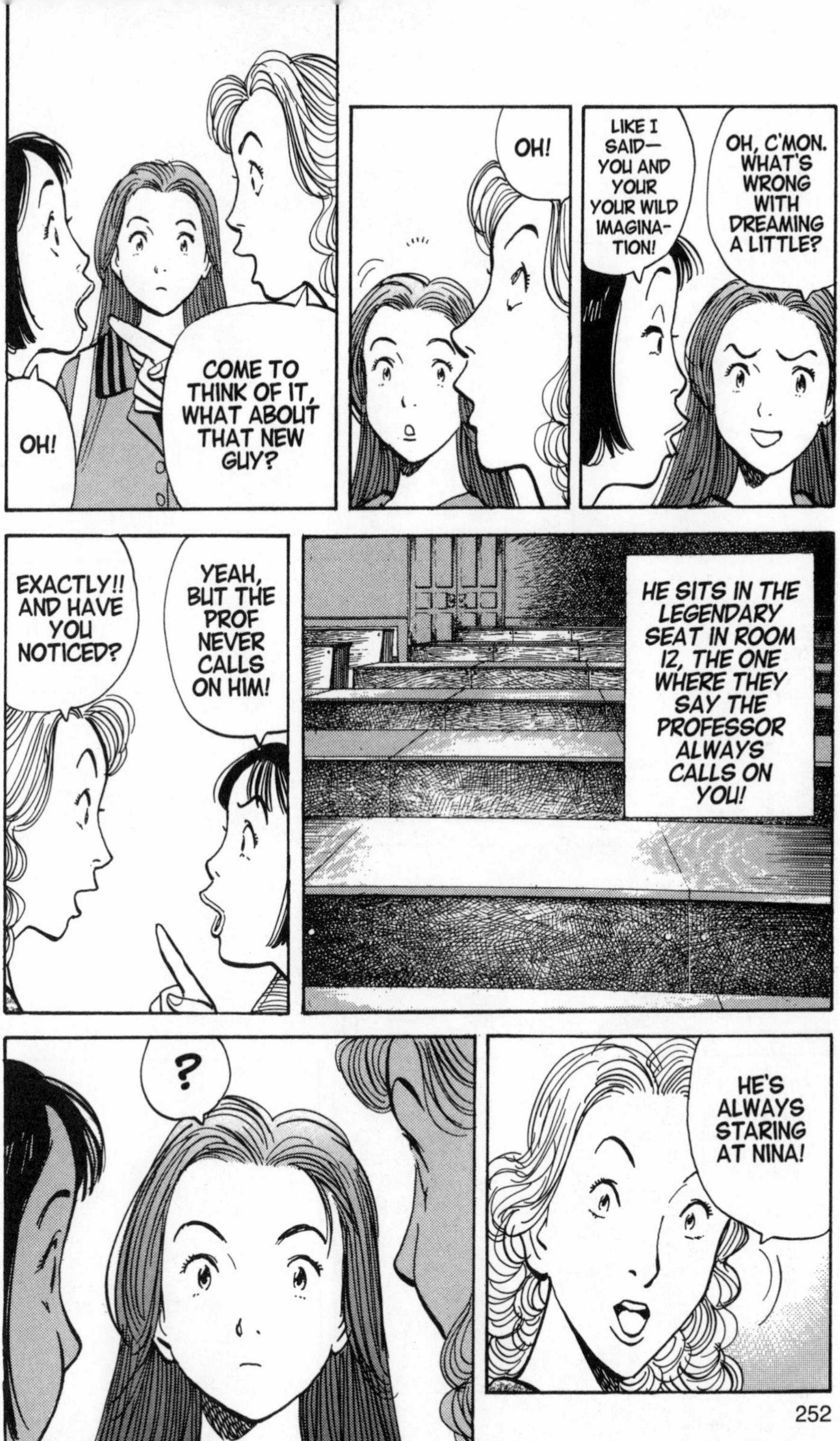
OH, C'MON. WHAT'S WRONG WITH DREAMING A LITTLE?
LIKE I SAID— YOU AND YOUR YOUR WILD IMAGINA-TION!
OH!
COME TO THINK OF IT, WHAT ABOUT THAT NEW GUY?
OH!
HE SITS IN THE LEGENDARY SEAT IN ROOM 12, THE ONE WHERE THEY SAY THE PROFESSOR ALWAYS CALLS ON YOU!
YEAH, BUT THE PROF NEVER CALLS ON HIM!
EXACTLY!! AND HAVE YOU NOTICED?
HE'S ALWAYS STARING AT NINA!
?

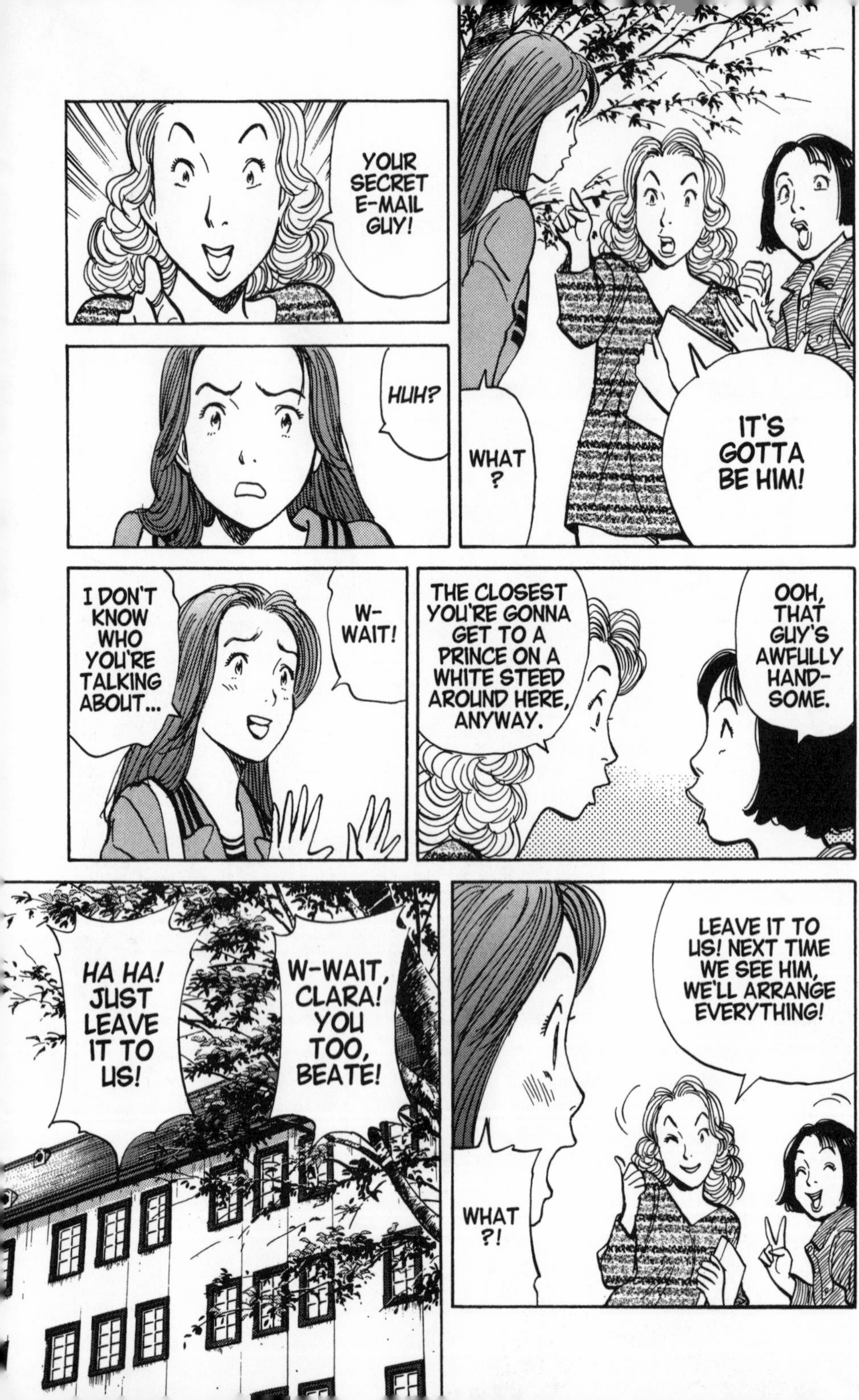
IT'S GOTTA BE HIM!
WHAT?
YOUR SECRET E-MAIL GUY!
HUH?
OOH, THAT GUY'S AWFULLY HAND-SOME.
THE CLOSEST YOU'RE GONNA GET TO A PRINCE ON A WHITE STEED AROUND HERE, ANYWAY.
W-WAIT!
I DON'T KNOW WHO YOU'RE TALKING ABOUT...
LEAVE IT TO US! NEXT TIME WE SEE HIM, WE'LL ARRANGE EVERYTHING!
WHAT?!
W-WAIT, CLARA! YOU TOO, BEATE!
HA HA! JUST LEAVE IT TO US!

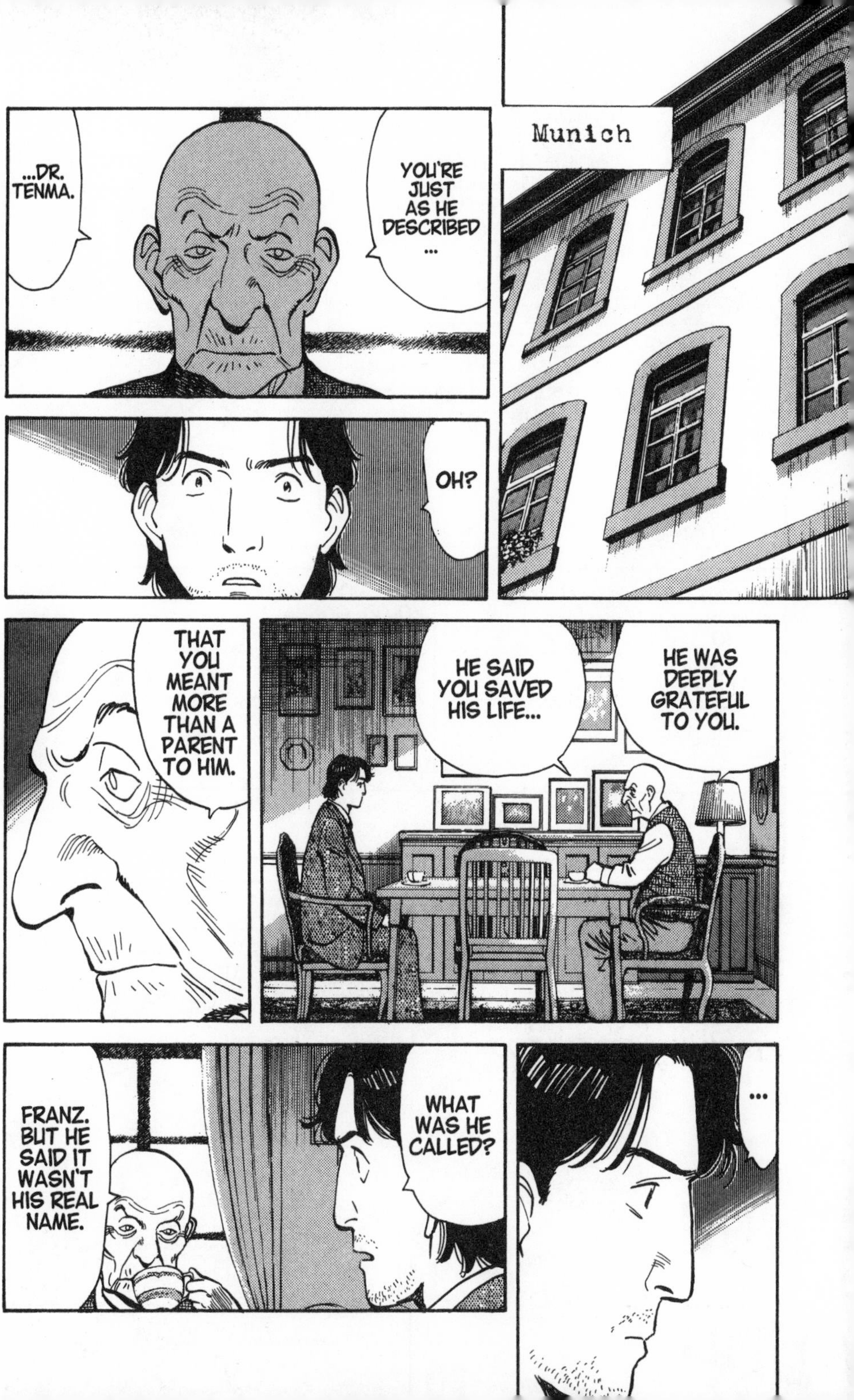
Munich
YOU'RE JUST AS HE DESCRIBED...
...DR. TENMA.
OH?
HE WAS DEEPLY GRATEFUL TO YOU.
HE SAID YOU SAVED HIS LIFE...
THAT YOU MEANT MORE THAN A PARENT TO HIM.
...
WHAT WAS HE CALLED?
FRANZ. BUT HE SAID IT WASN'T HIS REAL NAME.

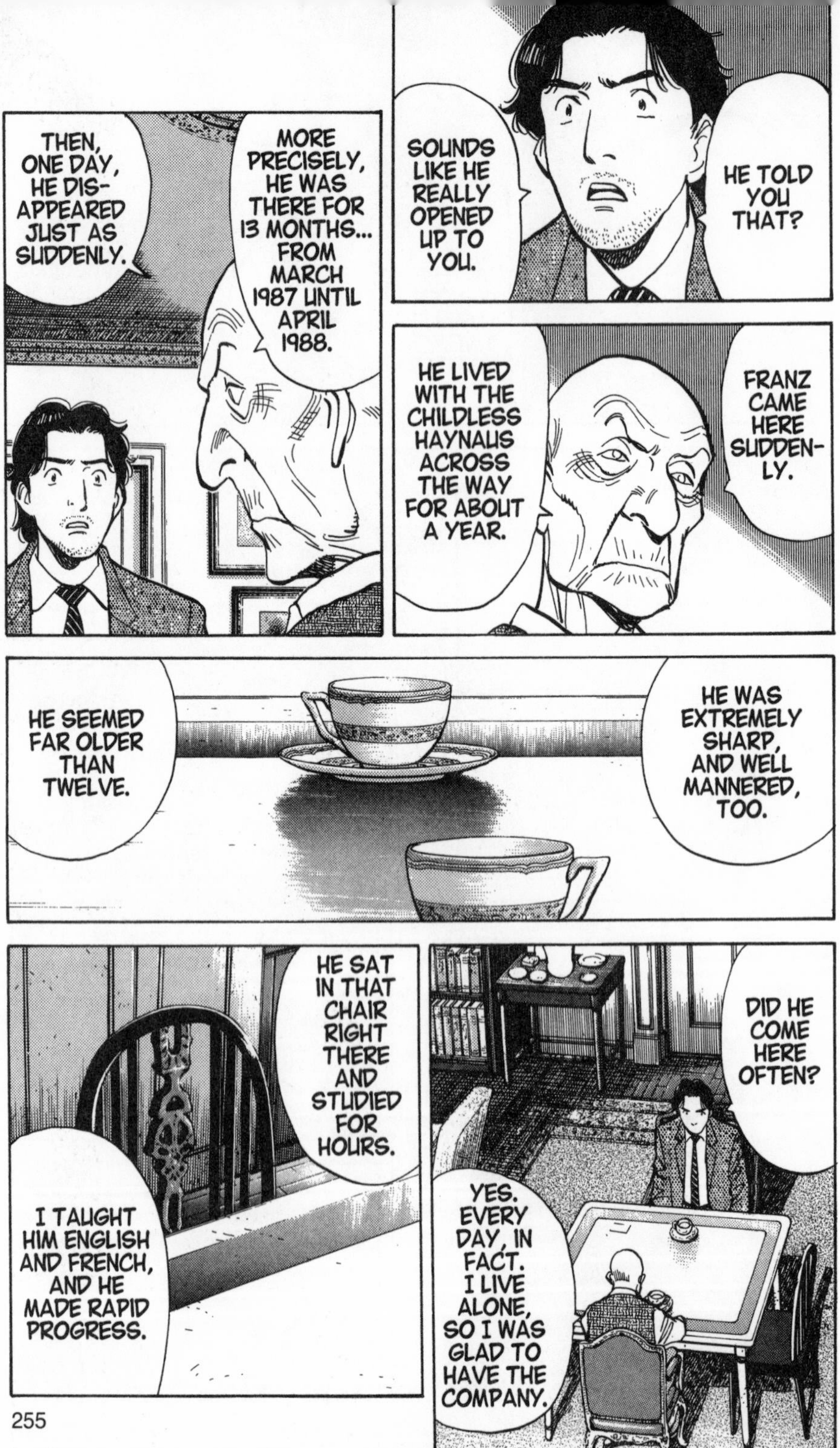
HE TOLD YOU THAT?
SOUNDS LIKE HE REALLY OPENED UP TO YOU.
FRANZ CAME HERE SUDDEN-LY.
HE LIVED WITH THE CHILDLESS HAYNAUS ACROSS THE WAY FOR ABOUT A YEAR.
MORE PRECISELY, HE WAS THERE FOR 13 MONTHS... FROM MARCH 1987 UNTIL APRIL 1988.
THEN, ONE DAY, HE DIS-APPEARED JUST AS SUDDENLY.
HE WAS EXTREMELY SHARP, AND WELL MANNERED, TOO.
HE SEEMED FAR OLDER THAN TWELVE.
DID HE COME HERE OFTEN?
YES. EVERY DAY, IN FACT. I LIVE ALONE, SO I WAS GLAD TO HAVE THE COMPANY.
HE SAT IN THAT CHAIR RIGHT THERE AND STUDIED FOR HOURS.
I TAUGHT HIM ENGLISH AND FRENCH, AND HE MADE RAPID PROGRESS.

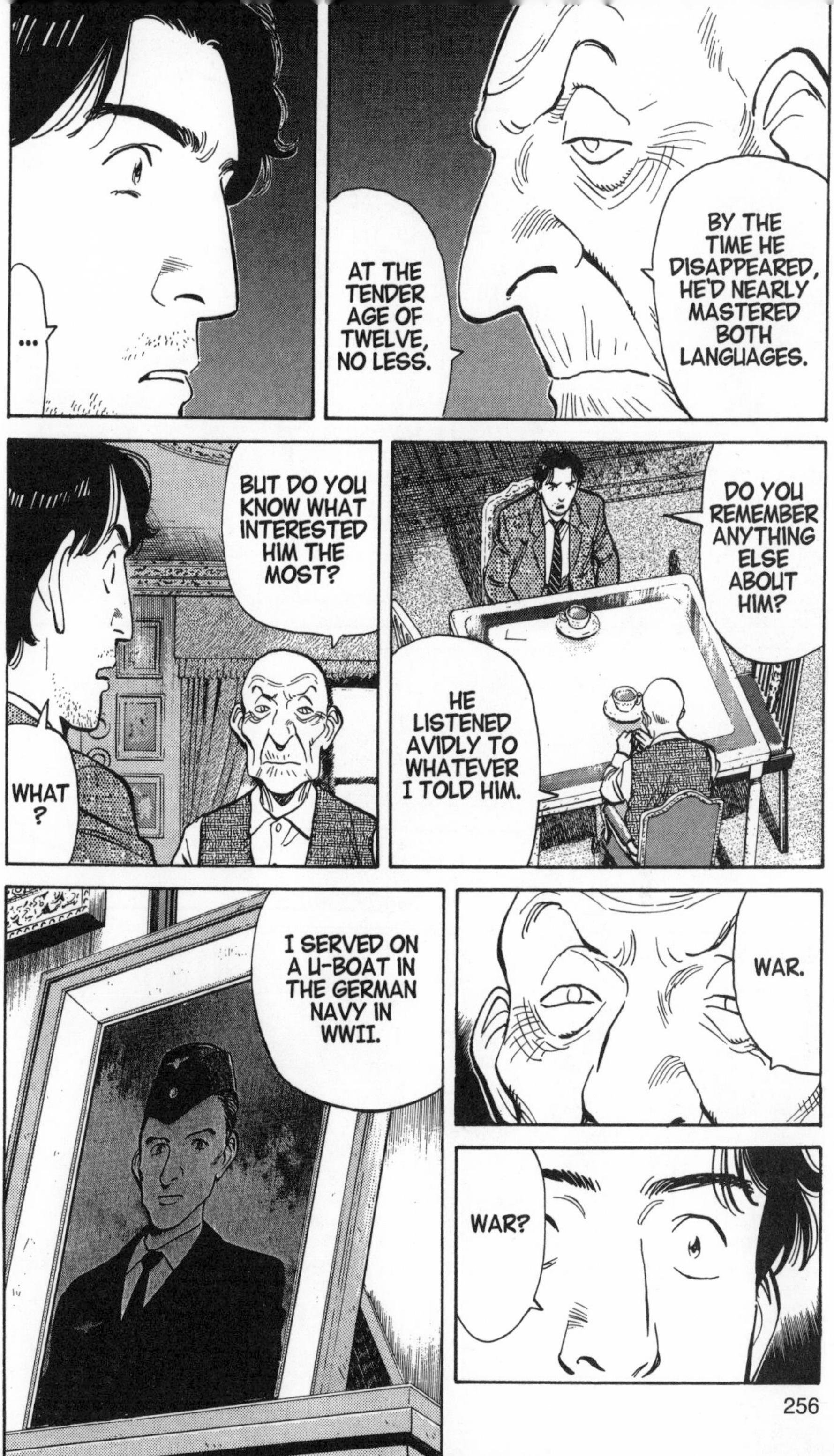
BY THE TIME HE DISAPPEARED, HE'D NEARLY MASTERED BOTH LANGUAGES.
AT THE TENDER AGE OF TWELVE, NO LESS.
...
DO YOU REMEMBER ANYTHING ELSE ABOUT HIM?
HE LISTENED AVIDLY TO WHATEVER I TOLD HIM.
BUT DO YOU KNOW WHAT INTERESTED HIM THE MOST?
WHAT?
WAR.
WAR?
I SERVED ON A U-BOAT IN THE GERMAN NAVY IN WWII.

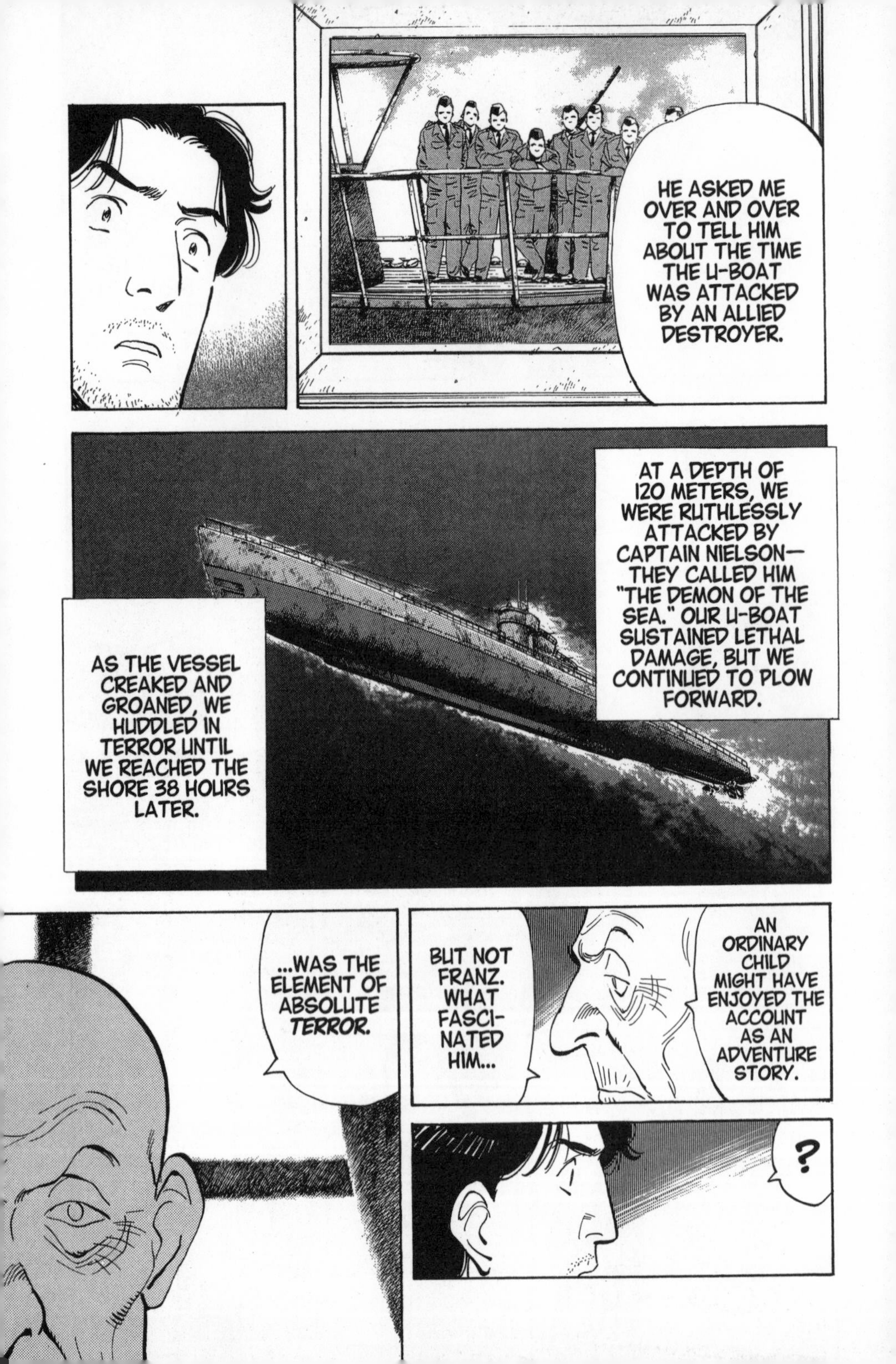
HE ASKED ME OVER AND OVER TO TELL HIM ABOUT THE TIME THE U-BOAT WAS ATTACKED BY AN ALLIED DESTROYER.
AT A DEPTH OF 120 METERS, WE WERE RUTHLESSLY ATTACKED BY CAPTAIN NIELSON—THEY CALLED HIM "THE DEMON OF THE SEA." OUR U-BOAT SUSTAINED LETHAL DAMAGE, BUT WE CONTINUED TO PLOW FORWARD.
AS THE VESSEL CREAKED AND GROANED, WE HUDDLED IN TERROR UNTIL WE REACHED THE SHORE 38 HOURS LATER.
AN ORDINARY CHILD MIGHT HAVE ENJOYED THE ACCOUNT AS AN ADVENTURE STORY.
BUT NOT FRANZ. WHAT FASCI-NATED HIM...
...WAS THE ELEMENT OF ABSOLUTE *TERROR.*
?

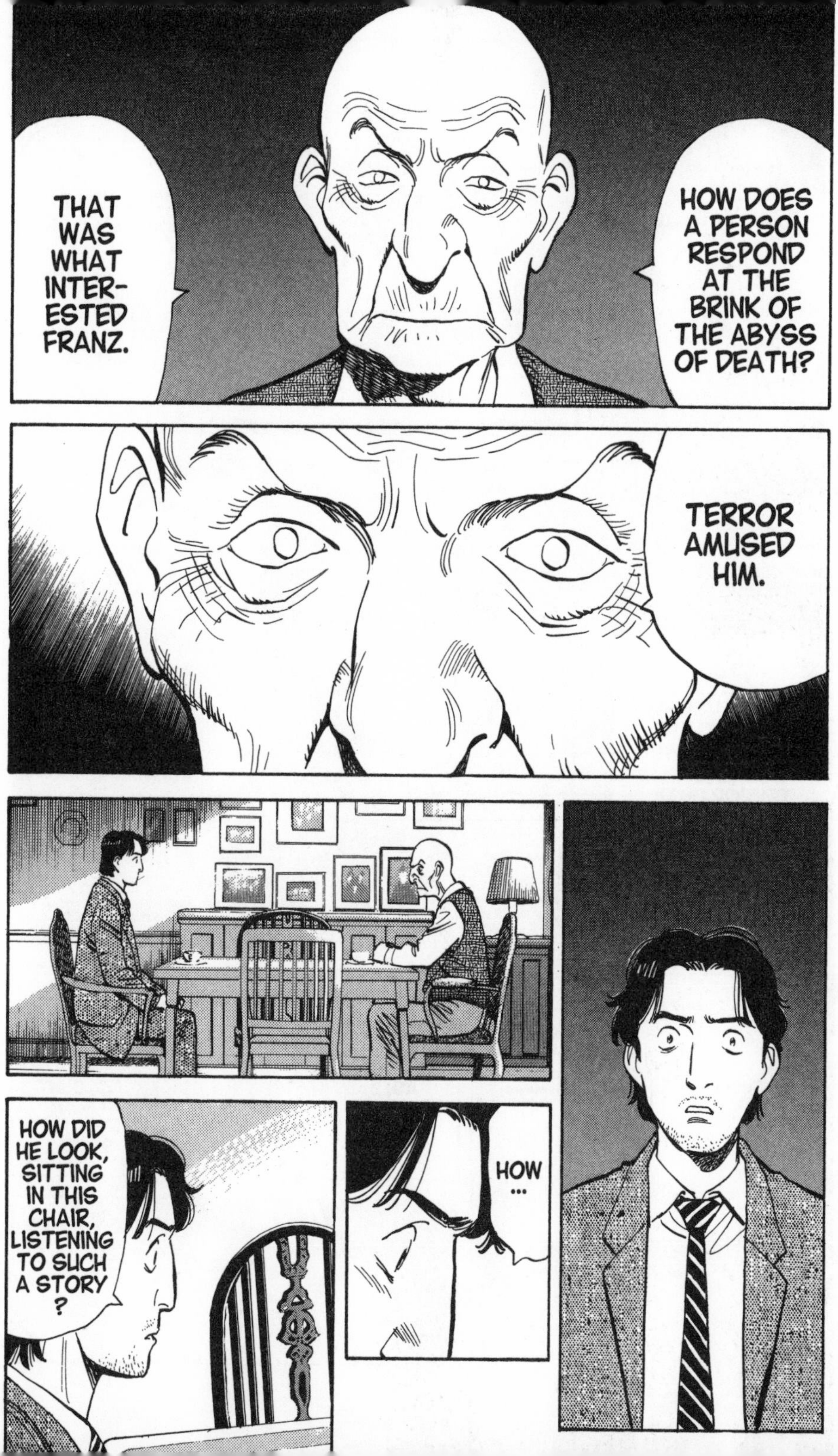
HOW DOES A PERSON RESPOND AT THE BRINK OF THE ABYSS OF DEATH?
THAT WAS WHAT INTER-ESTED FRANZ.
TERROR AMUSED HIM.
HOW ...
HOW DID HE LOOK, SITTING IN THIS CHAIR, LISTENING TO SUCH A STORY ?

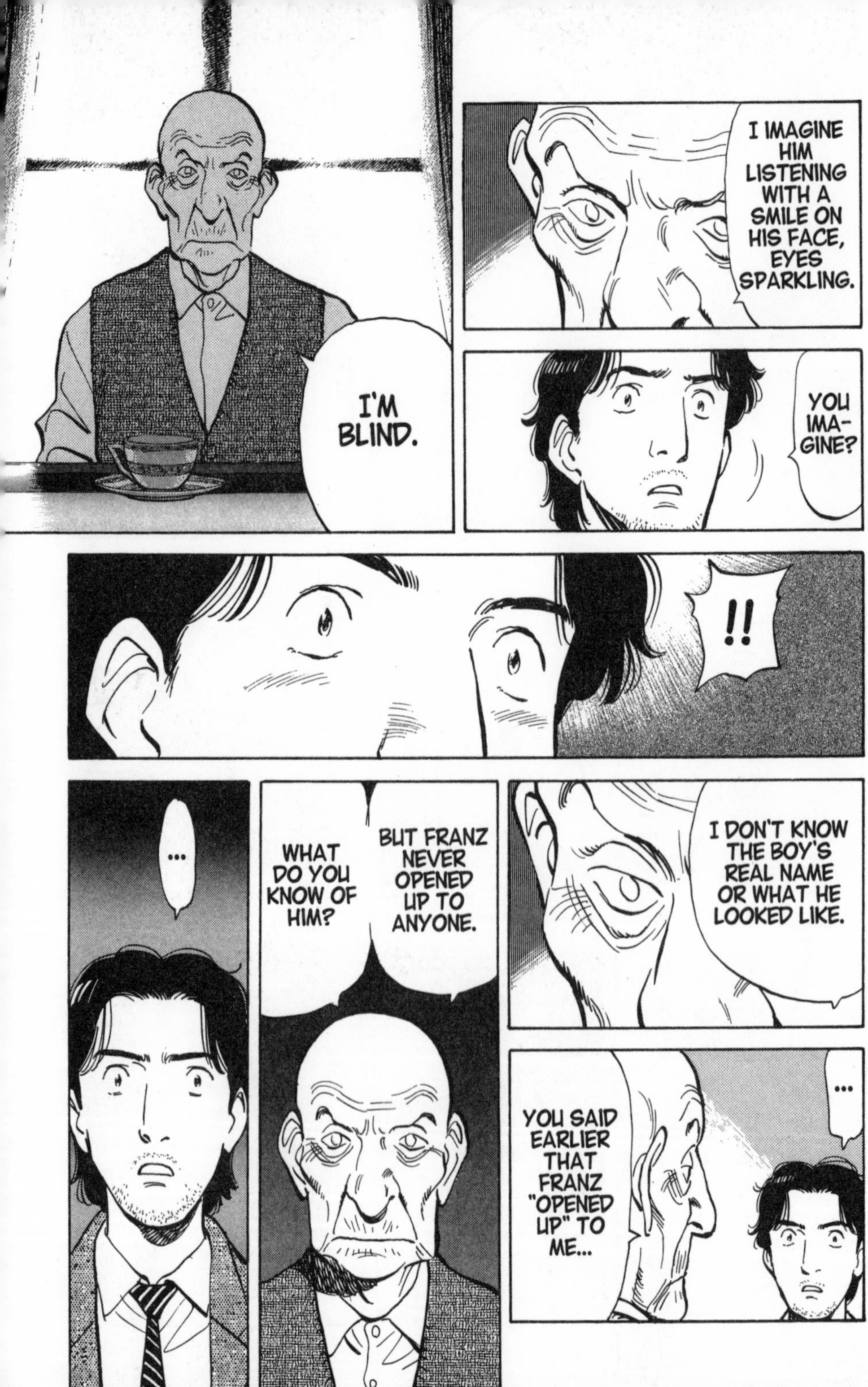
I IMAGINE HIM LISTENING WITH A SMILE ON HIS FACE, EYES SPARKLING.
YOU IMAGINE?
I'M BLIND.
!!
I DON'T KNOW THE BOY'S REAL NAME OR WHAT HE LOOKED LIKE.
...
YOU SAID EARLIER THAT FRANZ "OPENED UP" TO ME...
BUT FRANZ NEVER OPENED UP TO ANYONE.
WHAT DO YOU KNOW OF HIM?
...

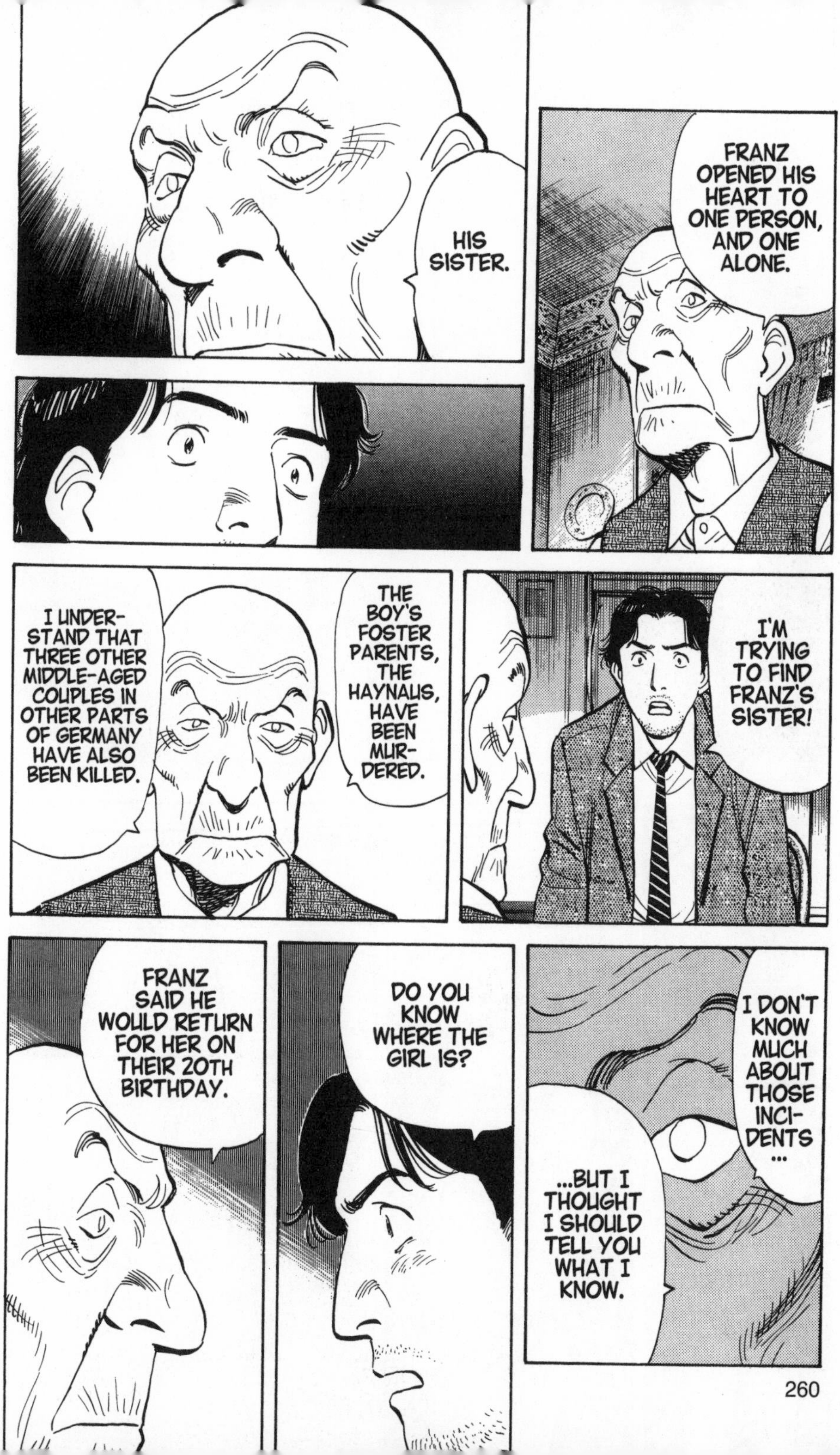
FRANZ OPENED HIS HEART TO ONE PERSON, AND ONE ALONE.
HIS SISTER.
I'M TRYING TO FIND FRANZ'S SISTER!
THE BOY'S FOSTER PARENTS, THE HAYNAUS, HAVE BEEN MUR-DERED.
I UNDER-STAND THAT THREE OTHER MIDDLE-AGED COUPLES IN OTHER PARTS OF GERMANY HAVE ALSO BEEN KILLED.
I DON'T KNOW MUCH ABOUT THOSE INCI-DENTS...
...BUT I THOUGHT I SHOULD TELL YOU WHAT I KNOW.
DO YOU KNOW WHERE THE GIRL IS?
FRANZ SAID HE WOULD RETURN FOR HER ON THEIR 20TH BIRTHDAY.

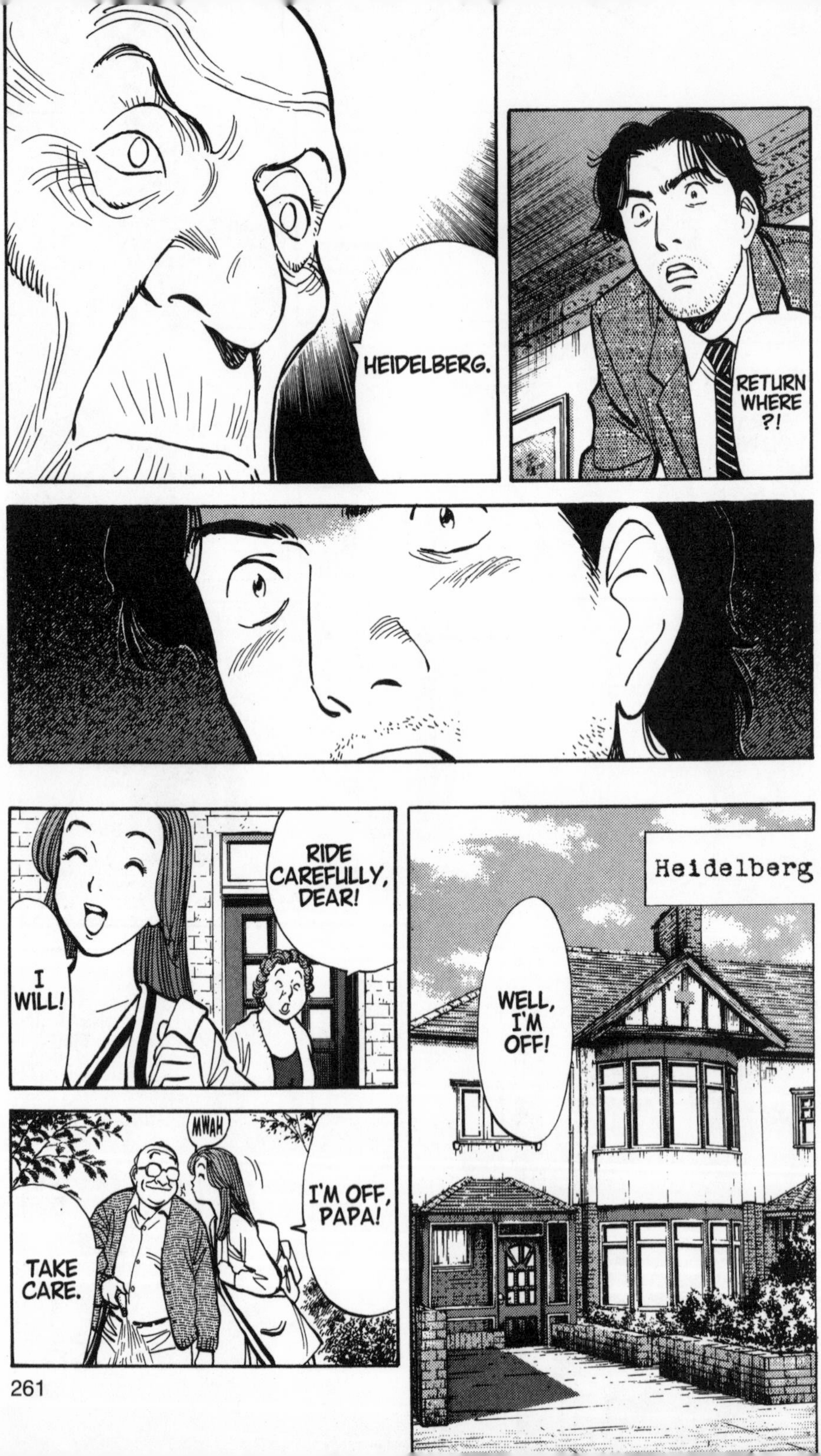
RETURN WHERE ?!
HEIDELBERG.
Heidelberg
WELL, I'M OFF!
RIDE CAREFULLY, DEAR!
I WILL!
I'M OFF, PAPA!
MWAH
TAKE CARE.

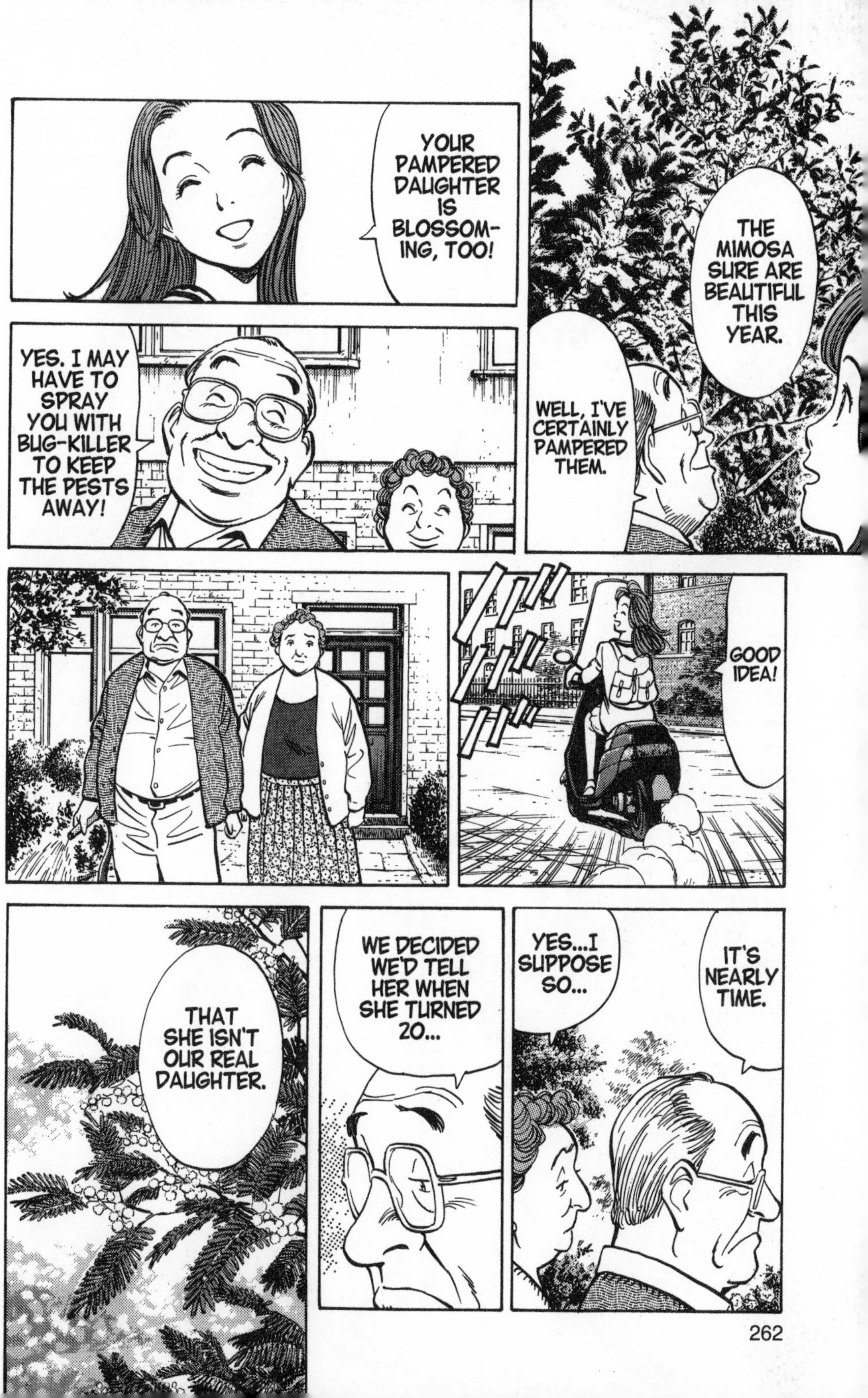
THE MIMOSA SURE ARE BEAUTIFUL THIS YEAR.
WELL, I'VE CERTAINLY PAMPERED THEM.
YOUR PAMPERED DAUGHTER IS BLOSSOM-ING, TOO!
YES. I MAY HAVE TO SPRAY YOU WITH BUG-KILLER TO KEEP THE PESTS AWAY!
GOOD IDEA!
IT'S NEARLY TIME.
YES...I SUPPOSE SO...
WE DECIDED WE'D TELL HER WHEN SHE TURNED 20...
THAT SHE ISN'T OUR REAL DAUGHTER.

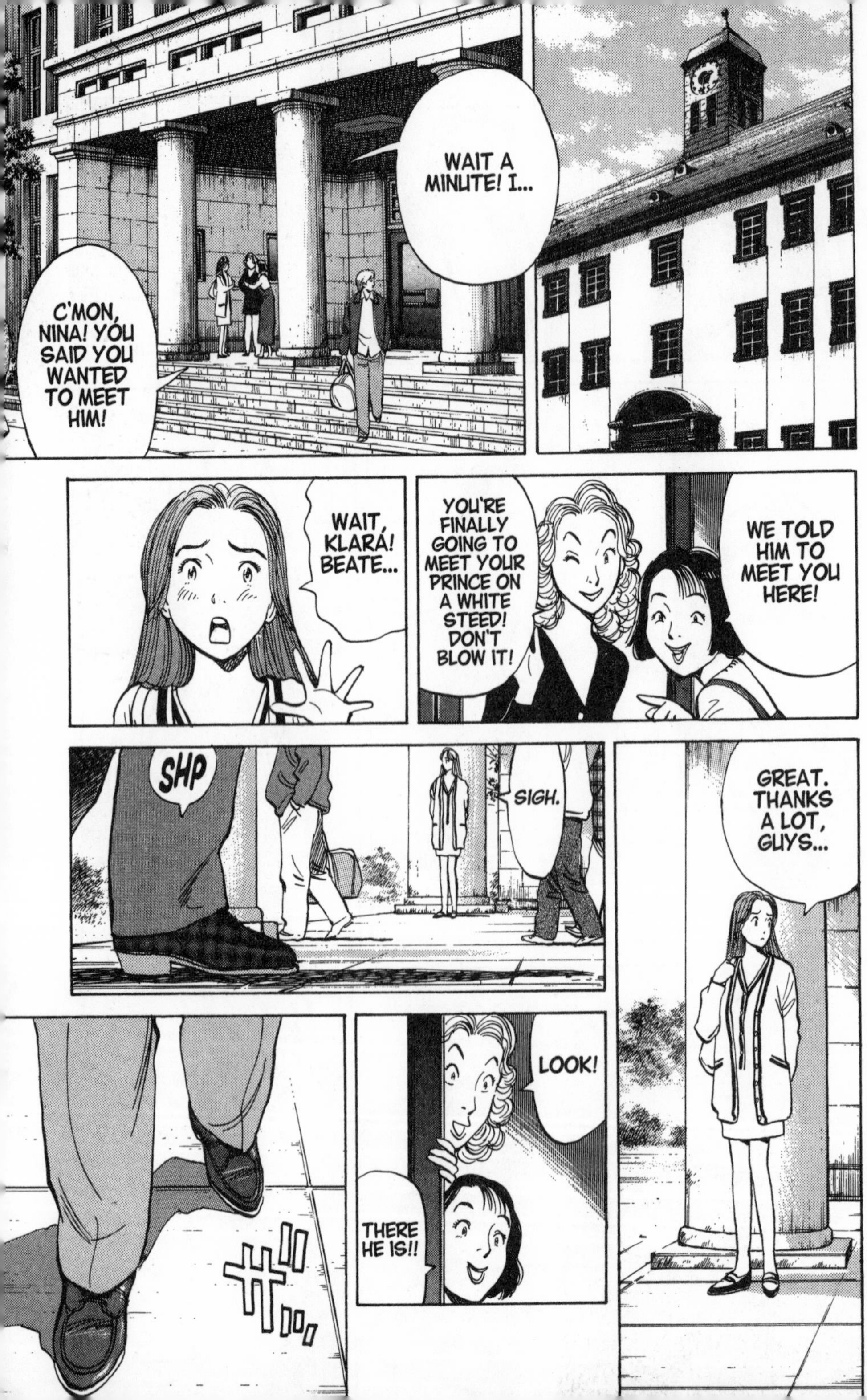

WAIT A MINUTE! I...
C'MON, NINA! YOU SAID YOU WANTED TO MEET HIM!
WE TOLD HIM TO MEET YOU HERE!
YOU'RE FINALLY GOING TO MEET YOUR PRINCE ON A WHITE STEED! DON'T BLOW IT!
WAIT, KLARA! BEATE...
GREAT. THANKS A LOT, GUYS...
SIGH.
SHP
LOOK!
THERE HE IS!!

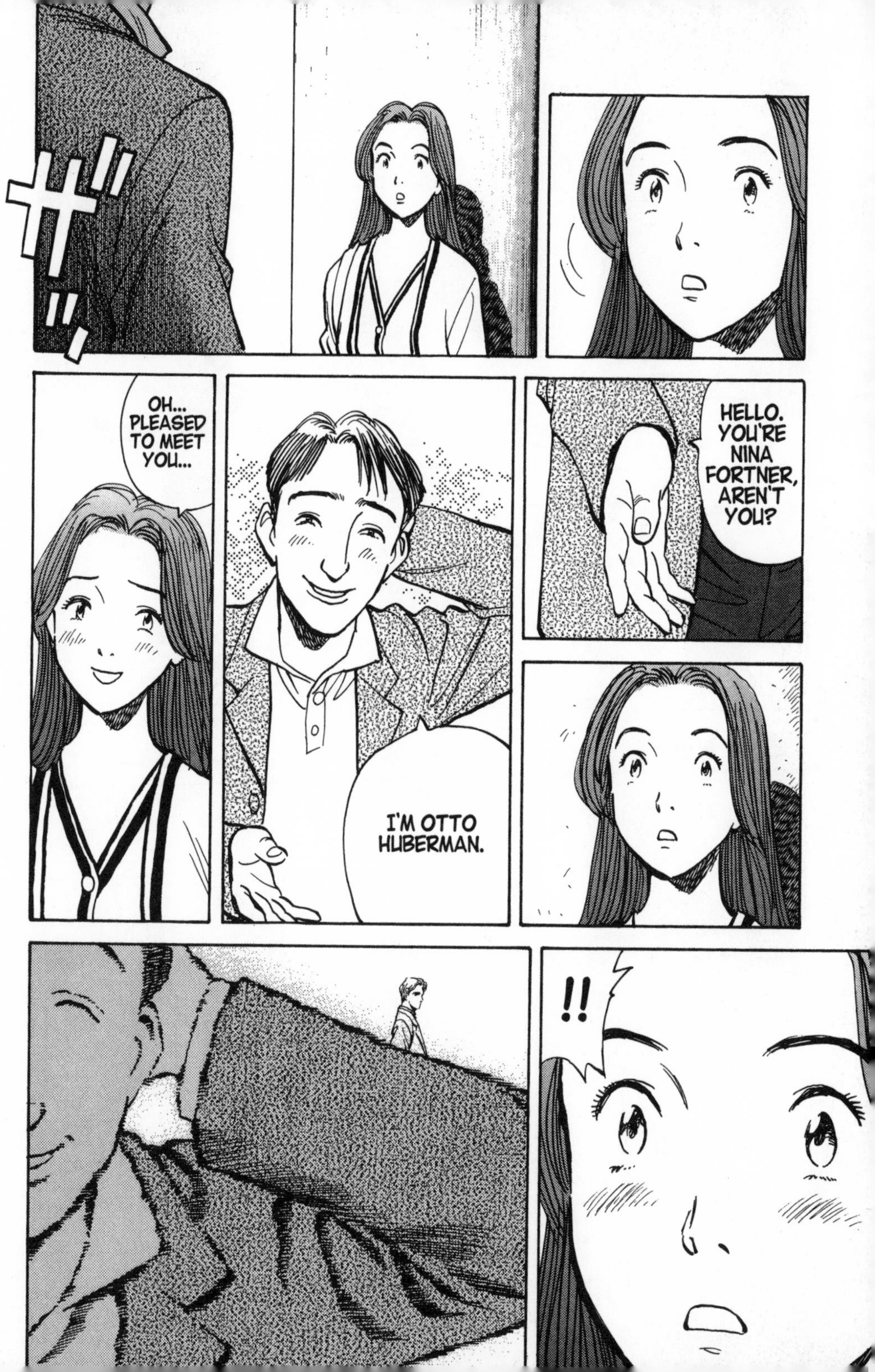
HELLO. YOU'RE NINA FORTNER, AREN'T YOU?
I'M OTTO HUBERMAN.
OH... PLEASED TO MEET YOU...
!!

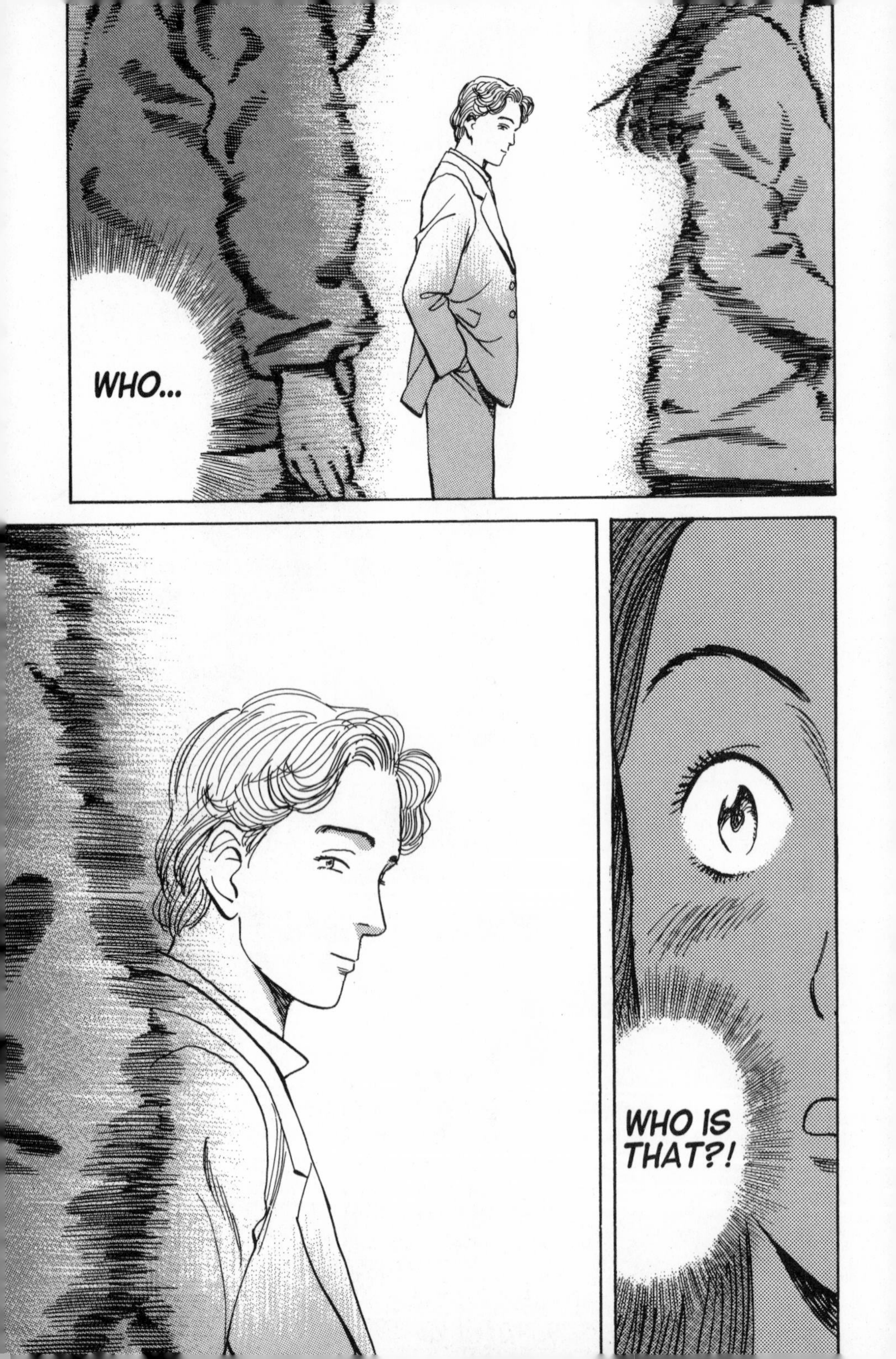
WHO...
WHO IS THAT?!

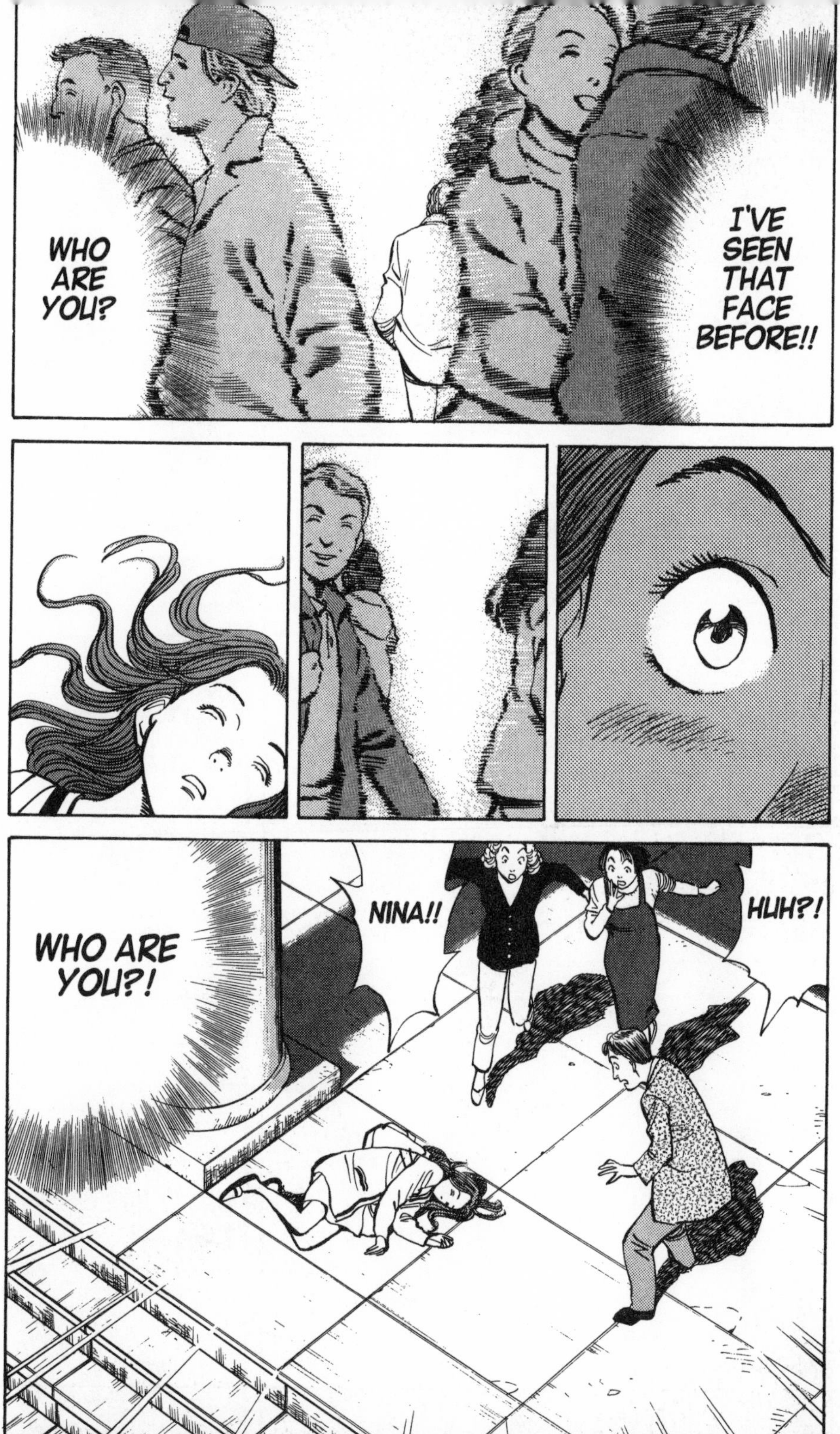
I'VE SEEN THAT FACE BEFORE!!
WHO ARE YOU?
HUH?!
NINA!!
WHO ARE YOU?!

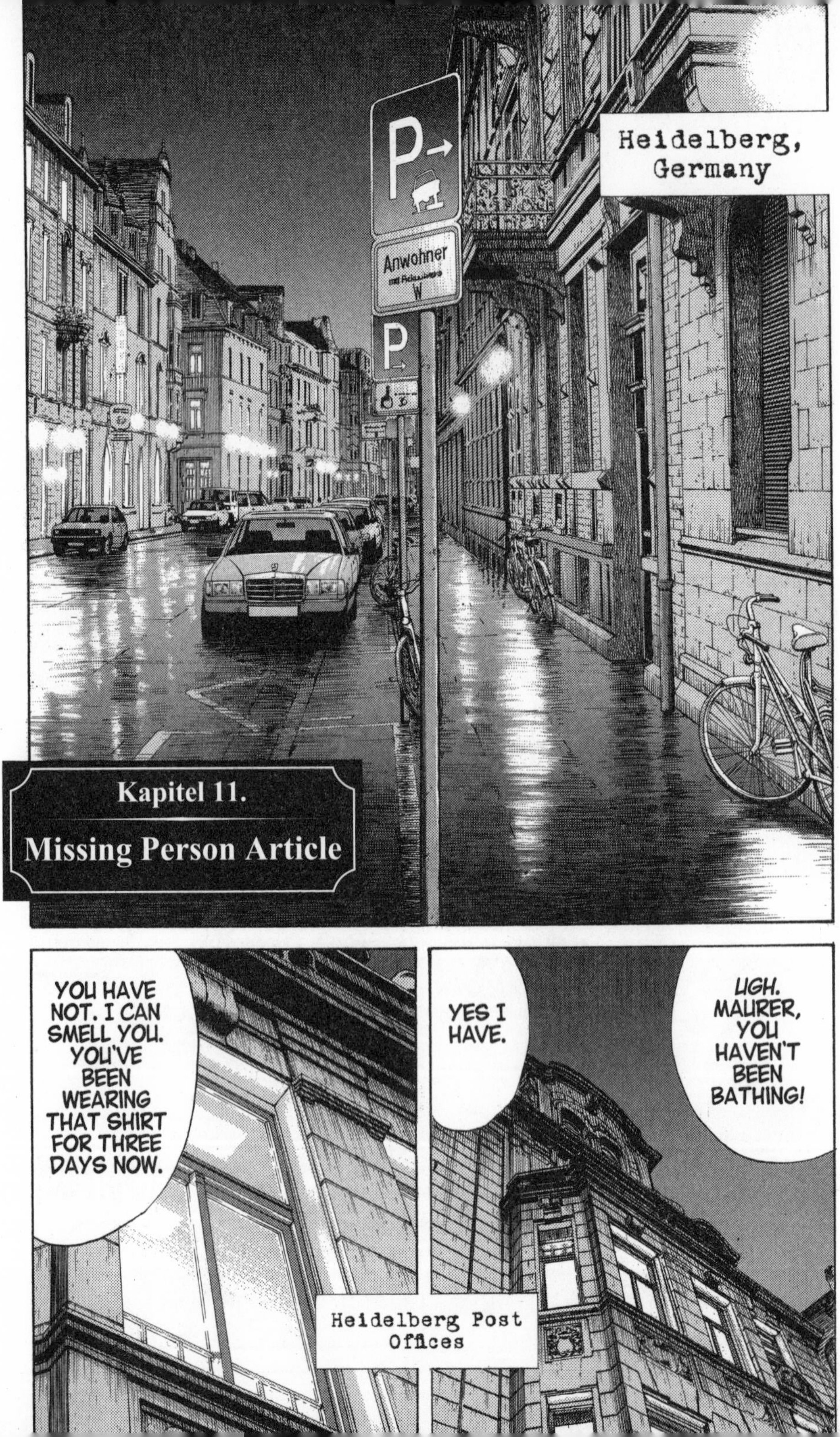
Heidelberg, Germany
Anwohner
Kapitel 11.
Missing Person Article
UGH. MAURER, YOU HAVEN'T BEEN BATHING!
YES I HAVE.
Heidelberg Post Offices
YOU HAVE NOT. I CAN SMELL YOU. YOU'VE BEEN WEARING THAT SHIRT FOR THREE DAYS NOW.

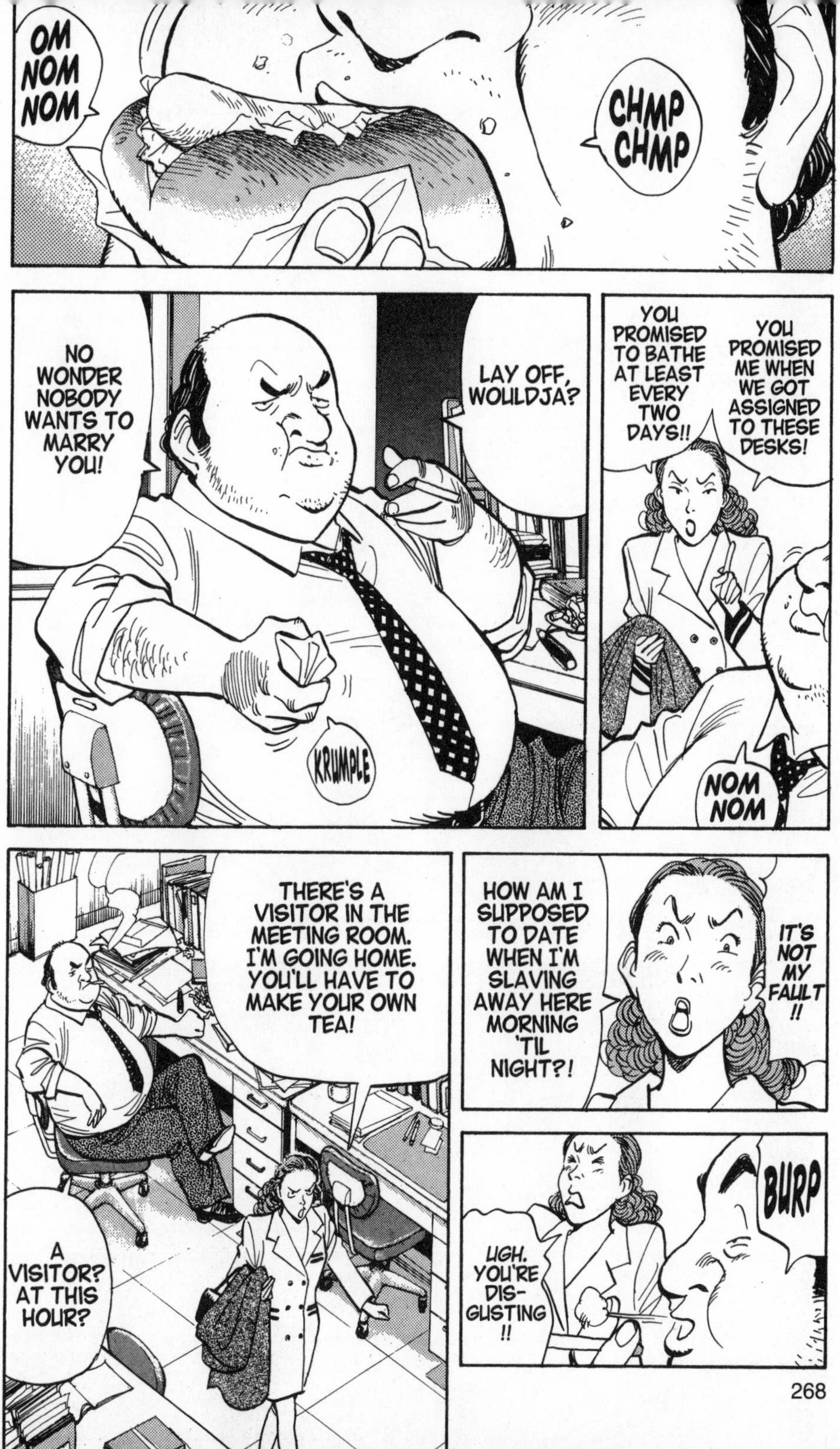
CHMP CHMP
OM NOM NOM
YOU PROMISED ME WHEN WE GOT ASSIGNED TO THESE DESKS!
YOU PROMISED TO BATHE AT LEAST EVERY TWO DAYS!!
NOM NOM
LAY OFF, WOULDJA?
NO WONDER NOBODY WANTS TO MARRY YOU!
KRUMPLE
IT'S NOT MY FAULT!!
HOW AM I SUPPOSED TO DATE WHEN I'M SLAVING AWAY HERE MORNING 'TIL NIGHT?!
BURP
UGH. YOU'RE DIS-GUSTING!!
THERE'S A VISITOR IN THE MEETING ROOM. I'M GOING HOME. YOU'LL HAVE TO MAKE YOUR OWN TEA!
A VISITOR? AT THIS HOUR?

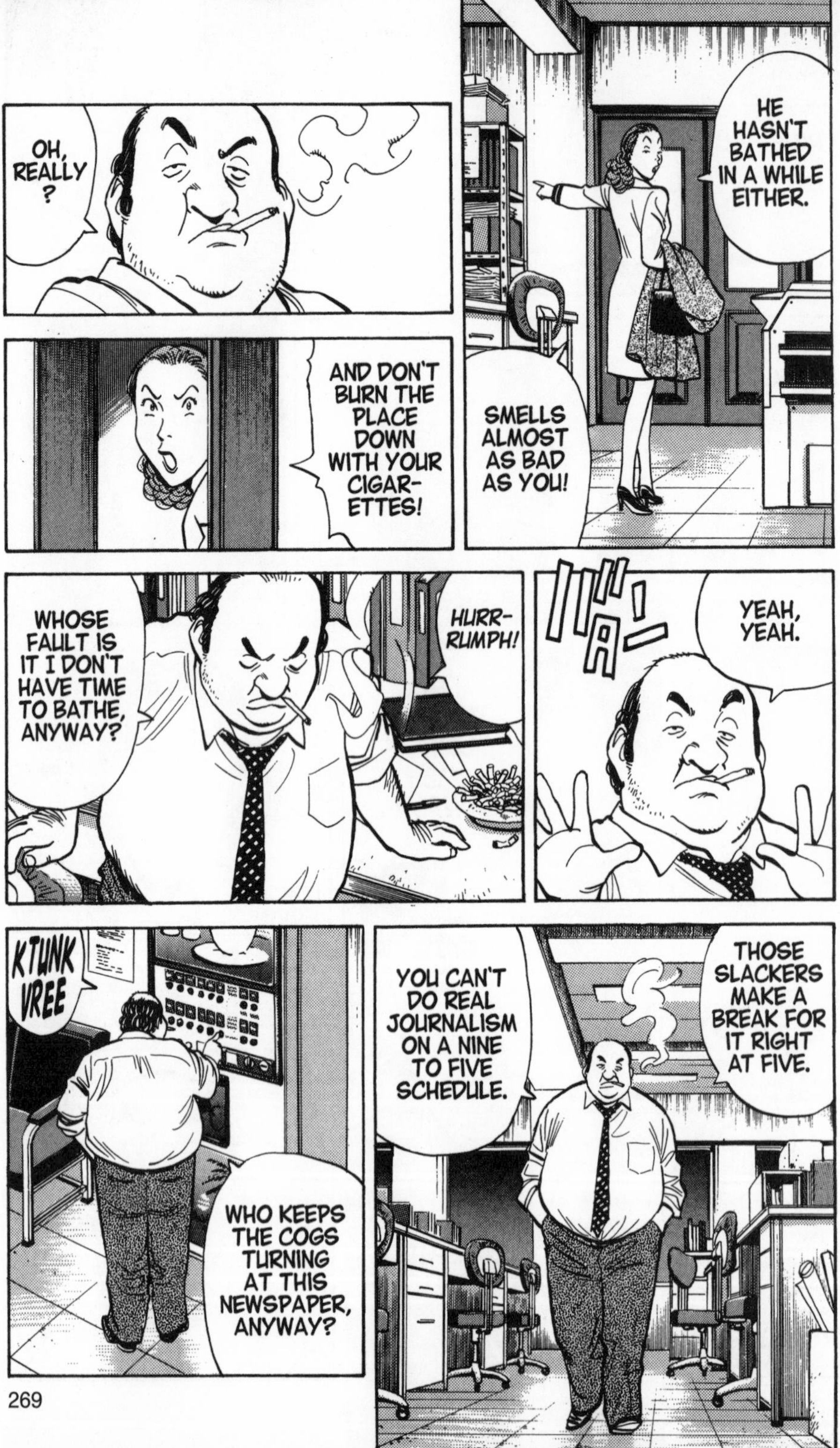
HE HASN'T BATHED IN A WHILE EITHER.
SMELLS ALMOST AS BAD AS YOU!
OH, REALLY?
AND DON'T BURN THE PLACE DOWN WITH YOUR CIGAR-ETTES!
YEAH, YEAH.
HURR-RUMPH!
WHOSE FAULT IS IT I DON'T HAVE TIME TO BATHE, ANYWAY?
THOSE SLACKERS MAKE A BREAK FOR IT RIGHT AT FIVE.
YOU CAN'T DO REAL JOURNALISM ON A NINE TO FIVE SCHEDULE.
KTUNK VREE
WHO KEEPS THE COGS TURNING AT THIS NEWSPAPER, ANYWAY?

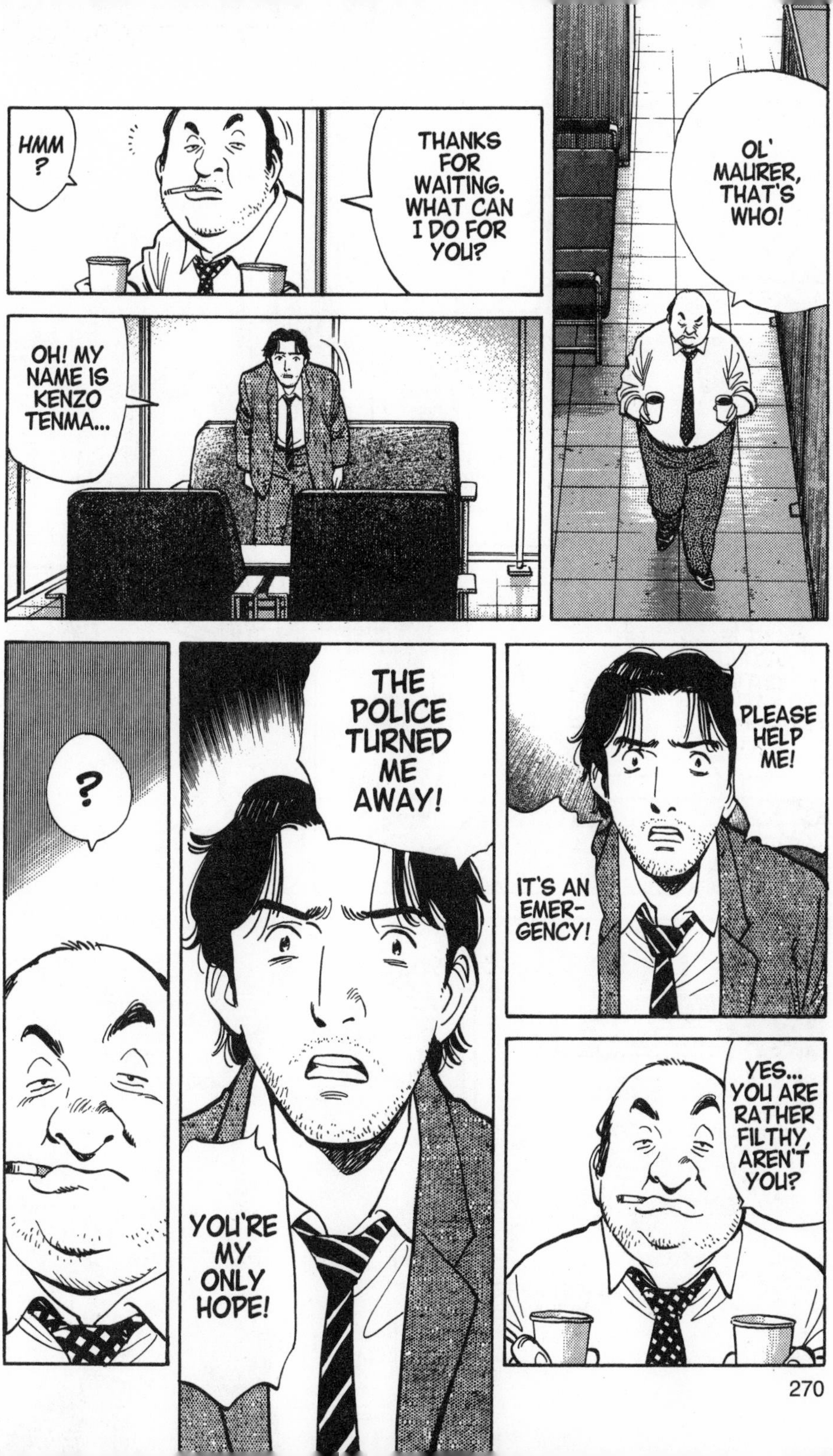
OL' MAURER, THAT'S WHO!
THANKS FOR WAITING. WHAT CAN I DO FOR YOU?
HMM?
OH! MY NAME IS KENZO TENMA...
PLEASE HELP ME!
IT'S AN EMERGENCY!
YES... YOU ARE RATHER FILTHY, AREN'T YOU?
THE POLICE TURNED ME AWAY!
YOU'RE MY ONLY HOPE!
?

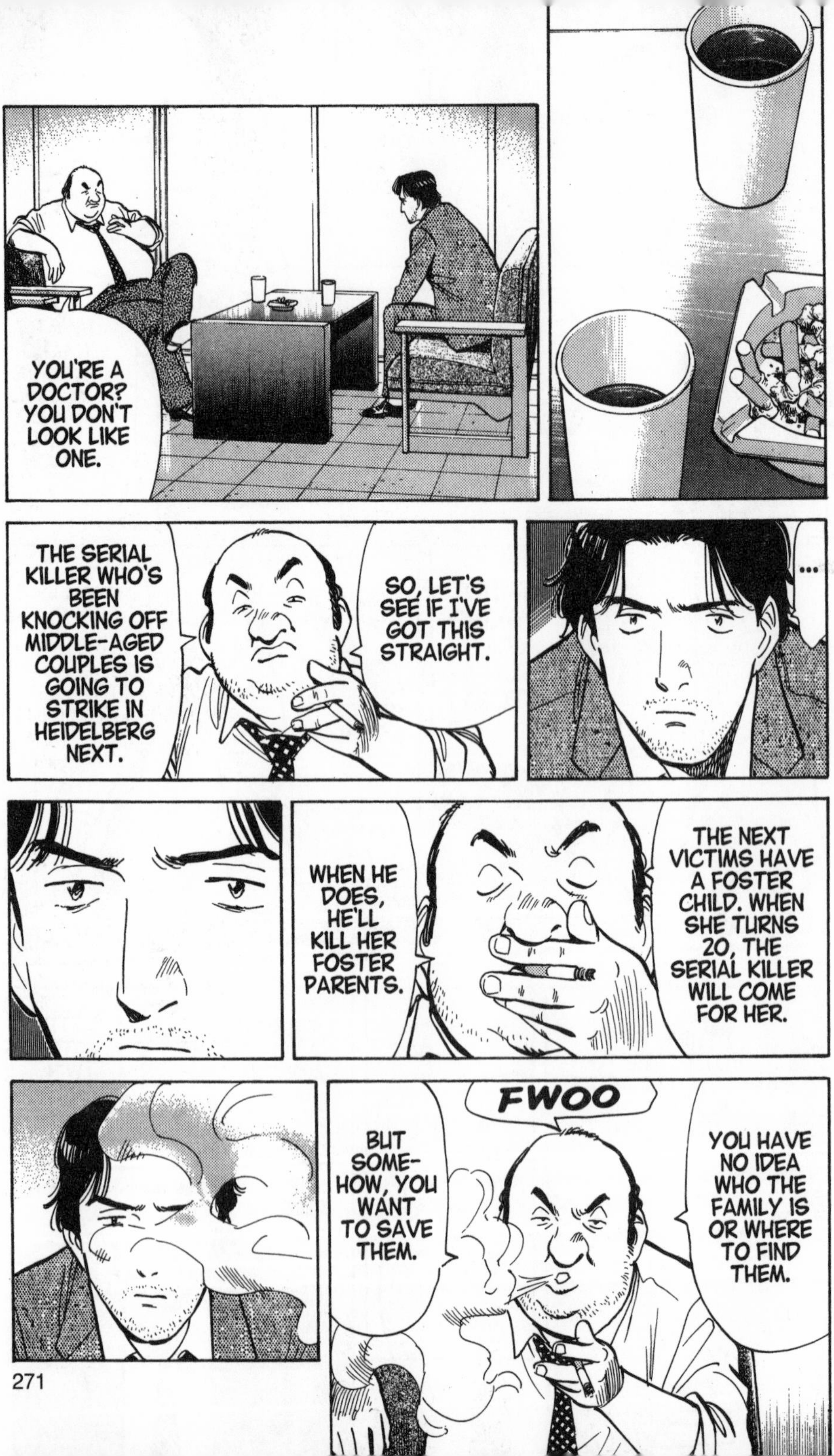
YOU'RE A DOCTOR? YOU DON'T LOOK LIKE ONE.
...
SO, LET'S SEE IF I'VE GOT THIS STRAIGHT.
THE SERIAL KILLER WHO'S BEEN KNOCKING OFF MIDDLE-AGED COUPLES IS GOING TO STRIKE IN HEIDELBERG NEXT.
THE NEXT VICTIMS HAVE A FOSTER CHILD. WHEN SHE TURNS 20, THE SERIAL KILLER WILL COME FOR HER.
WHEN HE DOES, HE'LL KILL HER FOSTER PARENTS.
FWOO
YOU HAVE NO IDEA WHO THE FAMILY IS OR WHERE TO FIND THEM.
BUT SOME-HOW, YOU WANT TO SAVE THEM.

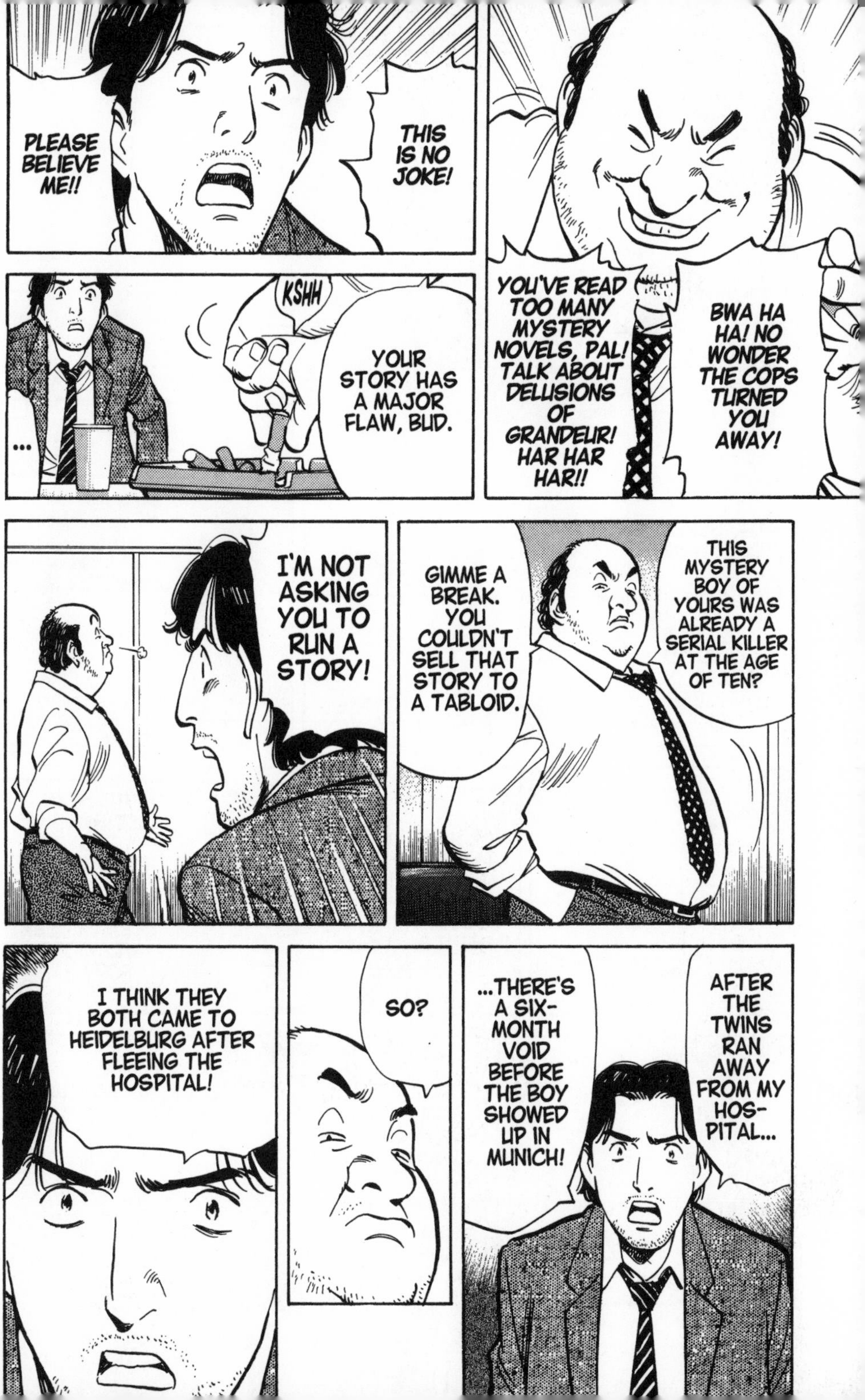
BWA HA HA! NO WONDER THE COPS TURNED YOU AWAY!
YOU'VE READ TOO MANY MYSTERY NOVELS, PAL! TALK ABOUT DELUSIONS OF GRANDEUR! HAR HAR HAR!!
THIS IS NO JOKE!
PLEASE BELIEVE ME!!
KSHH
YOUR STORY HAS A MAJOR FLAW, BUD.
...
THIS MYSTERY BOY OF YOURS WAS ALREADY A SERIAL KILLER AT THE AGE OF TEN?
GIMME A BREAK. YOU COULDN'T SELL THAT STORY TO A TABLOID.
I'M NOT ASKING YOU TO RUN A STORY!
AFTER THE TWINS RAN AWAY FROM MY HOS-PITAL...
...THERE'S A SIX-MONTH VOID BEFORE THE BOY SHOWED UP IN MUNICH!
SO?
I THINK THEY BOTH CAME TO HEIDELBURG AFTER FLEEING THE HOSPITAL!

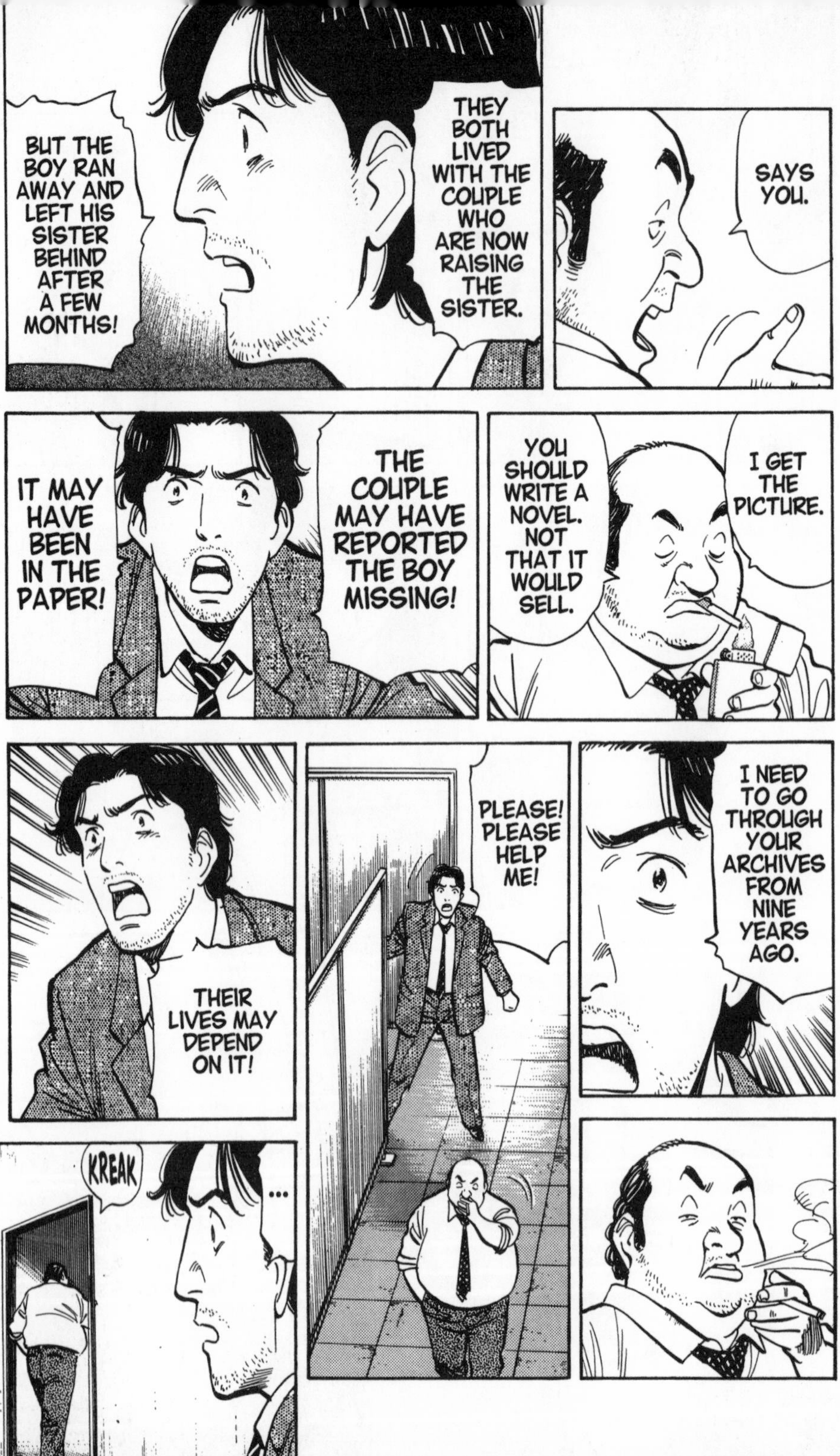
SAYS YOU.
THEY BOTH LIVED WITH THE COUPLE WHO ARE NOW RAISING THE SISTER.
BUT THE BOY RAN AWAY AND LEFT HIS SISTER BEHIND AFTER A FEW MONTHS!
I GET THE PICTURE.
YOU SHOULD WRITE A NOVEL. NOT THAT IT WOULD SELL.
THE COUPLE MAY HAVE REPORTED THE BOY MISSING!
IT MAY HAVE BEEN IN THE PAPER!
I NEED TO GO THROUGH YOUR ARCHIVES FROM NINE YEARS AGO.
PLEASE! PLEASE HELP ME!
THEIR LIVES MAY DEPEND ON IT!
KREAK
...

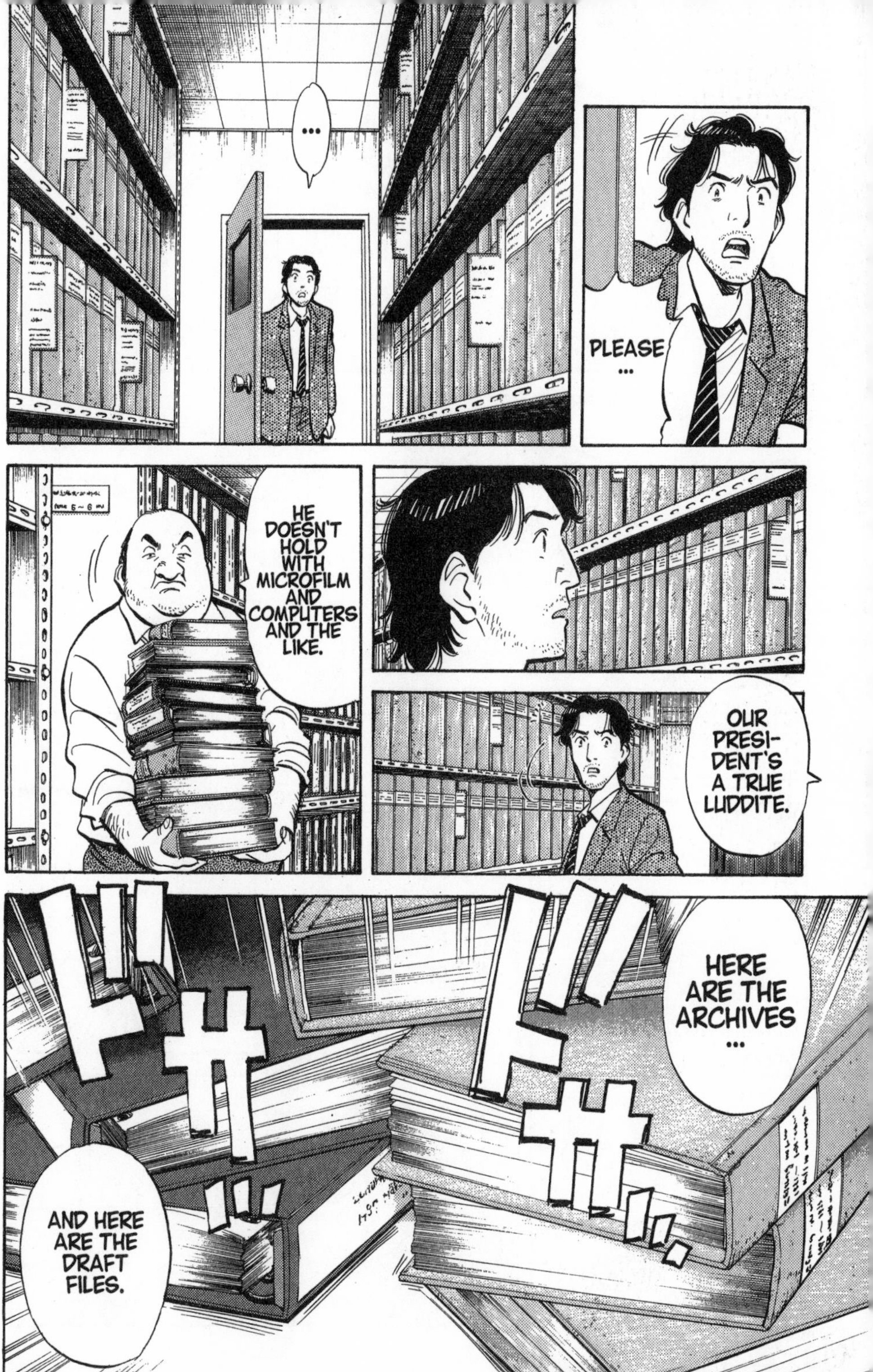
PLEASE ...
...
OUR PRESI-DENT'S A TRUE LUDDITE.
HE DOESN'T HOLD WITH MICROFILM AND COMPUTERS AND THE LIKE.
HERE ARE THE ARCHIVES ...
ドサッ
ドサッ
AND HERE ARE THE DRAFT FILES.

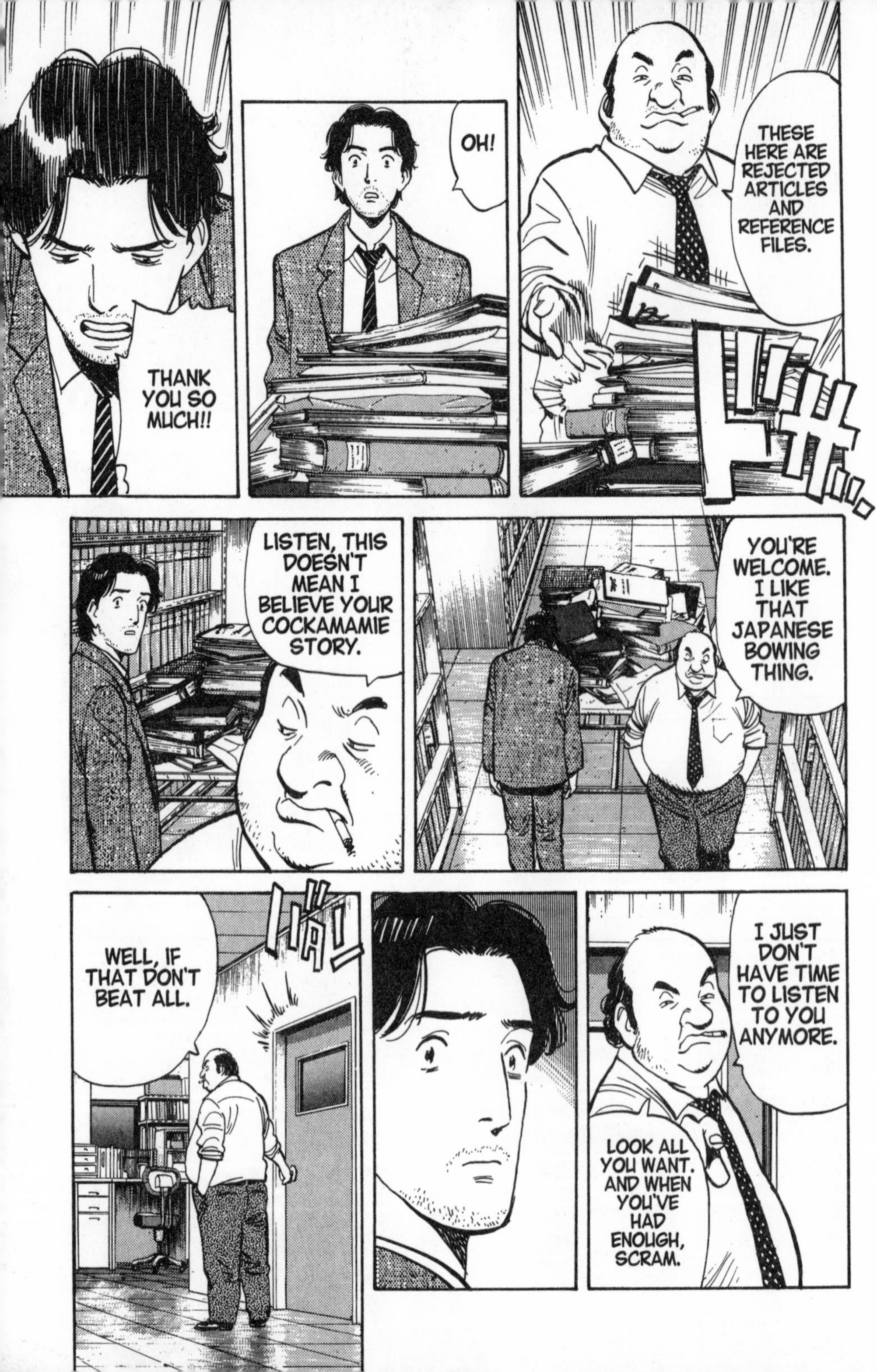
THESE HERE ARE REJECTED ARTICLES AND REFERENCE FILES.
OH!
THANK YOU SO MUCH!!
YOU'RE WELCOME. I LIKE THAT JAPANESE BOWING THING.
LISTEN, THIS DOESN'T MEAN I BELIEVE YOUR COCKAMAMIE STORY.
I JUST DON'T HAVE TIME TO LISTEN TO YOU ANYMORE.
LOOK ALL YOU WANT. AND WHEN YOU'VE HAD ENOUGH, SCRAM.
WELL, IF THAT DON'T BEAT ALL.

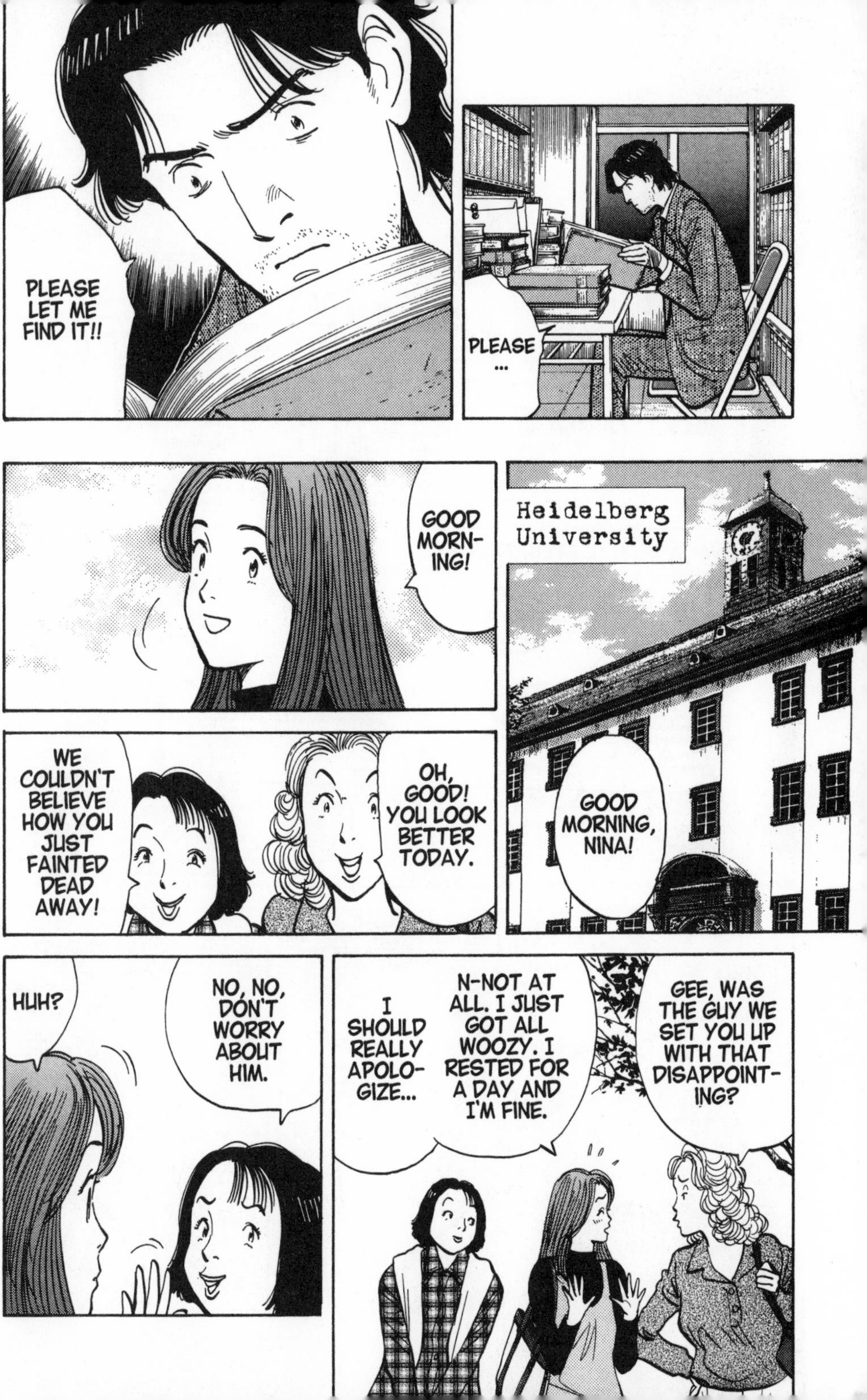
PLEASE ...
PLEASE LET ME FIND IT!!
Heidelberg University
GOOD MORNING, NINA!
GOOD MORNING!
OH, GOOD! YOU LOOK BETTER TODAY.
WE COULDN'T BELIEVE HOW YOU JUST FAINTED DEAD AWAY!
GEE, WAS THE GUY WE SET YOU UP WITH THAT DISAPPOINTING?
N-NOT AT ALL. I JUST GOT ALL WOOZY. I RESTED FOR A DAY AND I'M FINE.
I SHOULD REALLY APOLOGIZE...
NO, NO, DON'T WORRY ABOUT HIM.
HUH?

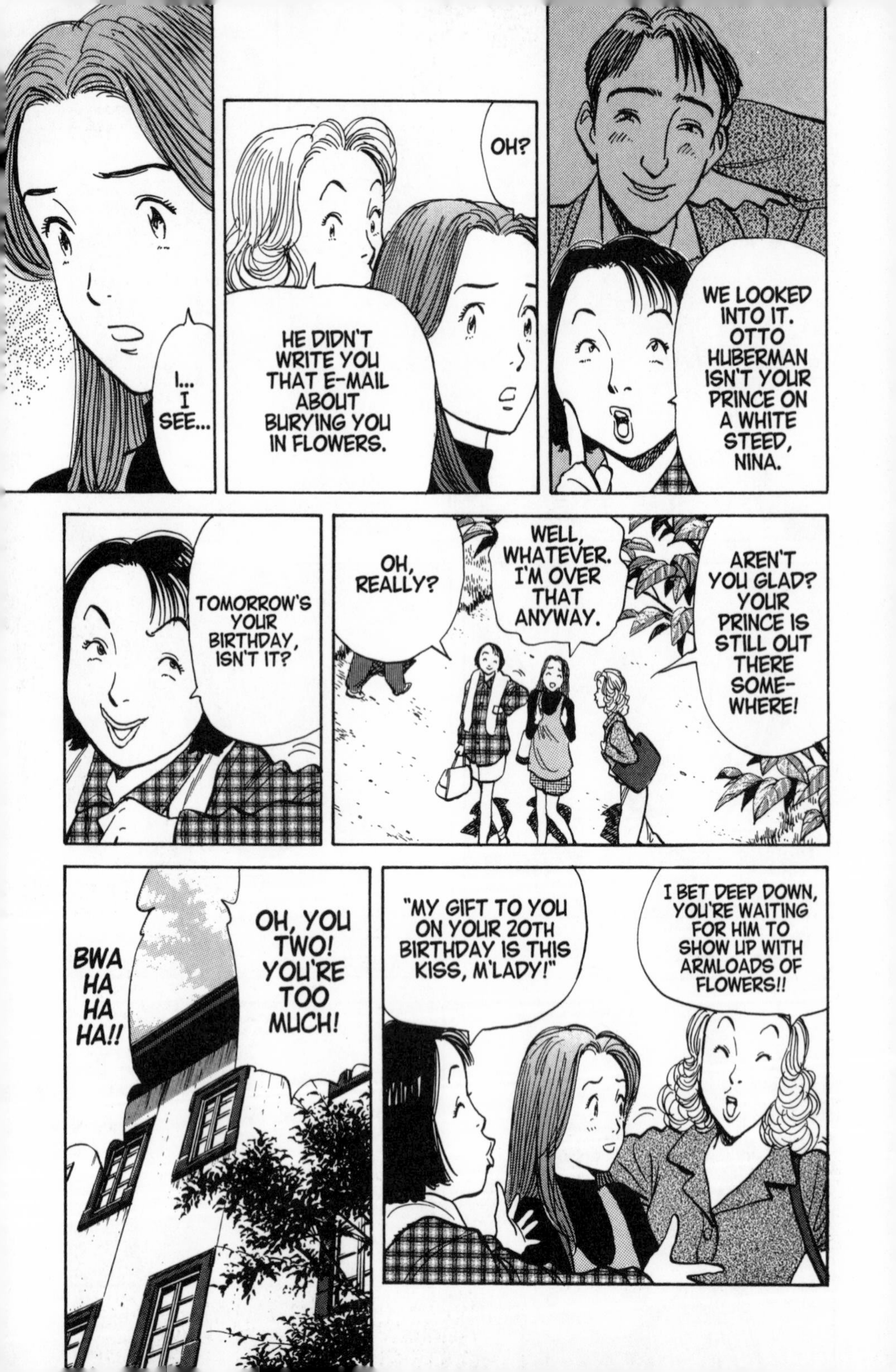
WE LOOKED INTO IT. OTTO HUBERMAN ISN'T YOUR PRINCE ON A WHITE STEED, NINA.
OH?
HE DIDN'T WRITE YOU THAT E-MAIL ABOUT BURYING YOU IN FLOWERS.
I... I SEE...
AREN'T YOU GLAD? YOUR PRINCE IS STILL OUT THERE SOME-WHERE!
WELL, WHATEVER. I'M OVER THAT ANYWAY.
OH, REALLY?
TOMORROW'S YOUR BIRTHDAY, ISN'T IT?
I BET DEEP DOWN, YOU'RE WAITING FOR HIM TO SHOW UP WITH ARMLOADS OF FLOWERS!!
"MY GIFT TO YOU ON YOUR 20TH BIRTHDAY IS THIS KISS, M'LADY!"
OH, YOU TWO! YOU'RE TOO MUCH!
BWA HA HA HA!!

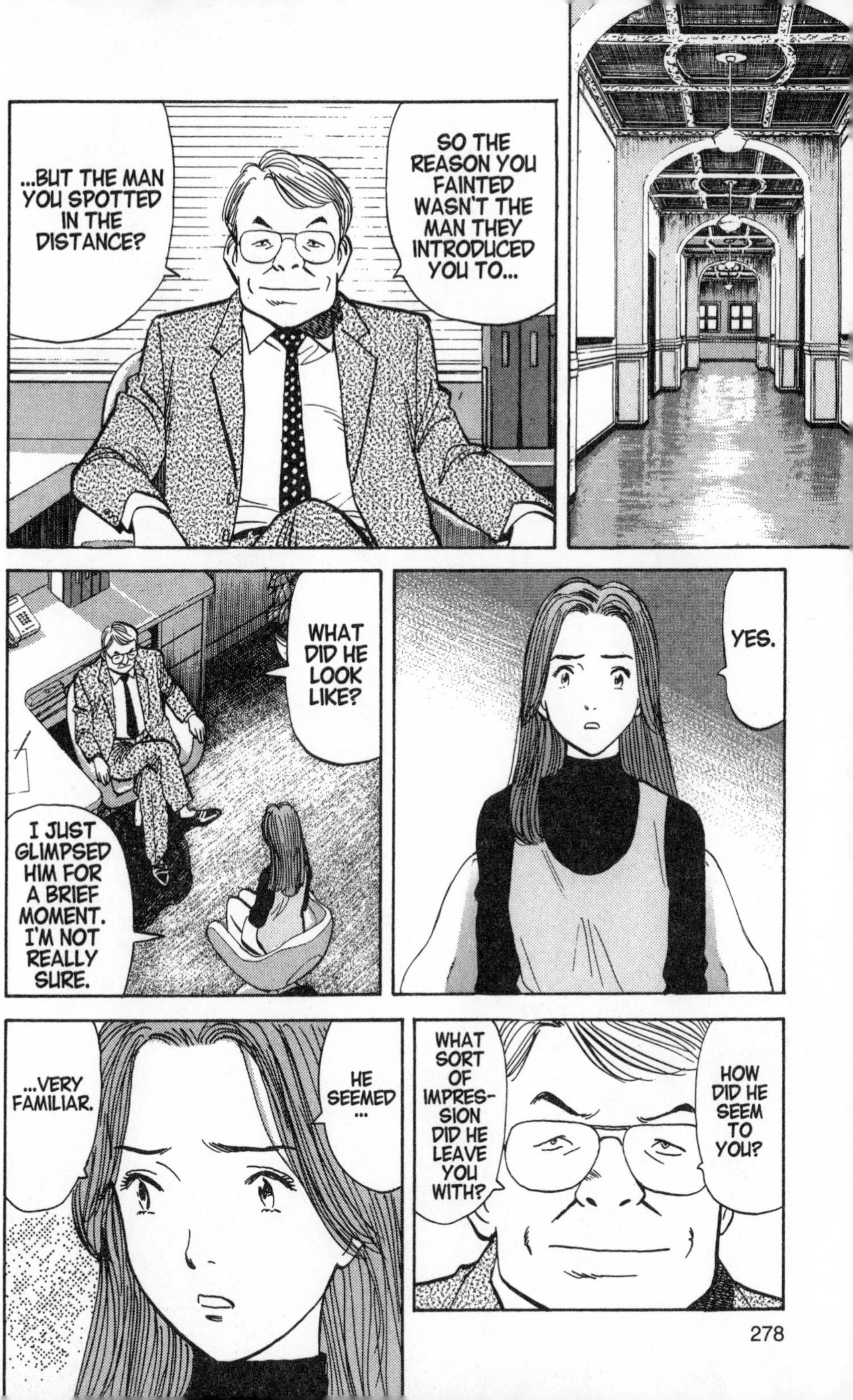
SO THE REASON YOU FAINTED WASN'T THE MAN THEY INTRODUCED YOU TO...
...BUT THE MAN YOU SPOTTED IN THE DISTANCE?
YES.
WHAT DID HE LOOK LIKE?
I JUST GLIMPSED HIM FOR A BRIEF MOMENT. I'M NOT REALLY SURE.
HOW DID HE SEEM TO YOU?
WHAT SORT OF IMPRES-SION DID HE LEAVE YOU WITH?
HE SEEMED...
...VERY FAMILIAR.

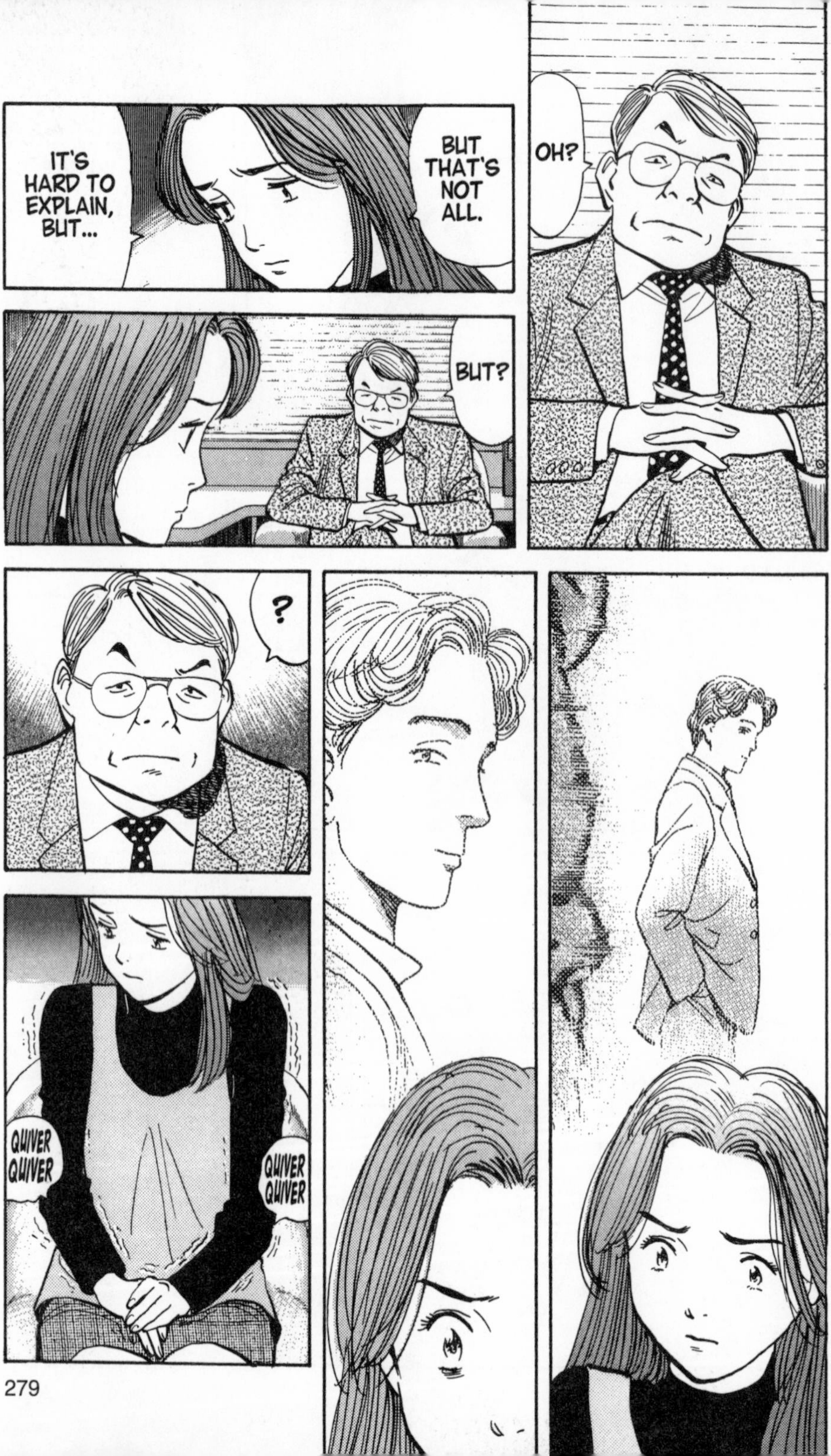
OH?
BUT THAT'S NOT ALL.
IT'S HARD TO EXPLAIN, BUT...
BUT?
?
QUIVER QUIVER
QUIVER QUIVER

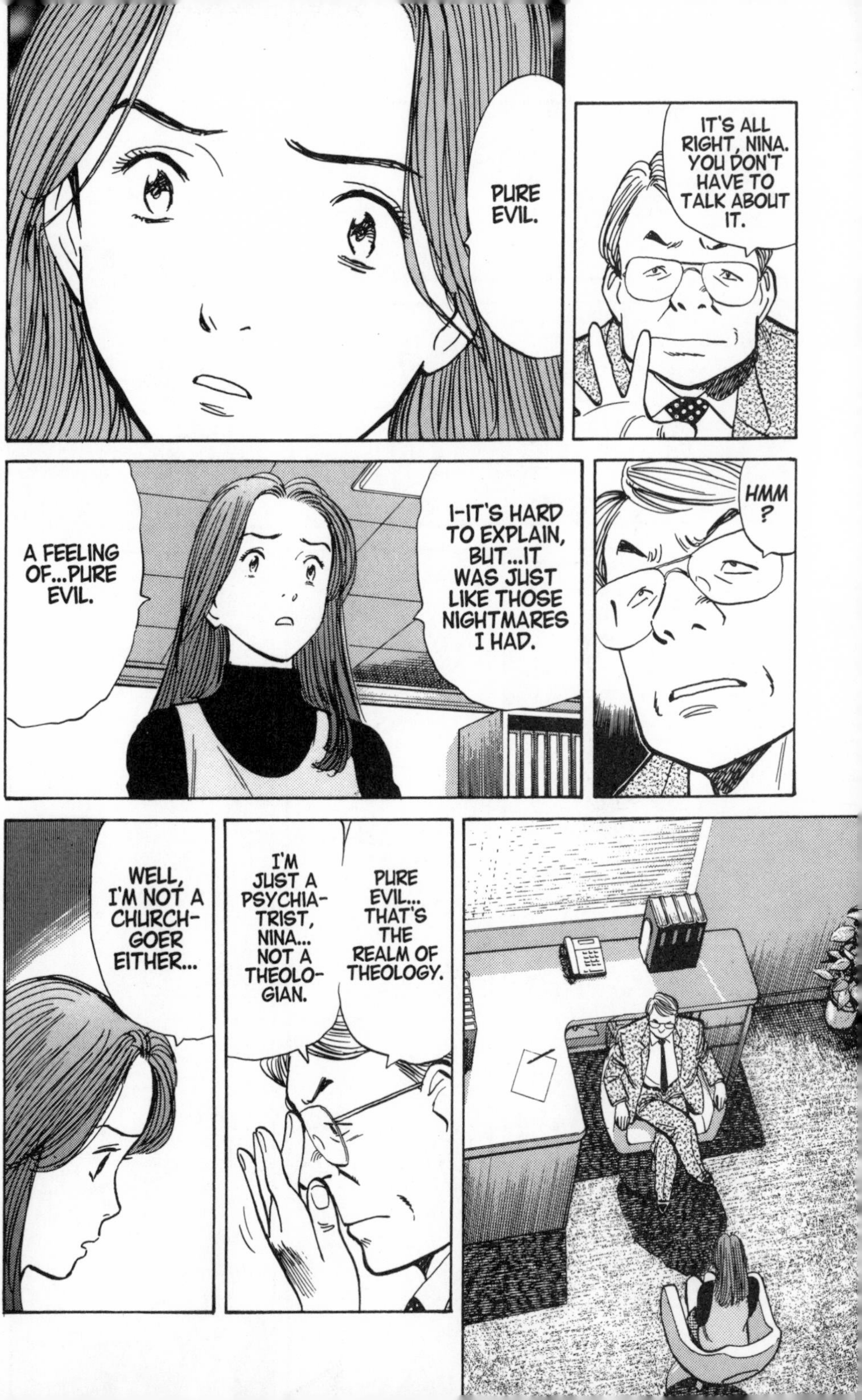
IT'S ALL RIGHT, NINA. YOU DON'T HAVE TO TALK ABOUT IT.
PURE EVIL.
HMM?
I-IT'S HARD TO EXPLAIN, BUT...IT WAS JUST LIKE THOSE NIGHTMARES I HAD.
A FEELING OF...PURE EVIL.
PURE EVIL... THAT'S THE REALM OF THEOLOGY.
I'M JUST A PSYCHIATRIST, NINA... NOT A THEOLOGIAN.
WELL, I'M NOT A CHURCHGOER EITHER...

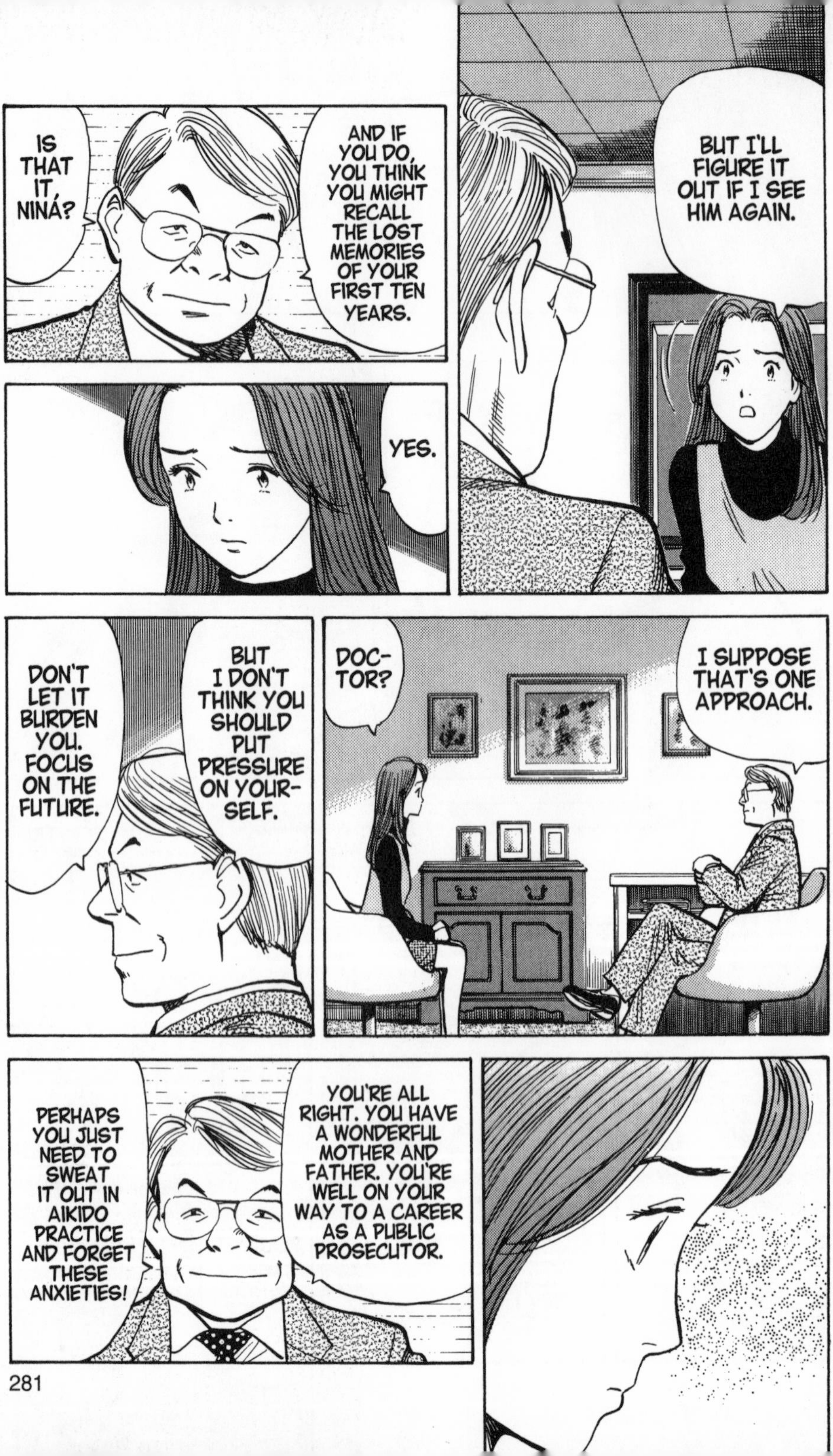
BUT I'LL FIGURE IT OUT IF I SEE HIM AGAIN.
AND IF YOU DO, YOU THINK YOU MIGHT RECALL THE LOST MEMORIES OF YOUR FIRST TEN YEARS.
IS THAT IT, NINA?
YES.
I SUPPOSE THAT'S ONE APPROACH.
DOC-TOR?
BUT I DON'T THINK YOU SHOULD PUT PRESSURE ON YOUR-SELF.
DON'T LET IT BURDEN YOU. FOCUS ON THE FUTURE.
YOU'RE ALL RIGHT. YOU HAVE A WONDERFUL MOTHER AND FATHER. YOU'RE WELL ON YOUR WAY TO A CAREER AS A PUBLIC PROSECUTOR.
PERHAPS YOU JUST NEED TO SWEAT IT OUT IN AIKIDO PRACTICE AND FORGET THESE ANXIETIES!

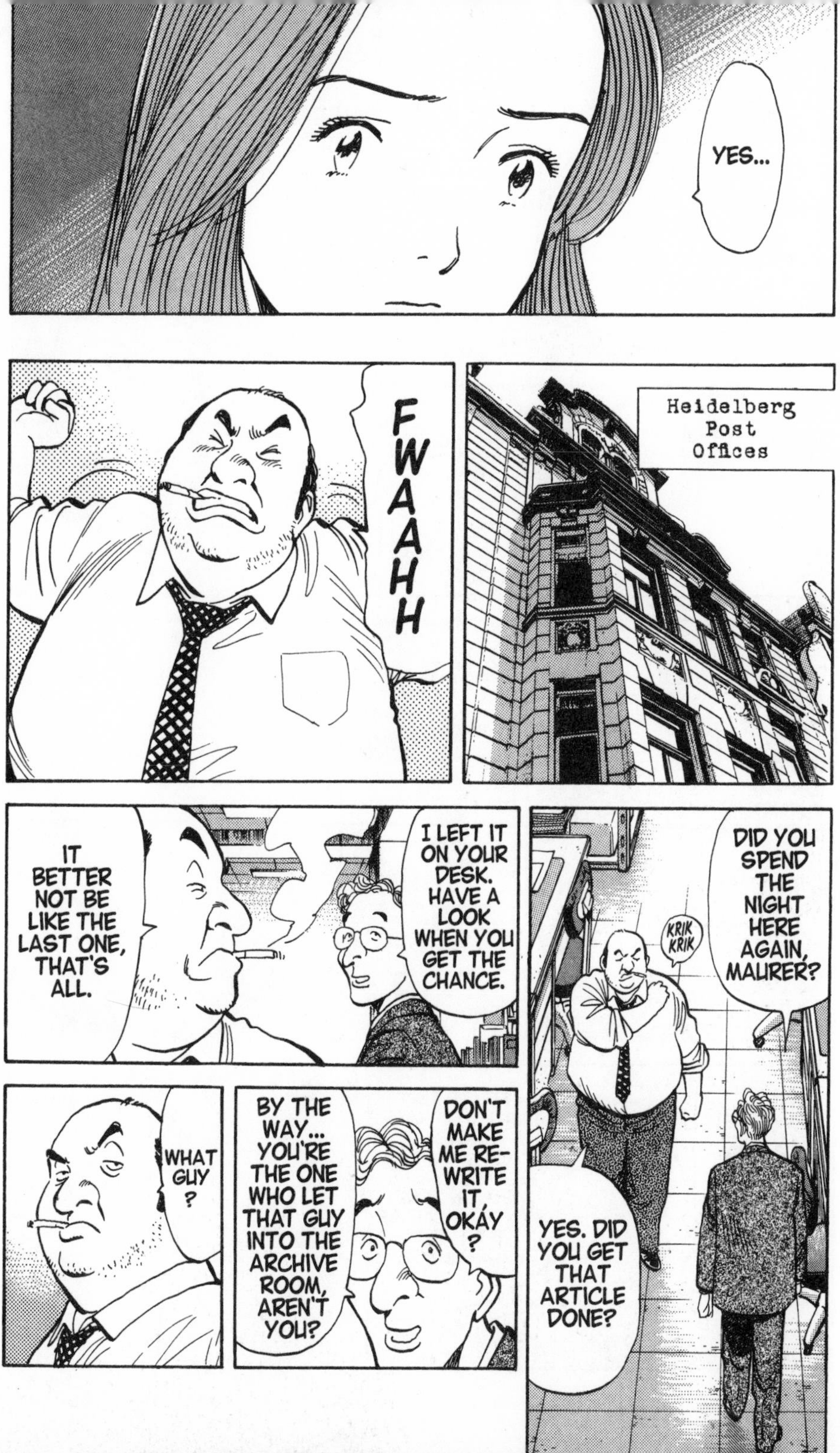

YES...
Heidelberg Post Offices
FWAAAHH
DID YOU SPEND THE NIGHT HERE AGAIN, MAURER?
KRIK KRIK
YES. DID YOU GET THAT ARTICLE DONE?
I LEFT IT ON YOUR DESK. HAVE A LOOK WHEN YOU GET THE CHANCE.
IT BETTER NOT BE LIKE THE LAST ONE, THAT'S ALL.
DON'T MAKE ME RE-WRITE IT, OKAY?
BY THE WAY... YOU'RE THE ONE WHO LET THAT GUY INTO THE ARCHIVE ROOM, AREN'T YOU?
WHAT GUY?

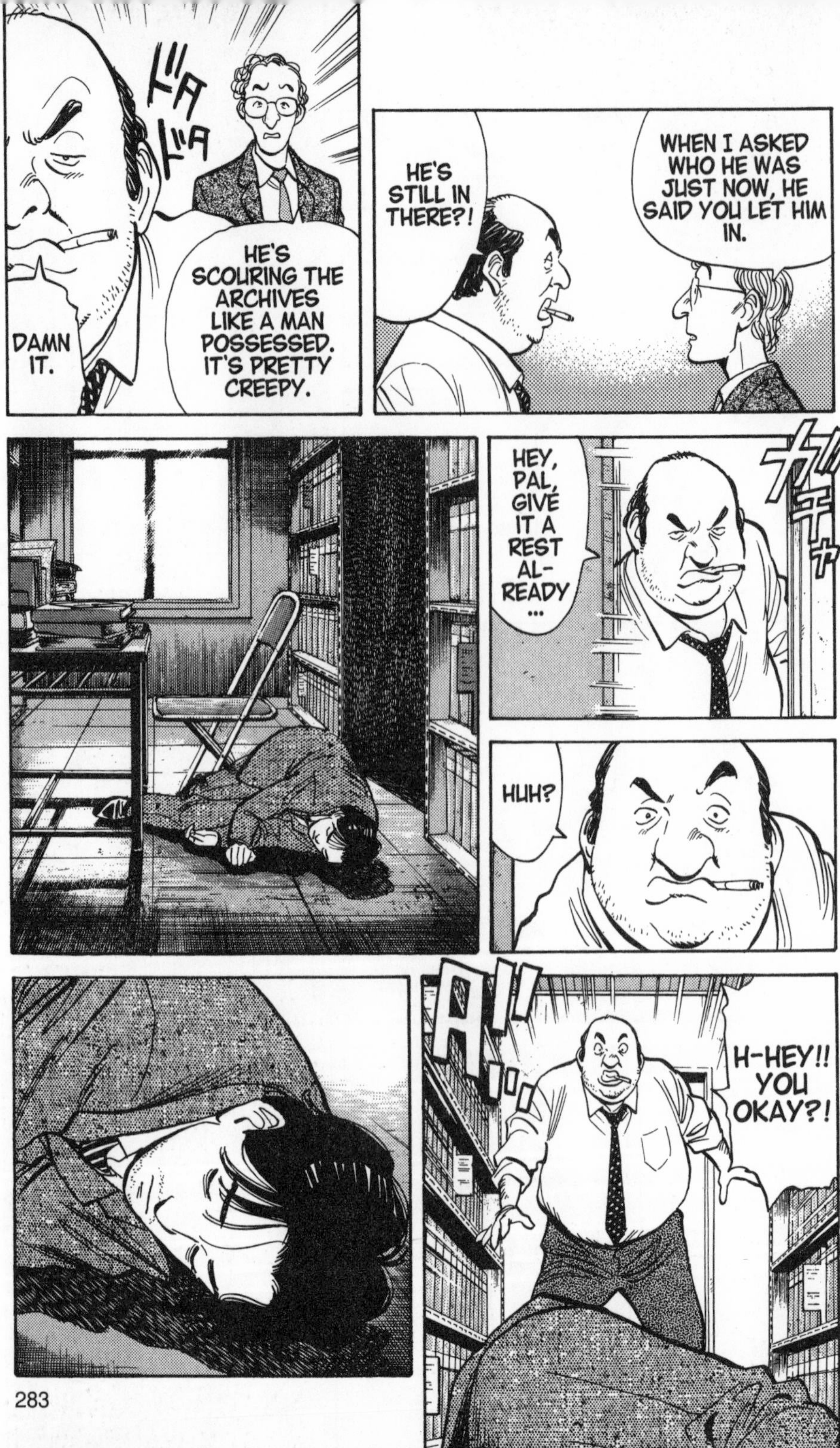
WHEN I ASKED WHO HE WAS JUST NOW, HE SAID YOU LET HIM IN.
HE'S STILL IN THERE?!
ドスドス
HE'S SCOURING THE ARCHIVES LIKE A MAN POSSESSED. IT'S PRETTY CREEPY.
DAMN IT.
ガチャ
HEY, PAL, GIVE IT A REST AL-READY...
HUH?
H-HEY!! YOU OKAY?!
A!!...

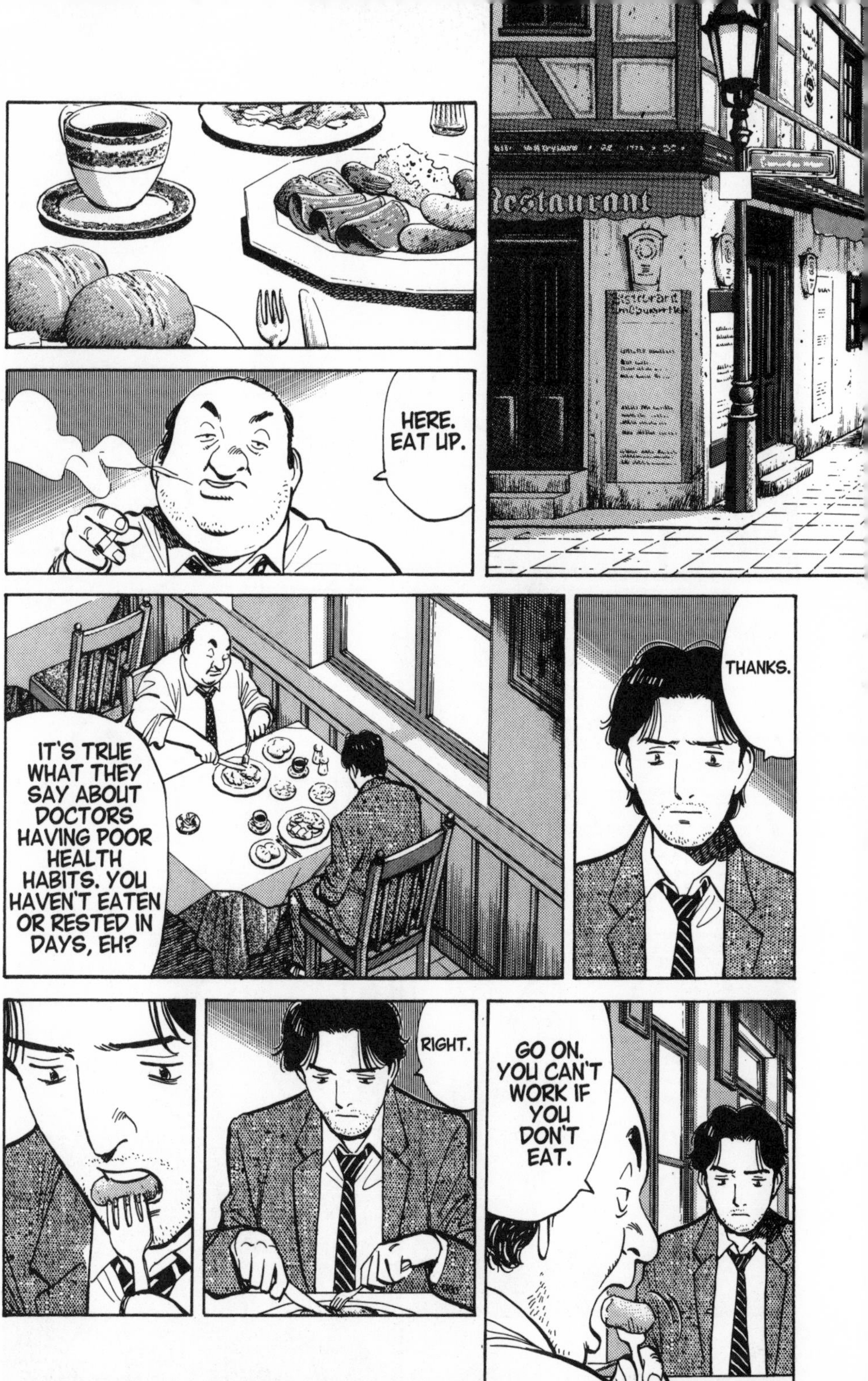
Restaurant
HERE. EAT UP.
THANKS.
IT'S TRUE WHAT THEY SAY ABOUT DOCTORS HAVING POOR HEALTH HABITS. YOU HAVEN'T EATEN OR RESTED IN DAYS, EH?
GO ON. YOU CAN'T WORK IF YOU DON'T EAT.
RIGHT.

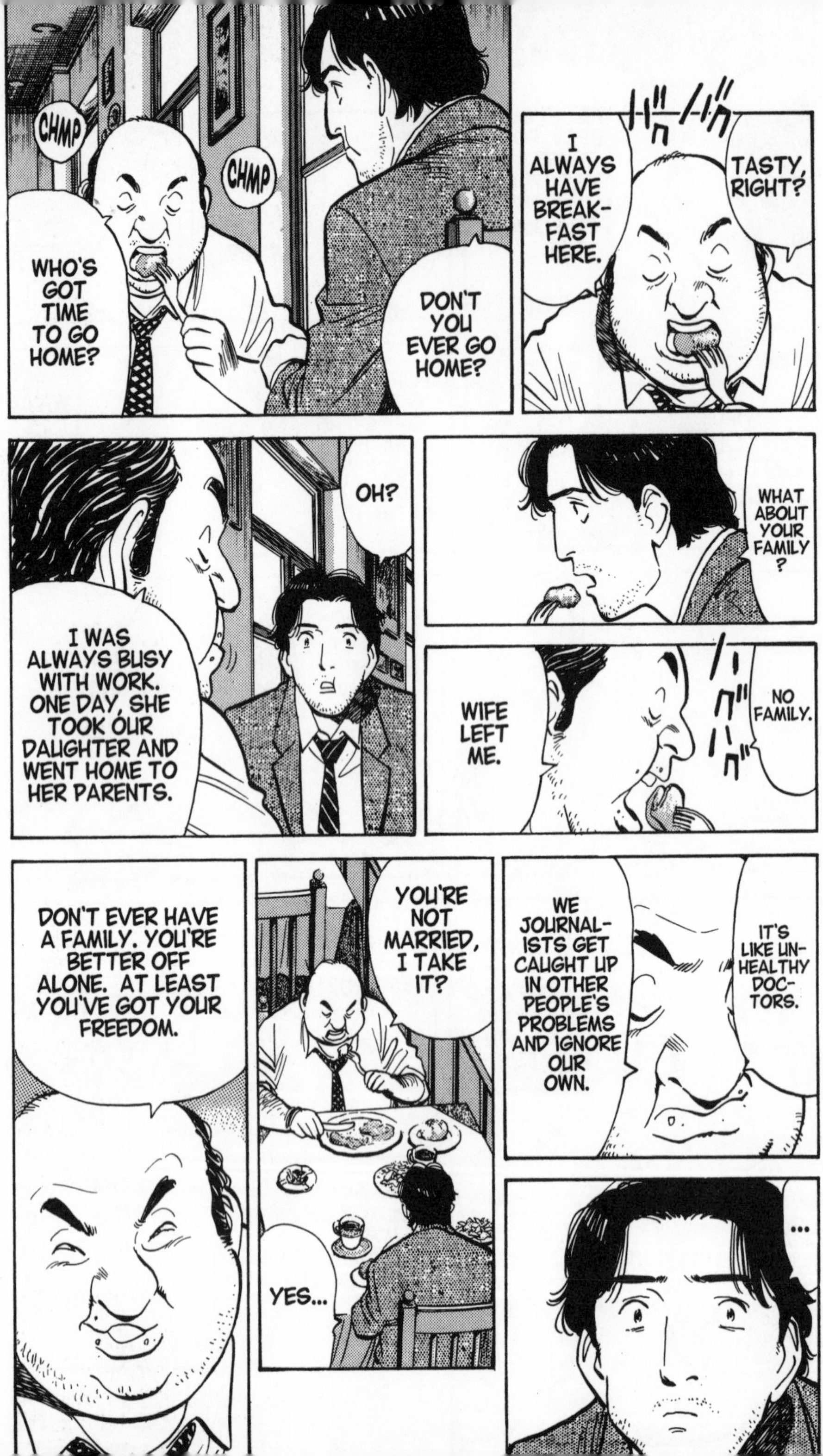

ハグ ハグ
TASTY, RIGHT?
I ALWAYS HAVE BREAK-FAST HERE.
CHMP
CHMP
DON'T YOU EVER GO HOME?
WHO'S GOT TIME TO GO HOME?
WHAT ABOUT YOUR FAMILY?
NO FAMILY.
WIFE LEFT ME.
OH?
I WAS ALWAYS BUSY WITH WORK. ONE DAY, SHE TOOK OUR DAUGHTER AND WENT HOME TO HER PARENTS.
IT'S LIKE UN-HEALTHY DOC-TORS.
WE JOURNAL-ISTS GET CAUGHT UP IN OTHER PEOPLE'S PROBLEMS AND IGNORE OUR OWN.
...
YOU'RE NOT MARRIED, I TAKE IT?
YES...
DON'T EVER HAVE A FAMILY. YOU'RE BETTER OFF ALONE. AT LEAST YOU'VE GOT YOUR FREEDOM.

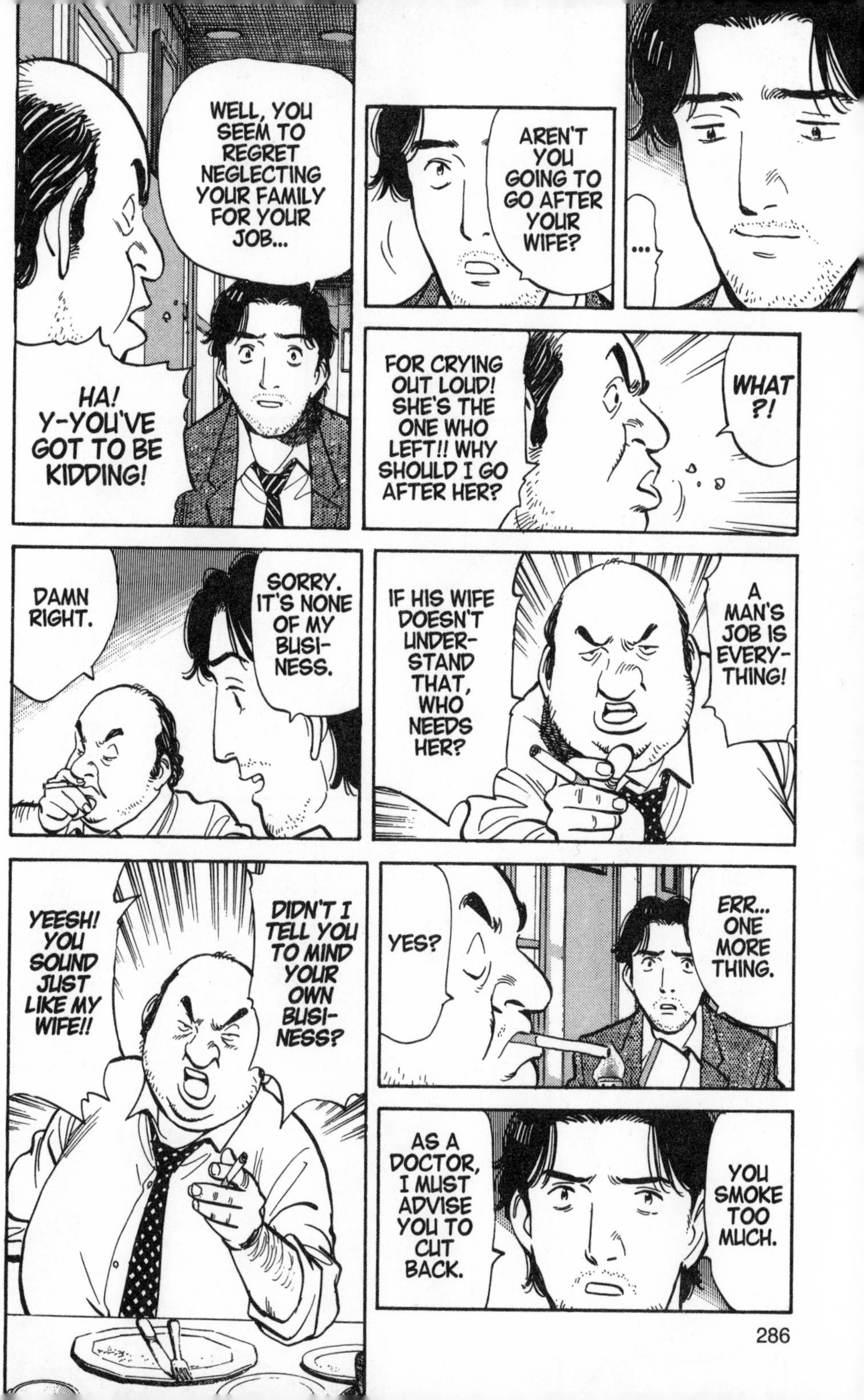
...
AREN'T YOU GOING TO GO AFTER YOUR WIFE?
WHAT ?!
FOR CRYING OUT LOUD! SHE'S THE ONE WHO LEFT!! WHY SHOULD I GO AFTER HER?
WELL, YOU SEEM TO REGRET NEGLECTING YOUR FAMILY FOR YOUR JOB...
HA! Y-YOU'VE GOT TO BE KIDDING!
A MAN'S JOB IS EVERY-THING!
IF HIS WIFE DOESN'T UNDER-STAND THAT, WHO NEEDS HER?
SORRY. IT'S NONE OF MY BUSI-NESS.
DAMN RIGHT.
ERR... ONE MORE THING.
YES?
YOU SMOKE TOO MUCH.
AS A DOCTOR, I MUST ADVISE YOU TO CUT BACK.
DIDN'T I TELL YOU TO MIND YOUR OWN BUSI-NESS?
YEESH! YOU SOUND JUST LIKE MY WIFE!!

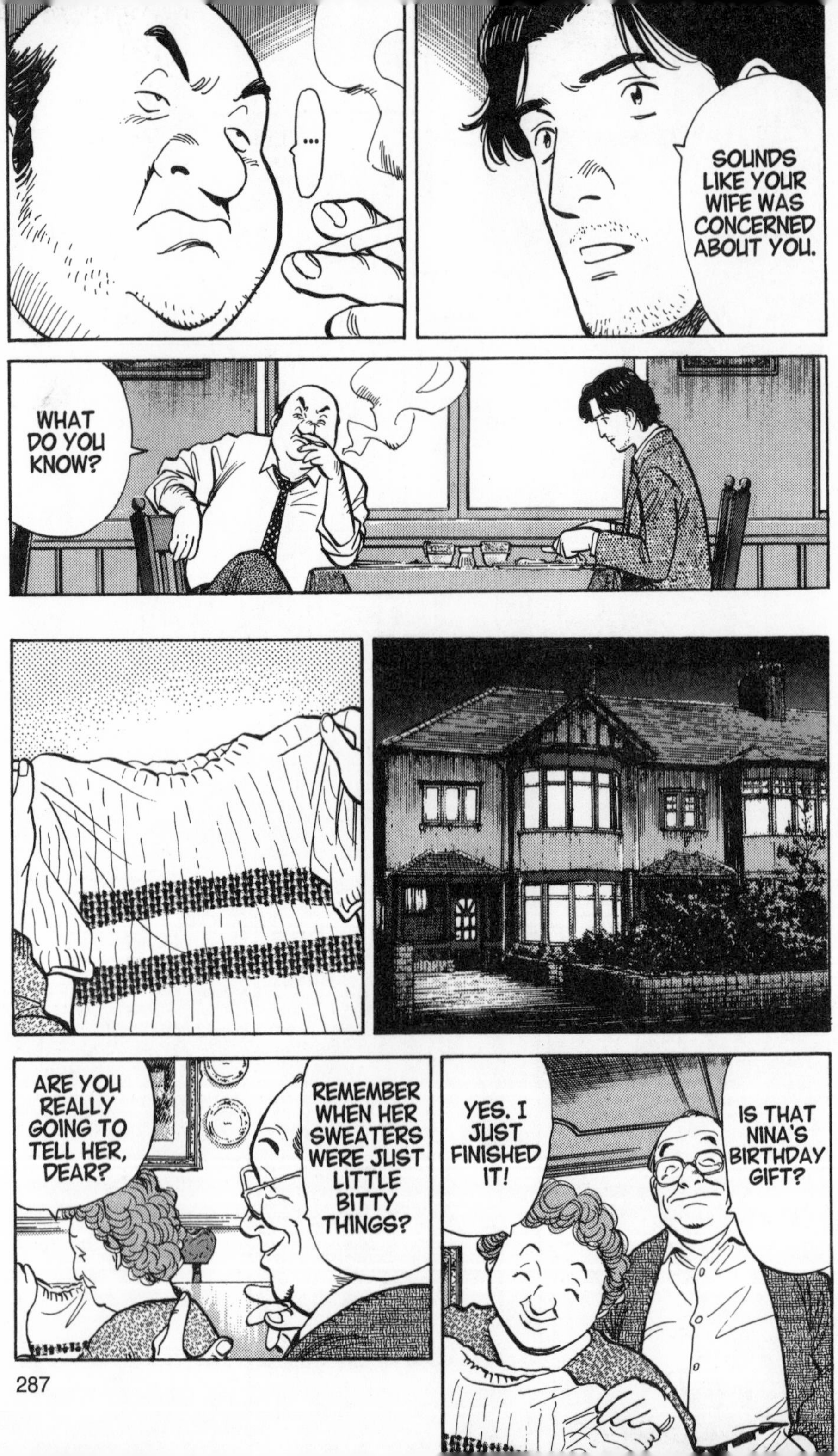
SOUNDS LIKE YOUR WIFE WAS CONCERNED ABOUT YOU.
...
WHAT DO YOU KNOW?
IS THAT NINA'S BIRTHDAY GIFT?
YES. I JUST FINISHED IT!
REMEMBER WHEN HER SWEATERS WERE JUST LITTLE BITTY THINGS?
ARE YOU REALLY GOING TO TELL HER, DEAR?

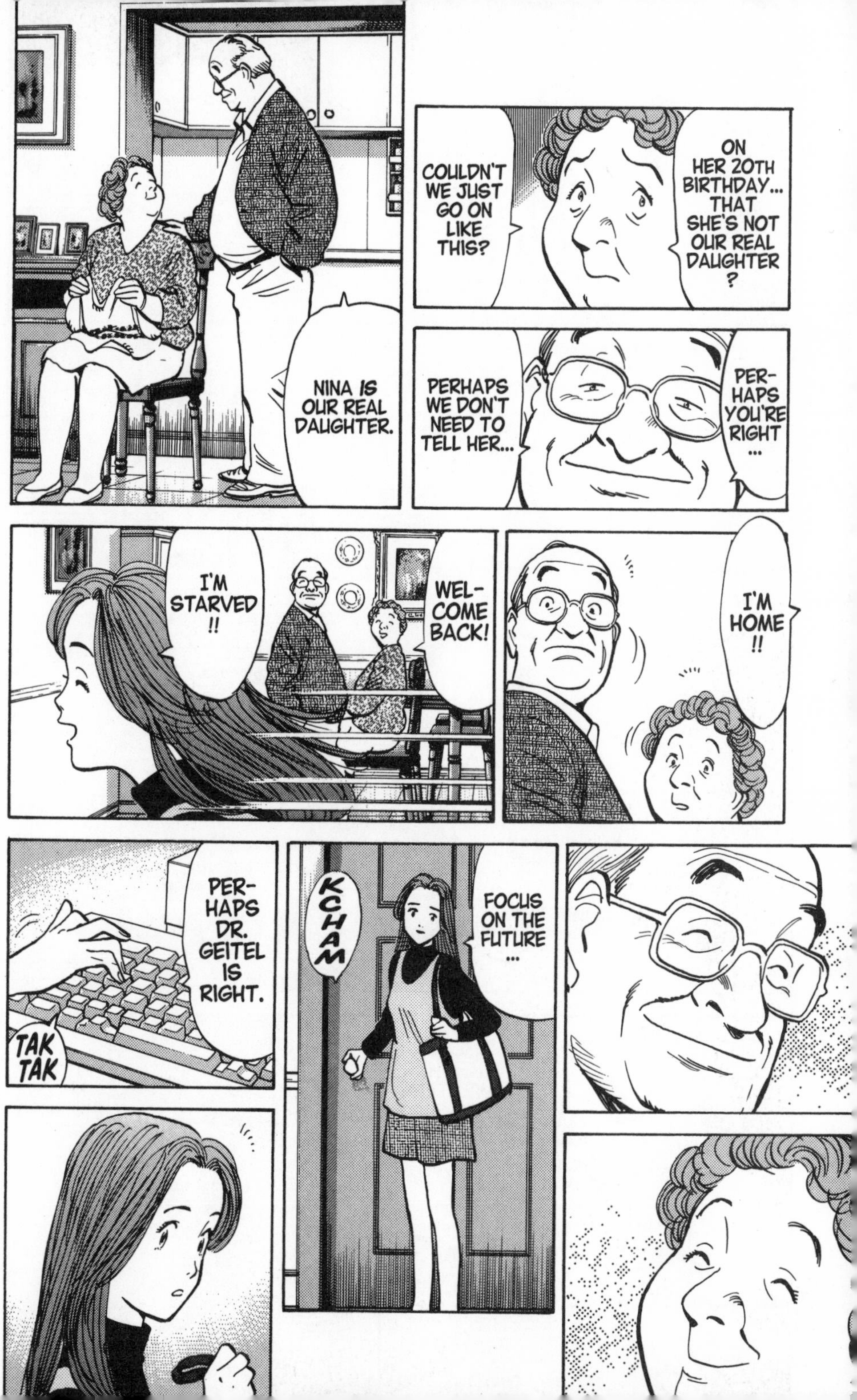
ON HER 20TH BIRTHDAY... THAT SHE'S NOT OUR REAL DAUGHTER?
COULDN'T WE JUST GO ON LIKE THIS?
PER-HAPS YOU'RE RIGHT...
PERHAPS WE DON'T NEED TO TELL HER...
NINA IS OUR REAL DAUGHTER.
I'M HOME!!
WEL-COME BACK!
I'M STARVED!!
FOCUS ON THE FUTURE...
KCHAM
PER-HAPS DR. GEITEL IS RIGHT.
TAK TAK

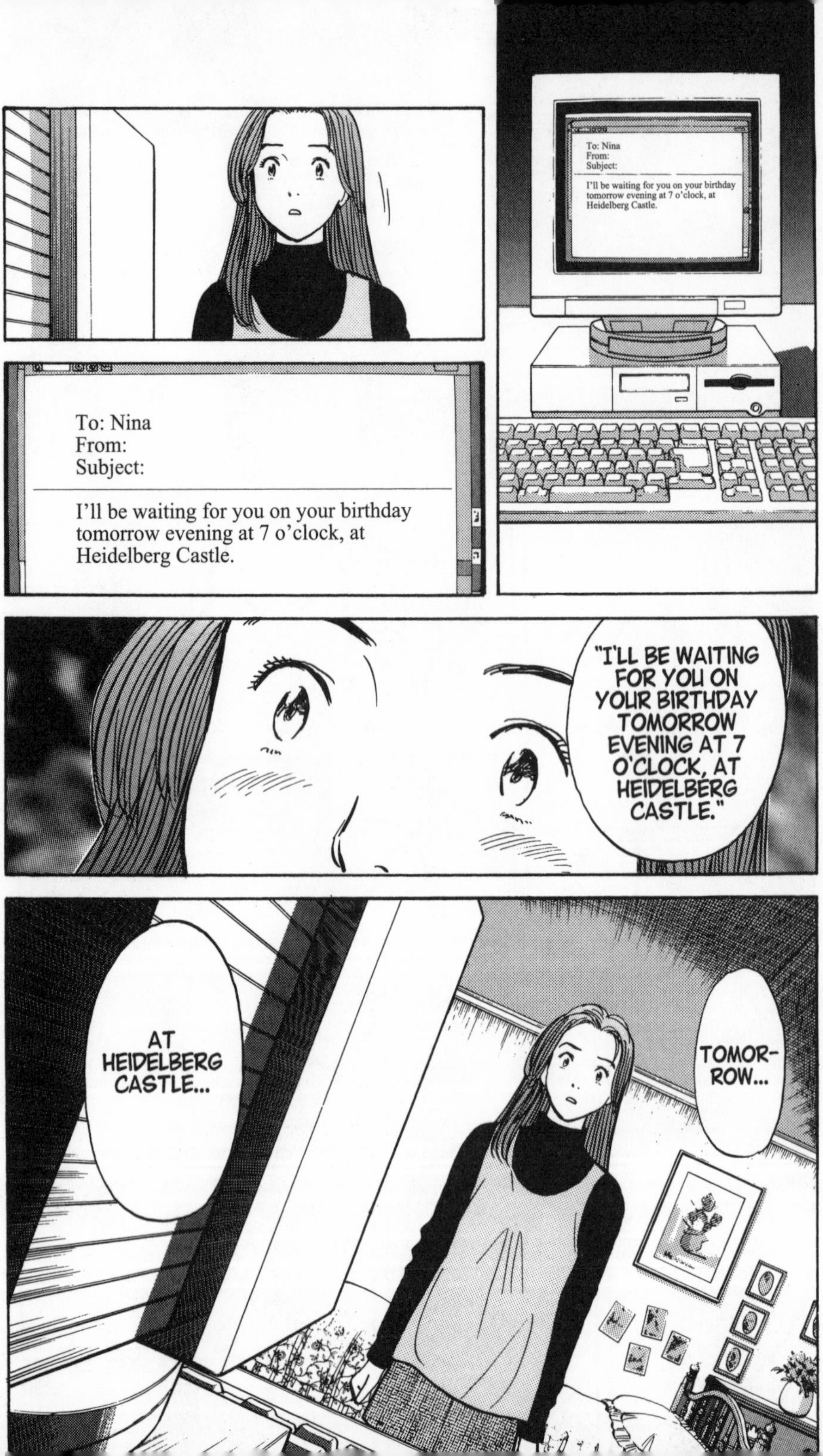
To: Nina
From:
Subject:
I'll be waiting for you on your birthday tomorrow evening at 7 o'clock, at Heidelberg Castle.
To: Nina
From:
Subject:
I'll be waiting for you on your birthday tomorrow evening at 7 o'clock, at Heidelberg Castle.
"I'LL BE WAITING FOR YOU ON YOUR BIRTHDAY TOMORROW EVENING AT 7 O'CLOCK, AT HEIDELBERG CASTLE."
TOMOR-ROW...
AT HEIDELBERG CASTLE...

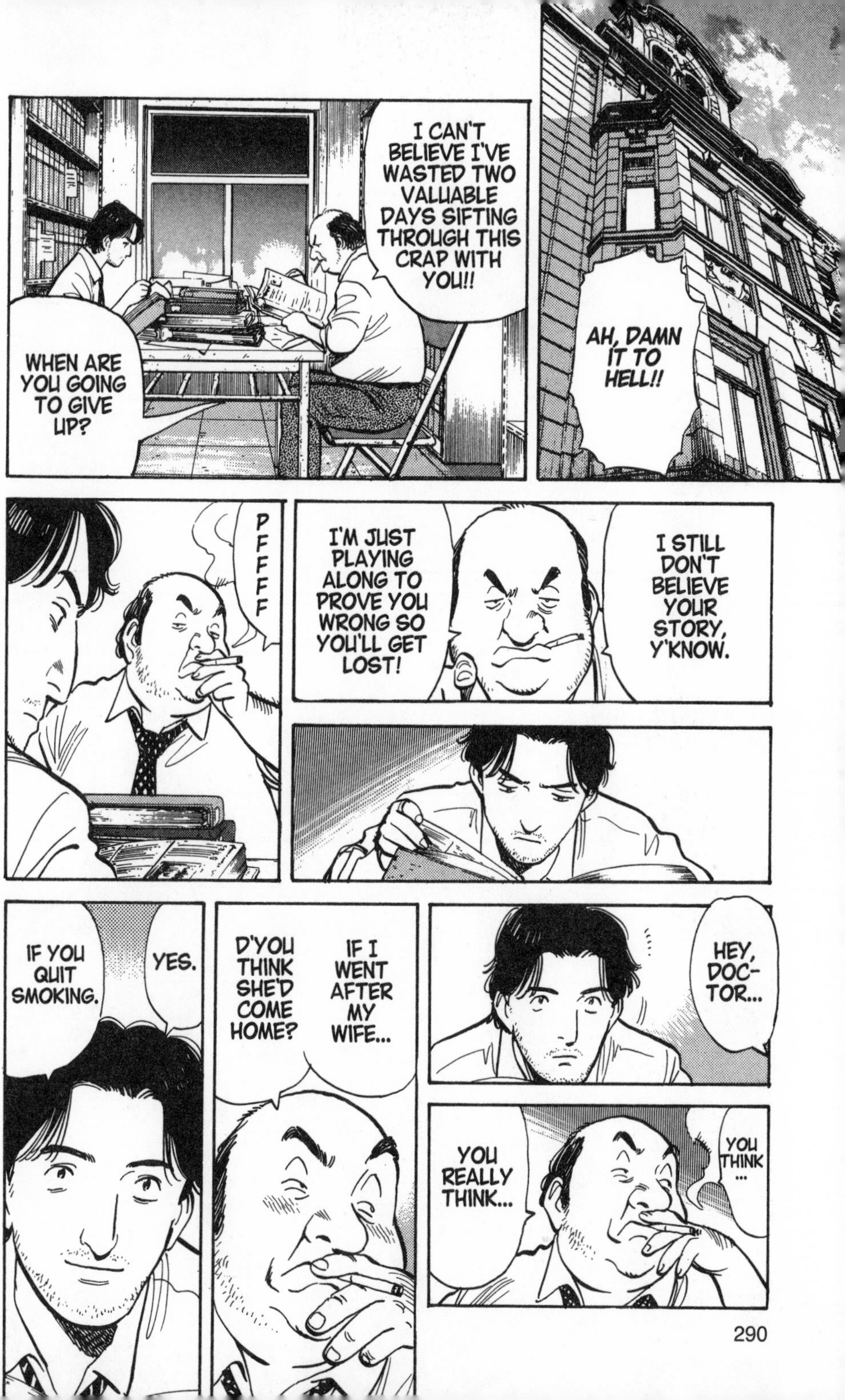
AH, DAMN IT TO HELL!!
I CAN'T BELIEVE I'VE WASTED TWO VALUABLE DAYS SIFTING THROUGH THIS CRAP WITH YOU!!
WHEN ARE YOU GOING TO GIVE UP?
I STILL DON'T BELIEVE YOUR STORY, Y'KNOW.
I'M JUST PLAYING ALONG TO PROVE YOU WRONG SO YOU'LL GET LOST!
PFFFFF
HEY, DOCTOR...
YOU THINK...
YOU REALLY THINK...
IF I WENT AFTER MY WIFE...
D'YOU THINK SHE'D COME HOME?
YES.
IF YOU QUIT SMOKING.

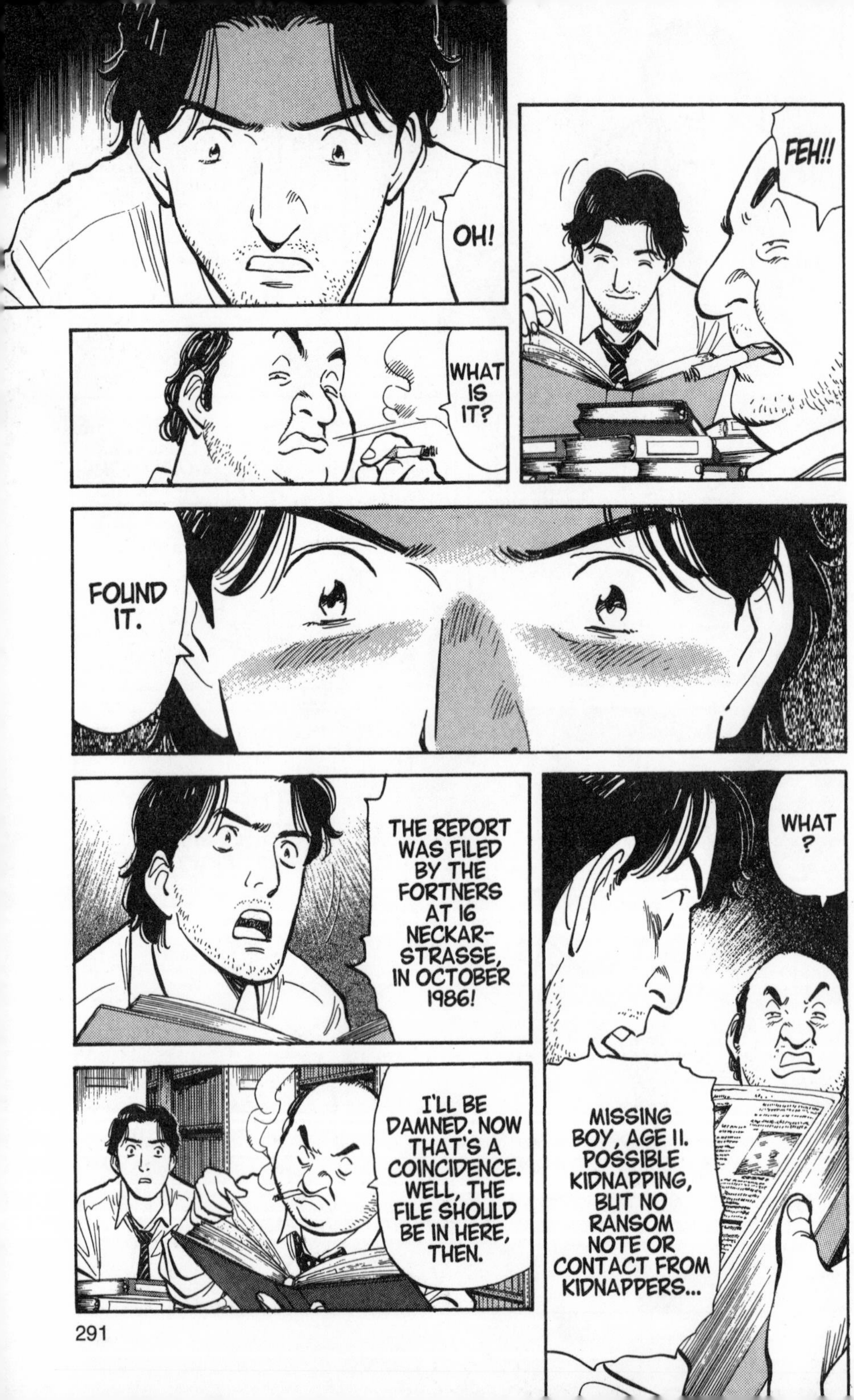

FEH!!
OH!
WHAT IS IT?
FOUND IT.
WHAT?
MISSING BOY, AGE 11. POSSIBLE KIDNAPPING, BUT NO RANSOM NOTE OR CONTACT FROM KIDNAPPERS...
THE REPORT WAS FILED BY THE FORTNERS AT 16 NECKAR-STRASSE, IN OCTOBER 1986!
I'LL BE DAMNED. NOW THAT'S A COINCIDENCE. WELL, THE FILE SHOULD BE IN HERE, THEN.

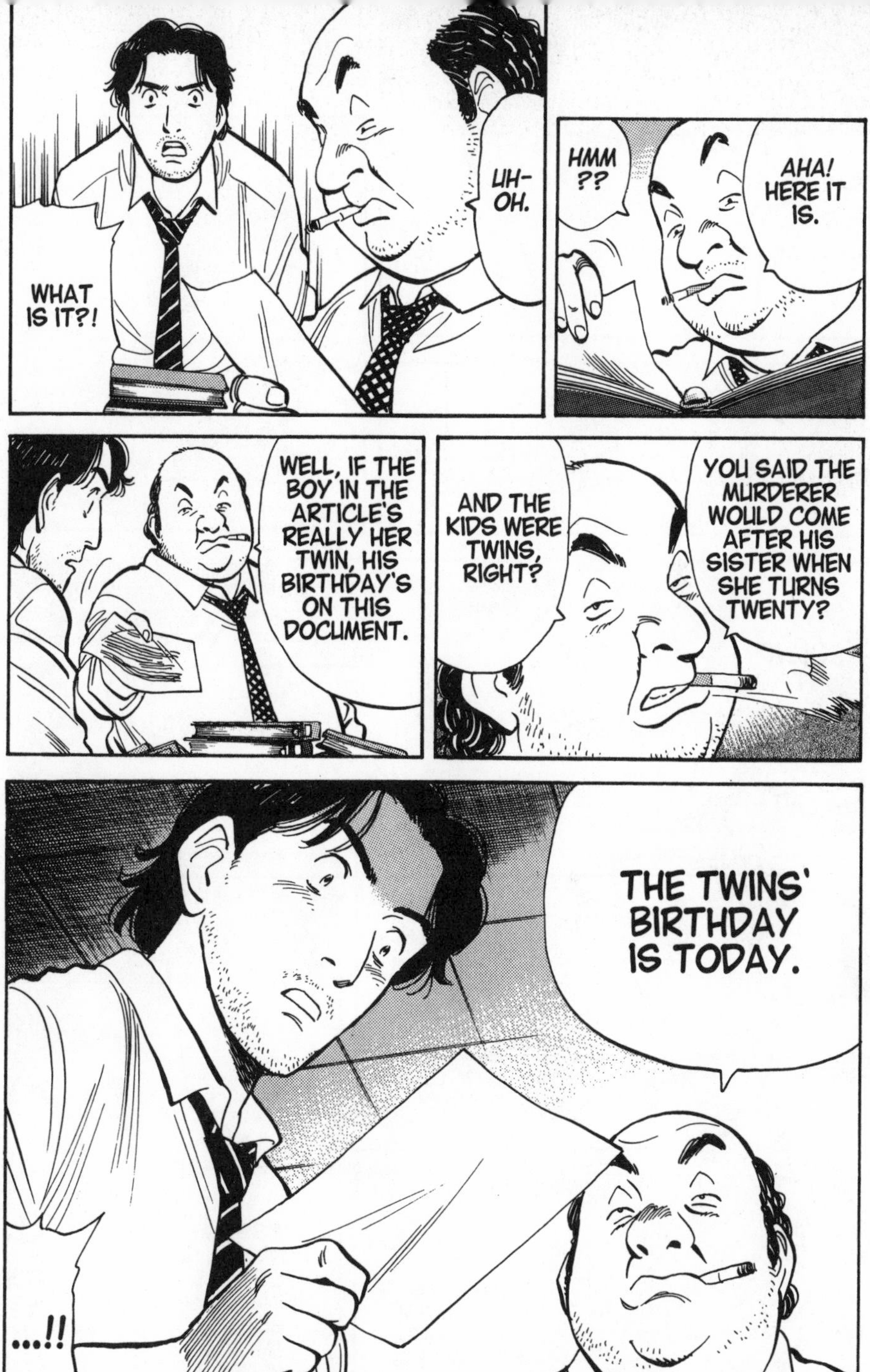
AHA! HERE IT IS.
HMM ??
UH-OH.
WHAT IS IT?!
YOU SAID THE MURDERER WOULD COME AFTER HIS SISTER WHEN SHE TURNS TWENTY?
AND THE KIDS WERE TWINS, RIGHT?
WELL, IF THE BOY IN THE ARTICLE'S REALLY HER TWIN, HIS BIRTHDAY'S ON THIS DOCUMENT.
THE TWINS' BIRTHDAY IS TODAY.
...!!

Kapitel 12. Birthday of Terror

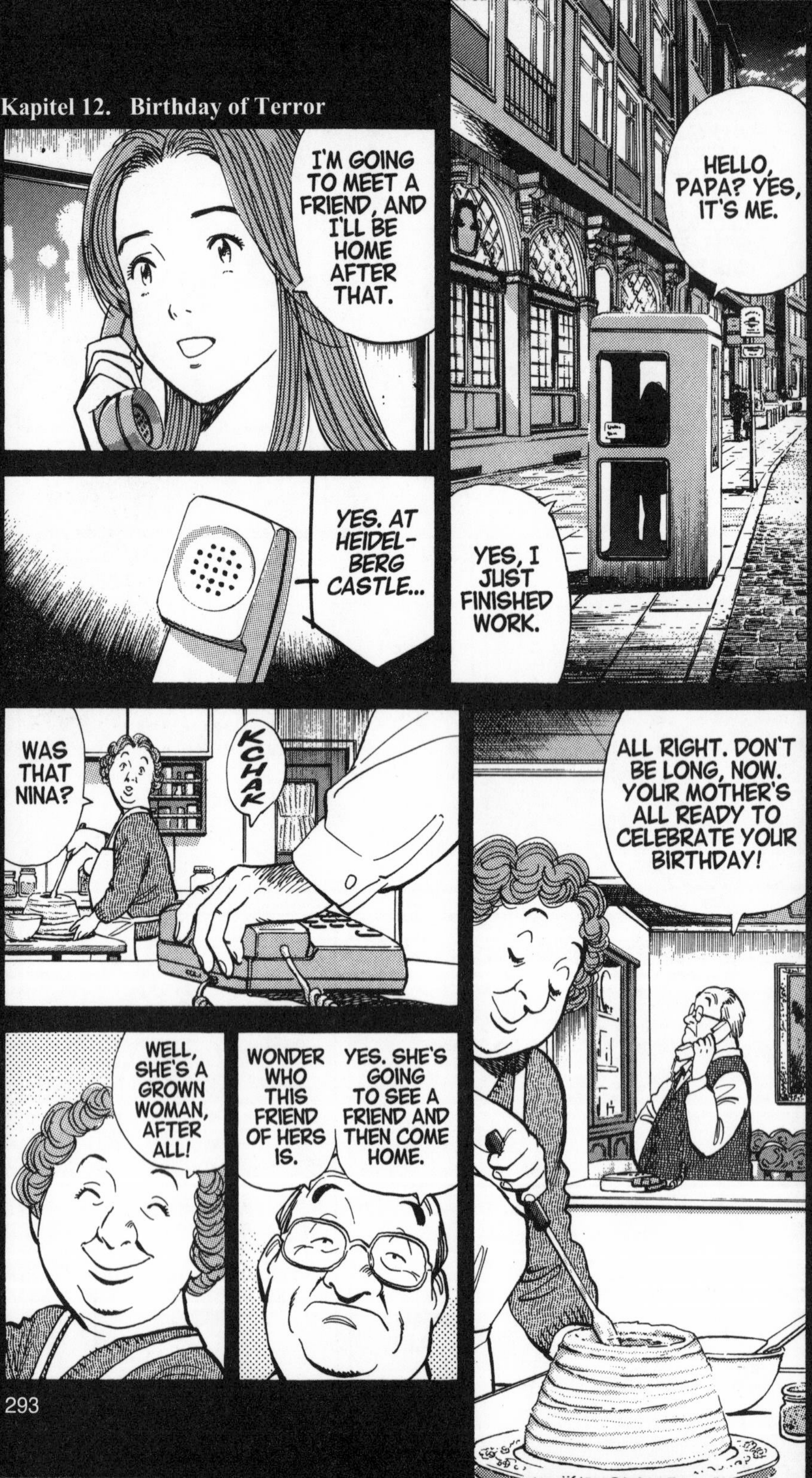
HELLO, PAPA? YES, IT'S ME.
YES, I JUST FINISHED WORK.
I'M GOING TO MEET A FRIEND, AND I'LL BE HOME AFTER THAT.
YES. AT HEIDEL-BERG CASTLE...
ALL RIGHT. DON'T BE LONG, NOW. YOUR MOTHER'S ALL READY TO CELEBRATE YOUR BIRTHDAY!
KCHAK
WAS THAT NINA?
YES. SHE'S GOING TO SEE A FRIEND AND THEN COME HOME.
WONDER WHO THIS FRIEND OF HERS IS.
WELL, SHE'S A GROWN WOMAN, AFTER ALL!

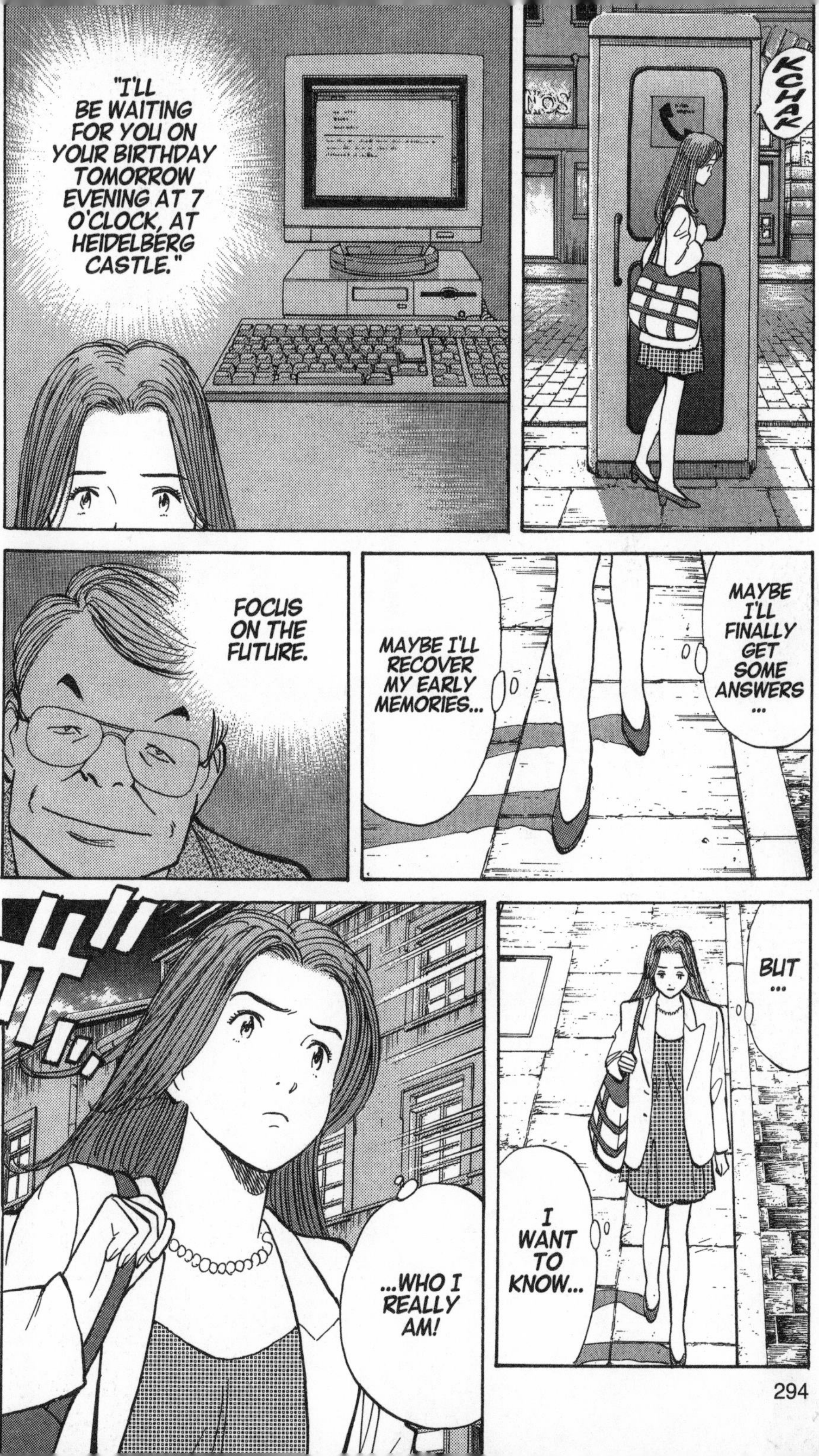

KCHAK
"I'LL BE WAITING FOR YOU ON YOUR BIRTHDAY TOMORROW EVENING AT 7 O'CLOCK, AT HEIDELBERG CASTLE."
MAYBE I'LL FINALLY GET SOME ANSWERS...
MAYBE I'LL RECOVER MY EARLY MEMORIES...
FOCUS ON THE FUTURE.
BUT...
I WANT TO KNOW...
...WHO I REALLY AM!

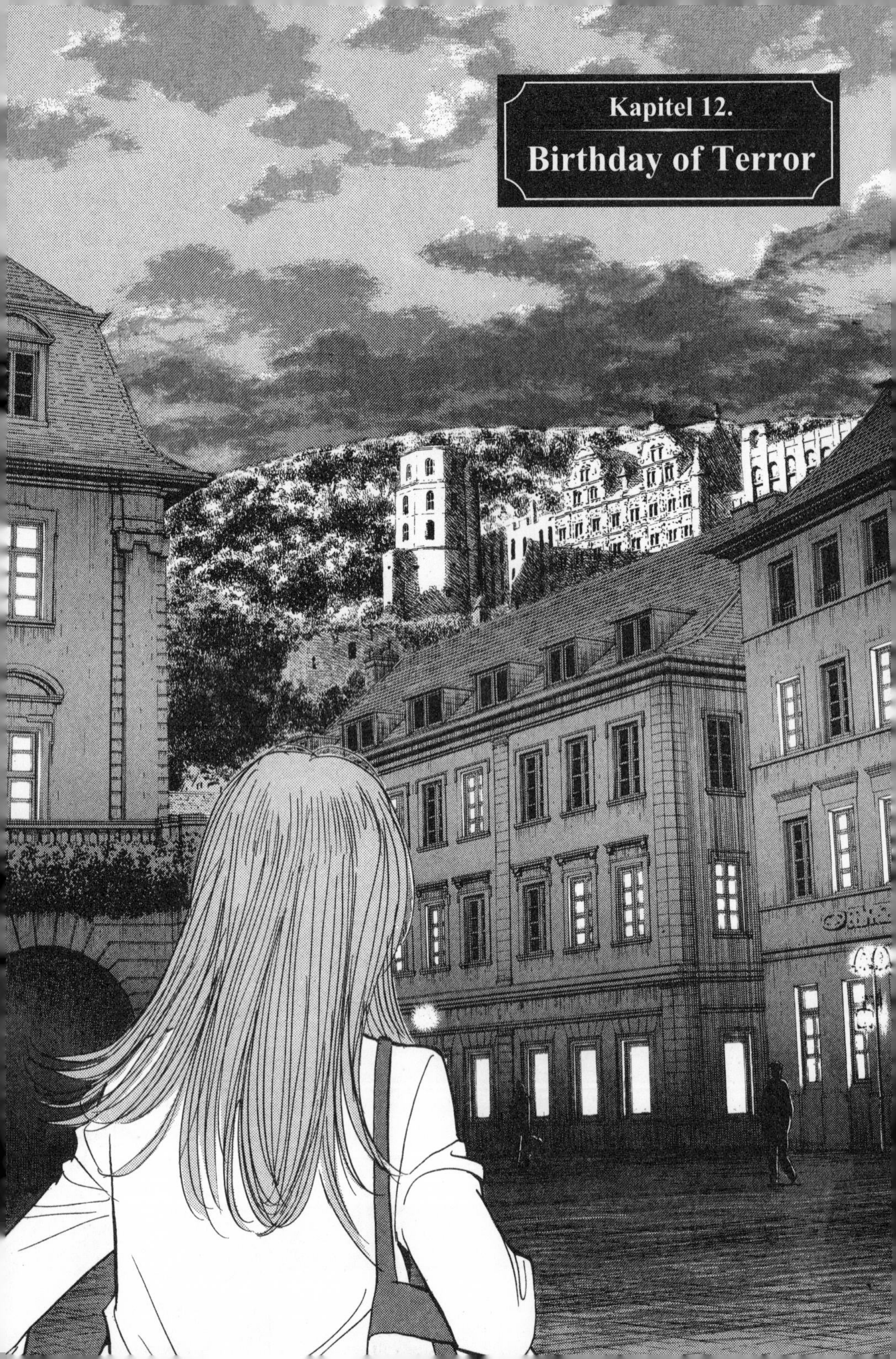
Kapitel 12.
Birthday of Terror

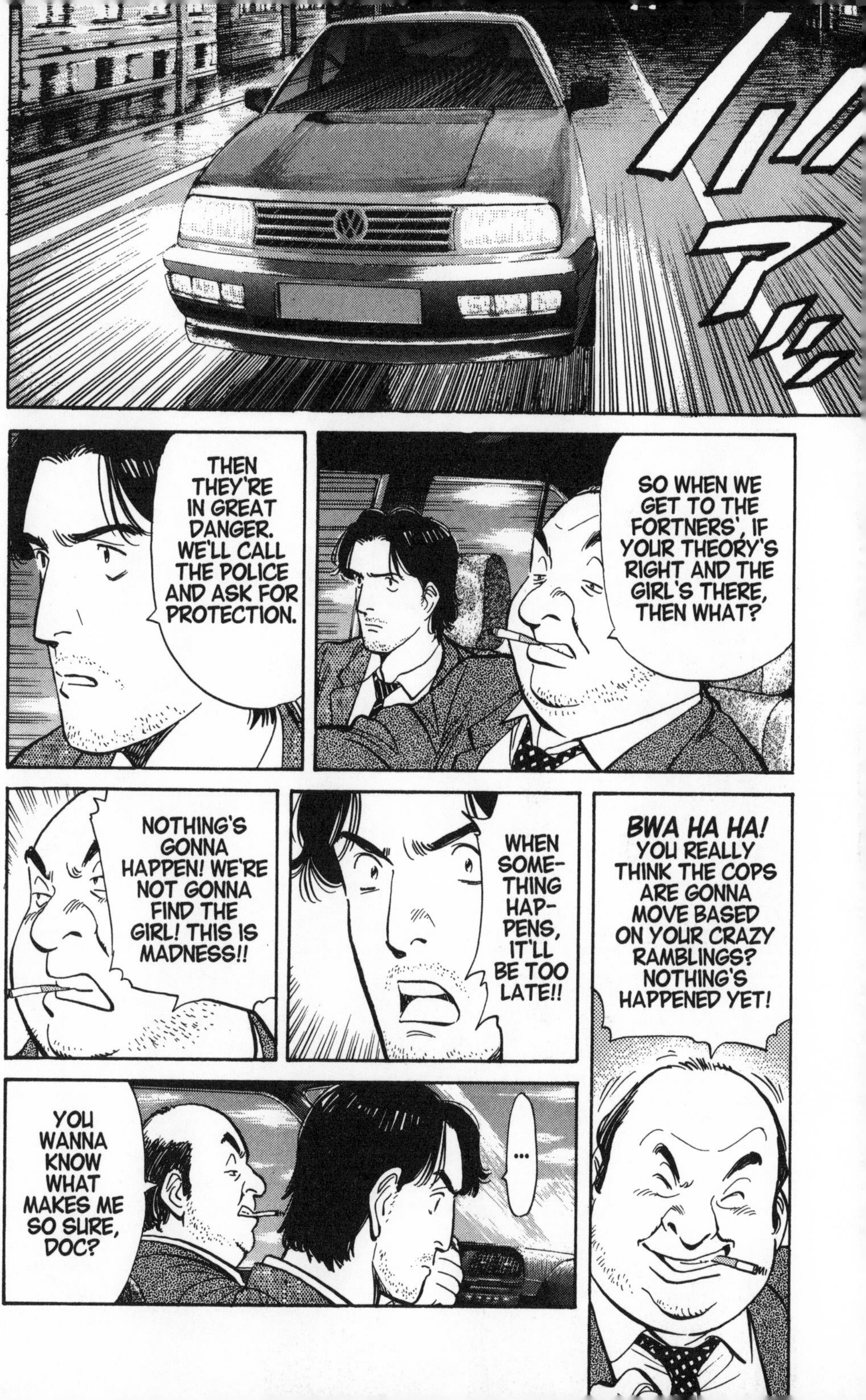
SO WHEN WE GET TO THE FORTNERS', IF YOUR THEORY'S RIGHT AND THE GIRL'S THERE, THEN WHAT?
THEN THEY'RE IN GREAT DANGER. WE'LL CALL THE POLICE AND ASK FOR PROTECTION.
BWA HA HA! YOU REALLY THINK THE COPS ARE GONNA MOVE BASED ON YOUR CRAZY RAMBLINGS? NOTHING'S HAPPENED YET!
WHEN SOME-THING HAP-PENS, IT'LL BE TOO LATE!!
NOTHING'S GONNA HAPPEN! WE'RE NOT GONNA FIND THE GIRL! THIS IS MADNESS!!
...
YOU WANNA KNOW WHAT MAKES ME SO SURE, DOC?

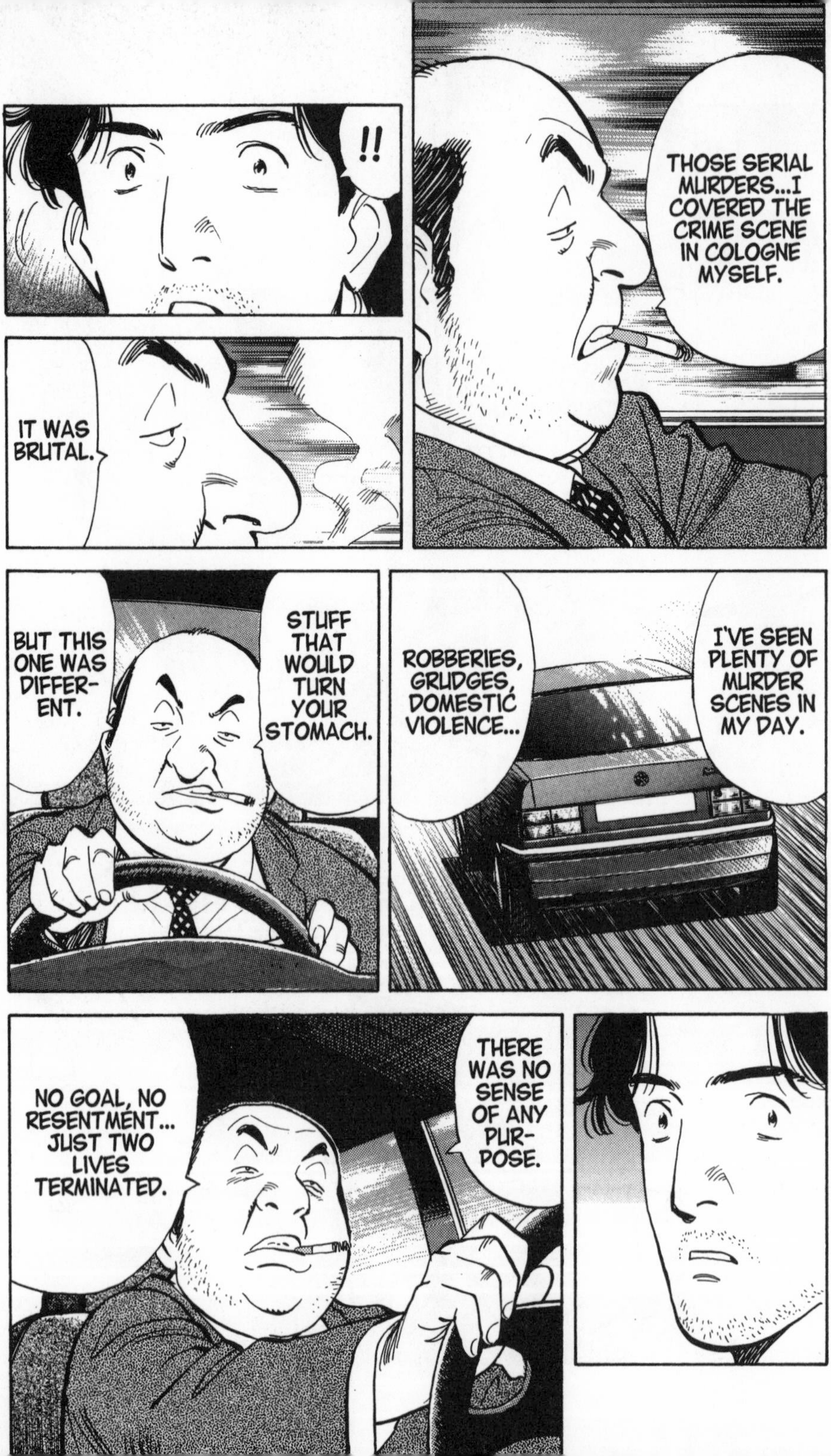
THOSE SERIAL MURDERS...I COVERED THE CRIME SCENE IN COLOGNE MYSELF.
!!
IT WAS BRUTAL.
I'VE SEEN PLENTY OF MURDER SCENES IN MY DAY.
ROBBERIES, GRUDGES, DOMESTIC VIOLENCE...
STUFF THAT WOULD TURN YOUR STOMACH.
BUT THIS ONE WAS DIFFER-ENT.
THERE WAS NO SENSE OF ANY PUR-POSE.
NO GOAL, NO RESENTMENT... JUST TWO LIVES TERMINATED.

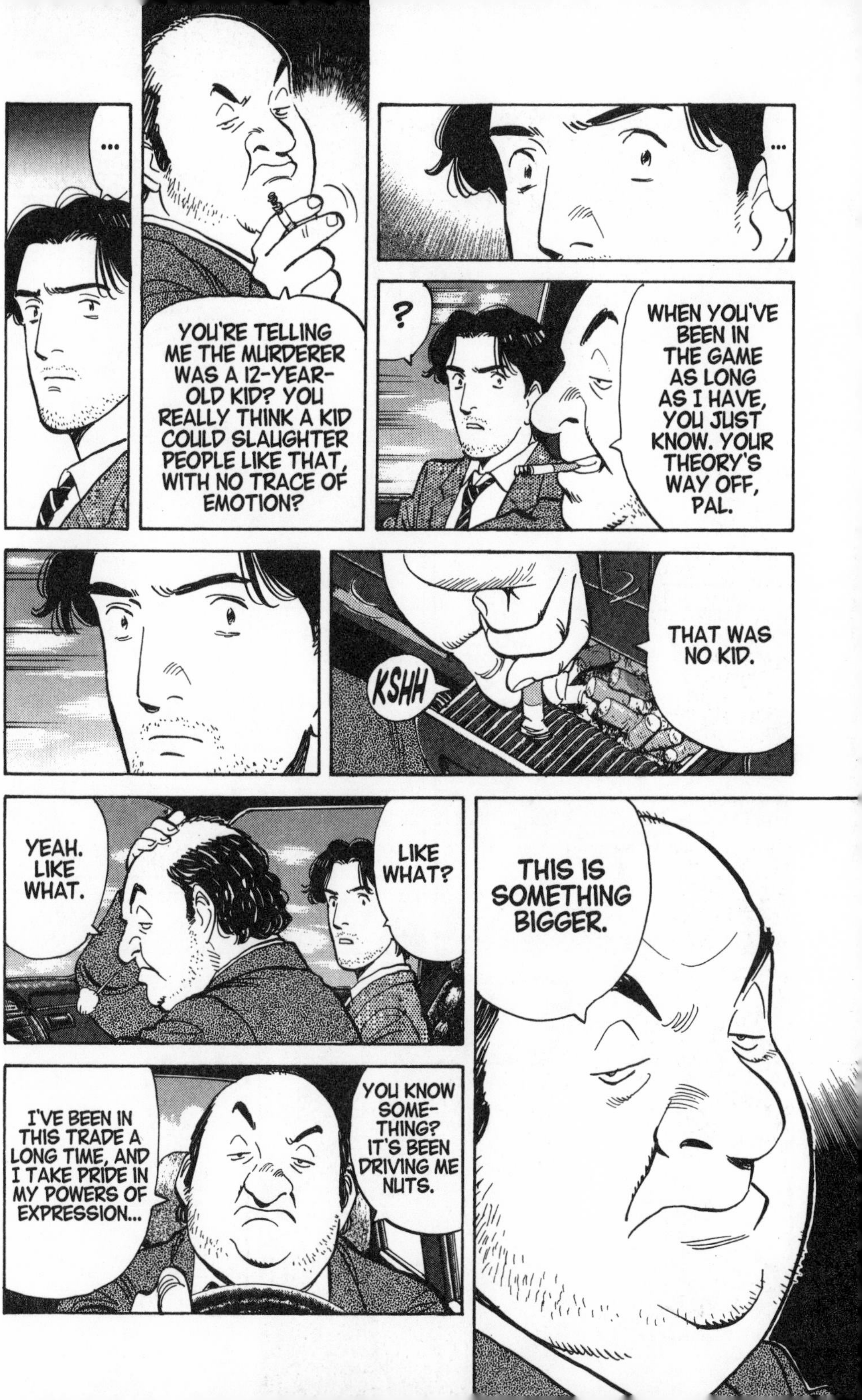
...
WHEN YOU'VE BEEN IN THE GAME AS LONG AS I HAVE, YOU JUST KNOW. YOUR THEORY'S WAY OFF, PAL.
?
YOU'RE TELLING ME THE MURDERER WAS A 12-YEAR-OLD KID? YOU REALLY THINK A KID COULD SLAUGHTER PEOPLE LIKE THAT, WITH NO TRACE OF EMOTION?
...
THAT WAS NO KID.
KSHH
THIS IS SOMETHING BIGGER.
LIKE WHAT?
YEAH. LIKE WHAT.
YOU KNOW SOME-THING? IT'S BEEN DRIVING ME NUTS.
I'VE BEEN IN THIS TRADE A LONG TIME, AND I TAKE PRIDE IN MY POWERS OF EXPRESSION...

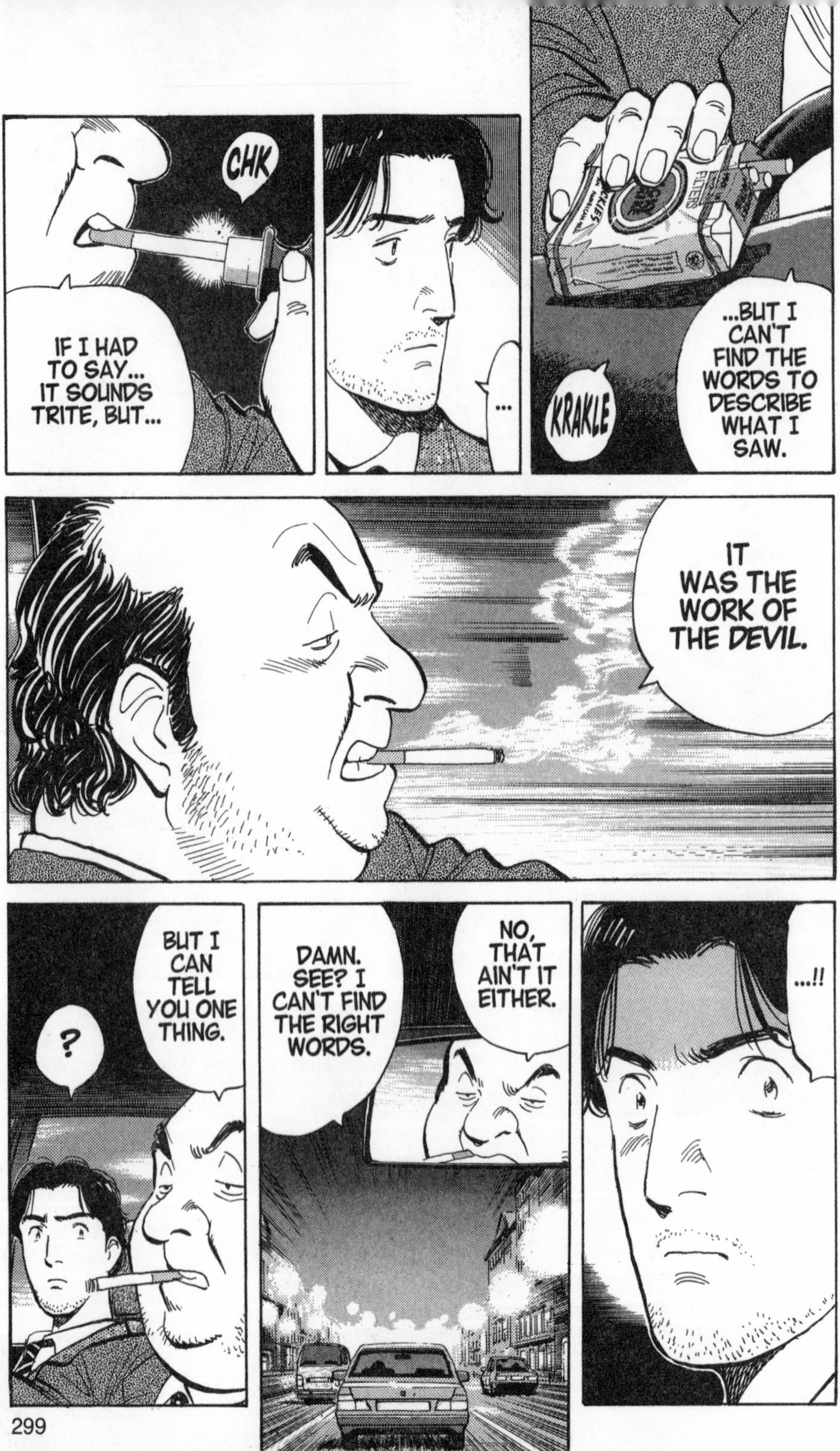
...BUT I CAN'T FIND THE WORDS TO DESCRIBE WHAT I SAW.
KRAKLE
...
CHK
IF I HAD TO SAY... IT SOUNDS TRITE, BUT...
IT WAS THE WORK OF THE DEVIL.
...!!
NO, THAT AIN'T IT EITHER.
DAMN. SEE? I CAN'T FIND THE RIGHT WORDS.
BUT I CAN TELL YOU ONE THING.
?

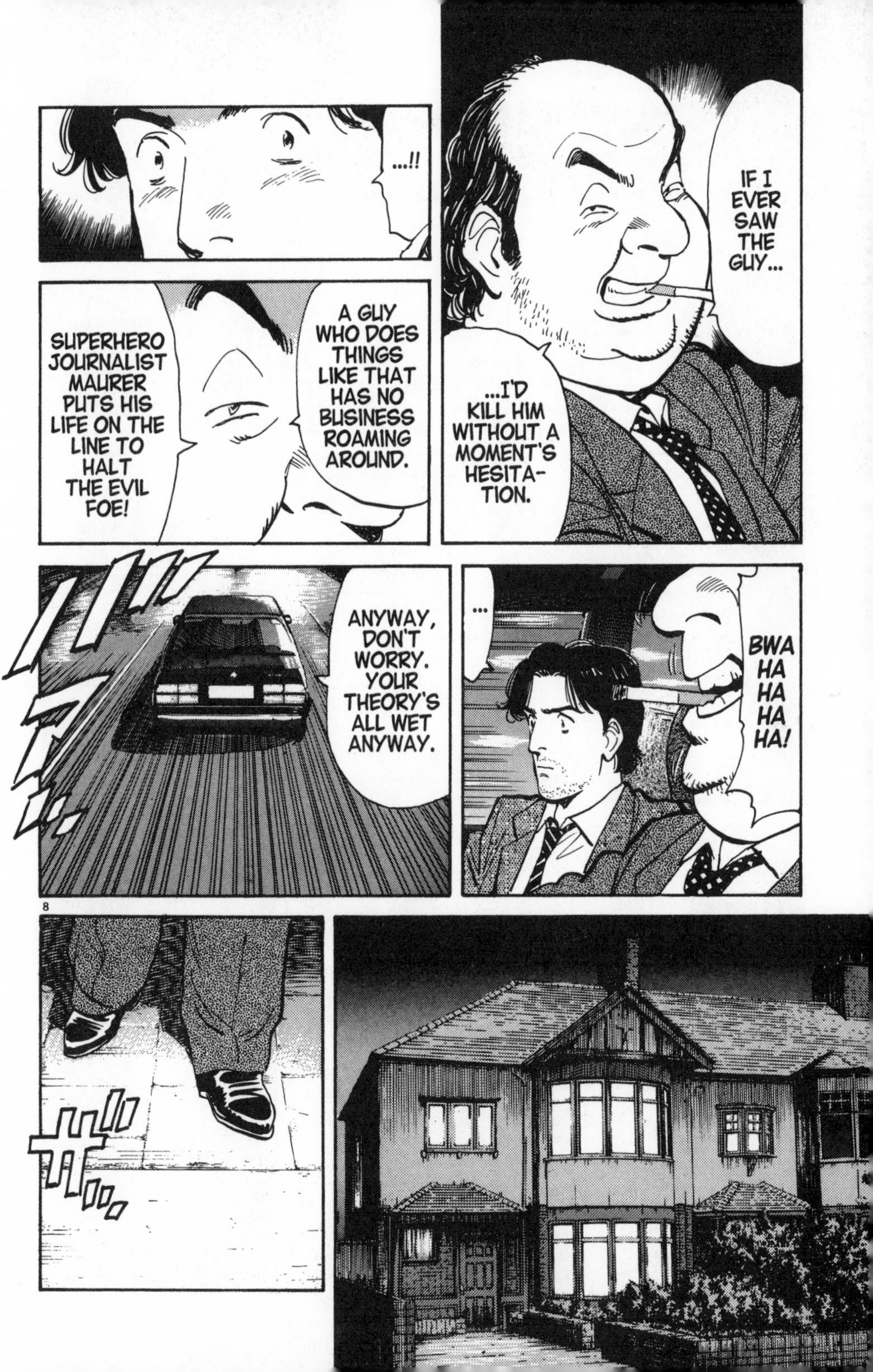
IF I EVER SAW THE GUY...
...I'D KILL HIM WITHOUT A MOMENT'S HESITA-TION.
...!!
A GUY WHO DOES THINGS LIKE THAT HAS NO BUSINESS ROAMING AROUND.
SUPERHERO JOURNALIST MAURER PUTS HIS LIFE ON THE LINE TO HALT THE EVIL FOE!
BWA HA HA HA HA!
...
ANYWAY, DON'T WORRY. YOUR THEORY'S ALL WET ANYWAY.

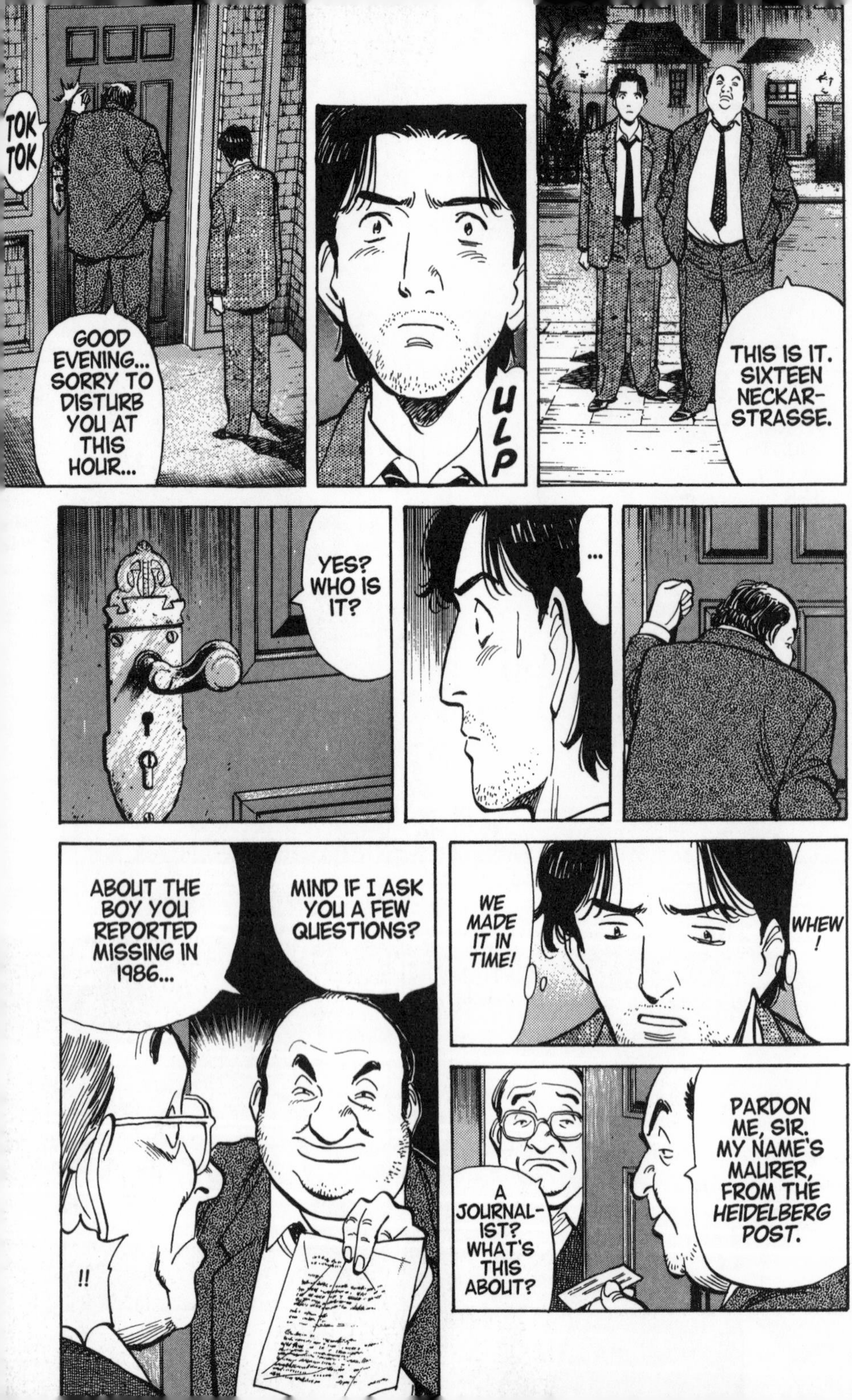
THIS IS IT. SIXTEEN NECKAR-STRASSE.
ULP
TOK TOK
GOOD EVENING... SORRY TO DISTURB YOU AT THIS HOUR...
...
YES? WHO IS IT?
WHEW!
WE MADE IT IN TIME!
PARDON ME, SIR. MY NAME'S MAURER, FROM THE HEIDELBERG POST.
A JOURNALIST? WHAT'S THIS ABOUT?
MIND IF I ASK YOU A FEW QUESTIONS?
ABOUT THE BOY YOU REPORTED MISSING IN 1986...
!!

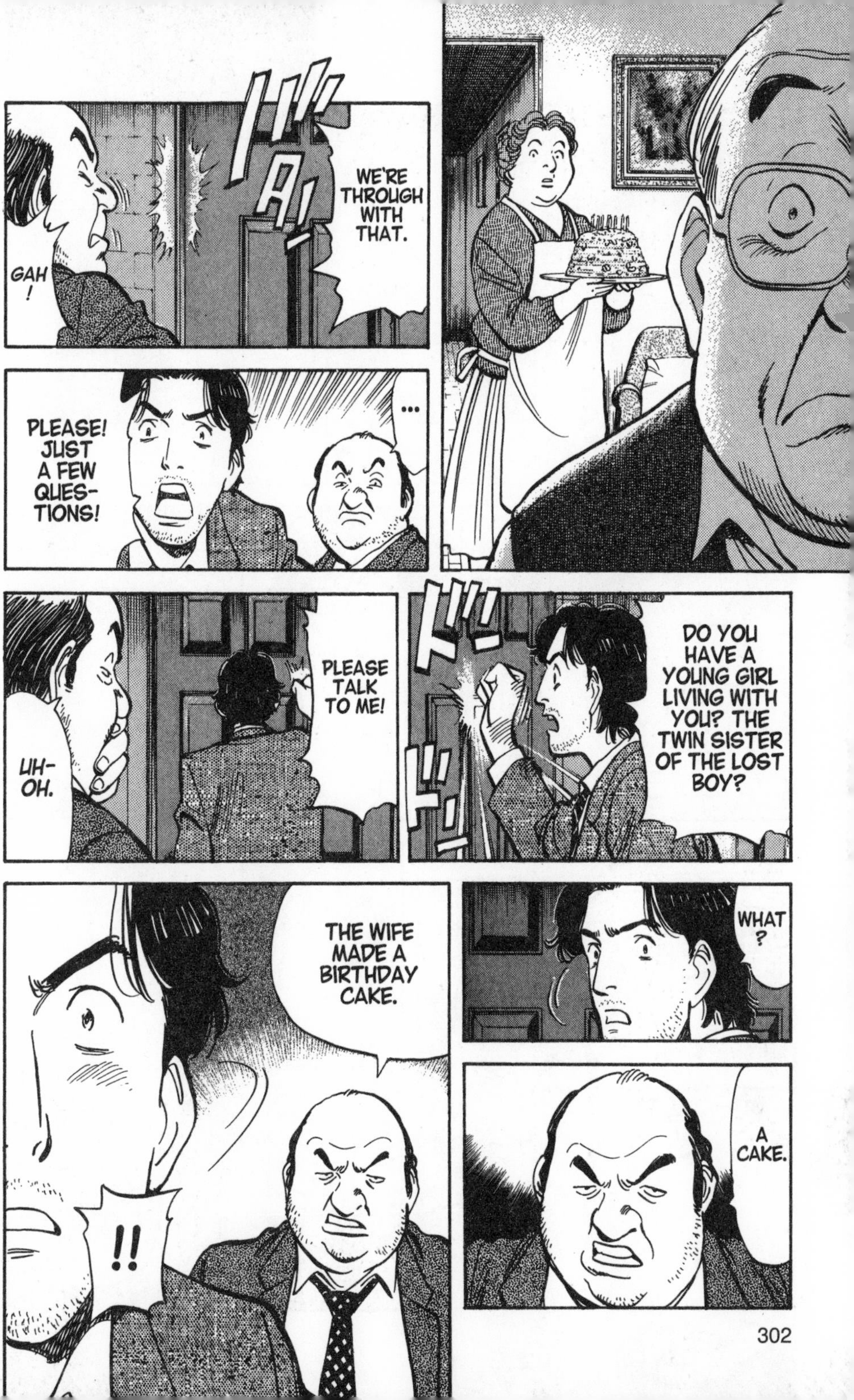
WE'RE THROUGH WITH THAT.
GAH!
...
PLEASE! JUST A FEW QUES-TIONS!
DO YOU HAVE A YOUNG GIRL LIVING WITH YOU? THE TWIN SISTER OF THE LOST BOY?
PLEASE TALK TO ME!
UH-OH.
WHAT?
A CAKE.
THE WIFE MADE A BIRTHDAY CAKE.
!!

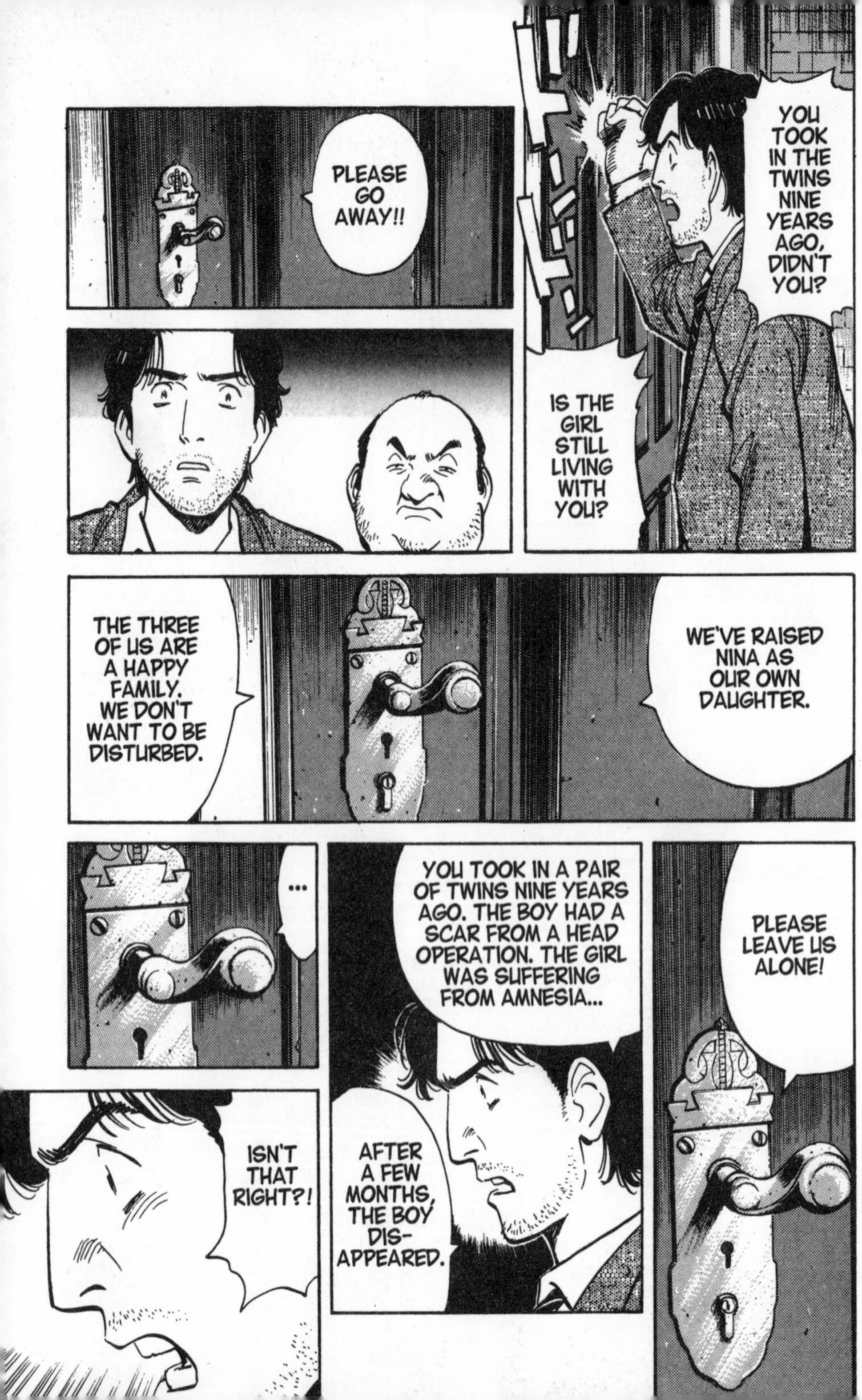
YOU TOOK IN THE TWINS NINE YEARS AGO, DIDN'T YOU?
IS THE GIRL STILL LIVING WITH YOU?
PLEASE GO AWAY!!
WE'VE RAISED NINA AS OUR OWN DAUGHTER.
THE THREE OF US ARE A HAPPY FAMILY. WE DON'T WANT TO BE DISTURBED.
PLEASE LEAVE US ALONE!
YOU TOOK IN A PAIR OF TWINS NINE YEARS AGO. THE BOY HAD A SCAR FROM A HEAD OPERATION. THE GIRL WAS SUFFERING FROM AMNESIA...
AFTER A FEW MONTHS, THE BOY DIS-APPEARED.
...
ISN'T THAT RIGHT?!

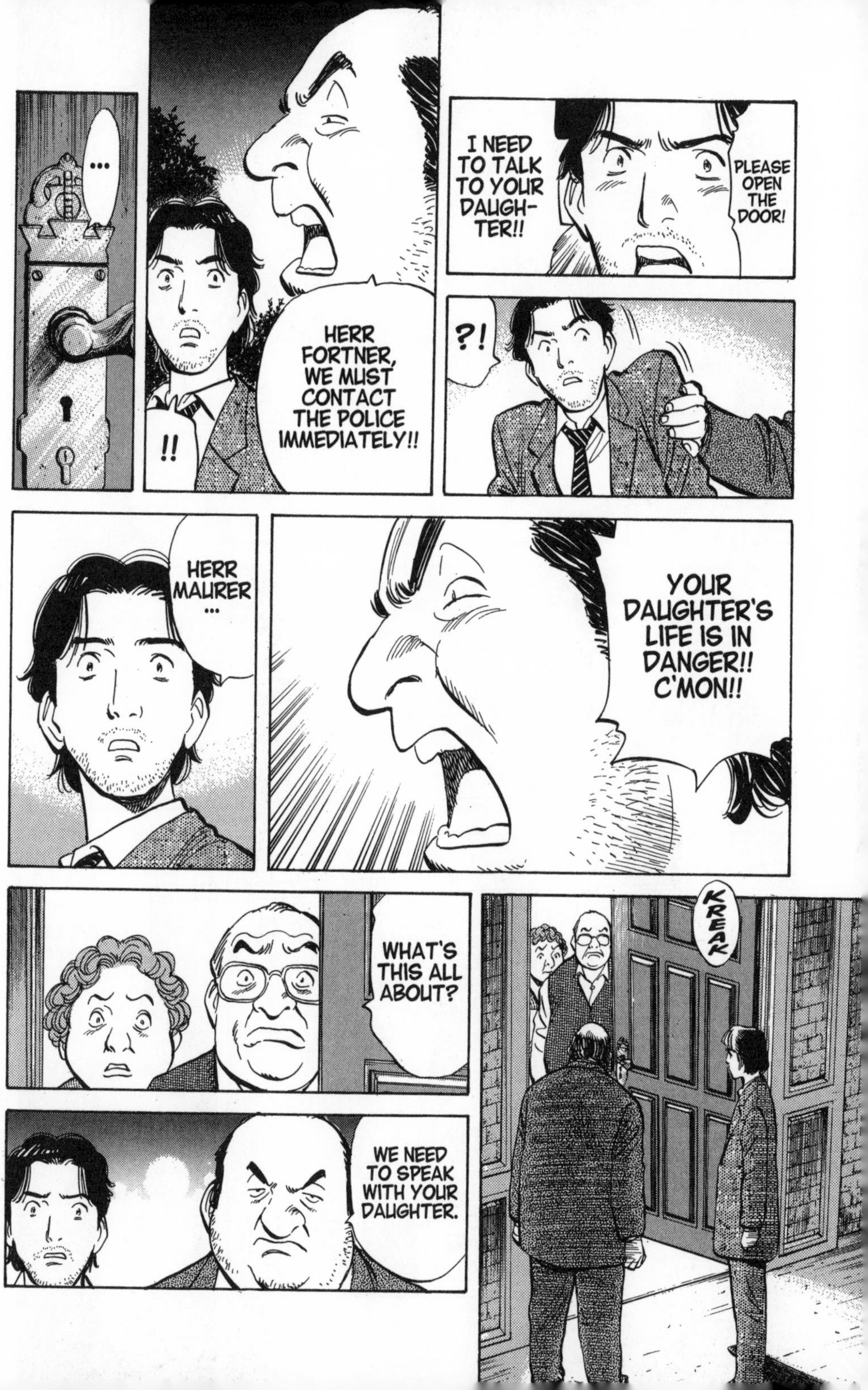
PLEASE OPEN THE DOOR!
I NEED TO TALK TO YOUR DAUGHTER!!
?!
HERR FORTNER, WE MUST CONTACT THE POLICE IMMEDIATELY!!
!!
...
YOUR DAUGHTER'S LIFE IS IN DANGER!! C'MON!!
HERR MAURER ...
KREAK
WHAT'S THIS ALL ABOUT?
WE NEED TO SPEAK WITH YOUR DAUGHTER.

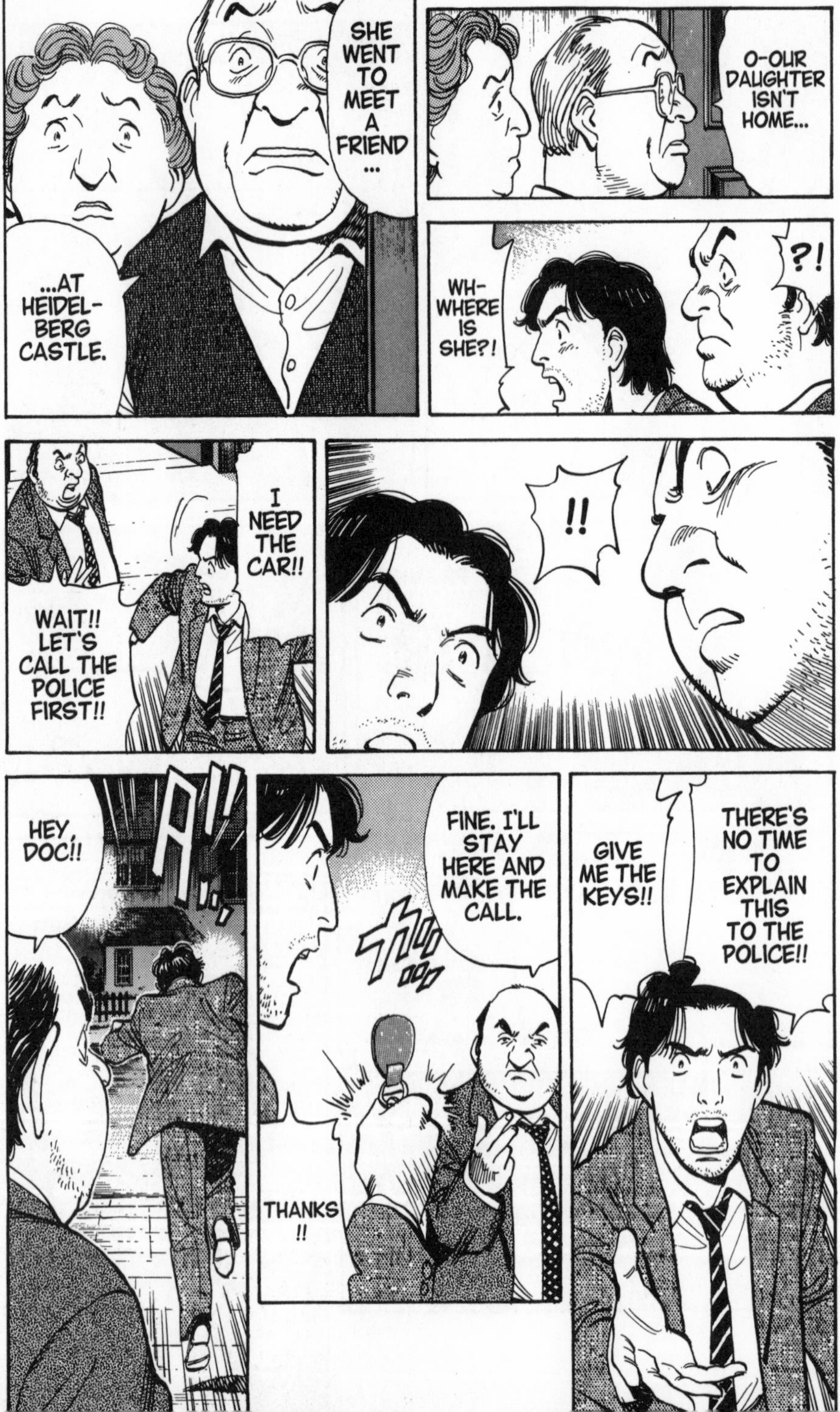
O-OUR DAUGHTER ISN'T HOME...
?!
WH-WHERE IS SHE?!
SHE WENT TO MEET A FRIEND...
...AT HEIDEL-BERG CASTLE.
!!
I NEED THE CAR!!
WAIT!! LET'S CALL THE POLICE FIRST!!
THERE'S NO TIME TO EXPLAIN THIS TO THE POLICE!!
GIVE ME THE KEYS!!
FINE. I'LL STAY HERE AND MAKE THE CALL.
THANKS!!
HEY, DOC!!

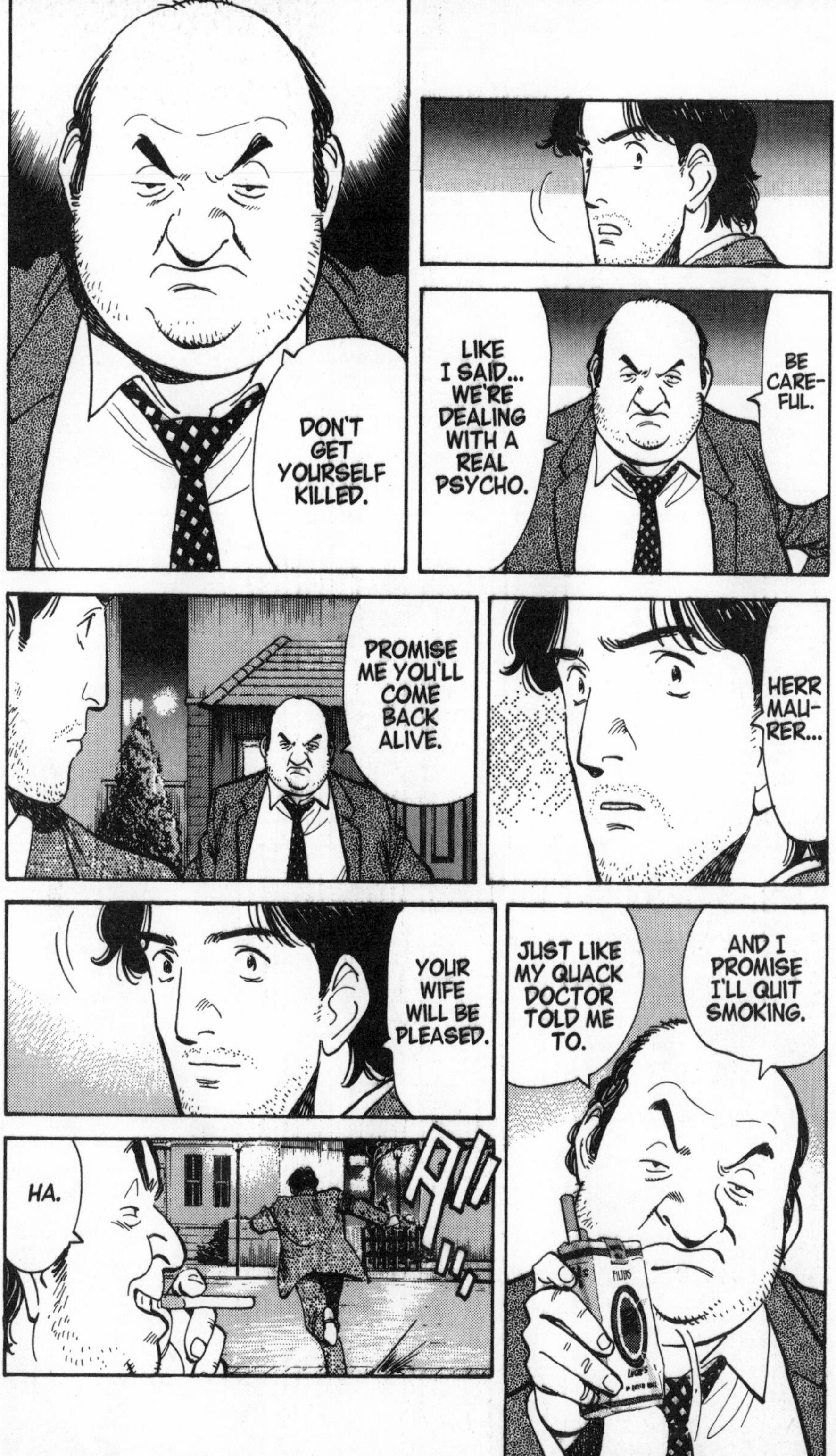
BE CAREFUL.
LIKE I SAID... WE'RE DEALING WITH A REAL PSYCHO.
DON'T GET YOURSELF KILLED.
HERR MAURER...
PROMISE ME YOU'LL COME BACK ALIVE.
AND I PROMISE I'LL QUIT SMOKING.
JUST LIKE MY QUACK DOCTOR TOLD ME TO.
YOUR WIFE WILL BE PLEASED.
HA.

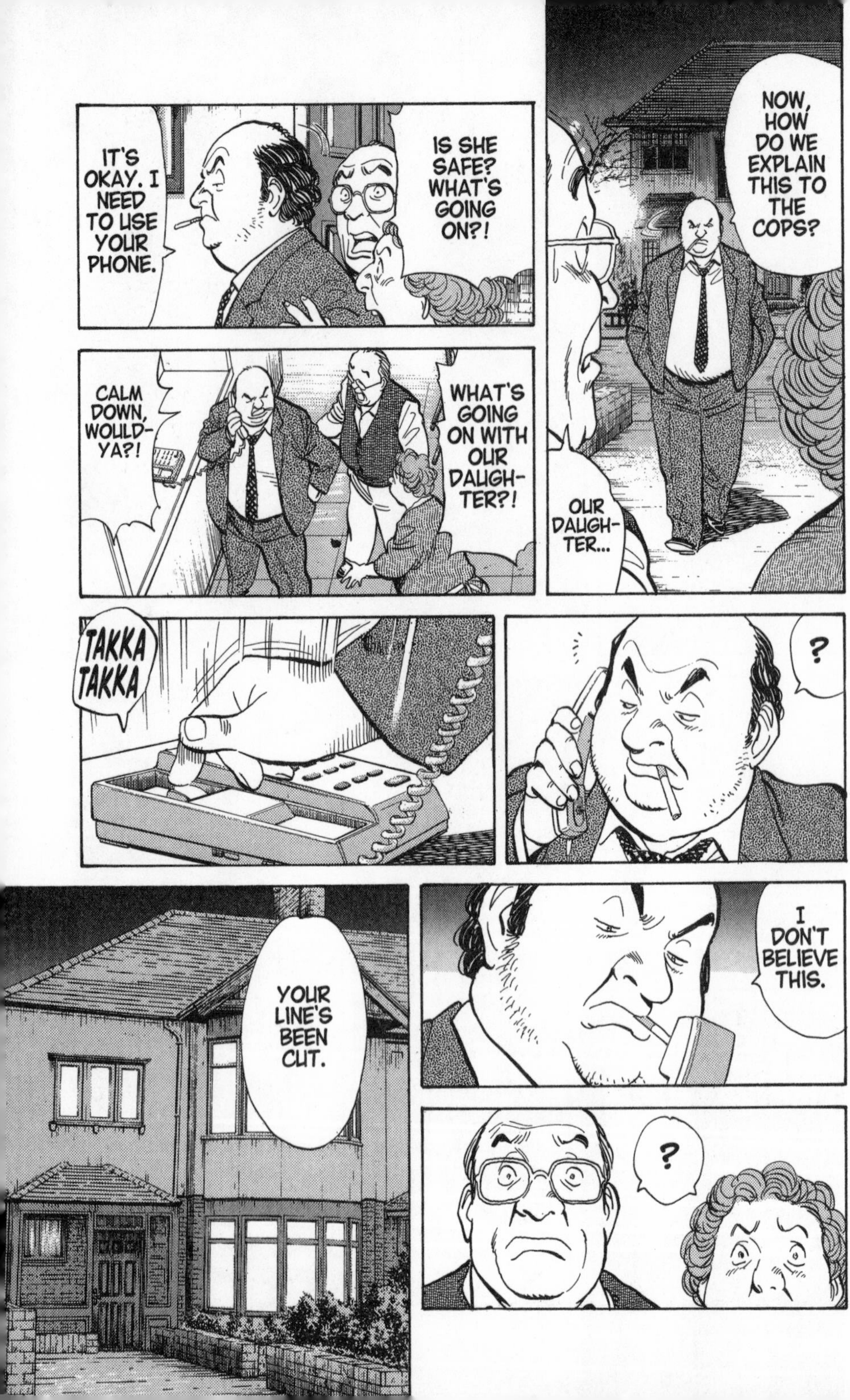
NOW, HOW DO WE EXPLAIN THIS TO THE COPS?
OUR DAUGHTER...
IS SHE SAFE? WHAT'S GOING ON?!
IT'S OKAY. I NEED TO USE YOUR PHONE.
WHAT'S GOING ON WITH OUR DAUGHTER?!
CALM DOWN, WOULD-YA?!
?
TAKKA TAKKA
I DON'T BELIEVE THIS.
?
YOUR LINE'S BEEN CUT.

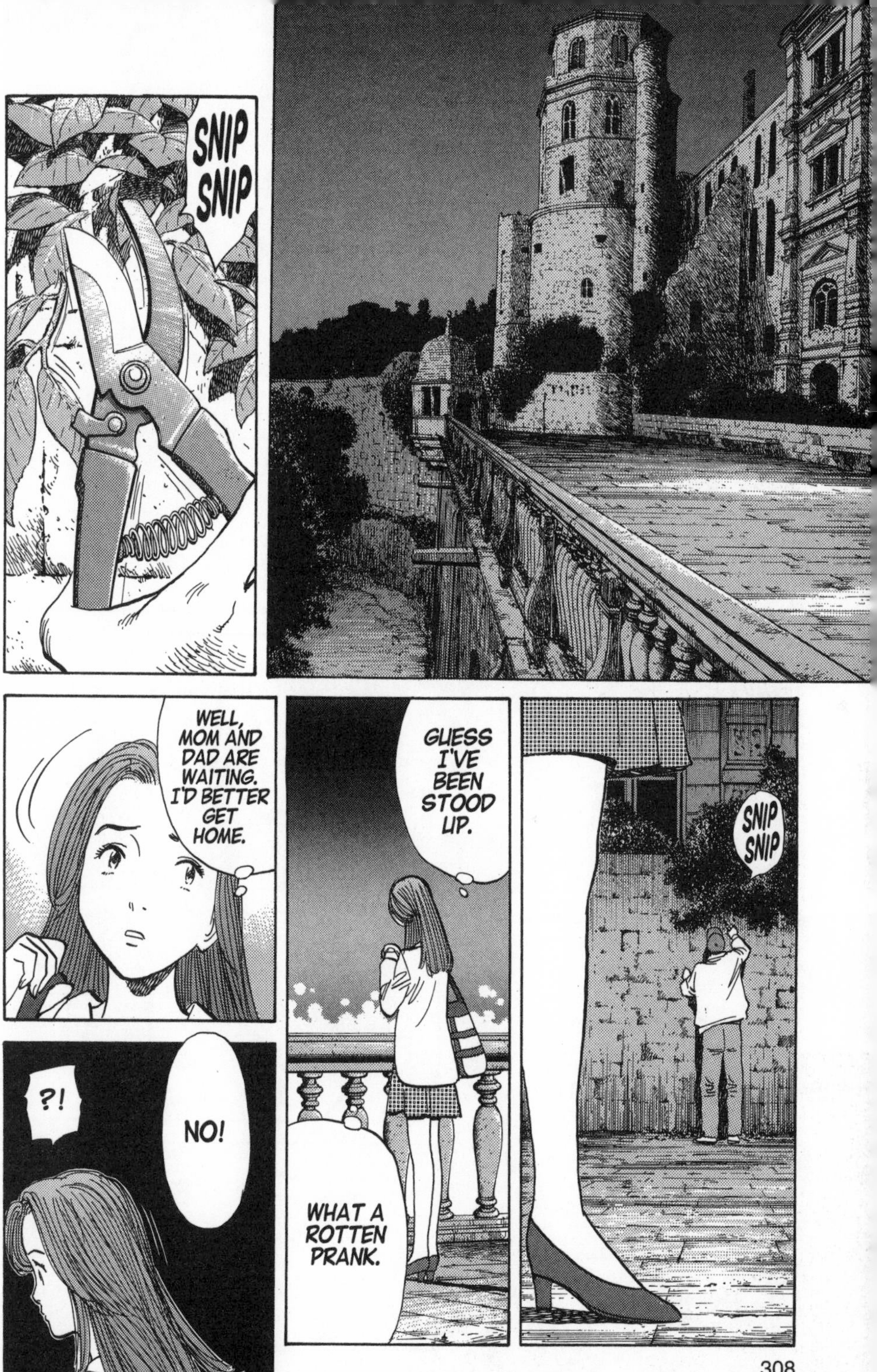
SNIP SNIP
SNIP SNIP
GUESS I'VE BEEN STOOD UP.
WHAT A ROTTEN PRANK.
WELL, MOM AND DAD ARE WAITING. I'D BETTER GET HOME.
NO!
?!

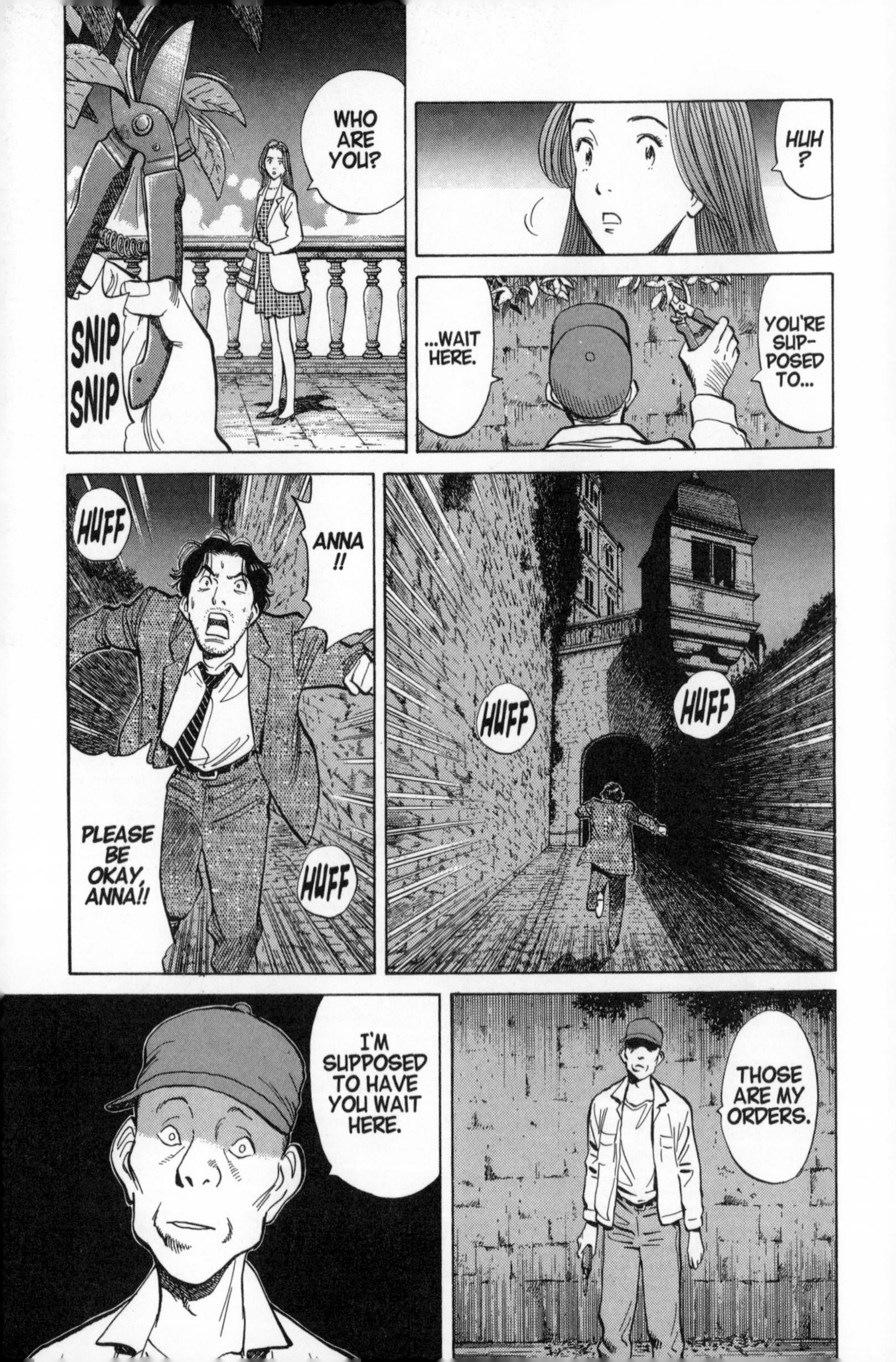
HUH ?
YOU'RE SUP-POSED TO...
...WAIT HERE.
WHO ARE YOU?
SNIP SNIP
HUFF
HUFF
HUFF
ANNA !!
PLEASE BE OKAY, ANNA!!
HUFF
THOSE ARE MY ORDERS.
I'M SUPPOSED TO HAVE YOU WAIT HERE.

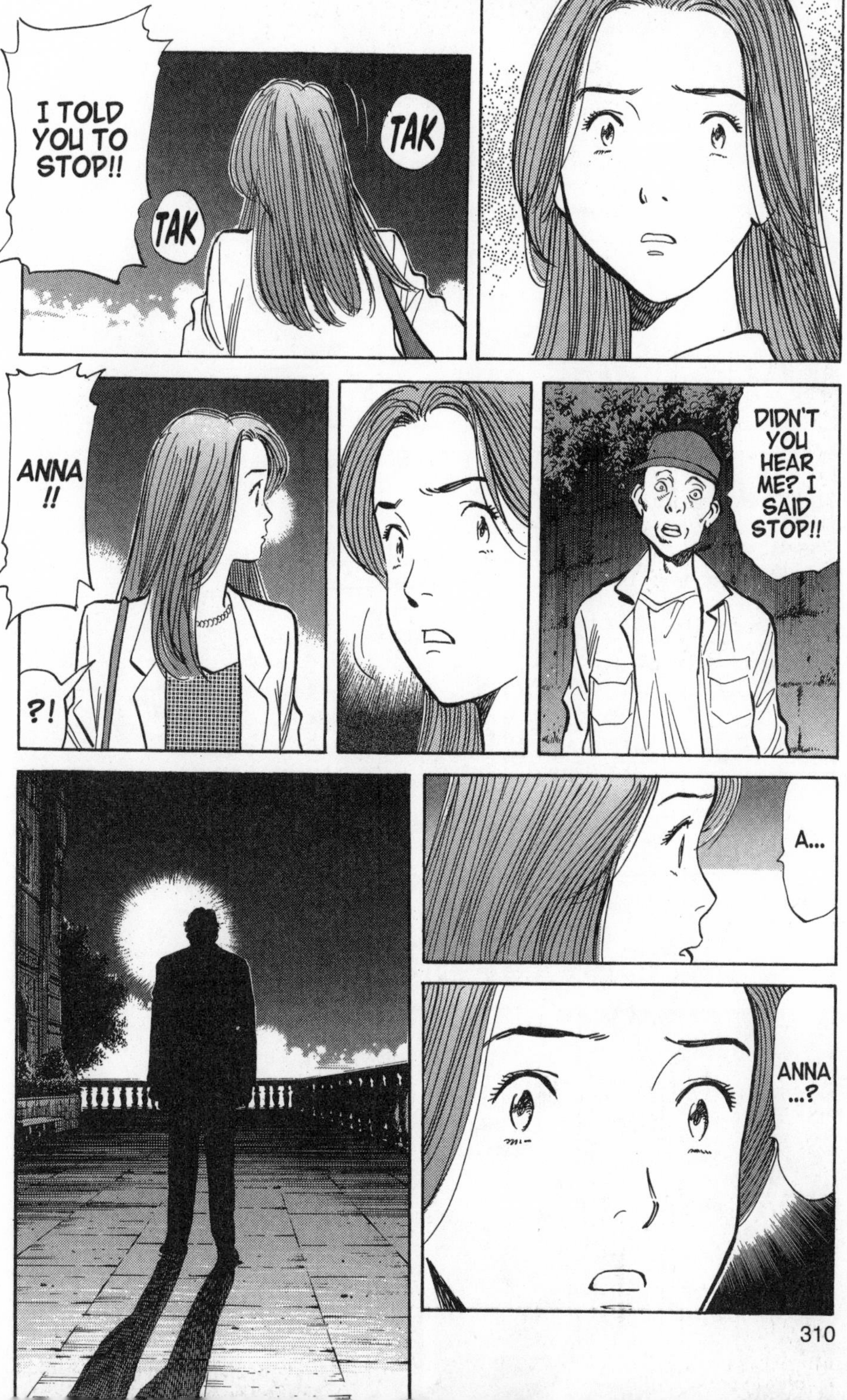
I TOLD YOU TO STOP!!
TAK
TAK
DIDN'T YOU HEAR ME? I SAID STOP!!
ANNA!!
?!
A...
ANNA...?

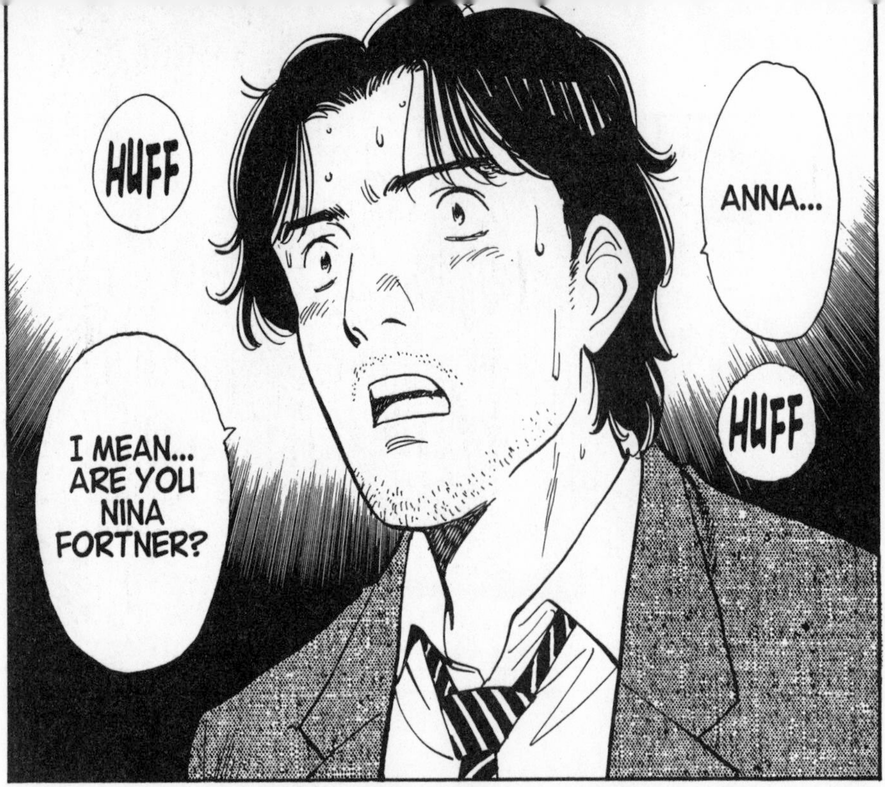
ANNA...
HUFF
HUFF
I MEAN... ARE YOU NINA FORTNER?

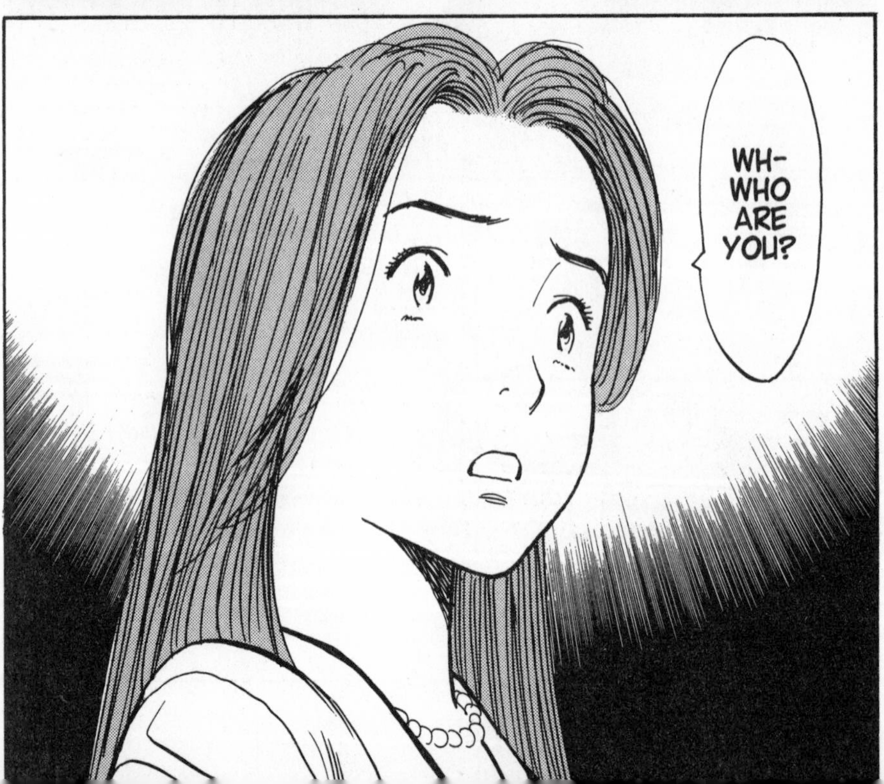
WH-WHO ARE YOU?

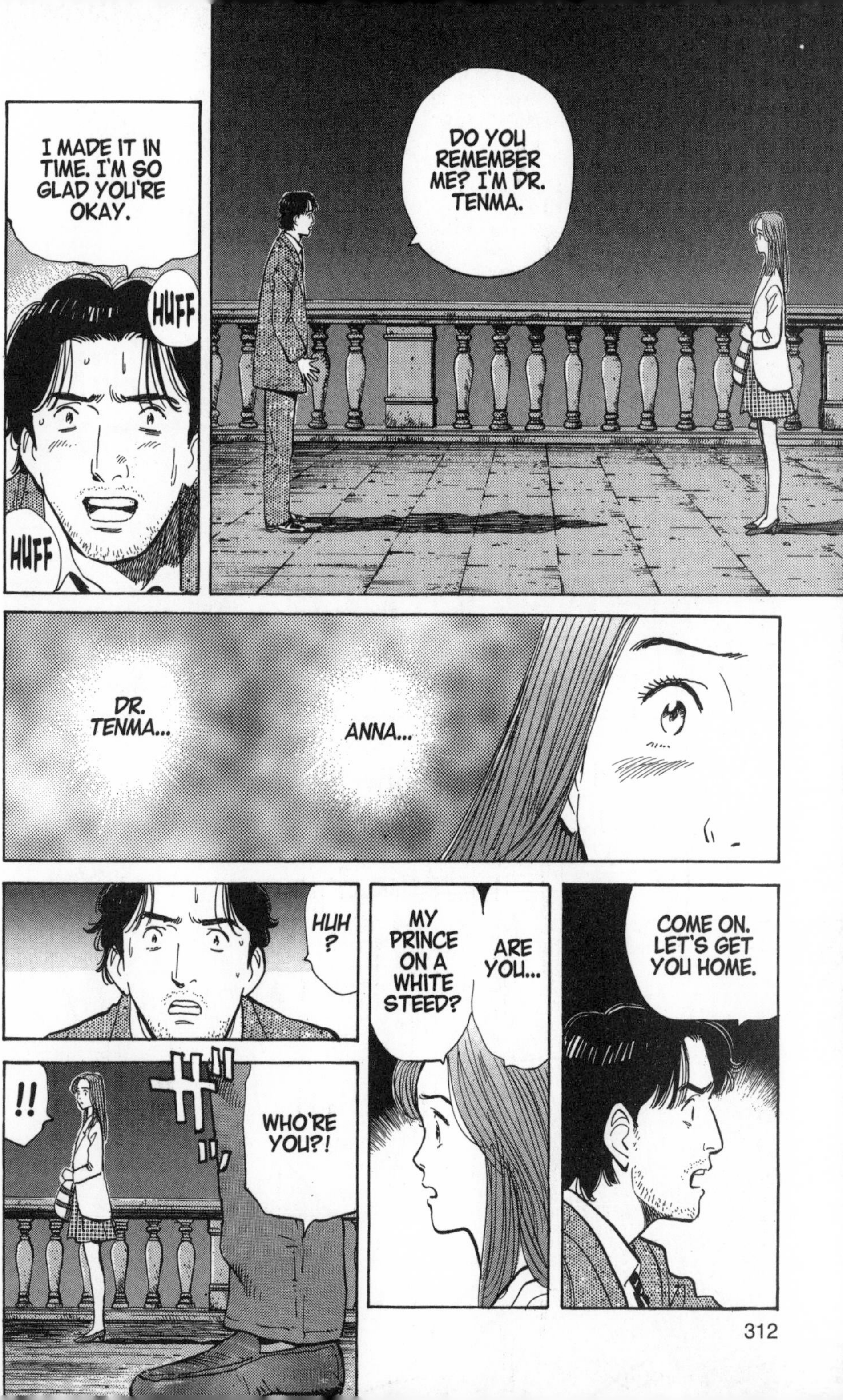
DO YOU REMEMBER ME? I'M DR. TENMA.
I MADE IT IN TIME. I'M SO GLAD YOU'RE OKAY.
HUFF
HUFF
ANNA...
DR. TENMA...
COME ON. LET'S GET YOU HOME.
ARE YOU...
MY PRINCE ON A WHITE STEED?
HUH?
!!
WHO'RE YOU?!

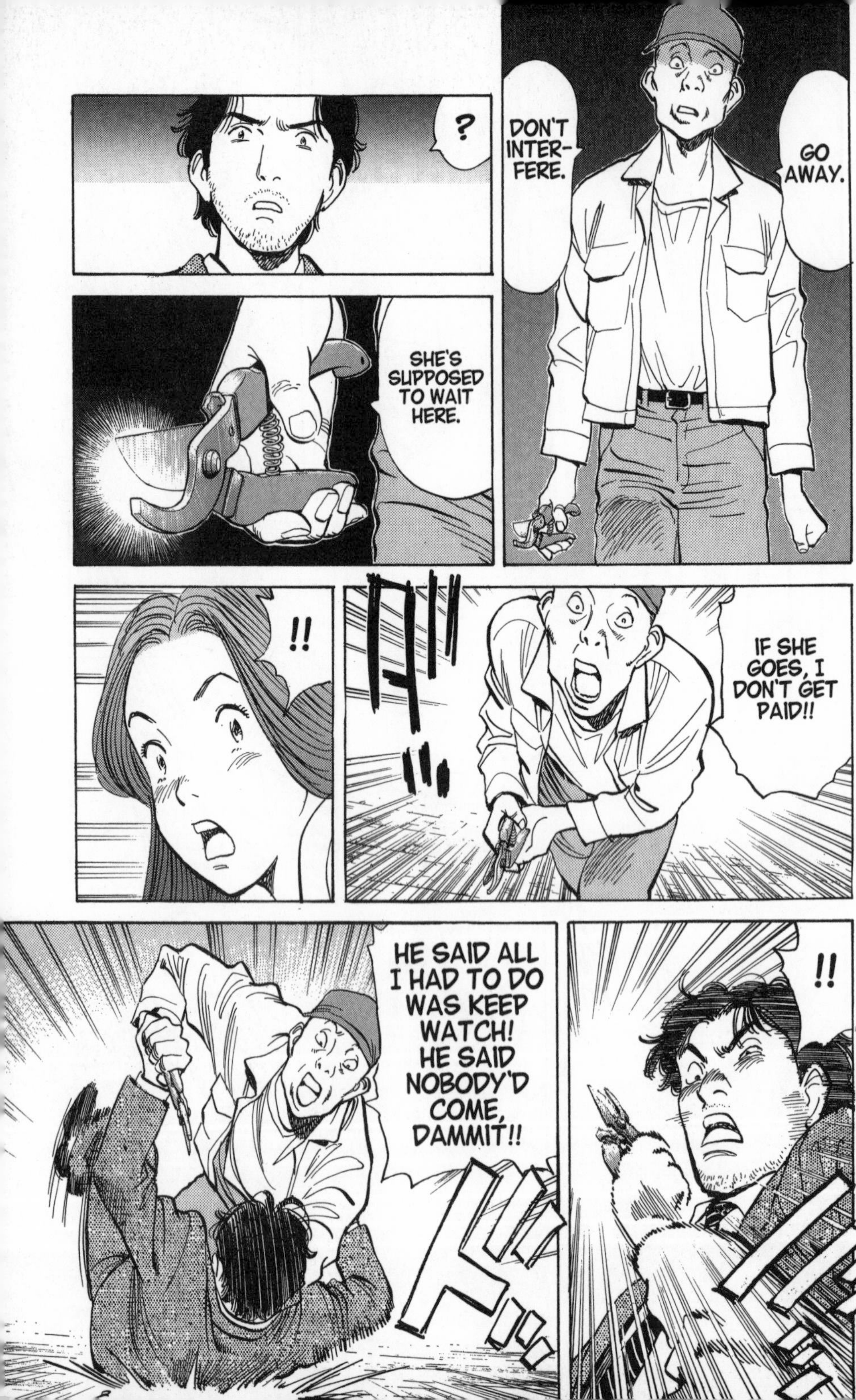
GO AWAY.
DON'T INTERFERE.
?
SHE'S SUPPOSED TO WAIT HERE.
IF SHE GOES, I DON'T GET PAID!!
!!
!!
HE SAID ALL I HAD TO DO WAS KEEP WATCH! HE SAID NOBODY'D COME, DAMMIT!!

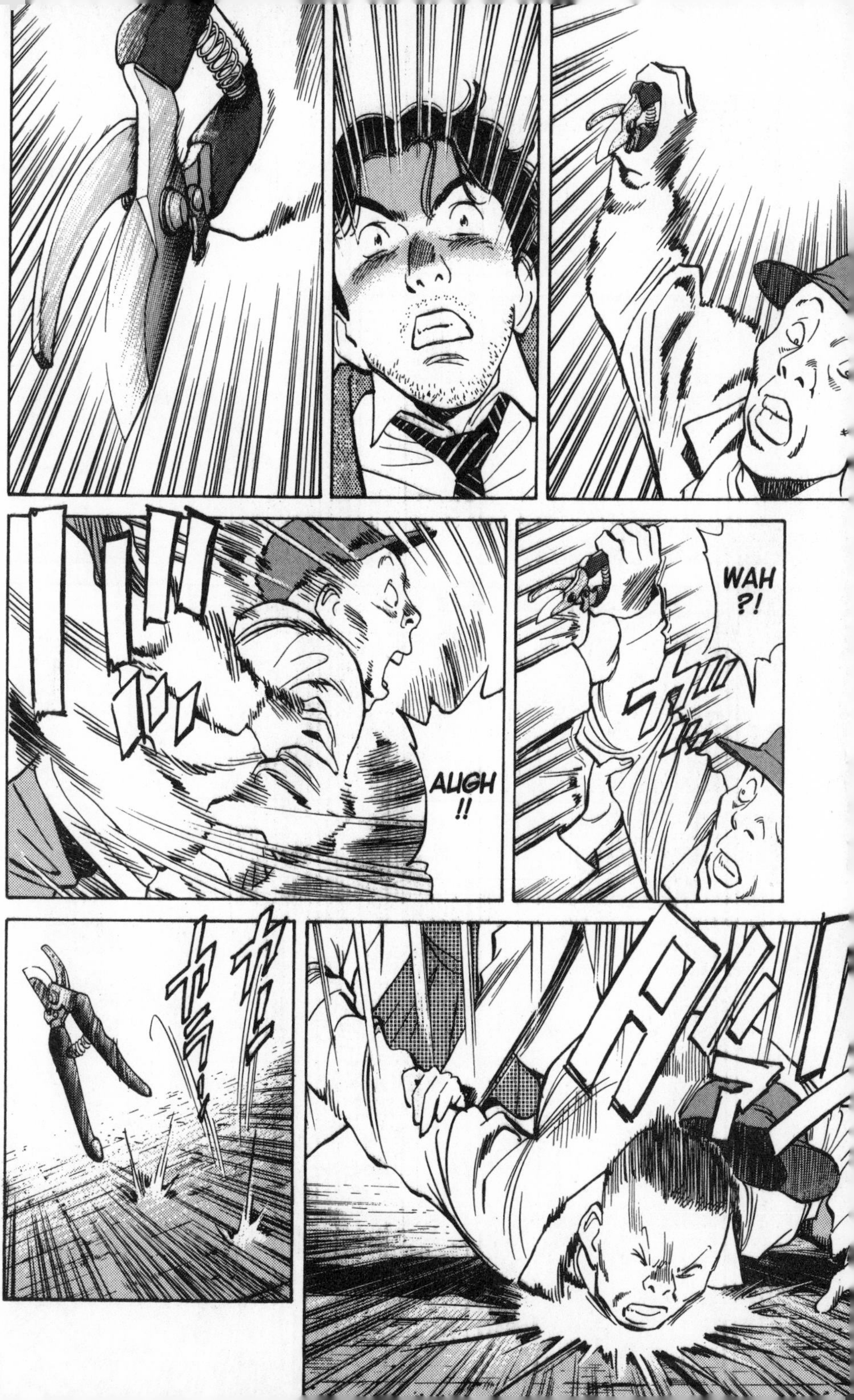
WAH ?!
AUGH !!

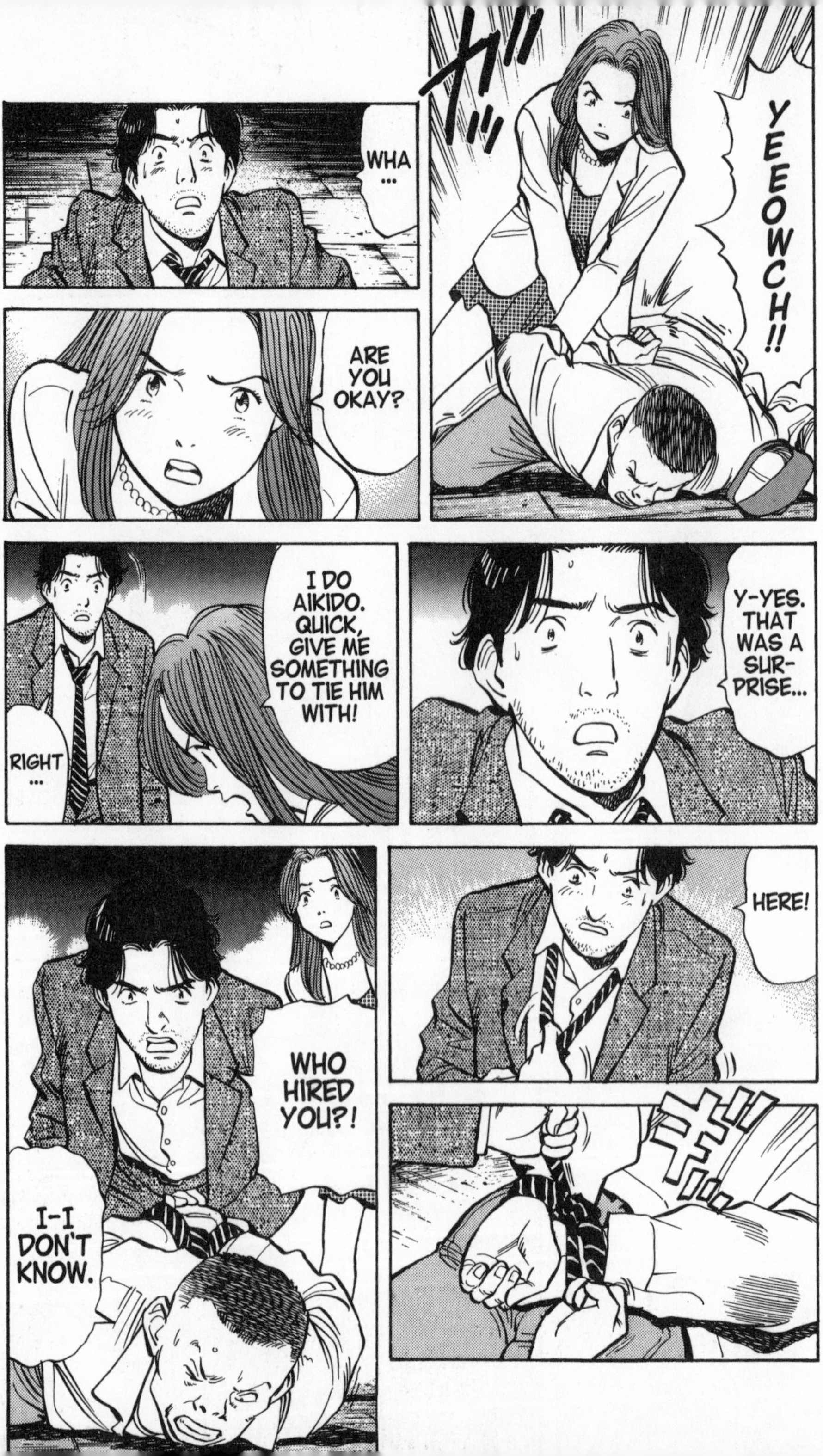
ガッ
YEEOWCH!!
WHA...
ARE YOU OKAY?
Y-YES. THAT WAS A SUR-PRISE...
I DO AIKIDO. QUICK, GIVE ME SOMETHING TO TIE HIM WITH!
RIGHT...
HERE!
WHO HIRED YOU?!
I-I DON'T KNOW.

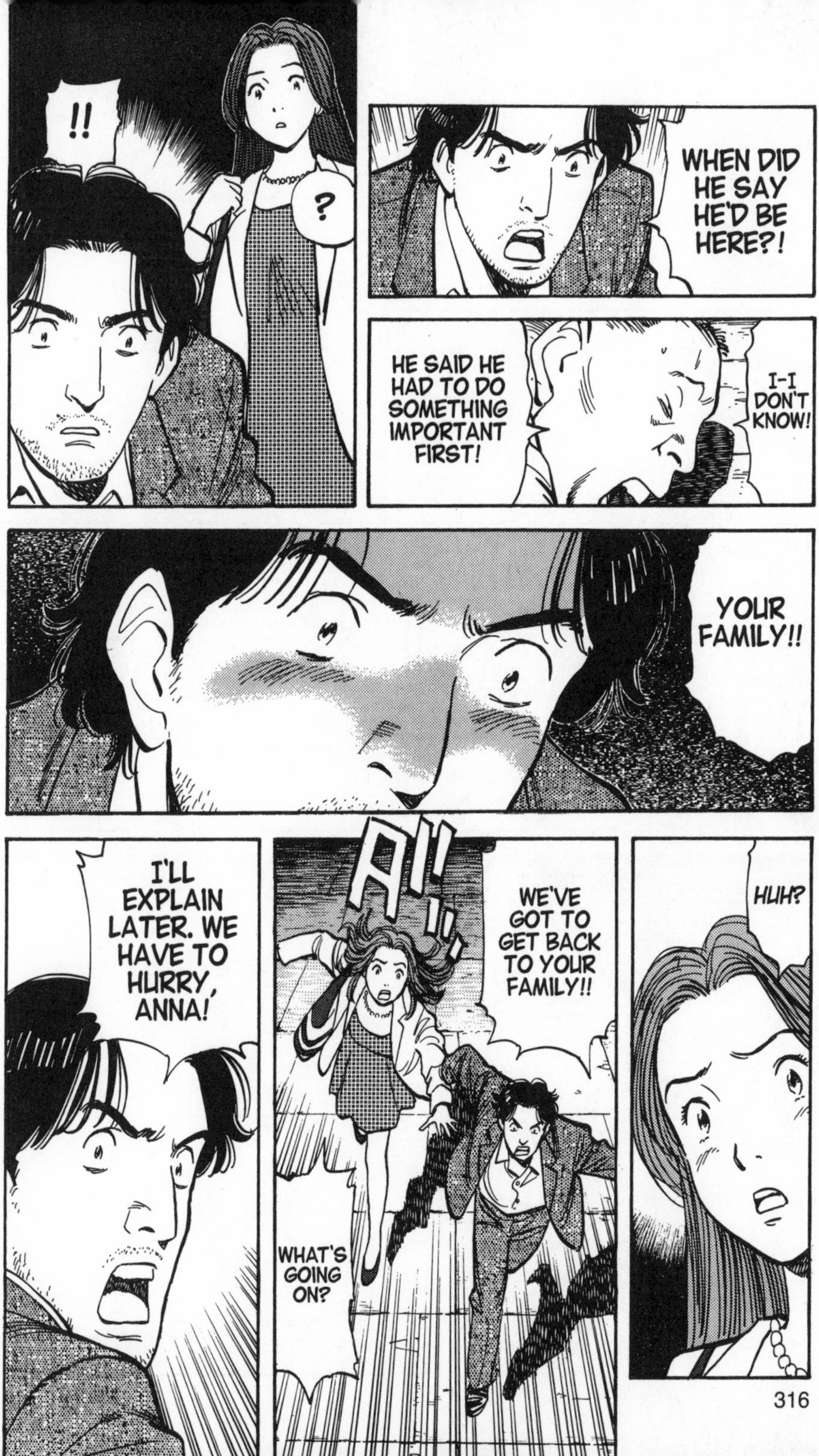
WHEN DID HE SAY HE'D BE HERE?!
I-I DON'T KNOW!
HE SAID HE HAD TO DO SOMETHING IMPORTANT FIRST!
!!
?
YOUR FAMILY!!
HUH?
A!!
WE'VE GOT TO GET BACK TO YOUR FAMILY!!
WHAT'S GOING ON?
I'LL EXPLAIN LATER. WE HAVE TO HURRY, ANNA!

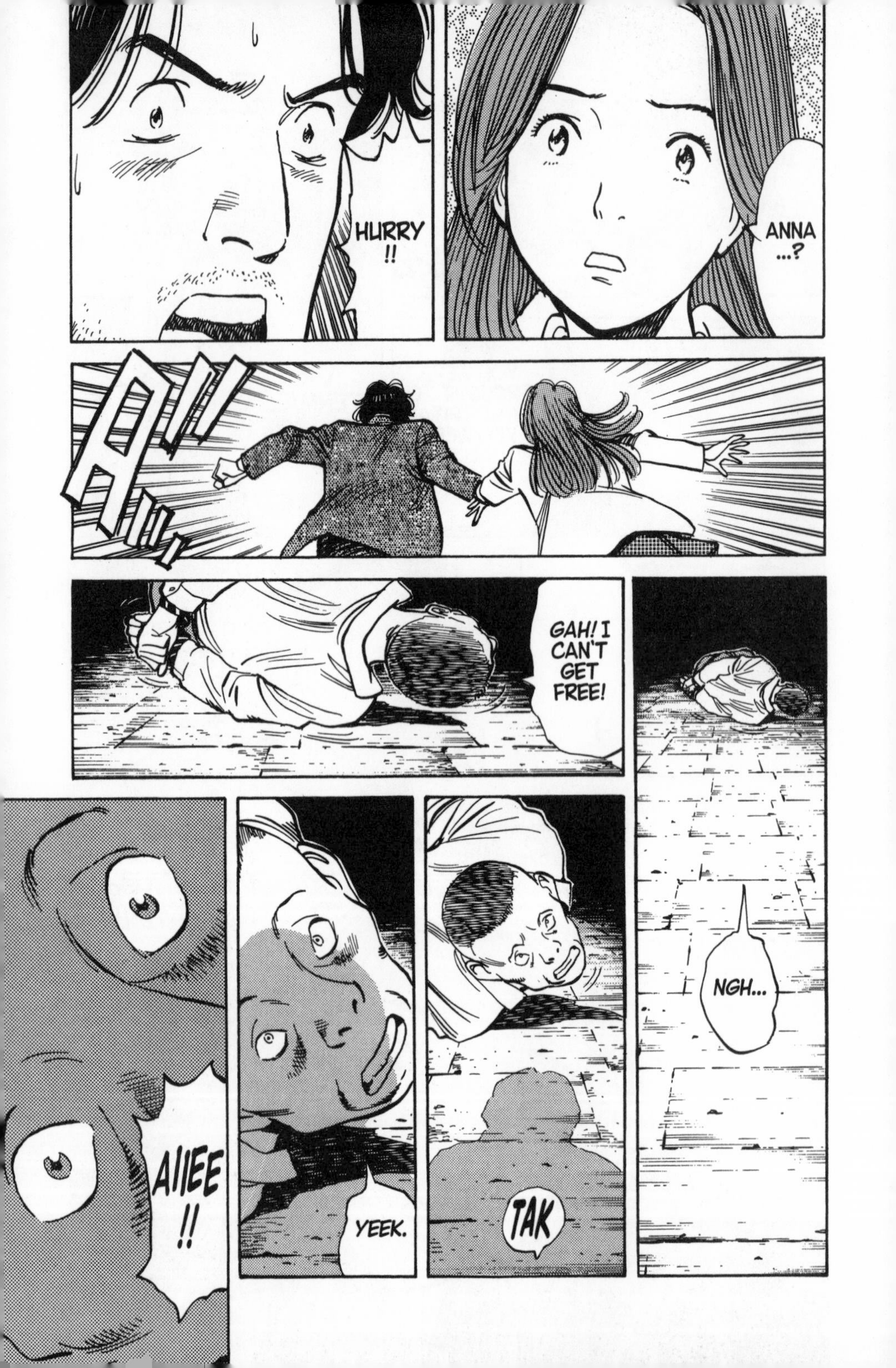
ANNA ...?
HURRY !!
ダッ
NGH...
GAH! I CAN'T GET FREE!
TAK
YEEK.
AIIEE !!

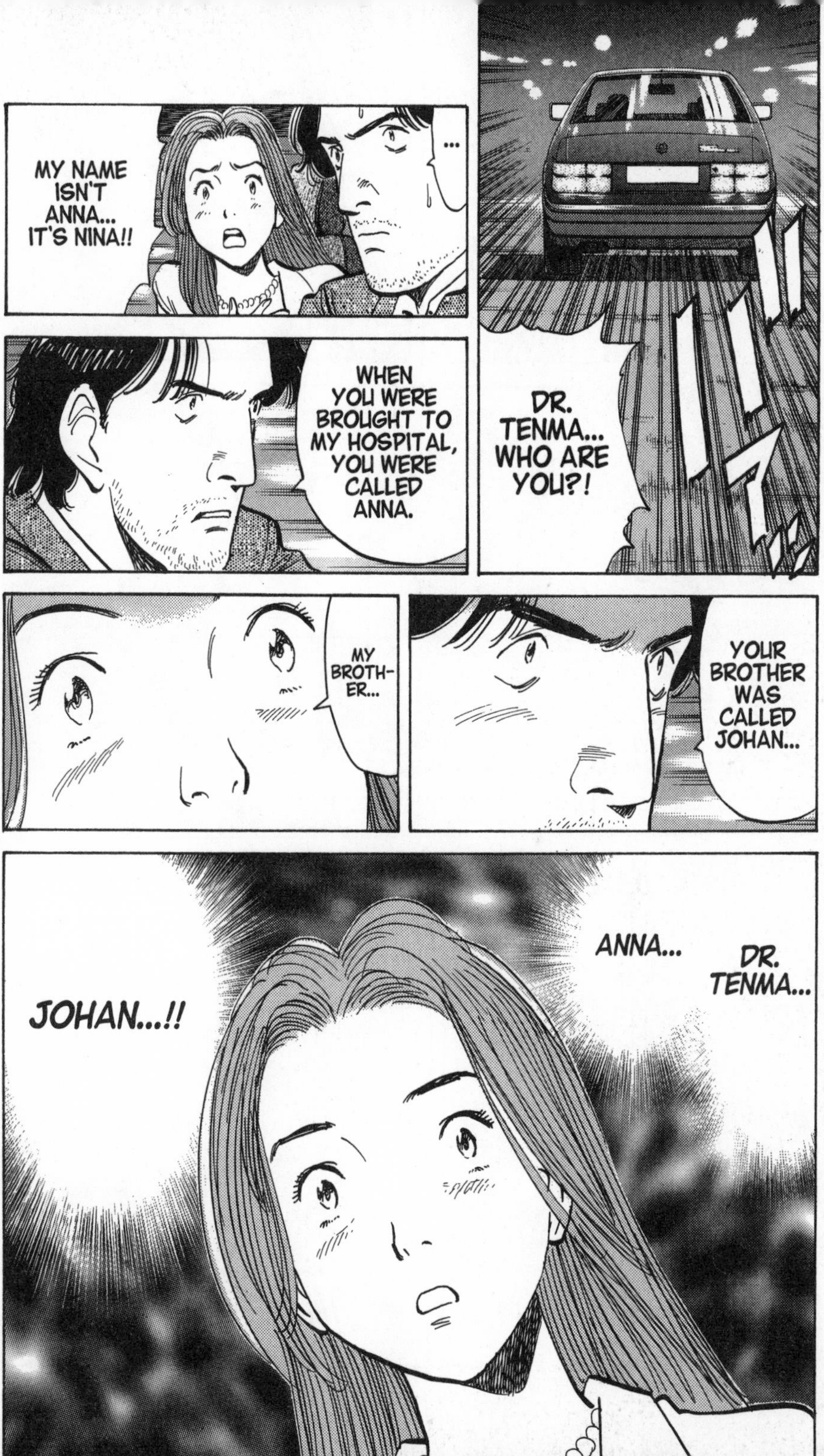
DR. TENMA... WHO ARE YOU?!
...
MY NAME ISN'T ANNA... IT'S NINA!!
WHEN YOU WERE BROUGHT TO MY HOSPITAL, YOU WERE CALLED ANNA.
YOUR BROTHER WAS CALLED JOHAN...
MY BROTH-ER...
DR. TENMA...
ANNA...
JOHAN...!!

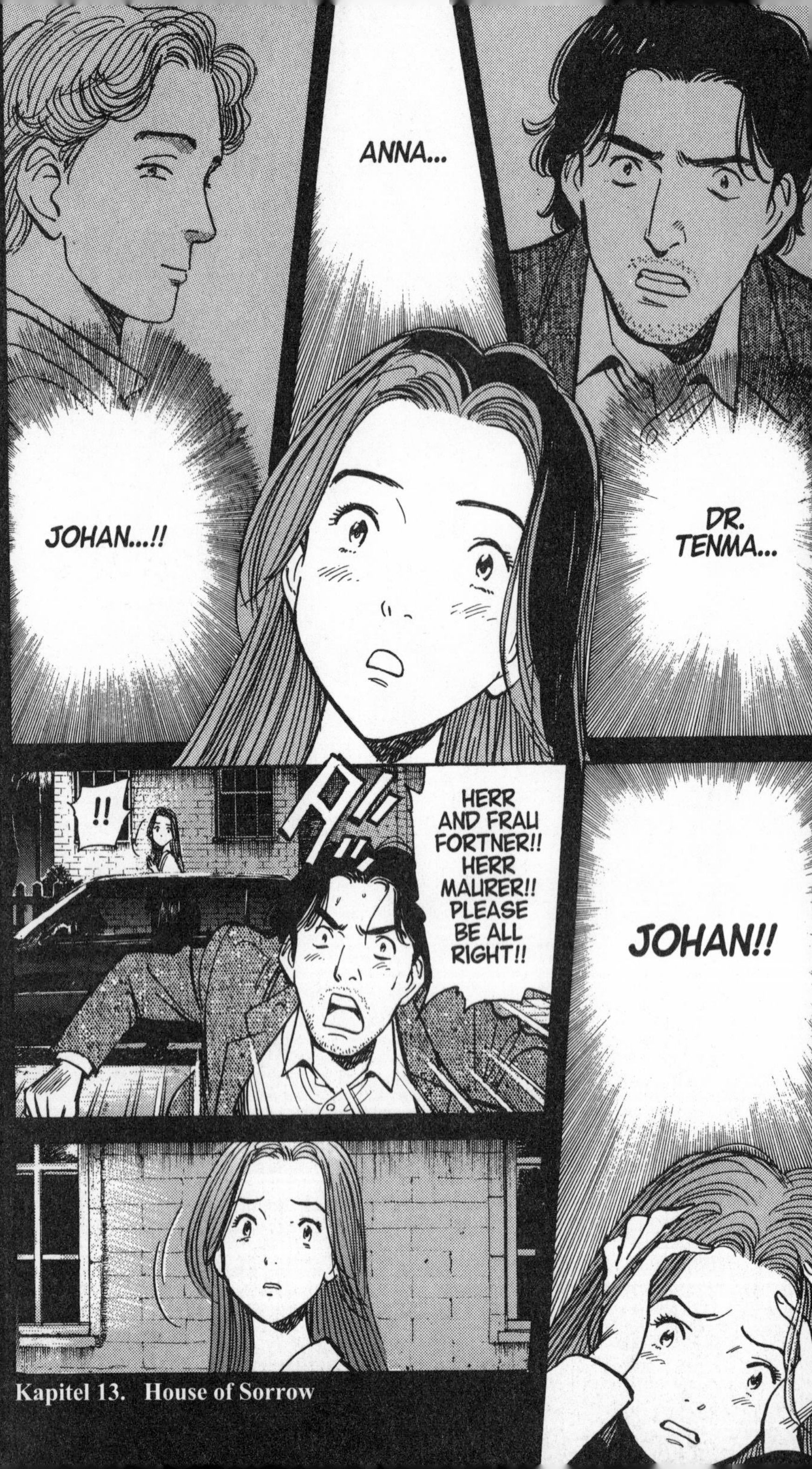
DR. TENMA...
ANNA...
JOHAN...!!
JOHAN!!
HERR AND FRAU FORTNER!! HERR MAURER!! PLEASE BE ALL RIGHT!!
!!

Kapitel 13. House of Sorrow

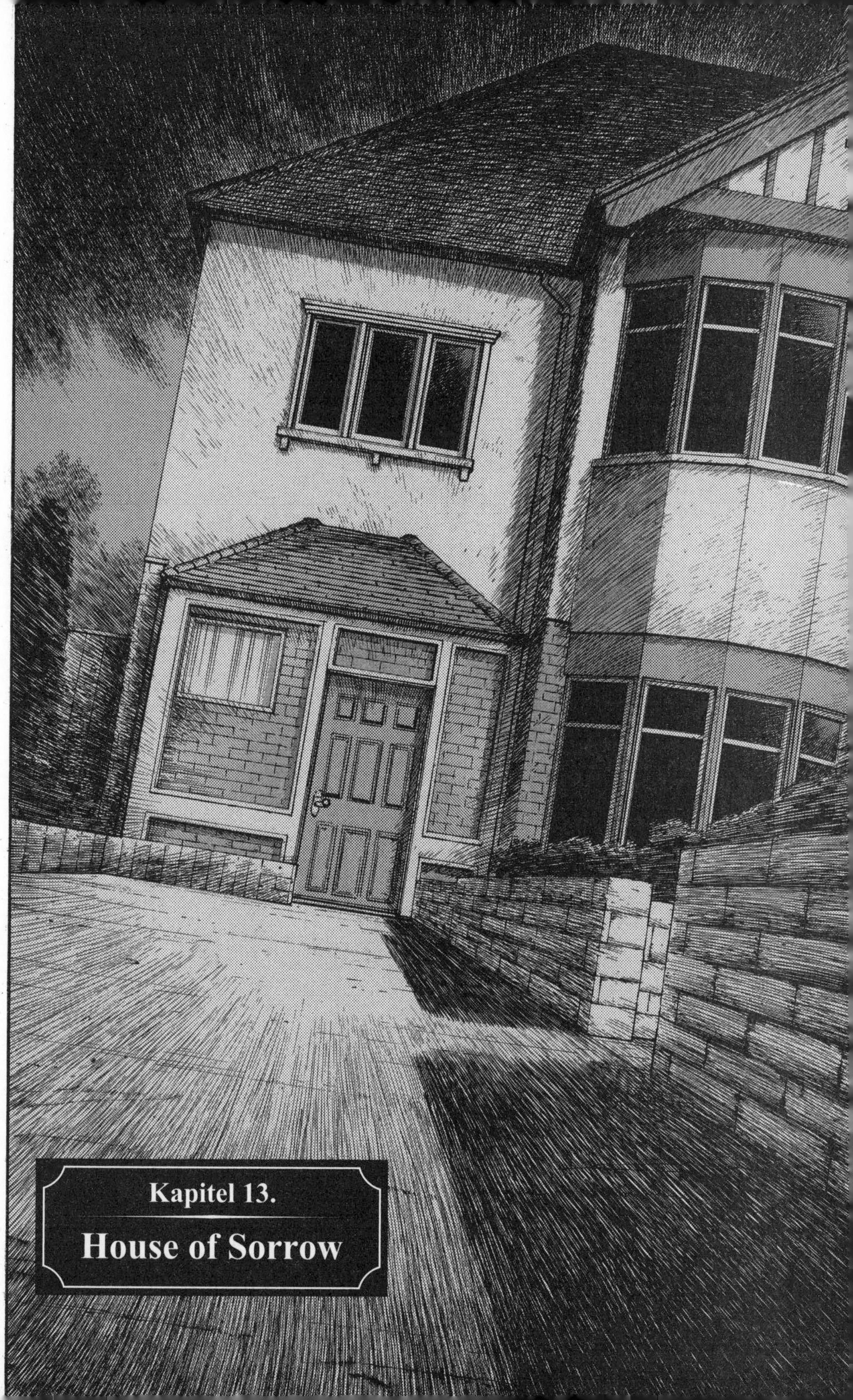
Kapitel 13.
House of Sorrow

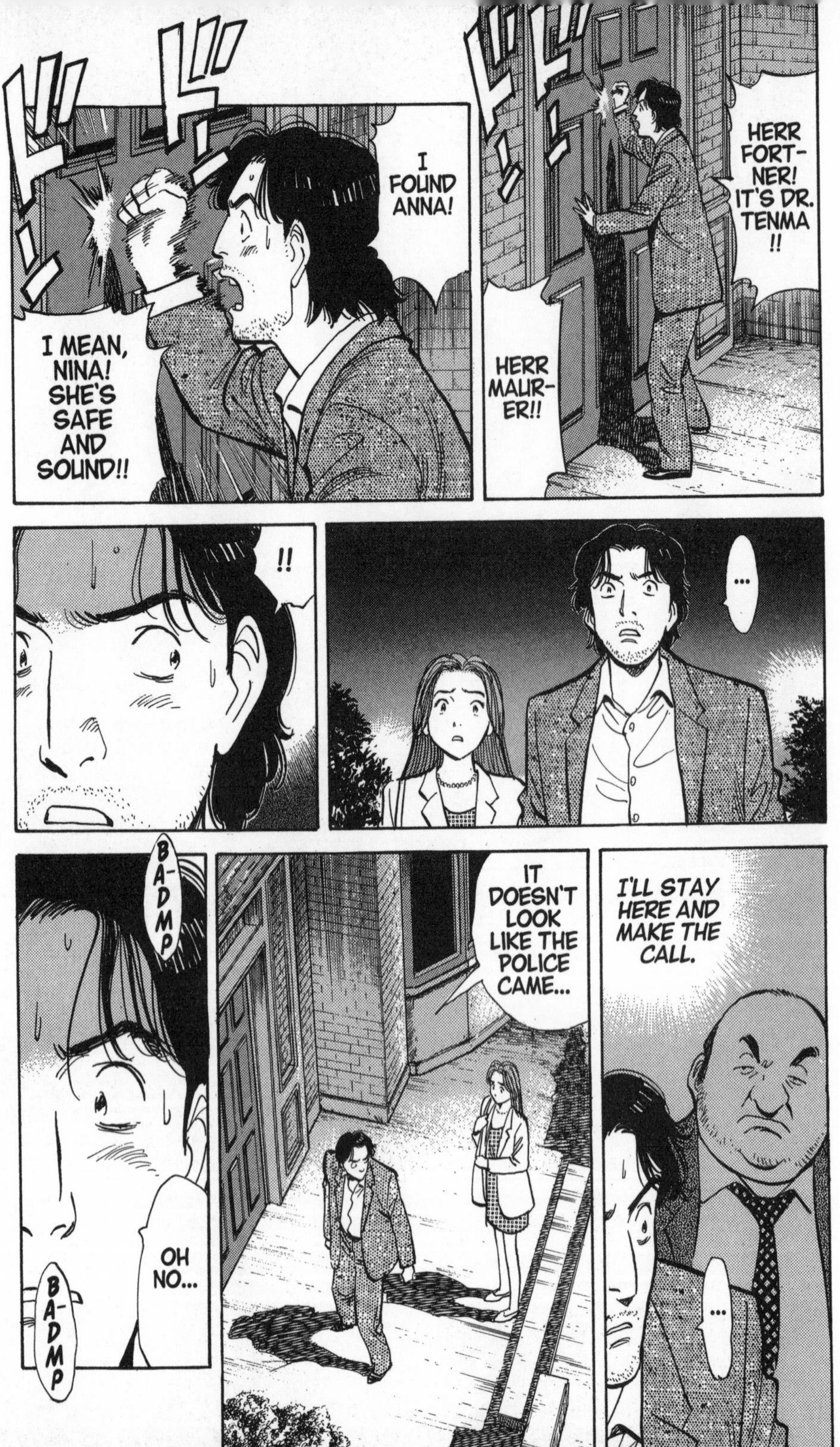
HERR FORTNER! IT'S DR. TENMA!!
HERR MAURER!!
I FOUND ANNA!
I MEAN, NINA! SHE'S SAFE AND SOUND!!
...
!!
I'LL STAY HERE AND MAKE THE CALL.
...
IT DOESN'T LOOK LIKE THE POLICE CAME...
BA-DMP
OH NO...
BA-DMP

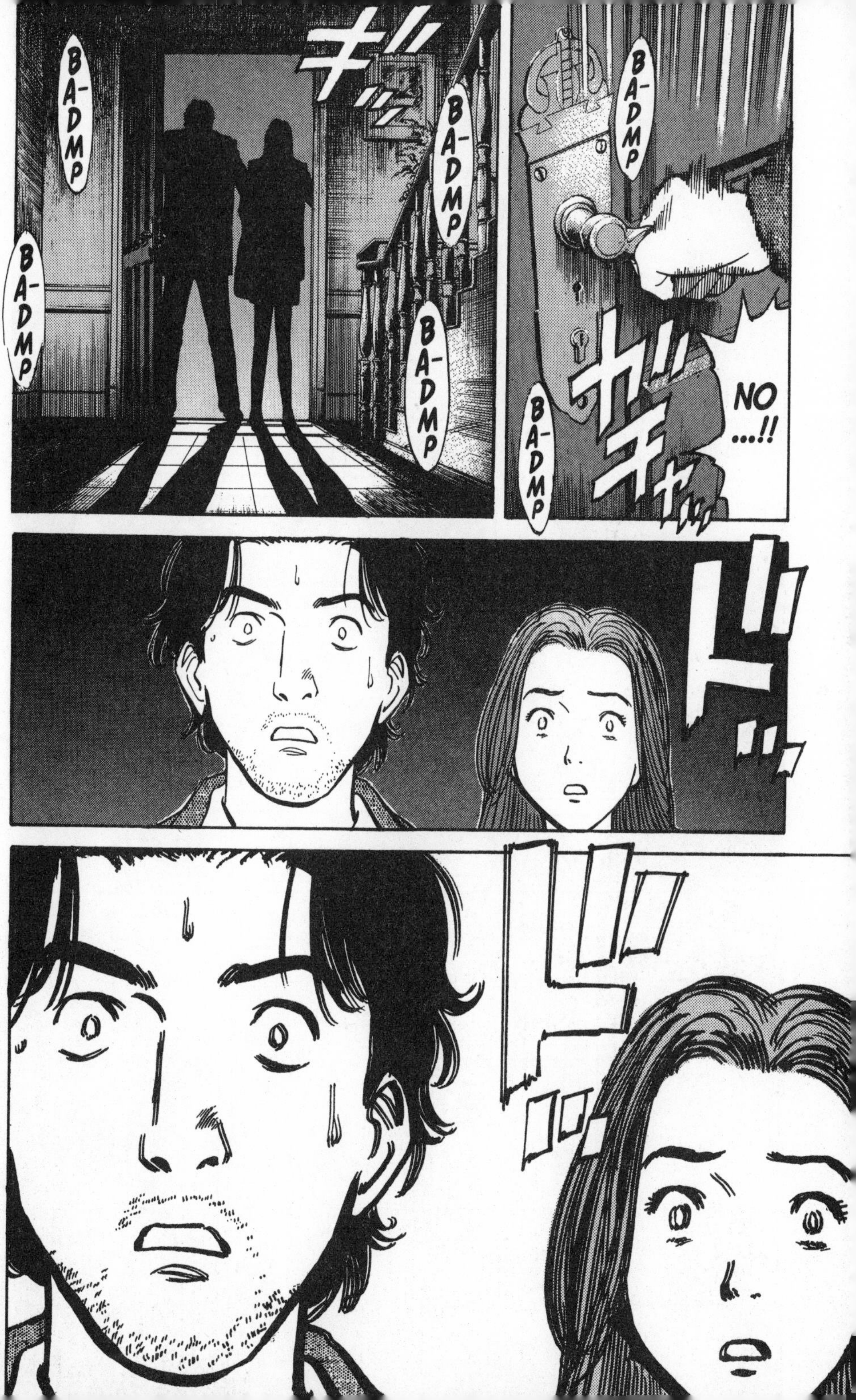

BA-DMP
BA-DMP
NO ...!!
BA-DMP
BA-DMP
BA-DMP
BA-DMP

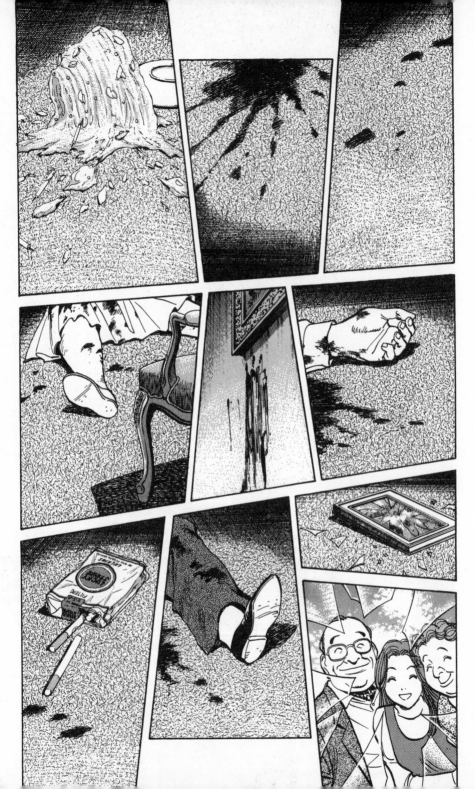

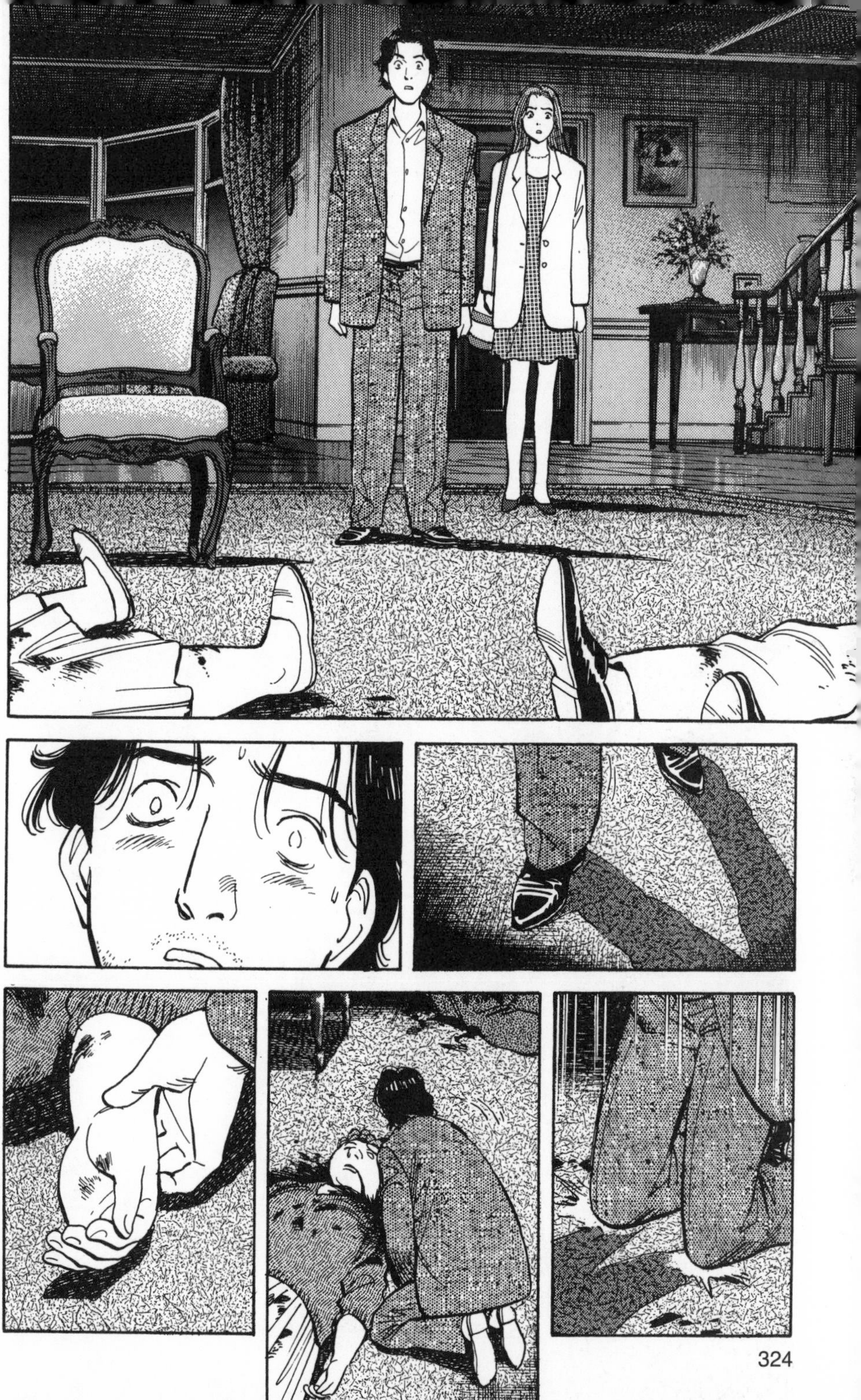

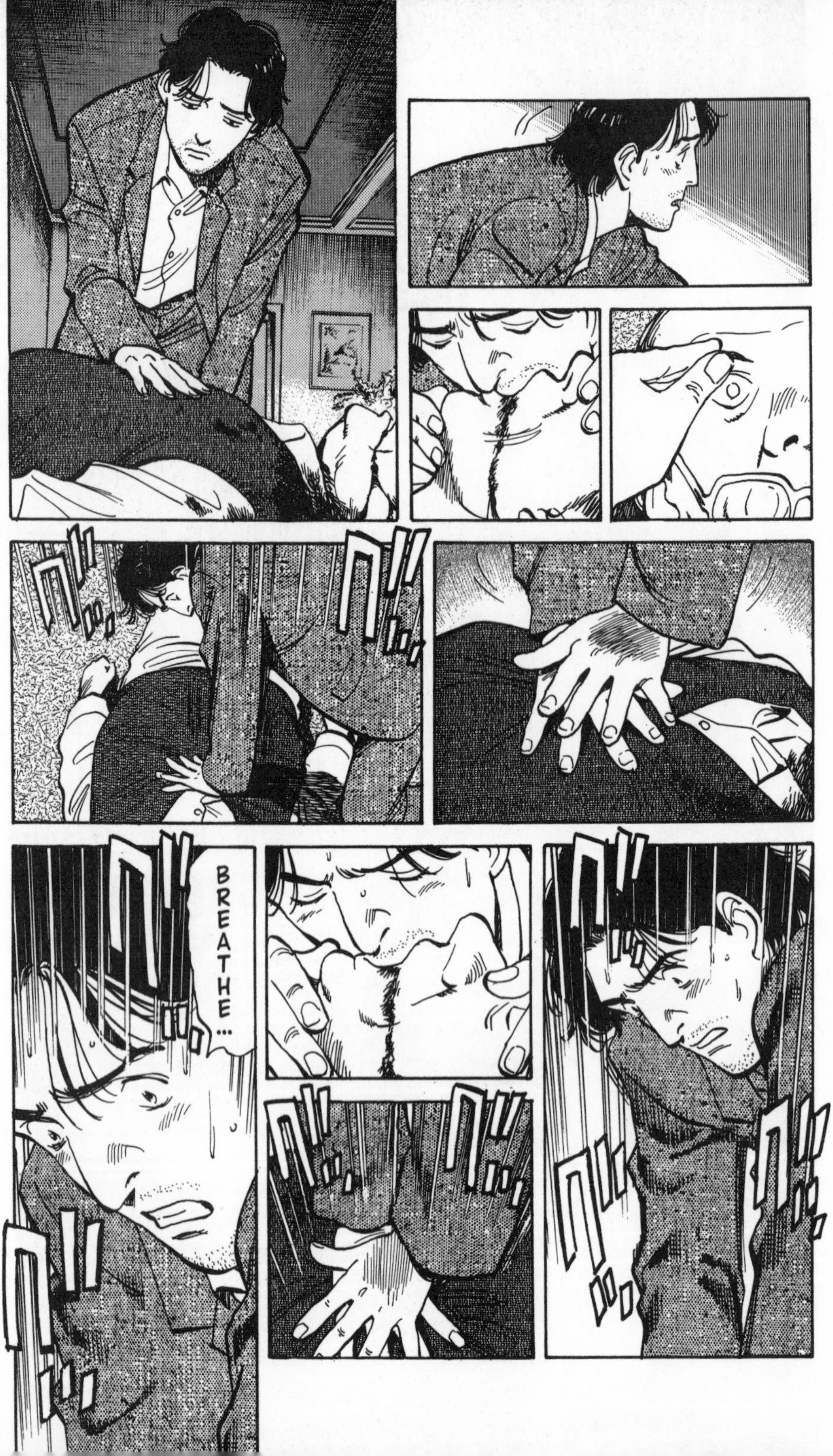
BREATHE...

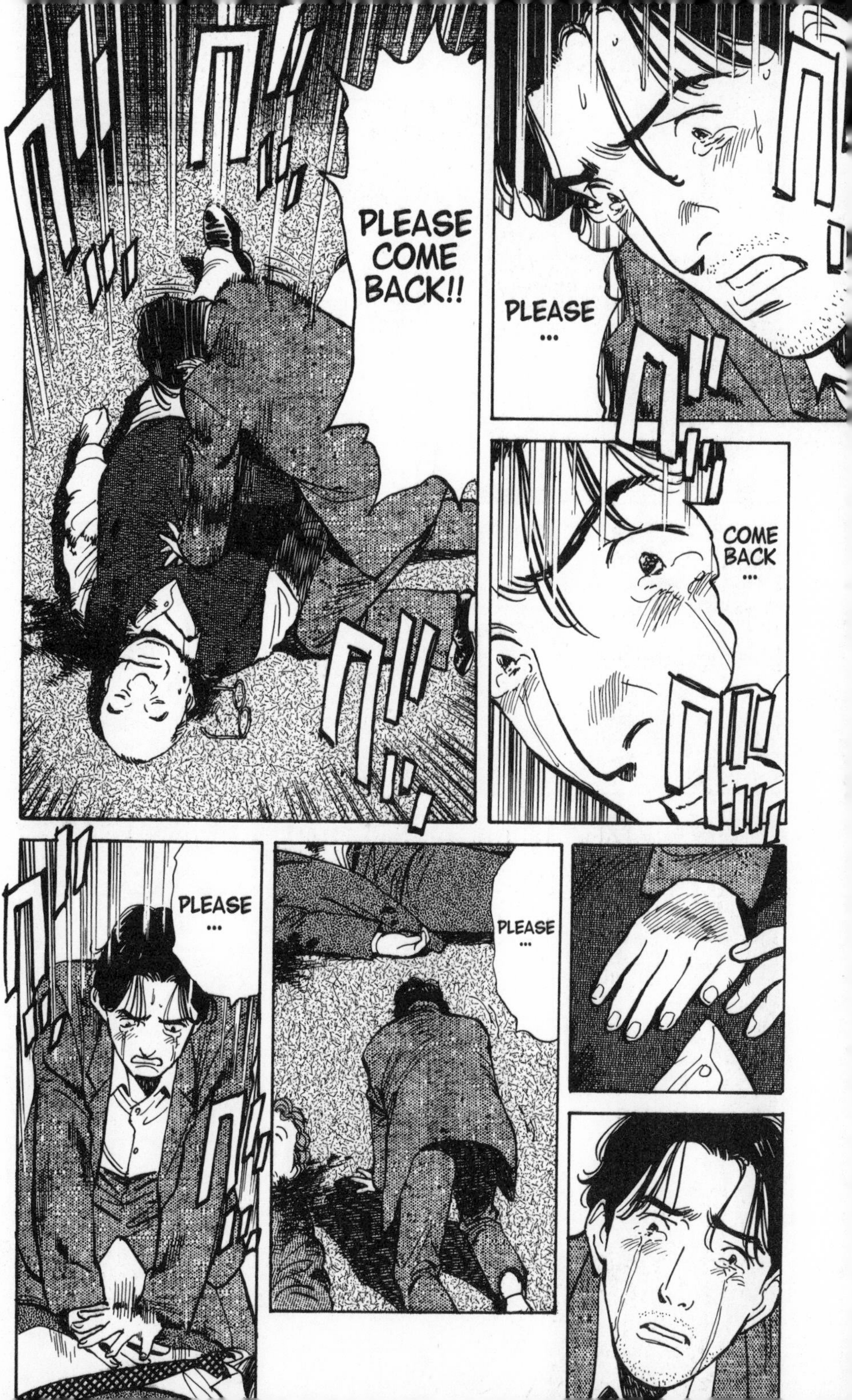
PLEASE ...
COME BACK ...
PLEASE COME BACK!!
PLEASE ...
PLEASE ...

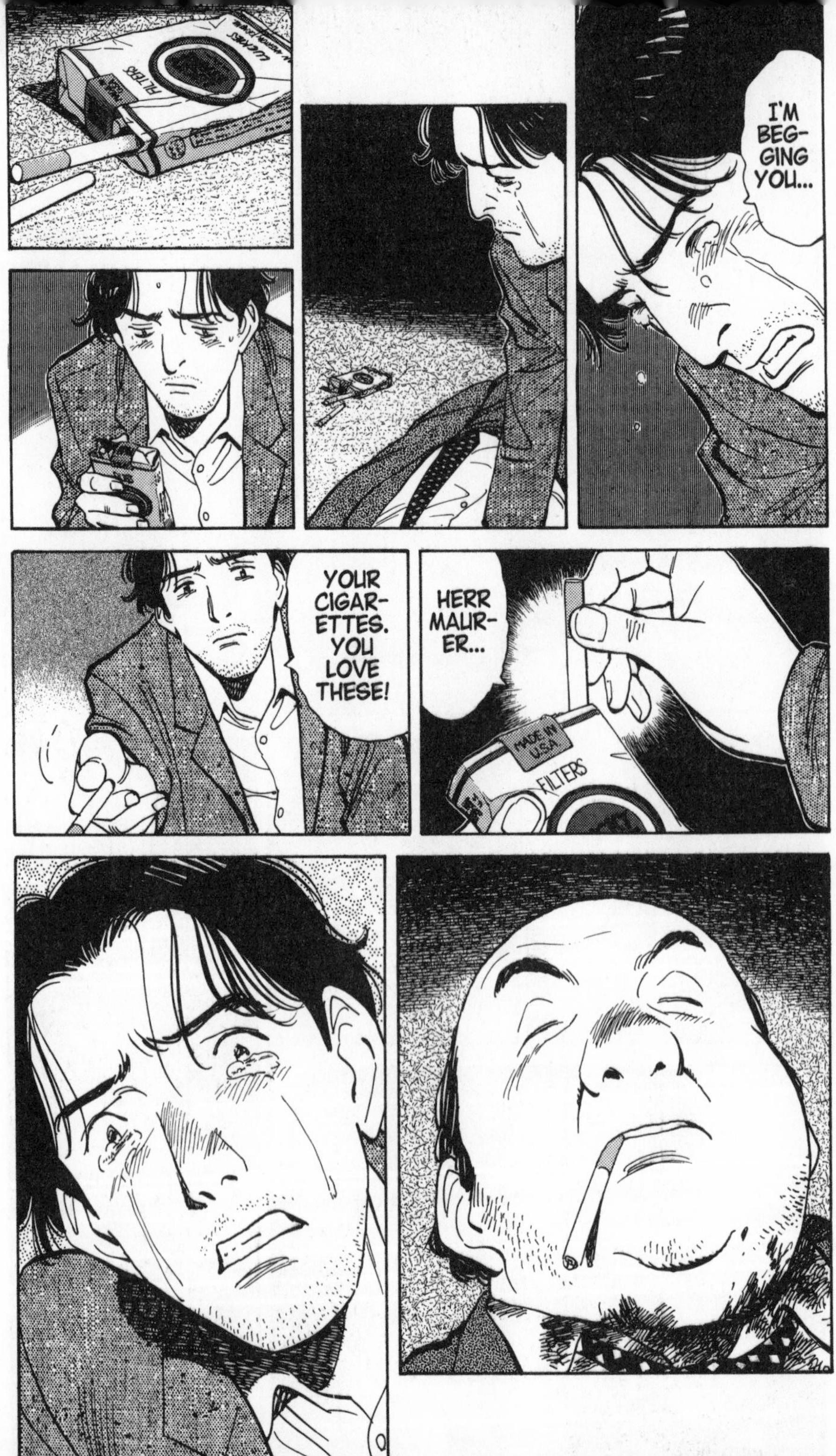
I'M BEG-GING YOU...
HERR MAURER-ER...
MADE IN U.S.A.
FILTERS
YOUR CIGAR-ETTES. YOU LOVE THESE!

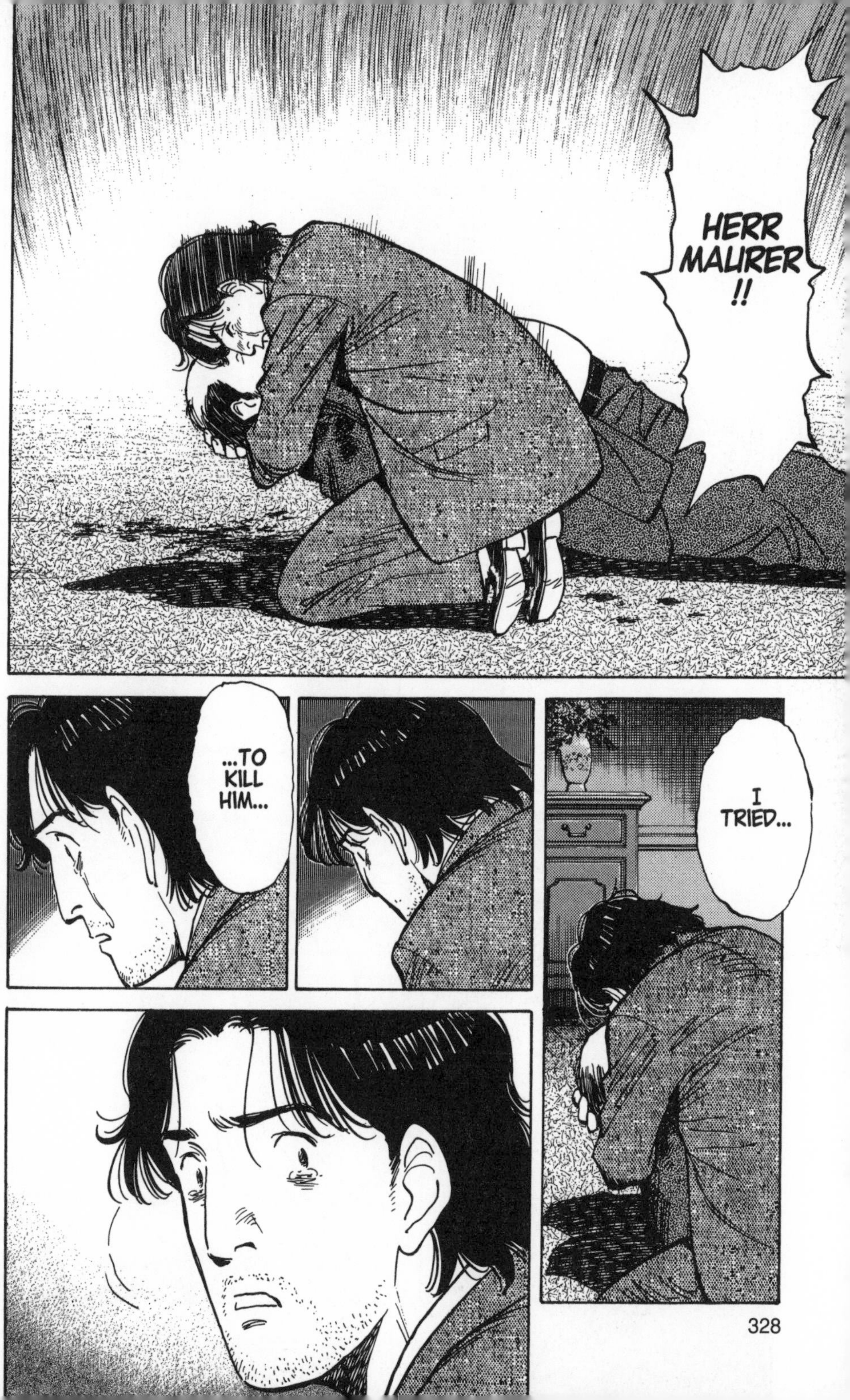
HERR MAURER!!
I TRIED...
...TO KILL HIM...

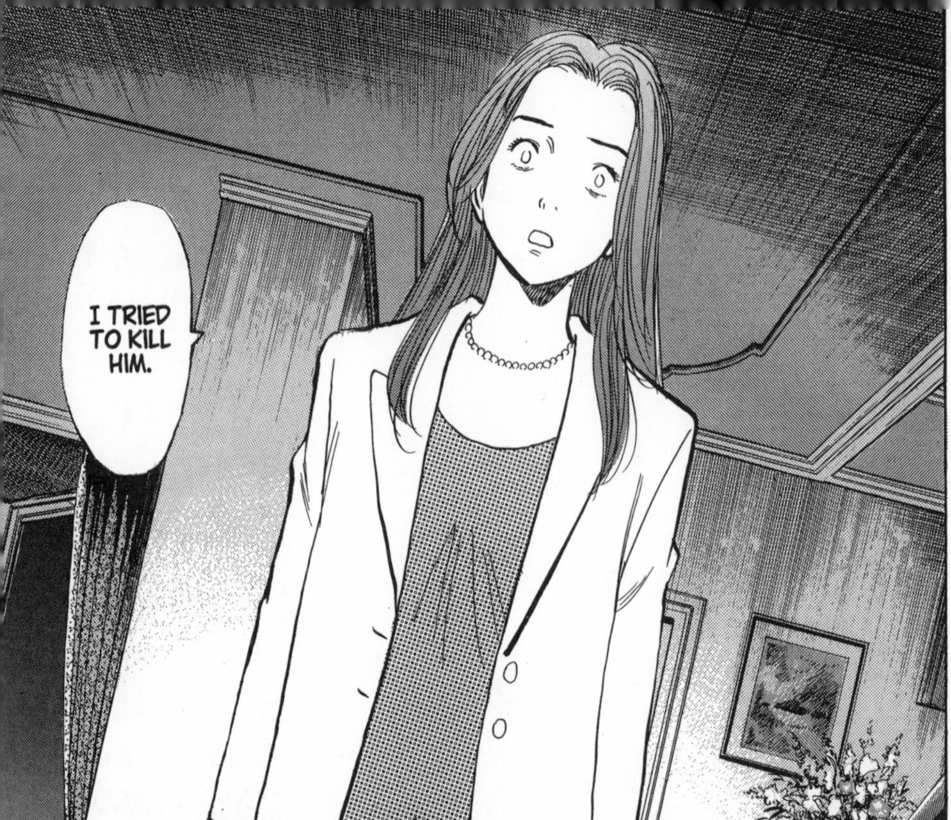
I TRIED TO KILL HIM.
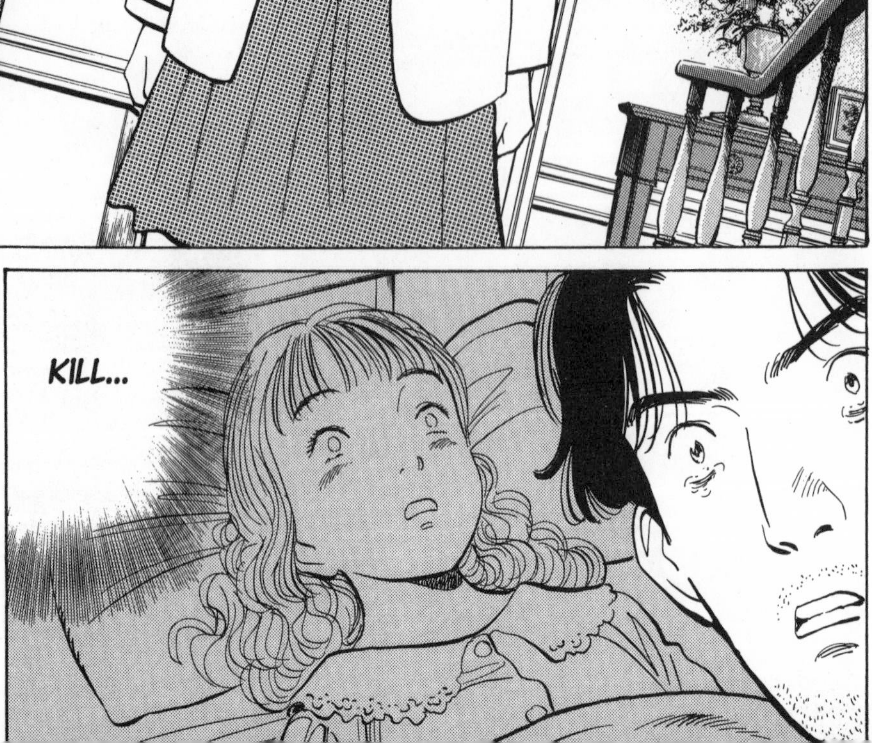
KILL...

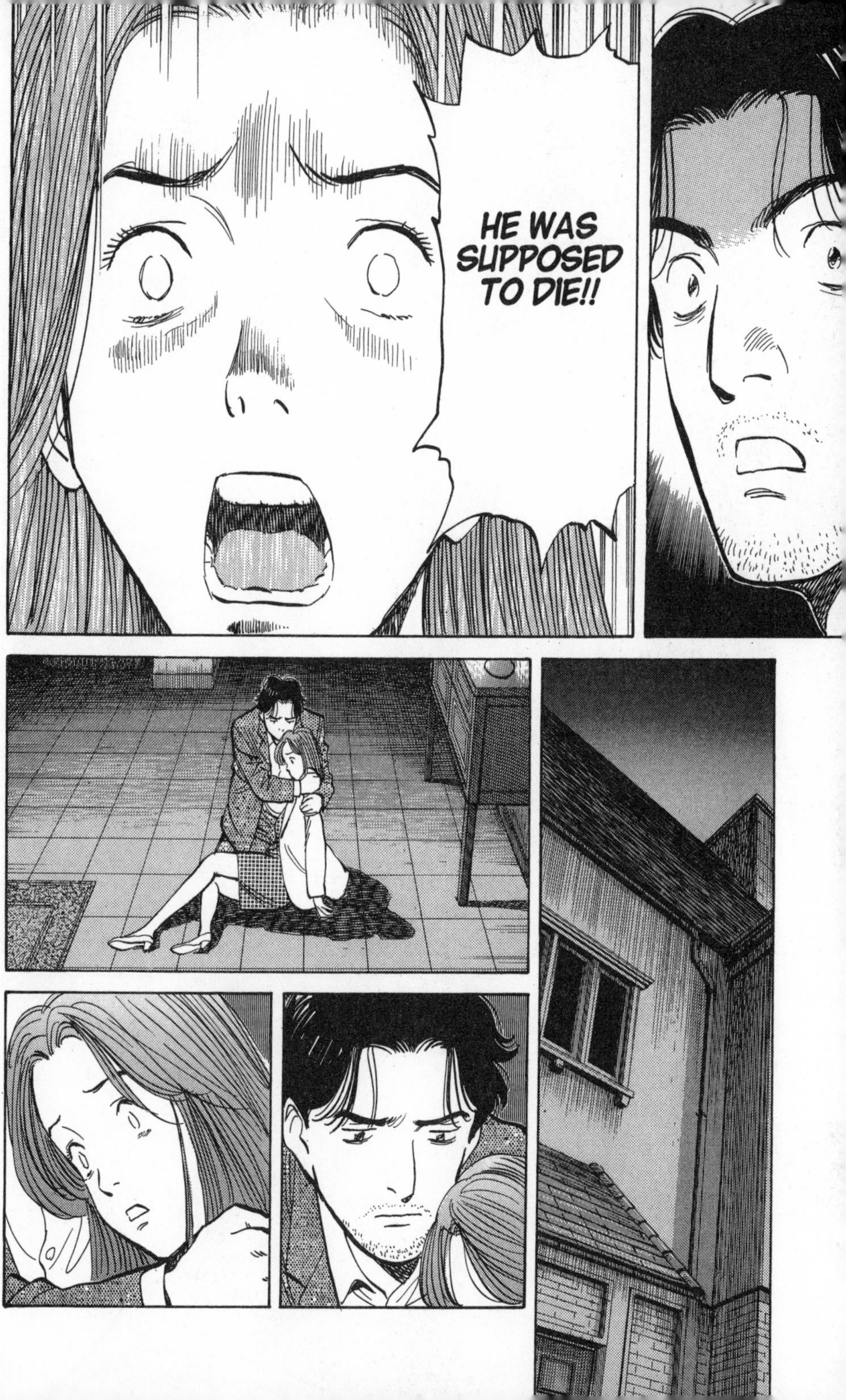
HE WAS SUPPOSED TO DIE!!

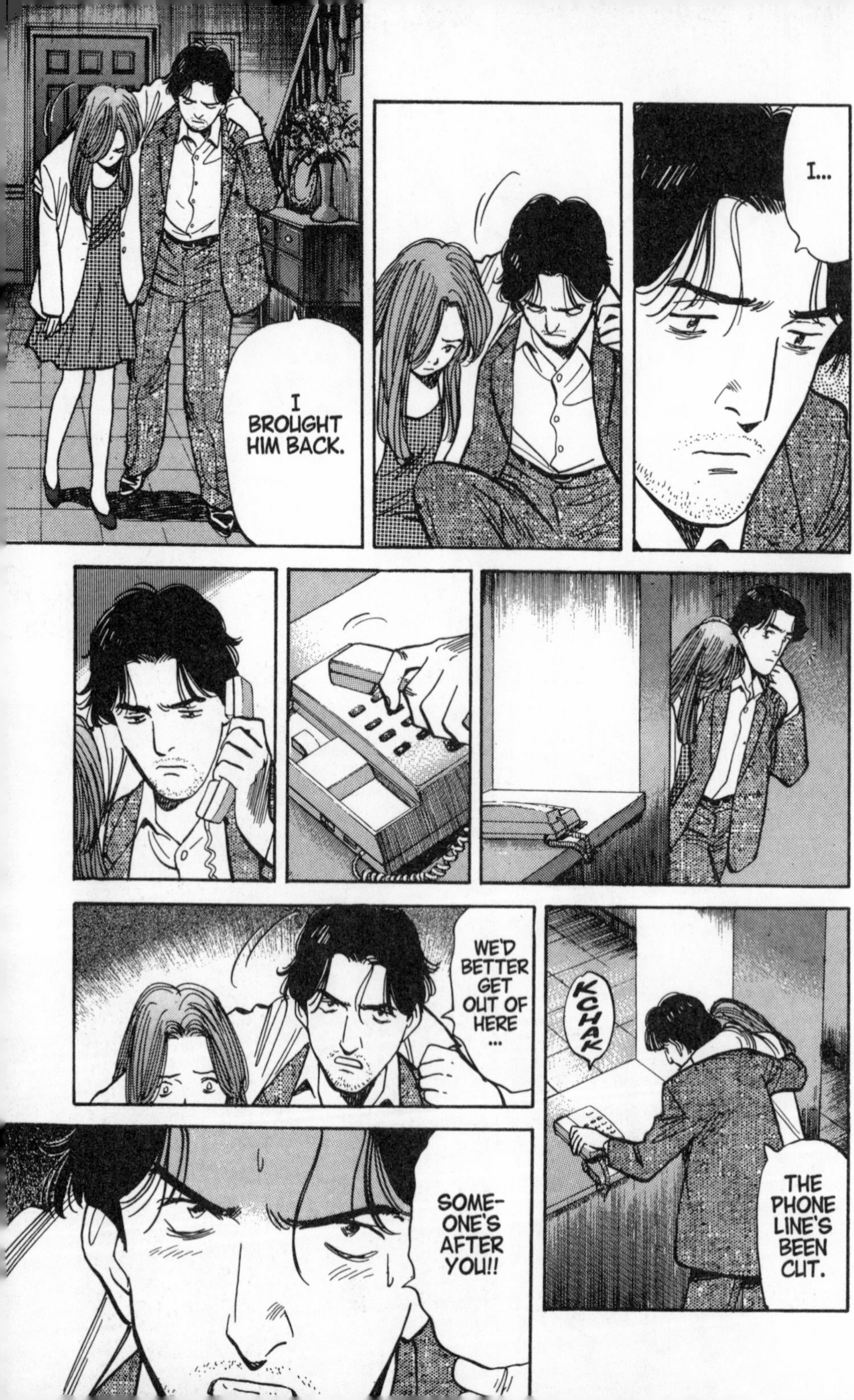
I...
I BROUGHT HIM BACK.
KCHAK
THE PHONE LINE'S BEEN CUT.
WE'D BETTER GET OUT OF HERE ...
SOME-ONE'S AFTER YOU!!

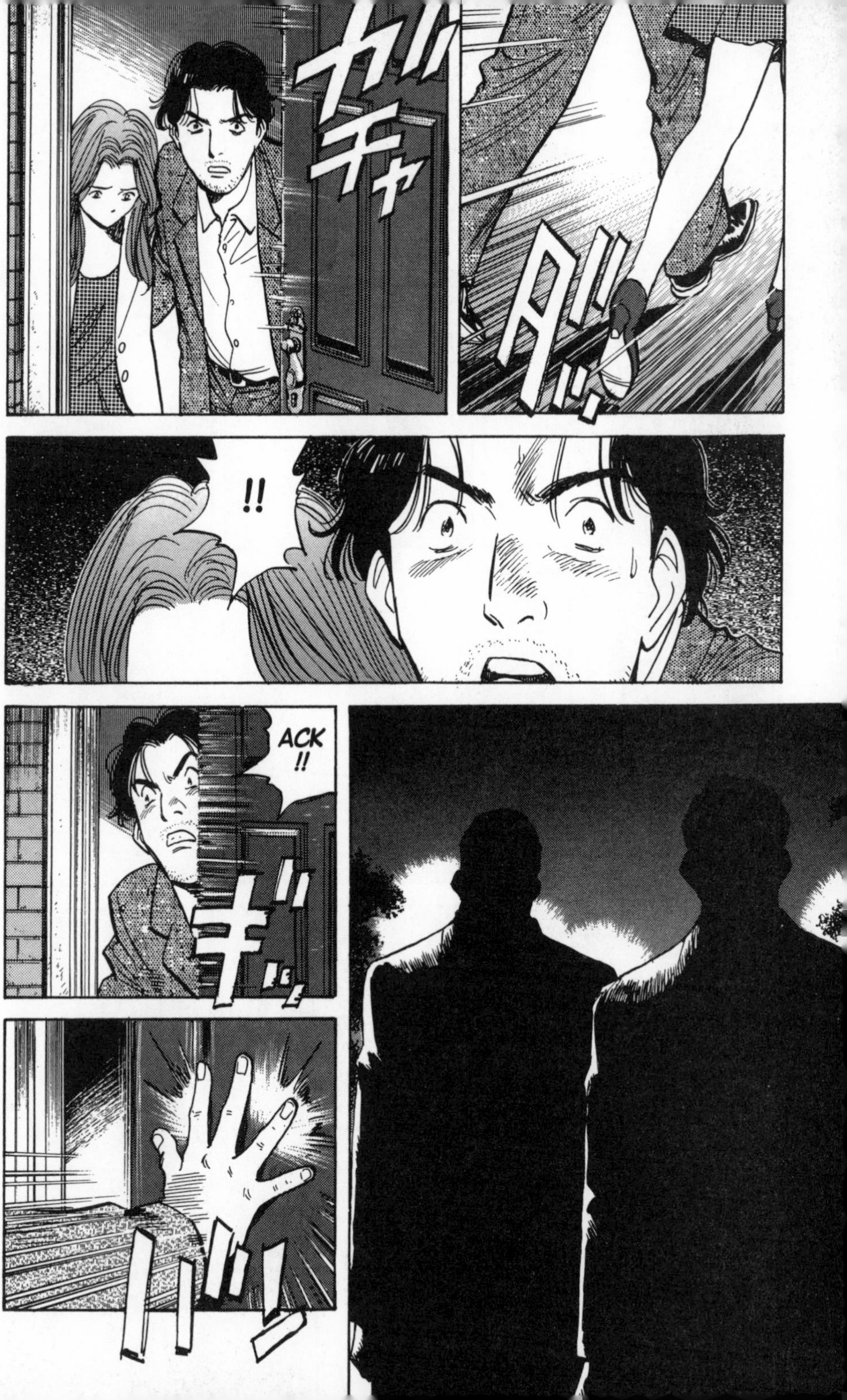
!!
ACK !!

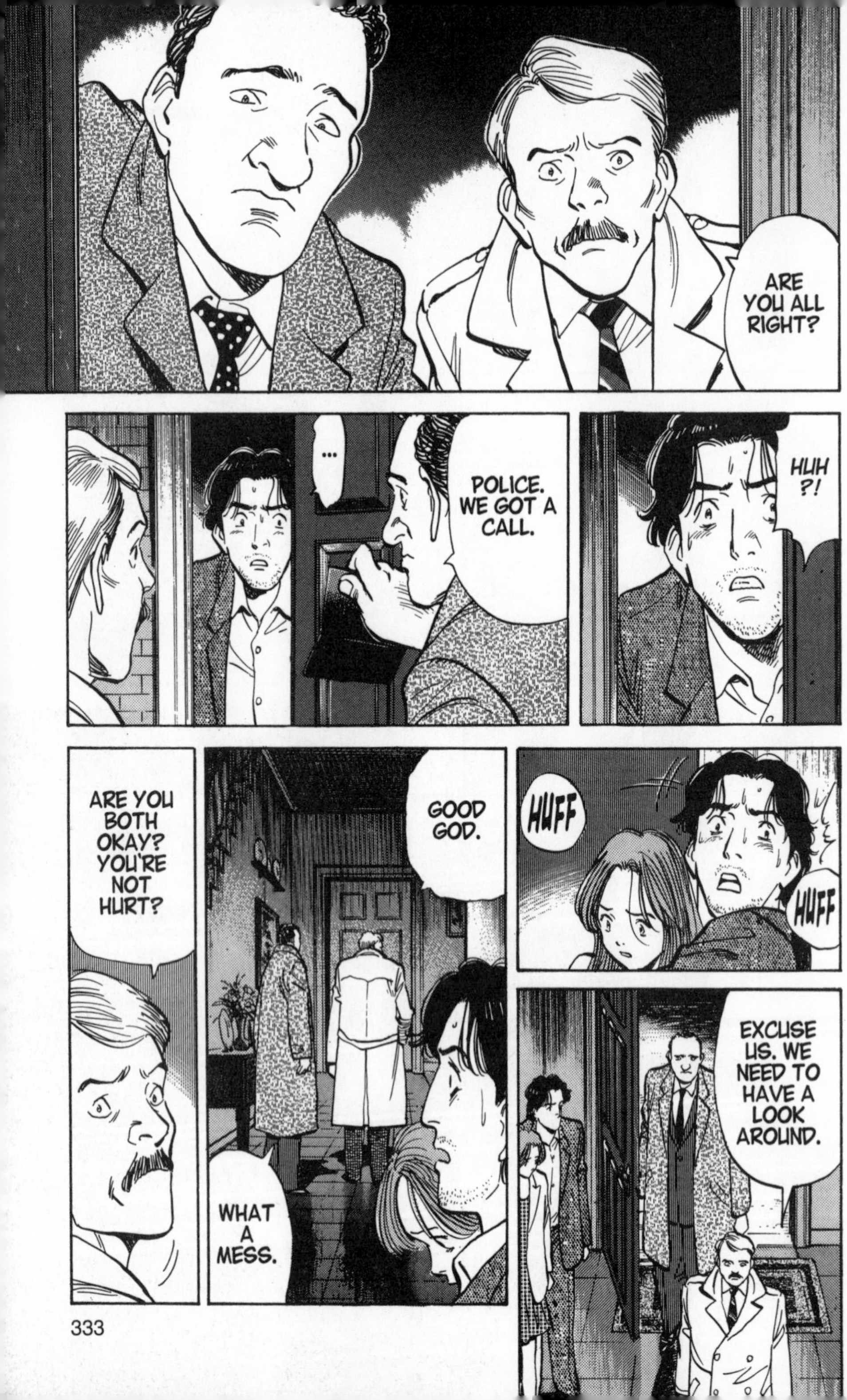
ARE YOU ALL RIGHT?
HUH ?!
POLICE. WE GOT A CALL.
...
HUFF
HUFF
EXCUSE US. WE NEED TO HAVE A LOOK AROUND.
GOOD GOD.
WHAT A MESS.
ARE YOU BOTH OKAY? YOU'RE NOT HURT?

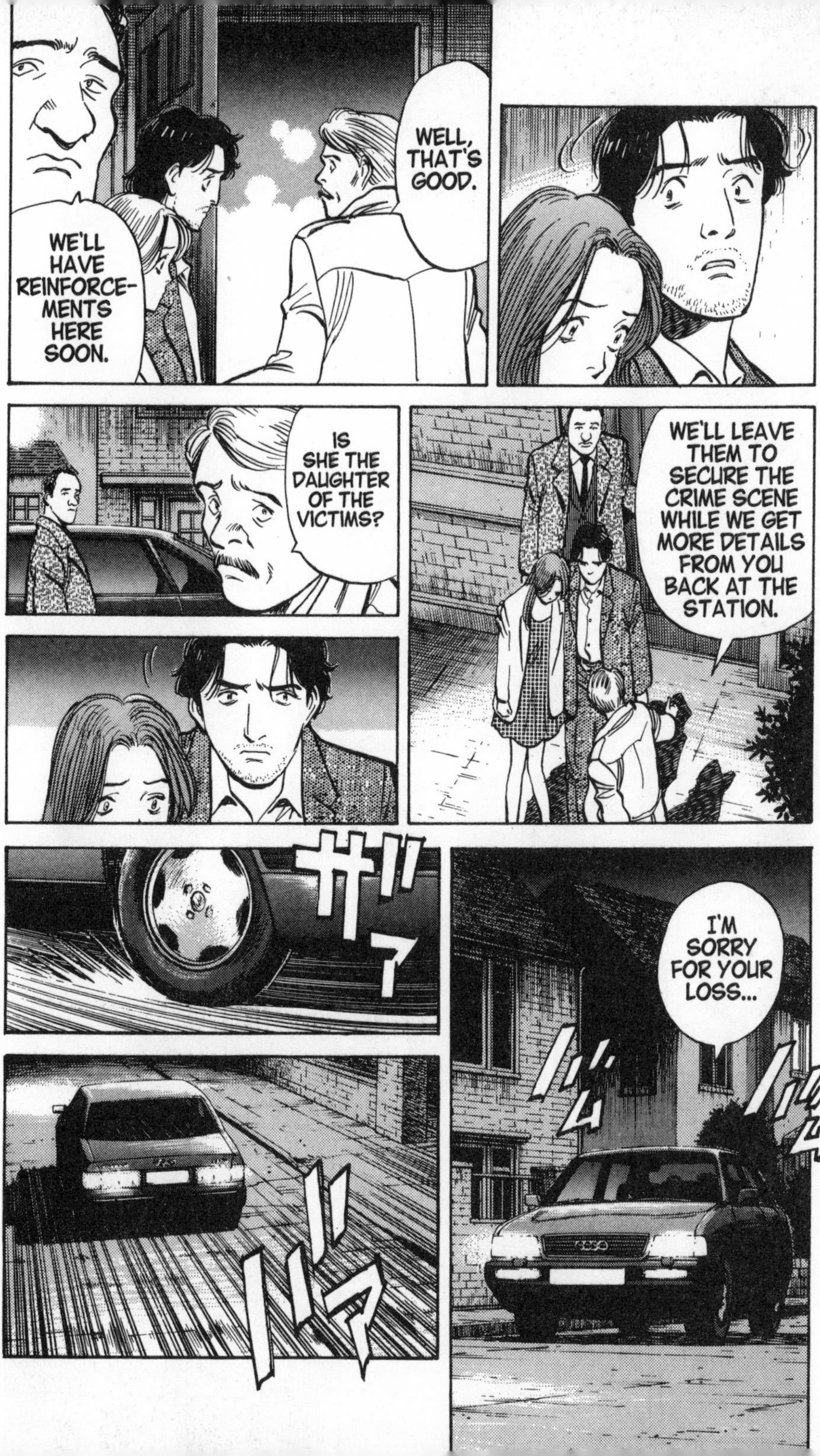
WELL, THAT'S GOOD.
WE'LL HAVE REINFORCEMENTS HERE SOON.
WE'LL LEAVE THEM TO SECURE THE CRIME SCENE WHILE WE GET MORE DETAILS FROM YOU BACK AT THE STATION.
IS SHE THE DAUGHTER OF THE VICTIMS?
I'M SORRY FOR YOUR LOSS...

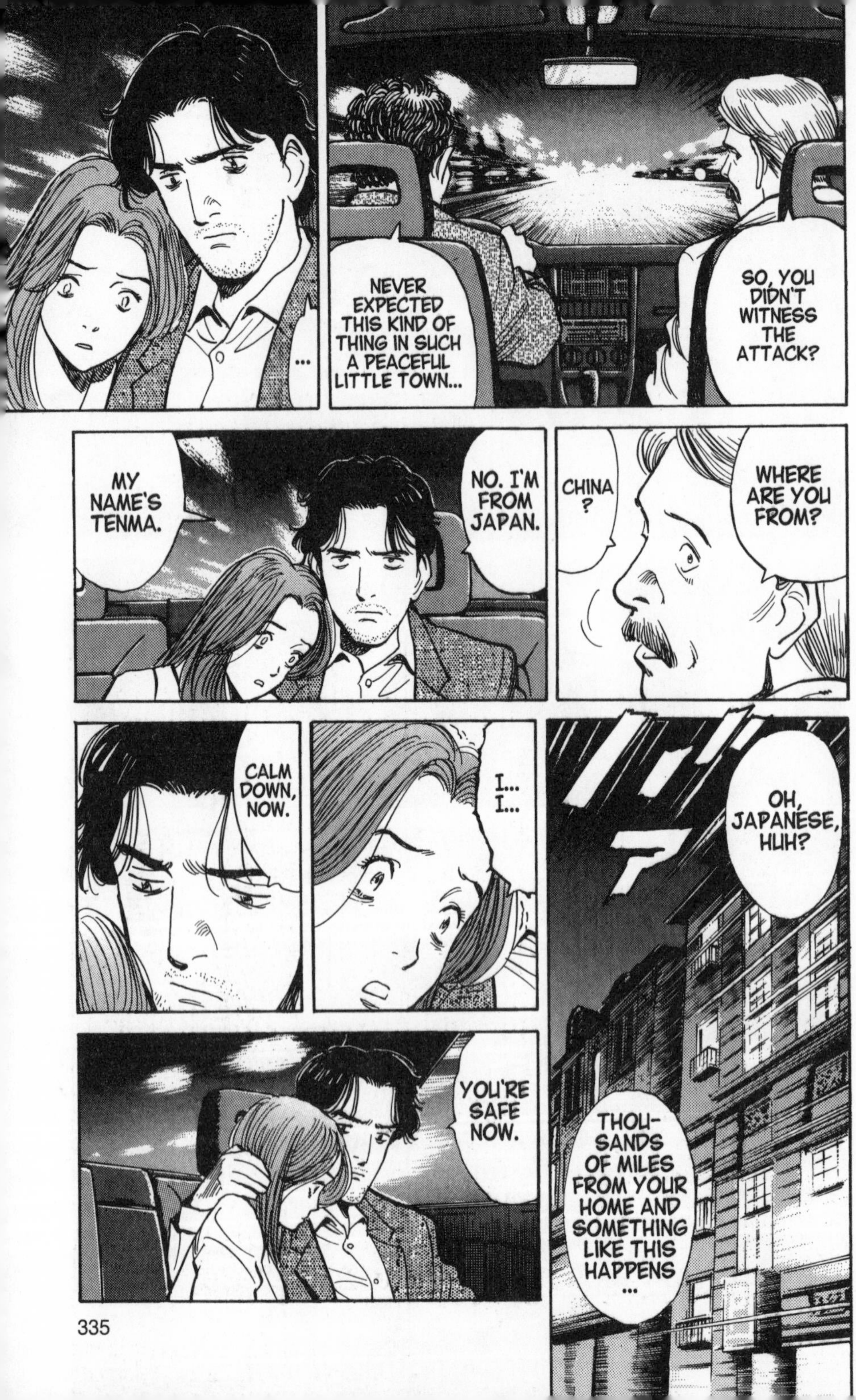
SO, YOU DIDN'T WITNESS THE ATTACK?
NEVER EXPECTED THIS KIND OF THING IN SUCH A PEACEFUL LITTLE TOWN...
...
WHERE ARE YOU FROM?
CHINA?
NO. I'M FROM JAPAN.
MY NAME'S TENMA.
OH, JAPANESE, HUH?
THOU-SANDS OF MILES FROM YOUR HOME AND SOMETHING LIKE THIS HAPPENS...
I... I...
CALM DOWN, NOW.
YOU'RE SAFE NOW.

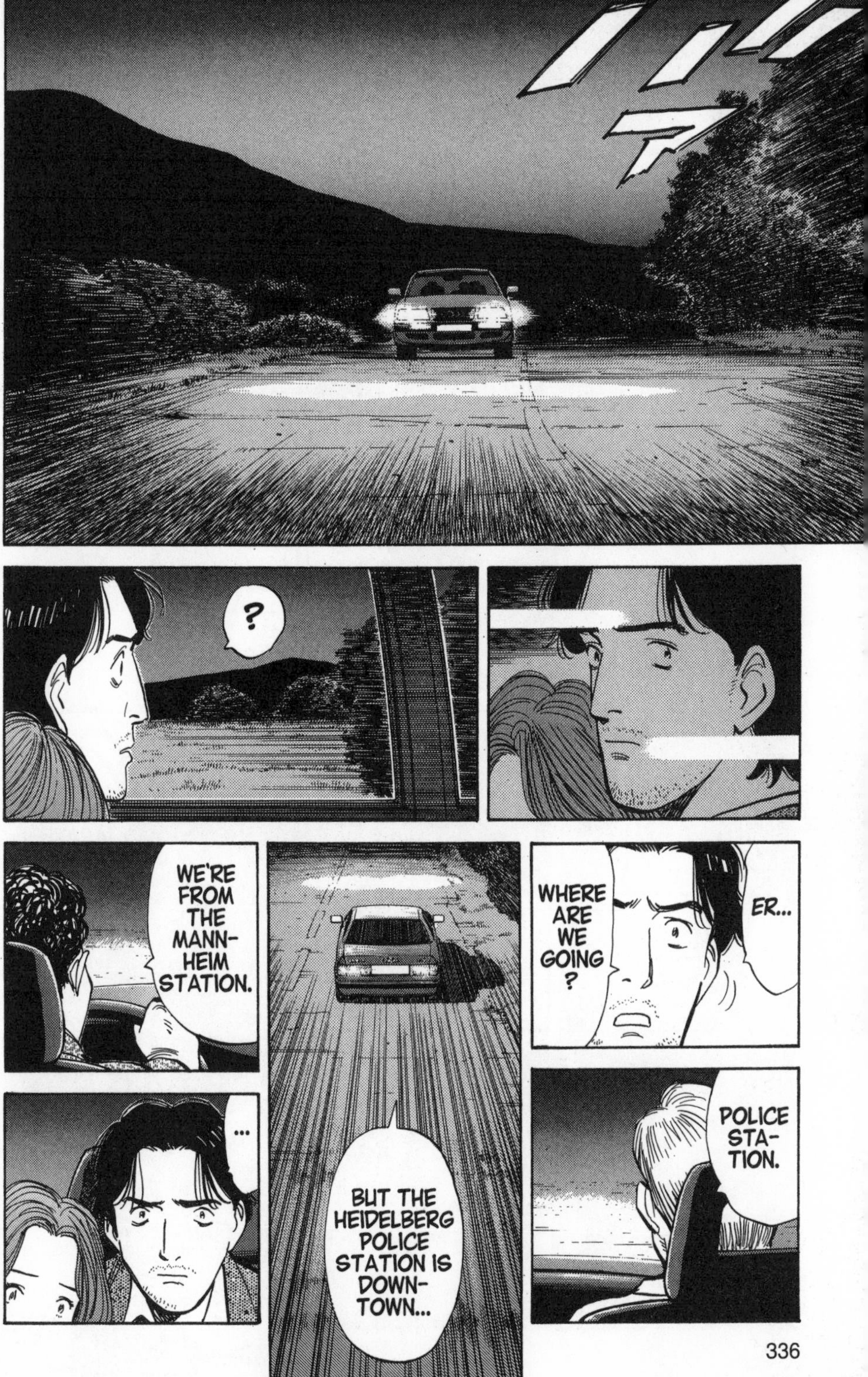
?
ER...
WHERE ARE WE GOING?
POLICE STATION.
BUT THE HEIDELBERG POLICE STATION IS DOWNTOWN...
WE'RE FROM THE MANNHEIM STATION.
...

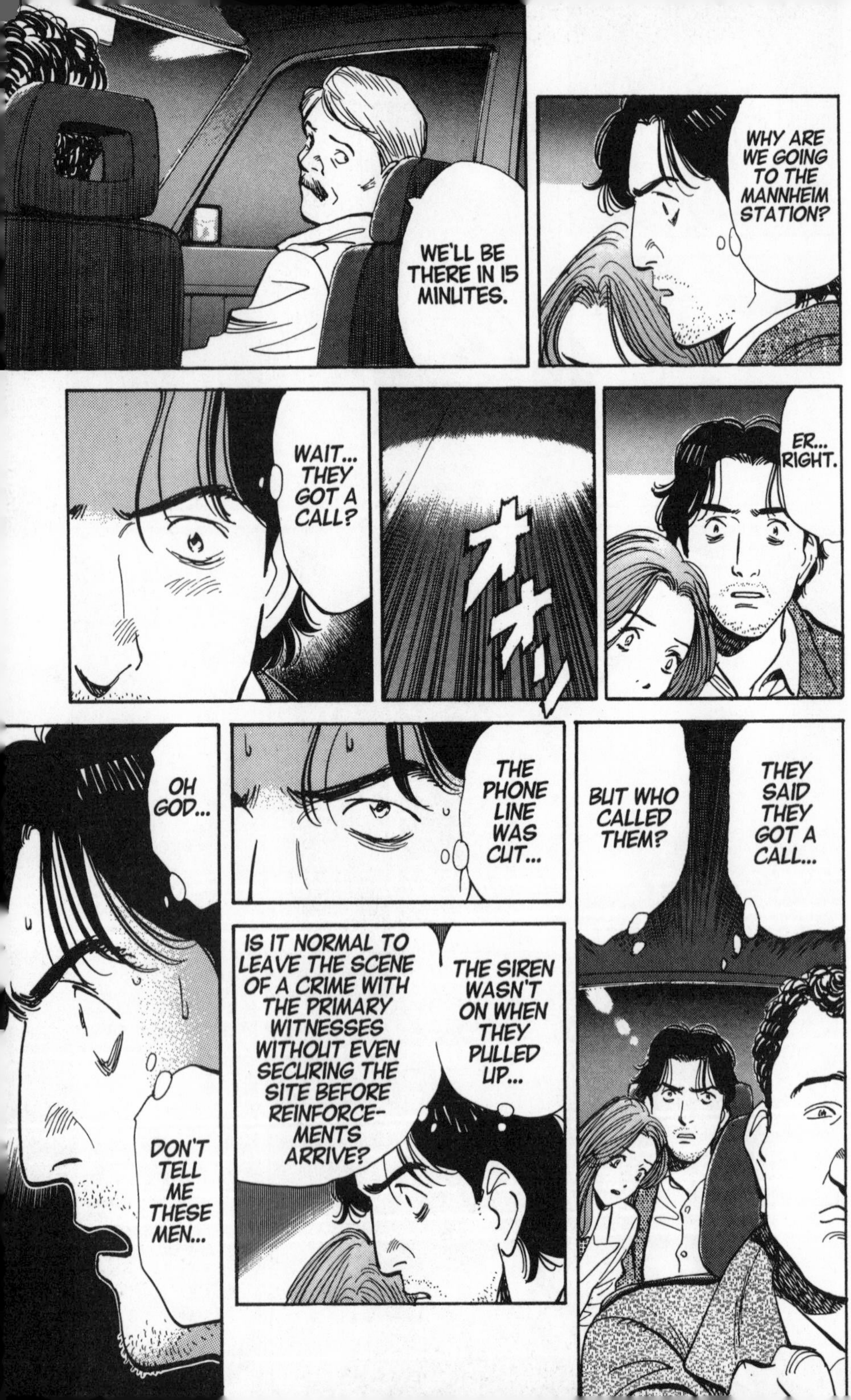
WHY ARE WE GOING TO THE MANNHEIM STATION?
WE'LL BE THERE IN 15 MINUTES.
ER... RIGHT.
WAIT... THEY GOT A CALL?
THEY SAID THEY GOT A CALL...
BUT WHO CALLED THEM?
THE PHONE LINE WAS CUT...
THE SIREN WASN'T ON WHEN THEY PULLED UP...
IS IT NORMAL TO LEAVE THE SCENE OF A CRIME WITH THE PRIMARY WITNESSES WITHOUT EVEN SECURING THE SITE BEFORE REINFORCEMENTS ARRIVE?
OH GOD...
DON'T TELL ME THESE MEN...

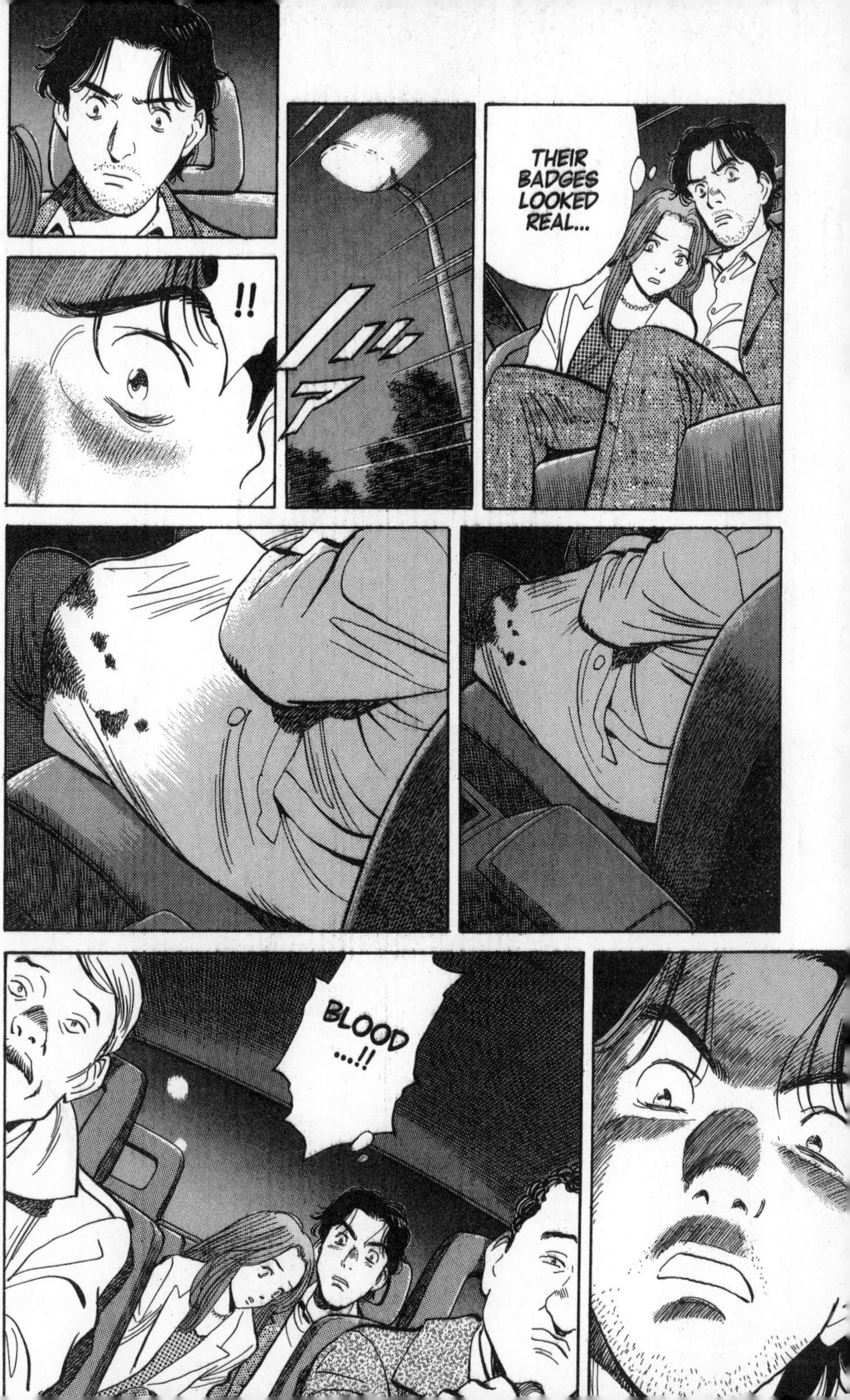
THEIR BADGES LOOKED REAL...
!!
BLOOD ...!!

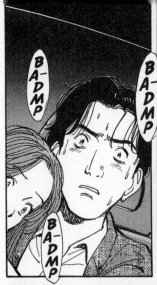
BA-DMP

BA-DMP

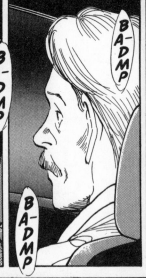
BA-DMP

BA-DMP

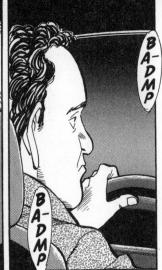
BA-DMP

BA-DMP

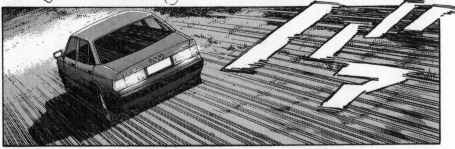

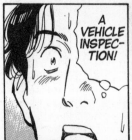
A VEHICLE INSPECTION!

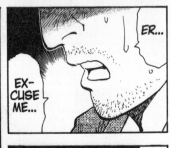
ER...

EXCUSE ME...

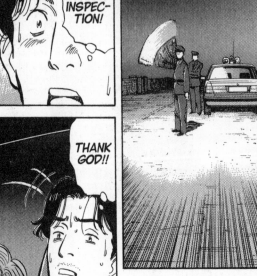

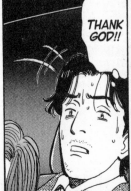
THANK GOD!!

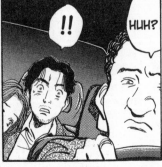
!!

HUH?

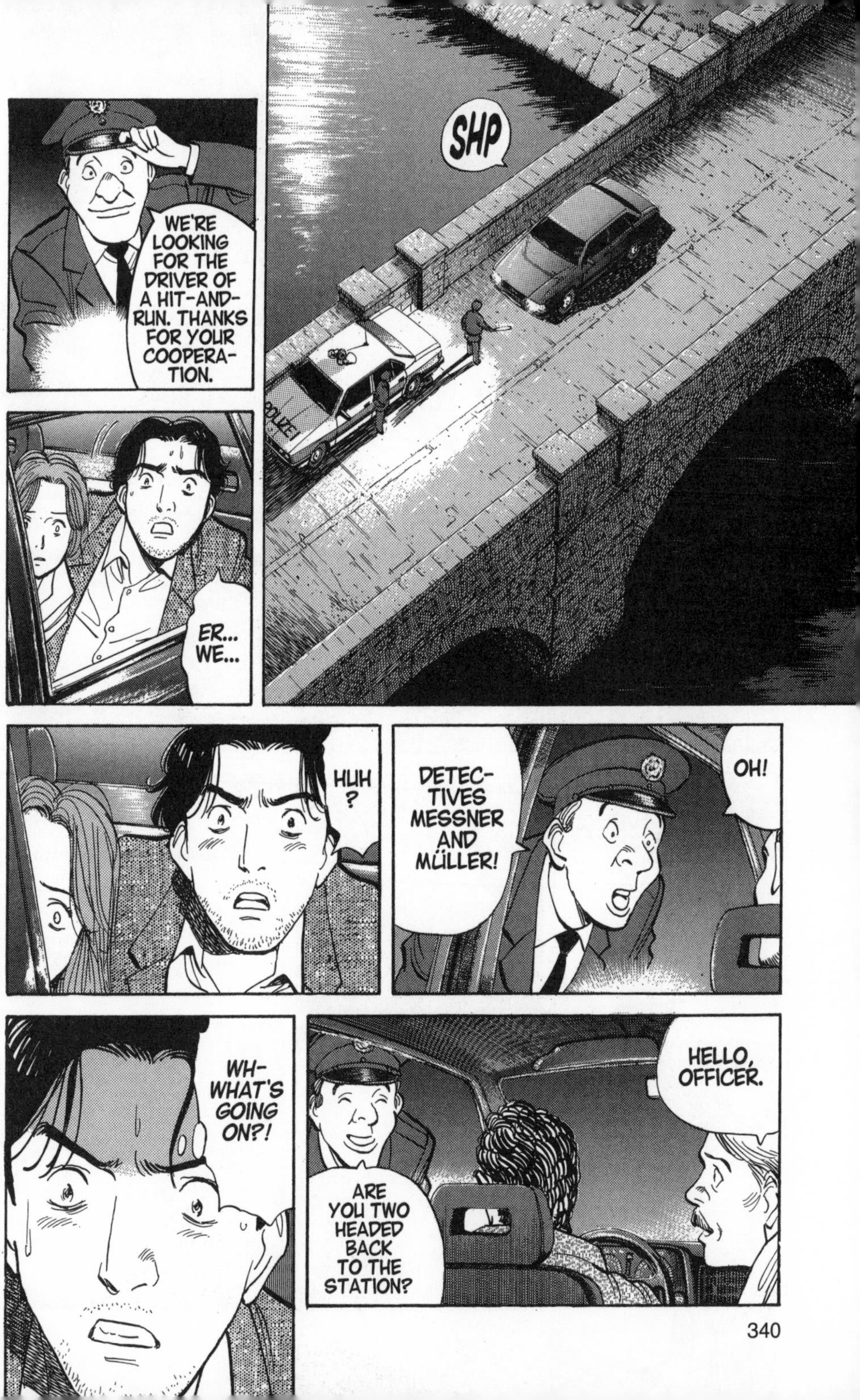
SHP
POLIZEI
WE'RE LOOKING FOR THE DRIVER OF A HIT-AND-RUN. THANKS FOR YOUR COOPERATION.
ER... WE...
OH!
DETECTIVES MESSNER AND MÜLLER!
HUH?
HELLO, OFFICER.
ARE YOU TWO HEADED BACK TO THE STATION?
WH-WHAT'S GOING ON?!

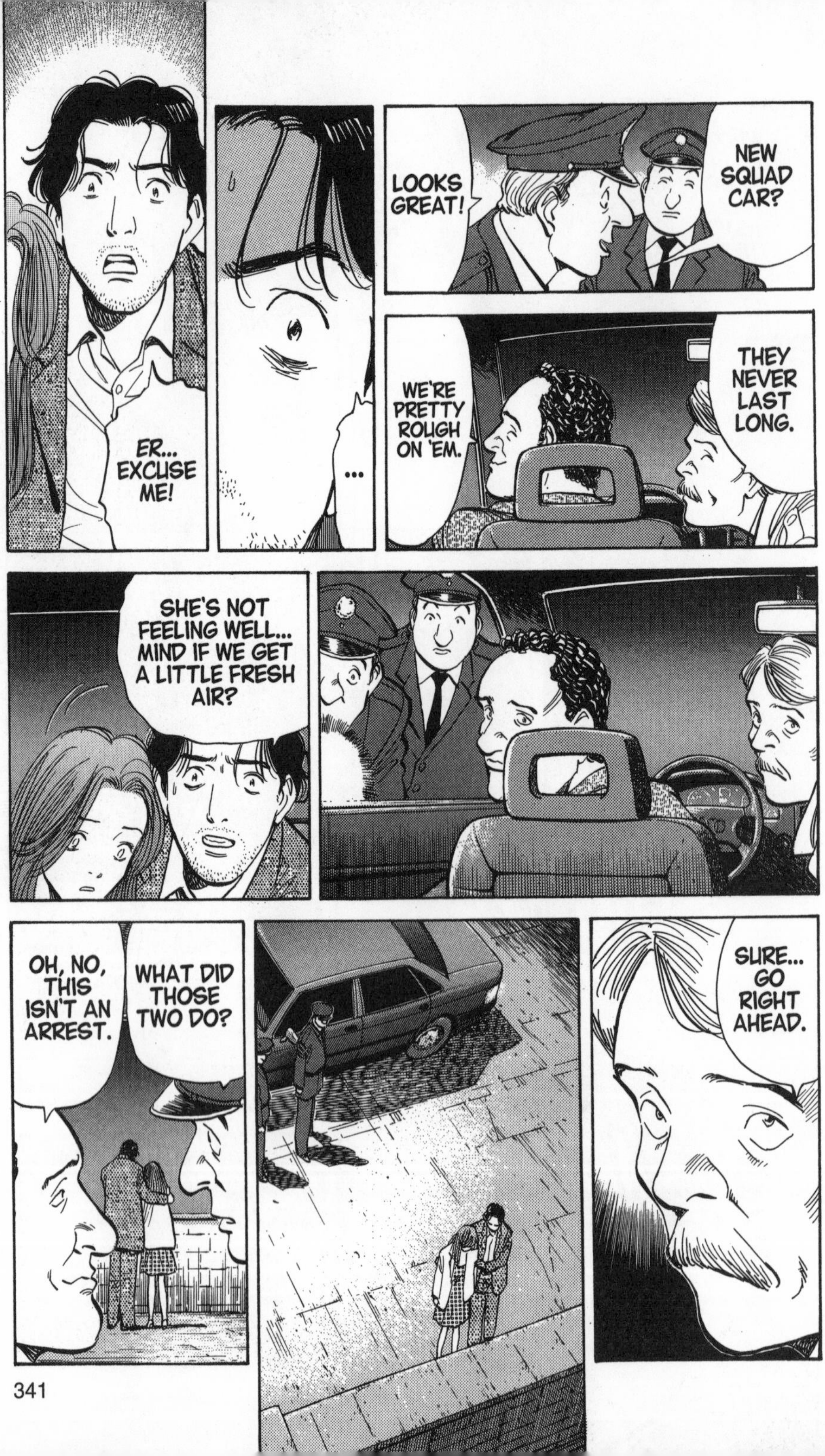
NEW SQUAD CAR?
LOOKS GREAT!
THEY NEVER LAST LONG.
WE'RE PRETTY ROUGH ON 'EM.
...
ER... EXCUSE ME!
SHE'S NOT FEELING WELL... MIND IF WE GET A LITTLE FRESH AIR?
SURE... GO RIGHT AHEAD.
WHAT DID THOSE TWO DO?
OH, NO, THIS ISN'T AN ARREST.

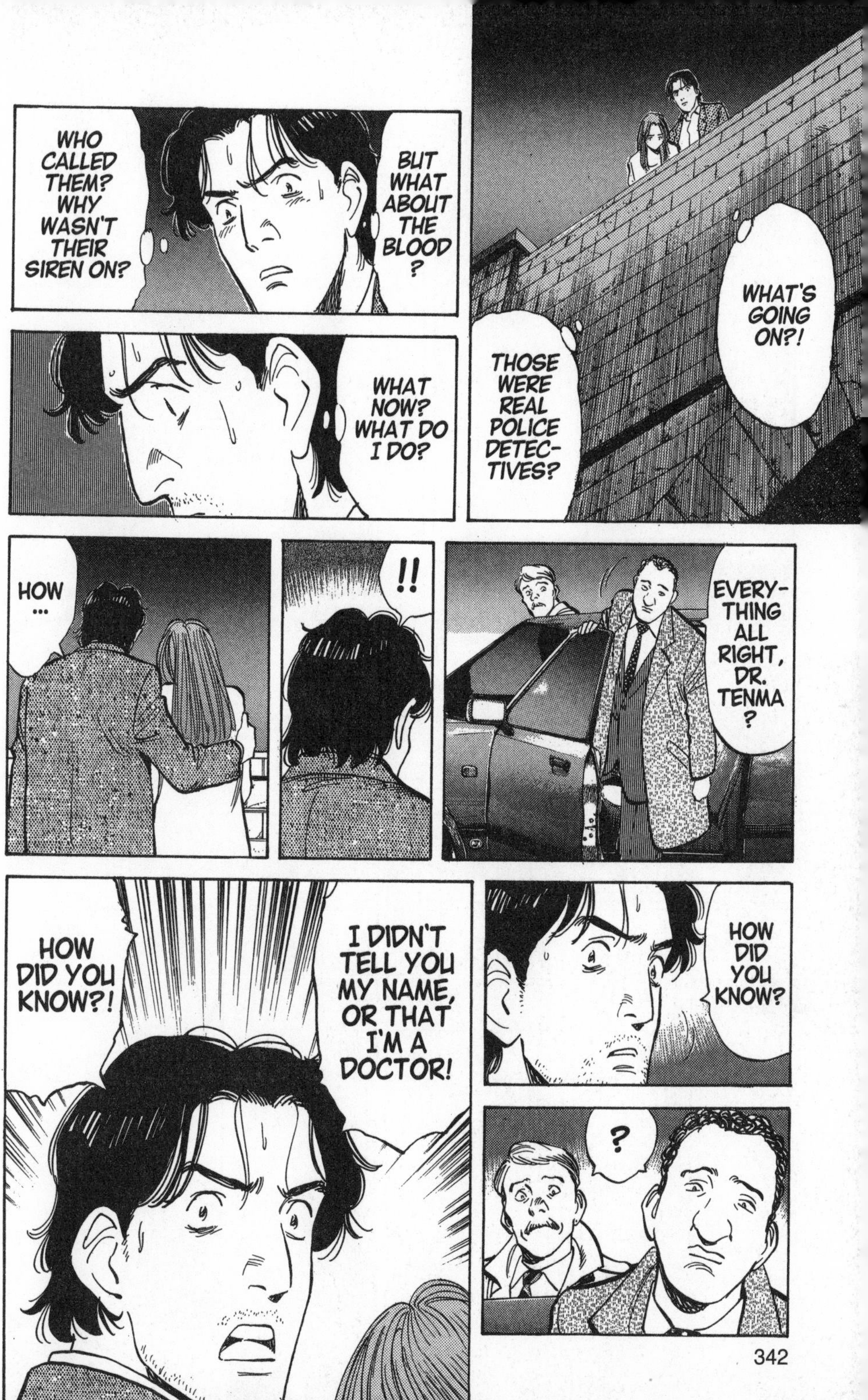
WHAT'S GOING ON?!
THOSE WERE REAL POLICE DETECTIVES?
BUT WHAT ABOUT THE BLOOD?
WHO CALLED THEM? WHY WASN'T THEIR SIREN ON?
WHAT NOW? WHAT DO I DO?
EVERYTHING ALL RIGHT, DR. TENMA?
!!
HOW ...
HOW DID YOU KNOW?
?
I DIDN'T TELL YOU MY NAME, OR THAT I'M A DOCTOR!
HOW DID YOU KNOW?!

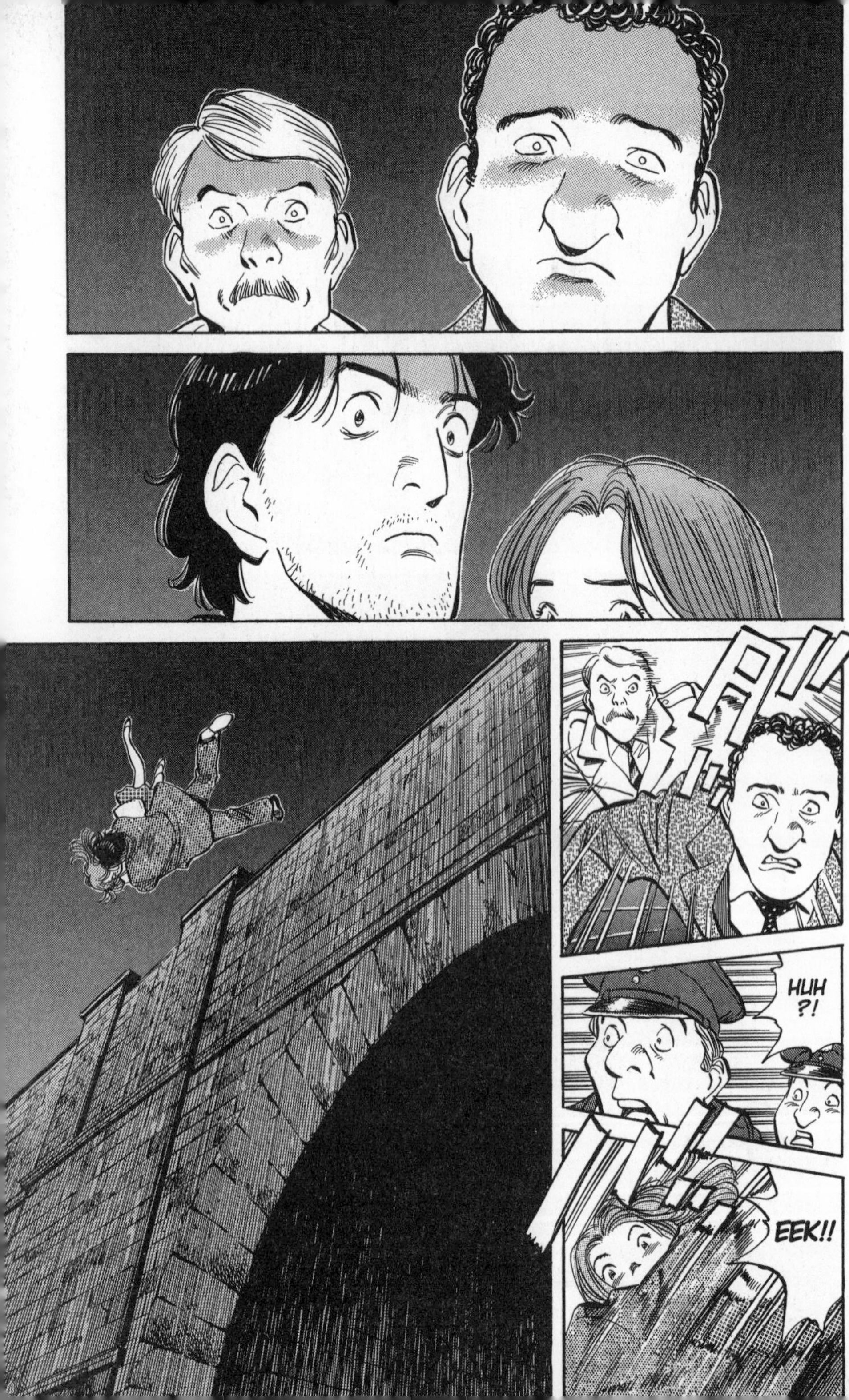
HUH ?!
EEK!!

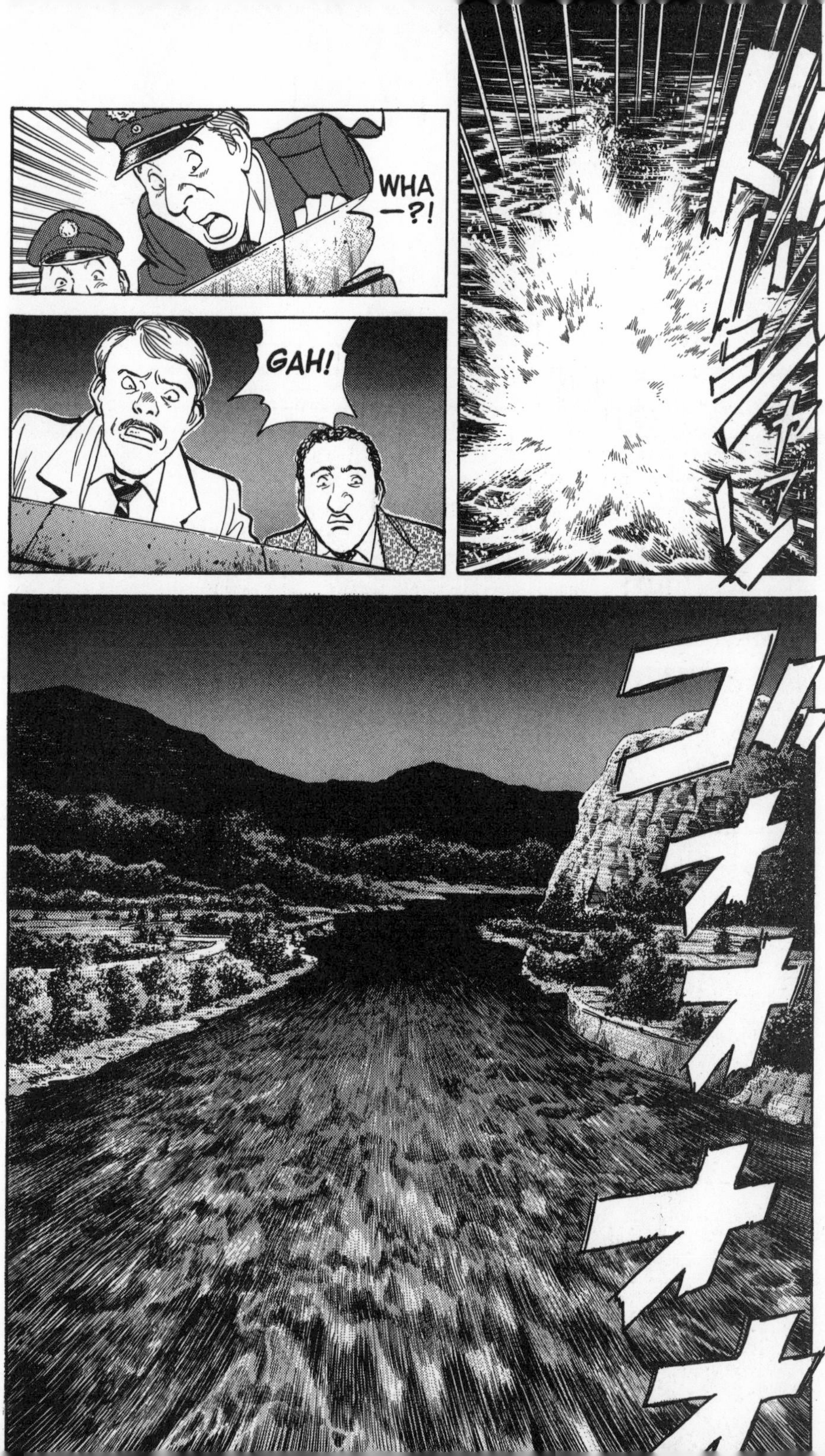
WHA—?!
GAH!

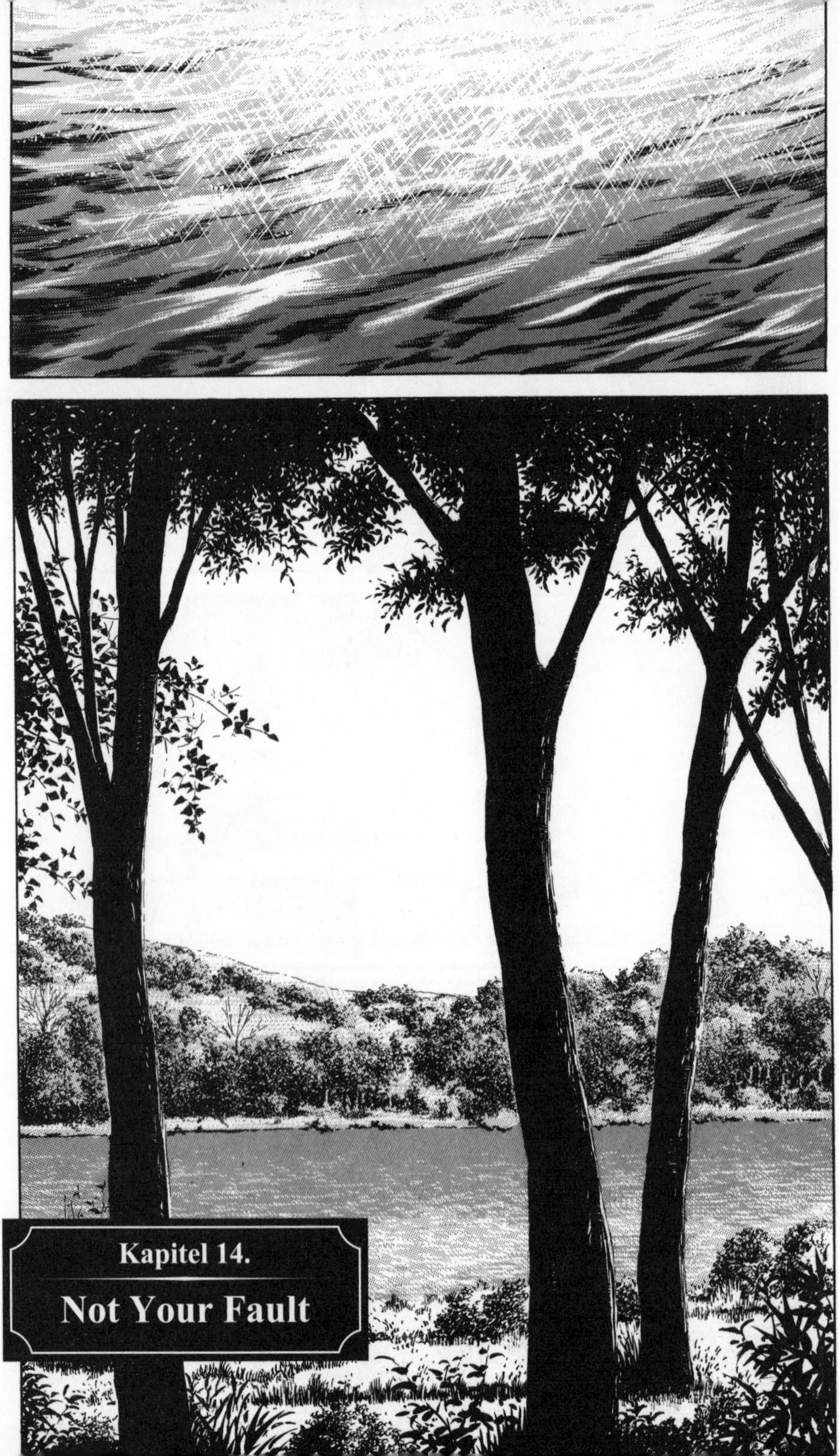
Kapitel 14.
Not Your Fault

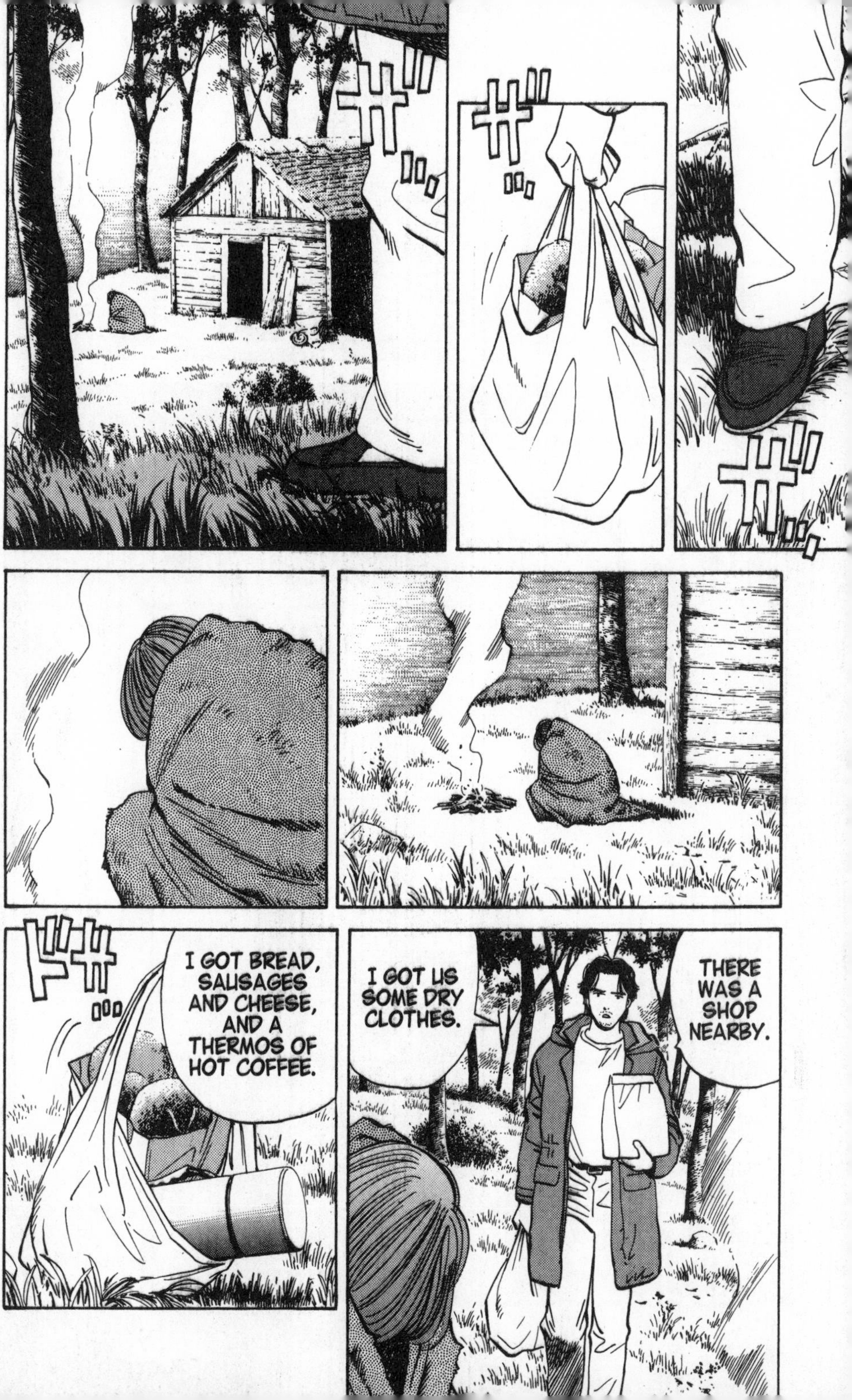
THERE WAS A SHOP NEARBY.
I GOT US SOME DRY CLOTHES.
I GOT BREAD, SAUSAGES AND CHEESE, AND A THERMOS OF HOT COFFEE.

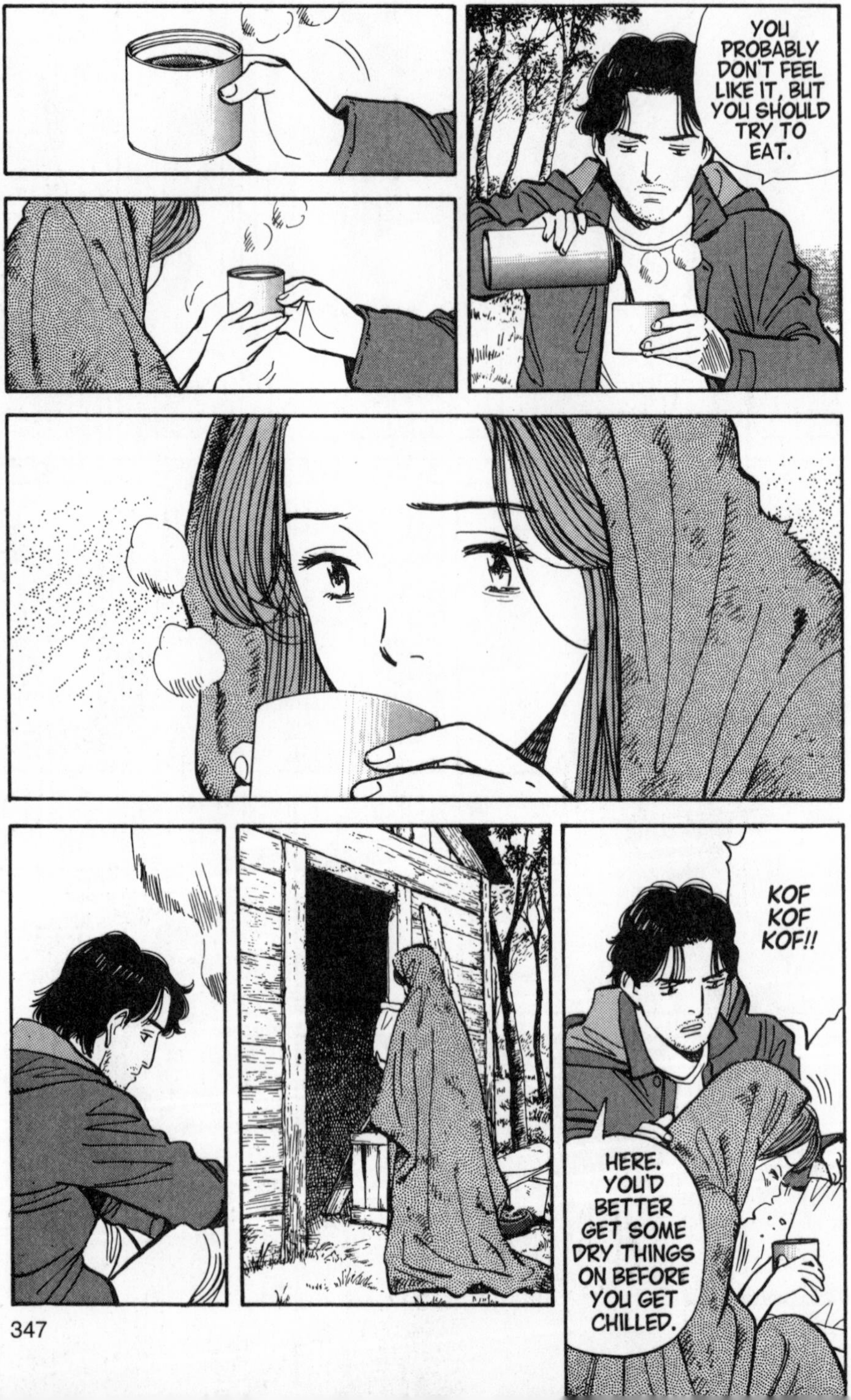
YOU PROBABLY DON'T FEEL LIKE IT, BUT YOU SHOULD TRY TO EAT.
KOF KOF KOF!!
HERE. YOU'D BETTER GET SOME DRY THINGS ON BEFORE YOU GET CHILLED.

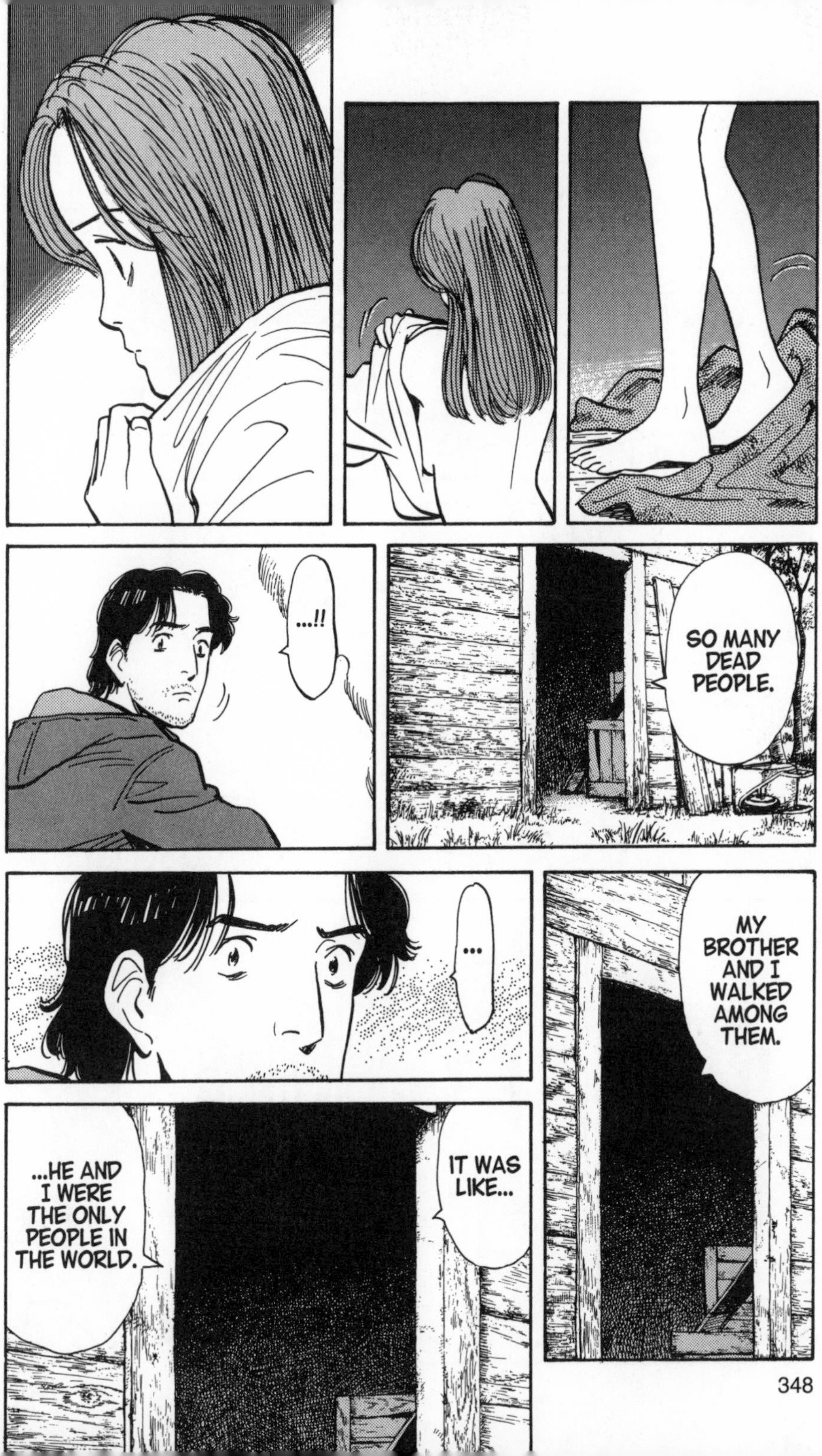
SO MANY DEAD PEOPLE.
...!!
MY BROTHER AND I WALKED AMONG THEM.
...
IT WAS LIKE...
...HE AND I WERE THE ONLY PEOPLE IN THE WORLD.

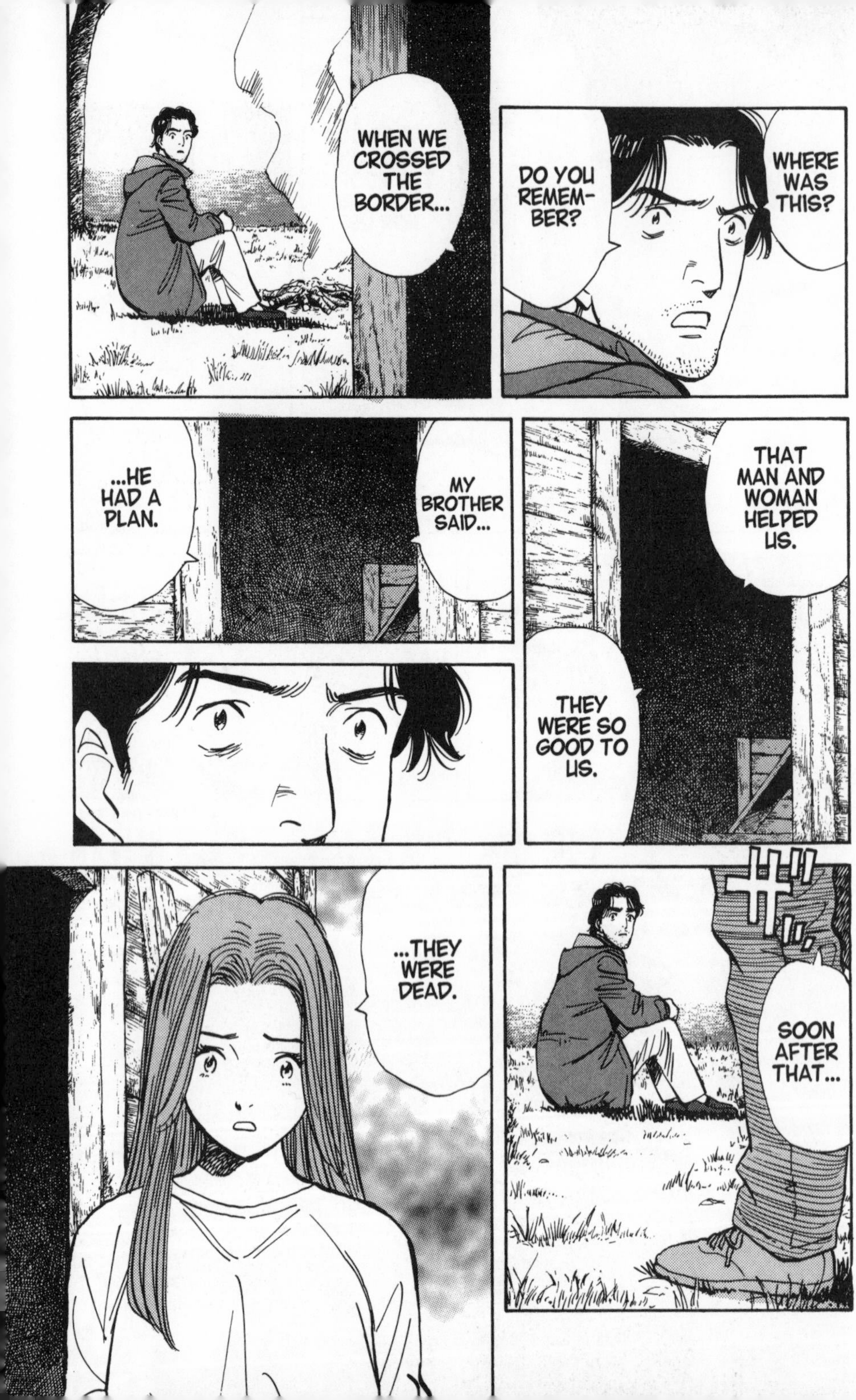
WHERE WAS THIS?
DO YOU REMEM-BER?
WHEN WE CROSSED THE BORDER...
THAT MAN AND WOMAN HELPED US.
THEY WERE SO GOOD TO US.
MY BROTHER SAID...
...HE HAD A PLAN.
ザッ
SOON AFTER THAT...
...THEY WERE DEAD.

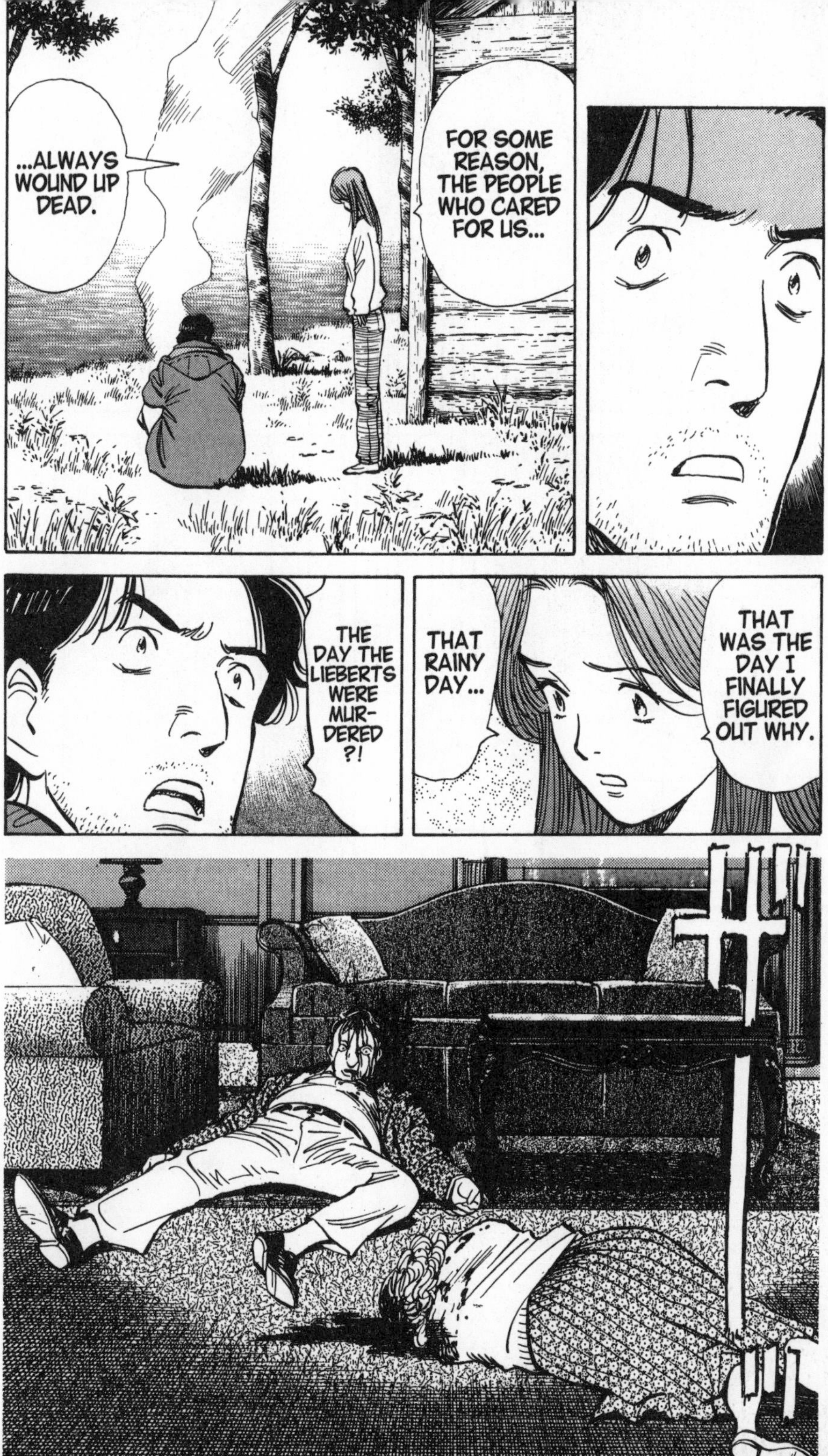
FOR SOME REASON, THE PEOPLE WHO CARED FOR US...
...ALWAYS WOUND UP DEAD.
THAT WAS THE DAY I FINALLY FIGURED OUT WHY.
THAT RAINY DAY...
THE DAY THE LIEBERTS WERE MUR-DERED?!

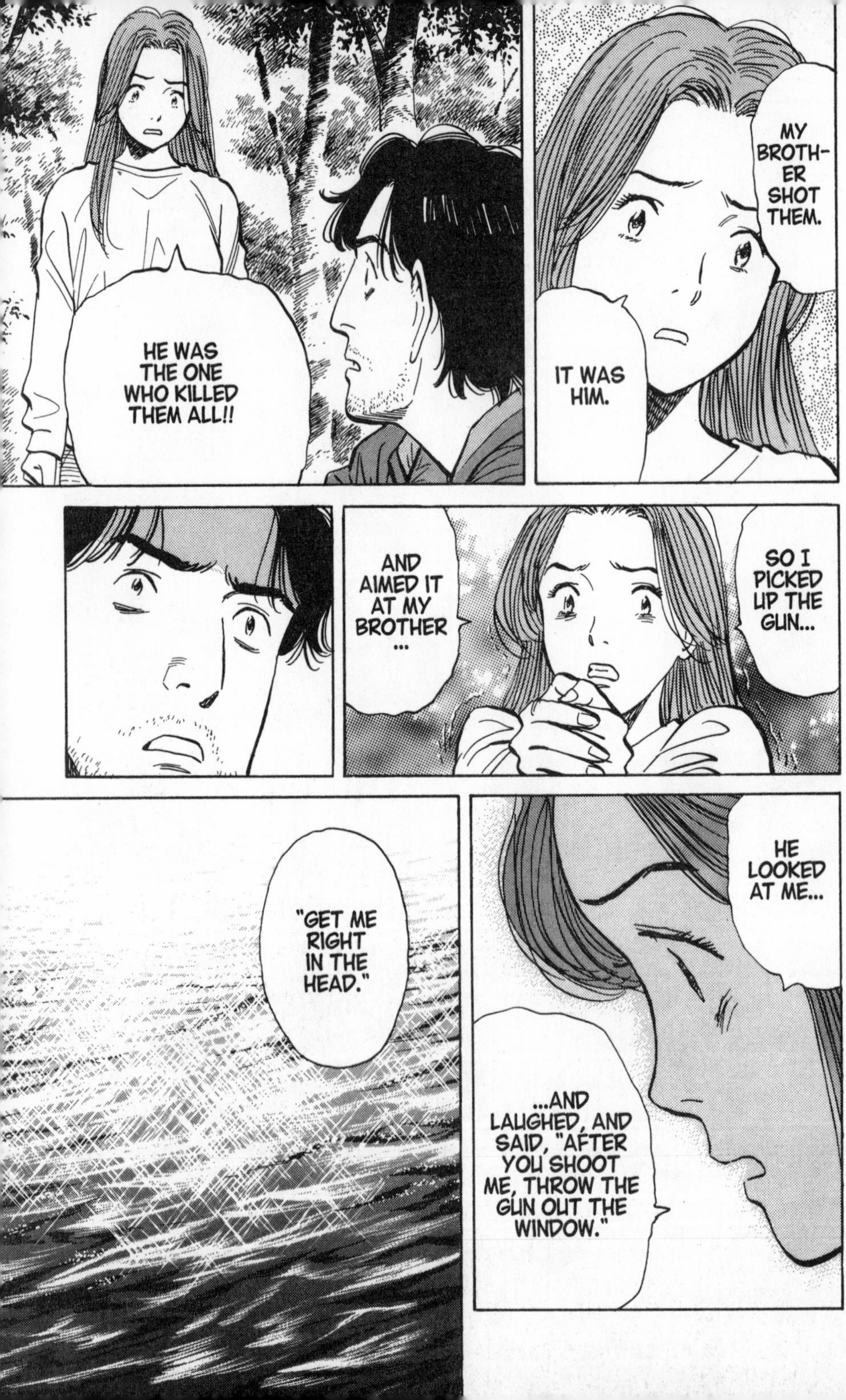
MY BROTHER SHOT THEM.
IT WAS HIM.
HE WAS THE ONE WHO KILLED THEM ALL!!
SO I PICKED UP THE GUN...
AND AIMED IT AT MY BROTHER ...
HE LOOKED AT ME...
...AND LAUGHED, AND SAID, "AFTER YOU SHOOT ME, THROW THE GUN OUT THE WINDOW."
"GET ME RIGHT IN THE HEAD."

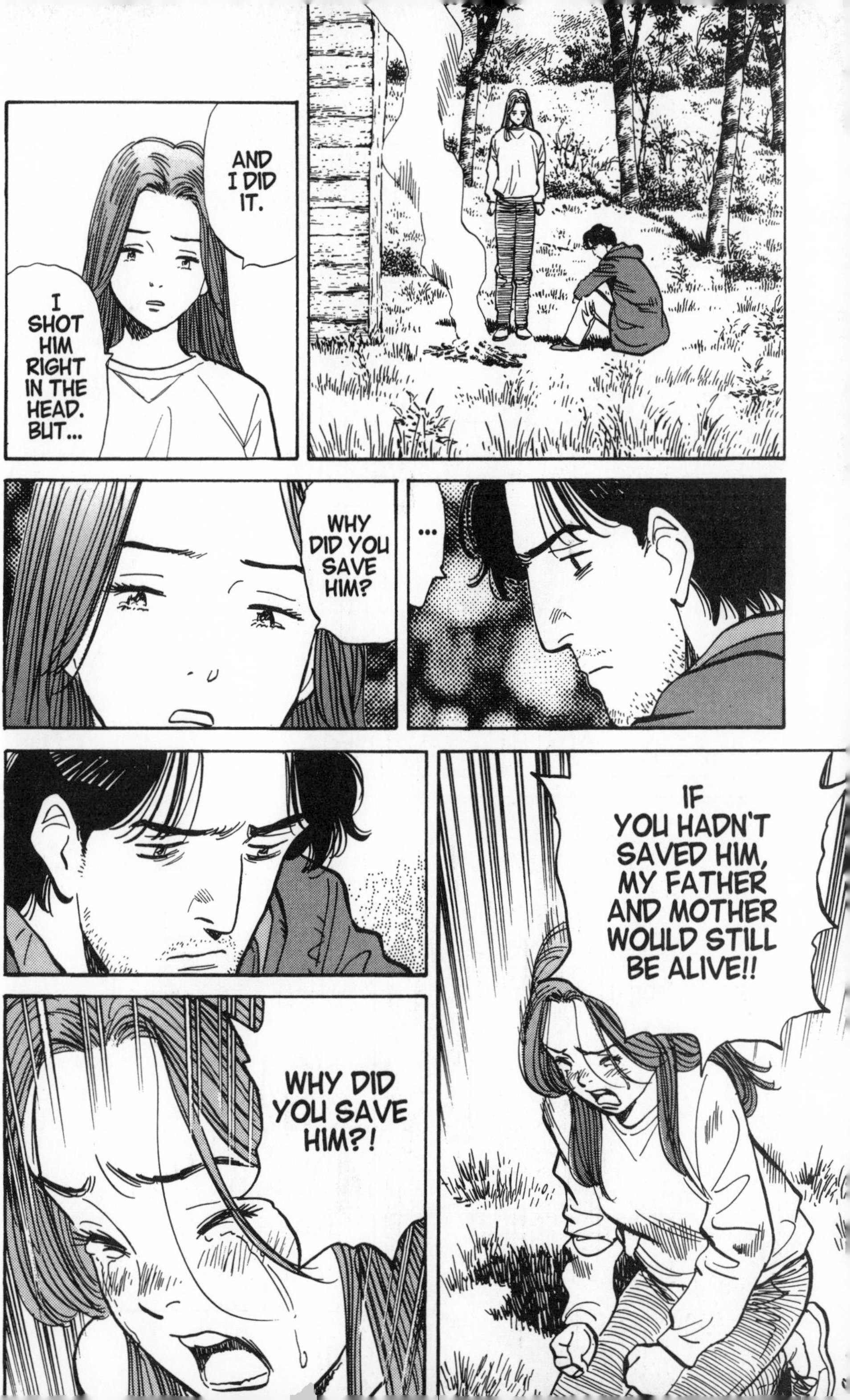
AND I DID IT.
I SHOT HIM RIGHT IN THE HEAD. BUT...
...
WHY DID YOU SAVE HIM?
IF YOU HADN'T SAVED HIM, MY FATHER AND MOTHER WOULD STILL BE ALIVE!!
WHY DID YOU SAVE HIM?!

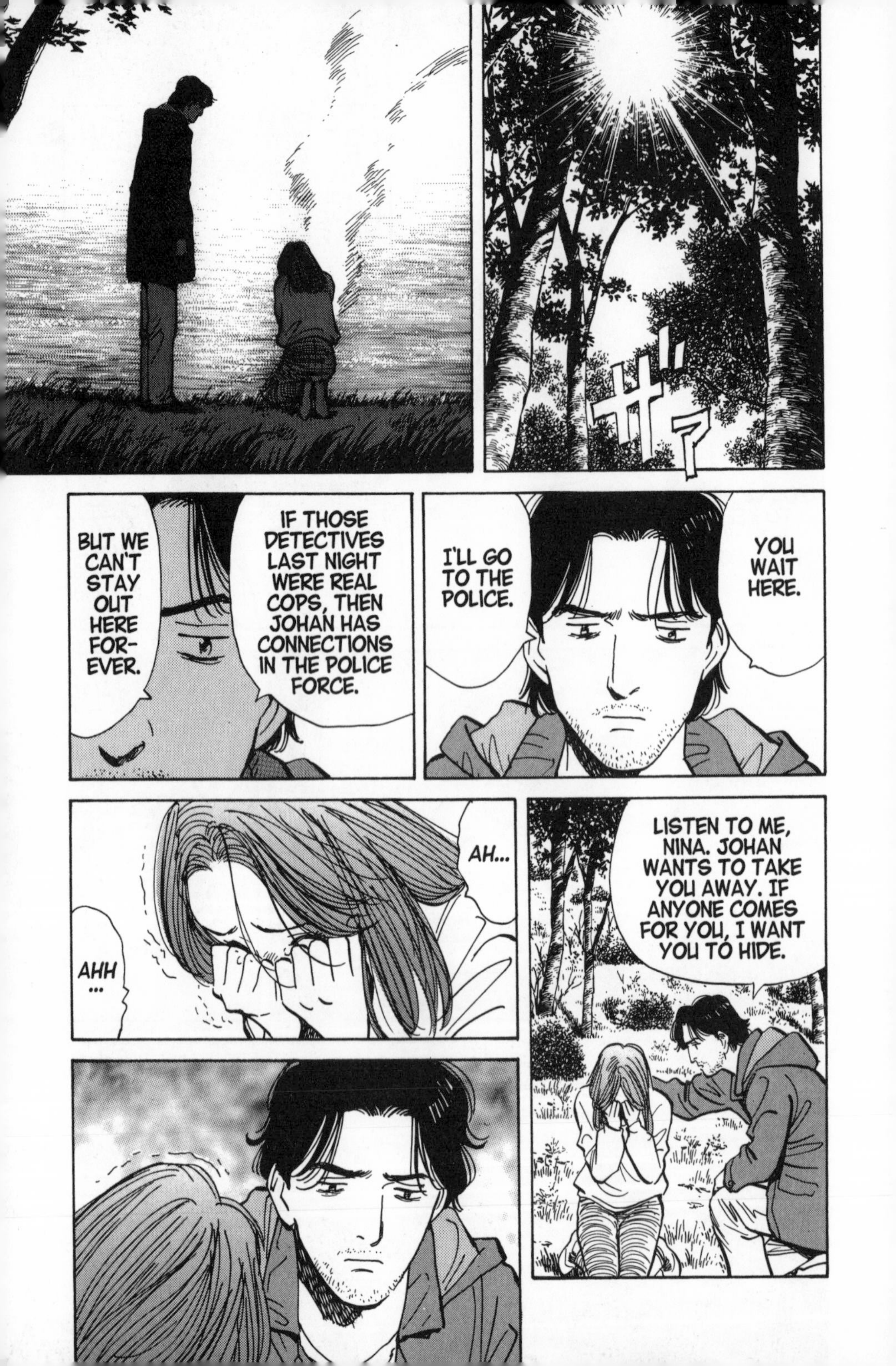
ザァ
YOU WAIT HERE.
I'LL GO TO THE POLICE.
IF THOSE DETECTIVES LAST NIGHT WERE REAL COPS, THEN JOHAN HAS CONNECTIONS IN THE POLICE FORCE.
BUT WE CAN'T STAY OUT HERE FOR-EVER.
LISTEN TO ME, NINA. JOHAN WANTS TO TAKE YOU AWAY. IF ANYONE COMES FOR YOU, I WANT YOU TO HIDE.
AH...
AHH ...

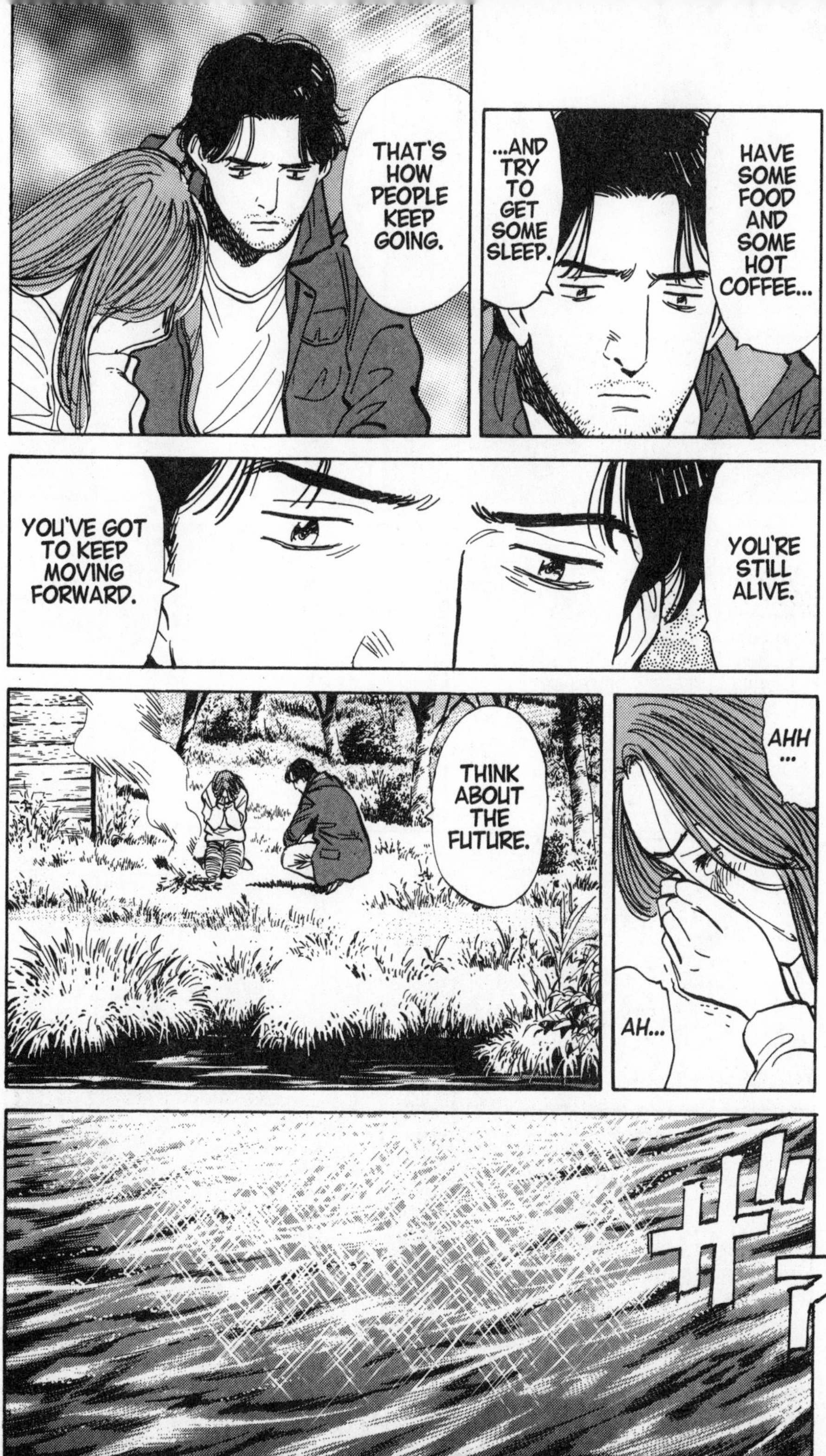
HAVE SOME FOOD AND SOME HOT COFFEE...
...AND TRY TO GET SOME SLEEP.
THAT'S HOW PEOPLE KEEP GOING.
YOU'RE STILL ALIVE.
YOU'VE GOT TO KEEP MOVING FORWARD.
AHH ...
AH...
THINK ABOUT THE FUTURE.
ザァ

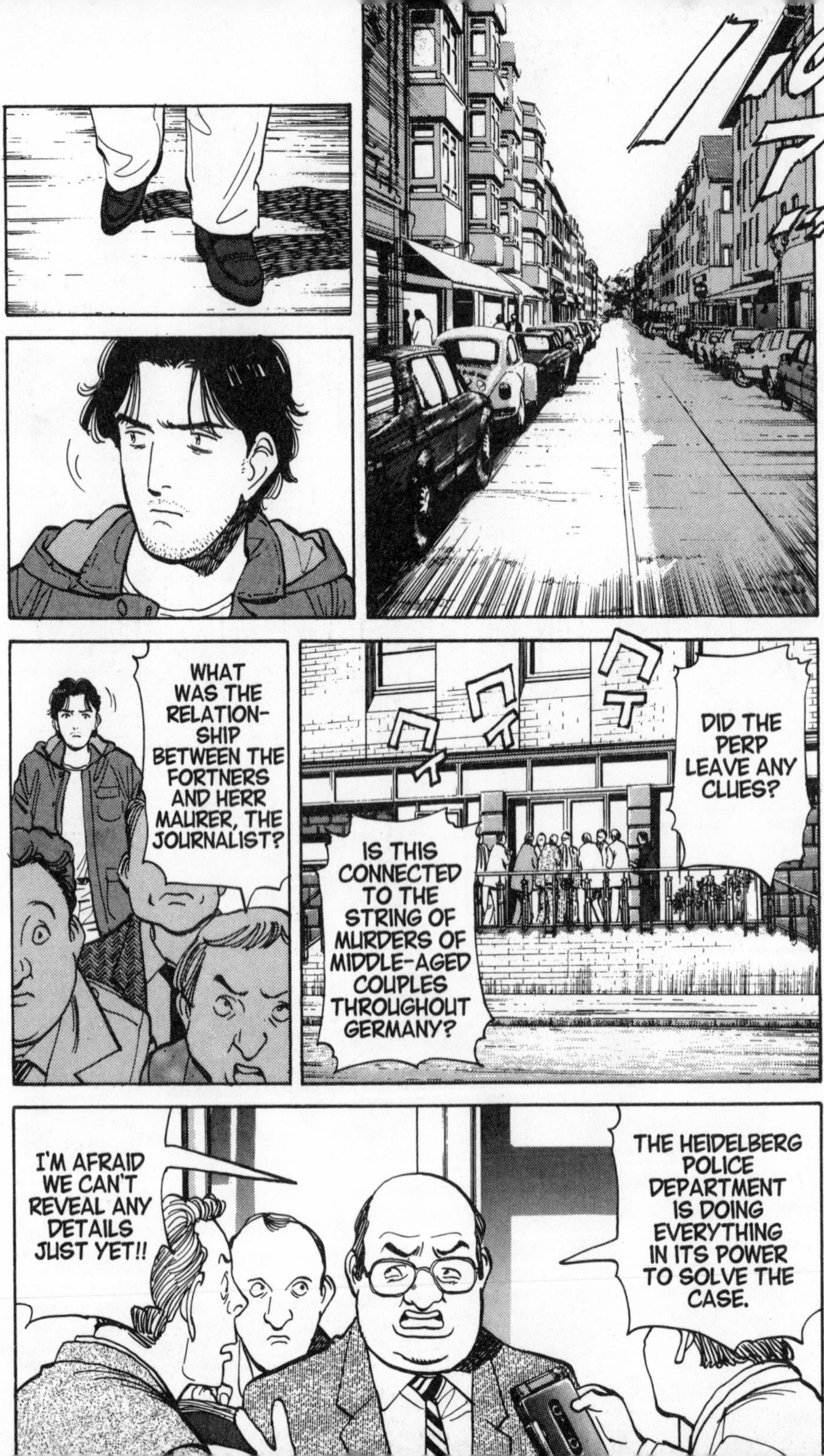
DID THE PERP LEAVE ANY CLUES?
IS THIS CONNECTED TO THE STRING OF MURDERS OF MIDDLE-AGED COUPLES THROUGHOUT GERMANY?
WHAT WAS THE RELATION-SHIP BETWEEN THE FORTNERS AND HERR MAURER, THE JOURNALIST?
THE HEIDELBERG POLICE DEPARTMENT IS DOING EVERYTHING IN ITS POWER TO SOLVE THE CASE.
I'M AFRAID WE CAN'T REVEAL ANY DETAILS JUST YET!!

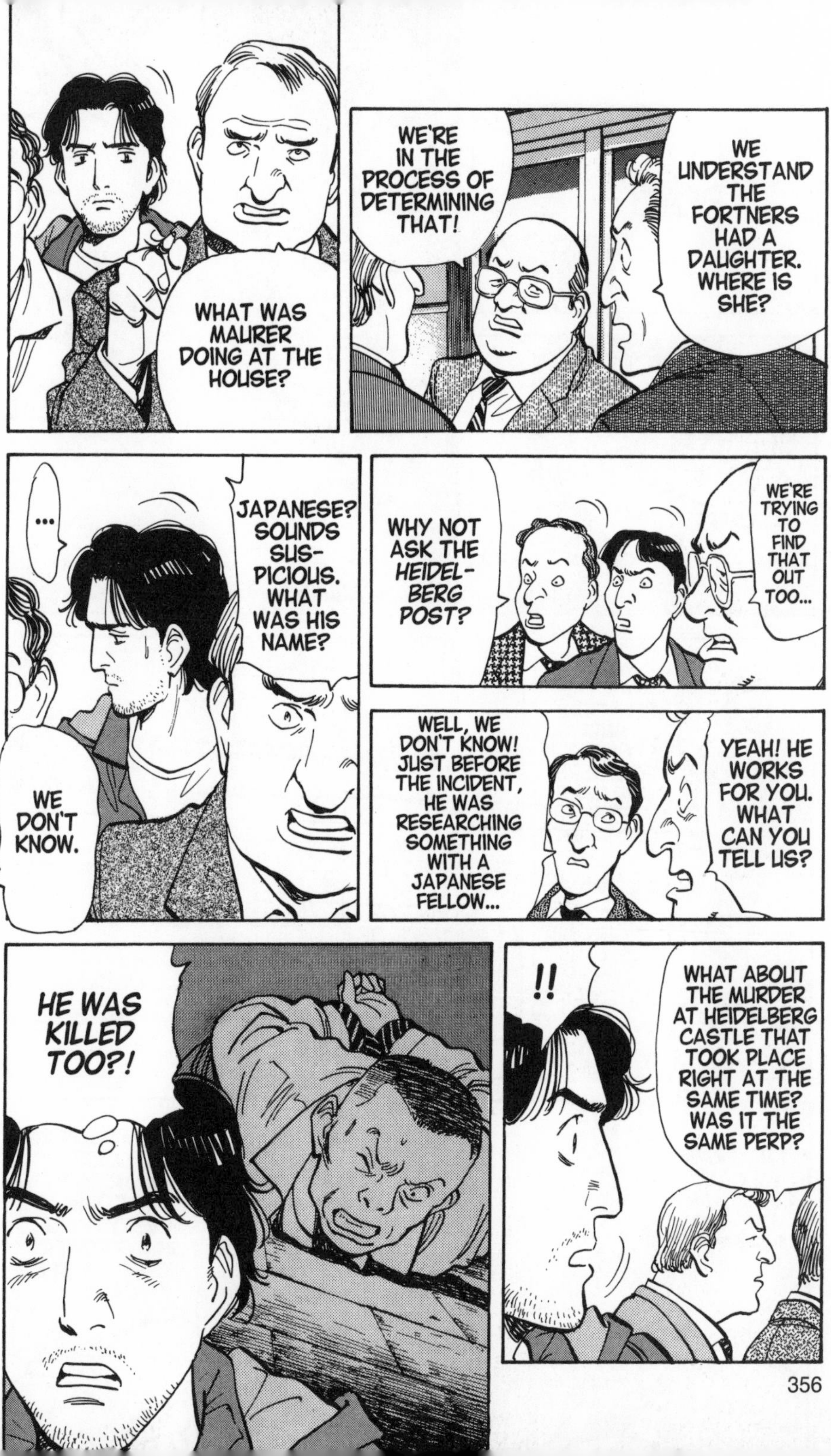
WE UNDERSTAND THE FORTNERS HAD A DAUGHTER. WHERE IS SHE?
WE'RE IN THE PROCESS OF DETERMINING THAT!
WHAT WAS MAURER DOING AT THE HOUSE?
WE'RE TRYING TO FIND THAT OUT TOO...
WHY NOT ASK THE HEIDEL-BERG POST?
YEAH! HE WORKS FOR YOU. WHAT CAN YOU TELL US?
WELL, WE DON'T KNOW! JUST BEFORE THE INCIDENT, HE WAS RESEARCHING SOMETHING WITH A JAPANESE FELLOW...
JAPANESE? SOUNDS SUS-PICIOUS. WHAT WAS HIS NAME?
...
WE DON'T KNOW.
WHAT ABOUT THE MURDER AT HEIDELBERG CASTLE THAT TOOK PLACE RIGHT AT THE SAME TIME? WAS IT THE SAME PERP?
!!
HE WAS KILLED TOO?!

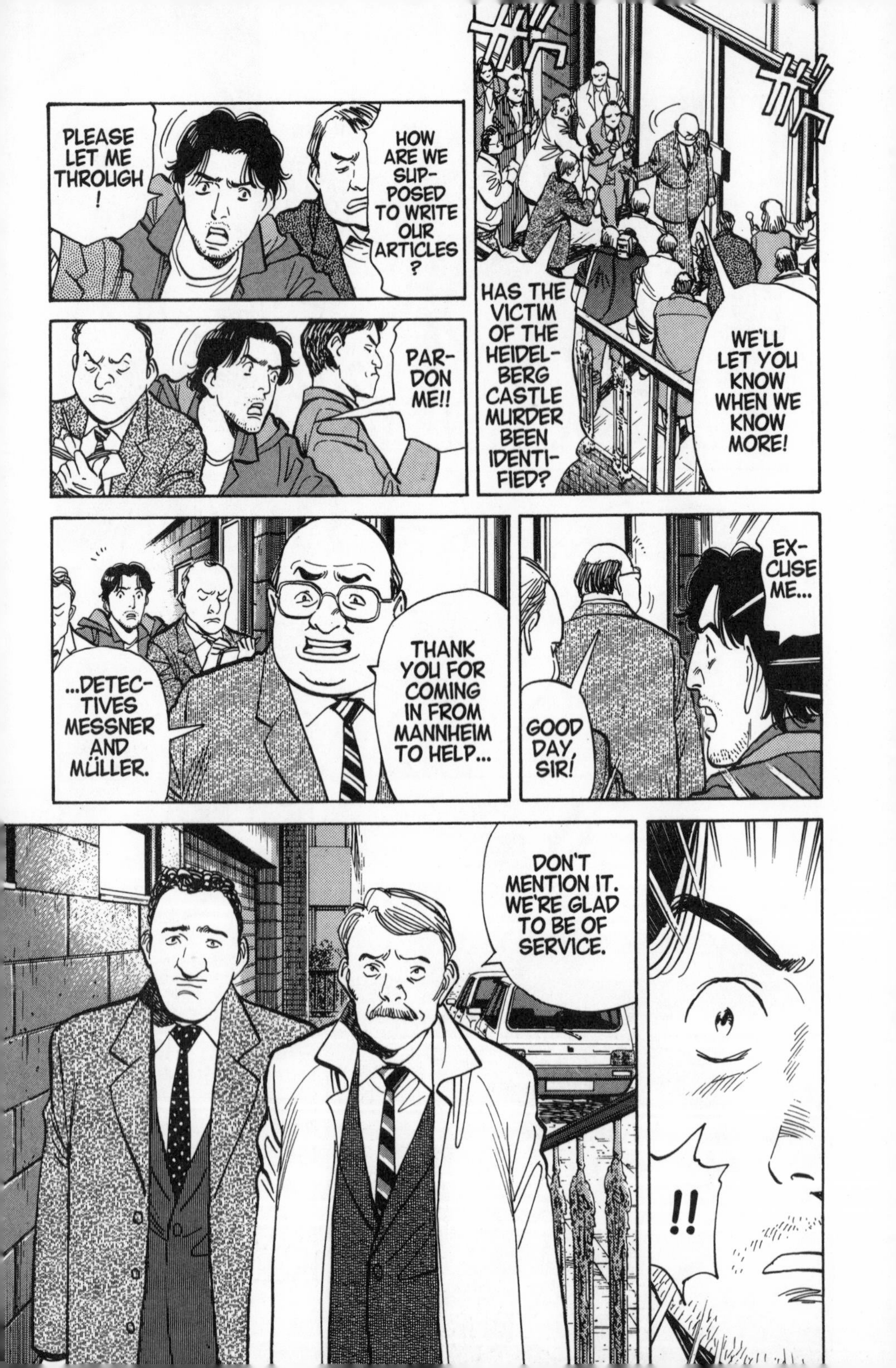

ガヤ
ガヤ
HAS THE VICTIM OF THE HEIDEL-BERG CASTLE MURDER BEEN IDENTI-FIED?
WE'LL LET YOU KNOW WHEN WE KNOW MORE!
HOW ARE WE SUP-POSED TO WRITE OUR ARTICLES ?
PLEASE LET ME THROUGH !
PAR-DON ME!!
EX-CUSE ME...
GOOD DAY, SIR!
THANK YOU FOR COMING IN FROM MANNHEIM TO HELP...
...DETEC-TIVES MESSNER AND MÜLLER.
!!
DON'T MENTION IT. WE'RE GLAD TO BE OF SERVICE.

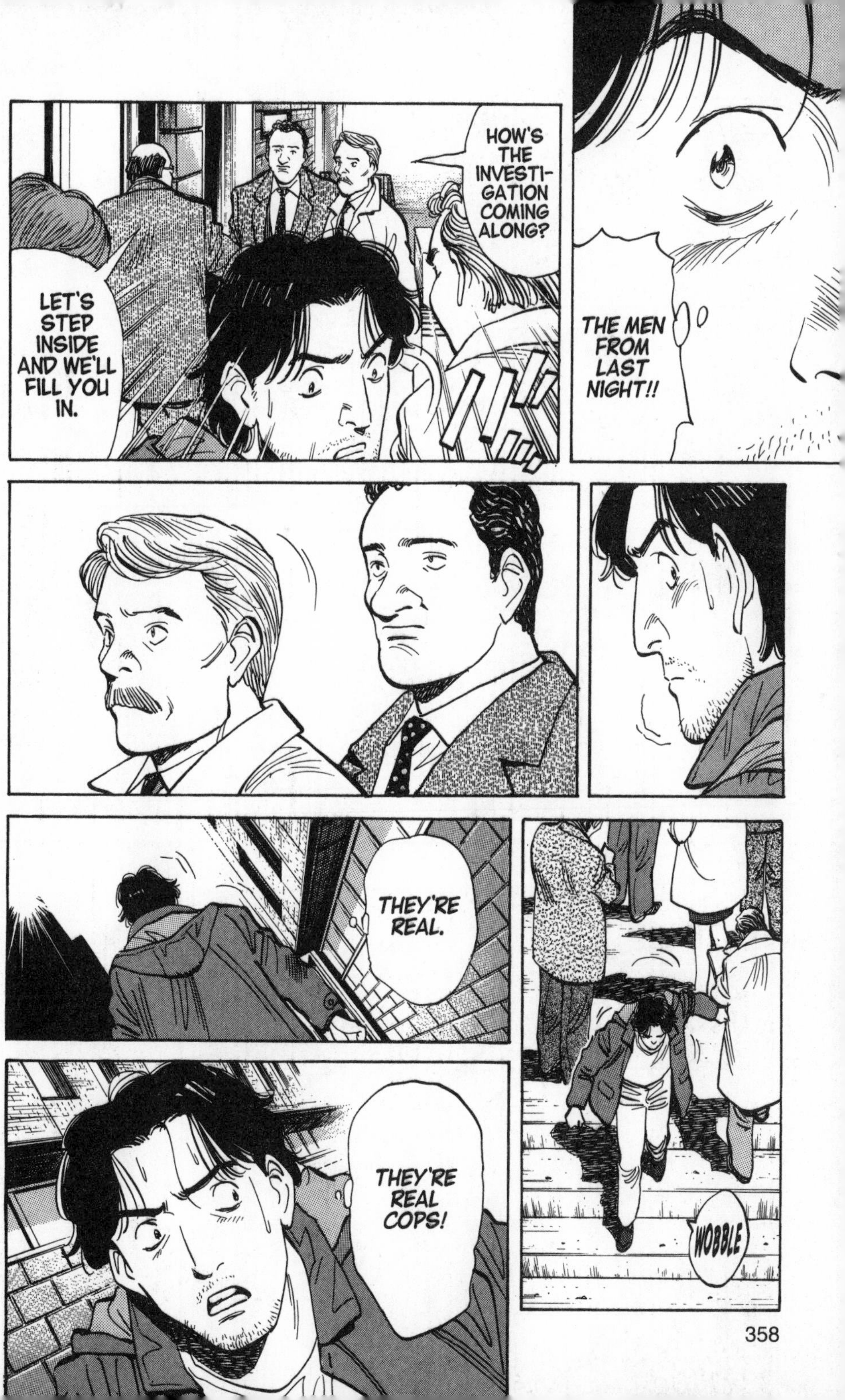
THE MEN FROM LAST NIGHT!!
HOW'S THE INVESTIGATION COMING ALONG?
LET'S STEP INSIDE AND WE'LL FILL YOU IN.
WOBBLE
THEY'RE REAL.
THEY'RE REAL COPS!

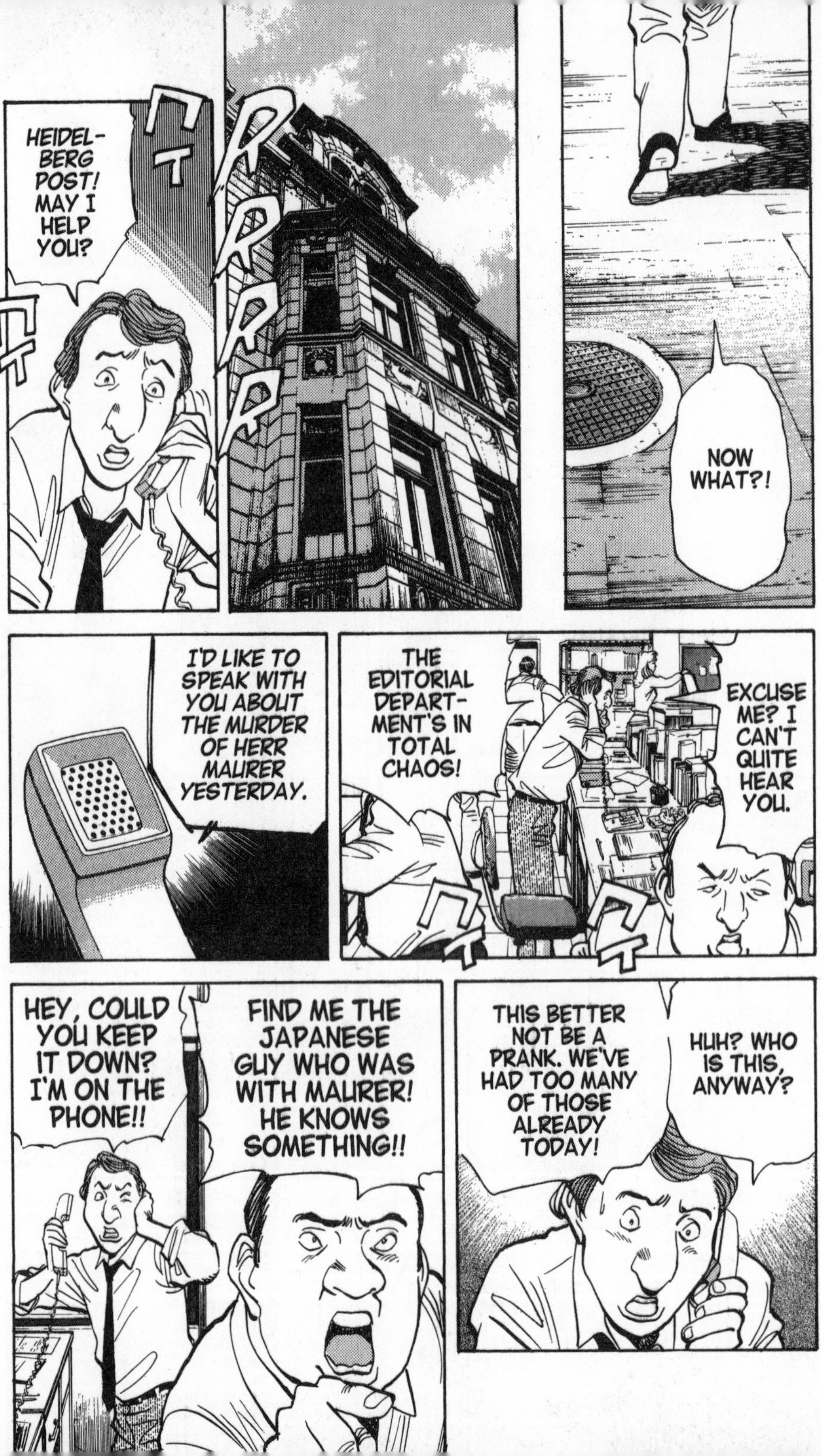
NOW WHAT?!
HEIDEL-BERG POST! MAY I HELP YOU?
EXCUSE ME? I CAN'T QUITE HEAR YOU.
THE EDITORIAL DEPART-MENT'S IN TOTAL CHAOS!
I'D LIKE TO SPEAK WITH YOU ABOUT THE MURDER OF HERR MAURER YESTERDAY.
HUH? WHO IS THIS, ANYWAY?
THIS BETTER NOT BE A PRANK. WE'VE HAD TOO MANY OF THOSE ALREADY TODAY!
FIND ME THE JAPANESE GUY WHO WAS WITH MAURER! HE KNOWS SOMETHING!!
HEY, COULD YOU KEEP IT DOWN? I'M ON THE PHONE!!

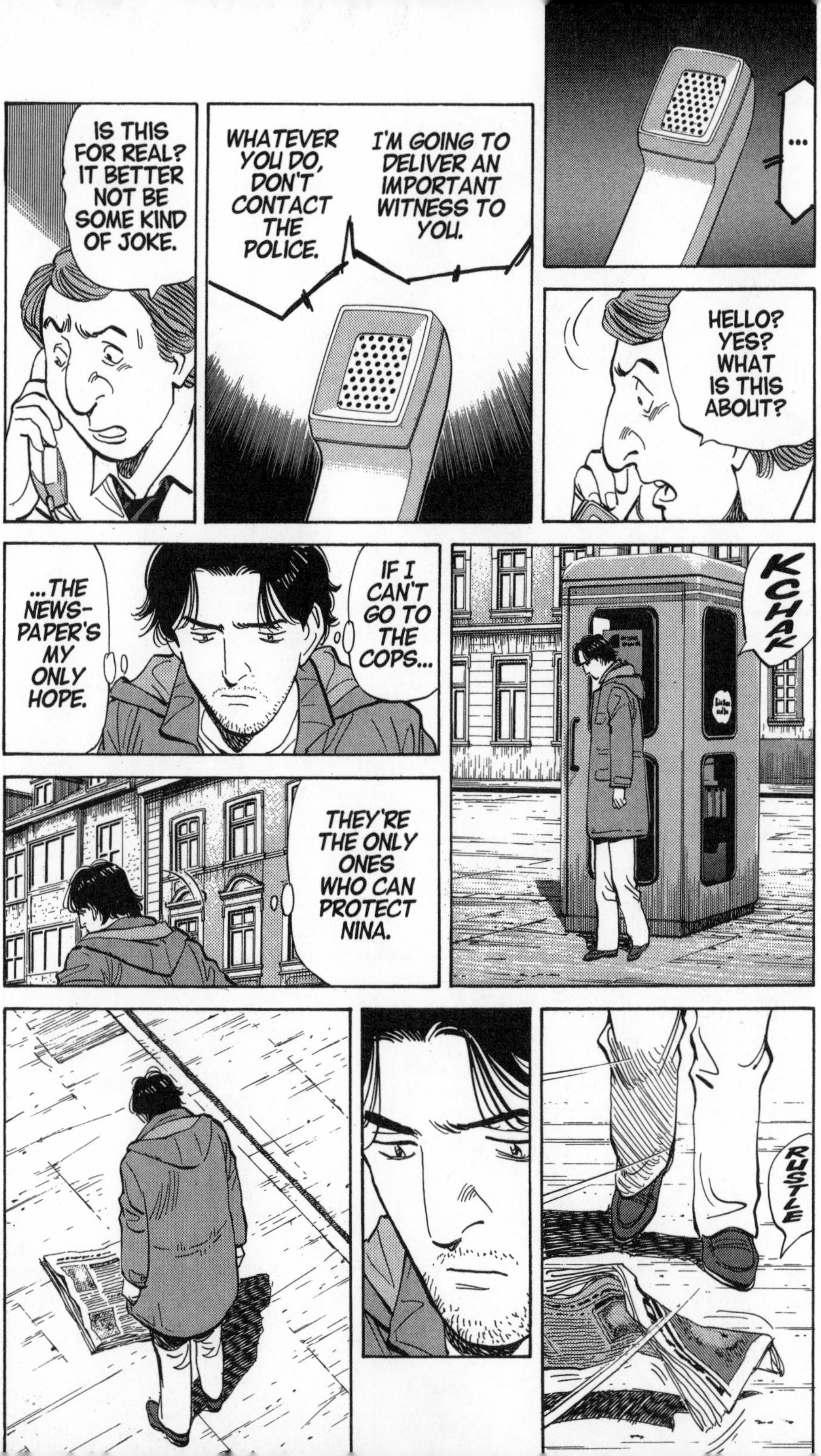
...
HELLO? YES? WHAT IS THIS ABOUT?
I'M GOING TO DELIVER AN IMPORTANT WITNESS TO YOU.
WHATEVER YOU DO, DON'T CONTACT THE POLICE.
IS THIS FOR REAL? IT BETTER NOT BE SOME KIND OF JOKE.
KCHAK
IF I CAN'T GO TO THE COPS...
...THE NEWSPAPER'S MY ONLY HOPE.
THEY'RE THE ONLY ONES WHO CAN PROTECT NINA.
RUSTLE

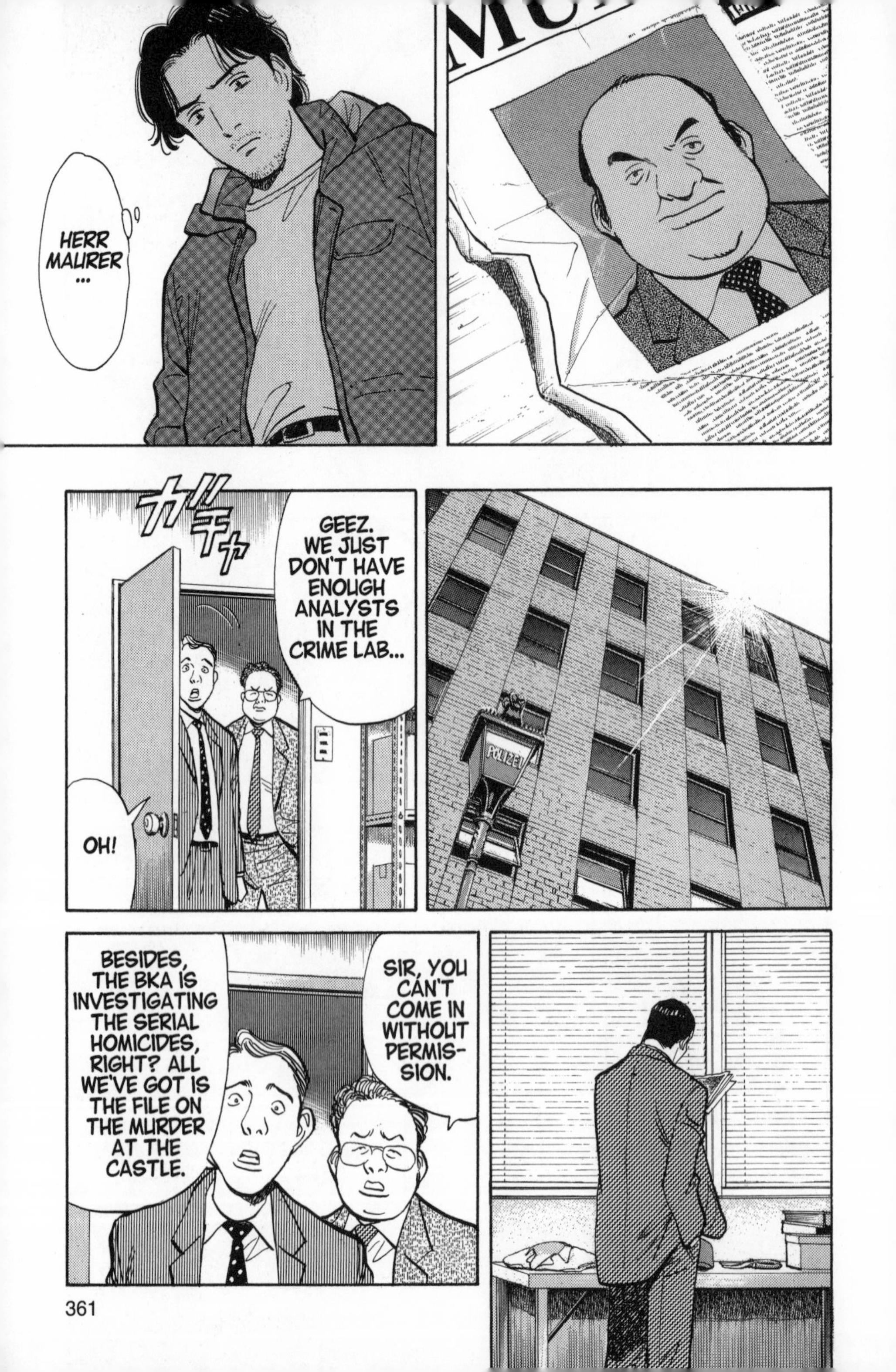
HERR MAURER ...
ガチャ
GEEZ. WE JUST DON'T HAVE ENOUGH ANALYSTS IN THE CRIME LAB...
OH!
POLIZEI
SIR, YOU CAN'T COME IN WITHOUT PERMISSION.
BESIDES, THE BKA IS INVESTIGATING THE SERIAL HOMICIDES, RIGHT? ALL WE'VE GOT IS THE FILE ON THE MURDER AT THE CASTLE.

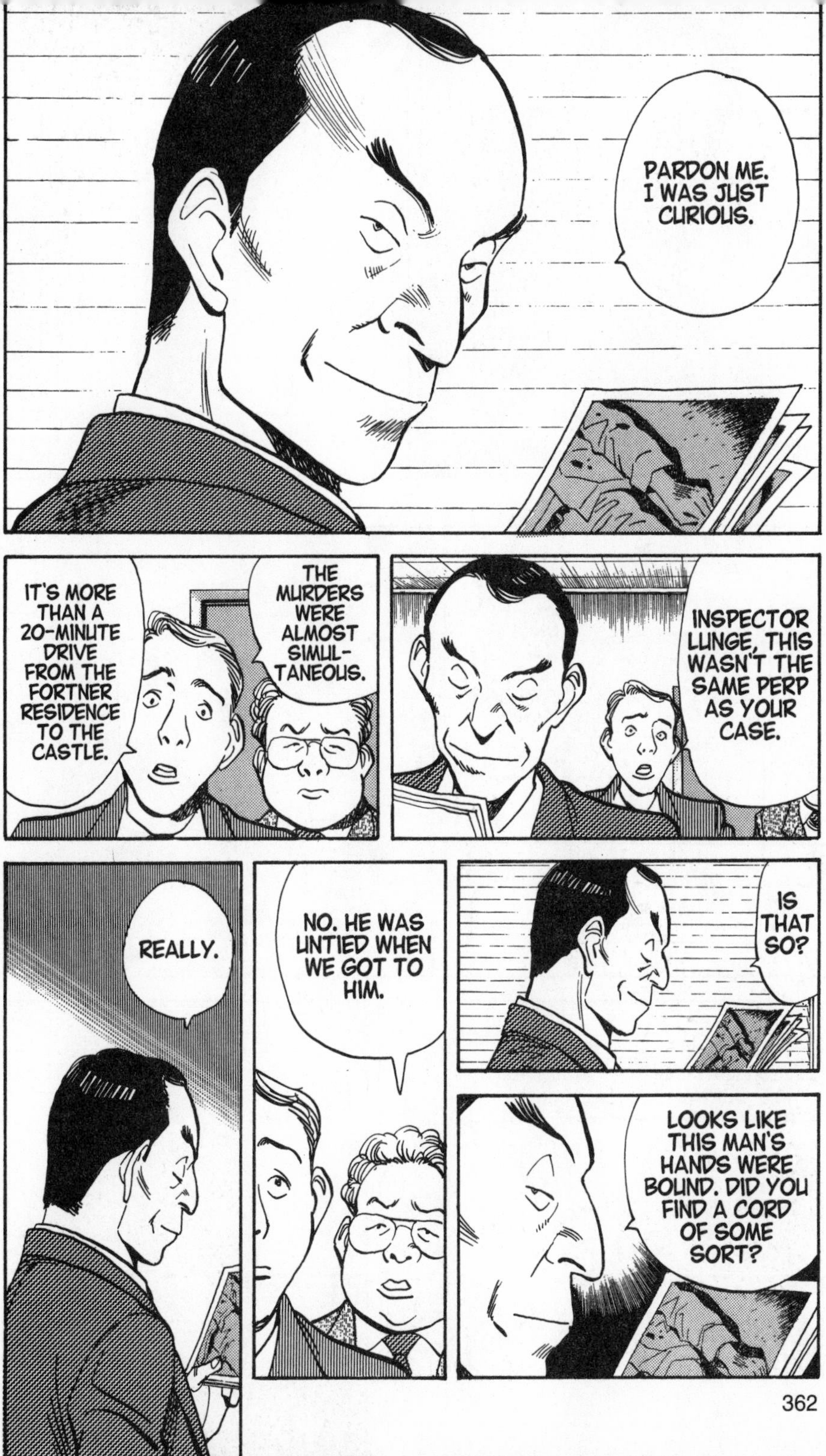
PARDON ME. I WAS JUST CURIOUS.
INSPECTOR LUNGE, THIS WASN'T THE SAME PERP AS YOUR CASE.
THE MURDERS WERE ALMOST SIMUL-TANEOUS.
IT'S MORE THAN A 20-MINUTE DRIVE FROM THE FORTNER RESIDENCE TO THE CASTLE.
IS THAT SO?
LOOKS LIKE THIS MAN'S HANDS WERE BOUND. DID YOU FIND A CORD OF SOME SORT?
NO. HE WAS UNTIED WHEN WE GOT TO HIM.
REALLY.

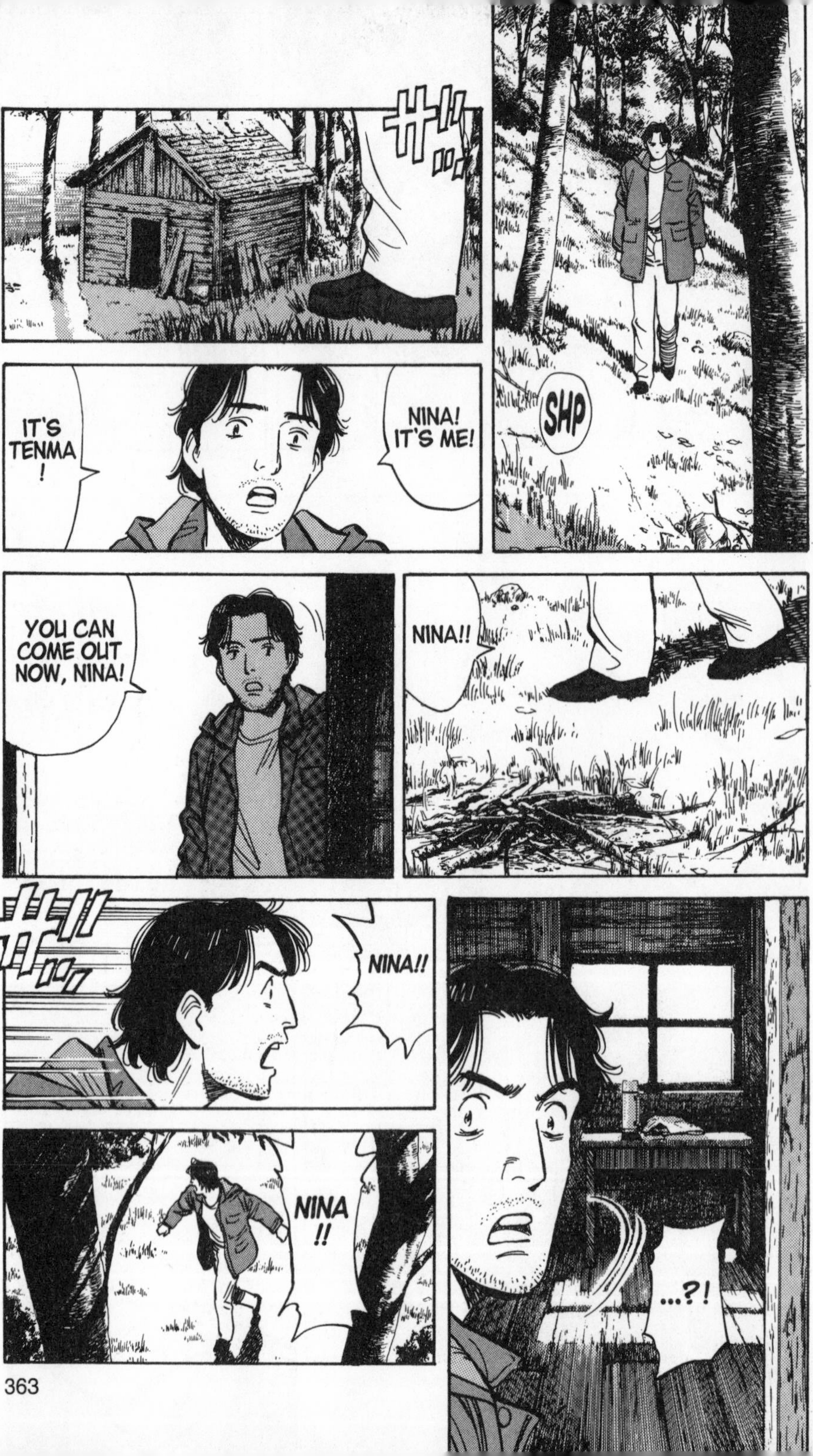
SHP
NINA! IT'S ME!
IT'S TENMA!
NINA!!
YOU CAN COME OUT NOW, NINA!
...?!
NINA!!
NINA !!

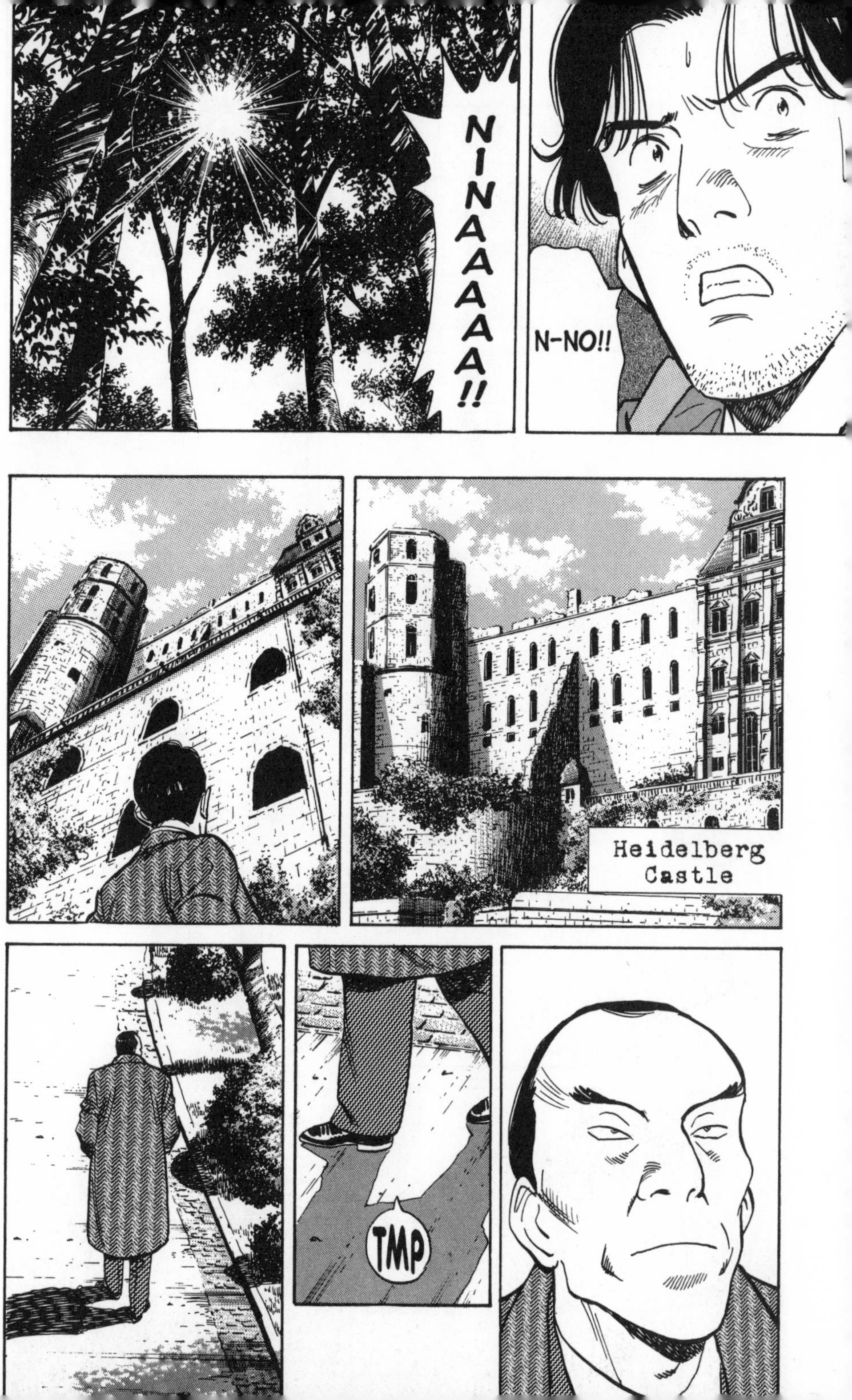
N-NO!!
NINAAAAA!!
Heidelberg Castle
TMP

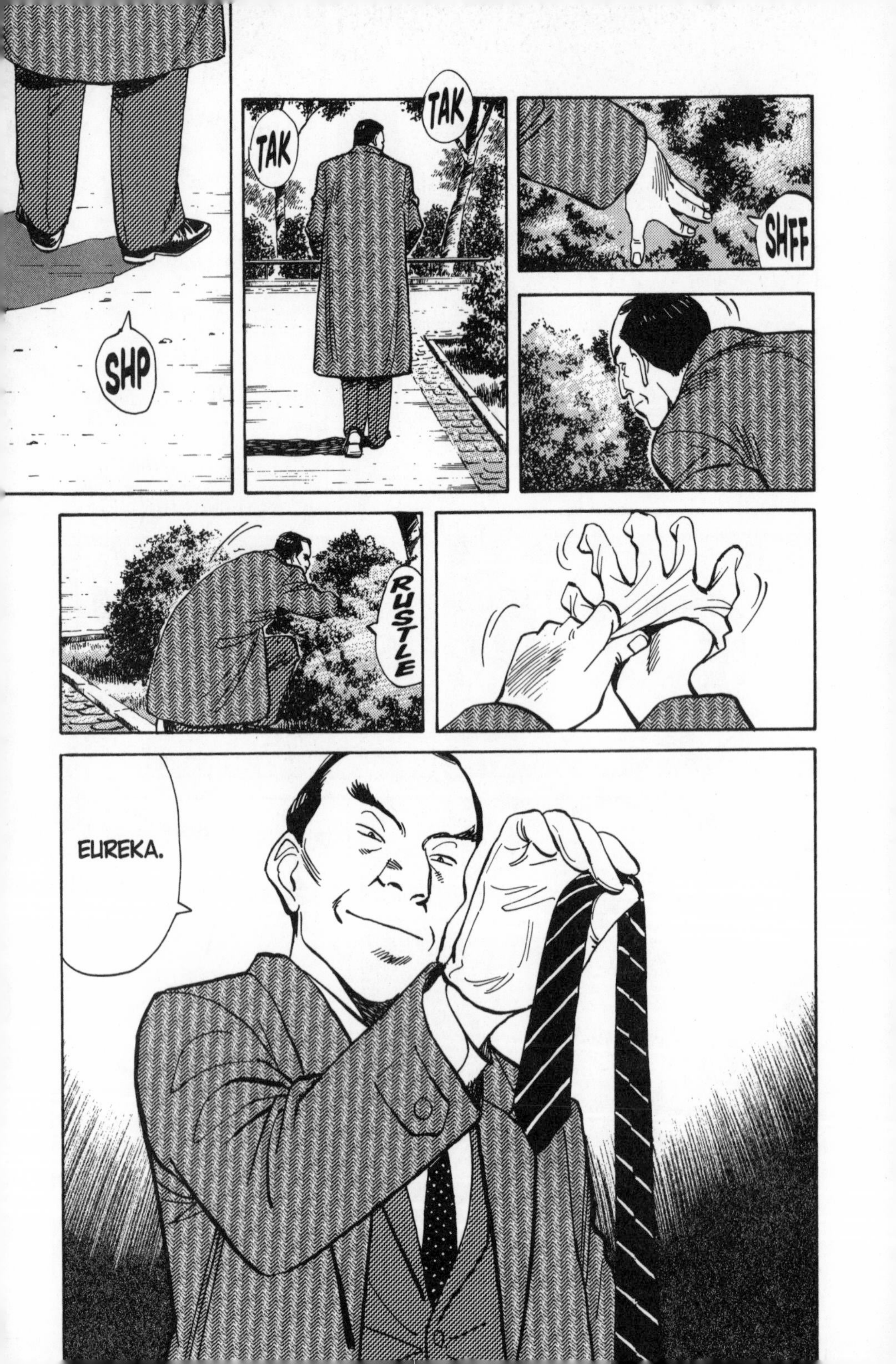
SHFF
TAK
TAK
SHP
RUSTLE
EUREKA.

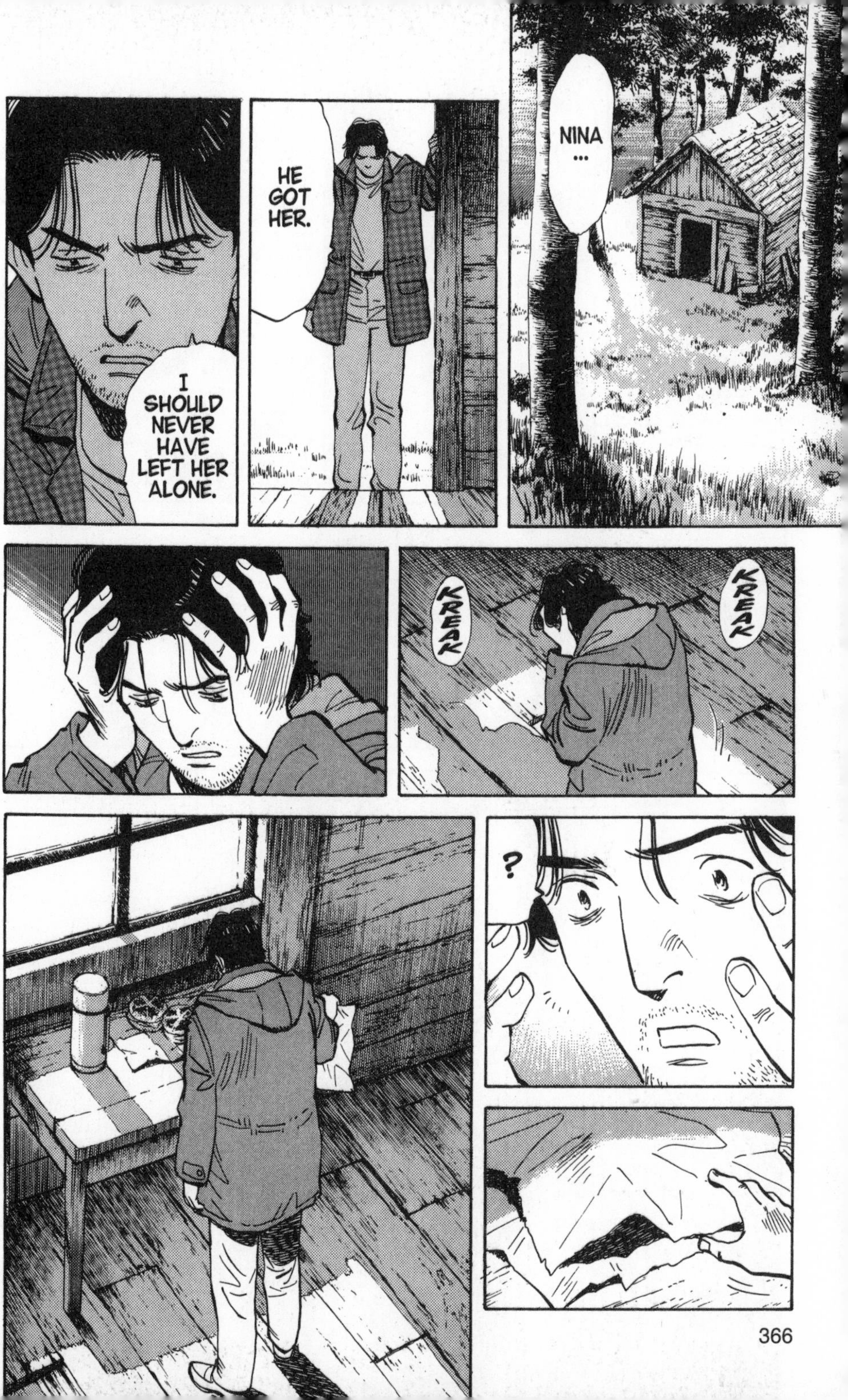
NINA ...
HE GOT HER.
I SHOULD NEVER HAVE LEFT HER ALONE.
KREAK
KREAK
?

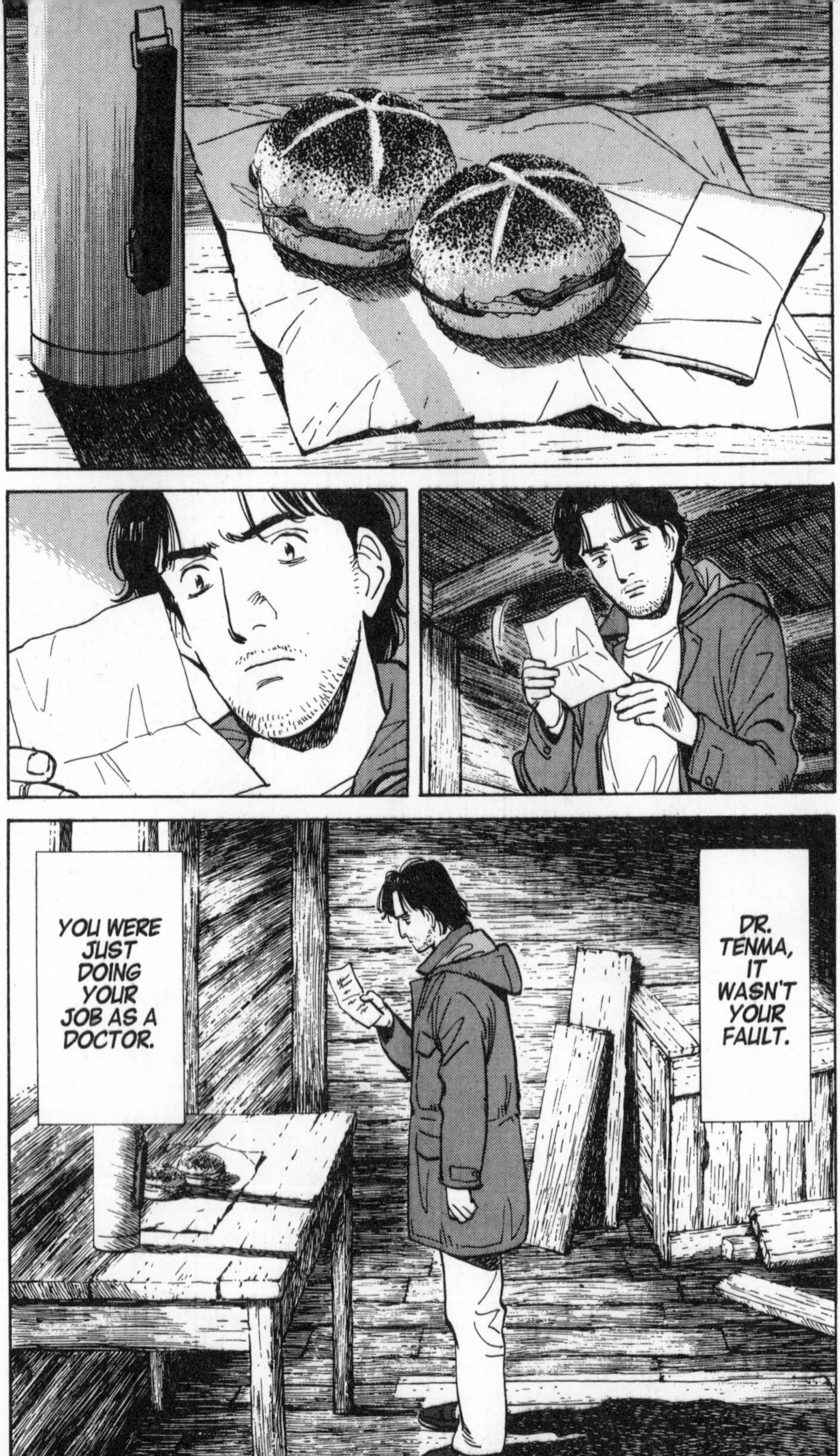
DR. TENMA, IT WASN'T YOUR FAULT.
YOU WERE JUST DOING YOUR JOB AS A DOCTOR.

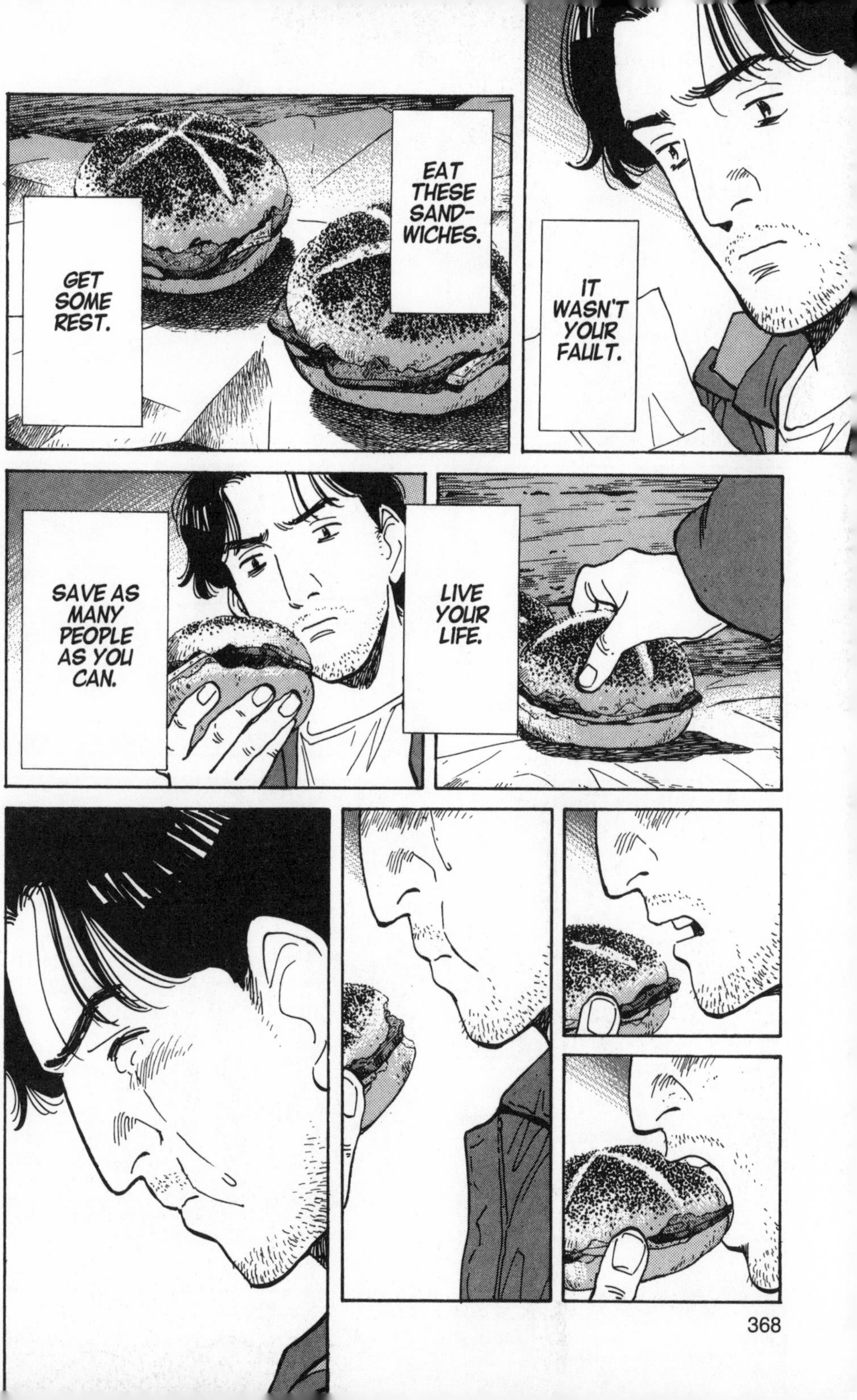
IT WASN'T YOUR FAULT.
EAT THESE SAND-WICHES.
GET SOME REST.
LIVE YOUR LIFE.
SAVE AS MANY PEOPLE AS YOU CAN.

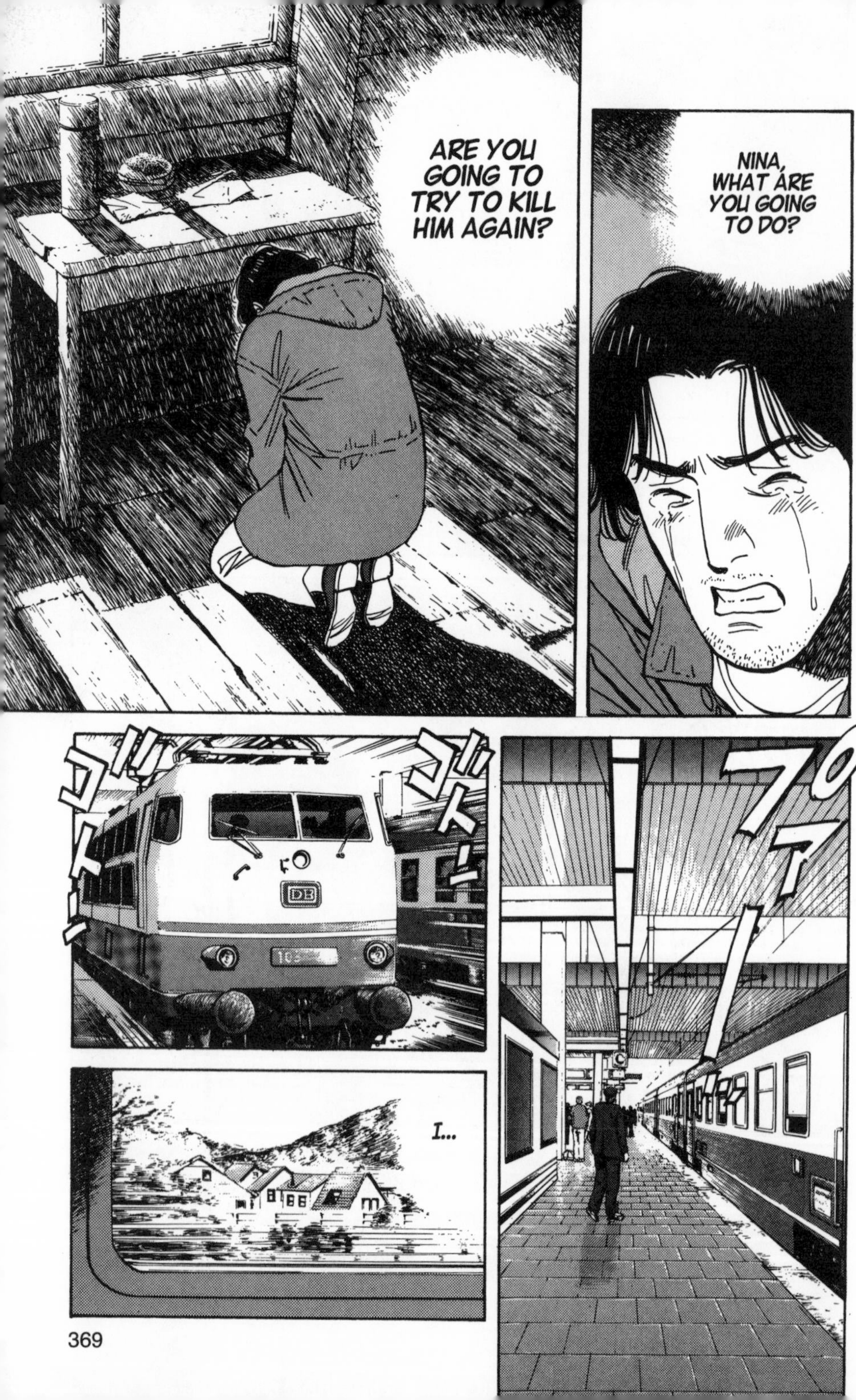
NINA, WHAT ARE YOU GOING TO DO?
ARE YOU GOING TO TRY TO KILL HIM AGAIN?
I...

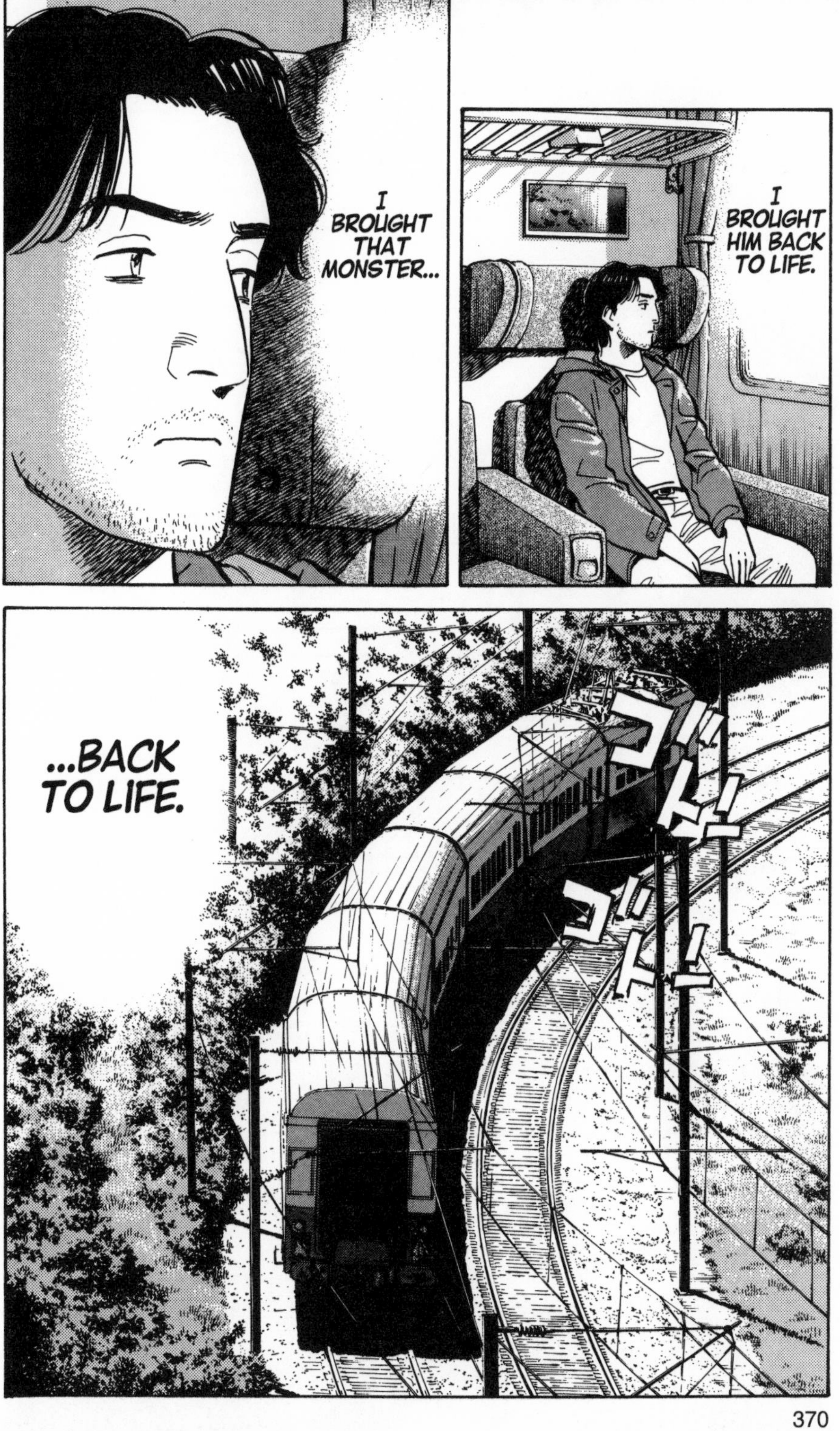
I BROUGHT HIM BACK TO LIFE.
I BROUGHT THAT MONSTER...
...BACK TO LIFE.

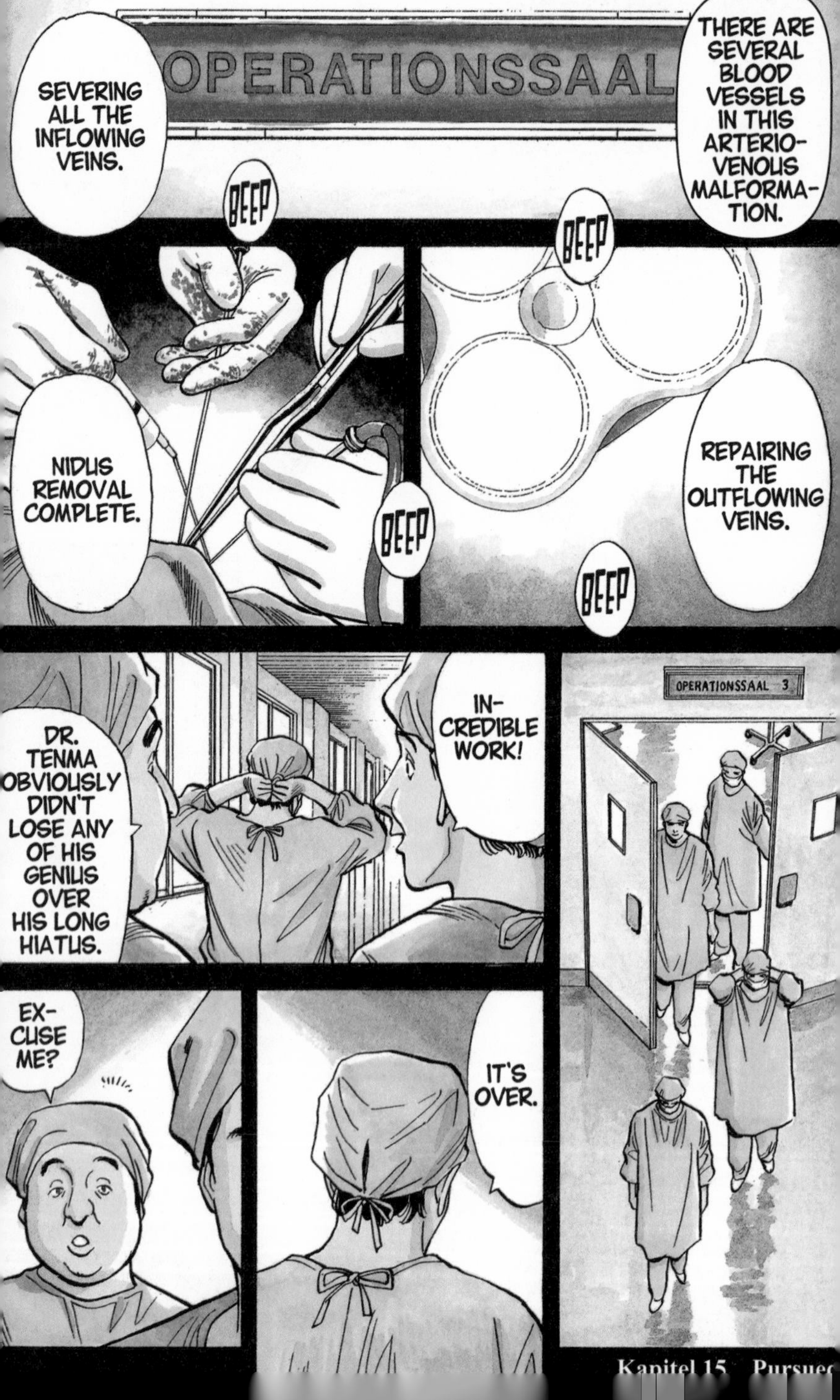
OPERATIONSSAAL
THERE ARE SEVERAL BLOOD VESSELS IN THIS ARTERIO-VENOUS MALFORMA-TION.
SEVERING ALL THE INFLOWING VEINS.
BEEP
BEEP
REPAIRING THE OUTFLOWING VEINS.
BEEP
BEEP
NIDUS REMOVAL COMPLETE.
OPERATIONSSAAL 3
IN-CREDIBLE WORK!
DR. TENMA OBVIOUSLY DIDN'T LOSE ANY OF HIS GENIUS OVER HIS LONG HIATUS.
IT'S OVER.
EX-CUSE ME?

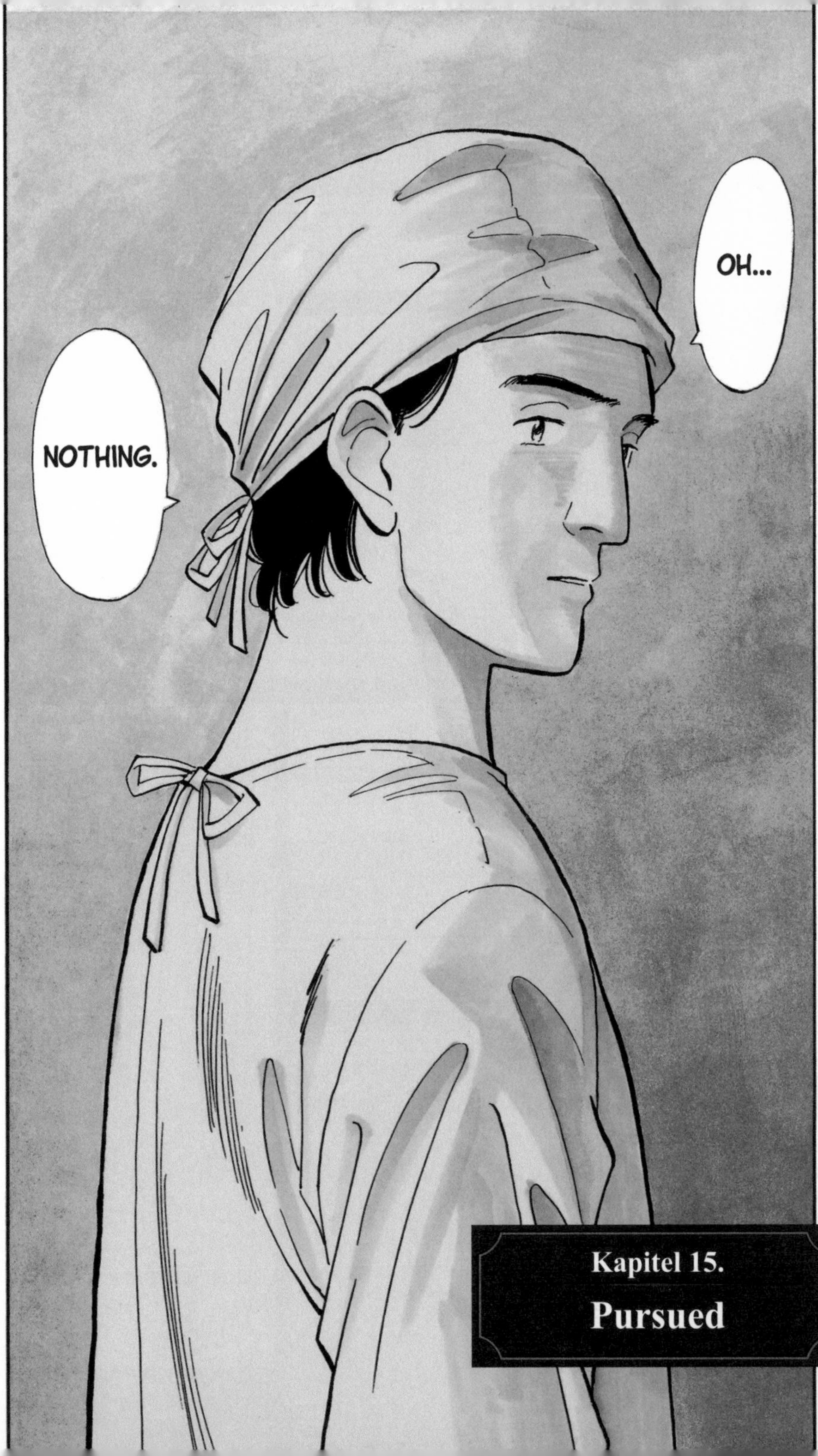
OH...
NOTHING.

Kapitel 15.
Pursued

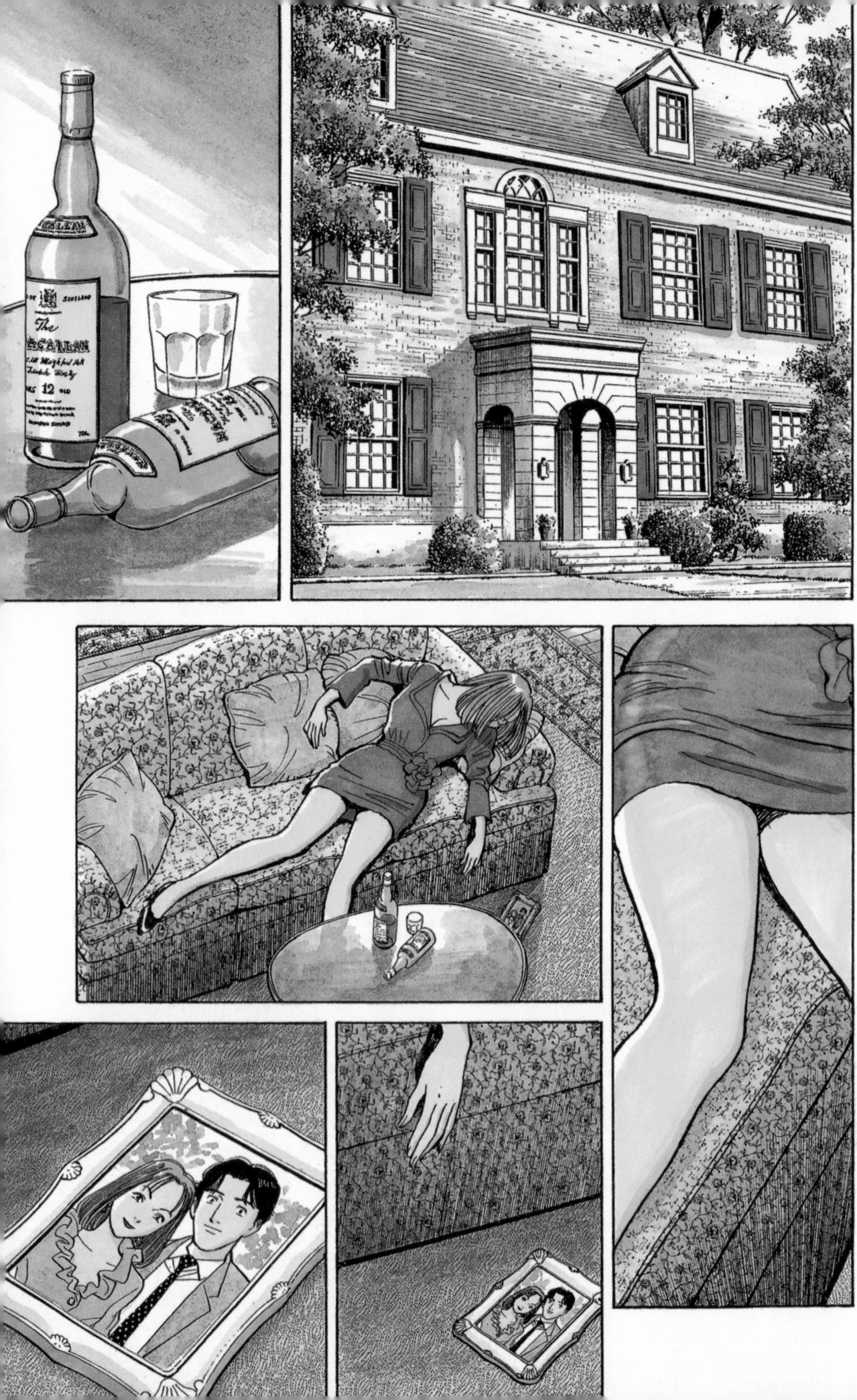

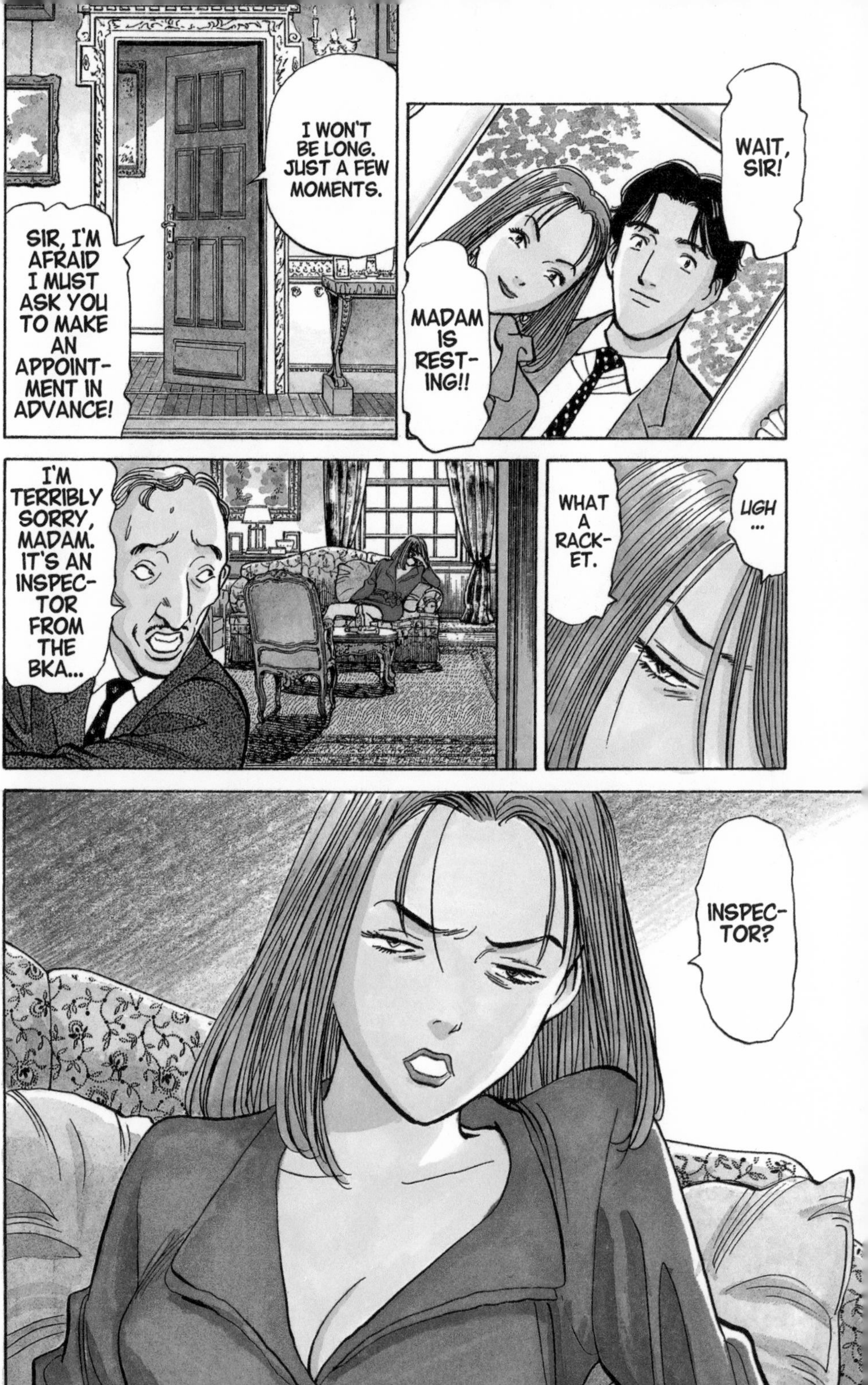
WAIT, SIR!
MADAM IS RESTING!!
I WON'T BE LONG. JUST A FEW MOMENTS.
SIR, I'M AFRAID I MUST ASK YOU TO MAKE AN APPOINTMENT IN ADVANCE!
UGH...
WHAT A RACKET.
I'M TERRIBLY SORRY, MADAM. IT'S AN INSPECTOR FROM THE BKA...
INSPECTOR?

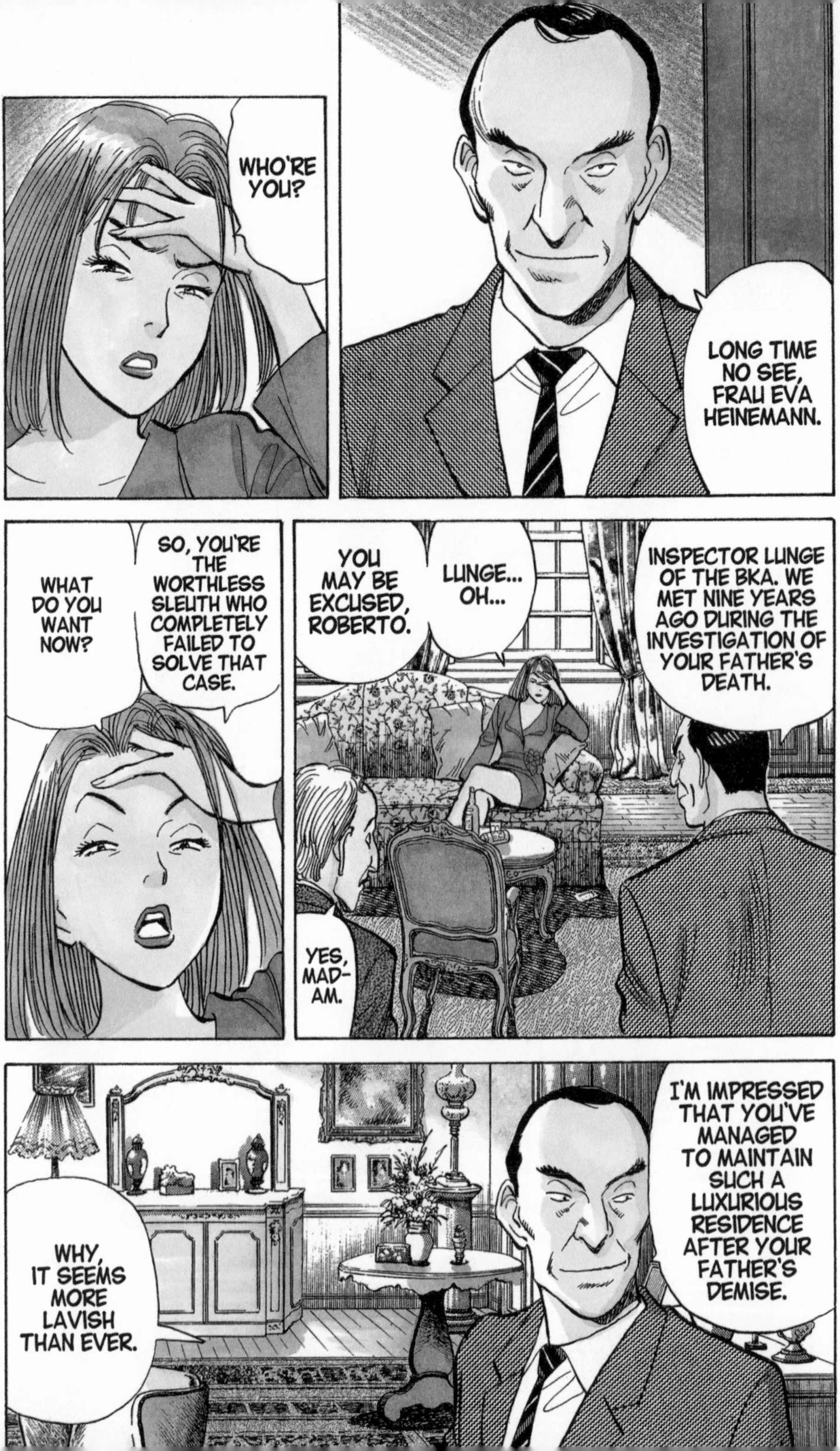
LONG TIME NO SEE, FRAU EVA HEINEMANN.
WHO'RE YOU?
INSPECTOR LUNGE OF THE BKA. WE MET NINE YEARS AGO DURING THE INVESTIGATION OF YOUR FATHER'S DEATH.
LUNGE... OH...
YOU MAY BE EXCUSED, ROBERTO.
YES, MAD-AM.
SO, YOU'RE THE WORTHLESS SLEUTH WHO COMPLETELY FAILED TO SOLVE THAT CASE.
WHAT DO YOU WANT NOW?
I'M IMPRESSED THAT YOU'VE MANAGED TO MAINTAIN SUCH A LUXURIOUS RESIDENCE AFTER YOUR FATHER'S DEMISE.
WHY, IT SEEMS MORE LAVISH THAN EVER.

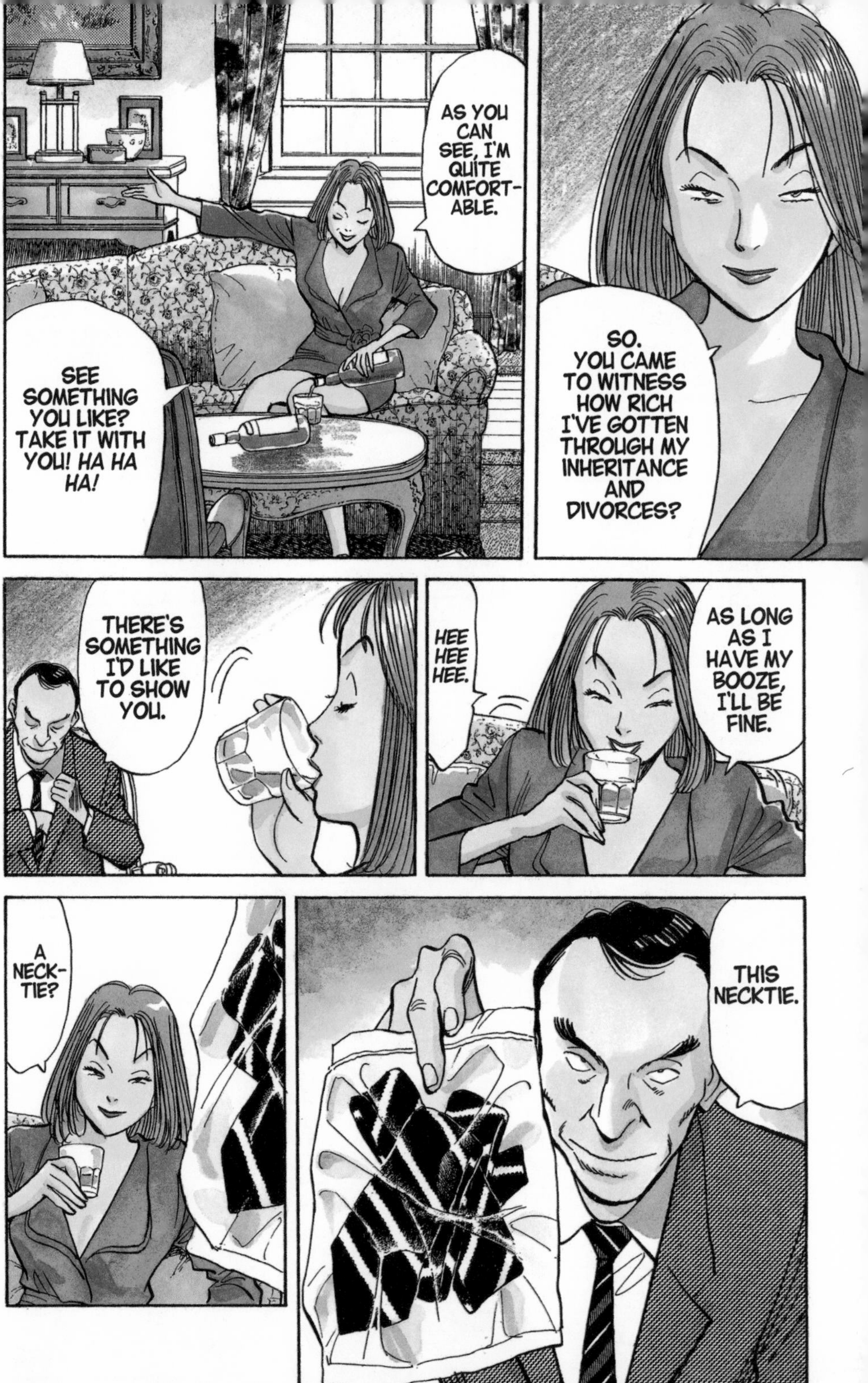
SO. YOU CAME TO WITNESS HOW RICH I'VE GOTTEN THROUGH MY INHERITANCE AND DIVORCES?
AS YOU CAN SEE, I'M QUITE COMFORTABLE.
SEE SOMETHING YOU LIKE? TAKE IT WITH YOU! HA HA HA!
AS LONG AS I HAVE MY BOOZE, I'LL BE FINE.
HEE HEE HEE.
THERE'S SOMETHING I'D LIKE TO SHOW YOU.
THIS NECKTIE.
A NECKTIE?

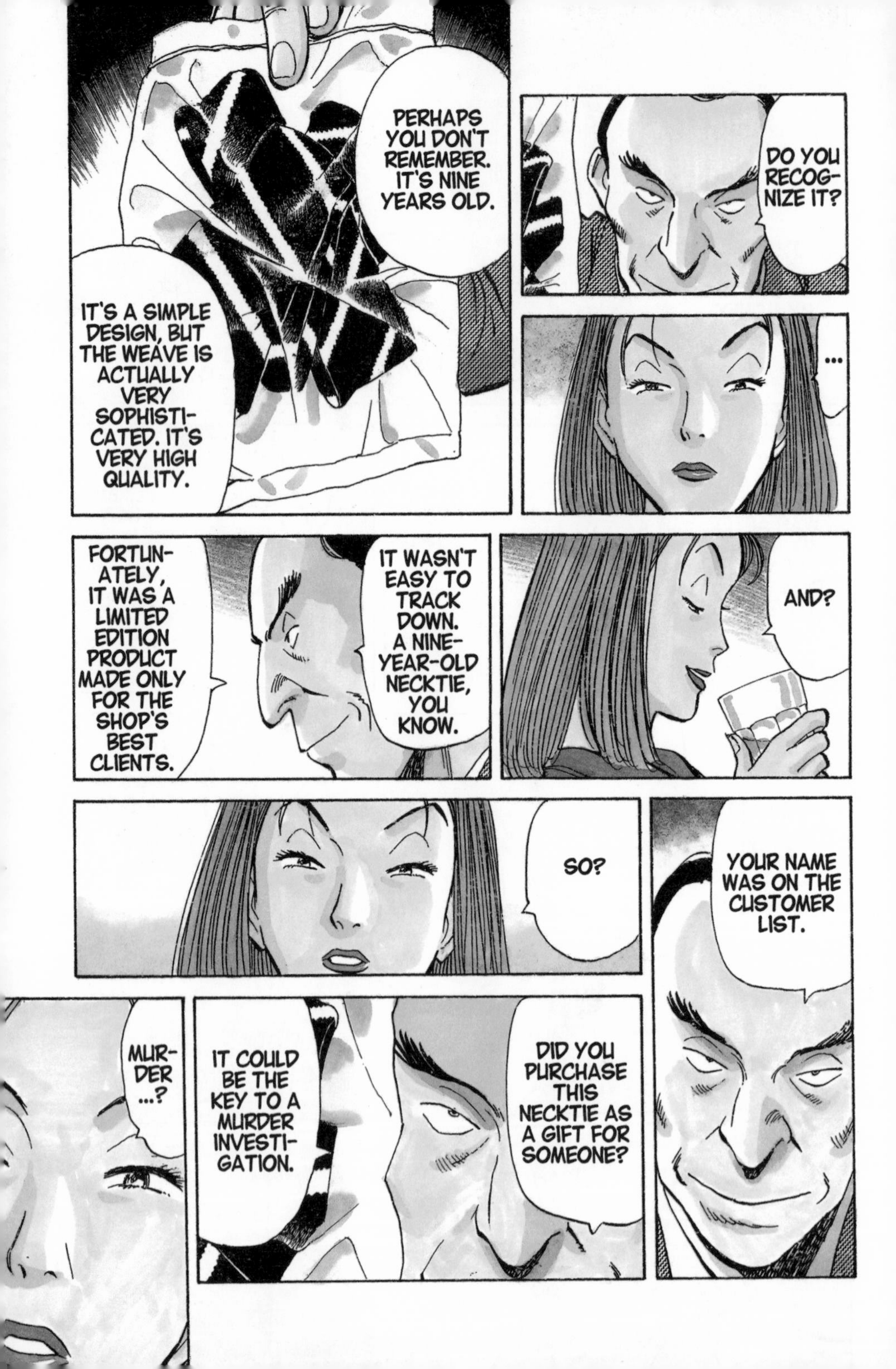
DO YOU RECOGNIZE IT?
...
PERHAPS YOU DON'T REMEMBER. IT'S NINE YEARS OLD.
IT'S A SIMPLE DESIGN, BUT THE WEAVE IS ACTUALLY VERY SOPHISTICATED. IT'S VERY HIGH QUALITY.
AND?
IT WASN'T EASY TO TRACK DOWN. A NINE-YEAR-OLD NECKTIE, YOU KNOW.
FORTUNATELY, IT WAS A LIMITED EDITION PRODUCT MADE ONLY FOR THE SHOP'S BEST CLIENTS.
YOUR NAME WAS ON THE CUSTOMER LIST.
SO?
DID YOU PURCHASE THIS NECKTIE AS A GIFT FOR SOMEONE?
IT COULD BE THE KEY TO A MURDER INVESTIGATION.
MURDER ...?

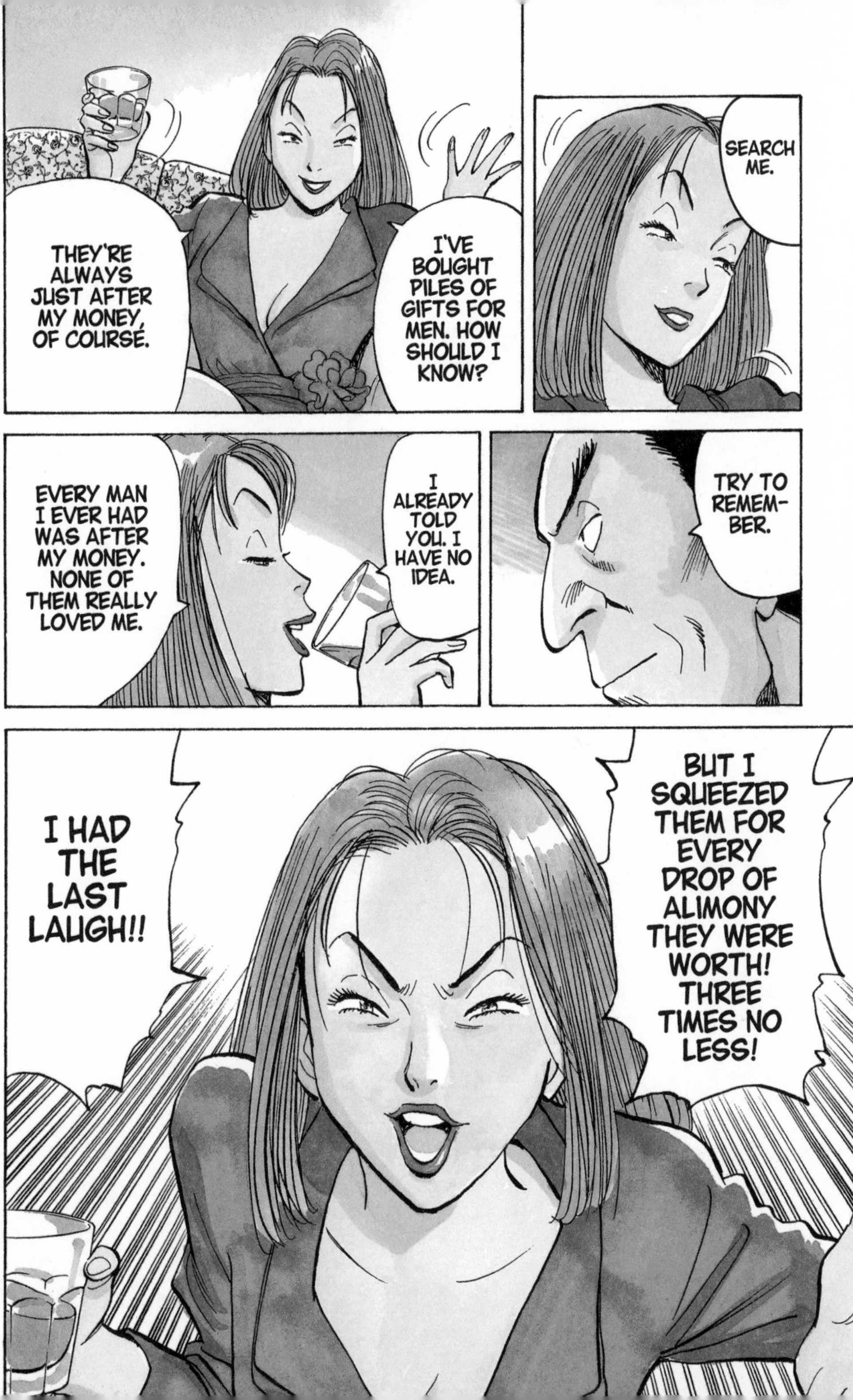
SEARCH ME.
I'VE BOUGHT PILES OF GIFTS FOR MEN. HOW SHOULD I KNOW?
THEY'RE ALWAYS JUST AFTER MY MONEY, OF COURSE.
TRY TO REMEMBER.
I ALREADY TOLD YOU. I HAVE NO IDEA.
EVERY MAN I EVER HAD WAS AFTER MY MONEY. NONE OF THEM REALLY LOVED ME.
BUT I SQUEEZED THEM FOR EVERY DROP OF ALIMONY THEY WERE WORTH! THREE TIMES NO LESS!
I HAD THE LAST LAUGH!!

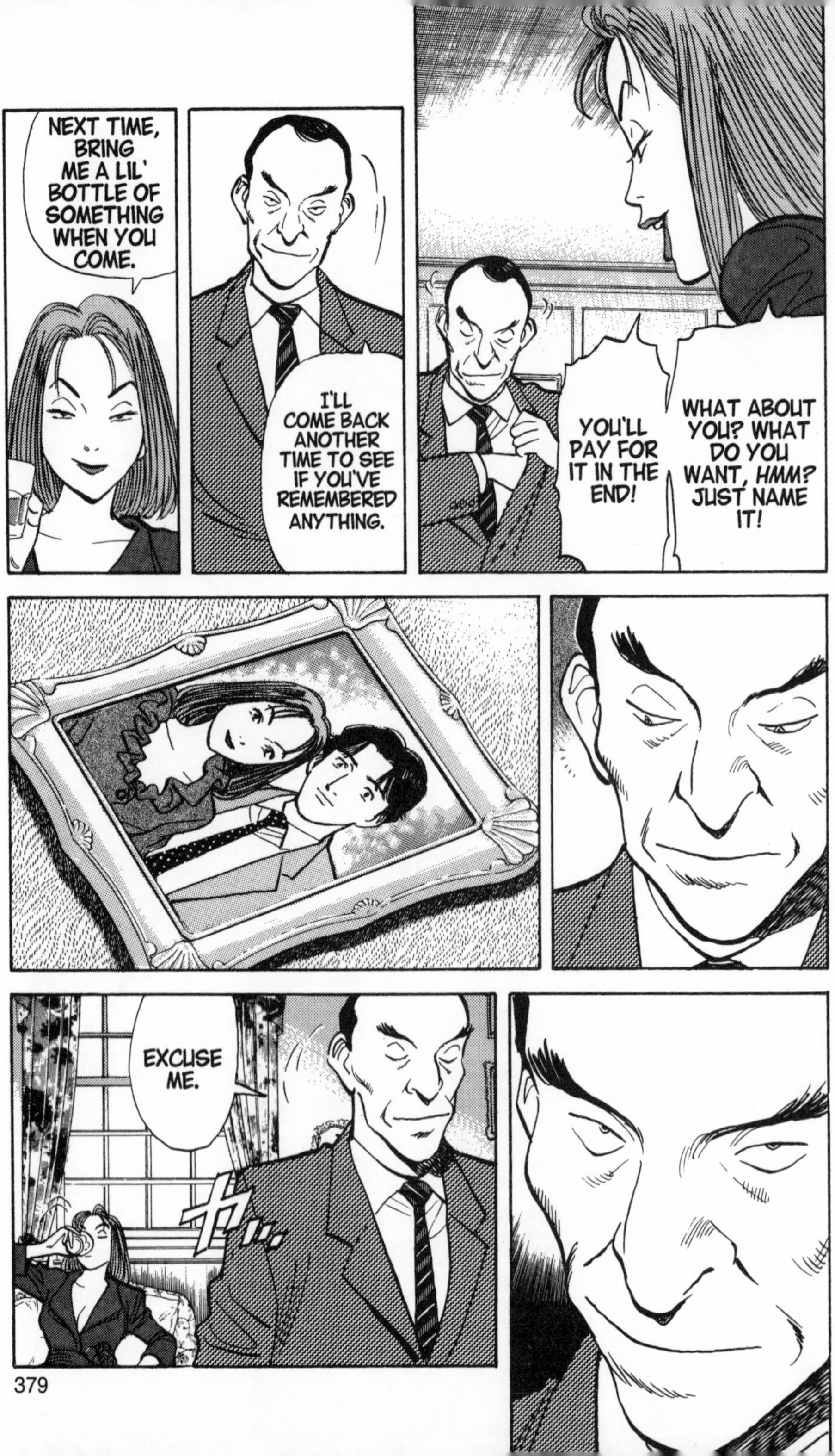
WHAT ABOUT YOU? WHAT DO YOU WANT, *HMM?* JUST NAME IT!
YOU'LL PAY FOR IT IN THE END!
I'LL COME BACK ANOTHER TIME TO SEE IF YOU'VE REMEMBERED ANYTHING.
NEXT TIME, BRING ME A LIL' BOTTLE OF SOMETHING WHEN YOU COME.
EXCUSE ME.

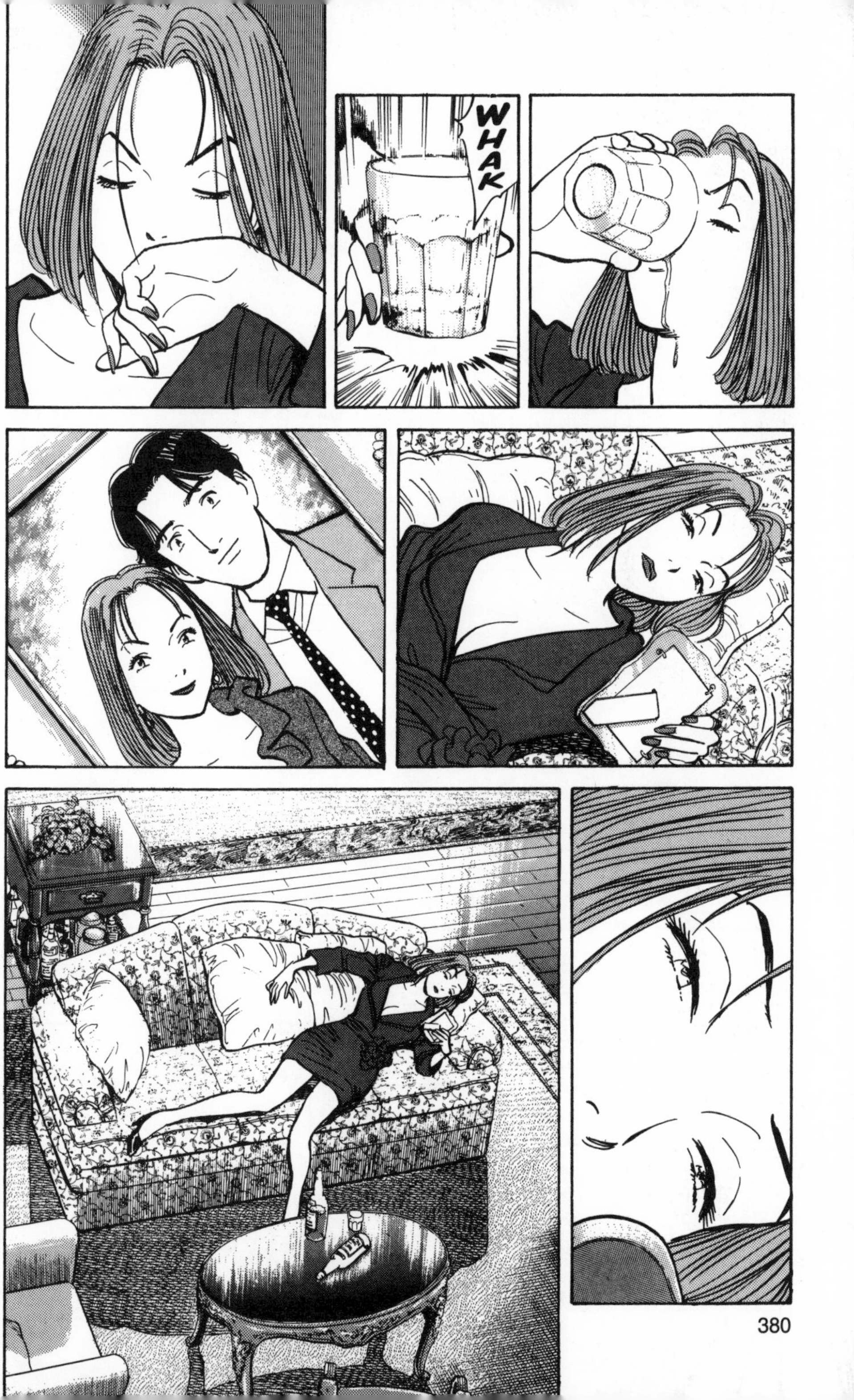
WHAK

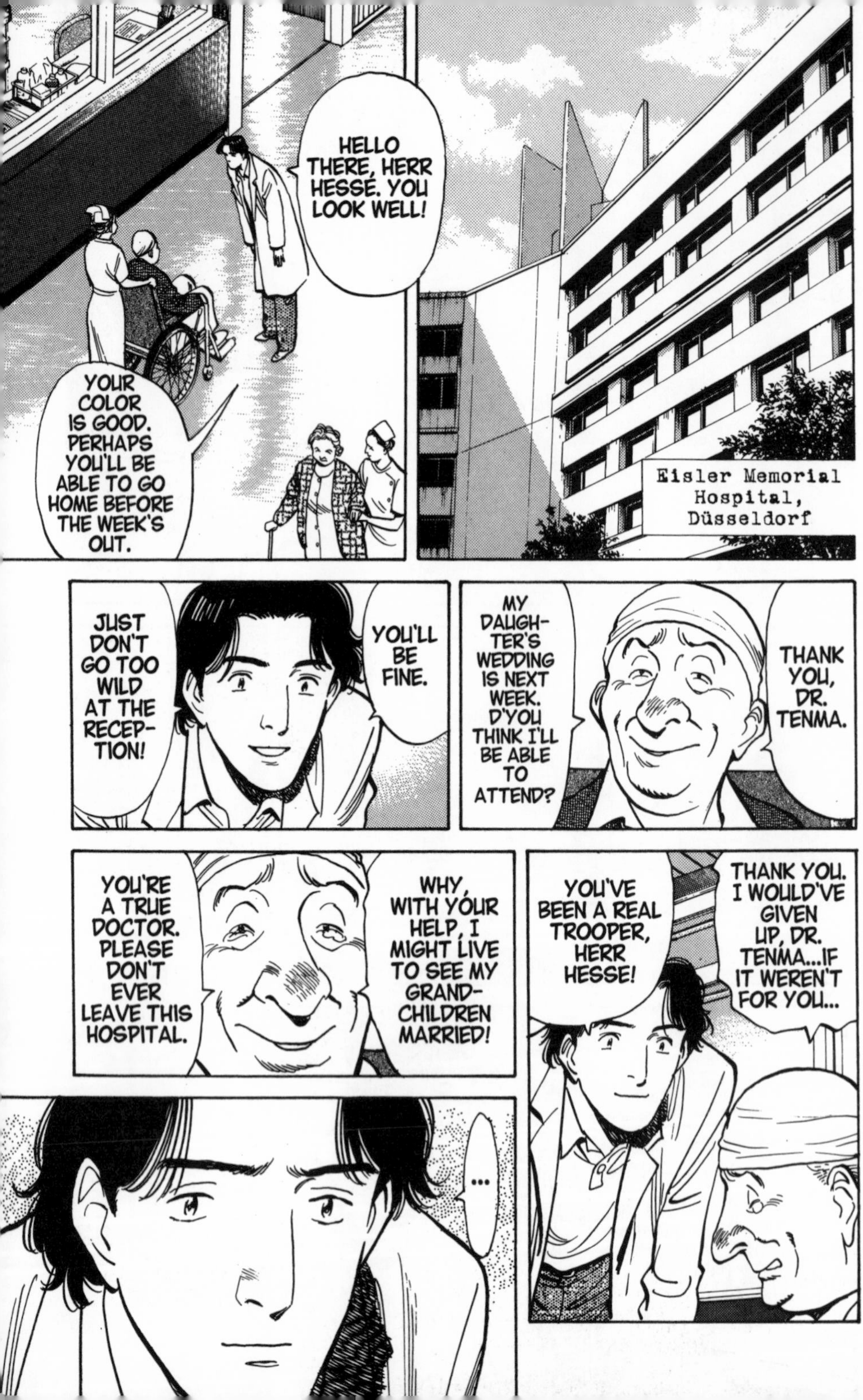
Eisler Memorial Hospital, Düsseldorf
HELLO THERE, HERR HESSE. YOU LOOK WELL!
YOUR COLOR IS GOOD. PERHAPS YOU'LL BE ABLE TO GO HOME BEFORE THE WEEK'S OUT.
THANK YOU, DR. TENMA.
MY DAUGHTER'S WEDDING IS NEXT WEEK. D'YOU THINK I'LL BE ABLE TO ATTEND?
YOU'LL BE FINE.
JUST DON'T GO TOO WILD AT THE RECEPTION!
THANK YOU. I WOULD'VE GIVEN UP, DR. TENMA...IF IT WEREN'T FOR YOU...
YOU'VE BEEN A REAL TROOPER, HERR HESSE!
WHY, WITH YOUR HELP, I MIGHT LIVE TO SEE MY GRANDCHILDREN MARRIED!
YOU'RE A TRUE DOCTOR. PLEASE DON'T EVER LEAVE THIS HOSPITAL.
...

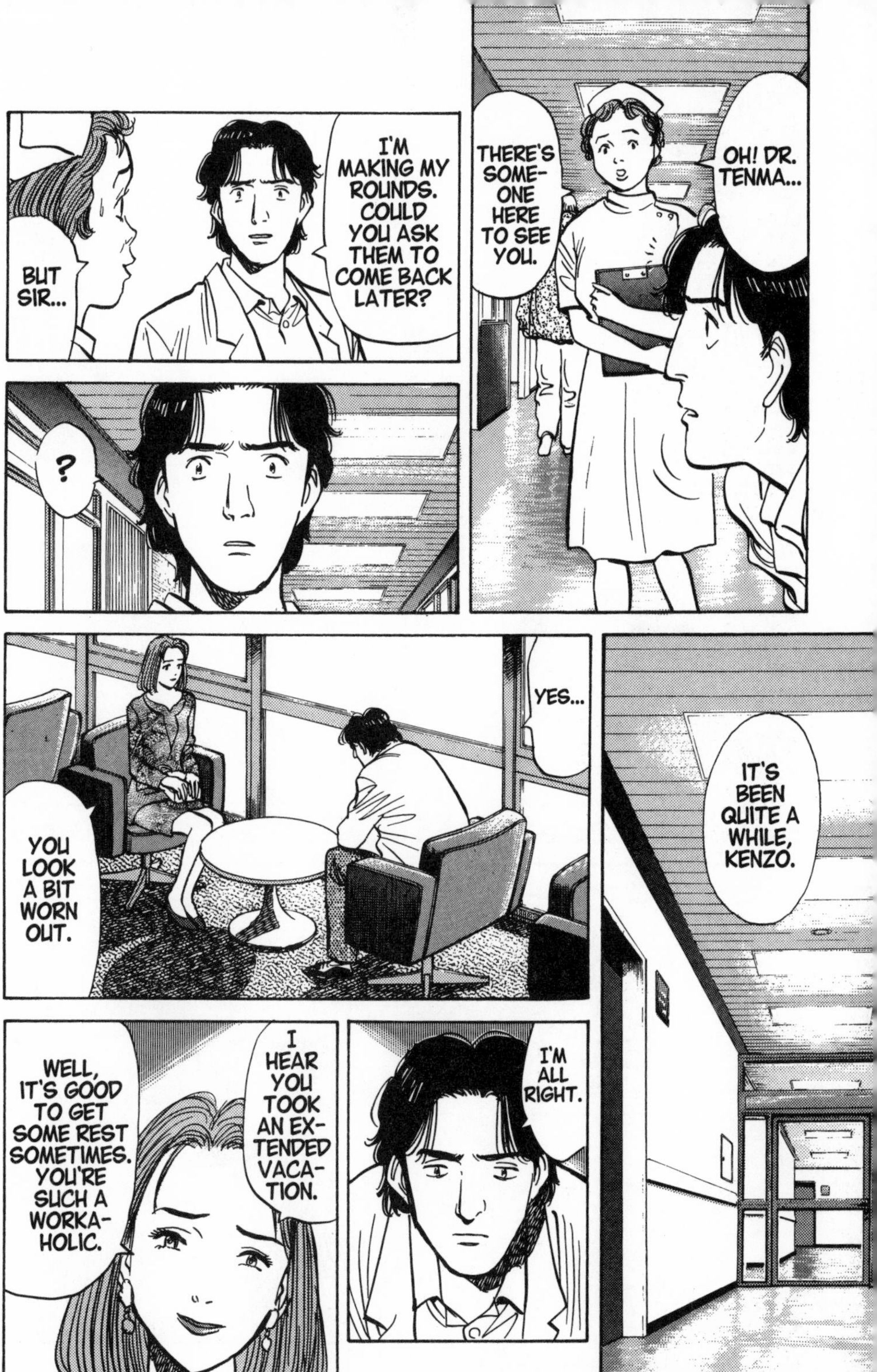
OH! DR. TENMA...
THERE'S SOMEONE HERE TO SEE YOU.
I'M MAKING MY ROUNDS. COULD YOU ASK THEM TO COME BACK LATER?
BUT SIR...
?
IT'S BEEN QUITE A WHILE, KENZO.
YES...
YOU LOOK A BIT WORN OUT.
I'M ALL RIGHT.
I HEAR YOU TOOK AN EXTENDED VACATION.
WELL, IT'S GOOD TO GET SOME REST SOMETIMES. YOU'RE SUCH A WORKAHOLIC.

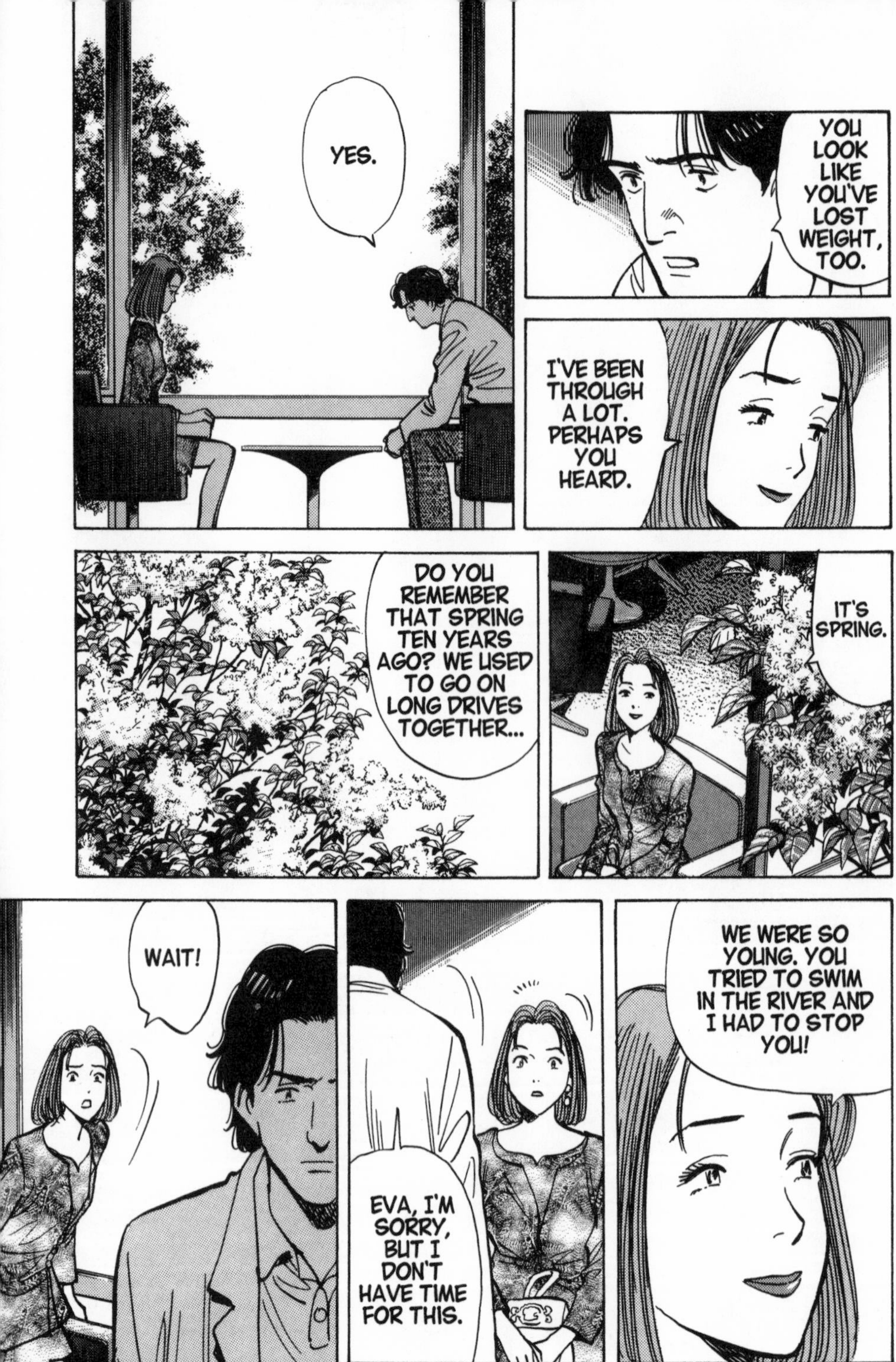
YOU LOOK LIKE YOU'VE LOST WEIGHT, TOO.
I'VE BEEN THROUGH A LOT. PERHAPS YOU HEARD.
YES.
IT'S SPRING.
DO YOU REMEMBER THAT SPRING TEN YEARS AGO? WE USED TO GO ON LONG DRIVES TOGETHER...
WE WERE SO YOUNG. YOU TRIED TO SWIM IN THE RIVER AND I HAD TO STOP YOU!
EVA, I'M SORRY, BUT I DON'T HAVE TIME FOR THIS.
WAIT!

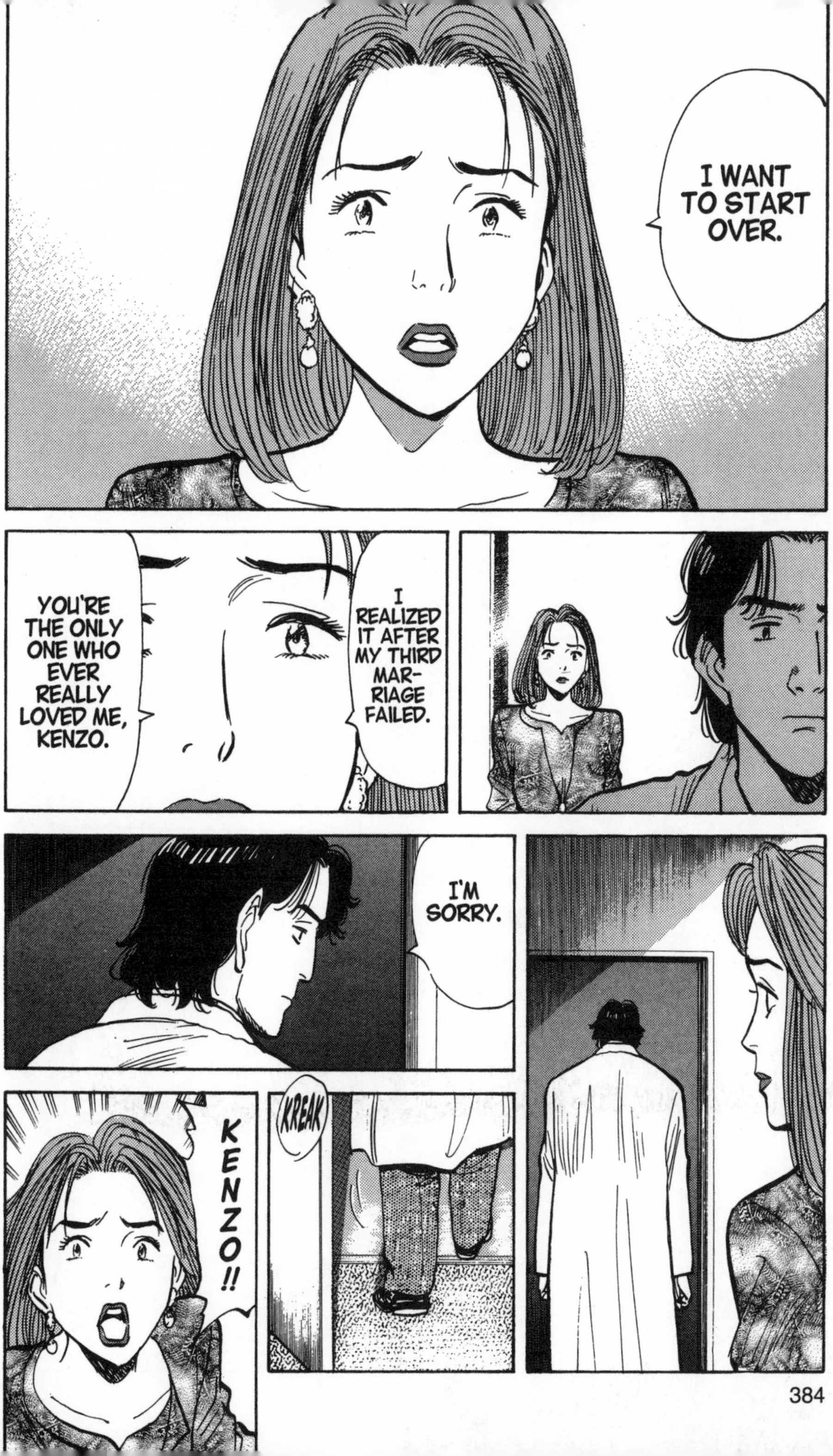
I WANT TO START OVER.
I REALIZED IT AFTER MY THIRD MAR-RIAGE FAILED.
YOU'RE THE ONLY ONE WHO EVER REALLY LOVED ME, KENZO.
I'M SORRY.
KREAK
KENZO!!

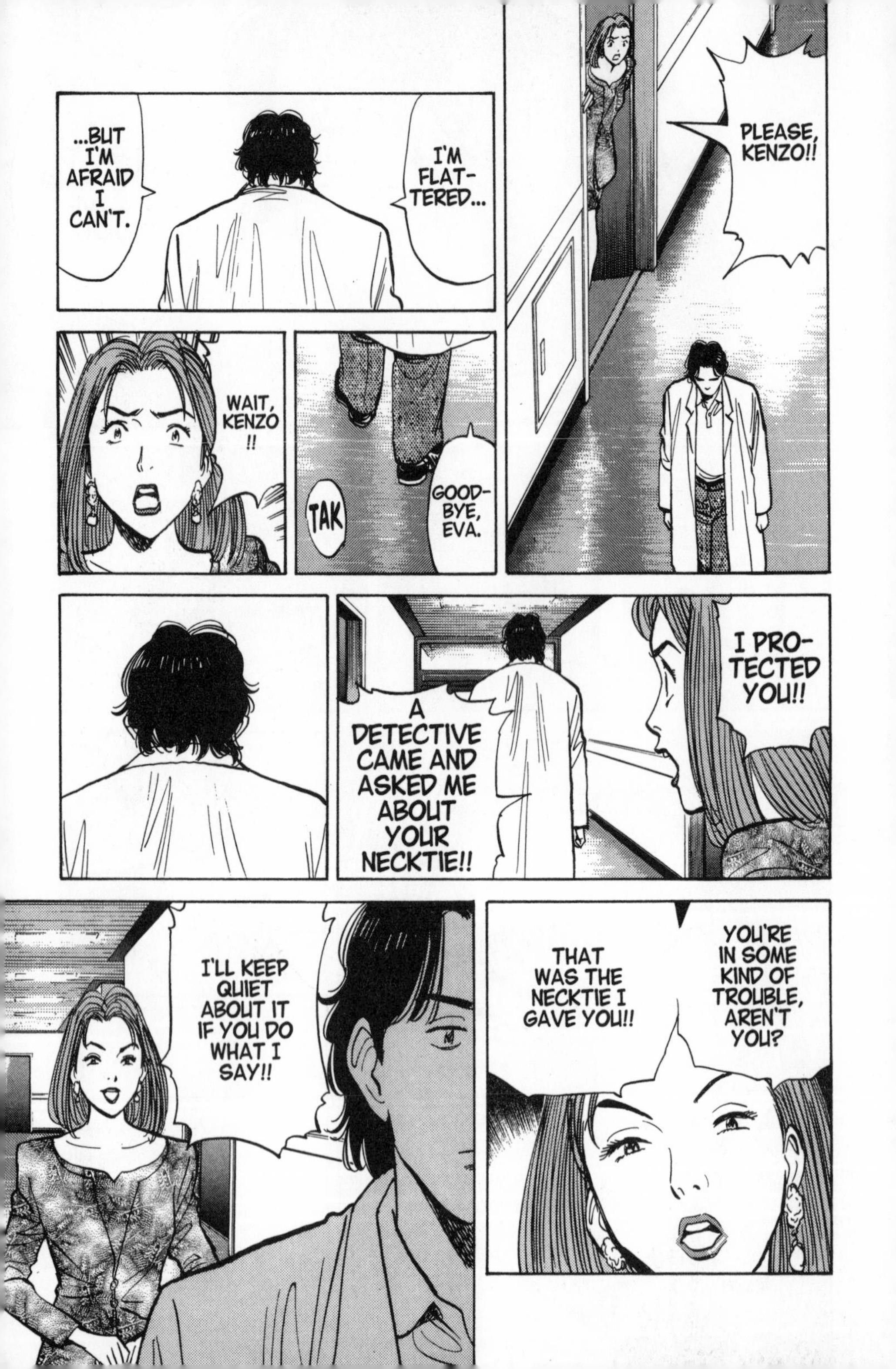
PLEASE, KENZO!!
I'M FLATTERED...
...BUT I'M AFRAID I CAN'T.
GOOD-BYE, EVA.
TAK
WAIT, KENZO!!
I PROTECTED YOU!!
A DETECTIVE CAME AND ASKED ME ABOUT YOUR NECKTIE!!
YOU'RE IN SOME KIND OF TROUBLE, AREN'T YOU?
THAT WAS THE NECKTIE I GAVE YOU!!
I'LL KEEP QUIET ABOUT IT IF YOU DO WHAT I SAY!!

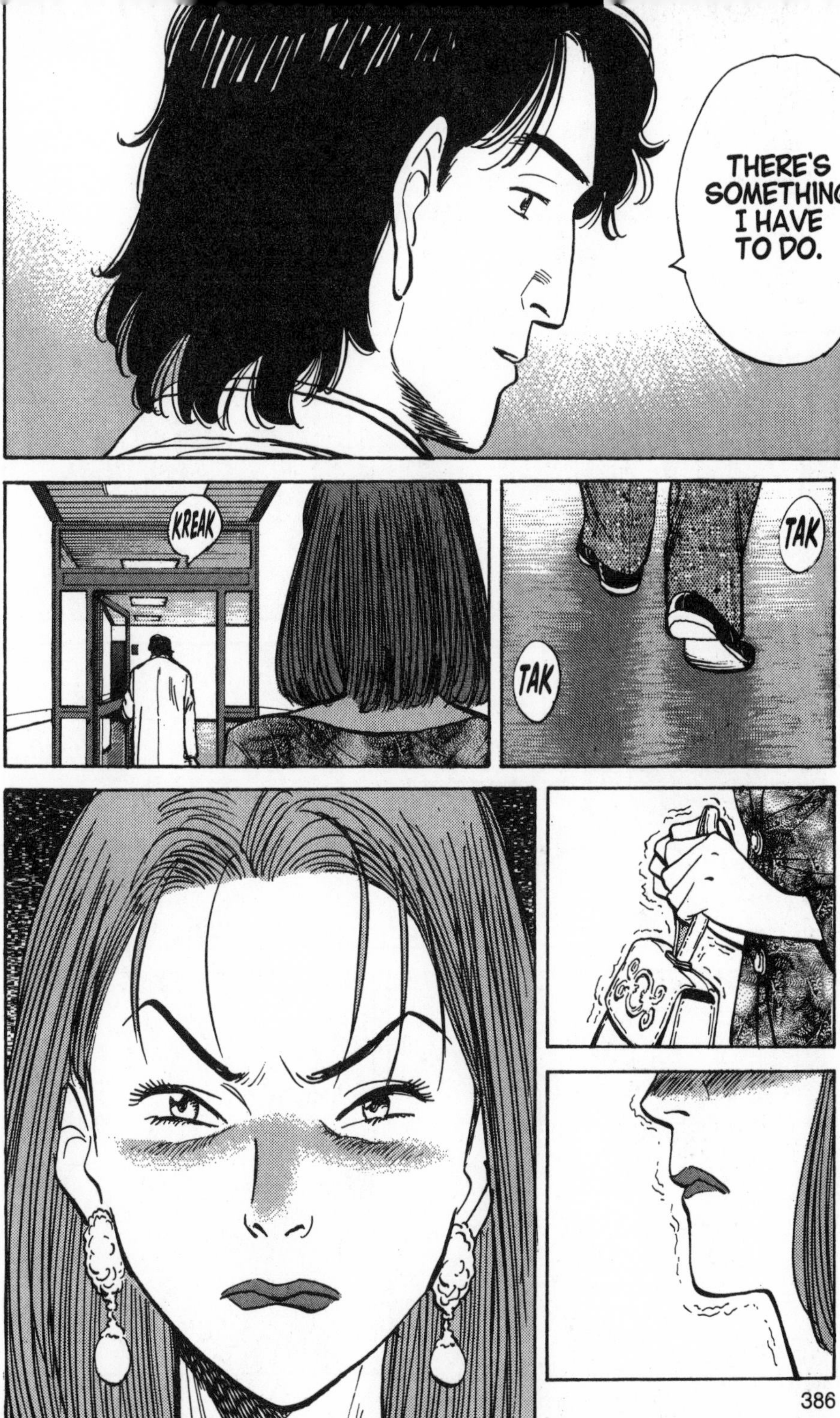
THERE'S SOMETHING I HAVE TO DO.
TAK
TAK
KREAK

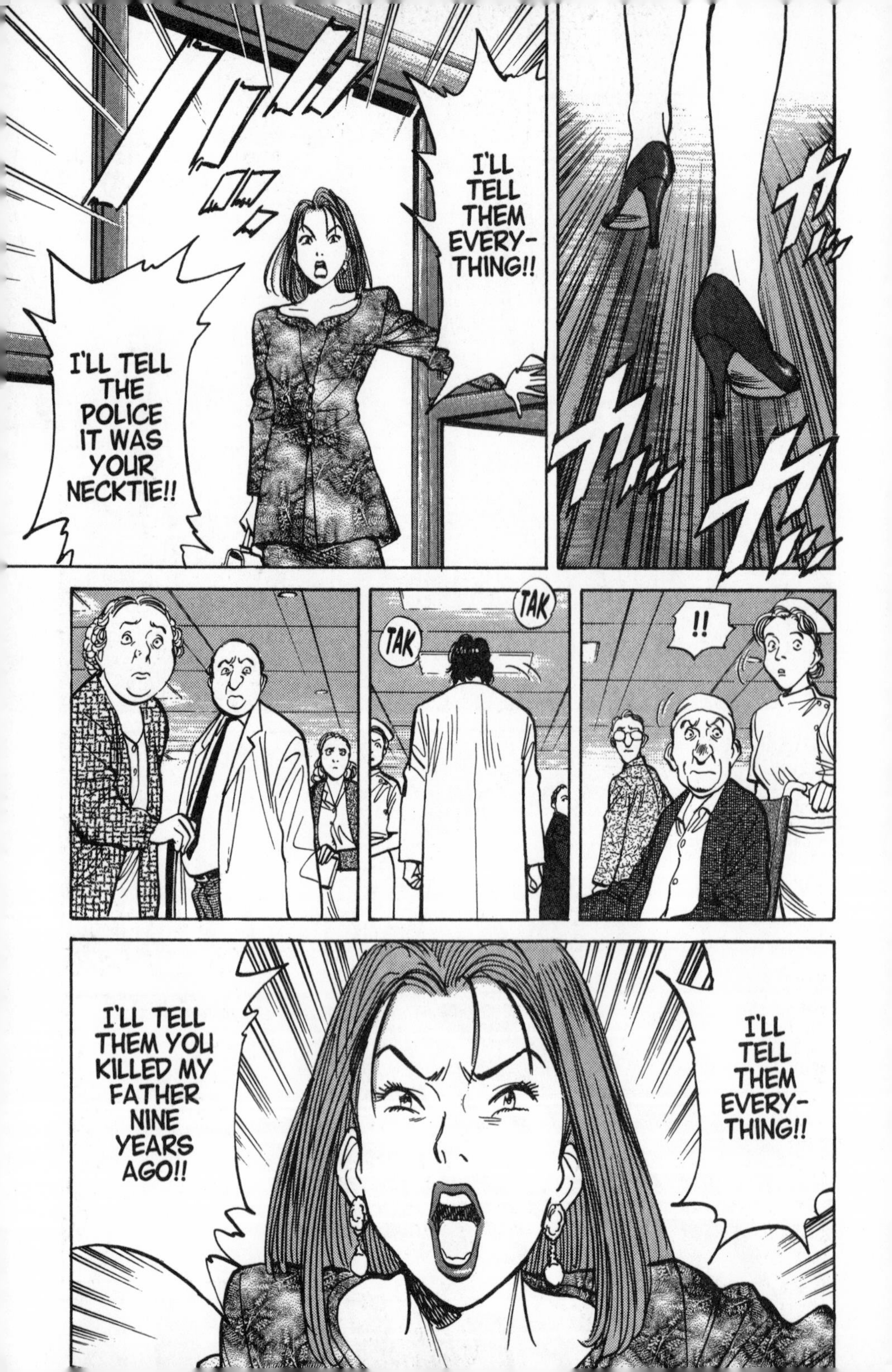
I'LL TELL THEM EVERY-THING!!
I'LL TELL THE POLICE IT WAS YOUR NECKTIE!!
!!
TAK
TAK
I'LL TELL THEM EVERY-THING!!
I'LL TELL THEM YOU KILLED MY FATHER NINE YEARS AGO!!

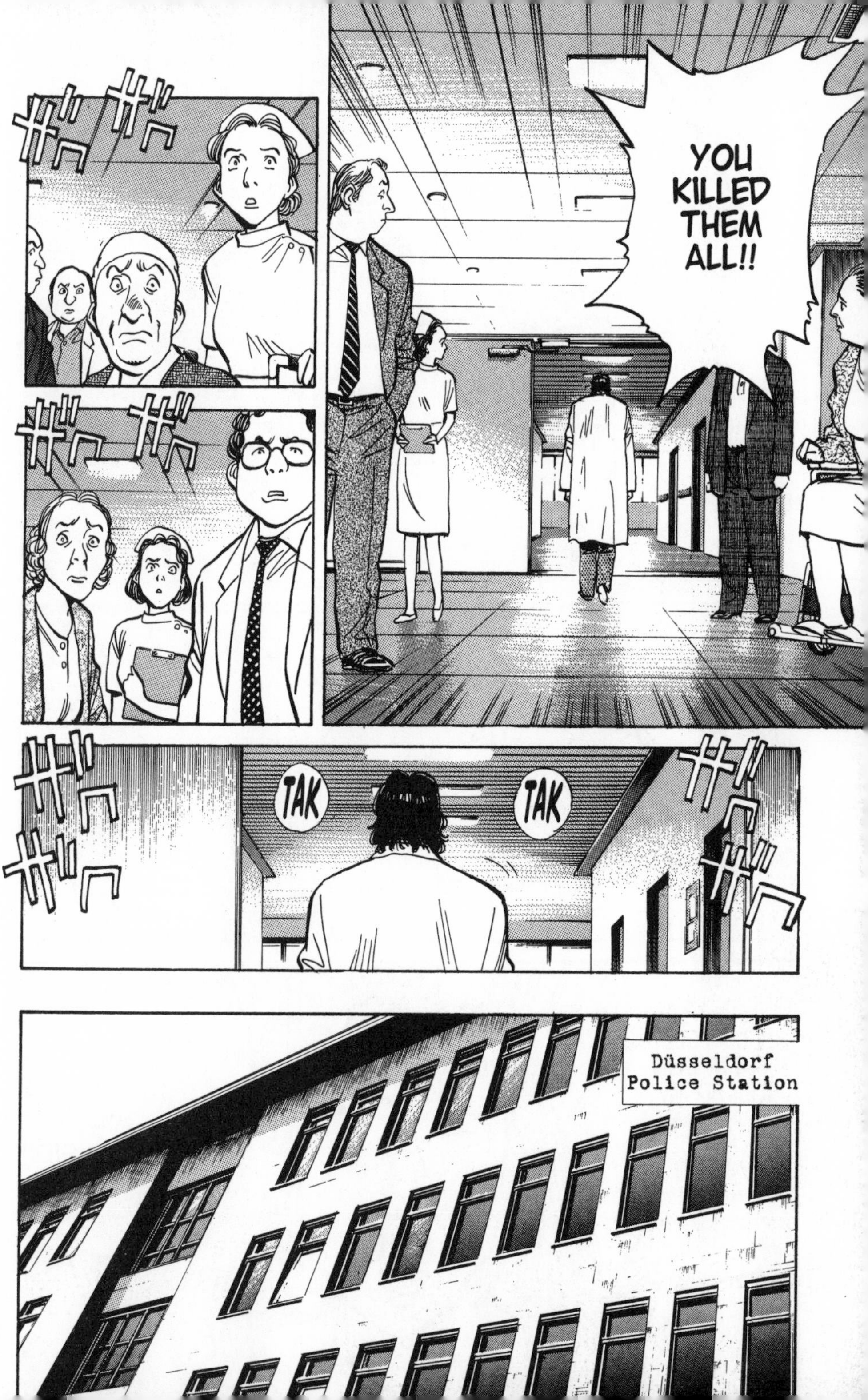
YOU KILLED THEM ALL!!
TAK
TAK
Düsseldorf Police Station

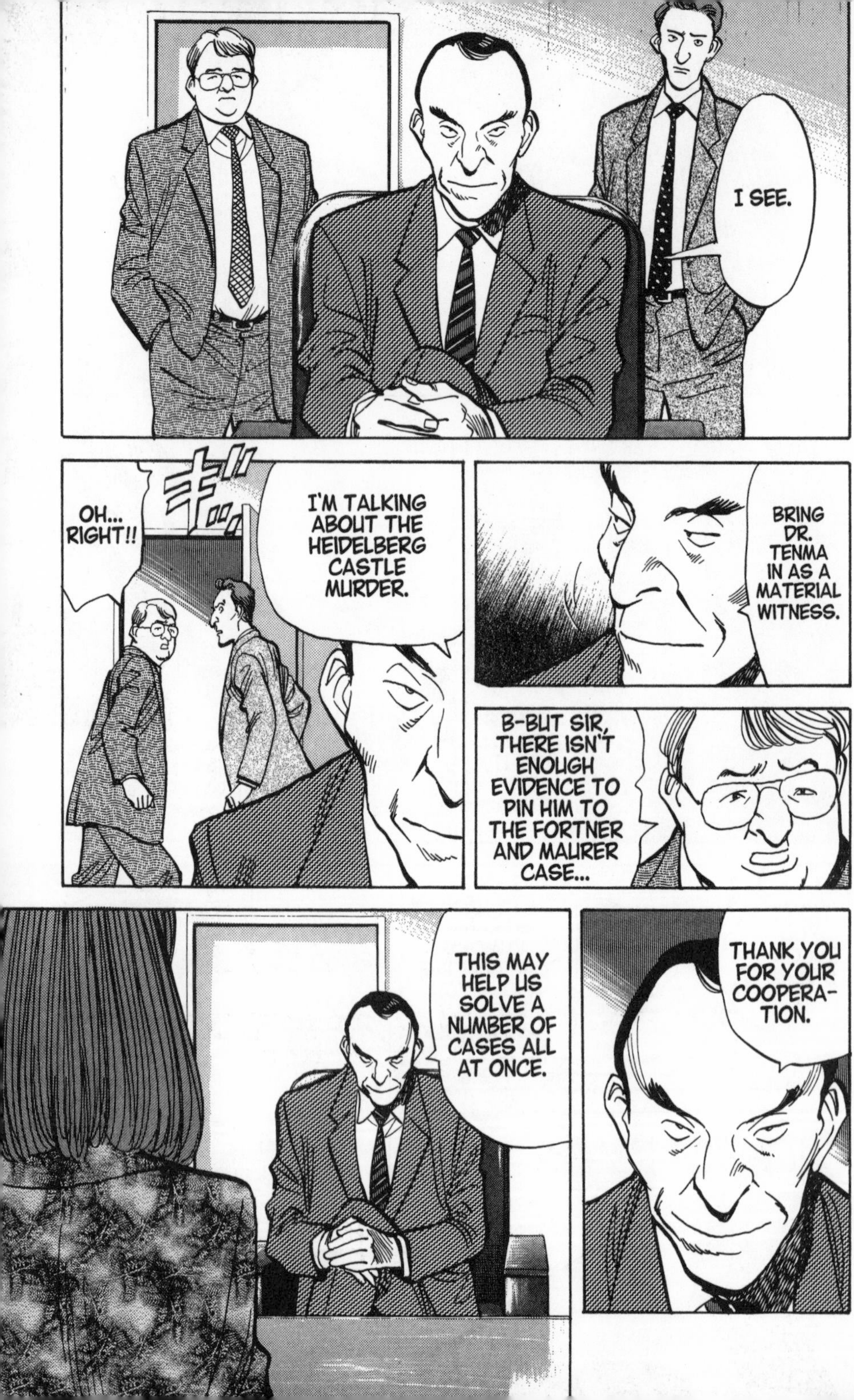
I SEE.
BRING DR. TENMA IN AS A MATERIAL WITNESS.
B-BUT SIR, THERE ISN'T ENOUGH EVIDENCE TO PIN HIM TO THE FORTNER AND MAURER CASE...
I'M TALKING ABOUT THE HEIDELBERG CASTLE MURDER.
OH... RIGHT!!
THANK YOU FOR YOUR COOPERATION.
THIS MAY HELP US SOLVE A NUMBER OF CASES ALL AT ONCE.

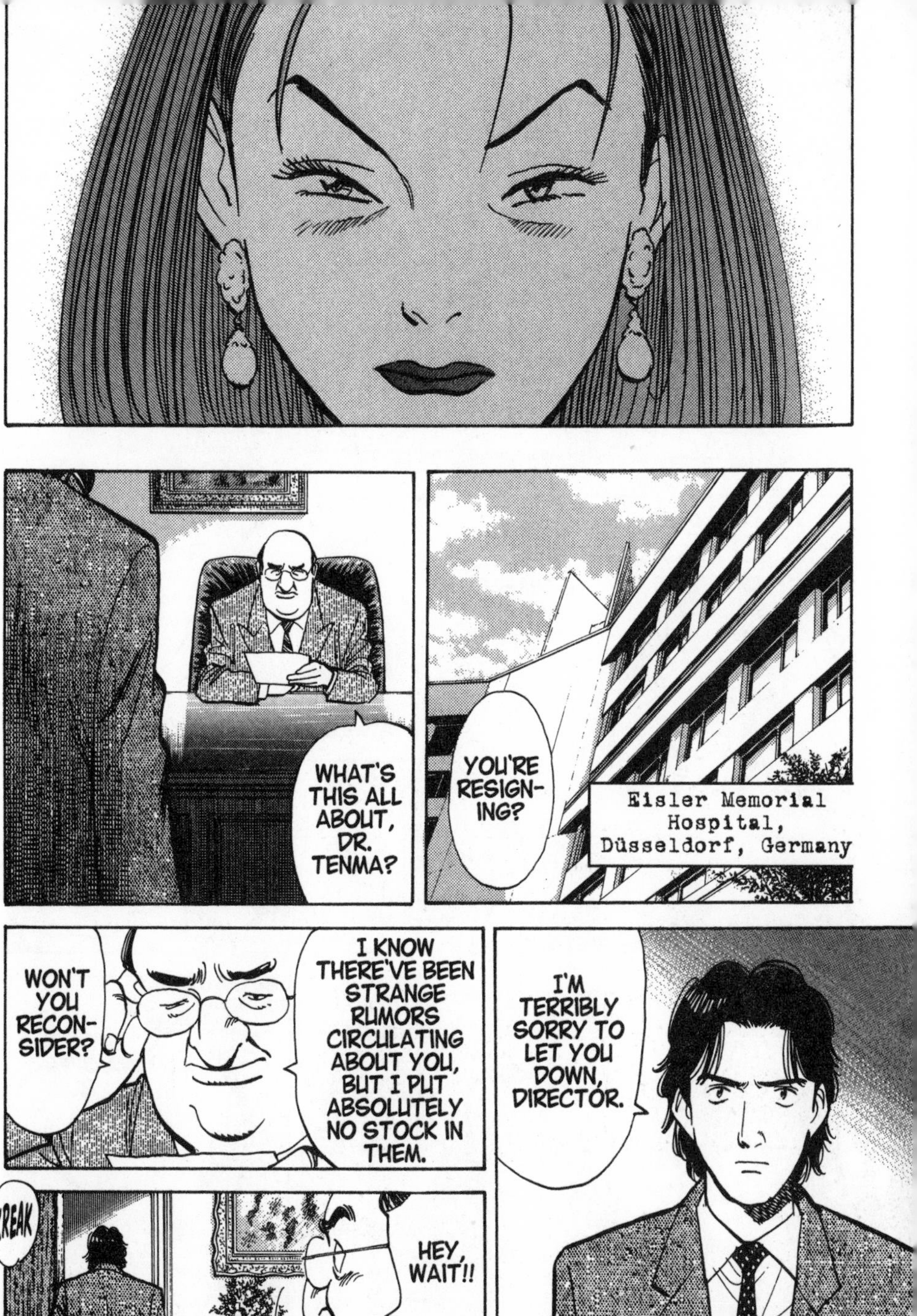

Eisler Memorial Hospital, Düsseldorf, Germany
YOU'RE RESIGNING?
WHAT'S THIS ALL ABOUT, DR. TENMA?
I'M TERRIBLY SORRY TO LET YOU DOWN, DIRECTOR.
I KNOW THERE'VE BEEN STRANGE RUMORS CIRCULATING ABOUT YOU, BUT I PUT ABSOLUTELY NO STOCK IN THEM.
WON'T YOU RECONSIDER?
HEY, WAIT!!
KREAK

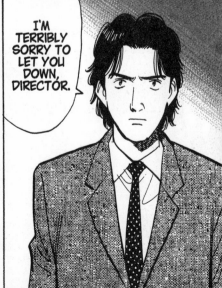

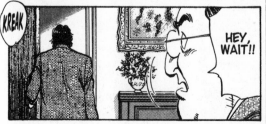

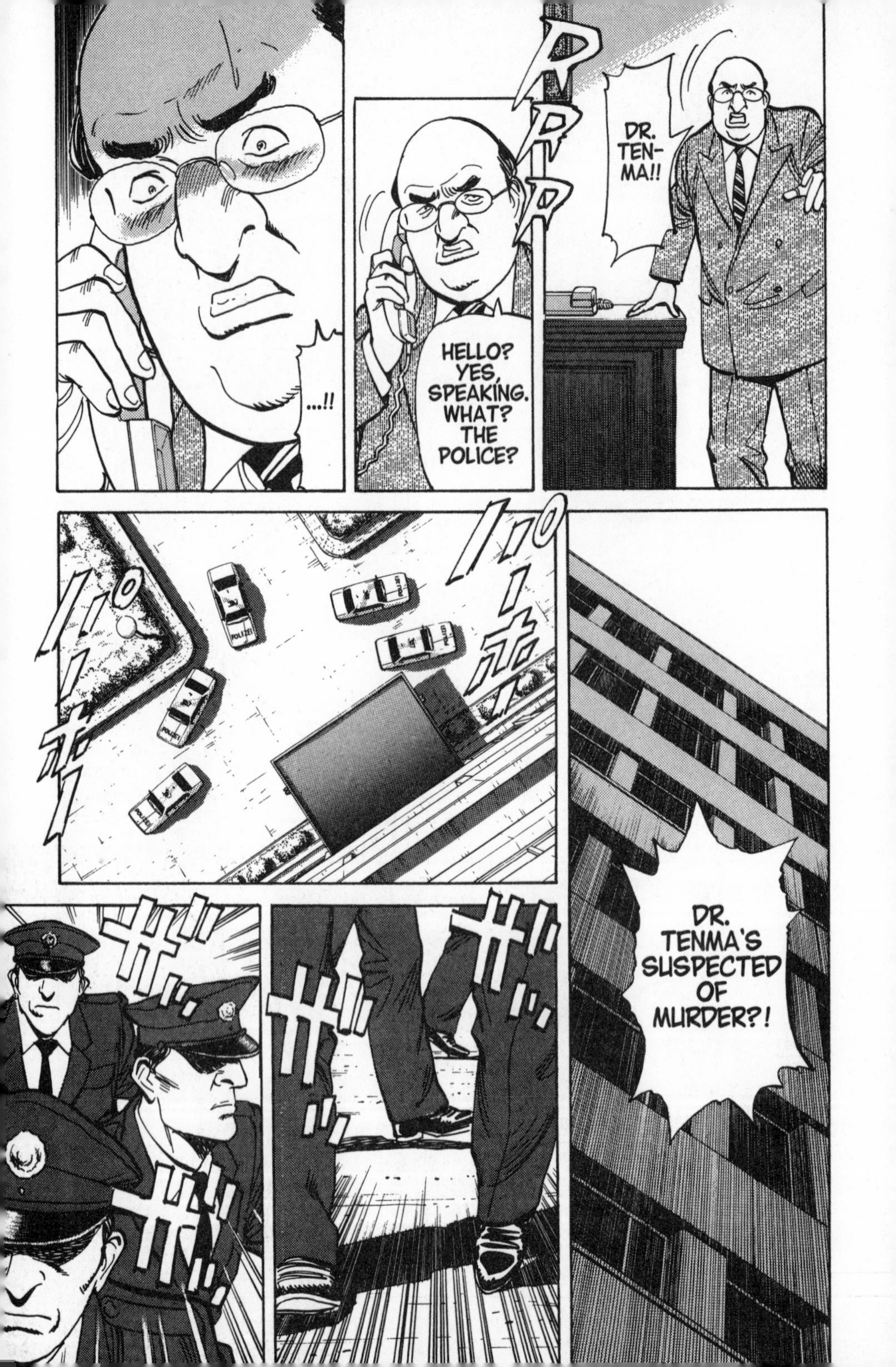
DR. TENMA!!
HELLO? YES, SPEAKING. WHAT? THE POLICE?
...!!
DR. TENMA'S SUSPECTED OF MURDER?!

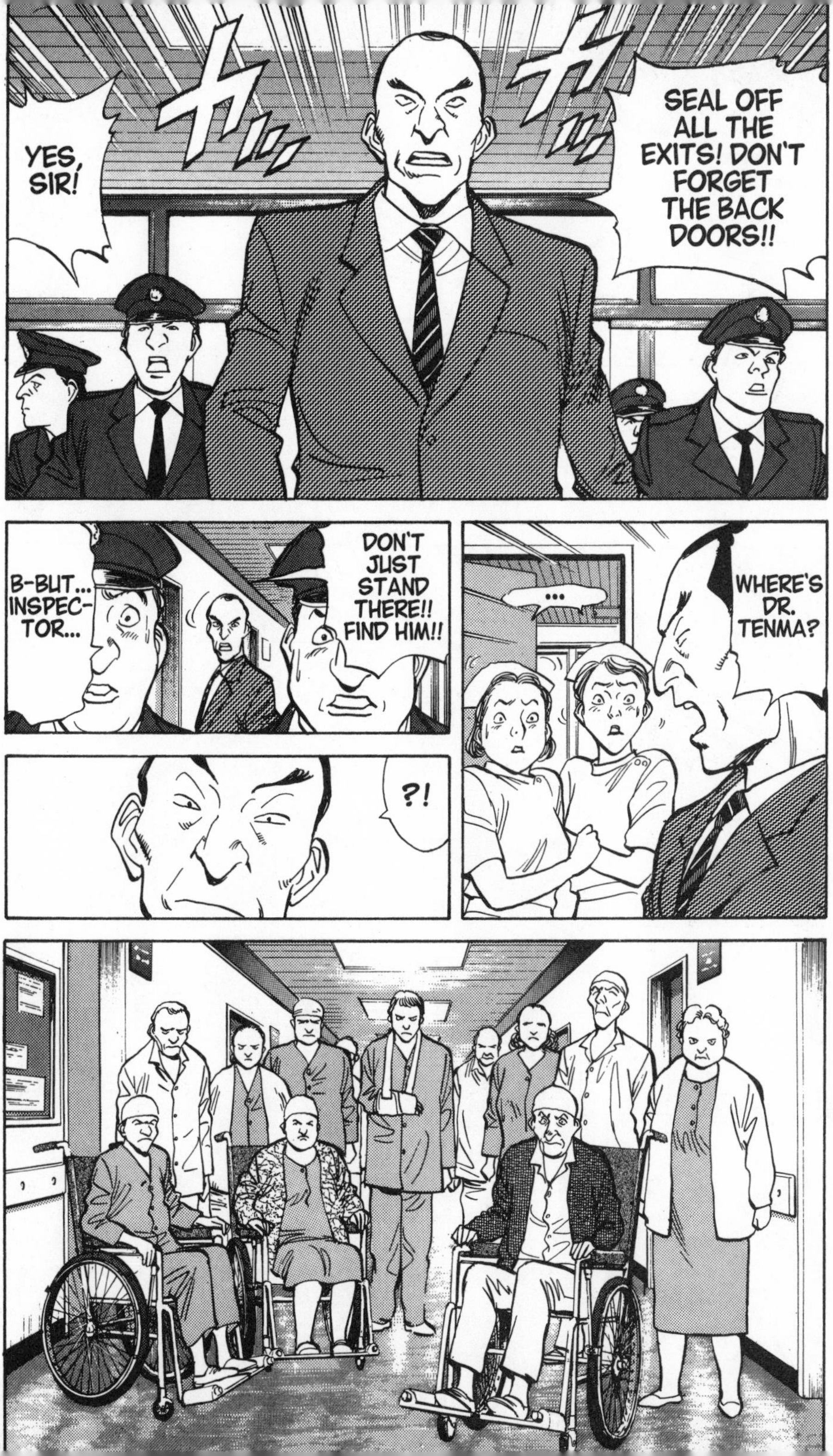
SEAL OFF ALL THE EXITS! DON'T FORGET THE BACK DOORS!!
YES, SIR!
WHERE'S DR. TENMA?
...
DON'T JUST STAND THERE!! FIND HIM!!
B-BUT... INSPEC-TOR...
?!

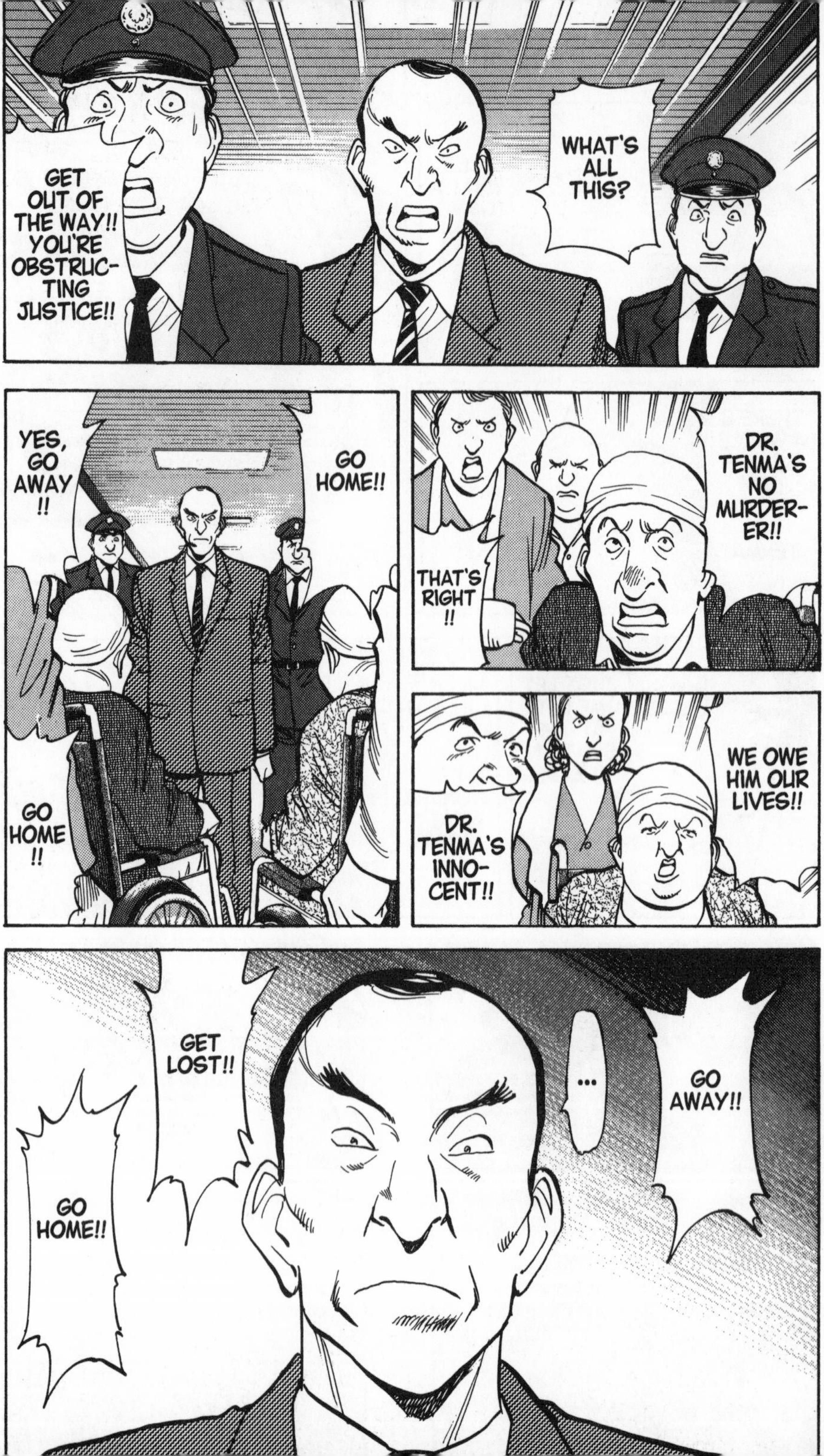
WHAT'S ALL THIS?
GET OUT OF THE WAY!! YOU'RE OBSTRUCTING JUSTICE!!
DR. TENMA'S NO MURDERER!!
THAT'S RIGHT!!
WE OWE HIM OUR LIVES!!
DR. TENMA'S INNOCENT!!
GO HOME!!
YES, GO AWAY!!
GO HOME!!
GO AWAY!!
...
GET LOST!!
GO HOME!!

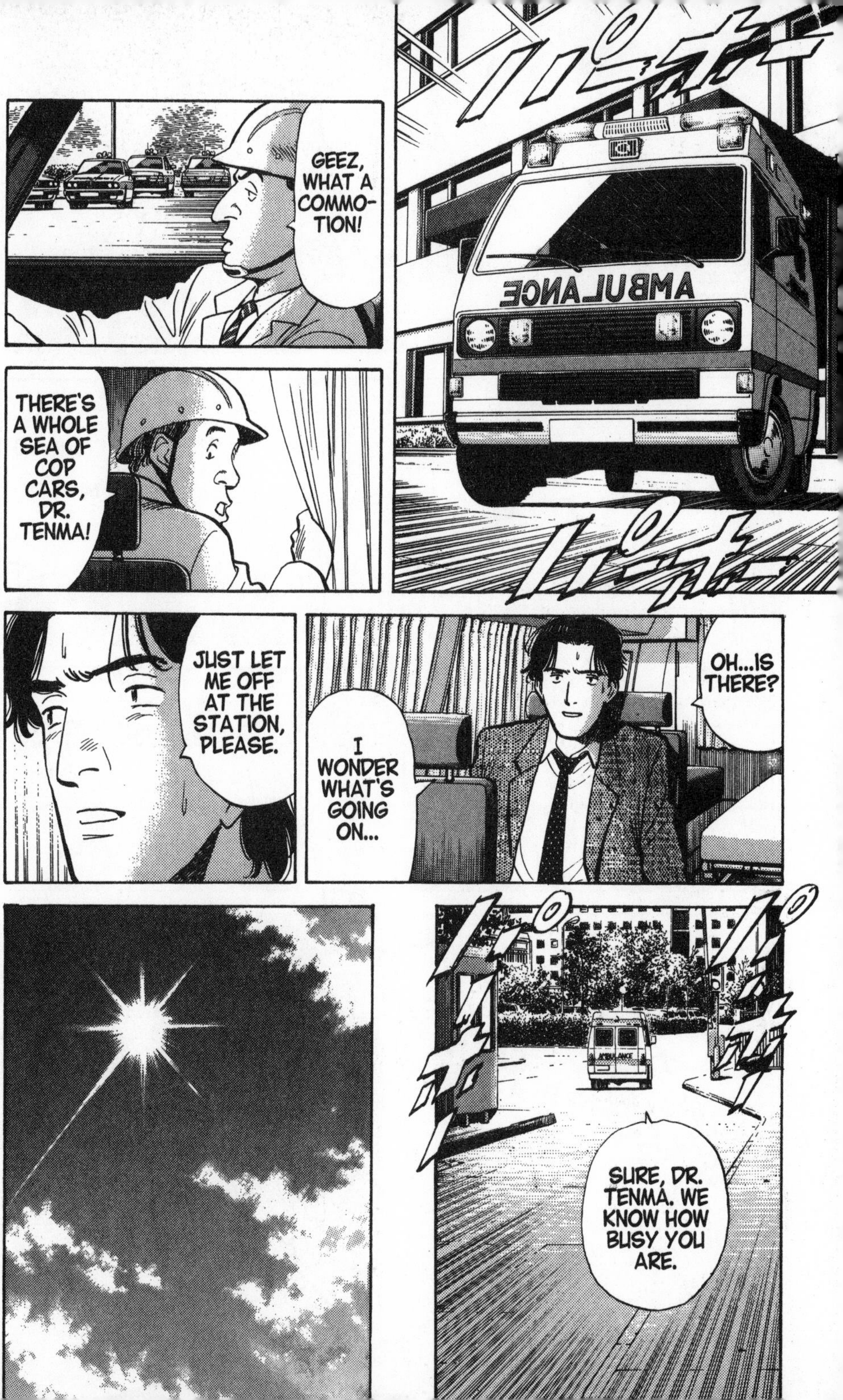
GEEZ, WHAT A COMMO-TION!
THERE'S A WHOLE SEA OF COP CARS, DR. TENMA!
OH...IS THERE?
I WONDER WHAT'S GOING ON...
JUST LET ME OFF AT THE STATION, PLEASE.
AMBULANCE
SURE, DR. TENMA. WE KNOW HOW BUSY YOU ARE.

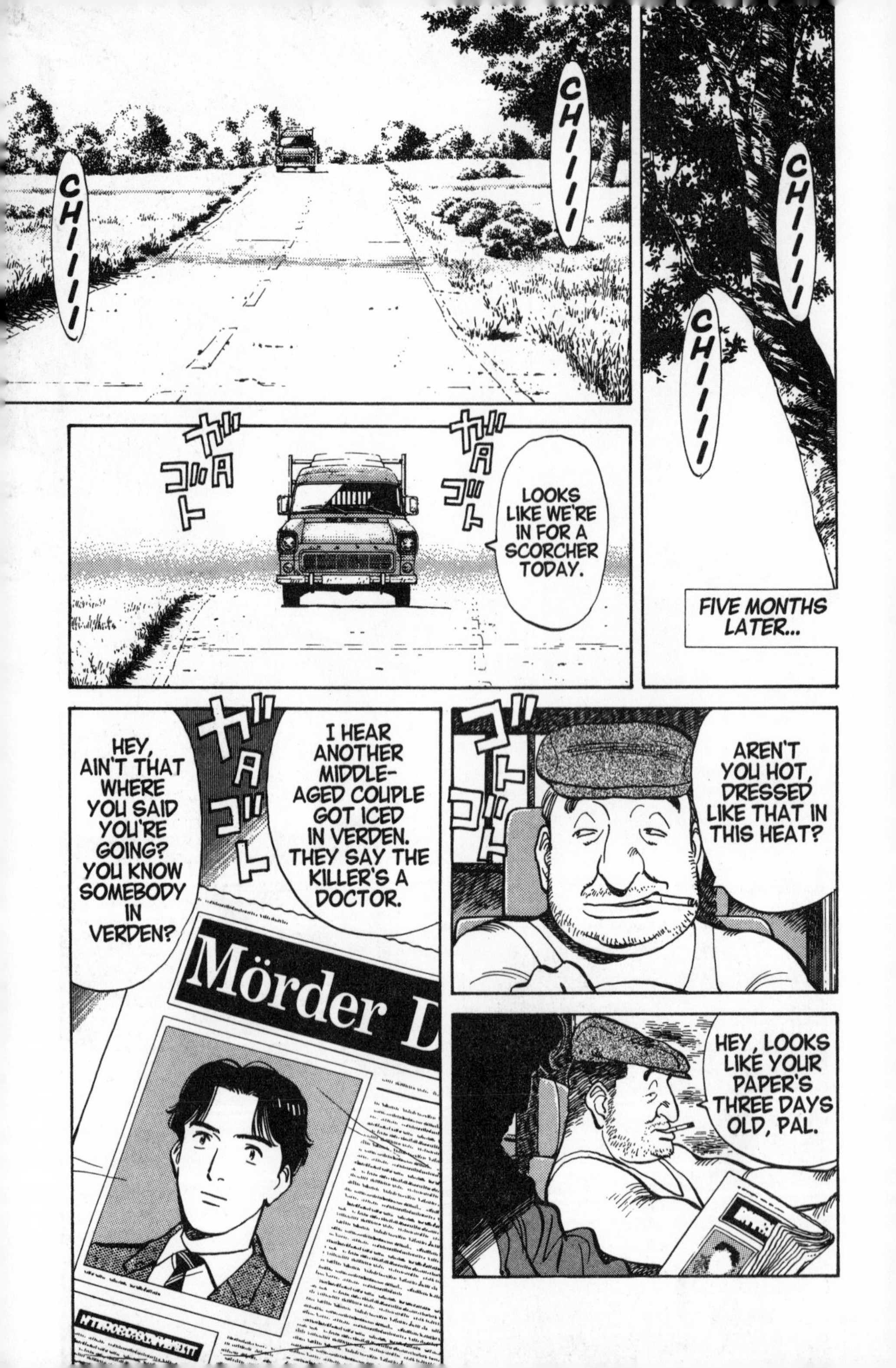
CHIIIIII
CHIIIIII
FIVE MONTHS LATER...
CHIIIIII
CHIIIIII
ガタゴト
ガタゴト
LOOKS LIKE WE'RE IN FOR A SCORCHER TODAY.
ゴトゴト
AREN'T YOU HOT, DRESSED LIKE THAT IN THIS HEAT?
HEY, LOOKS LIKE YOUR PAPER'S THREE DAYS OLD, PAL.
ガタゴト
I HEAR ANOTHER MIDDLE-AGED COUPLE GOT ICED IN VERDEN. THEY SAY THE KILLER'S A DOCTOR.
HEY, AIN'T THAT WHERE YOU SAID YOU'RE GOING? YOU KNOW SOMEBODY IN VERDEN?
Mörder D

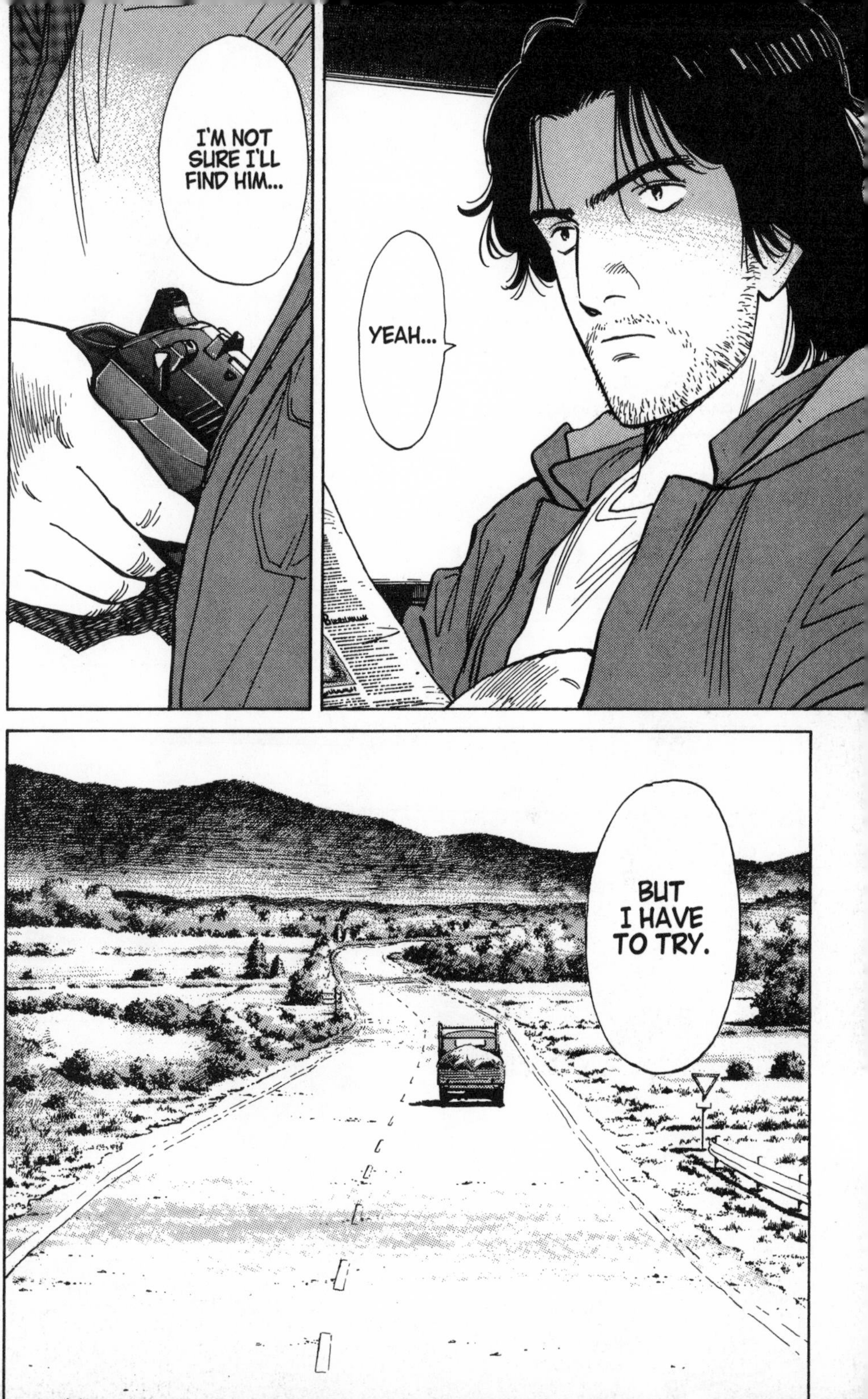
YEAH...
I'M NOT SURE I'LL FIND HIM...
BUT I HAVE TO TRY.

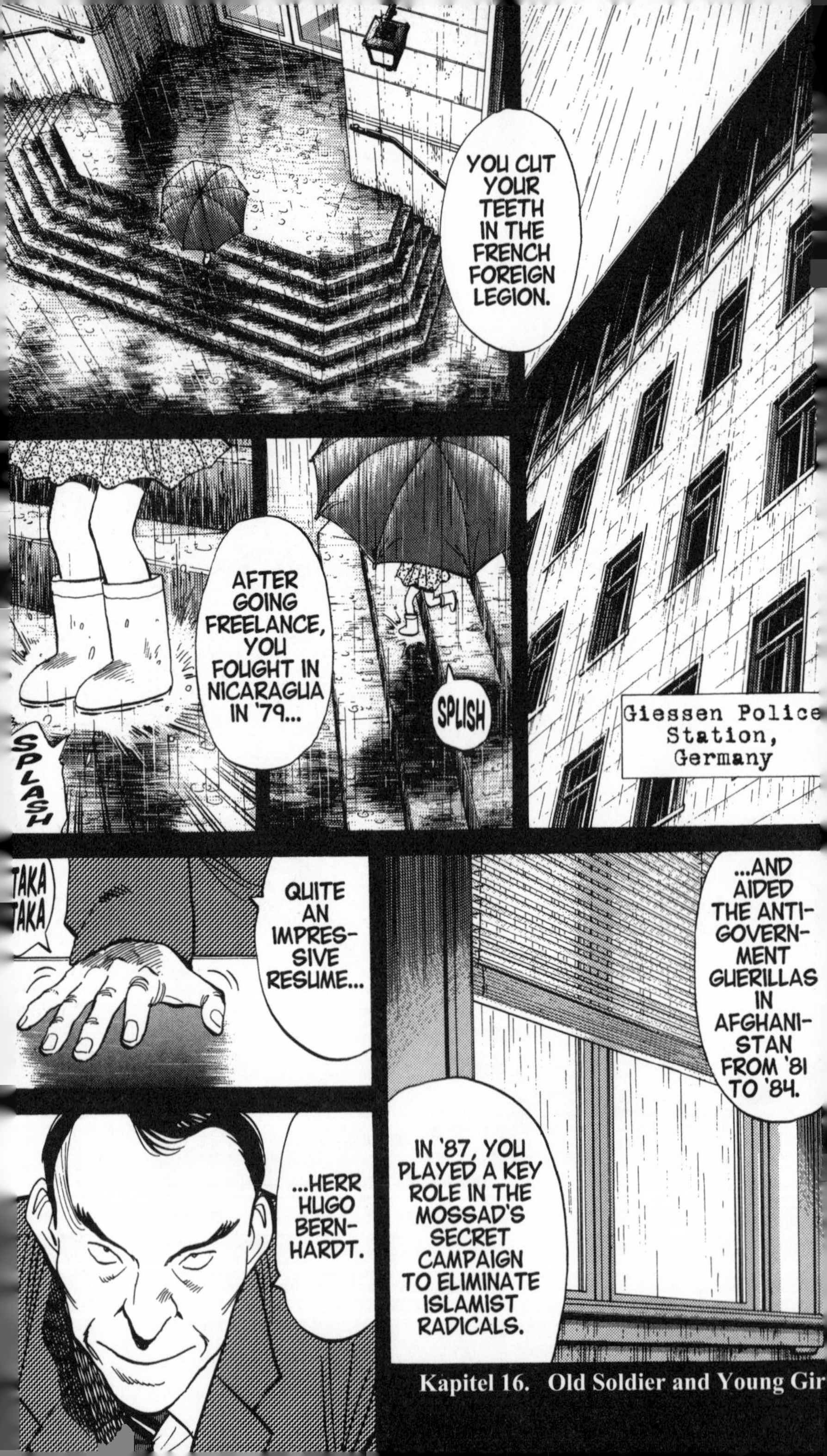
Giessen Police Station, Germany
YOU CUT YOUR TEETH IN THE FRENCH FOREIGN LEGION.
AFTER GOING FREELANCE, YOU FOUGHT IN NICARAGUA IN '79...
SPLISH
SPLASH
...AND AIDED THE ANTI-GOVERNMENT GUERILLAS IN AFGHANISTAN FROM '81 TO '84.
IN '87, YOU PLAYED A KEY ROLE IN THE MOSSAD'S SECRET CAMPAIGN TO ELIMINATE ISLAMIST RADICALS.
TAKA TAKA
QUITE AN IMPRESSIVE RESUME...
...HERR HUGO BERNHARDT.
Kapitel 16. Old Soldier and Young Gir

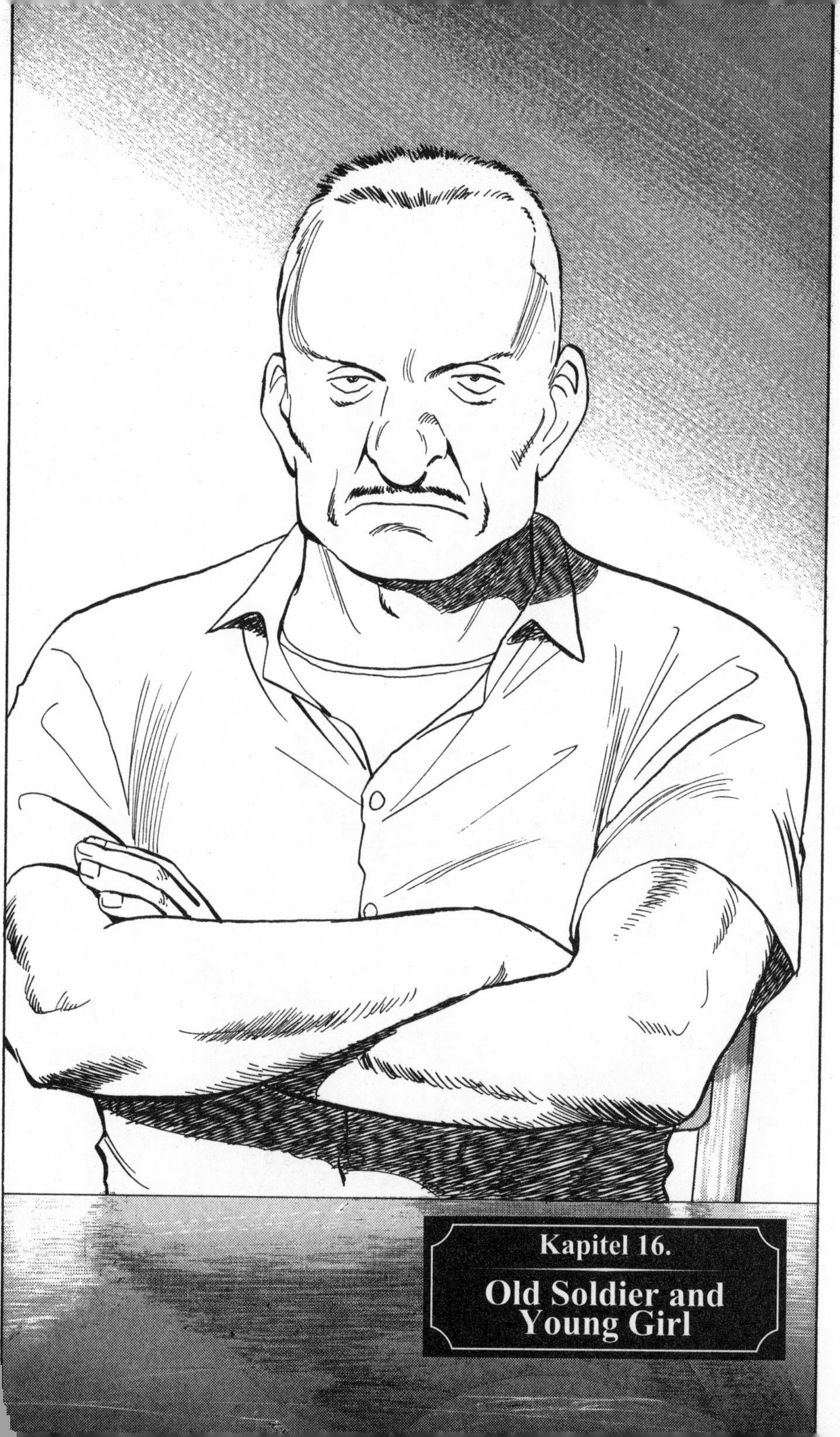
Kapitel 16.
Old Soldier and Young Girl

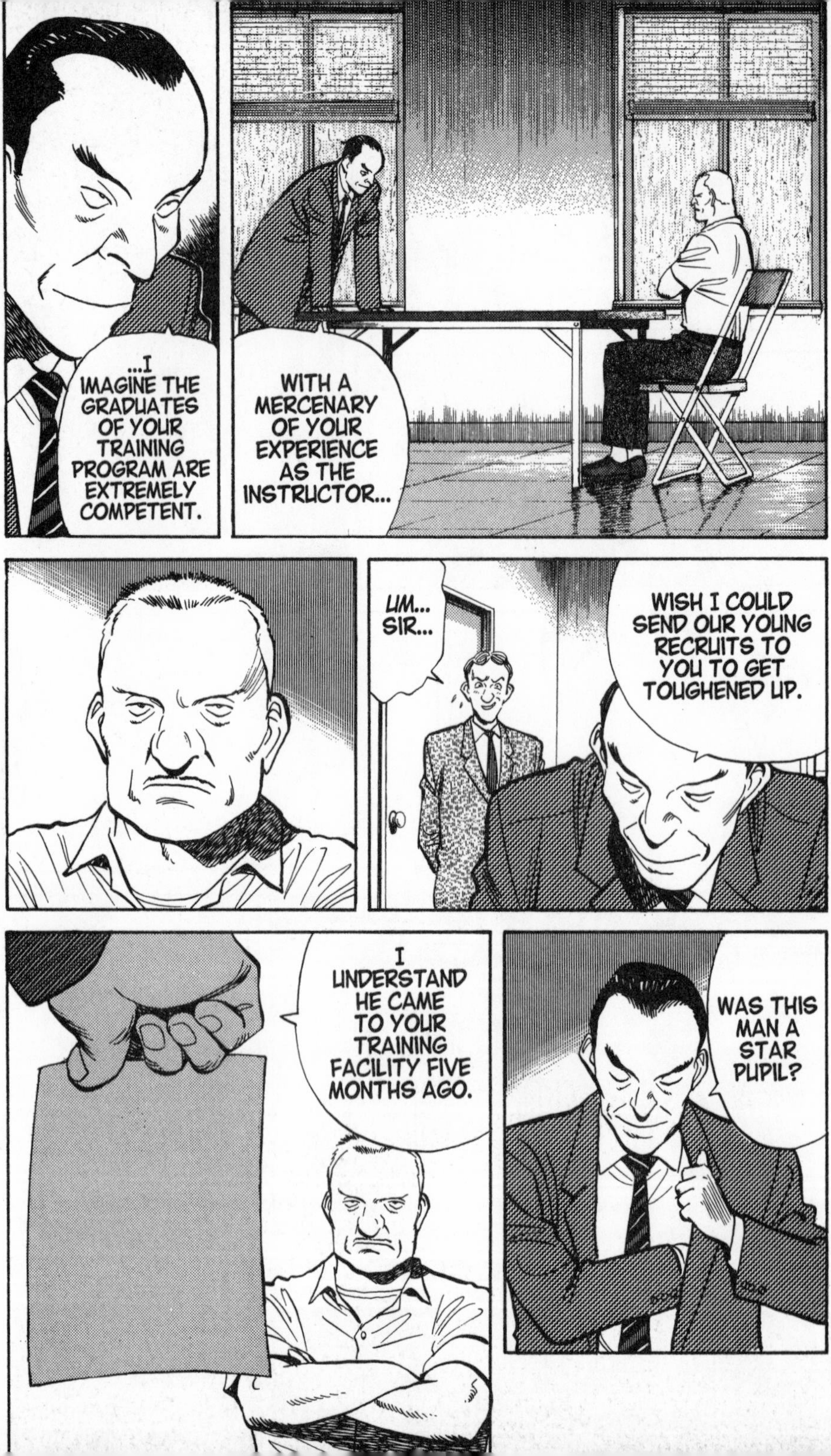
WITH A MERCENARY OF YOUR EXPERIENCE AS THE INSTRUCTOR...
...I IMAGINE THE GRADUATES OF YOUR TRAINING PROGRAM ARE EXTREMELY COMPETENT.
WISH I COULD SEND OUR YOUNG RECRUITS TO YOU TO GET TOUGHENED UP.
UM... SIR...
WAS THIS MAN A STAR PUPIL?
I UNDERSTAND HE CAME TO YOUR TRAINING FACILITY FIVE MONTHS AGO.

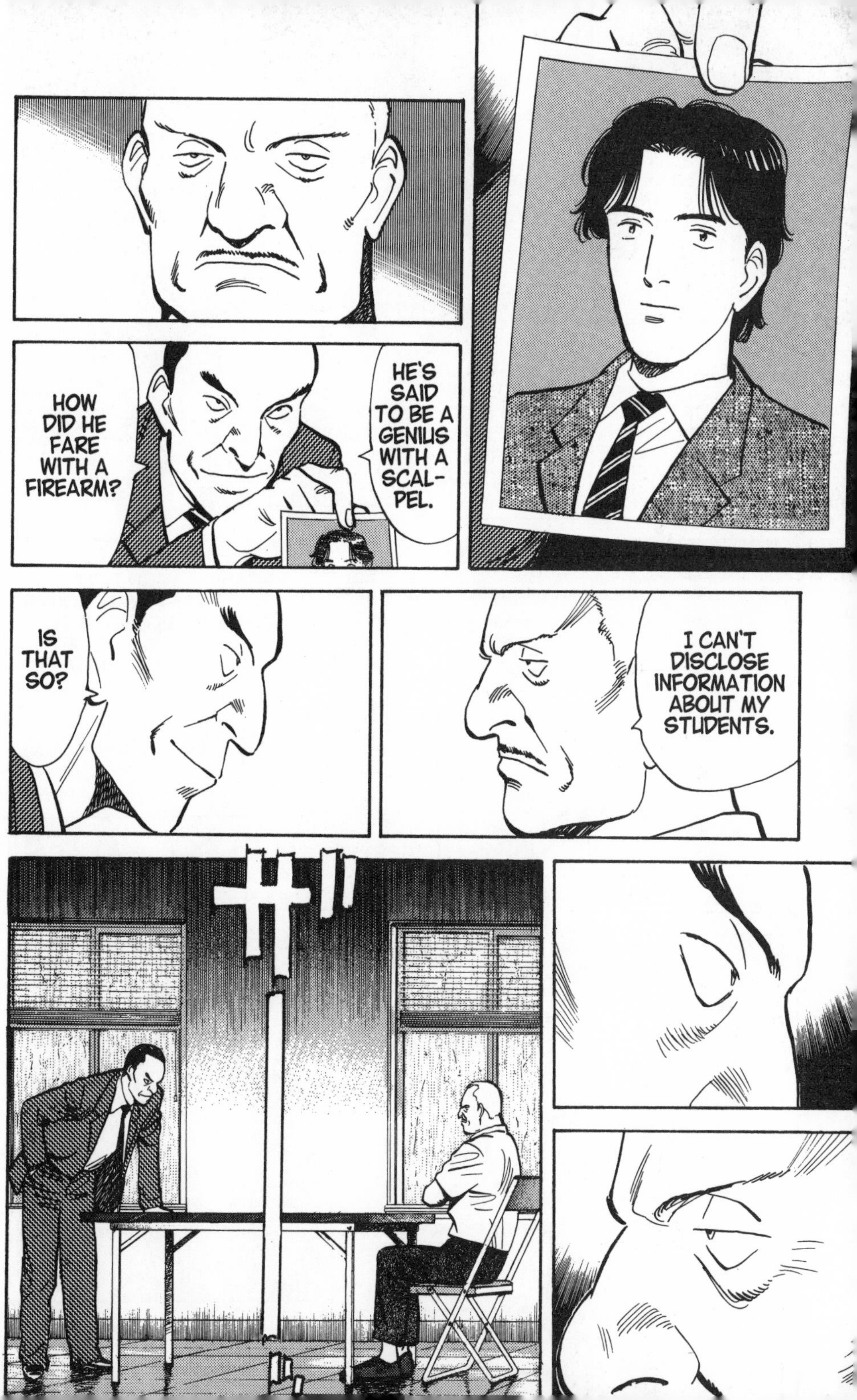
HE'S SAID TO BE A GENIUS WITH A SCALPEL.
HOW DID HE FARE WITH A FIREARM?
I CAN'T DISCLOSE INFORMATION ABOUT MY STUDENTS.
IS THAT SO?
ギリ

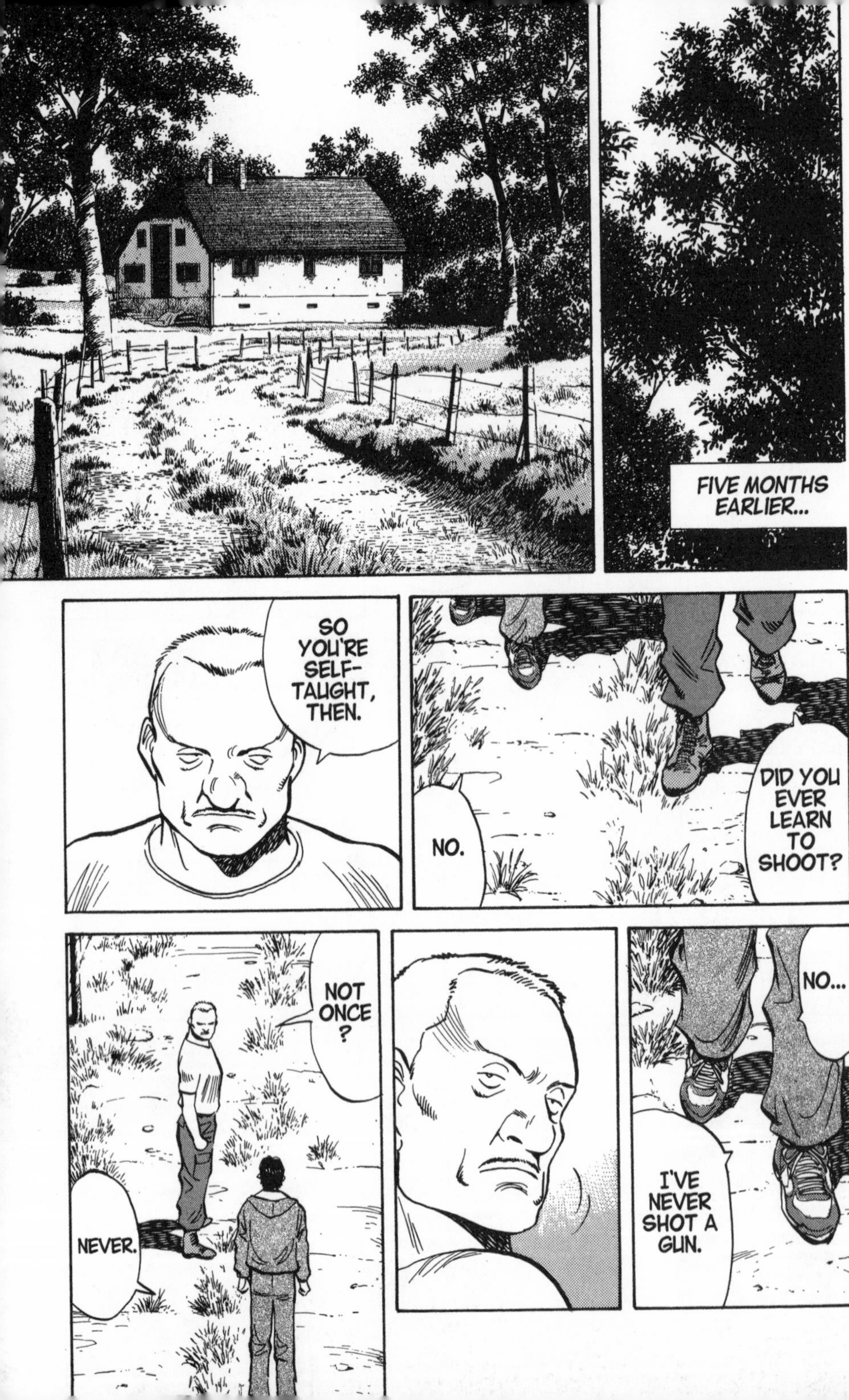
FIVE MONTHS EARLIER...
DID YOU EVER LEARN TO SHOOT?
NO.
SO YOU'RE SELF-TAUGHT, THEN.
NO...
I'VE NEVER SHOT A GUN.
NOT ONCE?
NEVER.

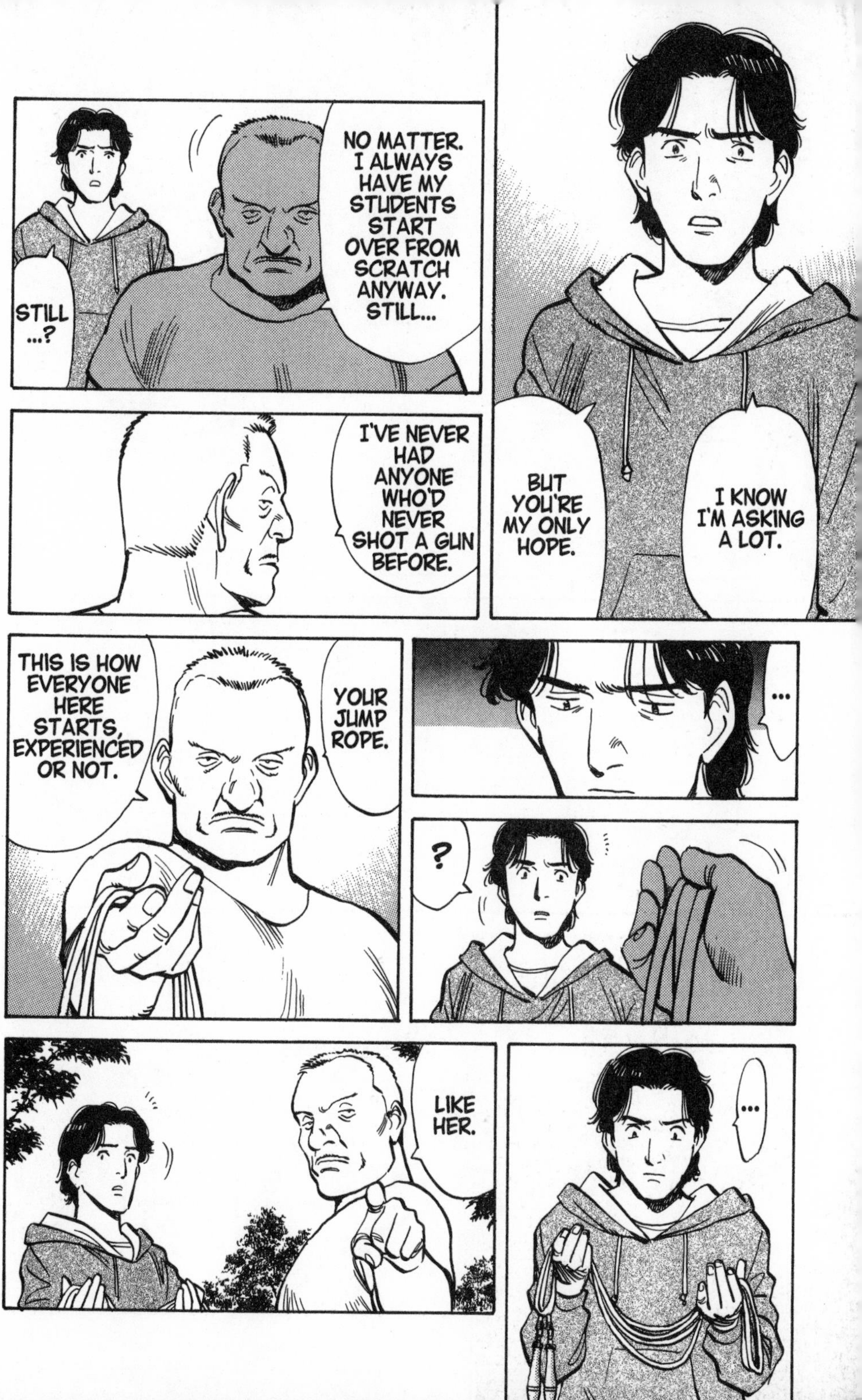
I KNOW I'M ASKING A LOT.
BUT YOU'RE MY ONLY HOPE.
NO MATTER. I ALWAYS HAVE MY STUDENTS START OVER FROM SCRATCH ANYWAY. STILL...
STILL ...?
I'VE NEVER HAD ANYONE WHO'D NEVER SHOT A GUN BEFORE.
...
?
YOUR JUMP ROPE.
THIS IS HOW EVERYONE HERE STARTS, EXPERIENCED OR NOT.
...
LIKE HER.

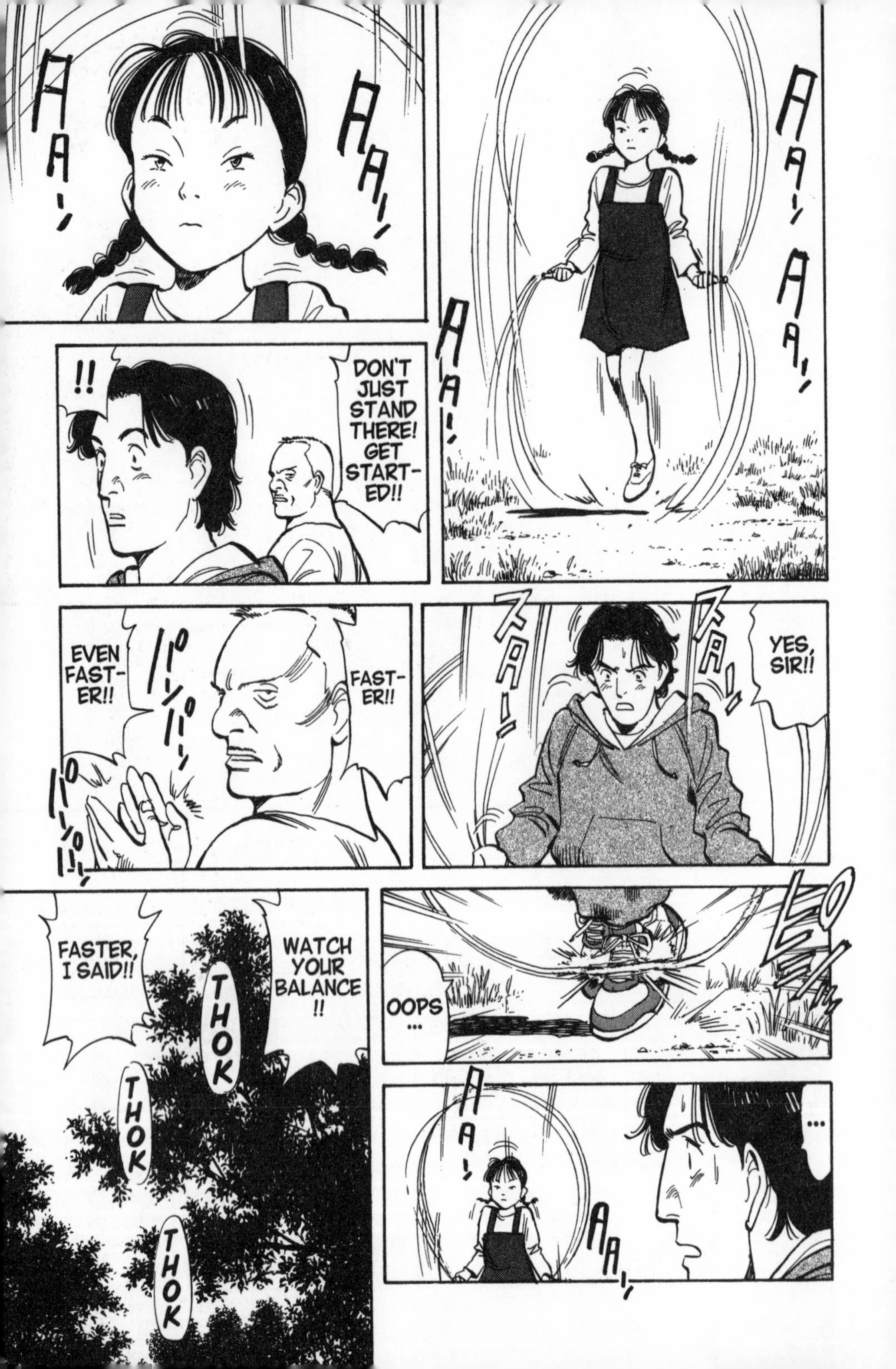
!!
DON'T JUST STAND THERE! GET STARTED-ED!!
YES, SIR!!
FASTER!!
EVEN FASTER!!
OOPS...
...
WATCH YOUR BALANCE!!
FASTER, I SAID!!
THOK
THOK
THOK

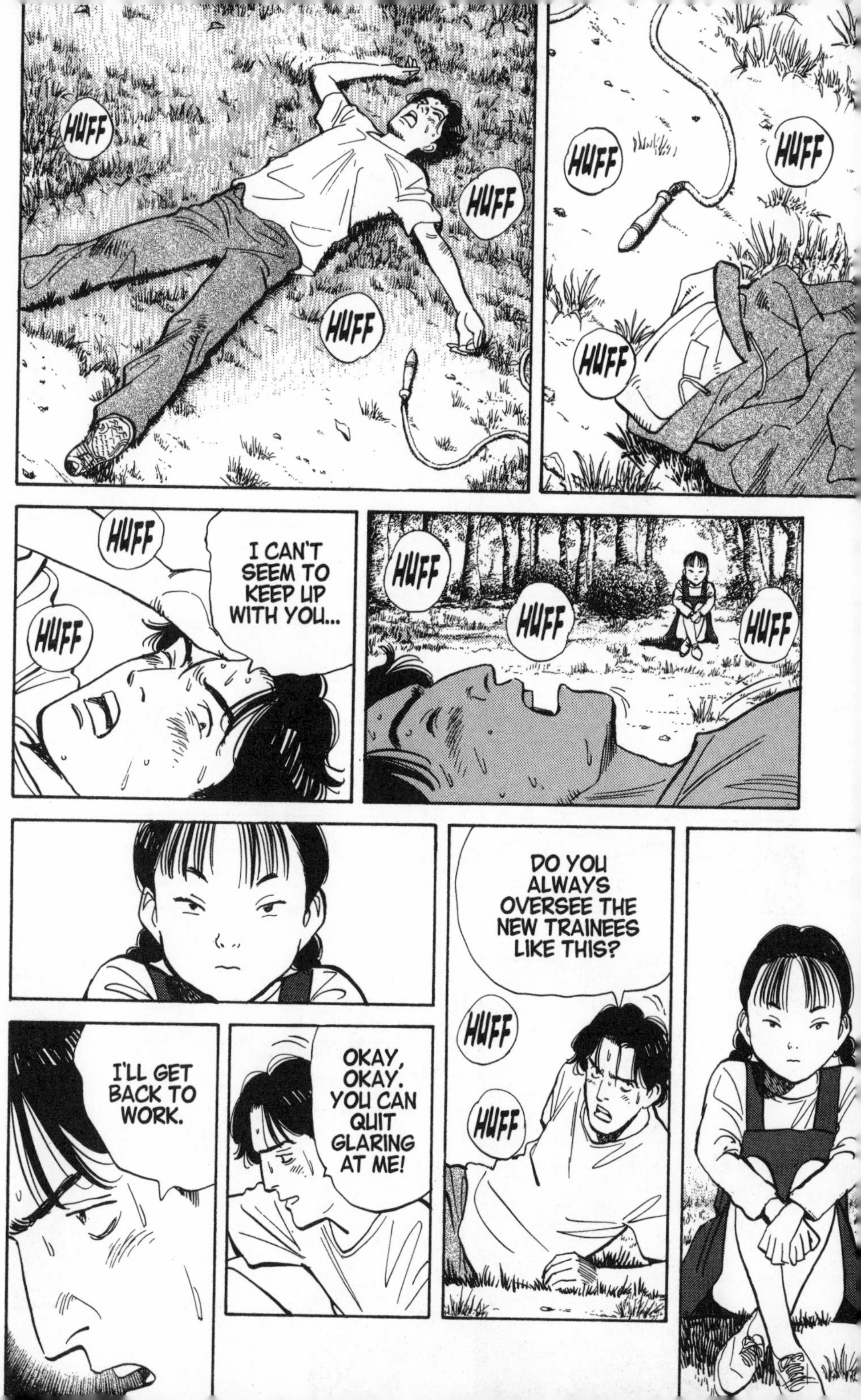
HUFF
HUFF
HUFF
HUFF
HUFF
HUFF
HUFF
HUFF
HUFF
I CAN'T SEEM TO KEEP UP WITH YOU...
HUFF
DO YOU ALWAYS OVERSEE THE NEW TRAINEES LIKE THIS?
HUFF
HUFF
OKAY, OKAY. YOU CAN QUIT GLARING AT ME!
I'LL GET BACK TO WORK.

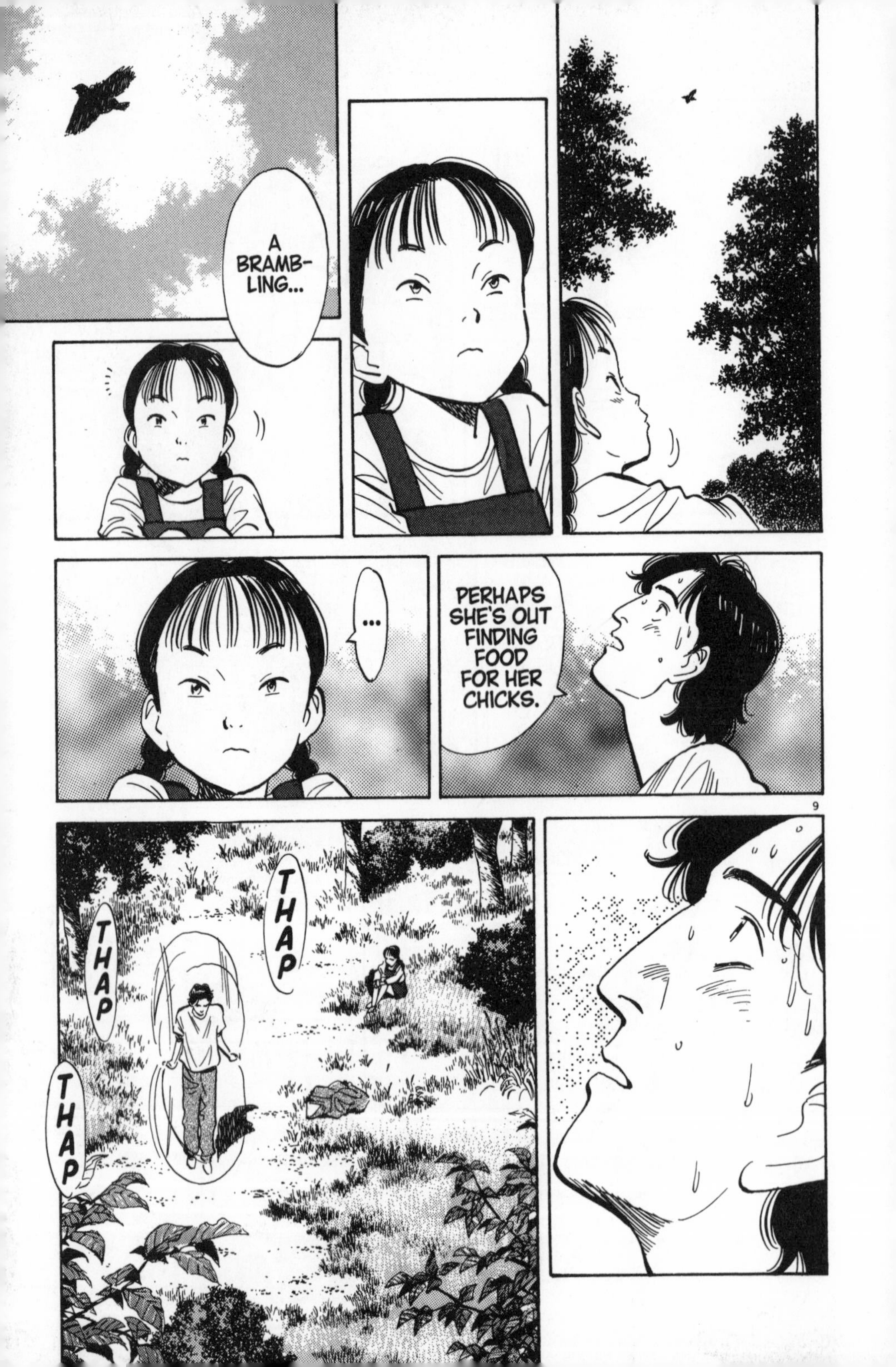
A BRAMBLING...
PERHAPS SHE'S OUT FINDING FOOD FOR HER CHICKS.
...
THAP
THAP
THAP
THAP

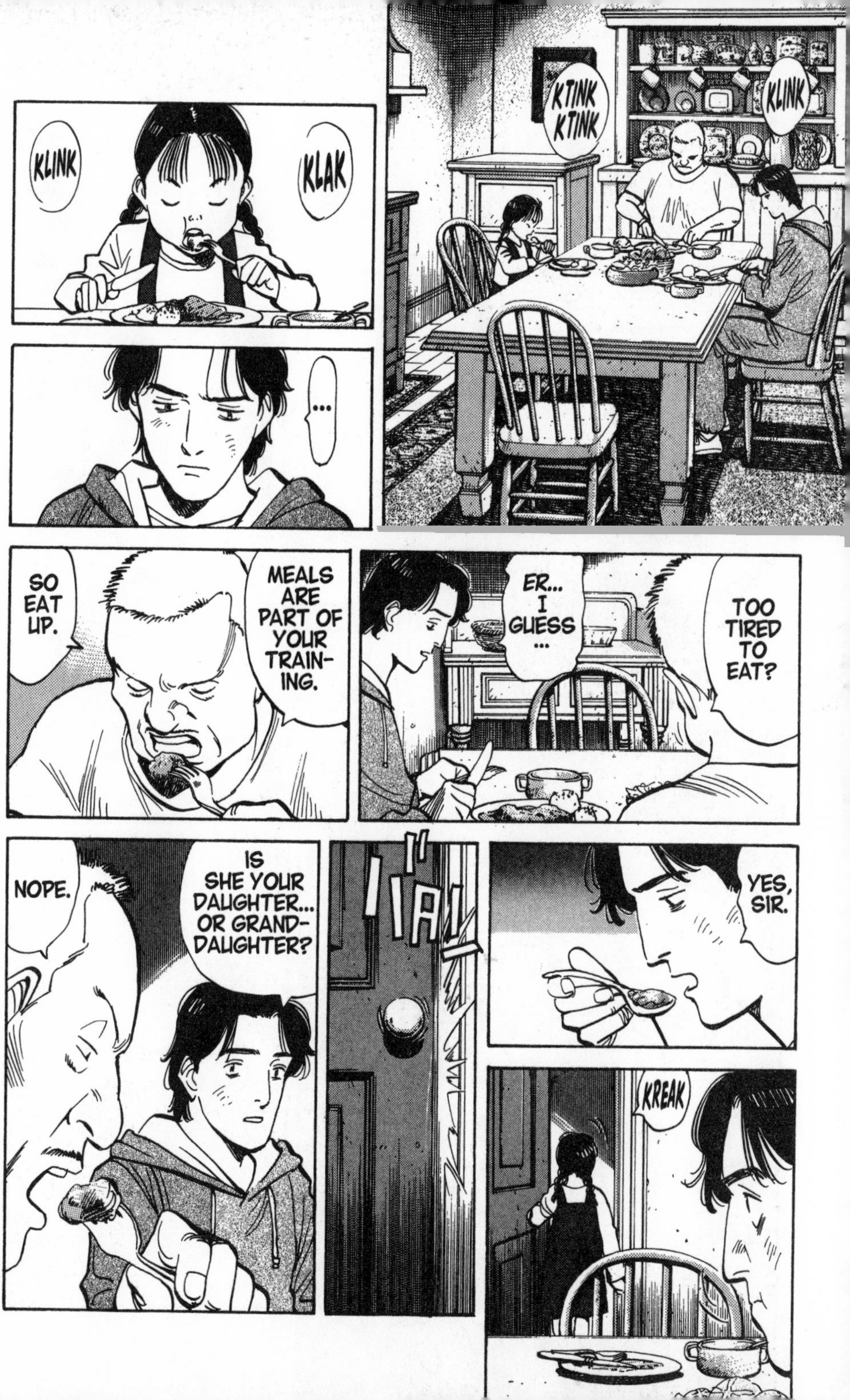
KLINK
KTINK KTINK
KLAK
KLINK
...
TOO TIRED TO EAT?
ER... I GUESS...
MEALS ARE PART OF YOUR TRAIN-ING.
SO EAT UP.
YES, SIR.
KREAK
IS SHE YOUR DAUGHTER... OR GRAND-DAUGHTER?
NOPE.

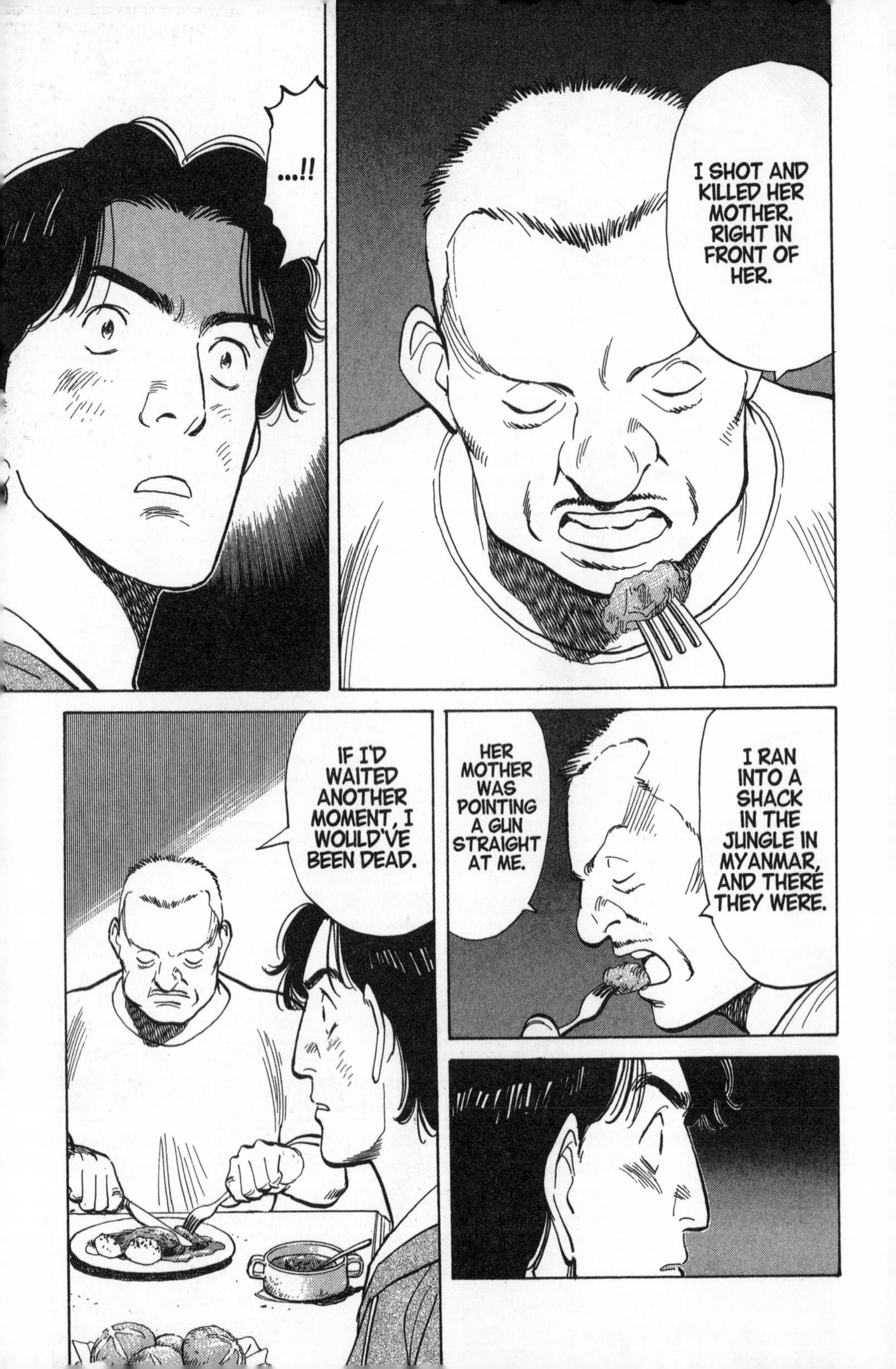
I SHOT AND KILLED HER MOTHER. RIGHT IN FRONT OF HER.
...!!
I RAN INTO A SHACK IN THE JUNGLE IN MYANMAR, AND THERE THEY WERE.
HER MOTHER WAS POINTING A GUN STRAIGHT AT ME.
IF I'D WAITED ANOTHER MOMENT, I WOULD'VE BEEN DEAD.

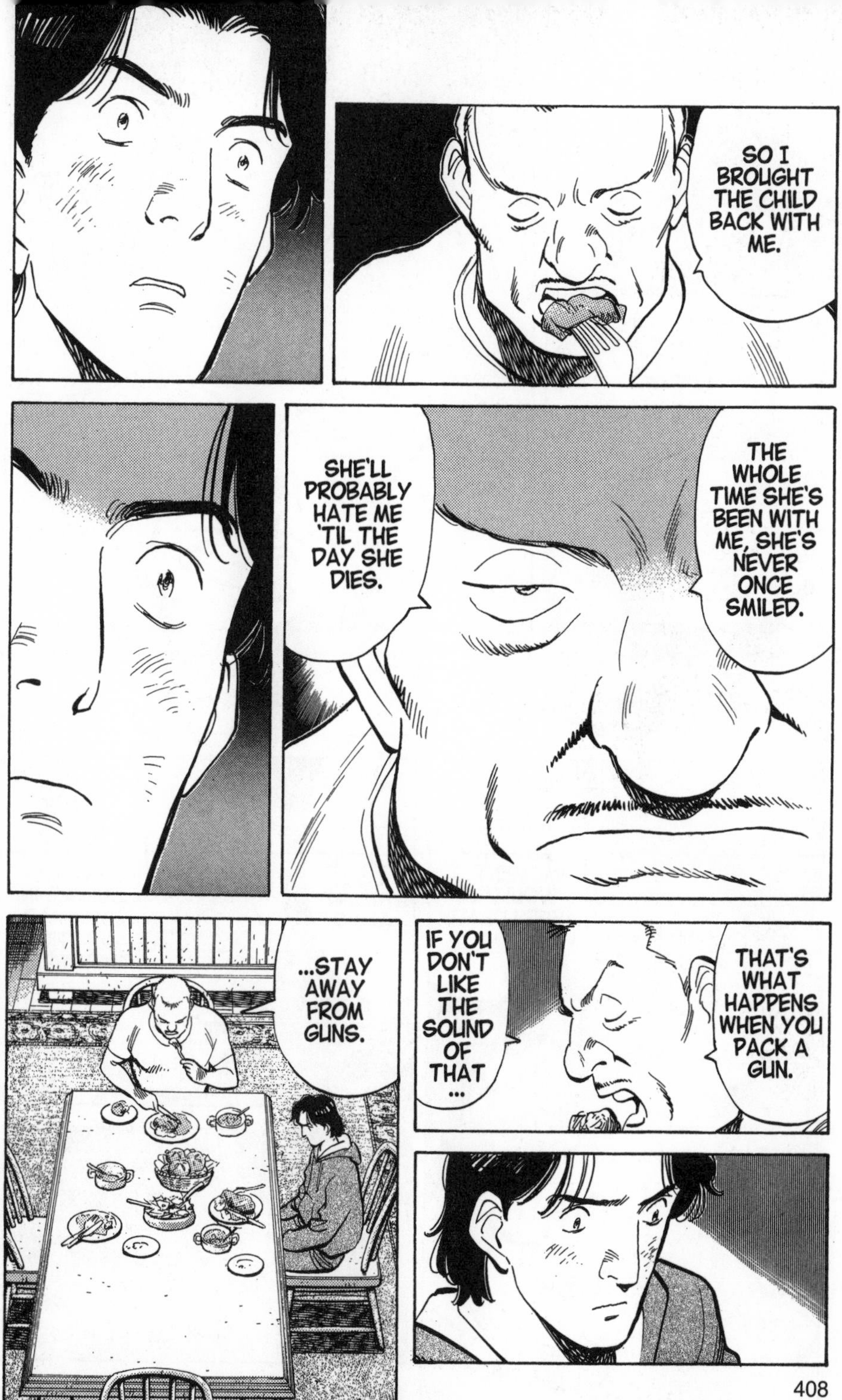
SO I BROUGHT THE CHILD BACK WITH ME.
THE WHOLE TIME SHE'S BEEN WITH ME, SHE'S NEVER ONCE SMILED.
SHE'LL PROBABLY HATE ME 'TIL THE DAY SHE DIES.
THAT'S WHAT HAPPENS WHEN YOU PACK A GUN.
IF YOU DON'T LIKE THE SOUND OF THAT ...
...STAY AWAY FROM GUNS.

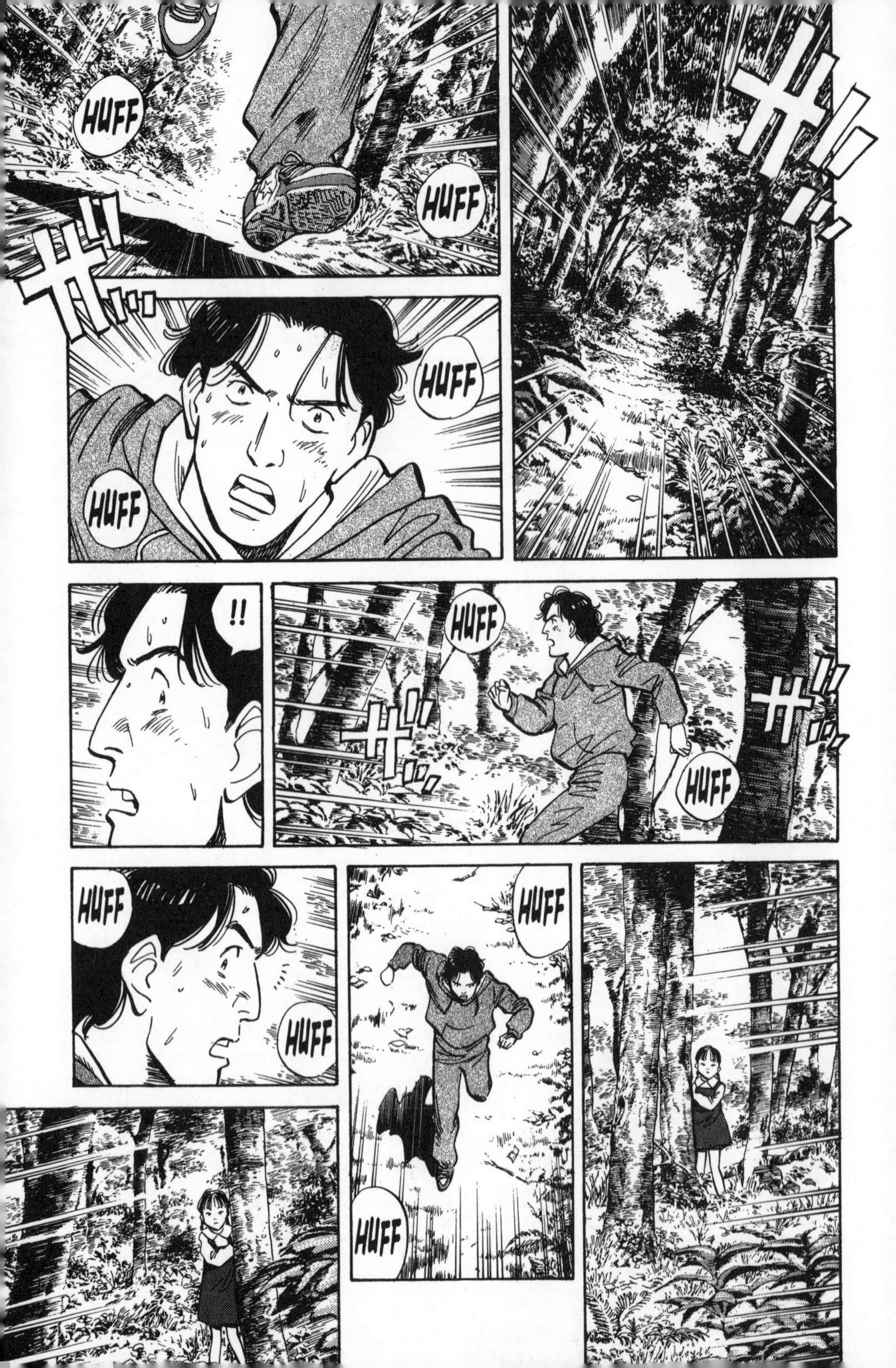
HUFF
HUFF
HUFF
HUFF
HUFF
HUFF
!!
HUFF
HUFF
HUFF
HUFF

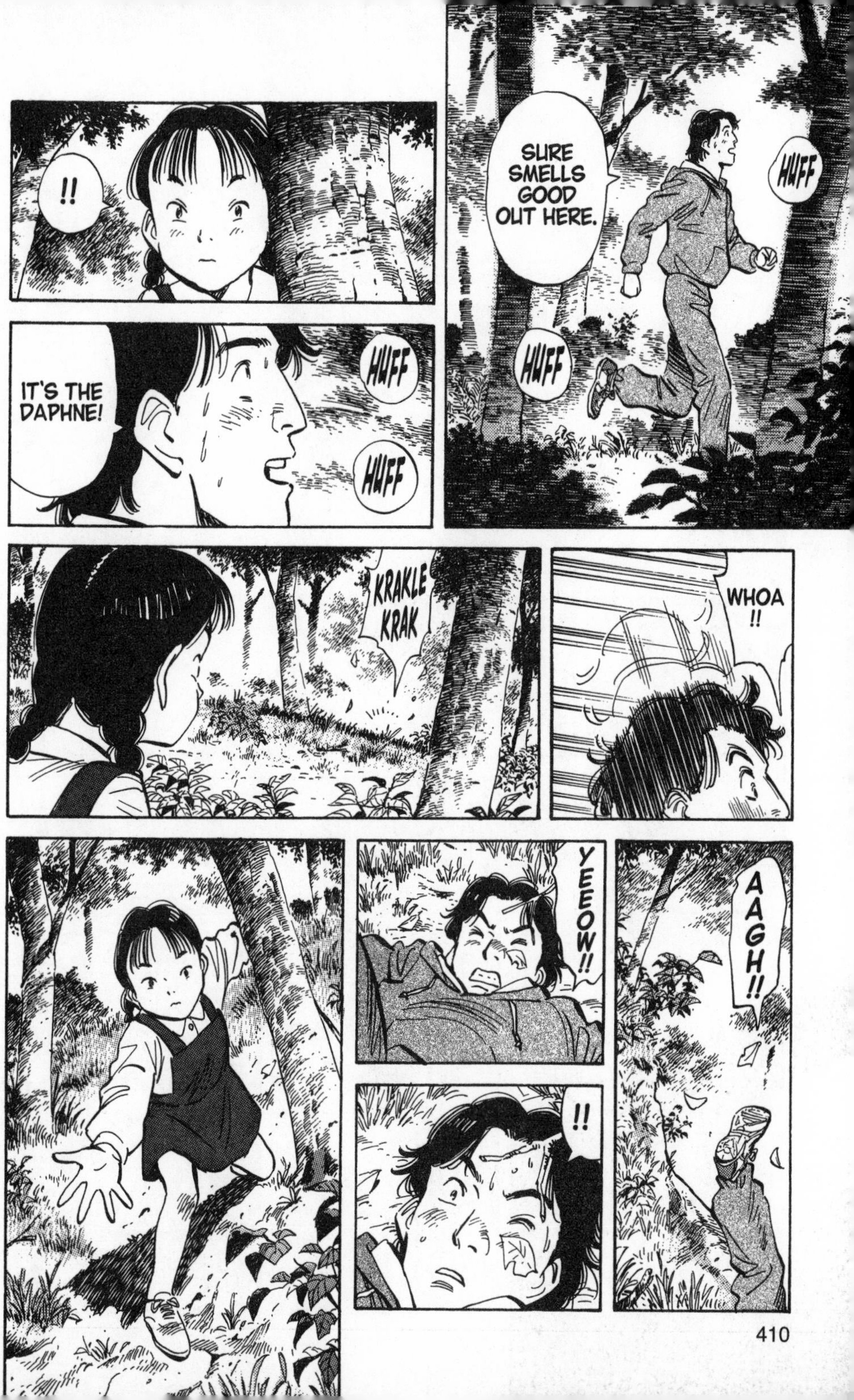
SURE SMELLS GOOD OUT HERE.
HUFF
HUFF
!!
IT'S THE DAPHNE!
HUFF
HUFF
WHOA !!
KRAKLE KRAK
AAGH!!
YEEEOW!!
!!

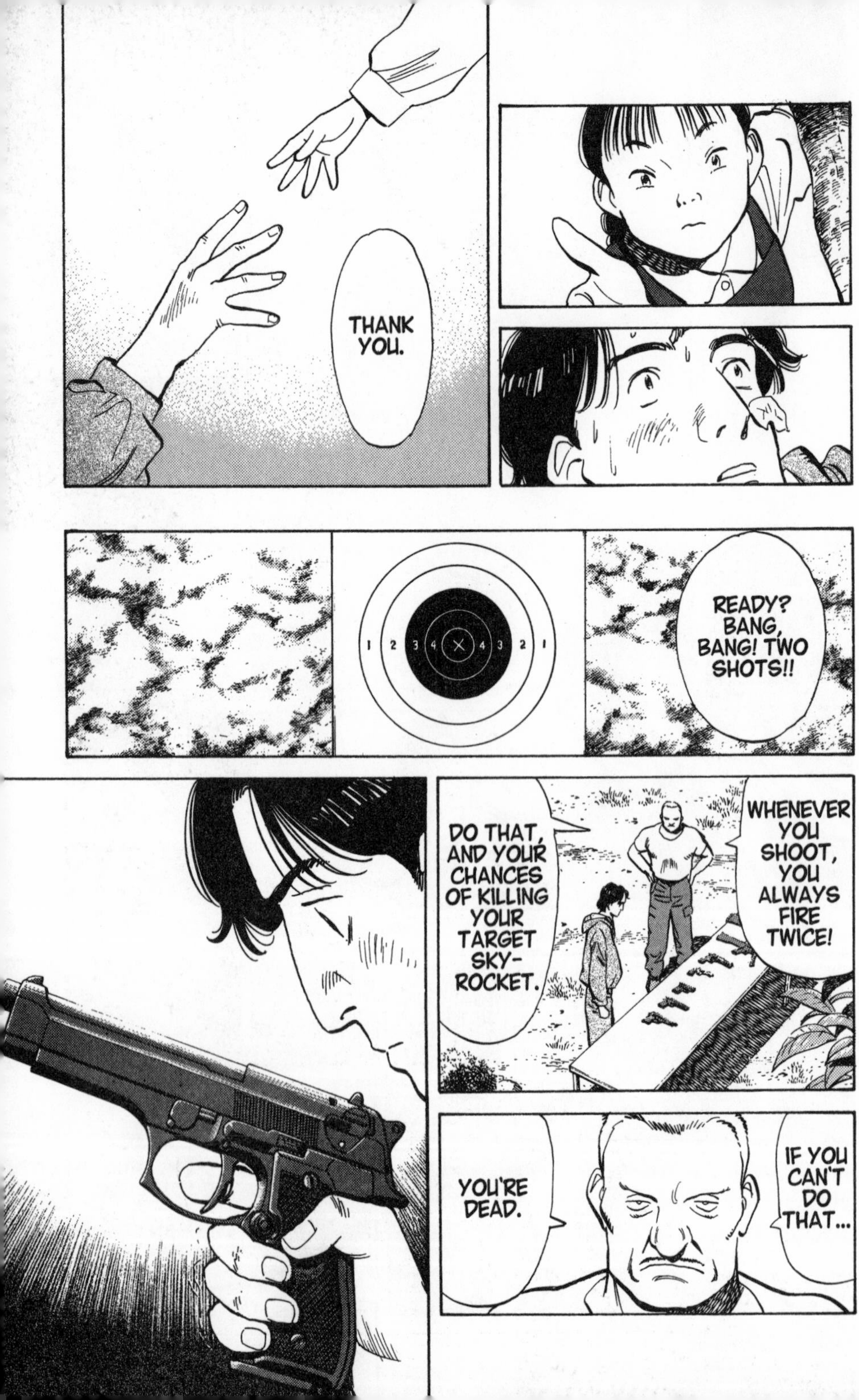
THANK YOU.
READY? BANG, BANG! TWO SHOTS!!
WHENEVER YOU SHOOT, YOU ALWAYS FIRE TWICE!
DO THAT, AND YOUR CHANCES OF KILLING YOUR TARGET SKY-ROCKET.
IF YOU CAN'T DO THAT...
YOU'RE DEAD.

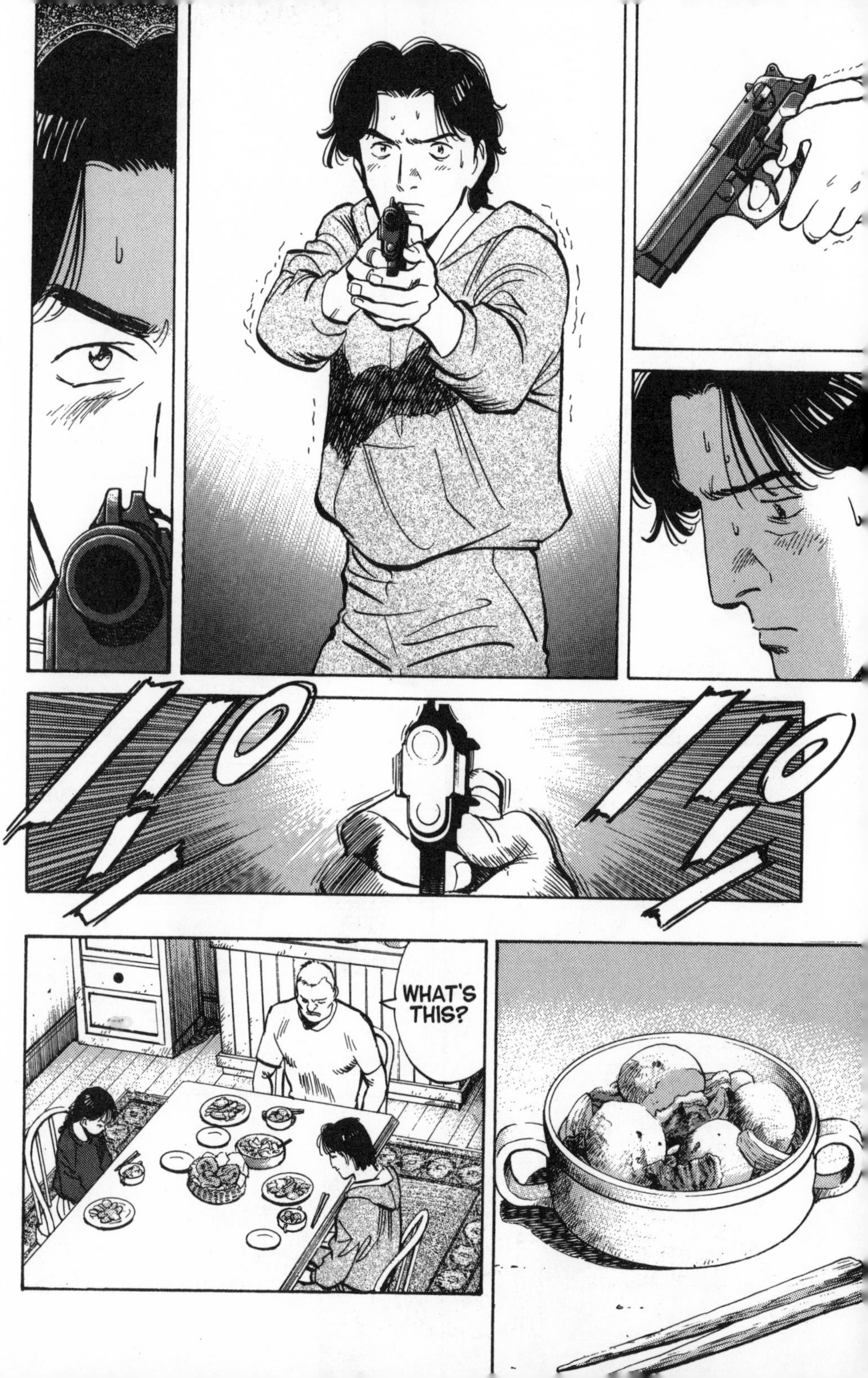
WHAT'S THIS?

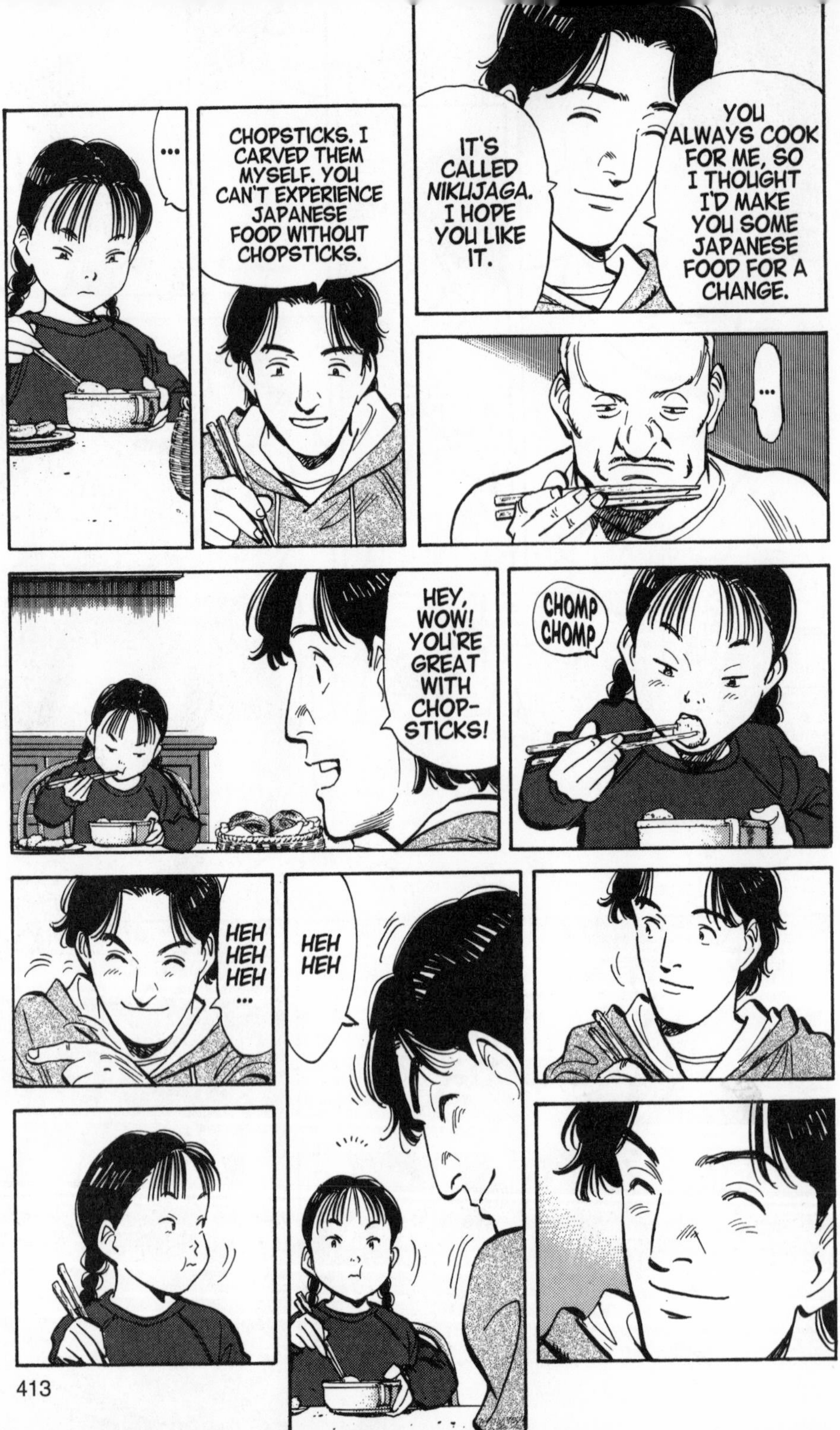
YOU ALWAYS COOK FOR ME, SO I THOUGHT I'D MAKE YOU SOME JAPANESE FOOD FOR A CHANGE.
IT'S CALLED NIKUJAGA. I HOPE YOU LIKE IT.
...
CHOPSTICKS. I CARVED THEM MYSELF. YOU CAN'T EXPERIENCE JAPANESE FOOD WITHOUT CHOPSTICKS.
...
CHOMP CHOMP
HEY, WOW! YOU'RE GREAT WITH CHOP-STICKS!
HEH HEH
HEH HEH HEH ...

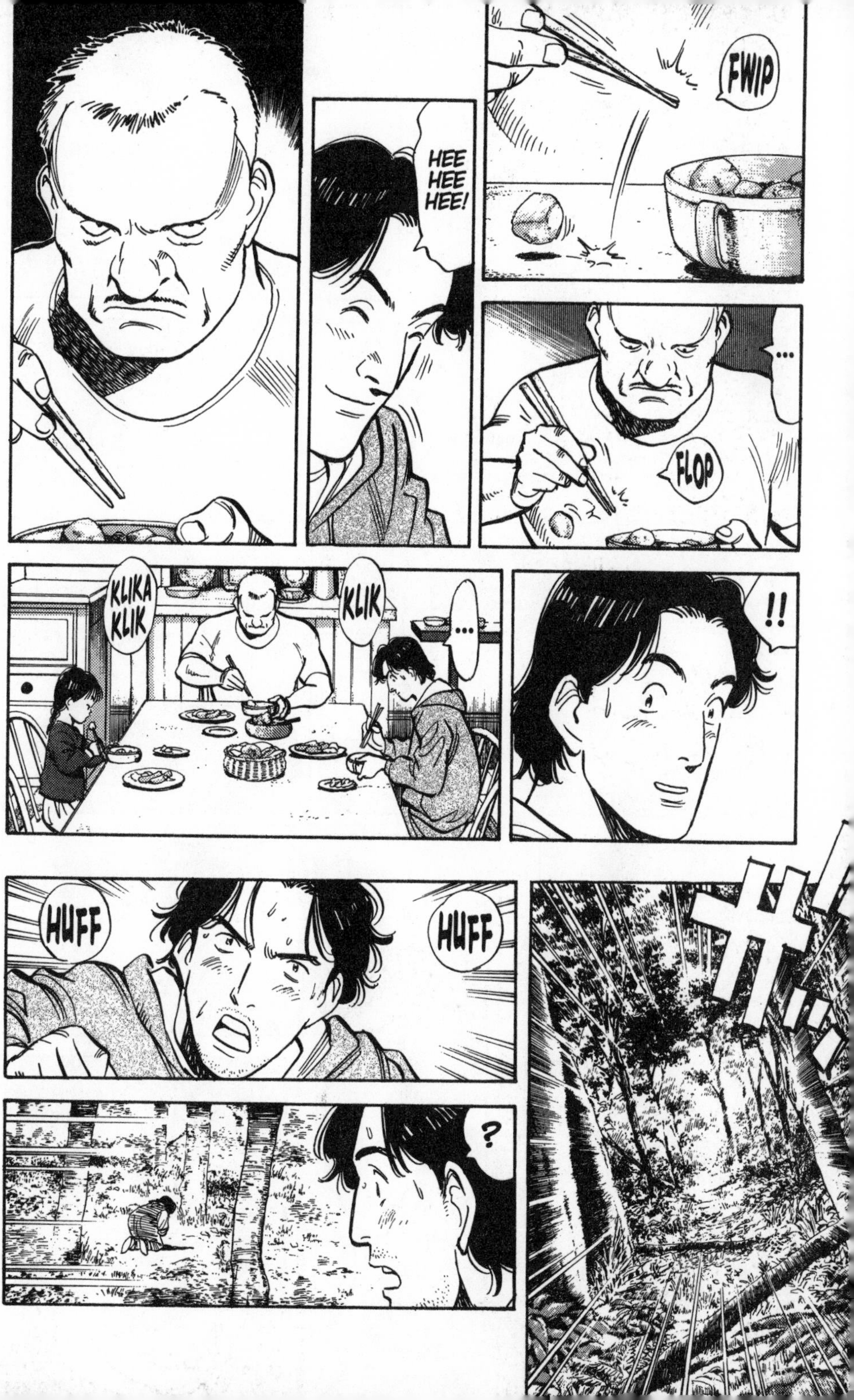
FWIP
...
FLOP
HEE HEE HEE!
!!
...
KLIK
KLIKA KLIK
ザ…
HUFF
HUFF
?

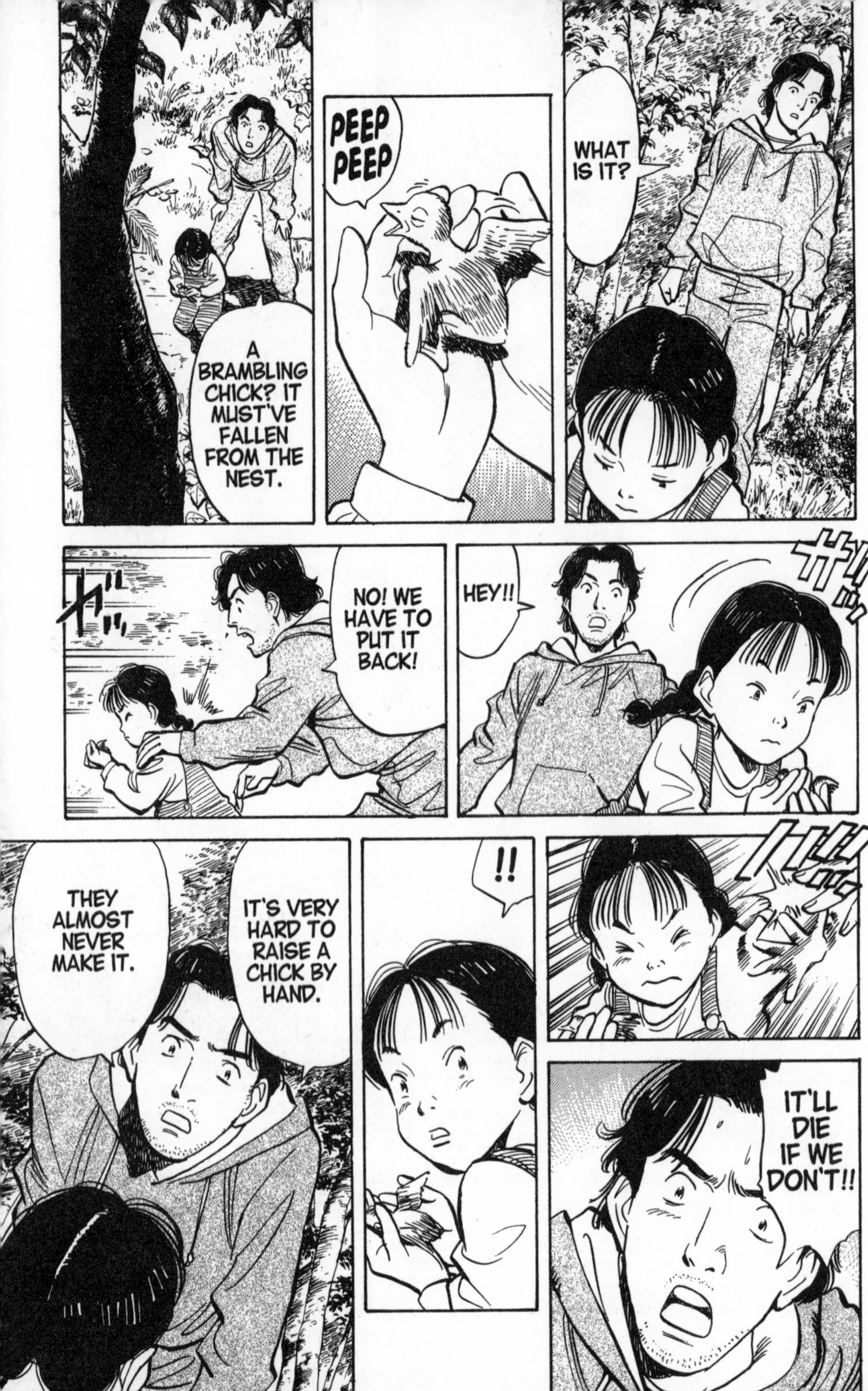
WHAT IS IT?
PEEP PEEP
A BRAMBLING CHICK? IT MUST'VE FALLEN FROM THE NEST.
HEY!!
NO! WE HAVE TO PUT IT BACK!
IT'LL DIE IF WE DON'T!!
!!
IT'S VERY HARD TO RAISE A CHICK BY HAND.
THEY ALMOST NEVER MAKE IT.

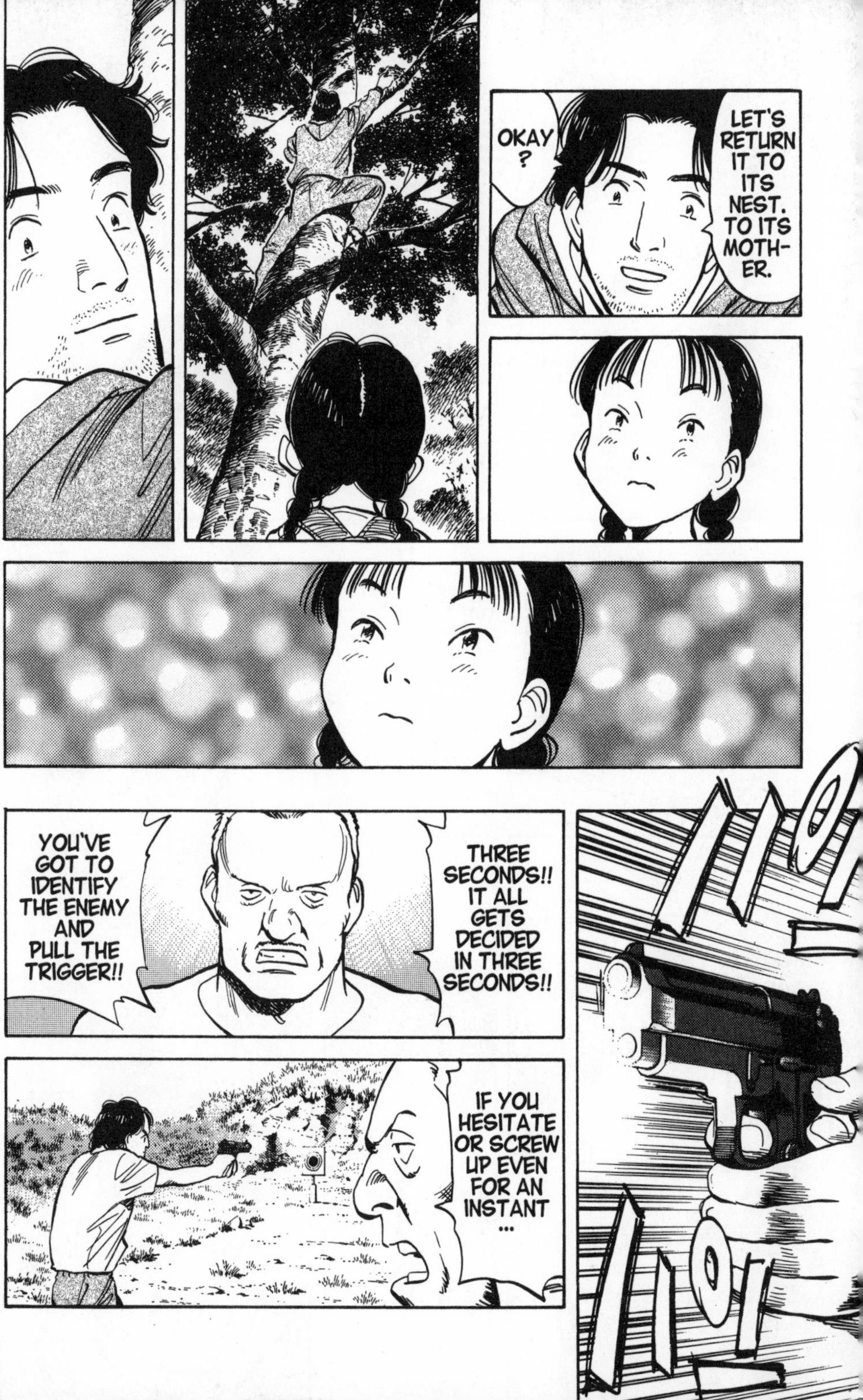
LET'S RETURN IT TO ITS NEST. TO ITS MOTHER.
OKAY?
THREE SECONDS!! IT ALL GETS DECIDED IN THREE SECONDS!!
YOU'VE GOT TO IDENTIFY THE ENEMY AND PULL THE TRIGGER!!
IF YOU HESITATE OR SCREW UP EVEN FOR AN INSTANT ...

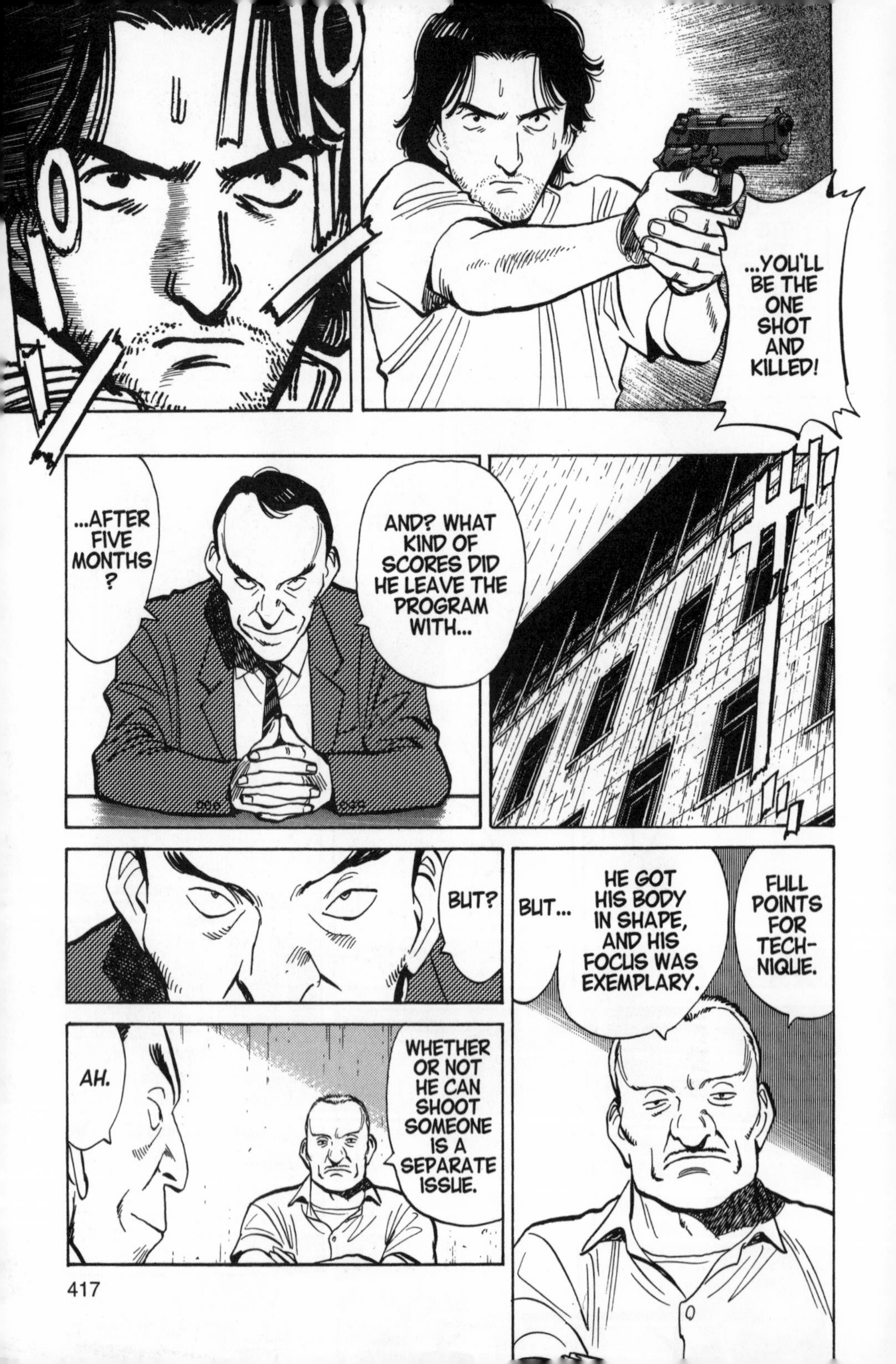
...YOU'LL BE THE ONE SHOT AND KILLED!
AND? WHAT KIND OF SCORES DID HE LEAVE THE PROGRAM WITH...
...AFTER FIVE MONTHS?
FULL POINTS FOR TECHNIQUE.
HE GOT HIS BODY IN SHAPE, AND HIS FOCUS WAS EXEMPLARY.
BUT...
BUT?
WHETHER OR NOT HE CAN SHOOT SOMEONE IS A SEPARATE ISSUE.
AH.

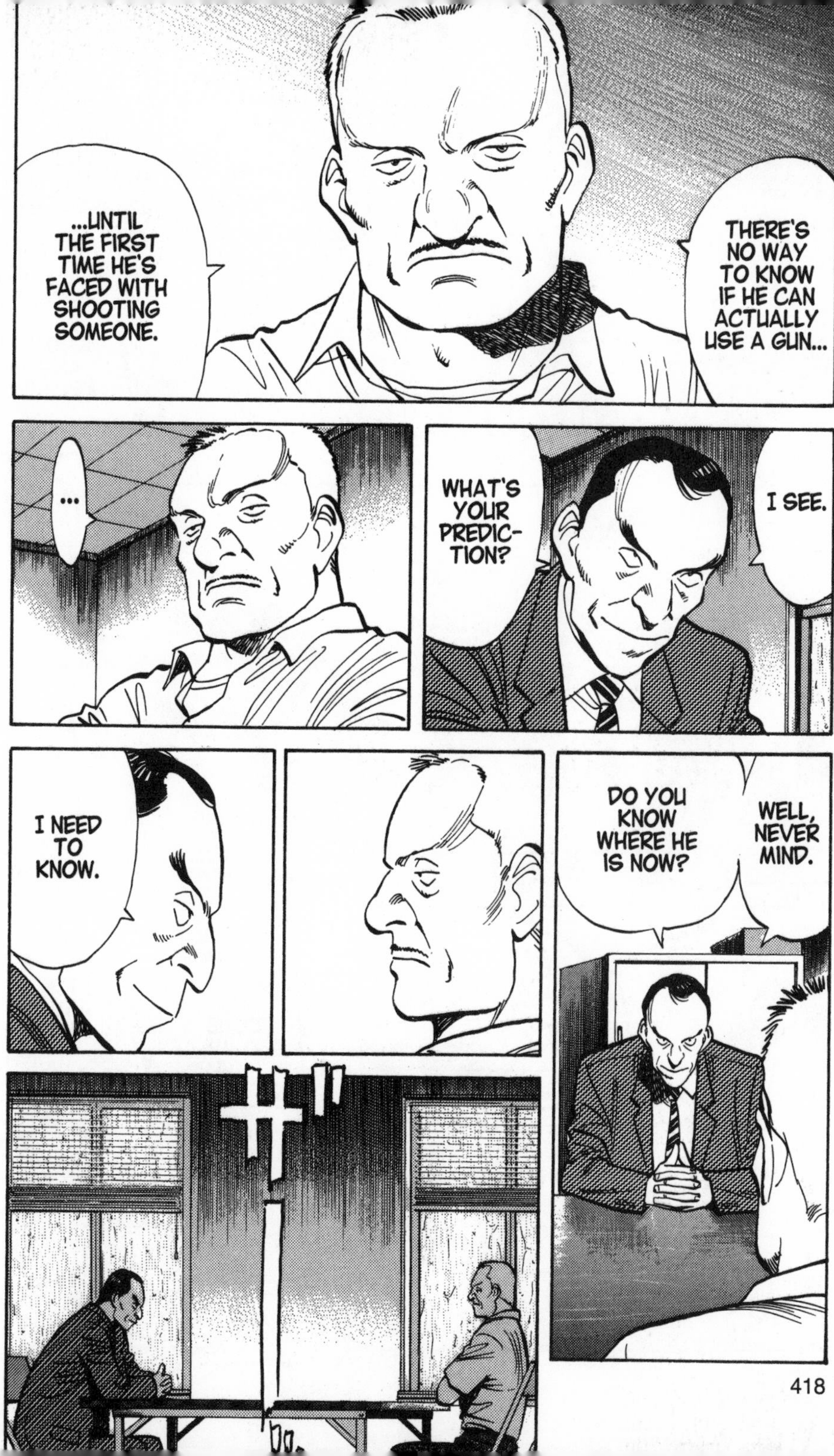
THERE'S NO WAY TO KNOW IF HE CAN ACTUALLY USE A GUN...
...UNTIL THE FIRST TIME HE'S FACED WITH SHOOTING SOMEONE.
I SEE.
WHAT'S YOUR PREDIC- TION?
...
WELL, NEVER MIND.
DO YOU KNOW WHERE HE IS NOW?
I NEED TO KNOW.

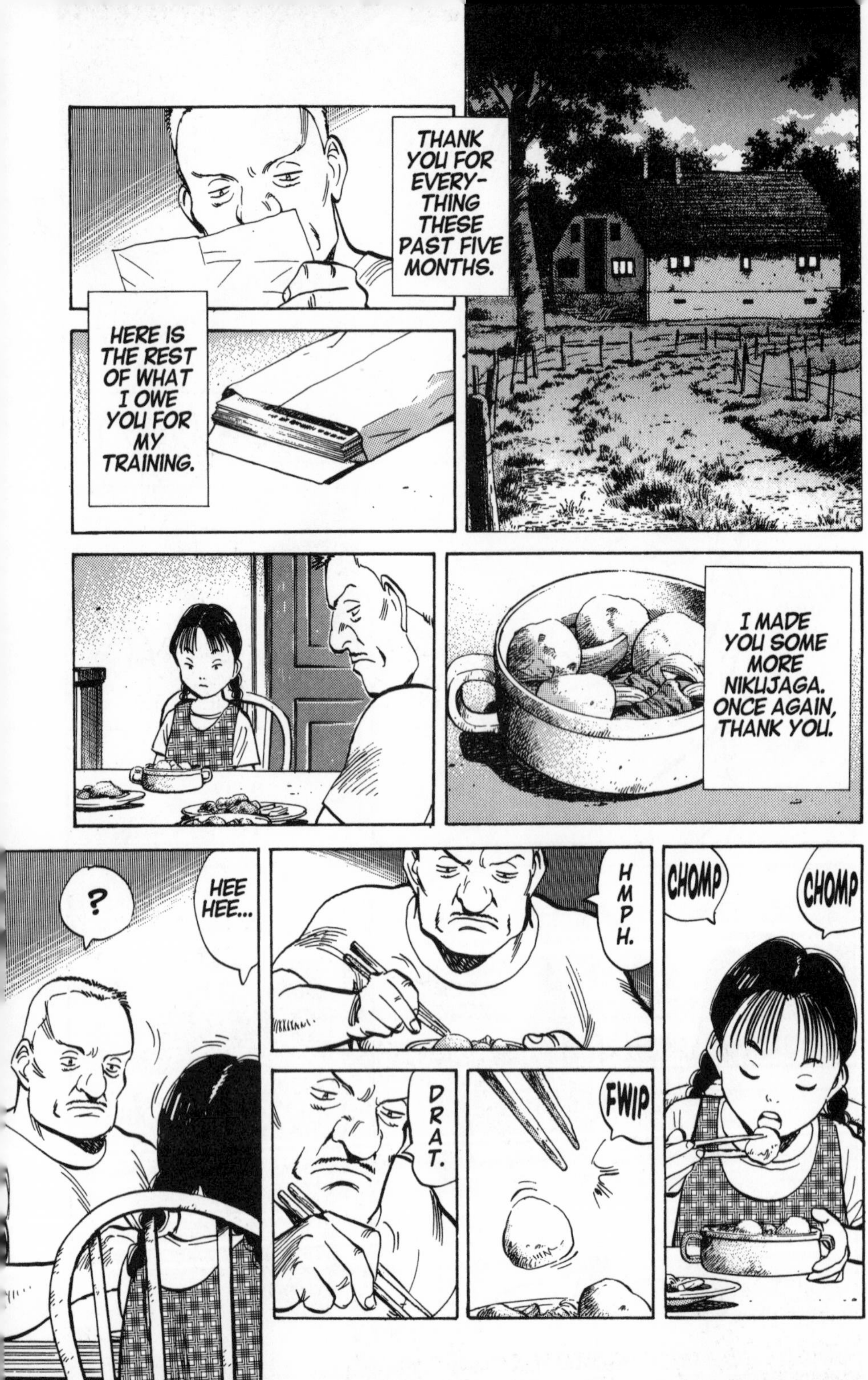
THANK YOU FOR EVERY-THING THESE PAST FIVE MONTHS.
HERE IS THE REST OF WHAT I OWE YOU FOR MY TRAINING.
I MADE YOU SOME MORE NIKUJAGA. ONCE AGAIN, THANK YOU.
CHOMP
CHOMP
HMPH.
FWIP
DRAT.
HEE HEE...
?

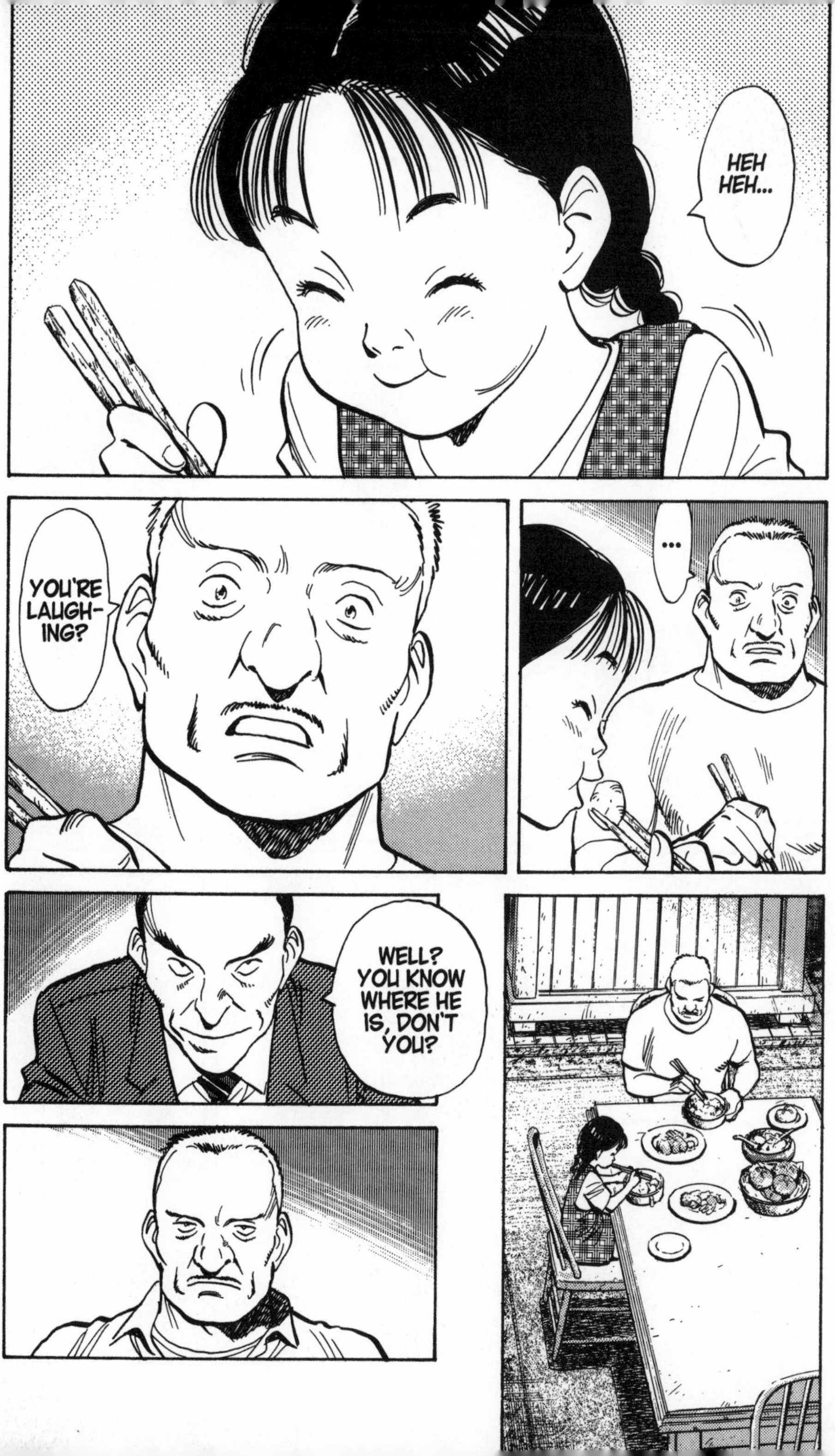
HEH HEH...
...
YOU'RE LAUGHING?
WELL? YOU KNOW WHERE HE IS, DON'T YOU?

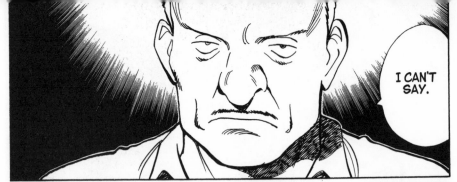

I CAN'T SAY.

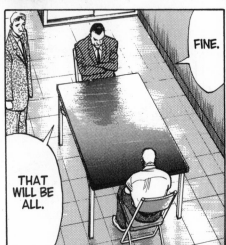

FINE.

THAT WILL BE ALL.

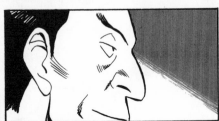

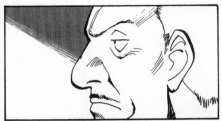

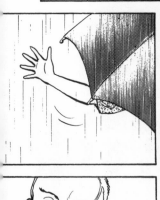

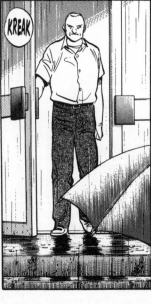

KREAK

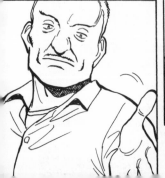

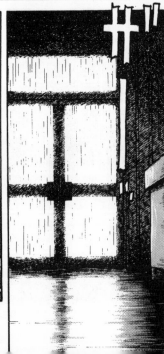

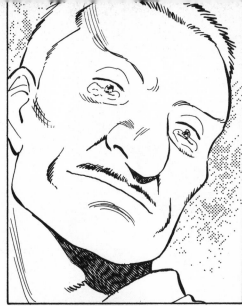
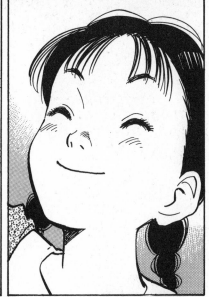
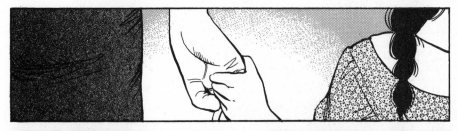
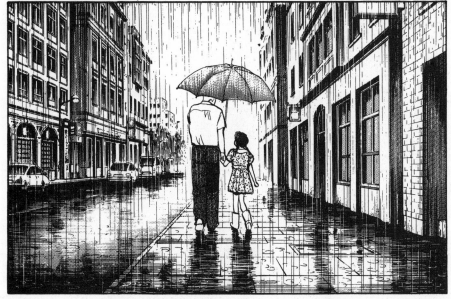

Monster—Volume 1—End

Naoki Urasawa

N aoki Urasawa's career as a manga artist spans more than twenty years and has firmly established him as one of the true manga masters of Japan. Born in Tokyo in 1960, Urasawa debuted with *BETA!* in 1983 and hasn't stopped his impressive output since. Well-versed in a variety of genres, Urasawa's oeuvre encompasses a multitude of different subjects, such as a romantic comedy (*Yawara! A Fashionable Judo Girl*), a suspenseful human drama about a former mercenary (*Pineapple ARMY*; story by Kazuya Kudo), a captivating psychological suspense story (*Monster*), a sci-fi adventure manga (*20th Century Boys*), and a modern reinterpretation of the work of the God of Manga, Osamu Tezuka (*Pluto: Urasawa × Tezuka*; co-authored with Takashi Nagasaki, supervised by Macoto Tezka, and with the cooperation of Tezuka Productions). Many of his books have spawned popular animated and live-action TV programs and films, and 2008 saw the theatrical release of the first of three live-action Japanese films based on *20th Century Boys*.

No stranger to accolades and awards, Urasawa received the 2011 and 2013 Eisner Award for Best U.S. Edition of International Material—Asia, and is a three-time recipient of the prestigious Shogakukan Manga Award, a two-time recipient of the Osamu Tezuka Cultural Prize, and also received the Kodansha Manga Award. Urasawa has also become involved in the world of academia, and in 2008 accepted a guest teaching post at Nagoya Zokei University, where he teaches courses in, of course, manga.

204.1 – kshh (zaa: rain)
204.5 – blam (don: gunshot)
205.1-2 – blam (don: gunshot)
206.1 – kshh (zaa: rain)
207.2 – kshh (zaa: rain)
209.3-4 – kshh (zaa: rain)
215.1-3 – tak (ka: footsteps)
216.4 – tak (ka: footsteps)
216.6 – kchak (ban: bursting through door)
220.1-2 – whap (ba: blow)
220.3 – vwap (ga: grabbing arm)
220.5 – wham (zutan: slamming)
220.6 – fwap fwap (ban ban: tapping out)
221.1 – wsh (za: quick movement)
221.2-3 – clappa clappa (pachi pachi: clapping)
222.5-7 – whap (ba: blow)
223.1-3 – brrrm (ba ba: engine)
232.1-2 – chomp chomp (ga ga: eating)
238.2 – tmp (za: footstep)
239.1 – brrrm (bwoo: engine)
239.1 – honk (paah: honking)
239.4 – honk (paah: honking)
247.3 – kchak (batan: door slamming)
262.4 – brrrm (ba ba: engine)
263.8 – shff (za: movement)
264.2 – shff (za: movement)
269.4 – kchak (batan: door slamming)
274.6 – whud whud (dosa dosa: thudding)
275.1 – whud (dosa: thudding)
275.8 – kchak (batan: door slamming)
283.2 – tak tak (dota dota: running)
283.3 – kchak (gacha: door opening)
283.6 – whsh (da: quick movement)
285.1 – mnch mnch (hagu hagu: chomping)
294.6 – shff (za: movement)
296.1 – brmm (baa: motor)
300.5 – brmm (baa: motor)
300.7 – shp (za: walking)
302.2 – kchak (batan: door slamming)
302.4 – bam bam (don don: thumping on door)
303.1 – bam bam (don don: thumping on door)
305.7 – chok (ga: catching keys)
305.8 – whsh (da: quick movement)
306.8 – whsh (da: quick movement)
312.7 – shp (za: movement)
313.4 – whsh (da: quick movement)
313.5 – fwhsh (ba: quick thrust)
313.6 – whud (do: thud)
314.4 – grab (ga: grab)
314.5 – whap (ba: throw)
314.6 – slam (da: impact)
314.7 – klink klunk (kan karan: clattering)
315.1 – yank (ga: yanking arm behind back)
315.7 – yoink (gi: tugging)
316.6 – tmp (da: running)
317.3 – tmp (da: running)
318.1 – vrmm (baa: engine)
319.5 – tmp (da: running)
321.1-2 – bam bam (don don: thumping on door)

322.1 – rattle (gacha: rattling door)
323.2 – kreak (gi: door hinges)
325.6-9 – whmp (gu: forceful pushing)
326.1-7 – whmp (gu: forceful pushing)
333.1 – tmp (da: running)
333.2 – klak (gacha: door latch)
333.5 – kreak (gi: door hinges)
333.6 – wham (ban: door slamming)
336.1 – swhoo (baa: fast movement)
337.4 – vrrmm (oon: car engine)
338.2 – swhoo (baa: fast movement)
339.4 – swhoo (baa: fast movement)
343.3 – dash (da: quick movement)
343.5 – whsh (da: quick movement)
344.1 – sploosh (dobashan: splash)
344.4 – fwshh (gooo: rushing water)
346.1-3 – zsh (za: footsteps in grass)
346.7 – shmp (dosa: setting down bag)
349.6 – zsh (za: footsteps in grass)
350.5 – kshh (zaa: downpour)
357.1 – yappa yappa (zawa zawa: clamor)
358.2 – whip (ba: fast movement)
359.2 – rring (RRRR: phone ringing)
359.3 – yappa yappa (wai wai: commotion)
361.4 – kchak (gacha: door opening)
363.2-6 – shp (za: footsteps in grass)
369.3 – voosh (faa: train whooshing past)
369.4 – ktunk ktunk (goton goton: wheels on tracks)
370.3 – ktunk ktunk (goton goton: wheels on tracks)
379.6 – tak (ka: footsteps)
387.1 – klop (ka: footsteps)
387.2 – voosh (ba: fast movement)
389.4 – kreak (gi: kreak)
391.2 – rring (RRR: phone ringing)
391.5 – eeoo eeoo (paapoo paapoo: sirens)
391.6-7 – tmp tmp (za za: footsteps)
392.1 – tmp tmp (ka ka: footsteps)
394.1 – eeoo eeoo (paapoo paapoo: sirens)
395.3 – bumpa bumpa (gata goto: bumping along)
395.4 – ktunk ktunk (goto goto: bumping along)
395.6 – bumpa bumpa (gata goto: bumping along)
440.8 – kshh (zaaa: rain)
403.1-3 – thok thok (tatan tatan: jumping)
403.4 – klap klap (pan pan: clapping)
403.5 – fwap (pishi: rope hitting feet)
403.6 – klap klap (pan pan: clapping)
406.8 – kchak (batan: door shutting)
409.2-4 – voosh (za: fast movement)
412.5 – blam blam (ban ban: shots)
414.7 – fwsh (za: fast movement)
415.4 – fwsh (za: fast movement)
415.6 – whsh (ba: pulling away)
415.7 – grab (ga: grabbing shoulder)
416.6 – blam blam (ban ban: shots)
417.2 – blam blam (ban ban: shots)
417.3 – kshh (zaaa: rain)
418.7 – kshh (zaaa: rain)
421.5 – kshh (zaaa: rain)

Sound Effects Glossary

The sound effects in this edition of Monster have been preserved in their original Japanese format. To avoid additional lettering cluttering up the panels, a list of the sound effects (FX) is provided here. Each FX is listed by page and panel number, so for example 3.4 would mean the FX is on page 3 in panel 4.

3.4 – tak tak (ka ka: footsteps)
3.5 – shp (ga: clasping hands)
4.3 – shah (ka: sunlight streaming in)
22.3-6 – whmp (don: thumping)
23.1 – whmp (don: thumping)
26.2 – chomp chomp (hagu: eating)
27.2 – shaaa (zaaa: downpour)
27.3 – wee-oo (paa-poo: siren)
27.4 – skree (kii: breaks squealing)
29.3 – dash (da: running)
29.7 – slam (ba: bursting in)
31.1 – wham (da: bursting in)
32.1-2 – zsshh (zaaa: downpour)
33.1 – shaaa (zaaa: downpour)
33.2 – fwish fwish (shakon shakon: wipers)
34.6 – shoop (bamu: emerging from car)
39.7 – vwaa (paa: oncoming truck)
40.2 – vrmmm (gohh: zooming truck)
40.2 – skree (kikii: breaks squealing)
40.5 – vwam (gan: thumping)
41.2 – tmp (da: running)
41.5 – tak tak (ka ka: footsteps)
42.5 – tak (ka: footstep)
44.7 – kchak (batam: door shutting)
46.1 – soosh (zaaa: water rushing)
46-7 – kreak (gi: squeaking door hinges)
47-3 – chik (ka: light coming on)
50.3 – tak (ka: footsteps)
50.4 – wmp (pon: thumping on shoulder)
50.5-6 – tak (ka: footsteps)
52.2 – whmp (don: thumping)
52.4 – whmp (don: thumping)
55.2-3 – tak (ka: footsteps)
56.1 – kreak (gi: squeaking door hinges)
56.2 – wham (bamu: door slamming)
56.3 – chik (ka: light coming on)
63.7 – tak (ka: footsteps)
71.3 – tak (ka: footsteps)
73.3-4 – clappa clappa (pachi pachi: applause)
74.2-3 – clappa clappa (pachi pachi: applause)
74.4 – chatter chatter (wai wai: talking)
74.5 – ha ha ha (ha ha ha: laughter)
76.2 – Ooh! (waaa: exclamations)
76.2-3 – clappa clappa (pachi pachi: applause)
77.7 – clappa clappa (pachi pachi: applause)
79.7 – chatter chatter (wai wai: talking)
82.6 – thump (don: thumping fist)
98.2 – tak (da: foot step)
99.1- tak (da: foot step)
101.2 – yoink (ga: yanking)
103.6 – whump (don: shove)
103.7 – kchak (batan: door slamming)

105.1 – shf (ka: quick movement)
106.2 – kreak (gi: door squeaking)
106.7 – ka-bash (don garagan: crashing)
107.5 – kreak (gi: door squeaking)
109.5 – kreak (gi: door squeaking)
111.3 – wobble (yoro: staggering)
111.4 – kreak (gi: door squeaking)
113.2 – clamor clamor (wai wai: shouting voices)
114.1 – tmp tmp (do do: running)
114.4 – tak (da: foot step)
114.5 – yappa yappa (zawa zawa: commotion)
115.2 – tak (ka: footsteps)
116.3 – shove (don: collision)
117.3 – tak (da: footstep)
117.4 – tak tak (da da: footsteps)
117.5 – fwam (ba: bursting through door)
121.2 – zsh (za: quick movement)
121.5 – whsh (ba: quick movement)
123.1 – whak (za: quick movement)
129.4 – kchak (kacha: door opening)
138.2 – tak tak (ka ka: footsteps)
138.4 – tak (ka: footsteps)
139.3 – splish (basha: splashing)
143.2 – shf (ta: quick movement)
143.3 – shoo (hyoon: falling)
145.8 – fwoo (da: running)
147.4 – shah (ka: light coming on)
147.5 – shp (kyu: putting on gloves)
149.3 – tmp (da: running)
150.1 – brmm (ooo: car's engine)
150.4-8 – skreee (gyagyagya: breaks squealing)
150.6 – vwam (don: impact)
151.3 – yappa yappa (zawa zawa: commotion)
152.2-3 – tak tak (ka ka: footsteps)
153.5 – voosh (zaa: fast movement)
153.6 – kchak (bamu: door shutting)
153.7 – tak (ka: footsteps)
157.6 – kchak (batan: door closing)
158.2 – shah (ka: light coming on)
169.1 – kchak (batan: door closing)
175.3-7 – quiver quiver (kata kata: shivering)
176.1 – quiver quiver (kata kata: shivering)
179.1 – kreak (gi: door opening)
181.2 – tmp (da: running)
181.8 – whsh (ba: quick movement)
182.1 – whsh (ba: quick movement)
182.4 – krash (gashan: clock smashing)
182.5 – tmp (da: running)
183.2 – tmp (da: running)
183.6 – kang kang (kan kan: running down stairs)
184.3 – whsh (ta: turning)
203.1 – kshh (zaa: rain)

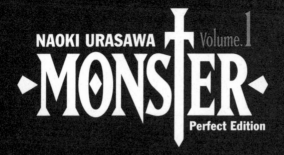

NAOKI URASAWA Volume.1

MONSTER

Perfect Edition

MONSTER
Volume 1
VIZ Signature Edition

Story & Art by NAOKI URASAWA
Story Coproduced with TAKASHI NAGASAKI

Translation & English Adaptation/Camellia Nieh
Lettering/Steve Dutro
Cover & Interior Design/King Clovis
Editor/Mike Montesa

MONSTER KANZENBAN Vol.1
by Naoki URASAWA/Studio Nuts
Story coproduced with Takashi NAGASAKI

Original Japanese edition published by SHOGAKUKAN.
English translation rights in the United States of America, Canada, United Kingdom, Ireland, Australia and New Zealand arranged with SHOGAKUKAN.
Original Art Direction by Kazuo UMINO
Original cover design by Mikiyo KOBAYASHI + Bay Bridge Studio

Printed in the U.S.A.

Published by VIZ Media, LLC
P.O. Box 77010
San Francisco, CA 94107

10 9 8 7 6 5 4 3
First printing, July 2014
Third printing, October 2017

viz media
www.viz.com

RATED T+ FOR OLDER TEEN

PARENTAL ADVISORY
MONSTER is rated T+ and is recommended for older teens. This volume contains scenes of violence and suggestive themes.
ratings.viz.com

VIZ SIGNATURE

D1503122